Lecture Notes in Computer Science 2024
Edited by G. Goos, J. Hartmanis and J. van Leeuwen

Springer
Berlin
Heidelberg
New York
Barcelona
Hong Kong
London
Milan
Paris
Singapore
Tokyo

Herbert Kuchen   Kazunori Ueda (Eds.)

Functional and Logic Programming

5th International Symposium, FLOPS 2001
Tokyo, Japan, March 7-9, 2001
Proceedings

Springer

Series Editors

Gerhard Goos, Karlsruhe University, Germany
Juris Hartmanis, Cornell University, NY, USA
Jan van Leeuwen, Utrecht University, The Netherlands

Volume Editors

Herbert Kuchen
Westfälische Wilhelms-Universität Münster, Institut für Wirtschaftsinformatik
Steinfurter Straße 109, 48149 Münster, Germany
E-mail: kuchen@uni-muenster.de

Kazunori Ueda
Waseda University, Department of Information and Computer Science
4-1, Okubo 3-chome, Shinjuku-ku, Tokyo 169-8555, Japan
E-mail: ueda@ueda.info.waseda.ac.jp

Cataloging-in-Publication Data applied for

Die Deutsche Bibliothek - CIP-Einheitsaufnahme

Functional and logic programming : 5th international symposium ; proceedings / FLOPS 2001, Tokyo, Japan, March 7 - 9, 2001. Herbert Kuchen ; Kazunori Ueda (ed.). - Berlin ; Heidelberg ; New York ; Barcelona ; Hong Kong ; London ; Milan ; Paris ; Singapore ; Tokyo : Springer, 2001
(Lecture notes in computer science ; Vol. 2024)
ISBN 3-540-41739-7

CR Subject Classification (1998): D.1.1, D.1.6, D.3, F.3, I.2.3

ISSN 0302-9743
ISBN 3-540-41739-7 Springer-Verlag Berlin Heidelberg New York

Springer-Verlag Berlin Heidelberg New York
a member of BertelsmannSpringer Science+Business Media GmbH
http://www.springer.de

Printed in Germany

Typesetting: Camera-ready by author, data conversion by PTP-Berlin, Stefan Sossna
Printed on acid-free paper SPIN: 10782353 06/3142 5 4 3 2 1 0

Preface

This volume contains the proceedings of the *Fifth International Symposium on Functional and Logic Programming*, FLOPS 2001, held in Tokyo, Japan, March 7–9, 2001, and hosted by Waseda University.

FLOPS is a forum for research on all issues concerning functional programming and logic programming. In particular, it aims to stimulate the cross-fertilization as well as the integration of the two paradigms. The previous FLOPS meetings took place in Fuji-Susono (1995), Shonan (1996), Kyoto (1998), and Tsukuba (1999). The proceedings of FLOPS'99 were published by Springer-Verlag as Lecture Notes in Computer Science, volume 1722.

There were 40 submissions, 38 of which were considered by the program committee. They came from Australia (5), Belgium ($^1/_3$), Denmark (3), Egypt (1), France ($^1/_2$), Germany ($2\,^1/_3$), Italy ($4\,^2/_3$), Japan (5), Korea ($1\,^1/_2$), Mexico (1), The Netherlands ($1\,^1/_6$), Spain ($10\,^1/_6$), Switzerland (1), UK ($1\,^5/_6$), and USA ($1\,^1/_2$). Each paper was reviewed by at least three, and mostly four, reviewers. The program committee meeting was conducted electronically for the period of two weeks in November 2000. As a result of active discussions, 21 papers (52.5%) were selected for presentation, which appear in this volume. In addition, we are very pleased to include in this volume full papers by three distinguished invited speakers, namely Gopalan Nadathur, George Necula, and Taisuke Sato.

On behalf of the program committee, the program chairs would like to thank the invited speakers who agreed to give talks and contribute papers, all those who submitted papers, and all the referees for their careful work in the reviewing and selection process. The support of our sponsors is also gratefully acknowledged. In particular, we would like to thank the Japan Society for Software Science and Technology (JSSST), Special Interest Group on Principles of Programming, and the Association for Logic Programming (ALP). Finally, we would like to thank the members of the organizing committee, notably Zhenjiang Hu, Yasuhiro Ajiro, Kazuhiko Kakehi, and Madoka Kuniyasu, for their invaluable support throughout the preparation and organization of the symposium.

January 2001

Herbert Kuchen
Kazunori Ueda

Symposium Organization

Program Chairs

Herbert Kuchen	University of Münster, Germany
Kazunori Ueda	Waseda University, Tokyo, Japan

Program Committee

Sergio Antoy	Portland State University, USA
Gopal Gupta	University of Texas at Dallas, USA
Michael Hanus	University of Kiel, Germany
Fergus Henderson	University of Melbourne, Australia
Zhenjiang Hu	University of Tokyo, Japan
Herbert Kuchen	University of Münster, Germany
Giorgio Levi	University of Pisa, Italy
Michael Maher	Griffith University, Brisbane, Australia
Dale Miller	Pennsylvania State University, USA
I. V. Ramakrishnan	State University of New York at Stony Brook, USA
Olivier Ridoux	IRISA, Rennes, France
Mario Rodríguez-Artalejo	Complutense University, Madrid, Spain
Colin Runciman	University of York, UK
Akihiko Takano	Hitachi, Ltd., Japan
Peter Thiemann	Freiburg University, Germany
Yoshihito Toyama	Tohoku University, Japan
Kazunori Ueda	Waseda University, Tokyo, Japan

Local Arrangements Chair

Zhenjiang Hu	University of Tokyo, Japan

List of Referees

The following referees helped the Program Committee in evaluating the papers. Their assistance is gratefully acknowledged.

Yohji Akama
Joseph Albert
Kenichi Asai
Gilles Barthe
Cristiano Calcagno
Manuel M. T. Chakravarty
Alessandra Di Pierro
Rachid Echahed
Moreno Falaschi
Adrian Fiech
Peter Flach
Maurizio Gabbrielli
Maria García de la Banda
Antonio Gavilanes
Robert Glück
Stefano Guerrini
Hai-feng Guo
Bill Harrison
Simon Helsen
Martin Henz
Hideya Iwasaki
Mark Jones
Kazuhiko Kakehi
Owen Kaser
Robert Kowalski
K. Narayan Kumar
Keiichirou Kusakari
Javier Leach-Albert
Francisco López-Fraguas
Wolfgang Lux
Narciso Martí-Oliet
Andrea Masini
Bart Massey
Hidehiko Masuhara
Aart Middeldorp
Yasuhiko Minamide
Luc Moreau
Shin-ya Nishizaki
Susana Nieva
Mizuhito Ogawa
Satoshi Okui
Fernando Orejas
Giridhar Pemmasani
Marek Perkowski
Enrico Pontelli
C. R. Ramakrishnan
Francesca Rossi
Salvatore Ruggieri
Masahiko Sakai
Chiaki Sakama
Takafumi Sakurai
R. Sekar
Don Smith
Tran Cao Son
Harald Søndergaard
Frank Steiner
Eijiro Sumii
Taro Suzuki
Izumi Takeuti
Naoyuki Tamura
Tetsuro Tanaka
David Wakeling

Table of Contents

Types

Program Analysis and Transformation

λ-Calculus

The Metalanguage λProlog and Its Implementation

Gopalan Nadathur

Department of Computer Science and Engineering
University of Minnesota
4-192 EE/CS Building, 200 Union Street SE
Minneapolis, MN 55455
gopalan@cs.umn.edu
Home Page: http://www.cs.umn.edu/~gopalan

Abstract. Stimulated by concerns of software certification especially as it relates to mobile code, formal structures such as specifications and proofs are beginning to play an explicit role in computing. In representing and manipulating such structures, an approach is needed that pays attention to the binding operation that is present in them. The language λProlog provides programming support for a higher-order treatment of abstract syntax that is especially suited to this task. This support is realized by enhancing the traditional strength of logic programming in the metalanguage realm with an ability for dealing directly with binding structure. This paper identifies the features of λProlog that endow it with such a capability, illustrates their use and and describes methods for their implementation. Also discussed is a new realization of λProlog called *Teyjus* that incorporates the implementation ideas presented.

1 Introduction

The language λProlog is based on the higher-order theory of hereditary Harrop formulas that embodies a rich interpretation of the abstract idea of logic programming [18]. Through a systematic exploitation of features present in the underlying logic, this language realizes several capabilities at the programming level such as ones for typing, scoping over names and procedure definitions, representing and manipulating complex formal structures, modularly constructing code and higher-order programming. Our interest in this paper is in one specific facet of λProlog: its role as a metalanguage.

The manipulation of symbolic expressions has been of longstanding interest and some of the earliest computational tasks to have been considered and systematically addressed have, in fact, concerned the realization of reasoning processes, the processing of human languages and the compilation and interpretation of programming languages. The calculations involved in these cases are typically metalinguistic and syntactic in nature and a careful study of their structure has produced a universally accepted set of concepts and tools relevant to this form of computing. An important component in this collection is the

H. Kuchen and K. Ueda (Eds.): FLOPS 2001, LNCS 2024, pp. 1–20, 2001.

idea of *abstract syntax* that moves away from concrete presentation and focuses instead on the essential relationships between the constituent parts of symbolic constructs. A complementary development has been that of languages that provide programming support for computing with abstract syntax. These languages, which include Lisp, ML and Prolog amongst them, contain mechanisms that simplify the representation, construction and deconstruction of abstract syntax and that permit the implicit management of space relative to such manipulations. Effort has also been invested in implementing these languages efficiently, thereby making them practical vehicles for realizing complex symbolic systems.

One may wonder against this backdrop if anything new really needs to be added to the capabilities already available for symbolic computation. The answer to this question revolves around the treatment of scope and binding. Many symbolic objects whose manipulation is of interest involve forms of these operations in their structure in addition to the compositionality that is traditionally treated in abstract syntax. This is true, for instance, of quantified formulas that are considered within reasoning systems and of procedures with arguments that are of interest to programming language compilers. The conventional approach in these cases has been to use auxiliary mechanisms to avoid explicit reference to binding in representation. Thus, reasoning systems eliminate quantifiers from formulas through a preprocessing phase and compilers utilize symbol tables to create binding environments when these are needed in the analysis of programs. While such methods have been successful in the past, there is now an increasing interest in formal constructs with sophisticated and diverse forms of scope whose uniform treatment requires a reflection of the binding operation into abstract syntax itself. The desire to reason in systems different from classical logic provides one example of this kind. The elimination of quantifiers may either not be possible or desirable in many of these cases, requiring them to be explicitly represented and dynamically treated by the reasoning process. In a similar vein, motivated by the proof-carrying-code approach to software certification [29], attention has been paid to the representation of proofs. The discharge of assumptions and the treatment of genericity are intrinsic to these formal structures and a convenient method for representing such operations involves the use of binding constructs that range over their subparts. As a final example, relationships between declarations and uses are an important part of program structure and a formal treatment of these in representation can influence new approaches to program analysis and transformation.

Driven by considerations such as these, much effort has recently been devoted to developing an explicit treatment of binding in syntax representation, culminating in what has come to be known as *higher-order abstract syntax* [31]. The main novelty of λProlog as a metalanguage lies in the support it offers for this new approach to encoding syntactic objects. It realizes this support by enriching a conventional logic programming language in three essential ways. First, it replaces first-order terms—the data structures of a logic programming language—by the terms of a typed lambda calculus. Attendant on these lambda terms is a notion of equality given by the α-, β- and η-conversion rules. The main difference in representational power between first-order terms and lambda terms is that the latter are capable of also capturing binding structure in a logically precise way. Thus, this enhancement in term structure endows λProlog with a means for representing higher-order abstract syntax. Second, λProlog uses a unification operation that builds in the extended notion of equality accompanying lambda terms. This change provides the language with a destructuring operation that can utilize information about binding structure. Finally, the language incorporates two new kinds of goals, these being expressions of the form $\forall x G$ and D => G, in which G is a goal and D is a conjunction of clauses.[1] A goal of the form $\forall x G$ is solved by replacing all free occurrences of x in G with a new constant and then solving the result and a goal of the form D => G is solved by enhancing the existing program with the clauses in D and then attempting to solve G. Thus, at a programming level, the new forms of goals, which are referred to as *generic* and *augment*, respectively, provide mechanisms for scoping over names and code. As we shall see presently, these scoping abilities can be used to realize recursion over binding structure.

Our objective in this paper is to show that the new features present in λProlog can simplify the programming of syntax manipulations and that they can be implemented with sufficient efficiency to be practical tools in this realm. Towards this end, we first motivate the programming uses of these features and then discuss the problems and approaches to realizing them in an actual system. The ideas we discuss here have been used in a recent implementation of λProlog called *Teyjus* [25] that we also briefly describe. We assume a basic familiarity with lambda calculus notions and logic programming languages and the methods for implementing them that are embedded, for instance, in the Warren Abstract Machine (WAM) [35]. Further, in keeping with the expository nature of the paper, we favor an informal style of presentation; all the desired formality can be found in references that are cited at relevant places.

2 Higher-Order Abstract Syntax in λProlog

A common refrain in symbolic computation is to focus on the essential functional structure of objects. This is true, for instance, of systems that manipulate programs. Thus, a compiler or interpreter that manipulates an expression of the form *if B then T else E* must recognize that this expression denotes a conditional involving three constituents: B, T and E. Similarly, a theorem prover that

[1] To recall terminology, a goal is what appears in the body of a procedure or as a top level query and is conventionally formed from atomic goals via conjunction, disjunction and existential quantification. Clauses correspond to procedure definitions. While a free variable in a clause is usually assumed to be implicitly universally quantified at the head of the clause, there is ambiguity about the scope and force of such quantification when the clause appears in an expression of the form D => G. λProlog interprets the scope in this case to be the entire expression of which D => G itself may only be a part, and it bases the force on whether this expression is a goal or a clause. All other interpretations need to be indicated through explicit quantification.

encounters the formula $P \wedge Q$, must realize that this is one representing the conjunction of P and Q. Conversely, assuming that we are not interested in issues of presentation, these are the *only* properties that needs to be recognized and represented in each case. The 'abstract syntax' of these expressions may therefore be captured by the expressions *cond(B,T,E)* and *and(P,Q)*, where *cond* and *and* are suitably chosen function symbols or constructors.

Another important idea in syntax based computations is that of structural operational semantics that advocates the description of computational content through rules that operate on abstract syntax. For example, using $\triangleright$ as an infix notation for the evaluation relation, the operational meaning of a conditional expression can be described through the rules

$$\frac{B \triangleright \mathit{true} \qquad T \triangleright V}{\mathit{cond}(B,T,E) \triangleright V}$$

$$\frac{B \triangleright \mathit{false} \qquad E \triangleright V}{\mathit{cond}(B,T,E) \triangleright V}$$

Similarly, assuming that $\Gamma \longrightarrow F$ represents the judgement that F follows from a set of assumptions Γ, the logical content of a conjunction can be captured in the rule

$$\frac{\Gamma \longrightarrow P \qquad \Gamma \longrightarrow Q}{\Gamma \longrightarrow \mathit{and}(P,Q)}$$

Rules such as these can be used in combination with some control regimen determining their order of application to actually evaluate programs or to realize reasoning processes.

The appropriateness of a logic programming language for symbolic computation arises from the fact that it provides natural expression to both abstract syntax and rule based specifications. Thus, expressions of the form *cond(B,T,E)* and *and(P,Q)* are directly representable in such a language, being first-order terms. Depending on what they are being matched with, the unification operation relative to these terms provides a means for constructing, deconstructing or recognizing patterns in abstract syntax. Structural operational rules translate directly to program clauses. The evaluation rules for conditional expressions can, for instance, be represented by the clauses

eval(cond(B,T,E),V) :- eval(B,true), eval(T,V).
eval(cond(B,T,E),V) :- eval(B,false), eval(E,V).

Using these rules to realize interpretation may require capturing additional control information, but this can be done through the usual programming devices.

2.1 The Explicit Representation of Binding

Many syntactic objects involve a form of binding and it may sometimes be necessary to reflect this explicitly in their representation. Binding structure can be represented only in an approximate manner using conventional abstract syntax or first order terms. For example, consider the formula $\forall x P(x)$. This formula may be represented by the expression $all(x, P(x))$. However, this representation misses important characteristics of quantification. Thus, the equivalence of $\forall x P(x)$ and $\forall y P(y)$ is not immediately present in the 'first-order' rendition and has to be built in through auxiliary processes. In a related sense, suppose it is necessary to instantiate the outer quantifier in the formula $\forall x \exists y P(x, y)$ with the term $t(y)$. The renaming required in carrying out this operation has to be explicitly programmed under the indicated representation.

The availability of lambda terms in λProlog provides a different method for dealing with these issues. A binding operator has two different characteristics: it determines a scope and it identifies a particular kind of term. In λProlog, the latter role may be captured by a suitably chosen constructor while the effect of scope may be reflected into a (metalanguage) abstraction. This form of representation is one of the main components of the higher-order approach to abstract syntax. Using this approach, the formula $\forall x P(x)$ might be rendered into the term *(all λx(P x))*, where *all* is a constructor chosen to represent the predicative force of the universal quantifier; we employ an infix, curried notation for application here and below as is customary for higher-order languages, but the correspondence to the first-order syntax should be evident. Similarly, the program fragment

*lambda (x) if (x = 0) then (x - 2) else (2 * x)*

in a Lisp-like language might be represented by the term

(abs λx(cond (eq x 0) (minus x 2) (times 2 x)))

where *abs* is a constructor that identifies an object language abstraction and *eq*, *plus*, *minus*, *0*, and *2* are constructors corresponding to the relevant programming language primitives. As a final, more involve example, consider the following code in a functional programming language:

*fact m n = if (m = 0) then n else (fact (m - 1) (m * n))*

This code identifies *fact* as a function of two arguments that is defined through a fixed point construction. Towards making this structure explicit, the given program fragment may be rewritten as

fact = (fixpt (f) (lambda (m) lambda (n)
*if (m = 0) then n else (f (m - 1) (m * n))))*

assuming that *fixpt* represents a binding operator akin to *lambda*. Now, using the constructor *fix* to represent this operator and *app* to represent object language application, the expression that is identified with *fact* may be rendered into the following λProlog term:[2]

[2] We are taking liberties with λProlog syntax here: the language employs a different notation for abstraction and all expressions in it are typed. In a more precise presen-

$(fix\ \lambda f(abs\ \lambda m(abs\ \lambda n$
$\quad (cond\ (eq\ m\ 0)\ n\ (app\ (app\ f\ (minus\ m\ 1))\ (times\ m\ n)))))).$

The higher-order abstract syntax representation of binding structure solves the problems that were discussed relative to the first-order encoding. The formulas $\forall x P(x)$ and $\forall y P(y)$ translate to $(all\ \lambda x(P\ x))$ and $(all\ \lambda y(P\ y))$, but these are really the same terms by virtue of the understanding of α-conversion present in the metalanguage. Similarly, the instantiation of the quantifier in a formula represented by *(all P)* with the term represented by t is given simply by $(P\ t)$; the correct substitution, with all the necessary renaming operations, is realized from this through the β-conversion rule. The real power of this approach arises from the fact that the *same* principles apply to many other situations where binding is present. The encoding of programs, for instance, manifests an insensitivity to the names of function arguments by virtue of the same α-conversion rule. Alternatively, consider the task of evaluating functional programs. Using the notation $F[f{:=}T]$ to depict the logically correct substitution of T for f in F, one of the rules relevant to this is the following:

$$\frac{F[f{:=}(fixpt\ (f)\ F)] \rhd V}{(fixpt\ (f)\ F) \rhd V}$$

This rule can be encoded in the following λProlog clause:

```
(eval (fix F) V) :- (eval (F (fix F)) V).
```

The required substitution is, once again, realized via the β-conversion rule.

2.2 Structure Analysis using Higher-Order Unification

Another useful property of the higher-order abstract syntax representation is that the unification operation over it provides for sophisticated forms of structure analysis. This observation has been used previously by Huet and Lang in recognizing program properties [9]. Consider, for example, the term

$(fix\ \lambda f(abs\ \lambda m(abs\ \lambda n$
$\quad (cond\ (C\ m\ n)\ (T\ m\ n)\ (app\ (app\ f\ (E1\ m\ n))\ (E2\ m\ n))))))$

in which the symbols C, T, $E1$ and $E2$ represent variables that may be instantiated to obtain terms that correspond to actual programs. Thus, the program term corresponding to *fact* is obtained from this term through the substitution of $\lambda m\lambda n(eq\ m\ 0)$, $\lambda m\lambda n\ n$, $\lambda m\lambda n(minus\ m\ 1)$ and $\lambda m\lambda n(times\ m\ n)$ for these respective variables. However, the logic places a restriction on what constitute correct instantiations: these cannot be carried out by terms that contain variables that get bound by the abstractions pertaining to f, m or n. Any dependencies in the subparts governed by C, T, $E1$ and $E2$ on the enclosing abstractions must,

tation the user would, for instance, identify a new sort *tm* to correspond to program terms and *fix* and *abs* would be given the types $(tm \rightarrow tm) \rightarrow tm$. We elide these aspects for paucity of space, referring the reader to, e.g., [24] for such details.

therefore, be realized through the arguments of these variables. As a consequence of this requirement, the abstracted variable f must appear in exactly one place in any program term that matches with the 'template' being considered—as the head of the right arm of the conditional. It is easy to see that any program that corresponds to such a term must be tail recursive. The displayed term functions, in this sense, as a recognizer for tail recursive programs.

Unfortunately, the template displayed is very limited in its applicability: any program it matches with must have a conditional as a body, must not contain nested conditionals, must have no recursive calls in the left branch of the conditional and must have a right branch that consists entirely of a recursive call. There are programs that violate all these requirements while still being tail recursive. A more important observation is that the limitation is inherent in any recognition scheme that uses templates alone: since conditionals can be arbitrarily nested, no finite collection of templates can be provided that recognize all tail recursive programs and only these. However, there is a recursive description of the relevant class of program terms that can be captured in a finite set of program clauses. In particular, consider the following, assuming that symbols beginning with uppercase letters denote instantiatable variables:

1. A program is tail recursive if it contains no recursive calls and its representation can be recognized by the term $(fix\ \lambda f\,(abs\ \lambda m\,(abs\ \lambda n\,(H\ m\ n))))$.
2. A program that consists solely of a recursive call with possibly modified arguments is also tail-recursive and its representation must match with the term $(fix\ \lambda f\,(abs\ \lambda m\,(abs\ \lambda n\,(app\ (app\ f\ (E1\ m\ n))\ (E2\ m\ n)))))$.
3. Finally, a program is tail-recursive if its body consists of a conditional in which there is no recursive call in the test and whose left and right branches themselves satisfy the requirements of tail-recursiveness. The representation of only such a program unifies with the term

   $$(fix\ \lambda f\,(abs\ \lambda m\,(abs\ \lambda n\,(cond\ (C\ m\ n)\ (T\ f\ m\ n)\ (E\ f\ m\ n)))))$$

   and in a way such that, under the instantiations determined for T and E,

   $$(fix\ \lambda f\,(abs\ \lambda m\,(abs\ \lambda n\,(T\ f\ m\ n))))\ \text{and}\ (fix\ \lambda f\,(abs\ \lambda m\,(abs\ \lambda n\,(E\ f\ m\ n))))$$

   represent tail-recursive programs.

These observations provide a complete characterization of the criterion for tail recursiveness under consideration, and they translate immediately into the following λProlog program:

```
(tailrec (fix λf (abs λm (abs λn (H m n))))).
(tailrec (fix λf (abs λm (abs λn (app (app f (E1 m n)) (E2 m n)))))).
(tailrec (fix λf (abs λm (abs λn (cond (C m n) (T f m n) (E f m n)))))) :-
      (tailrec (fix λf (abs λm (abs λn (T f m n))))),
      (tailrec (fix λf (abs λm (abs λn (E f m n))))).
```

Given a program term *Prog*, we can determine whether or not this represents a tail recursive program through a query of the form

?- *tailrec Prog.*

Higher-order unification will play an important computational role in this recognition task. In particular, this operation will determine which of the terms in the heads of the clauses matches an incoming program term and, in the case of the last clause, will also aid in destructuring and subsequently constructing terms needed in the recursive calls.

2.3 Recursion over Binding Structure

The program for recognizing tail recursiveness just discussed has an obvious defect: it is applicable only to *binary* recursive functions. A question to ask is if we can write a program to carry out such a recognition over *arbitrary* arity functions. Templates are not going to be very useful in this task since these must already anticipate the number of arguments for the function in their structure. A general solution to the problem must instead embody a systematic method for descending under the abstraction corresponding to each function argument; this method can then be applied as many times as is needed in any particular instance before conducting an analysis over the function body.

The scoping primitives present in λProlog provide a means for realizing the necessary recursion over binding structure. The overall computation may, in fact, be structured as follows: The expression that has to be dealt with at the outset has the form *(fix* $\lambda f F$*)*. The objective in this case is to ensure that the free occurrences of f in F are all of a properly restricted kind. Such a check can be carried out by introducing a new constant c, annotating this constant so that it can be easily identified later, replacing all free occurrences of f in F with c and analyzing the resulting structure. A *generic* goal can be used to introduce the needed constant, its annotation can be realized by using an *augment* goal to make a special predicate true of this constant and substitution can be realized by application. At the next step, the expression encountered is of the form *(abs* $\lambda x B$*)*. The objective now is to analyze B, noting that x may appear freely within this structure. Towards this end, a new constant may be temporarily added to the signature of the object language, the free occurrences of x in B may be replaced with this constant and the resulting term may be further examined. These computations can, once again, be realized using a *generic* and an *augment* goal and function application. After a few repetitions of this step, the 'body' of the function would be reached. This is essentially a first-order structure the needed recursive analysis over which can be specified through Horn clauses.

Assuming a definition for the predicate *term* that allows it to recognize terms corresponding to programs in the object language, the ideas just described translate into the following λProlog program:

(tailrec (fix M)) :- $\forall f$*((recfn f)* => *(trfn (M f)))*.
(trfn (abs R)) :- $\forall x$*((term x)* => *(trfn (R x)))*.
(trfn B) :- *(trbody B)*.
(trbody (cond C M N)) :- *(term C), (trbody M), (trbody N)*.

(trbody M) :- (recfn M).
(trbody (app M N)) :- (trbody M), (term N).

The computation resulting from a use of the above clauses actually mimics the way the recognition task would have been structured had a conventional abstract syntax representation been used. In such a case, it would still be necessary to traverse the body of the function definition, checking the apparent uses of recursion. The advantage with the higher-order abstract syntax style of programming is that tedious bookkeeping steps—such as recording the function name and identifying its free occurrences—receive a simple and logically precise treatment. The practical use of this approach depends, of course, on how efficiently the features supporting it can be realized. In the computation being considered, for example, several substitutions are performed over the function body by forming and contracting beta redexes. Carrying out these substitutions eagerly will result in several walks over the body of the function. Acceptable efficiency is dependent on mechanisms for delaying these substitutions so that they can performed in the same walk that analyzes the function body.

The ideas that we have discussed in this section are quite general in their applicability and they have, amongst other things, been used in encoding computations that arise in theorem proving and manipulation of proofs [2,6], type checking [13] and the specification of programming language semantics [7]. Moreover, the features that support these ideas have also been widely exploited relative to the metalanguage Elf [30] and its successor Twelf [32]. Thus, the programming benefits of these features seem to be significant, making questions of their implementability important ones to address.

3 Implementation Issues and Their Resolution

The computational model underlying λProlog shares many features with the one used for Prolog: the goal to be solved at intermediate stages typically consists of a sequence of simpler ones, there may be choices in clauses to use in solving atomic goals and unification provides the basis for matching an atomic goal with the head of a clause. Logic programming implementations embody mechanisms for dealing with all these aspects: sequential goal structure is realized with structure sharing using environment records and pointers to continuation code, a stack of choice point records is used to succinctly record alternative paths that may be followed on backtracking, the static information present in clause heads is used to compile significant parts of the unification computation and an understanding of how data may become redundant is used to manage the allocation and reclamation of space. Much of this methodology is applicable to λProlog as well. However, there are differences in detail. Considering only the features of the language presently of interest, terms with a richer structure have to be represented, a more sophisticated unification computation has to be realized and different signatures and programs may be relevant to the solution of distinct atomic goals. We discuss the new concerns that arise from these aspects below and outline approaches to their proper treatment within the broader framework.

3.1 Representation of Lambda Terms

The usual requirement of a representation for lambda terms is that this support the operation of β-reduction efficiently. Our special use of these as data structures raises additional concerns. Since it may be necessary to compare or destructure terms during execution, their intensions must be easy to access at run-time. At a logical level, two terms are considered to be equal if they differ only in the names of bound variables. The underlying representation must, therefore, support the rapid determination of α-convertibility. With respect to β-reduction, it is desirable to be able to perform substitutions arising from this operation lazily and also to be able to combine several such substitutions so that they can be performed in the same walk over term structure. Functional programming language implementations embody a simple solution to this problem, and also to questions of α-convertibility, but one that gives up an ability that is important in our context: that of examining structure within abstraction contexts.

Explicit substitution notations for lambda calculi that build on the de Bruijn method for eliminating bound variable names provide the conceptual basis for an adequate treatment of these representational questions. A popular version of such a notation is the $\lambda\sigma$-calculus [1]. Our implementation of λProlog uses a different version called the *suspension notation* [21, 28] that we believe is better suited to actual implementation. There are three categories of expressions in this notation that are referred to as terms, environments and environment terms and are given by the following syntax rules:

$$\begin{array}{lll} \langle Term \rangle & ::= & \langle Cons \rangle \mid \langle Var \rangle \mid \#\langle Index \rangle \mid (\langle Term \rangle\ \langle Term \rangle) \mid \\ & & (\lambda \langle Term \rangle) \mid [\![\langle Term \rangle, \langle Nat \rangle, \langle Nat \rangle, \langle Env \rangle]\!] \\ \langle Env \rangle & ::= & nil \mid \langle ETerm \rangle :: \langle Env \rangle \\ \langle ETerm \rangle & ::= & @\langle Nat \rangle \mid (\langle Term \rangle, \langle Nat \rangle) \end{array}$$

In these rules, $\langle Cons \rangle$ and $\langle Var \rangle$ represent constructors and instantiatable variables, $\langle Index \rangle$ is the category of positive numbers and $\langle Nat \rangle$ is the category of natural numbers. Terms correspond to lambda terms. In keeping with the de Bruijn scheme, $\#i$ corresponds to a variable bound by the ith abstraction looking back from the occurrence. The expression $[\![t, ol, nl, e]\!]$, referred to as a *suspension*, constitutes a new form of terms that encodes a term with a 'suspended' substitution: intuitively, this corresponds to the term t whose first ol variables have to be substituted for in the way determined by e and whose remaining bound variables have to be renumbered to reflect the fact that t used to appear within ol abstractions but now appears within nl of them. Nominally, the elements of an environment either indicate the retention of an abstraction or are terms generated by a contraction. However, to encode the renumbering of indices needed during substitution, these are annotated by a relevant abstraction level.

In addition to the syntactic expressions, the suspension notation includes a collection of rewrite rule schemata whose purpose is to simulate β-reduction. These schemata are presented in Figure 1. Of these, the ones labelled (β_s) and (β_s') generate the substitutions corresponding to the β-contraction rule on de

(β_s) $((\lambda t_1)\ t_2) \to [\![t_1, 1, 0, (t_2, 0) :: nil]\!]$

(β_s') $((\lambda [\![t_1, ol+1, nl+1, @nl :: e]\!])\ t_2) \to [\![t_1, ol+1, nl, (t_2, nl) :: e]\!]$

(r1) $[\![c, ol, nl, e]\!] \to c$, provided c is a constant.

(r2) $[\![x, ol, nl, e]\!] \to x$, provided x is a free variable.

(r3) $[\![\#i, 0, nl, nil]\!] \to \#(i + nl)$.

(r4) $[\![\#1, ol, nl, @l :: e]\!] \to \#(nl - l)$.

(r5) $[\![\#1, ol, nl, (t, l) :: e]\!] \to [\![t, 0, nl - l, nil]\!]$.

(r6) $[\![\#i, ol, nl, et :: e]\!] \to [\![\#(i-1), ol-1, nl, e]\!]$, provided $i > 1$.

(r7) $[\![(t_1\ t_2), ol, nl, e]\!] \to ([\![t_1, ol, nl, e]\!]\ [\![t_2, ol, nl, e]\!])$.

(r8) $[\![(\lambda t), ol, nl, e]\!] \to (\lambda [\![t, ol+1, nl+1, @nl :: e]\!])$.

Fig. 1. Rule schemata for rewriting terms in the suspension notation

Bruijn terms and the rules (r1)-(r8), referred to as the *reading rules*, serve to actually carry out these substitutions. The (β_s') schema has a special place in the calculus: it is the only one that makes possible the combination of substitutions arising from different β-contractions.

Unification and other comparison operations on terms require these to be first reduced to *head-normal forms*, i.e. to terms that have the structure

$$(\lambda \ldots (\lambda (\ldots (h\ t_1)\ \ldots\ t_m)) \ldots)$$

where h, called the head of the term, is a constant, a de Bruijn index or an instantiatable variable. By exploiting the atomic nature of the rules in Figure 1, it is possible to describe a stack based procedure to realize reduction to such a form [20] and to embed this procedure and its use naturally into the structure of a logic programming implementation [23]. Furthermore, the rewriting order can be arranged so as to exploit the (β_s') schema to combine all the substitutions that need to be performed on a term into a single environment. Following this course has measurable advantages: in preliminary studies we have observed benefits in time from following this course as opposed to never using the (β_s') schema that range from 25% to 500% over the entire computation.

We mention a few other salient issues relating to term representation. One of these relates to the internal encoding of applications. With reference to the head-normal form just displayed, there is a choice between representing the subterm under the abstractions as m iterations of applications as the curried presentation indicates or as one application with m arguments. There are practical advantages to the latter: access to the head, with which most structure examination begins, is immediate, the arguments, over which operations have to typically be iterated, are available as a vector and a close parallel to the WAM representation can be used for first-order terms. Our implementation of λProlog therefore uses this representation. In the realization of reduction, there is a choice between destructive, graph-based, rewriting and a copying based one. The former seems to be conservative in both space and time and can be realized using a value trailing mechanism within a WAM-like scheme. Finally, the terms in the suspension notation can be annotated in a way that indicates whether or not substitutions generated by contracting external β-redexes can affect them. These annotations can permit reading steps to be carried out trivially in certain cases, leading also to a conservation of space and, possibly, a greater sharing in graph-based reduction. Benefits such as these have been noted to be significant in practice [3], a fact confirmed also by our early studies using the *Teyjus* system.

3.2 Supporting Higher-Order Unification

The framework for organizing the unification computation relating to lambda terms is given by a procedure due to Huet [8].[3] This procedure considers a set of pairs of terms of the same type with the objective of making the two terms in each pair identical; the set is called a disagreement set and each pair in it is a disagreement pair. Progress towards a solution is made by the repeated application of two different kinds of steps, both of which are based on the normal forms of the terms in a chosen disagreement pair. Referring to a term as flexible if the head of its head-normal form is an instantiatable variable and rigid otherwise, the first kind of step is one that simplifies a pair of rigid-rigid terms. In particular, if the normal forms of these terms are

$$(\lambda \ldots (\lambda (\ldots (h_1\ t_1)\ \ldots\ t_m)) \ldots) \text{ and } (\lambda \ldots (\lambda (\ldots (h_2\ s_1)\ \ldots\ s_n)) \ldots),$$

where the abstractions at the front have been arranged to be of equal length possibly by using the η-conversion rule, the simplification step concludes that no unifiers exist if h_1 and h_2 are distinct and replaces the pair with the pairs $\langle t_1, s_1 \rangle, \ldots, \langle t_m, s_m \rangle$ otherwise; we note that if h_1 and h_2 are identical, typing constraints that we have left implicit up to this point dictate that $n = m$. The second kind of step deals with a flexible-rigid disagreement pair and it posits a finite set of substitutions for the variable at the head of the normal form of the flexible term that might be tried towards unifying the two terms. All substitutions must be tried for completeness, leading to a unification process that in general has a branching character.

A useful special case of the application of the simplification step is the one where there are no abstractions at the front of the normal forms of the terms in the disagreement pair. In this situation, this step is similar to the term simplification carried out in first-order unification. Further, when one of the terms is known ahead of time, the repeated application of the step to the pair and, subsequently, to the pairs of subterms it produces can actually be compiled. Finally, if the instantiatable variables within terms appear not as the heads of applications but, rather, as leaves, the simplification process either indicates non-unifiability or produces a disagreement set in which at least one element or each pair is a variable. A generalization of the occurs-check procedure of first-order unification

[3] Huet's original procedure pertains to unifying the *simply typed* lambda terms that are used in λProlog. However, its structure has been utilized for unifying lambda terms with other typing regimens as well.

usually succeeds in the latter case in determining non-unifiability or in finding a most general unifier. The empirical study in [14] concludes that a large percentage of the terms encountered in a λProlog-like language fit the 'first-order' description just considered. Unification of these terms can be treated efficiently and deterministically and it is important to reflect this into an implementation.

There are other situations in which determinism in unification can be recognized and exploited and many of these are embedded in the *Teyjus* system. However, a full treatment of higher-order unification has to eventually contend with branching and structures are needed to realize a depth-first, backtracking based search. The information that is needed for trying a different substitution for a flexible-rigid disagreement pair at a later time can be divided into two parts. One part corresponds to resetting program state to a point prior to making a choice in substitution; in a WAM-oriented model, this includes the values in the argument registers, the program pointer and the continuation pointer. The other part contains information for generating as yet untried substitutions and, if these are unsuccessful, for finding earlier backtracking possibilities. The computation model that is used in λProlog attempts to solve unification problems as completely as is possible before returning to goal simplification. In light of this, the state component of backtracking information will likely be common to more than one unification branch point. A representation and processing scheme can be designed that takes advantage of this situation to create only one record of the state information that is subsequently shared between all the relevant branch point records.

The disagreement set representing a unification problem consists in certain situations of only flexible-flexible pairs. While solutions can be proposed for such problems, this cannot be done without significant redundancy. The most prudent course, therefore, is to treat such sets as constraints on the solution process that are to be resolved when they get more refined. An explicit representation of disagreement sets is necessary for realizing this strategy. The following factors affect the design of a satisfactory representation for this purpose:

1. Disagreement sets change incrementally: they change when substitutions are made for variables, but these typically affect only a few pairs. For this reason, in representing a newly generated set it would be best if unchanged portions of the old set were reused.
2. Backtracking may require a return to a disagreement set that was in existence at some earlier computation point. For efficiency reasons, it should be possible to achieve such a reinstatement rapidly.

Both requirements can be met by using a heap-based doubly linked list representation for the set. The removal of a pair from this list can be realized by modifying pointers in the elements that appear before and after it. For backtracking purposes, it suffices to trail a pointer to the pair. To minimize bookkeeping, the addition of new pairs as a result of simplification must be done conservatively. Structures that may be used to support this are described in [23].

3.3 Realizing Generic Goals

The treatment of generic goals on the surface appears to be quite simple: whenever such a goal is encountered, we simply generate a new constant, instantiate the goal with this and solve the resulting goal using the usual logic programming mechanisms. The problem, however, is that scope restrictions have also to be honored. To understand the specific issues, consider the situation in which the program consists of the single clause $\forall x(p\ x\ x)$ and the desire is to solve the goal $\exists y \forall z(p\ y\ z)$. Using the usual treatment of existential goals in logic programming and the suggested one for generic goals, the given goal reduces to one of the form $(p\ Y\ c)$ where c is a new constant and Y is an instantiatable variable. The attempt to solve this atomic goal must now take recourse to matching it with the program clause. If the usual notion of unification is used for this purpose, success will result with Y being bound to c. The problem is that this success is not legitimate since the binding for Y allows the new constant to escape out of its scope. Unification must therefore be constrained to prevent such solutions.

The usual logical method for capturing restrictions arising out of quantifier scope is to instantiate universal quantifiers not with new constants but with Skolem functions of the existential quantifiers whose scope they appear within; occurs-check in unification then prevents illegal bindings of the sort just discussed. There is a dual to Skolemization called raising [16] that applies to higher-order logics and this has, in fact, been used in some λProlog implementations. Unfortunately, the logic underlying λProlog is such that the needed Skolem functions (and their duals) cannot be statically determined [19, 34], requiring lists of existential variables to be carried around and used in constructing the needed functions at runtime. Such a scheme is difficult to implement at a low level and certainly cannot be embedded well in an abstract machine.

There is, however, an alternative way to view the instantiation restrictions [19] that does admit an elegant implementation. The central idea is to think of the term universe as being constructed in levels, each new level being determined by a generic goal that is dynamically encountered. Thus, suppose we are given the goal $\exists x \forall y(p\ (f\ x)\ a\ y)$ and that our signature initially consists of only the constructors f and a. The collection of terms at the first level consists of only those that can be built using f and a. Processing the existential quantifier in the given goal reduces it one of the form $\forall y(p\ (f\ X)\ a\ y)$, where X is a new instantiatable variable. Treating the generic goal now introduces a new constant c and transforms the goal to be solved into $(p\ (f\ X)\ a\ c)$. However, c and all the terms that contain it belong to the second level in the term universe. Furthermore, X can only be instantiated with terms belonging to the first level. A way to encode these constraints is to label constants and variables with level numbers. For a constant, this denotes the stage at which it enters the term universe. For a variable, the label determines the level by which a term must be in the universe for it to constitute a legal instantiation.

An implementation of this scheme amounts to the following. A designated universe level is associated with each computation point and is maintained in a special register. A generic goal increments this register on entry and decrements it on exit; special instructions can realize these effects in a compilation model. Constants and variables that result from generic and existential goals are labelled with the existing universe level at their point of creation. These labels are used whenever a variable needs to be bound during unification. At this time, an occurs-check process ensures that the binding is consummated only if no constant in the instantiation term has a higher label value than that of the variable. The same process also modifies the label on variables in the term to have a value no higher than that on the one being instantiated. This is needed to ensure that refinements to the instantiation term also respect the relevant constraints.

3.4 Realizing Augment Goals

Augment goals have the effect of parameterizing the solution of each goal in a sequence by a program. In a sequential implementation, this parameterization can be realized by modifying a central program as computation proceeds. Note that the program may have to change not only as a result of commencing or completing an augment goal, but also as a result of backtracking. From the perspective of efficient implementation, the following are important: Programs should have succinct descriptions that can be recorded easily in choice points. The addition of code upon entering an augment goal should be rapid as also the removal of code. Access to procedure definitions operative at any point in computation should be fast. Finally, compilation of predicate definitions that appear in augment goals should be possible.

We outline here the scheme developed in [22] for realizing all these requirements. The essence of this scheme is in viewing a program as a composite of compiled code and a layered access function to this code, with each augment goal causing a new layer to be added to an existing access function. Thus, consider a goal of the form $(C_1 \wedge \ldots \wedge C_n) \supset G$ where, for $1 \leq i \leq n$, C_i is a program clause with no free variables; this is not the most general situation that needs to be treated, and we will discuss the fully general case shortly. This goal requires the clauses $C_1, \ldots, C_n$ to be added to (the front of) the program before an attempt is made to solve G. Now, these clauses can be treated as an independent program fragment and compiled as such. Let us suppose that the clauses define the predicates $p_1, \ldots, p_r$. Compilation then produces a segment of code with r entry points, each indexed by the name of a predicate. In addition, we require compilation to generate a procedure that we call $find\_code$ that performs the following function: given a predicate name, it returns the appropriate entry point in the code segment if the name is one of $p_1, \ldots, p_r$ and fails otherwise.[4] The execution of the augment goal results in a new access function that behaves as follows. Given a predicate name, $find\_code$ is invoked with it. If this function succeeds, then the code location that it produces is the desired result. Otherwise the code location is determined by using the access function in existence earlier.

[4] In the *Teyjus* implementation, $find\_code$ amounts to pointers to a generic search function and a hash-table or a binary search tree.

The described method for enhancing program context is incomplete in one respect: rather than constituting completely new definitions, the clauses provided for $p_1, \ldots, p_r$ may be adding to existing definitions for some of these predicates. Given this, compilation must produce code for each of these predicates that, instead of failing eventually, looks for code for the predicate using the access function existing earlier. Assuming that the last lookup occurs more than once, its effect may be precomputed. In particular, we may associate a vector of size r with the augment goal, the ith entry of which corresponds to the predicate p_i. One of the actions to be performed on entering the augment goal is then that of using the existing access function with each of the predicates to place pointers to the relevant entry points into this vector.

In a WAM-like implementation, the layered access function can be realized through a structure called an *implication point record* that is allocated on the local stack and that stores the following items:

1. a pointer to an enclosing implication point record representing the previous access function,
2. the *find_code* procedure for the antecedent of the augment goal,
3. a positive integer r indicating the number of predicates defined by the program clauses in the antecedent, and
4. a vector of size r that indicates the next clause to try for each of the predicates defined in the antecedent of the augment goal.

The program context at any stage is completely characterized by a pointer to an implication point record that may be stored in a specially designated *program register*. The goal $(C_1 \wedge \ldots \wedge C_n) \supset G$ may be compiled into code of the form

push_impl_point t
  { Compiled code for G }
pop_impl_point

where *push_impl_point* and *pop_impl_point* are special instructions that realize the beginning and ending actions of an augment goal and t is the address of a statically created table that stores the *find_code* function for this augment goal and also the numbers and names of the predicates defined. The *push_impl_point* instruction uses its table parameter and the program register to create a new implication point record in an entirely obvious way. The *pop_impl_point* instruction restores the old program context by using the pointer to the enclosing implication point record stored in the one currently pointed to by the program register.

The scheme that we have discussed provides for a particularly simple realization of backtracking behavior as it concerns program context. Since this is given at any point by the contents of the program register, saving these contents in a choice point record at the time of its creation and retaining implication point records embedded under choice points ensures the availability of all the information that is needed for context switching.

The structure we have assumed for augment goals up to this point embodies a simplification. In the most general case, a goal of the form $(C_1 \wedge \ldots \wedge C_n) \supset G$

may appear within the scope of universal quantifiers and the C_is may contain free, non-local, variables. Non-local variables can be treated by viewing a program clause as a combination of compiled code and a binding environment—in effect, as a *closure*—in the scheme described and leaving other details unchanged. Universal quantification over procedure names can lead to two different improvements. First, it may be possible to translate calls to such procedures from within G into a transfer of control to a fixed address rather than to one that is determined dynamically by the procedure $find\_code$. Second, the definitions of such procedures within $(C_1 \wedge \ldots \wedge C_n)$ cannot be extended, leading to a determinism that can be exploited in compiling these definitions and obviating entries for such procedures in the next clause vector stored in implication points.

4 The Teyjus System

The full λProlog language includes a typing regimen [26], facilities for conventional higher-order programming [24] and a modules notion for structuring large programs [17] in addition to the features considered in this paper. A curious aspect about the types in the language is that they influence computations. They must, therefore, be present during execution and efficient methods are needed for constructing and carrying them around. In work not discussed here, we have addressed the implementation problems that arise from these other features [10, 23, 27] and have incorporated all our ideas into a virtual machine for λProlog.

An implementation of λProlog based on our ideas envisages four software subsystems: a compiler, a loader, an emulator for the virtual machine and a user interface. The function of the compiler is to process any given module of λProlog code, to certify its internal consistency and to ensure that it satisfies a promise determined by an associated signature and, finally, to translate it into a byte code form consisting of a 'header' part relevant to realizing module interactions and a 'body' containing sequences of instructions that can be run on the virtual machine. The purpose of the loader is to read in byte code files for modules, to resolve names and absolute addresses using the information in the header parts of these files and to eventually produce a structure consisting of a block of code together with information for linking this code into a program context when needed. The emulator provides the capability of executing such code after it has been linked. Finally, the user interface allows for a flexibility in the compilation, loading and use of modules in an interactive session.

The *Teyjus* system embodies all the above components and comprises about 50,000 lines of C code. The functionality outlined above is realized in its entirety in a development environment. Also supported is the use of the compiler on the one hand and the loader and emulator on the other in standalone mode. The system architecture actually makes byte code files fully portable. Thus, λProlog modules can be distributed in byte code form, to be executed later using only the loader/emulator. The source code for the system and associated documentation is available from the URL `http://teyjus.cs.umn.edu/`.

5 Conclusion

We have discussed the use and implementation of features of λProlog that provide support for a higher-order approach to abstract syntax. We believe that there are many promising applications for these features, an observation that is accentuated by the extensive use that has been made recently of λProlog and the related language Twelf in prototyping experiments related to the proof-carrying code paradigm. The research we have described here also encompasses issues that are of broad interest to logic programming: matters related to typing, modular development of code and richer notions of equality between terms are important to other interpretations of this paradigm as well and the implementation ideas that we have developed should find applicability in these contexts.

Considerable work remains to be done relative to the *Teyjus* system. Many design choices have been made with little empirical guidance in this first implementation and it is important now to understand their practical implications and to refine them as needed. One category of choices concerns the representation of lambda terms. Explicit substitution notations provide only a framework for this and an actual realization has to address many additional issues such as sharing and optimality in reduction [11, 12], the extent of laziness and destructive versus non-destructive realization. Another possibility not discussed at all here is that of lifting higher-order unification directly to such a notation [5]. Doing this simplifies the construction and application of substitutions but also necessitates bookkeeping steps that may be difficult to realize well in a virtual machine. The *Teyjus* system provides a means to study the pragmatic impact of such choices, a matter often downplayed in theoretical studies related to the lambda calculus. Along another direction, it appears important to improve on the module system and its realization so that it offers stronger support for separate compilation, permits dynamic linking and can be used as a basis for interfacing with foreign code. Another issue relates to garbage collection. The memory management built into a WAM-like implementation has its limitations and these are especially exposed by our use of the heap in carrying out β-reductions in the *Teyjus* system. An auxiliary system therefore needs to be designed to reclaim disused space. A final question concerns the kind of support to provide for higher-order unification. The present realization of this operation uses a branching search but it may be possible to finesse this, using the ideas in [15] as is done in the Twelf system. Following this course has the additional advantage that the use of types can be limited to compile-time checking, leading to a significant simplification of the virtual machine structure.

We are addressing these and other related questions in ongoing research. We also mention here that λProlog has received other implementations, one of these being the *Prolog/Mali* system [4, 33]. Preliminary experiments with this system indicate a complementary behavior to that of *Teyjus*, with the former being more adept in the treatment of first-order computations and the latter with that of higher-order abstract syntax. This matter needs to be understood better and, where possible, the ideas in *Prolog/Mali* need to be exploited towards enhanced overall performance.

6 Acknowledgements

B. Jayaraman, K. Kwon and D.S. Wilson assisted in the design of the λProlog abstract machine and L. Headley, D.J. Mitchell, S.-M. Perng and G. Tong helped in the implementation of the *Teyjus* system. Support for this work has been provided by NSF at different stages under the grants CCR-8905825, CCR-9208465, CCR-9596119, CCR-9803849 and CCR-0096322.

References

1. M. Abadi, L. Cardelli, P.-L. Curien, and J.-J. Lévy. Explicit substitutions. *Journal of Functional Programming*, 1(4):375–416, 1991.
2. A. W. Appel and A. P. Felty. Lightweight lemmas in λProlog. In *International Conference on Logic Programming*, pages 411–425. MIT Press, November 1999.
3. P. Brisset and O. Ridoux. Naive reverse can be linear. In K. Furukawa, editor, *Eighth International Logic Programming Conference*, pages 857–870. MIT Press, June 1991.
4. P. Brisset and O. Ridoux. The compilation of λProlog and its execution with MALI. Publication Interne 687, IRISA, 1992.
5. G. Dowek, T. Hardin, and C. Kirchner. Higher-order unification via explicit substitutions. *Information and Computation*, 157:183–235, 2000.
6. A. Felty. Implementing tactics and tacticals in a higher-order logic programming language. *Journal of Automated Reasoning*, 11(1):43–81, August 1993.
7. J. Hannan and D. Miller. From operational semantics to abstract machines. *Mathematical Structures in Computer Science*, 2(4):415–459, 1992.
8. G. Huet. A unification algorithm for typed λ-calculus. *Theoretical Computer Science*, 1:27–57, 1975.
9. G. Huet and B. Lang. Proving and applying program transformations expressed with second-order patterns. *Acta Informatica*, 11:31–55, 1978.
10. K. Kwon, G. Nadathur, and D.S. Wilson. Implementing polymorphic typing in a logic programming language. *Computer Languages*, 20(1):25–42, 1994.
11. J. Lamping. An algorithm for optimal lambda calculus reduction. In *Seventeenth Annual ACM Symposium on Principles of Programming Languages*, pages 16–30. ACM Press, 1990.
12. J.-J. Lévy. Optimal reductions in the lambda-calculus. In J.P. Seldin and J.R. Hindley, editors, *To H.B. Curry: Essays on Combinatory Logic, Lambda Calculus and Formalism*, pages 159–191. Academic Press, 1980.
13. C. Liang. Let-polymorphism and eager type schemes. In *TAPSOFT '97: Theory and Practice of Software Development*, pages 490–501. Springer Verlag LNCS Vol. 1214, 1997.
14. S. Michaylov and F. Pfenning. An empirical study of the runtime behavior of higher-order logic programs. In D. Miller, editor, *Proceedings of the Workshop on the λProlog Programming Language*, pages 257–271, July 1992. Available as University of Pennsylvania Technical Report MS-CIS-92-86.
15. D. Miller. A logic programming language with lambda-abstraction, function variables, and simple unification. *Journal of Logic and Computation*, 1(4):497–536, 1991.
16. D. Miller. Unification under a mixed prefix. *Journal of Symbolic Computation*, 14:321–358, 1992.

17. D. Miller. A proposal for modules in λProlog. In R. Dyckhoff, editor, *Proceedings of the 1993 Workshop on Extensions to Logic Programming*, pages 206–221. Springer-Verlag, 1994. Volume 798 of Lecture Notes in Computer Science.
18. D. Miller, G. Nadathur, F. Pfenning, and A. Scedrov. Uniform proofs as a foundation for logic programming. *Annals of Pure and Applied Logic*, 51:125–157, 1991.
19. G. Nadathur. A proof procedure for the logic of hereditary Harrop formulas. *Journal of Automated Reasoning*, 11(1):115–145, August 1993.
20. G. Nadathur. An explicit substitution notation in a λProlog implementation. Technical Report TR-98-01, Department of Computer Science, University of Chicago, January 1998.
21. G. Nadathur. A fine-grained notation for lambda terms and its use in intensional operations. *Journal of Functional and Logic Programming*, 1999(2), March 1999.
22. G. Nadathur, B. Jayaraman, and K. Kwon. Scoping constructs in logic programming: Implementation problems and their solution. *Journal of Logic Programming*, 25(2):119–161, November 1995.
23. G. Nadathur, B. Jayaraman, and D.S. Wilson. Implementation considerations for higher-order features in logic programming. Technical Report CS-1993-16, Department of Computer Science, Duke University, June 1993.
24. G. Nadathur and D. Miller. Higher-order logic programming. In D. Gabbay, C. Hogger, and A. Robinson, editors, *Handbook of Logic in Artificial Intelligence and Logic Programming*, volume 5, pages 499–590. Oxford University Press, 1998.
25. G. Nadathur and D.J. Mitchell. System description: Teyjus—a compiler and abstract machine based implementation of λProlog. In H. Ganzinger, editor, *Automated Deduction–CADE-16*, number 1632 in Lecture Notes in Artificial Intelligence, pages 287–291. Springer-Verlag, July 1999.
26. G. Nadathur and F. Pfenning. The type system of a higher-order logic programming language. In F. Pfenning, editor, *Types in Logic Programming*, pages 245–283. MIT Press, 1992.
27. G. Nadathur and G. Tong. Realizing modularity in λProlog. *Journal of Functional and Logic Programming*, 1999(9), April 1999.
28. G. Nadathur and D. S. Wilson. A notation for lambda terms: A generalization of environments. *Theoretical Computer Science*, 198(1-2):49–98, 1998.
29. G.C. Necula. Proof-carrying code. In *24th Annual ACM Symposium on Principles of Programming Languages*, pages 106–119. ACM Press, January 1997.
30. F. Pfenning. Logic programming in the LF logical framework. In G. Huet and G.D. Plotkin, editors, *Logical Frameworks*, pages 149–181. Cambridge University Press, 1991.
31. F. Pfenning and C. Elliott. Higher-order abstract syntax. In *Proceedings of the ACM-SIGPLAN Conference on Programming Language Design and Implementation*, pages 199–208. ACM Press, June 1988.
32. F. Pfenning and C. Schürmann. System description: Twelf — a meta-logical framework for deductive systems. In H. Ganzinger, editor, *Proceedings of the 16th International Conference on Automated Deduction (CADE-16)*, pages 202–206, Trento, Italy, July 1999. Springer-Verlag LNAI 1632.
33. O. Ridoux. MALIv06: Tutorial and reference manual. Publication Interne 611, IRISA, 1991.
34. N. Shankar. Proof search in the intuitionistic sequent calculus. In D. Kapur, editor, *Automated Deduction – CADE-11*, number 607 in Lecture Notes in Computer Science, pages 522–536. Springer Verlag, June 1992.
35. D.H.D. Warren. An abstract Prolog instruction set. Technical Note 309, SRI International, October 1983.

A Scalable Architecture for Proof-Carrying Code

George C. Necula

Department of Electrical Engineering and Computer Sciences
University of California, Berkeley, CA 94720, USA
necula@cs.berkeley.edu

Abstract. Proof-Carrying Code (PCC) is a general mechanism for verifying that a code fragment can be executed safely on a host system. The key technical detail that makes PCC simple yet very powerful is that the code fragment is required to be accompanied by a detailed and precise explanation of how it satisfies the safety policy. This leaves the code receiver with the simple task of verifying that the explanation is correct and that it matches the code in question.
Previous implementations of PCC used safety explanations in the form of explicit formal proofs of code safety, thus gaining leverage from a substantial amount of previous research in the area of proof representation and checking, but at the expense of poor scalability due to large proof sizes. In this paper we describe a series of changes that are necessary to achieve a truly scalable architecture for PCC. These include a new proof representation form along with a better integration of the various components of a PCC checker. We also present experimental results that show this architecture to be effective for checking the type safety of even very large programs expressed as machine code.

1 Introduction

More an more software systems are designed and build to be extensible and configurable dynamically. The proportion of extensions can range from a software upgrade, to a third-party add-on or component, to an applet. On another dimension, the trust relationship with the producer of the extension code can range from completely trusted, to believed-not-malicious, to completely unknown and untrusted. In such a diverse environment there is a need for a general mechanism that can be used to allow even untrusted system extensions to be integrated into an existing software system without compromising the stability and security of the host system.

Proof-Carrying Code (PCC) [NL96, Nec97] was designed to be a *general* mechanism that allows the receiver of code (referred to as the **host**) to check

This research was supported in part by the National Science Foundation Grants No. CCR-9875171, CCR-0085949 and CCR-0081588 and by gifts from AT&T and Microsoft Corporation. The information presented here does not necessarily reflect the position or the policy of the Government and no official endorsement should be inferred.

H. Kuchen and K. Ueda (Eds.): FLOPS 2001, LNCS 2024, pp. 21–39, 2001.

quickly and *easily* that the code (referred to as the **agent**) has certain safety properties. The key technical detail that makes PCC very general yet very simple is a requirement that the agent producer cooperates with the host by attaching to the agent code an "explanation" of why the agent complies with the safety policy. Then all that the host has to do to ensure the safe execution of the agent is to define a framework in which the "explanation" must be conducted, along with a simple yet sufficiently strong mechanism for checking that (a) the explanation is acceptable (i.e., is within the established framework), that (b) the explanation pertains to the safety policy that the host wishes to enforce, and (c) that the explanation matches the actual code of the agent.

Below is a list of the most important ways in which PCC improves over other existing techniques for enforcing safe execution of untrusted code:

- PCC operates at **load time** before the agent code is installed in the host system. This is in contrast with techniques that enforce the safety policy by relying on extensive run-time checking or even interpretation. As a result PCC agents run at native-code speed, which can be ten times faster than interpreted agents (written for example using Java bytecode) or 30% faster than agents whose memory operations are checked at run time.
  Additionally, by doing the checking at load time it becomes possible to enforce certain safety policies that are hard or impossible to enforce at run time. For example, by examining the code of the agent and the associated "explanation" PCC can verify that a certain interrupt routine terminates within a given number of instructions executed or that a video frame rendering agent can keep up with a given frame rate. Run-time enforcement of timing properties of such fine granularity is hard.
- PCC is **small**. PCC is simple and small because it has to do a relatively simple task. In particular, PCC does not have to discover on its own whether and why the agent meets the safety policy.
- For the same reason, PCC can operate even on agents expressed in native-code form. And because PCC can verify the code after compilation and optimization, the checked code is ready to run without needing an additional interpreter or compiler on the host. This has serious software engineering advantages since it reduces the amount of security critical code and it is also a benefit when the host environment is too small to contain an interpreter or a compiler, such as is the case for many embedded software systems.
- PCC is **general**. All PCC has to do is to verify safety explanations and to match them with the code and the safety policy. By standardizing a language for expressing the explanations and a formalism for expressing the safety policies it is possible to implement a single algorithm that can perform the required check, for any agent code, any valid explanation and a large class of safety policies. In this sense a single implementation of PCC can be used for checking a variety of safety policies.

The combination of benefits that PCC offers is unique among the techniques for safe execution of untrusted code. Previously one had to sacrifice one or more of these benefits because it is impossible to achieve them all in a system that examines just the agent code and has to discover on its own why the code is safe.

The PCC infrastructure is designed to complement a cryptographic authentication infrastructure. While cryptographic techniques such as digital signatures can be used by the host to verify external properties of the agent program, such as freshness and authenticity, or the author's identity, the PCC infrastructure checks internal semantic properties of the code such as what the code does and what it does not do. This enables the host to prevent safety breaches due to either malicious intent (for agents originating from untrusted sources) or due to programming errors (for agents originating from trusted sources).

The description of PCC so far has been in abstract terms without referring to a particular form of safety explanations. There are a number of possible forms of explanations each with its own advantages and disadvantages. In any implementation the safety explanations must be precise and comprehensive, just like formal proofs. In fact, in the first realization of a PCC architecture [Nec98] the explanations were precisely formal proofs represented as terms in a variant of the dependently-typed λ-calculus called the Edinburgh Logical Framework (LF) [HHP93]. The major advantage of this approach is that proof checking can be accomplished using a relatively simple and well understood LF type checker.

The proof-based realization of PCC was very useful for gaining initial experience with the PCC technique in various applications. However, when we attempted to try out PCC for medium and large examples it quickly became apparent that the size of the LF representation of proofs grows roughly quadratically with the size of the program. (All experiments referred to in this paper are in the context of type-safety policies, for which the proof certifies that the machine code is well typed in a given, usually first-order, type system.) In an attempt to address this issue we first devised a simple extension of the LF type checker that enables it to reconstruct certain small but numerous fragments of proofs while type checking [NL98]. This variant of LF, which we call LF_i (for implicit LF), allows us to omit those fragments from the representation of proofs with the major benefit that proof sizes and the checking times are now growing linearly with the size of the program. This allows us to process examples up to several thousands of line of code with proof sizes averaging 2.5 to 5 times the size of the code. But even LF_i-based proof representations are too large for the hundred-thousand line examples that we want to process.

In this paper we describe a series of improvements to the PCC architecture that together allow us to process even the largest examples. These improvements range from major changes in the representation and checking of proofs to changes in the way different components of the PCC system communicate. We start in Section 2 with a description, in general terms, of the new proof representation technique that we use. Then, in Section 3 we demonstrate in the context of an example both the new proof representation technique and the way in which the various checker components communicate with each other. Although most of this paper focuses on the code-receiving end, we observed that for better scaling the code producer must also cooperate. We describe in Section 4 one way in which a compiler that produces PCC agents can speed up the checking process. Finally, in Section 5 we discuss experimental evidence that substantiates the claim that this combination of techniques does indeed scale to very large examples.

2 A Hint-Based Representation of Proofs

One of the main impediments to scalability in the original proof-based realization of PCC is that proofs can be very large. Our solution to this problem is motivated by the observation that PCC proof checking is not able to exploit domain-specific knowledge in order to reduce the size of the proofs. For example, the PCC proofs of type safety are an order of magnitude larger than the size of the typing annotations that the Typed Assembly Language (TAL) system [MWCG99] uses. The overhead in TAL is smaller because TAL is less general than PCC and targets a specific type-safety policy, for a specific language and type system. The TAL type checker can be viewed as a proof checker specialized and optimized for a specific logic.

What we need is a different PCC implementation strategy that allows the size of PCC proofs to adapt automatically to the complexity of the property being checked. As a result, we should not have to pay a proof-size price for the generality of PCC in those instances when we check relatively simple properties. There are several components to our new strategy. First is a slightly different view on how the proofs in PCC can assist the verification on the host side. We assume that the host uses a non-deterministic checker for the safety policy. Then, a proof can essentially be replaced by an oracle guiding the non-deterministic checker. Every time the checker must make a choice between N possible ways to proceed, it consults the next $\lceil \log_2 N \rceil$ bits from the oracle. There are several important points that this new view of PCC exposes:

- The possibility of using non-determinism simplifies the design of the checker and enables the code receiver to use a simple checker even for checking a complex property.
- This view of verification exposes a three-way tradeoff between the complexity of the safety policy, the complexity and "smartness" of the checker, and the oracle size. If the verification problem is highly directed, as is the case with typical type-checking problems, the number of non-deterministic choices is usually small, and thus the required oracles are small. If the checker is "smart" and can narrow down further the choices, the oracle becomes even smaller. At an extreme, the checker might explore by itself small portions of the search space and require guidance from the oracle only in those situations when the search would be either too costly or not guaranteed to terminate.
- In the particular case of type-checking, even for assembly language, the checking problem is so directed that in many situations there is only one applicable choice, meaning that no hand-holding from the oracle is needed. This explains the large difference between the size of the typing derivation (i.e. the size of the actual proof) and the size of the oracles in our experiments.

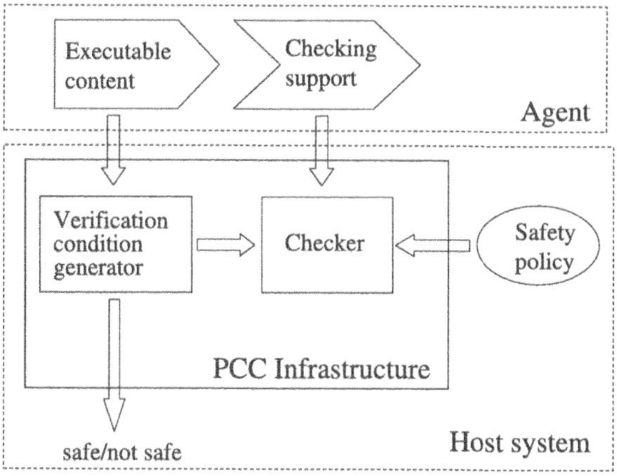

Fig. 1. The high-level structure of the PCC architecture.

- This view of PCC makes direct use of the defining property of the complexity class NP. This suggests that one of the benefits of PCC is that it allows the checker to check the solutions of problems in NP in polynomial time (with help from the oracle). But PCC can also help with checking even of solutions for semi-decidable problems, provided the checker and the oracle negotiate before hand a limit on the number of inference steps to be carried during verification.
- Since oracles are just streams of bits and no lookahead is necessary, they can be used in an online fashion, which is harder to do with syntactic representations of proofs. This leads to a smaller memory footprint for the checker, which is important in certain applications of PCC for embedded devices.

A high-level view of an oracle-based architecture for PCC is shown in Figure 1. The untrusted code is first inspected by a verification condition generator (VCGen) that checks simple syntactic conditions (e.g. that direct jumps are within the code boundary). Each time VCGen encounters an instruction whose execution could violate the safety policy, it asks the Checker module to verify that in the current context the instruction actually behaves safely. For this purpose, VCGen encodes the property to be checked as a simple symbolic formula. Our choice for the implementation of the Checker module is as a nondeterministic logic interpreter whose goals are the formulas produced by VCGen and whose logic program is an encoding of the host's safety policy. The next section describes in more details these components in the context of a simple example.

```
bool forall(bool *data, int dlast) {
  int i;
  for(i=dlast; i >= 0; i --)
    if(! data[i]) return false;
  return true;
}
```

Fig. 2. The C code for a function that computes the conjunction of all elements in an array of booleans.

3 An Extended Example

In this section we describe the operation of the PCC checking infrastructure in the context of verifying a simple type-safety policy for an agent written in a generic assembly language. Due to space limits and to keep the presentation concise we consider here only a trivial agent consisting of a function that computes the boolean value representing the conjunction of all elements in an array of booleans. The C source code for the function is shown in Figure 2. The inputs consist of a pointer to the start of an array of booleans along with the index of the last element. To simplify the presentation somewhat the array is scanned backwards.

```
                                 /* r_d=data, r_l=dlast */
      r_i = r_l
L0:
      r_t = ge r_i, 0
      jfalse r_t, L1
      r_t = add r_d, r_i
      r_t = load t
      jfalse r_t, L2
      r_i = sub r_i, 1
      jump L0
L1:    ret 1
L2:    ret 0
```

Fig. 3. The assembly language code for the function shown in Figure 2.

In Figure 3 we show one possible compilation of the `forall` function into a generic assembly language. The resulting program uses four registers, r_d and r_l to hold respectively the start address and the index of the last element of the array, a register r_i to hold the value of the local variable i and a temporary register r_t.

3.1 The Safety Policy

Before the code producer and the host can exchange agents they must agree on a safety policy. Setting up the safety policy is mostly the host's responsibility. For our example, the safety policy is a variant of type safety and requires that all memory accesses be contained in a memory range whose starting value and last-element index are being passed by the host in the input argument registers r_d and r_l. Furthermore, only boolean values may be written to that memory range and the agent may assume that the values read from that memory range are themselves boolean values. The safety policy further specifies that the function's return value must be a boolean value. Finally, the safety policy specifies that only the values 0 and 1 are valid boolean values.

It is obvious that this safety policy is tailored to our example and thus is not very general. To alleviate this problem we allow the host to define a language of types along with their meaning and the agent to customize the safety policy by declaring the type of the arguments that it expects and the type of the return value. This constitutes the interface of the agent and in our system is expressed as a pair of a function precondition and postcondition formulas constructed by the code producer using a number of type constructors defined by the host's safety policy.

In the case of our example the agent declares the following specification:

$$\begin{aligned} \mathtt{Pre}_{\mathtt{forall}} &= r_d\!: \mathtt{array}(\mathtt{bool}, r_l) \\ \mathtt{Post}_{\mathtt{forall}} &= \mathtt{res} : \mathtt{bool} \end{aligned}$$

which is a straightforward transcription of the function type. This specification uses the infix binary predicate constructor ":" to denote that a certain register contains value of a certain type, along with two type constructors, `array` and `bool`. Somewhat unusual for a type, the `array` type constructor declares the index of the last element of the array along with the type of the array elements. In the postcondition, the name `res` refers to the result value.

These predicate and type constructors are declared as part of the trusted safety policy along with inference rules (or typing rules) that specify how the constructors can be used. We show in Figure 4 the rules of inference that are necessary for our example. In order to understand these rules we preview briefly the operation of the VCGen. We do so here with only enough details to motivate the form of the rules. More details on VCGen follow in Section 3.3.

When VCGen encounters a memory read at an address E_a, it asks the Checker module to verify that the predicate $\mathtt{saferd}(E_a)$ holds according to the trusted rules of inference. The first rule of inference from Figure 4 says that one instance in which a memory read is considered safe is when it falls within the boundaries of an array. The rule `mem` goes even further and says that the value read from an array has the same type as the declared array element type.[1]

[1] Since the contents of memory does not change in our example we can introduce a constructor `mem` such that $\mathtt{mem}(E)$ denotes the contents of memory at address E. In general, a different mechanism must be used to keep track of the memory contents in the presence of memory writes. The reader is invited to consult [Nec98] for details.

$$\frac{A : \texttt{array}(T,\ L) \quad I \geq 0 \quad I \leq L}{\texttt{saferd}(\texttt{add}(A,\ I))}\ \texttt{rd}$$

$$\frac{A : \texttt{array}(T,\ L) \quad I \geq 0 \quad I \leq L}{\texttt{mem}(\texttt{add}(A,\ I)) : T}\ \texttt{mem} \qquad \frac{A : \texttt{array}(T,\ L) \quad I \geq 0 \quad I \leq L \quad E : T}{\texttt{safewr}(\texttt{add}(A,\ I),\ E)}\ \texttt{wr}$$

$$\frac{}{0 : \texttt{bool}}\ \texttt{bool0} \qquad \frac{}{1 : \texttt{bool}}\ \texttt{bool1}$$

$$\frac{}{E = E}\ \texttt{eqid} \qquad \frac{}{E \leq E}\ \texttt{leqid} \qquad \frac{I \leq E \quad \texttt{ge}(I,\ 0)}{\texttt{sub}(I,\ 1) \leq E}\ \texttt{dec} \qquad \frac{\texttt{ge}(E, 0)}{E \geq 0}\ \texttt{geq0}$$

Fig. 4. The rules of inference that constitute the safety policy for our example.

Similarly, the predicate $\texttt{safewr}(E_a, E)$ is generated by VCGen to request a verification that a memory write of value E at address E_a is safe. The third rule of inference in our safety policy can prove such a predicate if E_a falls inside an array and if E has the array element type. Notice that in all of these rule the function add has been used instead of the usual mathematical function "+". This is because we want to preserve the distinction between the mathematical functions and their approximate implementation in a processor.

The rules bool0 and bool1 specify the representation of booleans. The last row of inference rules in Figure 4 are a sample of the rules that encode the semantics of arithmetic and logic machine instructions. Consider for example the rule dec rule. Here ge and sub are the predicate constructors that encode the result of the machine instructions with the same name. VCGen uses such predicate constructors to encode the result of the corresponding instructions, leaving their interpretation to the safety policy. The rule dec says that the result of performing a machine subtraction of 1 from the value I is less or equal to some other value E if I itself is known to be less-or-equal to E and also if the test $\texttt{ge}(I, 0)$ is successful. This rule deserves an explanation. If we could assume that the machine version of subtraction is identical in behavior to the standard subtraction operation then the rule would be sound even without the second hypothesis. However, the second hypothesis must be added to prevent the case when I is the smallest representable integer value and the sub operation underflows. (A weaker hypothesis would also work but this one is sufficient for our example.) The rule geq0 say that in comparisons with zero the meaning of the machine ge operation is the same as that of the mathematical greater-or-equal comparison.

The rules of Figure 4 constitute a representative subset of a realistic safety policy. The safety policy used for the experiments discussed in Section 5 for the type system of the Java language consists of about 140 such inference rules.

3.2 The Role of Program Annotations

The VCGen module attempts to execute the untrusted program symbolically in order to signal all potentially unsafe operations. To make this execution possible in finite time and without the need for conservative approximations on the part of VCGen, we require that the program be annotated with invariant predicates. At least one such invariant must be specified for each cycle in the program's control-flow graph. To further simplify the work of VCGen each such invariant must also declare those registers that are live at the invariant point and are guaranteed to preserve their values between two consecutive times that the execution reaches the invariant point. We call these registers the *invariant registers.*

For our example, at least one invariant must be specified for some point inside the loop that starts at label L_0. We place the following invariant at label L_0:

$$L_0 : \quad \texttt{INV} = r_i \leq r_l \;\; \texttt{REGS} = \{r_d, r_l\}$$

The invariant annotation says that whenever the execution reaches the label L_0 the contents of register r_i is less-or-equal to the contents of register r_l and also that in between two consecutive hits of the program point the register r_d and r_l are the only ones among the live registers that are guaranteed to preserve their values.

A valid question at this point is who discovers this annotation and how. There are several possibilities. First, annotations can be inserted by hand by the programmer. This is the only alternative when the agent code is programmed in assembly language or when the programmer wants to hand-optimize the output of a compiler. It is true that this method does not scale well, but it is nevertheless a feature of PCC that the checker does not care whether the code is produced by a trusted compiler and will gladly accept code that was written or optimized by hand.

Another possibility is that the annotations can be produced automatically by a certifying compiler. Such a compiler first inserts bounds checks for all array accesses. In the presence of these checks the invariant predicates must include only type declarations for those live registers that are not declared invariant. An exception are those registers that contain integers, for which no declaration is necessary or useful since the integer data type contains all representable values. In our example, the reader can verify that in the presence of bounds checks preceding the memory read the invariant predicate `true` is sufficient. In general, the invariant predicates that are required in the absence of optimizations are very easy to generate by a compiler.

An optimizing compiler might analyze the program and discover that the lower bound check is entailed by the loop termination test and the upper bound check is entailed by a loop invariant "$r_i \leq r_l$". With this information the optimizing compiler can eliminate the bounds checks but it must communicate through the invariant predicate what are the loop invariants that it discovered and used in optimization. This is the process by which the code and annotations of Figure 3 could have been produced automatically. The reader can consult [Nec98] for the detailed description of a certifying compiler for a safe subset of C and [CLN+00] for the description of a certifying compiler for Java.

Finally, note that the invariant annotations are required but cannot be trusted to be correct as they originate from the same possibly untrusted source as the code itself. Nevertheless, VCGen can still use them safely, as described in the next section.

3.3 The Verification Condition Generator

The verification condition generator (VCGen) is implemented as a symbolic evaluator for the program being checked. It scans the program in a forward direction and at each program point it maintains a symbolic value for each register in the program. These symbolic values are then used at certain program points (e.g. memory operations, function calls and returns) to formulate checking goals for the Checker module. To assist the checker in verifying these goals VCGen also records for each goal that is submitted to the Checker a number of assumptions that the Checker is allowed to make. These assumptions are generated from the control-flow instructions (essentially informing the Checker about the location of the current program point) or from the program-supplied invariants. Figure 5 shows a summary of the sequence of actions performed by VCGen for our example.

First, VCGen initializes the symbolic values of all four registers with fresh new symbolic values to denote unknown initial values in all registers. But the initial values of the registers r_d and r_l are constrained by the precondition. To account for this, VCGen takes the specified precondition and, without trying to interpret its meaning, substitutes in it the current symbolic values of the registers. The result is the symbolic predicate formula "$d_0 : \texttt{array}(\texttt{bool}, l_0)$" that is added to a stack of assumptions. (These assumptions are shown underlined in Figure 5 and with an indentation level that corresponds to their position in the stack.)

After these initial steps VCGen proceeds to consider each instruction in turn. The assignment instruction of line 2 is modeled as a assignment of symbolic values. On line 3, VCGen notices that it hit an invariant. Since the invariant is not trusted VCGen asks the Checker to verify first that the invariant predicate holds at this point. To do this VCGen substitutes the current symbolic register values in the invariant predicate and the resulting predicate "$l_0 \leq l_0$" is submitted to the Checker for verification. (Such verification goals are shown in Figure 5 right-justified and boxed.)

Then, VCGen simulates symbolically an *arbitrary* iteration through the loop. To achieve this VCGen generates fresh new symbolic values for all registers, except the invariant ones. Next VCGen adds to the assumption stack the predicate "$i_1 \leq l_0$" obtained from the invariant predicate after substitution of the new symbolic values for registers.

When VCGen encounters a conditional branch it simulates both possible outcomes. First, the branch is assumed to be taken and a corresponding assumption is placed on the assumption stack. When that symbolic execution of that branch

1: Generate fresh values $r_d = d_0$, $r_l = l_0$, $r_i = i_0$ and $r_t = t_0$

1: Assume Precondition — d_0 : array(bool, l_0) (assumption)

2: Set $r_i = l_0$

3: Invariant (first hit) — $l_0 \leq l_0$ (goal)

3: Generate fresh values $r_i = i_1$, $r_t = t_1$

3: Assume invariant — $i_1 \leq l_0$ (assumption)

4: Set $r_t =$ ge(i_1, 0)

5: Branch 5 taken — not (ge(i_1, 0)) (assumption)

11: Check postcondition — 1 : bool (goal)

5: Branch 5 not taken — ge(i_1, 0) (assumption)

6: Set $r_t =$ add(d_0, i_1)

7: Check load — saferd(add(d_0, i_1)) (goal)

7: Set $r_t =$ mem(add(d_0, i_1))

8: Branch 8 taken — not (mem(add(d_0, i_1))) (assumption)

10: Check postcondition — 0 : bool (goal)

8: Branch 8 not-taken — mem(add(d_0, i_1)) (assumption)

9: Set $r_i =$ sub(i_1, 1)

3: Invariant (second hit) — sub(i_1, 1) $\leq l_0$, $d_0 = d_0$, $l_0 = l_0$ (goal)

4: Done

Fig. 5. The sequence of actions taken by VCGen. We show on the left the program points and a brief description of each action. Some actions result in extending the stack of assumptions that the Checker is allowed to make. These assumptions are shown underlined and with an indentation level that encodes the position in the stack of each assumption. Thus an assumption at a given indentation level implicitly discards all previously occurring assumptions at the same or larger indentation level. Finally, we show right-justified and boxed the checking goals submitted to the Checker.

terminates (e.g. when hitting a return instruction or an invariant for the second time), VCGen restores the state of the assumption stack and processes in a similar way the case when the branch is not taken.

Consider for example the branch of line 5. In the case when the branch is taken, VCGen pushes the assumption "`not` $(\mathrm{ge}(i_1, 0))$" and continues the execution from line 11. There a return instruction is encountered and VCGen asks the Checker to verify that the postcondition is verified. The precise verification goal is produced by substituting the actual symbolic return value (the literal 1 in this case) for the name `res` in the postcondition $\mathtt{Post}_{\mathtt{forall}}$. Once the Checker module verifies this goal, VCGen restores the symbolic values of registers and the state of the assumption stack to their states from before the branch was taken and then simulates the case when the branch is not taken. In this case, the memory read instruction is encountered and VCGen produces a `saferd` predicate using the symbolic value of the registers to construct a symbolic representation of the address being read.

The final notable item in Figure 5 is what happens when VCGen encounters the invariant for the second time. In this case VCGen instructs the Checker to verify that the invariant predicate still holds. At this point VCGen also asks the Checker to verify that the symbolic values of those registers that were declared invariant are equal to their symbolic values at the start of the arbitrary iteration thorough the loop. In our case, since the registers declared invariant were not assigned at all, their symbolic values before and after the iteration are not only equal but identical.

This completes our simplified account of the operation of VCGen. For details on how VCGen deals with more complex issues such as function calls and memory updates, the reader is invited to consult [Nec98]. Note that in the VCGen used in previous versions of PCC (such as that described in [Nec98]) the result of the verification condition generator is a single large predicate that encodes all of the goals (using conjunctions) and all of the assumptions (using implications). This means that the VCGen runs first to completion and produces this predicate which is then consumed by the Checker. This approach, while natural, turned out to be too wasteful. For large examples it became quite common for this monolithic predicate to require hundreds of megabytes for storage slowing down the checking process considerably. In some of the largest examples not even a virtual address space of 1Gb could hold the whole predicate. In the architecture that we propose here VCGen produces one small goal at a time and then passes the control to the Checker. Once a goal is validated by the Checker, it is discarded and the symbolic evaluation continues. This optimization might not seem interesting from a scientific point of view but it is illustrative of a number of purely engineering details that we had to address to make PCC scalable.

3.4 The Checker Module

The Checker module in the proposed architecture is simply a non-deterministic logic interpreter whose logic program consists of the safety policy rules of inference formulated as Horn clauses and whose goals are the formulas produced by VCGen. For example, the rd inference rule of Figure 4 is expressed as the following clause written in Prolog notation:

$$\texttt{saferd(add(}A,\ I\texttt{))}\ \ \text{:–}\ \ \texttt{of(}A,\ \texttt{array(}T,\ L\texttt{)},\ \ I \geq 0,\ \ I \leq L.$$

There are two major differences between a traditional logic interpreter and our Checker. One is that in PCC the logic program is dynamic since assumptions (represented as logic facts) are added and retracted from the system as the symbolic execution follows different paths through the agent. However, this happens only in between two separate invocations of the Checker. The second and more important difference is that while a traditional interpreter selects clauses by trying them in order and backtracking on failure, the Checker is a non-deterministic logic interpreter meaning that it "guesses" the right clause to use at each step. This means that the Checker can avoid backtracking and it is thus significantly simpler and generally faster than a traditional interpreter. In essence the Checking contains a first-order unification engine and a simple control-flow mechanism that records and processes all the subgoals in a depth-first manner. The last element of the picture is that the "guesses" that the Checker makes are actually specified as a sequence of clause names as part of the "explanation" of safety that accompanies the code. In this sense the proof is replaced by an oracle that guides the non-deterministic interpreter to success.

As an example of how this works, consider the invocation of the Checker on the goal "$\texttt{saferd(add(}d_0,\ i_1\texttt{))}$". For this invocation the active assumptions are:

$$\begin{aligned} A_0 &= \texttt{of}(d_0,\ \texttt{array(bool},\ l_0)) \\ A_1 &= i_1 \leq l_0 \\ A_2 &= \texttt{ge}(i_1,\ 0) \end{aligned}$$

The fragment of oracle for this checking goal is the following sequence of clause names "rd, A_0, geq0, A_2, A_1". To verify the current goal the Checker obtains the name of the next clause to be used (rd) from the oracle and unifies its head with the current goal. This leads to the following subgoals, where T and L are not-yet-instantiated logic variables:

$$\begin{aligned} &\texttt{of}(d_0,\ \texttt{array(T, L)}) \\ &i_1 \geq 0 \\ &i_1 \leq \mathrm{L} \end{aligned}$$

To solve the first subgoal the Checker extracts the next clause name (A_0) from the oracle and unifies the subgoal with its head. The unification succeeds and it instantiates the logic variables T and L to bool and l_0 respectively. Then the oracle guides the interpreter to use the rule geq0 followed by assumption A_2 to validate the subgoal "$i_1 \geq 0$" and assumption A_1 to validate the subgoal "i1 $\leq l_0$". The oracle for checking all of the goals pertaining to our example is:

leqid, bool1, rd, A_0, geq0, A_2, A_1, bool0, dec, A_1, A_2, eqid, eqid

3.5 An Optimized Checker

So far we have not yet achieved a major reduction in the size of the "explanation". Since the oracle contains mentions of every single proof rule its size is comparable with that of a proof. What we need now is to make the Checker "smarter" and ask it to narrow down the number of clauses that could possibly match the current goal, before consulting the oracle. If this number turns out to be zero then the Checker can reject the goal thus terminating the verification. In the fortunate case when the number of usable clauses is exactly one then the Checker can proceed with that clause without needing assistance from the oracle. And in the case when the number of usable clauses is larger than one the Checker needs only enough bits from the oracle to address among these usable clauses.

Such an optimization is also useful for a traditional logic interpreter because it reduces the need for backtracking. By having phrased the checking problem as a logic interpretation problem we can simply use off-the-shelf logic program optimizations to reduce the amount of non-determinism and thus to reduce the size of the necessary oracle.

Among the available logic program optimizations we selected automata-driven term indexing(ATI) [RRW95] because it has a relatively small complexity and good clause selectivity. The basic idea behind ATI is that the conclusions of all the active clauses are scanned and a decision tree is build from them. Intuitively, the leaves of the decision tree are labeled with sets of clauses whose conclusions could match a goal whose structure is encoded by the path corresponding to the goal. This allows the quick computation of the set of clauses the could match a goal. For details on how the ATI technique is used in the implementation of the Checker the reader can consult [NR01].

In our example the ATI optimization works almost perfectly. For nearly all goals and subgoals it manages to infer that exactly one clause is usable. However, for three of the subgoals involving the predicate "$\leq$" the ATI technique confuses the correct clause (either A_1 or `dec`) with the `leqid` rule. This is because ATI is not able to encode exactly in the decision tree conclusions involving duplicate logical variables. Thus the conclusion of the `leqid` rule is encoded as "$E_1 \leq E_2$", which explains why ATI would think that this conclusion matches all subgoals involving the $\leq$ predicate.

Even with this minor lack of precision the oracle for our example is reduced to just 3 bits. This constitutes a major saving. The original oracle consisted of 13 clause names and since we never had more than 16 active clauses in our example, we could use 52 bits to encode the entire oracle. In practice we observe savings of more than 30 times over the uncompressed oracles. This is because it is not uncommon to have even 1000 clauses active at one point. This would happen in deeply nested portions of the code where there are many assumptions active. And the ATI technique is so selective that even in these cases it is able to filter out most of the clauses.

4 Compiler Support for Scalability

So far we have described two techniques that proved essential for obtaining a scalable architecture for PCC: an oracle-based encoding of proofs and an interleaved execution of the VCGen and the Checker modules. Both of these techniques are implemented on the code-receiver end. But it would be incorrect to draw the conclusion that scalability can be achieved without cooperation from the code-producer end.

To see how the code producer can and should help, recall that VCGen considers both branches for each conditional and that symbolic execution stops when a return instruction is encountered or when an invariant is encountered for the second time. VCGen does verify that each cycle through the code has at least one invariant thus ensuring the termination of the symbolic evaluation.

But consider a program without loops and with a long sequence of conditionals, such as the following:

$$\begin{array}{l} \text{if}(c_1)\ s_1 \text{ else } s_1'; \\ \ldots \\ \text{if}(c_n)\ s_n \text{ else } s_n'; \\ \text{return x} \end{array}$$

VCGen considers each of the 2^n paths through this function because it might actually be the case that each such path has a different reason (and proof) to be safe. In most cases (and in all cases involving type safety) the verification can be modularized by placing an invariant annotation after each conditional. Then VCGen will have to verify only $2n$ path fragments from one invariant to another. Thus the code producer should place more than the minimum necessary number of invariants. If it fails to do so then the number of verification goals, and consequently the size of the oracle and the duration of the verification process can quickly become very large. We have verified in our experiments that this optimization is indeed very important for scalability.

5 Experimental Results

The experiments discussed in this section are in the context of a PCC system that checks Intel x86 binaries for compliance with the Java type-safety policy. The binaries are produced using a bytecode-to-native optimizing compiler [CLN+00]. This compiler is responsible for generating the invariant annotations. The oracle is produced on the code producer side in a manner similar to oracle checking. The VCGen is used as usual to produce a sequence of goals and assumptions. Each of these goals is submitted to a modified Checker engine that first uses the ATI engine to compute a small set of usable clauses and then tries all such clauses in order, using backtracking. Then this modified Checker emits an oracle that encodes the sequence of clauses that led to success for each goal.

We carried out experiments on a set of nearly 300 Java packages of varying sizes. Some of the larger ones are described in Figure 6. The running times

Program	Description	Source Size (LOC)	Code Size (bytes)
gnu-getopt	Command-line parser	1588	12644
linpack	Linear algebra routines	1050	17408
jal	SGI's Java Algorithm Library	3812	27080
nbody†	N-body simulation	3700	44064
lexgen	Lexical analyzer generator	7656	109196
ocaml†	Ocaml byte code interpreter	9400	112060
raja	Raytracer	8633	126364
kopi†	Java development tools	71200	760548
hotjava	Web browser	229853	2747548

Fig. 6. Description of our test cases, along with the size of the Java source code and the machine-code size. † indicates that source code was not available and the Java source size is estimated based on the size of the bytecode.

Program	LF_i Size (bytes)	LF_i Checking Time (ms)	Oracle Size (bytes)	Logic Interpretation Time (ms)
gnu-getopt	49804	82	1936	223
linpack	65008	117	2360	319
jal	53328	84	1698	314
nbody†	187026	373	7259	814
lexgen	413538	655	15726	1948
ocaml†	415218	641	13607	1837
raja	371276	747	11854	2030
kopi†	3380054	5321	96378	14693
hotjava	10813894	19757	354034	53491

Fig. 7. For each of the test cases, the size and time to check the LF_i representation of proofs, the size of the oracles and the logic interpretation time using oracles.

were averaged over a sufficient number of iterations of the checker on a 400MHz Pentium II machine with 128MB RAM.

Based on the data shown in Figure 6 we computed, for each example, how much smaller are the oracles compared to LF_i proofs (shown in Figure 8), what percentage of the code size are the oracles (shown in Figure 9) and how much slower is the logic interpreter compared to the LF_i checker (shown in Figure 10). These figures also show the geometric means for the corresponding ratios over these examples.

We observe that oracles are on average nearly 30 times smaller than LF_i proofs, and about 12% of the size of the machine code. While the binary representation of oracles is straightforward, for LF_i it is more complicated. In particular, one has to decide how to represent various syntactic entities. For the purpose of computing the size of LF_i proofs, we streamline LF_i terms as 16-bit tokens, each containing tag and data bits. The data can be the deBruijn index [DeB72] for a

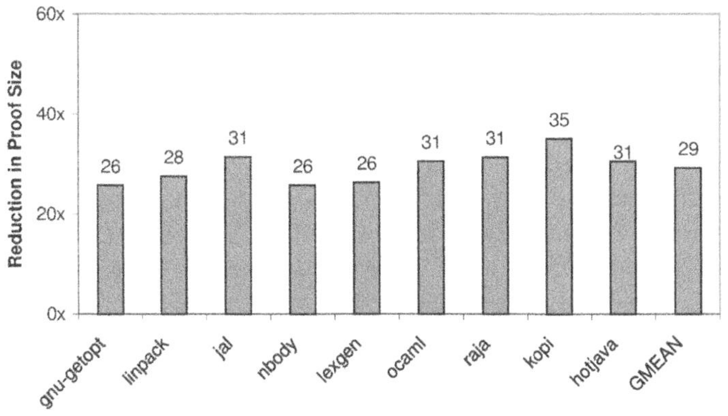

Fig. 8. Ratio between LF_i proof size and oracle size.

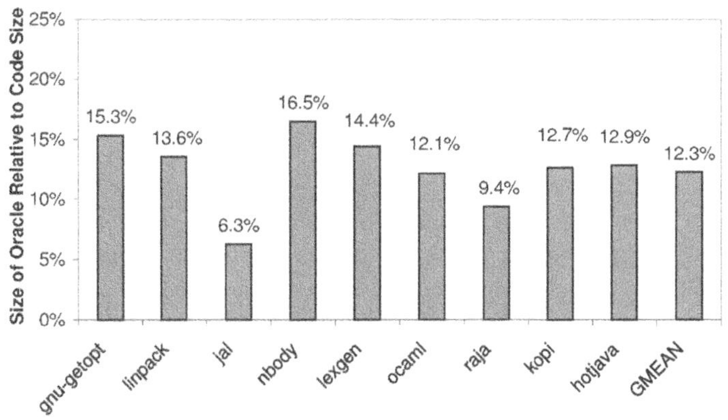

Fig. 9. Ratio between oracle size and machine code.

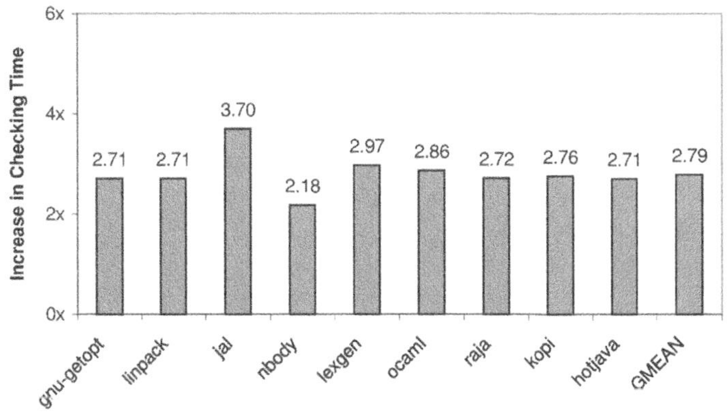

Fig. 10. Ratio between logic-interpretation time and LF_i type-checking time.

variable, the index into the signature for constants, or the number of elements in an application or abstraction.

We also compared the performance of our technique with that obtained by using a popular off-the-shelf compression tool, namely `gzip`. We do more than 3 times better than `gzip` with maximum compression enabled, without incurring the decompression time or the addition of about 8000 lines of code to the server side of the PCC system. That is not to say that oracles could not benefit from further compression. There could be opportunities for Lempel-Ziv compression in oracles, in those situations when sequences of deduction rules are repeated. Instead, we are looking at the possibility of compressing these sequences at a semantic level, by discovering lemmas whose proof can be factored out.

It is also interesting to note that logic interpretation is about 3 times slower than LF_i type checking. This is due to the overhead of constructing the decision trees used by ATI. There are some simple optimizations that one can do to reduce the checking time. For example, the results shown here are obtained by using an ATI truncated to depth 3. This saves time for the maintenance of the ATI but also loses precision thus leading to larger oracles. If we don't limit the size of the ATI we can save about 8% in the size of the oracles at the cost of increasing the checking time by 24%.

One interesting observation is that while LF_i checking is faster than oracle checking, it also uses a lot more memory. While oracles can be consumed a few bits at a time, the LF_i syntactic representation of a proof must be entirely brought in memory for checking. While we have not measured precisely the memory usage we encountered examples whose oracles can be checked using less than 1Mbyte of memory while the checking of the corresponding LF_i terms could not be performed even with 1Gbyte of virtual memory.

6 Conclusion

We presented in this paper an architecture for Proof-Carrying Code where proofs are replaced by an oracle guiding a non-deterministic checker for a given safety policy. The luxury of using non-determinism in the checker allows a simple checker to enforce even complex safety policies. Since many safety policies are relatively simple, the amount of non-determinism is low and this leads to small oracles that are required for checking compliance with such policies. In this sense the proposed PCC architecture is able to adapt the cost of verification to the complexity of the safety policy.

In designing this architecture we struggled to preserve a useful property of the previous implementation of PCC, namely that it can be easily configured to check different safety policies without changing the implementation. This has great software-engineering advantages and contributes to the trustworthiness of a PCC infrastructure since code that changes rarely is less likely to have bugs. To support this feature our choice for a non-deterministic checker is a non-deterministic logic interpreter that can be configured with the safety policy encoded as a logic program.

To achieve true scalability we had to solve several engineering problems, such as to design a low-cost interaction model between the various modules that compose the infrastructure. The code producer also must play an active role in ensuring that the verification process is quick. Through the combination of such techniques we have produced the first implementation of PCC that scales well to large programs at least in the context of a fairly simple type safety policy. What remains now to be seen is if Proof-Carrying Code can be practically applied to more complex safety policies.

Acknowledgments

We would like to thank Shree Rahul for the help with the collection of the experimental data presented in this paper and to Peter Lee, Mark Plesko, Chris Colby, John Gregorski, Guy Bialostocki and Andrew McCreight from Cedilla Systems Corporation who have implemented the certifying compiler for Java used in these experiments.

References

[CLN+00] Christopher Colby, Peter Lee, George C. Necula, Fred Blau, Mark Plesko, and Kenneth Cline. A certifying compiler for Java. *ACM SIGPLAN Notices*, 35(5):95–107, May 2000.

[DeB72] N. DeBruijn. Lambda-calculus notation with nameless dummies, a tool for automatic formula manipulation. *Indag. Mat.*, 34:381–392, 1972.

[HHP93] Robert Harper, Furio Honsell, and Gordon Plotkin. A framework for defining logics. *Journal of the Association for Computing Machinery*, 40(1):143–184, January 1993.

[MWCG99] Greg Morrisett, David Walker, Karl Crary, and Neal Glew. From system F to typed assembly language. *ACM Transactions on Programming Languages and Systems*, 21(3):527–568, May 1999.

[Nec97] George C. Necula. Proof-carrying code. In *The 24th Annual ACM Symposium on Principles of Programming Languages*, pages 106–119. ACM, January 1997.

[Nec98] George C. Necula. *Compiling with Proofs*. PhD thesis, Carnegie Mellon University, September 1998. Also available as CMU-CS-98-154.

[NL96] George C. Necula and Peter Lee. Safe kernel extensions without run-time checking. In *Second Symposium on Operating Systems Design and Implementations*, pages 229–243. Usenix, October 1996.

[NL98] George C. Necula and Peter Lee. Efficient representation and validation of proofs. In *Thirteenth Annual Symposium on Logic in Computer Science*, pages 93–104, Indianapolis, June 1998. IEEE Computer Society Press.

[NR01] George C. Necula and Shree P. Rahul. Oracle-based checking of untrusted programs. In *The 28th Annual ACM Symposium on Principles of Programming Languages*. ACM, January 2001. To appear.

[RRW95] R. Ramesh, I. V. Ramakrishnan, and David Scott Warren. Automata-driven indexing of Prolog clauses. *Journal of Logic Programming*, 23(2):151–202, May 1995.

Parameterized Logic Programs where Computing Meets Learning

Taisuke SATO*

Dept. of Computer Science
Tokyo Institute of Technology
2-12-1 Ôokayama Meguro-ku Tokyo Japan 152

Abstract. In this paper, we describe recent attempts to incorporate learning into logic programs as a step toward adaptive software that can learn from an environment. Although there are a variety of types of learning, we focus on parameter learning of logic programs, one for statistical learning by the EM algorithm and the other for reinforcement learning by learning automatons. Both attempts are not full-fledged yet, but in the former case, thanks to the general framework and an efficient EM learning algorithm combined with a tabulated search, we have obtained very promising results that open up the prospect of modeling complex symbolic-statistical phenomena.

1 Introduction

We start by assuming that reproducing intelligence in a computer constitutes a great challenge to human intelligence in the 21st century. We on the other hand recall that the assumption held by AI researchers in the late seventies was such that it would be achieved by writing a huge program with a huge knowledge base (though no one knew how large they would be). The first assumption is taken undebatable in this paper but the second one, once thought to be undebatable, raises a serious question in light of the fact that OS, software comprising tens of millions of codes, is far short of being intelligent. We must admit that the size of a program has little to do with its intelligence. It is also recognized that intelligence is something very complex and the most feasible way of building a very complex object comprised of tens of millions of components is to write a program. So we are trapped in a kind of dilemma that writing a huge program may not be a solution to building intelligence, but we seem to have no way other than that (at least at the moment).

One way out is to note that programs can be smarter if they are born with the ability of learning, and it might be possible, instead of writing a huge complete program from the beginning, to let them learn how to behave more intelligently. Think of the following. Why is a program called a program? Because it specifies things to happen beforehand. And people have been taking it for granted that programs never change spontaneously regardless of how many times they are

* email: sato@mi.cs.titech.ac.jp

H. Kuchen and K. Ueda (Eds.): FLOPS 2001, LNCS 2024, pp. 40–60, 2001.

used. Aside from the positive side, the negative side of this property is well-known; once an error occurs, the same error recurs indefinitely many times under the same condition. This stubbornness, "once built, no change," of programs exhibits a striking contrast to human beings who grow with time and learn from mistakes. After learning, we expect that something changes for the better, but programs lack any means of learning as they are designed to be just symbolic constructs for defining recursive functions, mathematically speaking.

The lack of learning ability is a common feature of deductive symbolic systems in general, and programs in particular, but there are well-established symbolic systems that have a close relationship to learning. For instance, there exist stochastic formal languages such as hidden Markov models (HMMs) [15].[1] HMMs are used in many fields from speech recognition to natural language processing to bioinformatics as a versatile modeling tool, and learning their parameters is a key step in their applications. Probabilistic context free grammars (PCFGs) [30, 9],[2] an extension of HMMs, have also statistical parameters learnable from linguistic data [1]. Turning to knowledge representation, we notice (discrete) Bayesian networks, a graphical representation of a finite joint distribution,[3] [4] are used to represent knowledge about uncertainty in the real world at propositional level [13, 2], and there is a standard way of statistically learning their parameters. Unfortunately, all these symbolic systems do not work as a program as they don't have a means of expressing control and data structures.

In the following,[5] we propose to integrate logic programs with parameter learning in hopes that they supply new building blocks for AI [16, 17, 7, 21, 22]. Resulting systems have the ability of expressing programs and the ability of learning at the same time. They can compute as they are logic programs and can learn parameters as well. There exist a couple of problems with this approach though. The most basic one is semantics. Notice that the basic principle

---

[1] A hidden Markov model is a stochastic finite automaton in which a transition is made probabilistically and a probabilistically chosen alphabet is output on each transition. The state transition is supposedly not observable from the outside.

[2] A probabilistic context free grammar is a CFG with probabilities assigned to each production rule. If a nonterminal A has N production rules $\{A \to \alpha_i \mid 1 \leq i \leq N\}$, probability p_i is assigned to each rule $A \to \alpha_i$ $(1 \leq i \leq N)$ in such a way that $\sum_{i=1}^{N} p_i = 1$. The probability of a sentence s is the sum of probabilities of each (leftmost) derivation of s. The latter is the product of probabilities of rules used in the derivation.

[3] By a joint distribution, we mean a joint probability density function [3].

[4] A Bayesian network is a graphical representation of a joint distribution $P(X_1 = x_1, \ldots, X_N = x_N)$ by a directed acyclic graph where each node is a random variable. A conditional probability table (CPT) representing $P(X_i = x_i \mid \boldsymbol{\Pi}_i = \boldsymbol{u}_i)$ $(1 \leq i \leq N)$ is associated with each node X_i where $\boldsymbol{\Pi}_i$ represents the parent nodes $(1 \leq i \leq N)$ and $\boldsymbol{u}_i$ are their values. When X_i has no parent, i.e. a topmost node in the graph, the table is just a marginal distribution $P(X_i = x_i)$. The whole joint distribution is given by $\prod_{i=1}^{N} P(X_i = x_i \mid \boldsymbol{\Pi}_i = \boldsymbol{u}_i)$.

[5] The content of Section 2 and Section 3 is based on [22]. Related work is omitted due to space limitations.

of logic is that "nothing is connected unless otherwise specified by axioms" while the general rule of thumb in statistics is that "everything is connected unless otherwise specified by independence assumptions." This fundamental difference is carried over to semantics in such a way that logic has a compositional semantics, i.e. the meaning of $A \wedge B$ is a function of the meaning of A and that of B, but probability is not compositional, i.e. $P(A \wedge B)$ is not a function of $P(A)$ and $P(B)$. We are going to synthesize a new semantics by mixing these somewhat conflicting semantics in the next section for a class of *parameterized logic programs*, definite clause programs with a parameterized distribution over facts.

The new semantics is called *distribution semantics* [16]. It considers a parameterized logic program as defining a joint distribution (of infinite dimensions), and subsumes the standard least model semantics and the above mentioned symbolic systems, HMMs, PCFGs and Bayesian networks [17, 22]. In the following, after having established distribution semantics for parameterized logic programs in Section 2, we apply it to symbolic-statistical modeling [17, 18] in Section 3 and show that three basic tasks, i.e.

Task-1: computing probabilities
Task-2: finding out the most likely computation path
Task-3: learning parameters from data

are solved efficiently[7, 20–22]. Furthermore, in the case of PCFGs, we experimentally discovered that our learning algorithm called *the graphical EM algorithm* outperforms the Inside-Outside algorithm [1], the standard parameter learning algorithm for PCFGs, by orders of magnitudes [22]. In Section 4, we investigate another direction of combining logic programming and learning by incorporating reinforcement learning. Reinforcement learning is a method of online training by reward and penalty [5]. We show that logic programs incorporating *learning automatons*, simple reinforcement learning devices [12, 14], can be trained to behave desirably for our purpose.

The reader is supposed to be familiar with the basics of logic programming [8, 4], probability theory [3], Bayesian networks [13, 2] stochastic grammars [15, 9], reinforcement learning [5] and learning automatons [12].

2 Semantic framework

In this section, we define *distribution semantics*. Although it was already explained in various places [16, 17, 21, 22], we repeat the definition for the sake of self-containedness. First of all, our program is a definite clause program $DB = F \cup R$ in a first-order language $\mathcal{L}$ with countably many constant symbols, function symbols and predicate symbols where F is a set of unit clauses and R, a set of non-unit clauses. To avoid mathematical complications, we pretend that DB consists of countably many ground clauses and no clause head in R appears in F. Our intention is that non-unit definite clauses represent eternal laws in the universe whereas unit clauses represent probabilistic facts which happen to be true or happen to be false. So we introduce a probability measure P_F over the set of ground atoms in F and extend it to a probability measure P_{DB} over the set of Herbrand interpretations for $\mathcal{L}$.

Let Ω_F be the set of Herbrand interpretations for the set of ground atoms in F and fix an enumeration $A_1, A_2, \ldots$ of ground atoms in F.[6] A Herbrand interpretation has a one-to-one correspondence to an infinite series $\langle x_1, x_2, \ldots \rangle$ of 1s and 0s by stipulating that $x_i = 1$ $(i = 1, 2, \ldots)$ (resp. $= 0$) if and only if A_i is true (resp. false). So Ω_F is identified with the direct product $\prod_{i=1}^{\infty} \{0, 1\}_i$ of $\{0, 1\}$s. The existence of a probability measure P_F over Ω_F is not self-evident but actually it is constructed freely from a collection of finite joint distributions $P_F^{(n)}(A_1 = x_1, \ldots, A_n = x_n)$ $(n = 1, 2, \ldots, x_i \in \{0, 1\}, 1 \leq i \leq n)$ such that

$$\begin{cases} 0 \leq P_F^{(n)}(A_1 = x_1, \ldots, A_n = x_n) \leq 1 \\ \sum_{x_1, \ldots, x_n} P_F^{(n)}(A_1 = x_1, \ldots, A_n = x_n) = 1 \\ \sum_{x_{n+1}} P_F^{(n+1)}(A_1 = x_1, \ldots, A_{n+1} = x_{n+1}) \\ \qquad\qquad = P_F^{(n)}(A_1 = x_1, \ldots, A_n = x_n) \end{cases} \tag{1}$$

It is proved [3] that if $P_F^{(n)}(\cdot)$s satisfy the three conditions of (1), there exists a σ-additive probability measure P_F such that for $(n = 1, 2, \ldots, x_i \in \{0, 1\}, 1 \leq i \leq n)$,

$$P_F(A_1 = x_1, \ldots, A_n = x_n) = P_F^{(n)}(A_1 = x_1, \ldots, A_n = x_n).$$

$P_F^{(n)}(\cdot)$s are presentable as an infinite binary tree like Figure 1. In the tree, $p_1, p_{21}, p_{22}, \ldots$ $(0 \leq p_1, p_{21}, p_{22}, \ldots \leq 1)$ are free parameters, and the tree specifies $P_F(A_1 = 1, A_2 = 0) = p_1(1 - p_{21})$ and so on.

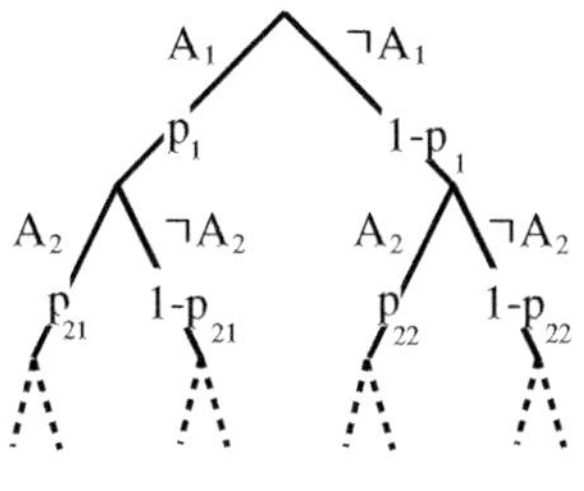

Fig. 1. Making a collection of finite distributions

Conversely, Figure 1 describes a general method of constructing $P_F^{(n)}$ but for practical reason, we assume that each probabilistic atom in F independently represents a probabilistic choice from a set of finitely many alternatives. So we introduce atoms of the form `msw(i,n,v)` which simulates a multi-ary random

[6] we assume that F contains countably many ground atoms.

switch whose name is i and whose outcome is v on trial n as a generalization of primitive probabilistic events such as coin tossing and rolling a dice. We henceforth assume that P_F is specified in the following way.

1. F consists of probabilistic atoms $\texttt{msw}(i,n,v)$. The arguments i and n are arbitrary ground terms. We assume that a finite set V_i of ground terms is associated with each i, and $v \in V_i$ holds.
2. Write V_i as $\{v_1, v_2, \ldots, v_m\}$ ($m = |V_i|$). Then, one of the ground atoms $\{\texttt{msw}(i,n,v_1),\ \texttt{msw}(i,n,v_2),\ \ldots,\ \texttt{msw}(i,n,v_m)\}$ becomes exclusively true (takes value 1) on each trial. With each i and ($v \in V_i$), a *parameter* $\theta_{i,v} \in [0,1]$ such that $\sum_{v \in V_i} \theta_{i,v} = 1$ is associated. $\theta_{i,v}$ is the probability of $\texttt{msw}(i,\cdot,v)$ being true.
3. For each ground terms i, i', n, n', $v \in V_i$ and $v' \in V_{i'}$, random variable $\texttt{msw}(i,n,v)$ is independent of $\texttt{msw}(i',n',v')$ if $n \neq n'$ or $i \neq i'$.

Speaking more formally, we introduce a family of parameterized finite distribution $P_{(i,n)}$ such that

$$P_{(i,n)}(\texttt{msw}(i,n,v_1) = x_1, \ldots, \texttt{msw}(i,n,v_m) = x_m \mid \theta_{i,v_1}, \ldots, \theta_{i,v_m}) \stackrel{\text{def}}{=} \begin{cases} \theta_{i,v_1}^{x_1} \cdots \theta_{i,v_m}^{x_m} & \text{if } \sum_{k=1}^{m} x_k = 1 \\ 0 & \text{o.w.} \end{cases} \quad (2)$$

where $m = |V_i|$, $x_k \in \{0,1\}$ ($1 \leq k \leq m$), and define P_F as the infinite-dimensional product measure

$$P_F \stackrel{\text{def}}{=} \prod_{i,n} P_{(i,n)}.$$

Based on P_F, another probability measureP_{DB} over the set of Herbrand interpretations Ω_{DB} for $\mathcal{L}$ is constructed as an extension of P_F by making use of the least Herbrand model semantics of logic programs [16]. Think of a Herbrand interpretation $\nu \in \Omega_F$. It defines a set F_ν of true atoms in F, and hence defines the least Herbrand model $M_{DB}(\nu)$ of $F_\nu \cup R$. $M_{DB}(\nu)$ determines all truth values of ground atoms in $\mathcal{L}$. A sampling ν from P_F thus determines all truth values of ground atoms. In other words, every ground atom in $\mathcal{L}$ becomes a random variable in this way. We formalize this idea. Enumerate *all ground atoms in* $\mathcal{L}$ and put it as $A_1, A_2, \ldots$ Then introduce a collection of finite disrtibutions $P_{DB}^{(n)}(A_1 = x_1,\ \ldots,\ A_n = x_n)$ ($n = 1, 2, \ldots$) by

$$[A_1^{x_1} \wedge \cdots \wedge A_n^{x_n}]_F \stackrel{\text{def}}{=} \{\nu \in \Omega_F \mid M_{DB}(\nu) \models A_1^{x_1} \wedge \cdots \wedge A_n^{x_n}\}$$

$$P_{DB}^{(n)}(A_1 = x_1, \ldots, A_n = x_n) \stackrel{\text{def}}{=} P_F([A_1^{x_1} \wedge \cdots \wedge A_n^{x_n}]_F)$$

where $A^x = A$ if $x = 1$ and $A^x = \neg A$ if $x = 0$. Note that $[A_1^{x_1} \wedge \cdots \wedge A_n^{x_n}]_F$ is P_F-measurable. Since $P_{DB}^{(n)}$ ($n = 1, 2, \ldots$) satisfies (1), there exists a probability measure P_{DB} over Ω_{DB}, an extension of P_F, such that

$$P_{DB}(A_1 = x_1, \ldots, A_n = x_n) = P_F(A_1 = x_1, \ldots, A_n = x_n)$$

for every finite sequence of atoms $A_1, \ldots, A_n$ in F and for every binary vector $\langle x_1, \ldots, x_n \rangle$ ($x_i \in \{0,1\}$, $1 \le i \le n$). We consider $P_{DB}(\cdot)$ as a joint distribution of countably infinite dimensions and define the *denotation* of the program $DB = F \cup R$ w.r.t. P_F as P_{DB} (*distribution semantics*). DB then becomes a random vector of infinite dimensions having the distribution P_{DB} whose sample realization is a Herbrand interpretation for $\mathcal{L}$.

Distribution semantics subsumes the least Herbrand semantics in logic programming as a special case in which P_F places all probability mass on one interpretation, i.e. making a specific set of ground atoms in F always true. On the contrary, it is also possible to define a uniform distribution over F (like the one over the unit interval $[0,1]$) in which every Herbrand interpretation for F is equally probable. Since the cardinality of interpretations is just that of real numbers (Ω_{DB} is isomorphic to Cantor set), each probability of an $M_{DB}(\nu)$ is 0 in this case. What we are interested in however is distributions between these extremes which better reflect our observations in the real world such as a corpus. The characteristics of distribution semantics are summarized as follows.

- It is applicable to any parameterized logic programs. The underlying first-order language is allowed to contain countably many symbols be they functions or predicates, and programs can be arbitrary.
- Since it is based on the least model semantics, both sides of the iff definition of a predicate[7] $p(x) \leftrightarrow \exists y_1(x = t_1 \wedge W_1) \vee \cdots \vee \exists y_n(x = t_n \wedge W_n)$ unconditionally coincide as a random variable for any ground instantiation $p(t)$.
- Unfold/fold transformation [25] preserves the denotation of parameterized logic programs.

Owing to P_{DB}, we may regard every ground atom (and closed formula) as a random variable on Ω_{DB}. We apply our semantics in two directions, one for symbolic-statistical modeling described in Section 3, and the other for reinforcement learning described in Section 4.

Before proceeding, we explain how to execute a parameterized logic program. Suppose $DB = F \cup R$ is a parameterized logic program such that $F = \{\texttt{msw}(i,n,v)\}$ has a distribution $P_F = \prod_{i,n} P_{(i,n)}$ mentioned before, and also suppose a goal $\leftarrow G$ is given. We execute $\leftarrow G$ w.r.t. DB by a special SLD interpreter whose only difference from the usual one is an action taken for a goal `msw(I,N,V)`. When it is called with ground `I` $= i$ and `N` $= n$, two cases occur.[8]

- `msw(`i`,`n`,V)` is called for the first time. The interpreter chooses some ground term v from V_i with probability $\theta_{i,v}$, instantiates `V` to v and returns successfully.

[7] Here x is a vector of new variables of length equal to the arity of p, $p(t_i) \leftarrow W_i$ ($1 \le i \le n, 0 \le n$), an enumeration of clauses about p in DB, and each y_i, a vector of variables occurring in $p(t_i) \leftarrow W_i$.

[8] If either `I` or `N` is non-ground, the execution of `msw(`i`,`n`,V)` is unspecified.

- `msw(`i`,`n`,V)` was called before, and the returned value was v. If `V` is a free variable, the interpreter instantiates `V` to v and returns successfully. If `V` is bound to some non-free variable v', the interpreter tries to unify v' with v and and returns successfully if the unification is successful, or fails otherwise.

Execution of this type is called *sampling execution* because it corresponds to sampling from P_{DB}.

3 Statistical learning and parameterized logic programs

3.1 Blood type example

Parameterized logic programs define probabilities of ground atoms. Our aim here is to express our observations of symbolic-statistical phenomena such as observations of blood types by ground atoms, and write a parameterized logic program for them and adjust their parameters so that the distribution defined by the program closely approximates to their empirical distribution. Let's take `ABO` blood types. Possible types are `'A'`, `'B'`, `'O'` and `'AB'`. We declaratively model by a parameterized logic program $DB_1 = F_1 \cup R_1$ in Figure 2 how these blood types are determined from inherited blood type genes $\{\mathtt{a}, \mathtt{b}, \mathtt{o}\}$. Note that we employ Prolog conventions [?]. So strings beginning with a upper-case letter are variables. Quoted atoms are constants. The underscore "_" is an anonymous variable. Apparently clauses in DB_1 are direct translation of genetic knowledge about blood types. `btype('A'):- (gtype(a,a) ; gtype(a,o) ; gtype(o,a))` for instance says one's blood type is `'A'` if the inherited genes are $\langle \mathtt{a}, \mathtt{a} \rangle$, $\langle \mathtt{a}, \mathtt{o} \rangle$ or $\langle \mathtt{o}, \mathtt{a} \rangle$.[9] `gene(fa,X)` (resp. `gene(mo,Y)`) means one inherits a blood type gene `X` from the father (resp. `Y` from the mother). `msw(gene,P,G)` represents an event that `G`, gene, is probabilistically chosen to be inherited from `P`, a parent.

$R_1 =$
```
btype('A'):-(gtype(a,a) ; gtype(a,o) ; gtype(o,a)).
btype('B'):-(gtype(b,b) ; gtype(b,o) ; gtype(o,b)).
btype('O'):-gtype(o,o).
btype('AB'):-(gtype(a,b) ; gtype(b,a)).
gtype(X,Y):-gene(fa,X),gene(mo,Y).
gene(P,G):-msw(gene,P,G).
```

$F_1 = \{$`msw(gene,P,a)`, `msw(gene,P,b)`, `msw(gene,P,o)`$\}$

Fig. 2. ABO blood type program DB_1

[9] The left gene (resp. the right gene) is supposed to come from the father (resp. from the mother).

P_{F_1}, a joint distribution over the set of $\{\mathtt{msw(gene,}t\mathtt{,}g\mathtt{)} \mid t \in \{\mathtt{fa},\mathtt{mo}\}, g \in \{\mathtt{a},\mathtt{b},\mathtt{o}\}\}$, is given as the product $P_{F_1} = P_{\mathtt{fa}} \cdot P_{\mathtt{mo}}$.

$$P_t(\mathtt{msw(gene,}t\mathtt{,a)} = x, \mathtt{msw(gene,}t\mathtt{,b)} = y, \\ \mathtt{msw(gene,}t\mathtt{,o)} = z \mid \theta_a, \theta_b, \theta_o) \stackrel{\text{def}}{=} \theta_a^x \theta_b^y \theta_c^z$$

Here $t \in \{\mathtt{fa},\mathtt{mo}\}$ and one of $\{x, y, z\}$ is 1 and the remaining two are 0. θ_a is the probability of inheriting gene a from a parent and so on. When $t \notin \{\mathtt{fa},\mathtt{mo}\}$, we put $P_{F_t}(\cdot,\cdot,\cdot \mid, \theta_a, \theta_b, \theta_o) = 0$.

Suppose we observed blood types. We represent such observations by atoms chosen from $obs(DB_1) = \{\mathtt{btype('A')}, \mathtt{btype('B')}, \mathtt{btype('O')}, \mathtt{btype('AB')}\}$. Our concern then is to estimate hidden parameters $\theta_a, \theta_b, \theta_o$ from the observed atoms. First we reduce an observed atom to a disjunction of conjunction of **msw** atoms by unfolding [25]. Take **btype('A')** for instance. $\leftarrow$ **btype('A')** is unfolded by $comp(R_1)$ [8,4] into $S_1 \vee S_2 \vee S_3$ such that

$$comp(R_1) \vdash \mathtt{btype('A')} \leftrightarrow S_1 \vee S_2 \vee S_3$$

where

$$S_1 = \mathtt{msw(gene,fa,a)} \wedge \mathtt{msw(gene,mo,a)}$$
$$S_2 = \mathtt{msw(gene,fa,a)} \wedge \mathtt{msw(gene,mo,o)}$$
$$S_3 = \mathtt{msw(gene,fa,o)} \wedge \mathtt{msw(gene,mo,a)}$$

Each S_i is called an *explanation* for **btype('A')** and $\{S_1, S_2, S_3\}$ is called the *support set* of **btype('A')**.[10] Taking into account that S_1, S_2 and S_3 are mutually exclusive and **msw** atoms are independent, $P_{DB_1}(\mathtt{btype('A')})$ is calculated as

$$P_{DB_1}(\mathtt{btype('A')} \mid \theta_a, \theta_b, \theta_o) = P_{F_b}(S_1) + P_{F_b}(S_2) + P_{F_b}(S_3) \\ = \theta_a^2 + 2\theta_a\theta_o$$

Hence, the values of θ_a, θ_b and θ_o are determined as the maximizers of $\theta_a^2 + 2\theta_a\theta_o$ (maximum likelihood (ML) estimation). When there are multiple observations, say T observations $G_1, \ldots, G_T$, all we need to do is to maximize of the likelihood $\prod_{t=1}^{T} P_{DB_1}(G_t \mid \theta_a, \theta_b, \theta_o)$, and this optimization problem is solvable by the EM algorithm [10], an iterative algorithm for ML estimation. We face a fundamental problem here however because the EM algorithm in statistics has been defined only for numerically represented distributions and no EM algorithm is available for parameterized logic programs. So we have to derive a new one. Fortunately, thanks to the rigorous mathematical foundation of distribution semantics, it is straightforward to derive a (naive) EM algorithm for parameterized logic programs [16, 6, 22].

Given T observations $\mathcal{G} = \langle G_1, \ldots, G_T \rangle$ of observable atoms and a parameterized logic program DB that models the distribution of observable atoms, the

[10] An *explanation* S for a goal G w.r.t. a parameterized logic program $DB = F \cup R$ is a minimal conjunction S ($\subseteq F$) of **msw** atoms such that $S, R \vdash G$. The *support set* $\psi_{DB}(G)$ of G is the set of all explanations for G.

parameter set $\boldsymbol{\theta}$ which (locally) maximizes the likelihood $\prod_{t=1}^{T} P_{DB_1}(G_t \mid \boldsymbol{\theta})$ is computed by an EM algorithm *learn-naive*$(DB, \mathcal{G})$ below [16,6]. Here $\psi_{DB}(G_t)$ $(1 \leq t \leq T)$ is the support set of G_t and $\boldsymbol{\theta}$ is the set of parameters associated with `msw` atoms appearing in some $\psi_{DB}(G_t)$. $\sigma_{i,v}(S)$ is $\left|\{ n \mid \texttt{msw}(i,n,v) \in S\}\right|$, the number of how many times an atom of the form $\texttt{msw}(i,n,v)$ appears in an explanation S.

---

procedure *learn-naive*$(DB, \mathcal{G})$ **begin**
Initialize $\boldsymbol{\theta}$ with appropriate values and ε with a small positive number ;
$\lambda^{(0)} := \sum_{t=1}^{T} \ln P_{DB}(G_t \mid \boldsymbol{\theta})$; % Compute the log-likelihood.
repeat
  foreach $i \in I, v \in V_i$ **do**

$$\eta[i,v] := \sum_{t=1}^{T} \frac{1}{P_{DB}(G_t \mid \boldsymbol{\theta})} \sum_{S \in \psi_{DB}(G_t)} P_F(S \mid \boldsymbol{\theta}) \sigma_{i,v}(S);$$

  foreach $i \in I, v \in V_i$ **do**

$$\theta_{i,v} := \frac{\eta[i,v]}{\sum_{v' \in V_i} \eta[i,v']}; \quad \text{\% Update the parameters.}$$

  $m := m + 1$;
  $\lambda^{(m)} := \sum_{t=1}^{T} \ln P_{DB}(G_t \mid \boldsymbol{\theta})$ % Compute the log-likelihood again.
until $\lambda^{(m)} - \lambda^{(m-1)} < \varepsilon$ % Terminate if converged.
end.

Our modeling process by a parameterized logic program DB of an observation G is summarized as follows (the case of multiple observations is analogous).

Search of all explanations for G
⇓
Support set $\psi_{DB}(G)$ for G
⇓
EM learning applied to $\psi_{DB}(G)$
⇓
Parameter values for `msw` atoms

3.2 OLDT and the graphical EM algorithm

Symbolic-statistical modeling by parameterized logic programs has been formulated, but the real problem is whether it scales up or not. This is because for example the first step in the modeling process includes the search of all explanations for G, and it can be prohibitively time consuming. If there are exponentially many explanations for G as is the case with HMMs, search by backtracking would take also exponential time. We circumvent this difficulty by employing OLDT search [26]. OLDT is a complete refutation procedure for definite clause programs which reuses previously computed results saved in a table. Because it avoids computing the same goal twice, the search of all explanations by OLDT often can be done in polynomial time. In case of HMMs, search time is $O(N^2L)$ (N the number of states, L the length of an input string) and in case of PCFGs, it is $O(N^3L^3)$ (N the number of non-terminals, L the length of an input sentence).

The adoption of OLDT search yields a very favorable side effect on achieving **Task-1**, **Task-2** and **Task-3** in Section 1.[11] Since OLDT search shares sub-refutations, corresponding partial explanations are factored out, which makes it possible to represent the support set $\psi_{DB}(G)$ compactly as a hierarchical graph called a *support graph* reflecting the sharing structure between explanations for G. Look at $learn\text{-}naive(DB, \mathcal{G})$, especially the computation of $P_{DB}(G_t \mid \boldsymbol{\theta})$ and $\sum_{S \in \psi_{DB}(G_t)} P_F(S \mid \boldsymbol{\theta})\sigma_{i,v}(S)$. The computation of $P_{DB}(G_t \mid \boldsymbol{\theta}) = \sum_{S \in \psi_{DB}(G_t)} P_F(S \mid \boldsymbol{\theta})$ takes time proportional to the number of explanations for G_t if it is implemented faithfully to this formula. We reorganize this computation by introducing *inside probabilities* for logic programs as a generalization of the backward algorithm for HMMs [15] and the inside probabilities for PCFGs [1] in order to share subcomputations in $\sum_{S \in \psi_{DB}(G_t)} P_F(S \mid \boldsymbol{\theta})$. They are just a probability $P_{DB}(A \mid \boldsymbol{\theta})$ but recursively computed from the set of iff definitions of predicates and efficiently perform **Task-1** in time proportional to the size of a support graph.

The same optimization can be done for the computation of $\sum_{S \in \psi_{DB}(G_t)} P_F(S \mid \boldsymbol{\theta})\sigma_{i,v}(S)$ by introducing *outside probabilities* for logic programs as a generalization of the forward algorithm for HMMs [15] and the outside probabilities for PCFGs [1]. They represent the probability of "context" in which a specific atom occurs. Inside probabilities and outside probabilities are recursively computed from a support graph and the computation takes time only proportional to the size of the graph. Thus a new EM algorithm called the *graphical EM algorithm* incorporating inside probabilities and outside probabilities that works on support graphs has been proposed in [7]. We omit the description of the graphical EM algorithm though (see [22] for the detailed description). When combined with OLDT search, it is shown [7, 22] that

OLDT search + (support graphs) + the graphical EM algorithm

is as efficient as specialized EM algorithms developed domain-dependently (the Baum-Welch algorithm for HMMs, the Inside-Outside algorithm for PCFGs and the one for singly connected Bayesian networks) complexity-wise.[12] So **Task-3** is efficiently carried out in our framework.

It is also easy to design an algorithm for **Task-2** that finds out the most likely explanation in time linear in the size of a support graph [20], which generalizes

[11] Detailed explanations are found in [7, 22].

[12] This is a bit surprising as the graphical EM algorithm is a single algorithm generally designed for definite clause programs (satisfying certain conditions [7, 22]) allowing recursion and infinite domains.

the Viterbi algorithm for HMMs [15]. We therefore can say that the introduction of support graphs (constructed from OLDT search) and that of inside probabilities and outside probabilities for logic programs computed from a support graph efficiently solve the three tasks laid in Section 1.

3.3 Learning experiments

It is appropriate here to report some performance data about the graphical EM algorithm. We conducted learning experiments to compare the performance of the graphical EM algorithm with that of the Inside-Outside algorithm, the standard parameter learning algorithm for PCFGs, by using a real corpus and a PCFG developed for it.

We used ATR corpus [28] containing 10,995 sentences whose minimum length, average length and maximum length are respectively 2, 9.97 and 49. The grammar, G_{ATR}, is a hand crafted CFG comprising 860 rules (172 nonterminals and 441 terminals) [27] developed for ATR corpus. G_{ATR}, being not in Chomsky normal form, was translated into CFG G^*_{ATR} in Chomsky normal form for the Inside-Outside algorithm to be applicable.[13] G^*_{ATR} contains 2,105 rules (196 nonterminals and 441 terminals).

We created subgroups S_L ($1 \leq L \leq 25$) of sentences with length L and $L+1$ by randomly choosing 100 sentences for each L from the corpus. Support graphs for S_Ls w.r.t. G_{ATR} and G^*_{ATR} were generated by Tomita (Generalized LR) parser by the way. After these preparations, for each S_L, we compared time per iteration for the Inside-Outside algorithm to update the parameters of G^*_{ATR}[14] with that for the graphical EM algorithm to update the parameters of G_{ATR} and G^*_{ATR}. The results are shown in Figure 3.

A vertical axis shows the required time. A horizontal axis is L, the length parameter of learned sentences. A curve labeled I-O in the left graph[15] is drawn by the Inside-Outside algorithm. It is cubic as $O(N^3L^3)$ predicts. The curves labeled gEM in the right graphs are drawn by the graphical EM algorithm. One with a comment "original" is for G_{ATR}. As seen from the graph, the graphical EM algorithm runs almost 850 times faster than the Inside-Outside algorithm at length 10 (the average sentence length in the ATR corpus is 9.97). The other one with "Chomsky NF" is the curve obtained by applying the graphical EM algorithm to G^*_{ATR}.[16] The graphical EM algorithm still runs 720 times faster than the the Inside-Outside algorithm. Further more, a closer inspection reveals that update time by the graphical EM algorithm is almost linearly dependent

[13] The Inside-Outside algorithms requires a CFG to be in Chomsky normal form while the graphical EM algorithm accepts every form of production rules.

[14] We used a somewhat improved version of the Inside-Outside algorithm that avoids apparently redundant computations. For instance $p \cdot \sum_x q(x)$ is immediately evaluated as 0 if $p = 0$.

[15] The right graph is an enlarged version of the left one.

[16] We would like to emphasize again that the graphical EM algorithm does not require a CFG in Chomsky normal form. This comparison is only made to measure time for updating parameters of a common PCFG.

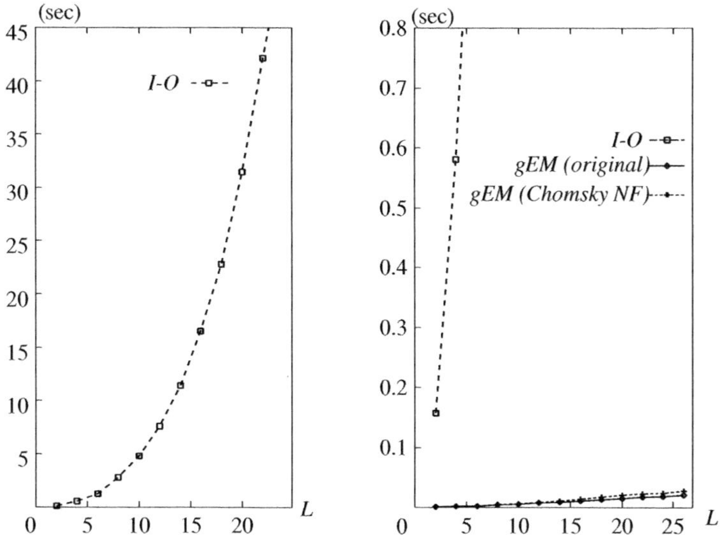

Fig. 3. The Inside-Outside algorithm vs. the graphical EM algorithm

on L, not on L^3. The conclusion is that although the graphical EM algorithm has the same time complexity as the Inside-Outside algorithm, the difference in their performances is enormous when applied to real data, and the almost linear dependency of the graphical EM on the sentence length suggests that it can cope with the learning of a complex stochastic grammar applied to a bigger corpus with longer sentences.

3.4 PRISM

As an implementation of distribution semantics, a symbolic-statistical modeling language PRISM (URL = `http://sato-www.cs.titech.ac.jp/prism/`) has been developed [16–18]. It is intended for modeling complex symbolic-statistical phenomena such as discourse interpretation in natural language processing, consumer behavior, gene inheritance interacting with complicated social rules [18]. As a programming language, it is an extension of Prolog with built-in predicates including `msw` predicate and other special predicates for manipulating `msw` atoms and their parameters.

A PRISM program is comprised of three parts, one for directives, one for modeling and one for utilities. The directive part contains declarations telling the system what `msw` atoms will be used in the program. The modeling part is a non-unit definite clause program like DB_1 that defines the denotation of the program containing `msw` atoms. The last part, the utility part, is an arbitrary Prolog program which refers to predicates defined in the modeling part. We can use there `learn` built-in predicate to carry out EM learning by *learn-naive*$(DB, \mathcal{G})$ from observed atoms. There are three modes of execution. The sampling execution corresponds to a random sampling drawn from the distribution defined by the modeling part. The second one computes the probability of a given atom. The third one returns the support set for a given goal. These modes of execution are available through built-in predicates. Currently the implementation of the graphical EM algorithm and the simplified OLDT search mechanism is underway.

4 Reinforcement learning and parameterized logic programs

4.1 Reinforcement learning

We turn our attention here to on-line learning, i.e. data come one by one and learning is done each time. The idea is to use reinforcement learning [24, 29] (see [5] for a survey) to reactively adjust parameters $\theta_{i,k}$ for $\texttt{msw}(i,n,v_k)$ $(1 \leq k \leq N)$. Reinforcement learning is a model of learning good behavior by trial and error, by receiving reward and penalty from a random environment.[17] For instance, in Q-learning [29], one of the most popular reinforcement learning methods based on MDP (Markov Decision Process) [11], an agent is expected to learn, while randomly or systematically walking in the environment, a best action among several ones at each state to maximize its discounted or total expected reward. In this paper however, we adopt *learning automatons* [12, 14] instead of MDP as an underlying theoretical framework because of their affinity with parameterized logic programs as a learning device for `msw` atoms.[18]

A *learning automaton* (henceforth referred to as LA) is a reactive learning device working in a random environment. On each execution, it selects an action in proportion to choice probabilities assigned to each action, and adjust them in response to the gained reward so that profitable actions are likely to be selected again. The point is that, while it just makes a random choice in the beginning, by repeatedly choosing an action and adjusting probabilities, it asymptotically converges to a stage where it only takes the most rewarding action (in average sense) [12, 14].

We embed LAs in a parameterized logic program to automatically adjust parameters of `msw` atoms. Aside from the theoretical question about convergence of their collective behavior, the learning ability of LAs added to logic programs makes them reactive to the environment. We call such programs as *reactive logic programs*. Reactive logic programs are intended to model an agent with rich background knowledge working in an uncertain world who learns from the environment how to behave optimally.

[17] By random, we mean the reward returned for taking an action is a random variable. In this paper, we assume the environment is stationary, i.e. the distribution of reward does not change with time. Also we leave out penalty as a type of response for convenience.

[18] They require neither the notion of state nor that of state change.

4.2 Learning Automaton

A learning automaton (LA) [12, 14][19] is a learning device applicable to a situation in which there are several possible actions with different probabilistic rewards, and we want to know the best one that maximizes the average reward. The most typical situation would be gambling. Imagine playing with a slot machine that has N levers (N-armed bandit). Pulling a lever gives us winnings if we are lucky. We want to know the best lever yielding the maximum average payoff while betting coins repeatedly. Which lever should we pull at nth time?

One way to solve this problem is to use an LA. Suppose there are N possible actions $\alpha_1, \ldots, \alpha_N$. We associate a choice probability $\theta_i(n)$ with each α_i ($1 \leq i \leq N$) so that α_i is chosen with probability $\theta_i(n)$ at time n. The distribution for actions at time n is expressed by a random vector $\boldsymbol{\theta}(n) = \langle \theta_1(n), \ldots, \theta_N(n) \rangle$ ($\sum_i \theta_i(n) = 1$). Suppose α_i is chosen. By executing α_i, we get a reward γ from an environment[20], with which we update $\boldsymbol{\theta}(n)$ by using L_{R-I} (Linear Reward-Inaction) scheme [12][21]

$$\theta_i(n+1) = \theta_i(n) + c_n\gamma(1 - \theta_i(n))$$
$$\theta_j(n+1) = (1 - c_n\gamma)\theta_j(n) \quad (j \neq i)$$

where c_n ($0 \leq c_n \leq 1$) is a *learning rate* at time n. The scheme says that if the reward γ is non-zero, we will give more chance of selection to action α_i. Since γ is a random variable, so are the $\theta_i(n)$s. Figure 4 illustrates an LA where edges denote actions and d_i is the average reward for action α_i ($1 \leq i \leq N$).

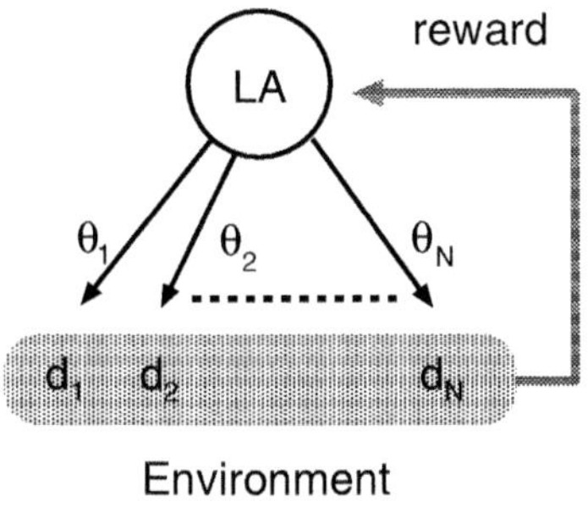

Fig. 4. A learning automaton

It is known that the L_{R-I} scheme can improve the average reward of the LA [12]. To see it, let $\boldsymbol{\theta}(n)$ be a current distribution. $M(n)$, the average reward at time n conditioned on $\boldsymbol{\theta}(n)$, is derived as

$$M(n) = E[\gamma \mid \boldsymbol{\theta}(n)]$$

---

[19] The type of LAs we use is called a variable-structure stochastic automaton in [12].
[20] We assume γ is normalized such that $0 \leq \gamma \leq 1$.
[21] There are other learning schemes [12]. The L_{R-I} scheme is the simplest one.

$$= \sum_{i=1}^{N} \theta_i(n) d_i \tag{3}$$

where $E[\cdot]$ denotes expectation and d_i is the average reward for taking action α_i $(1 \leq i \leq N)$. $M(n)$ is a random variable as a function of $\boldsymbol{\theta}(n)$. $E[M(n+1) \mid \boldsymbol{\theta}(n)]$, the average reward at time $n+1$ conditioned on $\boldsymbol{\theta}(n)$, then comes out as

$$\begin{aligned} E[M(n+1) \mid \boldsymbol{\theta}(n)] &= E[\sum_{i=1}^{N} \theta_i(n+1) d_i) \mid \boldsymbol{\theta}(n)] \\ &= M(n) + \frac{c_n \gamma}{2} \sum_{i,j} (d_i - d_j)^2 \theta_i(n) \theta_j(n) &(4) \\ &\geq M(n) &(5) \end{aligned}$$

By taking expectation of both sides in (5), we conclude

$$E[M(n+1)] \geq E[M(n)] \tag{6}$$

i.e. the average reward is increasing at every time step.

It is also important to note that $\{M(n)\}_{n=1,2,\ldots}$ forms a submartingale. Since $E[M(n)] \leq 1$ holds for all n, $\{M(n)\}$ has an a.s.(almost sure) convergence, which in turn implies, when the learning rate c_n is kept constant c, we see $\theta_j(n) \xrightarrow{\text{a.s.}} 0$ or 1 for every $\theta_j(n)$ $(1 \leq j \leq N)$. Regrettably, this does not necessarily mean that the probability $\theta_i(n)$ corresponding to the maximum average reward d_i will converge to 1 with probability 1 after infinite trials. However, it was proved that the probability of $\theta_i(n)$ not converging to 1 is made arbitrarily small by setting c small enough [12]. Also, recently it also has been proved that if we decay the learning rate c_n like $c_n = \frac{b}{n+a}$ $(a > b, 1 > b > 0)$, and if initial probabilities are positive, i.e. $\theta_j(1) > 0$ $(1 \leq j \leq N)$ and $d_i > d_j$ for $j \neq i$, we have $\theta_i(n) \xrightarrow{\text{a.s.}} 1$ [14].

4.3 LA networks

In reactive logic programming, parameters $\theta_{i,k}$ $(1 \leq k \leq N)$ associated with `msw`$(i,n,\cdot)$ in a parameterized logic program are trained by an LA. The embedded LAs in the program as a whole constitute a tree, a dag (directed acyclic graph) or a more general graph structure. Unfortunately, unlike a single LA, not much has been known about the convergent behavior of the graph-structured LAs.[22] So we here introduce *LA networks*, the class of LAs organized as a dag and discuss their mathematical properties. Although we are aware that our reactive logic programming sometimes requires the use of a more general graph

[22] When there are multiple LAs connected with each other, the analysis becomes much harder. The reason is that for a given LA, other LAs are part of the environment and the average reward for a selected action becomes non-stationary, i.e. changes with time as the learning of the other LAs proceed, which prevents the derivation of formulas (5) which entails (6).

structures containing loops, we introduce LA networks because they are relatively expressive but yet analyzable.

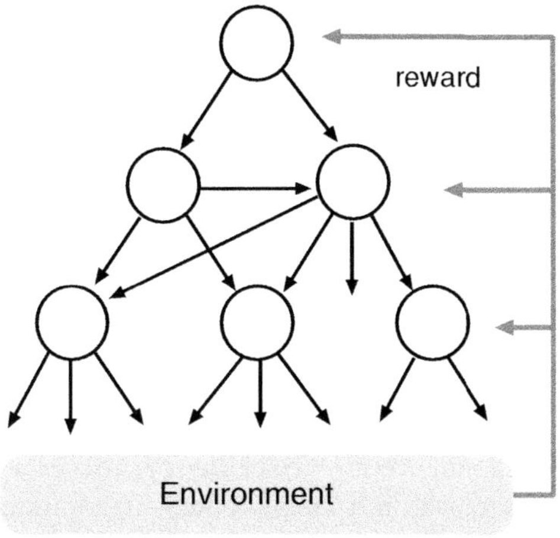

Fig. 5. A LA network

Formally, a *LA network* is a connected dag (Figure 5) such that a node and its outgoing edges comprise an LA and there is the only one node with no incoming edges called the *root* LA. A node which has no descendent node is called a *leaf* LA. Each edge is labeled by an action and by the probability associated with it (see Figure 4). Actions are chosen sequentially from the root LA to a leaf LA in an obvious way and the reward is simultaneously given to each LA on the path from the root to the leaf to update choice probabilities.

Let $\boldsymbol{\theta}(n)$ be probabilities for all edges in the graph at time n, and $M(n)$ the average reward at time n conditioned on $\boldsymbol{\theta}(n)$. When the shape of the LA network is a tree, we can prove (6) w.r.t. the root LA by setting learning rates differently for each LA and for each trial (hierarchical systems [12]). On the other hand, the need of computing different learning rates is computationally disadvantageous compared to using a common constant learning rate, for which case we can still prove (5) (and hence (6)) under the condition that the reward is binary i.e. $\{0,1\}$ (proof omitted).

For LA networks which are not trees, we do not know at the moment if (5) holds w.r.t. the root LA for a constant learning rate. However, we proved in [19] that (5), the increase of the average reward, holds for arbitrary LA networks as long as a common learning rate $\frac{1}{n+a}$ with large enough a is used by all LAs at time n. That is, with this decaying learning rate, an LA network gains more reward on average every time the program is executed. What is disappointing about it is that it gives too slow convergence, experimentally. So we decided instead to use a constant learning rate set by a user.

4.4 LA library

We built a library called *LA library* so that various built-in predicates are available to manipulate LAs in a parameterized logic program. We here explain some of them. First `new_choice(`i`,`*list*`)` creates `msw` atoms $\{$`msw(`i`,`t`,`v`)` $\mid (v \in list)\}$ with an LA attached to them with equal values for vs. We use fresh t every on every execution of such `msw` atom. `new_choice(sanfrancisco, [neworleans, chicago])` for instance sets up a new LA named `sanfrancisco` that outputs equiprobably `neworleans` or `chicago`. *list* is a list containing arbitrary terms but i must be a ground term. `choice(`i`,V)` executes an LA named i with a current distribution and the output is returned in `V`. `reinforce_choice(`c`,`*list*`)` adjusts according to the L_{R-I} learning scheme choice probabilities in all LAs contained in *list* using the base line cost c (see Section 4.5).

4.5 Reinforcement condition

It must be emphasized that we are a tackling optimization problem. We use a reactive logic program expecting that by repeatedly running it, the parameters of LAs are automatically adjusted, and the most rewarding choice sequence will eventually gain the highest execution probability. In view of this, we should not apply `reinforce_choice/2` unconditionally every time computation is done, because we are not seeking for a correct answer but for a better answer that corresponds to a more rewarding choice sequence and there is no reason for giving out a reward to whatever answer is computed.

We try to obtain a better answer by comparing a new one and the old ones. Suppose we run a program and the computed answer is judged better than the old ones. We reinforce every LA involved in the computation by invoking `reinforce_choice/2`. The criterion for invocation is called a *reinforcement condition*. We can conceive of several reinforcement conditions depending on the type of problem, but in this paper, we use the following heuristic condition.[23]

$$\frac{C_s + C_a}{2} > C$$

where C is the cost of the computed answer, C_s the least cost achieved so far and C_a the average cost in the past M trials ($M = 50$ is used in this paper).

4.6 Going to the East

Now we present a very simple reactive logic program for a stochastic optimization problem. The problem is to find a route in Figure 6 from San Francisco to New York but a traveling cost between adjacent cities (cost attached to edges in Figure 6) is supposed to vary randomly for various reasons on each trial. The task is to find a route giving the least average cost.

We first define `travel/2` predicate to compute the route and cost of traveling from the current city (`Now`) to New York.

[23] Note that the condition is stated in terms of cost, so the lesser, the better.

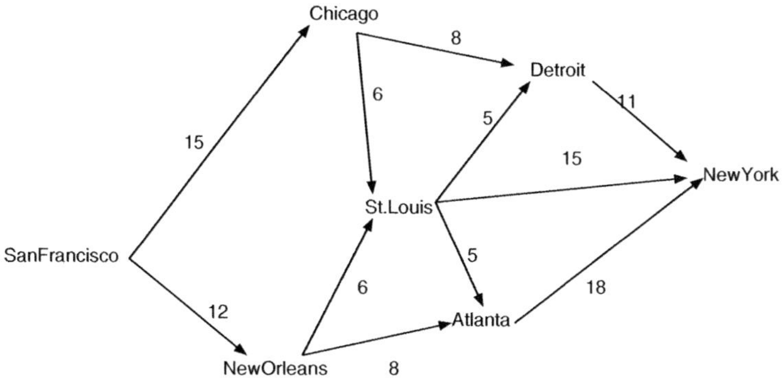

Fig. 6. Going to the East

```
% Destination = New York
 travel(newyork,0,[newyork]).
 travel(Now,Cost,[Now|Route]) :-
    choice(Now,Next),
    travel(Next,C1,Route),
    link_cost(Now,Next,C2),
    Cost is C1 + C2.
```

`link_cost/2` returns the traveling cost of adjacent two cities. It consists of a basic cost plus a random increment (uniform distribution, max 20%) determined by `random_float/2`.

```
 link_cost(Now,Next,Cost) :-
    cost(Now,Next,C1),
    random_float(0.2,C2),
    Cost is C1 * (1+C2).
```

A table of basic cost is given by unit clauses (numbers are artificial).

```
 cost(sanfrancisco, neworleans, 10).
 cost(sanfrancisco, chicago, 15).
 cost(sanfrancisco, stlouis, 12).
 ...
 cost(stlouis, newyork, 15).
 cost(atlanta, newyork, 18).
```

After 10,000 trials of `?- travel(sanfrancisco,_,Route)` with a learning rate 0.01 and the reinforcement condition previously stated, we obtained the following route. As can be seen, the recommended route (`San Francisco, New Orleans, St. Louis, New York`) gives the least average cost. How learning converges is depicted in Figure 8. It plotted the average cost in the past 50 trials. We see that the average cost decreases rapidly in the initial 1,000 trials and then slowly. Theoretically speaking however, there is no guarantee of the

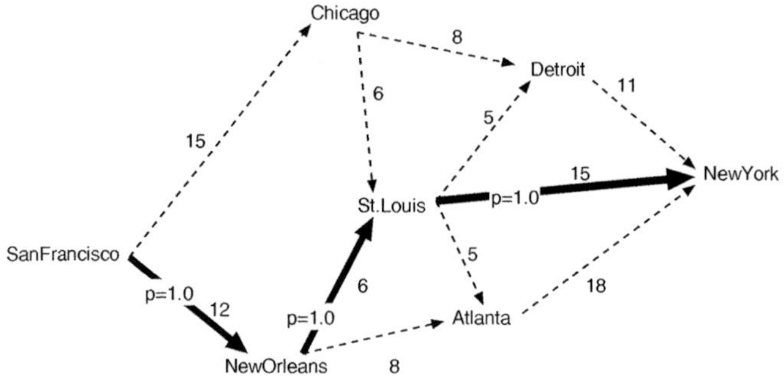

Fig. 7. A route to New York

decreasing average cost when the learning rate is kept constant in an LA network with loops, but taking into account the fact that the average cost decreases with a decaying learning rate (Section 4.3), we may reasonably expect it happens as well provided the learning rate is kept sufficiently small.

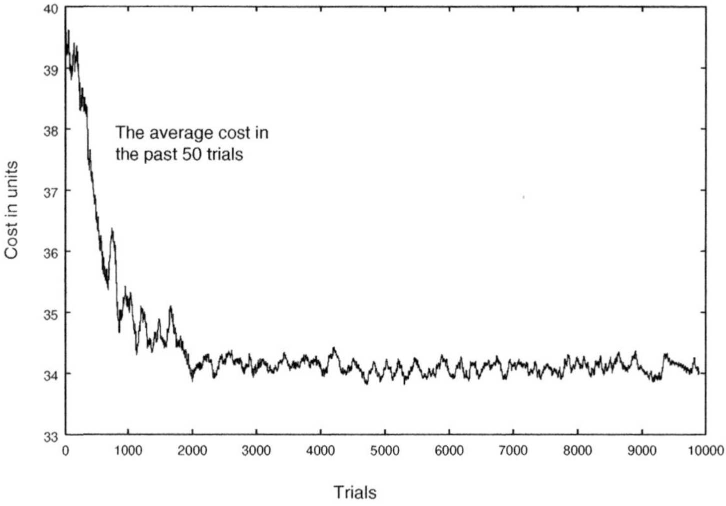

Fig. 8. Learning curve

5 Conclusion

We have presented attempts to make programs more adaptive by adding learning ability. In order to unify computing and learning at semantic level, distribution semantics is introduced for parameterized logic programs that contain probabilistic facts with a parameterized distribution. The new semantics is a generalization of the least model semantics for definite clause programs to possible world semantics with a distribution. We then apply the semantics to statistical modeling in Section 3 and to reactive programming in Section 4. It is shown that efficient symbolic-statistical modeling is made possible by the graphical EM algorithm working on a new data structure called support graphs. The learning experiments have shown that the graphical EM algorithm combined with OLDT search is not only as competitive as existing specialized EM algorithms complexity-wise, but in the case of PCFGs, runs 850 times faster than the Inside-Outside algorithm, a rather pleasant surprise. We also applied distribution semantics to reinforcement learning of parameterized logic programs by learning automatons, and showed a simple reactive programming example applied to a stochastic search problem.

References

1. Baker, J. K., Trainable grammars for speech recognition, *Proc. of Spring Conference of the Acoustical Society of America*, pp.547–550, 1979.
2. Castillo, E., Gutierrez, J.M., and Hadi, A.S., *Expert Systems and Probabilistic Network Models*, Springer-Verlag, 1997.
3. Chow,Y.S. and Teicher, H., *Probability Theory* (3rd ed.), Springer, 1997.
4. Doets, K., *From Logic to Logic Programming*, MIT Press, Cambridge, 1994.
5. Kaelbling,L.P. and Littman,M.L., Reinforcement Learning: A Survey, *J. of Artificial Intelligence Research*, Vol.4, pp.237–285, 1996.
6. Kameya, Y., Ueda, N. and Sato, T., A graphical method for parameter learning of symbolic-statistical models, *Proc. of DS'99*, LNAI 1721, pp.264–276, 1999.
7. Kameya, Y. and Sato, T., Efficient EM learning for parameterized logic programs, *Proc. of CL2000*, LNAI 1861, pp.269–294, 2000.
8. Lloyd, J. W., *Foundations of Logic Programming*, Springer-Verlag, 1984.
9. Manning, C. D. and Schütze, H., *Foundations of Statistical Natural Language Processing*, The MIT Press, 1999.
10. McLachlan, G. J. and Krishnan, T., The EM Algorithm and Extensions, Wiley Interscience, 1997.
11. Monahan,G.E., A Survey of Partially Observable Markov Decision Processes: Theory, Models, and Algorithms, *Management Science* Vol.28 No.1, pp.1–16, 1982.
12. Narendra,K.S. and Thathacher,M.A.L., *Learning Automata: An Introduction*, Prentice-Hall Inc., 1989.
13. Pearl, J., *Probabilistic Reasoning in Intelligent Systems*, Morgan Kaufmann, 1988.
14. Poznyak,A.S. and Najim,K., *Learning Automata and Stochastic Optimization*, Lecture Notes in Control and Information Sciences 225, Springer, 1997.
15. Rabiner, L. R. and Juang, B., *Foundations of Speech Recognition*, Prentice-Hall, 1993.
16. Sato, T., A statistical learning method for logic programs with distribution semantics, *Proc. of ICLP'95*, pp.715-729, 1995.
17. Sato, T. and Kameya, Y., PRISM:A Language for Symbolic-Statistical Modeling, *Proc. of IJCAI'97*, pp.1330–1335, 1997.
18. Sato, T., Modeling Scientific Theories as PRISM Programs, *ECAI Workshop on Machine Discovery*, pp.37–45, 1998.

19. Sato, T., On Some Asymptotic Properties of Learning Automaton Networks, Techinical report TR99-0003, Dept. of Computer Science, Tokyo Institute of Technology, 1999.
20. Sato,T. and Kameya, Y., A Viterbi-like algorithm and EM learning for statistical abduction", *Proc. of UAI2000 Workshop on Fusion of Domain Knowledge with Data for Decision Support*, 2000.
21. Sato,T., Statistical abduction with tabulation, submitted for publication, 2000.
22. Sato,T. and Kameya, Y., Parameter Learning of Logic Programs for Symbolic-statistical Modeling, submitted for publication, 2000.
23. Sterling, L. and Shaprio, E. *The Art of Prolog*, The MIT Press, 1986.
24. Sutton,R.S., Learning to predict by the method of temporal difference, *Machine Learning*, Vol.3 No.1, pp.9–44, 1988.
25. Tamaki, H. and Sato, T., Unfold/Fold Transformation of Logic Programs, *Proc. of ICLP'84*, Uppsala, pp.127–138, 1984.
26. Tamaki, H. and Sato, T., OLD resolution with tabulation, *Proc. of ICLP'86*, London, LNCS 225, pp.84–98, 1986.
27. Tanaka, H. and Takezawa, T. and Etoh, J., Japanese grammar for speech recognition considering the MSLR method (in Japanese), *Proc. of the meeting of SIG-SLP (Spoken Language Processing)*, 97-SLP-15-25, Information Processing Society of Japan, pp.145–150, 1997.
28. Uratani, N. and Takezawa, T. and Matsuo, H. and Morita, C., ATR Integrated Speech and Language Database (in Japanese), TR-IT-0056, ATR Interpreting Telecommunications Research Laboratories, 1994.
29. Watkins,J.C.H. and Dayan,P., Q-learning, *Machine Intelligence*, Vol.8, No.3, pp.279–292, 1992.
30. Wetherell, C.S., Probabilistic languages: a review and some open questions, *Computing Surveys*, Vol.12, No.4, pp.361–379, 1980.

Proving Syntactic Properties of Exceptions in an Ordered Logical Framework *

Jeff Polakow[1] and Kwangkeun Yi[2]

[1] jpolakow@cs.cmu.edu
Department of Computer Science
Carnegie Mellon University
[2] kwang@cs.kaist.ac.kr
ROPAS***
Department of Computer Science
Korea Advanced Institute of Science & Technology

Abstract. We formally prove the stackability and linearity of exception handlers with ML-style semantics using a novel proof technique via an ordered logical framework (OLF). We first transform exceptions into continuation-passing-style (CPS) terms and formalize the exception properties as a judgement on the CPS terms. Then, rather than directly proving that the properties hold for terms, we prove our theorem for the representations of the CPS terms and transform in OLF. We rely upon the correctness of our representations to transfer the results back to the actual CPS terms and transform.
Our work can be seen as two-fold: we present a theoretical justification of using the stack mechanism to implement exceptions of ML-like semantics; and we demonstrate the value of an ordered logical framework as a conceptual tool in the theoretical study of programming languages.

1 This Work

We formally prove a folklore property of exceptions of ML-like semantics: exception handlers are used at most once (linearity) in a stack-like-manner (stackability) (i.e., installing an exception handler and handling an exception respectively amounts to "push" and "pop."). Furthermore we show that the ordering properties investigated in [DDP99,DP95] for results of the conventional continuation-passing-style (CPS) transformation [DF92,Plo75,Ste78]— stackability of both continuation identifiers and continuation parameters— also hold for results of an extended CPS transform[KYD98,App97] which replaces exception-raise and -handle expressions by function (continuation) calls and constructions in higher-order programs.

We prove the two properties as follows:

* This work is supported by Creative Research Initiatives of the Korean Ministry of Science and Technology.

*** Research On Program Analysis System (http://ropas.kaist.ac.kr), National Creative Research Initiative Center, KAIST, Korea.

H. Kuchen and K. Ueda (Eds.): FLOPS 2001, LNCS 2024, pp. 61–77, 2001.

1. In order to expose the semantics of exceptions in the program text, we encode exceptions in source programs with continuations by using the extended CPS transformation.
2. We then formalize the properties of interest as a judgement on CPS terms.
3. We then prove that all terms resulting from the transformation satisfy our judgement.

We carry out the main portion of our proof (pt. 3 above) in a novel fashion—via an ordered logical framework (OLF) [PP00], a new formalism which is particularly well-suited for our purpose. Rather than directly proving that the properties hold for terms (which would require a rather tedious logical-relations style argument [DDP99]), we directly prove our theorem for representations of the CPS terms and transform in OLF. By working in OLF we can take advantage of known properties of OLF terms (e.g. substitution properties) which simplify our task. We then rely upon the correctness of our representations to transfer the results back to the actual CPS terms and transformation.

Our work can be seen as a theoretical justification of existing compilers that use the stack mechanism to implement exceptions. Our work also demonstrates the value of a (ordered) logical framework as a conceptual tool in the theoretical study of programming languages. We believe that working inside OLF greatly simplifies our proof. Of course such simplification comes at the cost of gaining familiarity with OLF. However, we feel the trade-off is advantageous. Logical frameworks have generally proven themselves to be useful tools for studying programming languages [Pfe96]; and we believe OLF, though still a new formalism, will likewise prove itself useful.

1.1 Overview

Section 2 introduces the ordered logical framework in which we will represent our terms and transform. In section 3.2 we define direct-style terms with exception raise and handle expressions, CPS terms, and the CPS transformation for encoding exception-raise and -handle expressions by continuations. We also define judgements on CPS terms for stackability (and linearity) of the exception handling mechanism. In section 4 we give OLF representations for direct-style terms and for CPS terms satisfying the stackability judgements. In section 5 we show the representation of the CPS transformation. This representation takes represented direct-style terms to represented CPS terms. The correctness of this representation completes our proof since represented CPS terms correspond to actual CPS terms satisfying the stackability judgements. Finally, we give a conclusion with some related and future work in section 7.

2 Ordered Logical Framework

OLF is a logical framework in the tradition of LF [HHP93] and its linear extension LLF [CP99]. Thus OLF is essentially a dependent type theory[1] for which

[1] Types can depend upon terms.

type checking is decidable and canonical forms exist. Since OLF has come under study quite recently, the remainder of this section provides the necessary background information to follow our proof.

OLF should be thought of as ordered linear types [PP99a] extended with dependent types. Thus, we will first review ordered linear logic, the logic corresponding to ordered linear types.

2.1 Ordered Linear Logic

Ordered linear logic (OLL) is a conservative extension of intuitionistic linear logic with ordered hypotheses. We begin with a review of the fragment of OLL which we will use. For a description of the full system see [PP99b,PP99a].

Types	$A ::= a$	atomic types
	$\mid A_0 \rightarrow A_1$	intuitionistic implication
	$\mid A_0 \twoheadrightarrow A_1$	ordered right implication
	$\mid A_0 \,\&\, A_1$	additive conjunction
	$\mid \top$	additive truth

Objects	$M ::= c$	constants
	$\mid x \mid z$	variables
	$\mid \lambda x{:}A.\ M \mid M_0\, M_1$	intuitionistic functions $(A \rightarrow B)$
	$\mid \overset{>}{\lambda} z{:}A.\ M \mid M_0 \,^{>}\, M_1$	right ordered functions $(A \twoheadrightarrow B)$
	$\mid \langle M\, ,\, N\rangle \mid \pi_1\, M \mid \pi_2\, M$	additive pairs $(A \,\&\, B)$
	$\mid \langle\rangle$	additive unit $(\top)$

We build typing rules for OLL objects from the following judgement

$$\Gamma; \Omega \vdash M : A$$

where Γ is a list of unrestricted hypotheses, Ω is a list of ordered hypotheses, and a signature containing constant declarations is left implicit. The inference rules will be structured to allow copying, discarding, and exchanging of unrestricted hypotheses. However, ordered hypotheses will not enjoy those structural properties— they must be used exactly once in their relative order.

Here are the rules for unrestricted functions.

$$\frac{}{(\Gamma_1, x{:}A, \Gamma_2); \cdot \vdash x : A}\,\mathbf{ivar} \qquad \frac{(\Gamma, x{:}A); \Omega \vdash M : B}{\Gamma; \Omega \vdash \lambda x{:}A.\ M : A \rightarrow B}\rightarrow I$$

$$\frac{\Gamma; \Omega \vdash M : A \rightarrow B \qquad \Gamma; \cdot \vdash N : A}{\Gamma; \Omega \vdash M\, N : B}\rightarrow E$$

Note that the ordered context in the minor premise of $\rightarrow_E$ must be empty. This ensures that unrestricted functions, which may use their argument arbitrarily, may not be applied to ordered arguments, which must be used exactly once.

The rules for ordered functions follow.

$$\frac{}{\Gamma; z{:}A \vdash z : A}\,\textbf{ovar} \qquad \frac{\Gamma; (\Omega, z{:}A) \vdash M : B}{\Gamma; \Omega \vdash \overset{>}{\lambda} z{:}A.\ M : A \twoheadrightarrow B}\twoheadrightarrow I$$

$$\frac{\Gamma; \Omega_1 \vdash M : A \twoheadrightarrow B \qquad \Gamma; \Omega_2 \vdash N : A}{\Gamma; (\Omega_1, \Omega_2) \vdash M\,\overset{>}{}\,N : B}\twoheadrightarrow E$$

Note that the argument to an ordered function may only depend upon ordered hypotheses to the right of those use by the body of the function—the order of the hypotheses constrains their use by ordered functions.

Finally we give the rules for pairs and unit.

$$\frac{\Gamma; \Omega \vdash M : A \qquad \Gamma; \Omega \vdash N : B}{\Gamma; \Omega \vdash \langle M\,,\, N\rangle : A \,\&\, B}\&_I \qquad \frac{}{\Gamma; \Omega \vdash \langle\rangle : \top}\top_I$$

$$\frac{\Gamma; \Omega \vdash M : A \,\&\, B}{\Gamma; \Omega \vdash \pi_1\, M : A}\&_{E1} \qquad \frac{\Gamma; \Omega \vdash M : A \,\&\, B}{\Gamma; \Omega \vdash \pi_2\, M : B}\&_{E2}$$

The reduction rules for OLL objects are simply β-reduction for both kinds of functions. The appropriate notion of equality of objects also includes η-conversion so that every well-typed object has an equivalent canonical form.

Our calculus enjoys subject reduction, as proved in [PP99a].

Theorem 1 (Subject Reduction).
If $M \Longrightarrow M'$ and $\Gamma; \Omega \vdash M : A$ then $\Gamma; \Omega \vdash M' : A$.

Proof: For each reduction, we apply inversion to the given typing derivation and then use a substitution lemma to obtain the typing derivation for the conclusion. □

Finally, we note that this calculus has canonical forms as shown in [PP99a]. Thus all terms of functional type may be converted to the form $\lambda x{:}A.\ M$ or $\overset{>}{\lambda} z{:}A.\ M$; all terms of conjunctive type may be converted to pairs $\langle M\,,\, N\rangle$; and all objects of atomic type may be reduced to a constant applied to zero or more canonical objects.

The existence of canonical forms for this simple implicational fragment of OLL provides a basis for an ordered logical framework. We conjecture that an ordered logical framework based on a full type theory can be constructed along the lines of the linear logical framework [CP99]. In this paper we only need a two-level fragment as explained in subsection 2.2.

2.2 Two-Level Framework

We extend the ordered λ-calculus from subsection 2.1 to a simple two-level logical framework where level-2 types will be allowed to depend upon level-1 objects.

Thus level-2 type families p are indexed by level 1 objects M, and we can quantify only over level 1 objects.

Level 2 types	*Level 2 objects*
$F ::= p\, M_1 \ldots M_n$	$D ::= c \mid w \mid y$
$\mid\ F_1 \rightarrow F_2$	$\mid\ \lambda w{:}F.\ D \mid D_1\, D_2$
$\mid\ F_1 \twoheadrightarrow F_2$	$\mid\ \overset{>}{\lambda} y{:}F.\ D \mid D_1 \overset{>}{\ } D_2$
$\mid\ F_1\ \&\ F_2$	$\mid\ \langle D_1\, ,\, D_2 \rangle \mid \pi_1\, D \mid \pi_2\, D$
$\mid\ \top$	$\mid\ \langle\rangle$
$\mid\ \Pi x{:}A.\ F$	$\mid\ \lambda x{:}A.\ D \mid D\, M$

The extended typing judgement now has the form $\Gamma; \Omega \vdash D : F$, where Γ may contain declarations of the form $x{:}A$ or $w{:}F$ and Ω contains declarations $y{:}F$. We omit the typing rules which are very similar to the propositional case, except that we now need rules for the dependent types:

$$\frac{\Gamma, x{:}A; \Omega \vdash D : F}{\Gamma; \Omega \vdash \lambda x{:}A.\ D : \Pi x{:}A.\ F} \qquad \frac{\Gamma; \Omega \vdash D : \Pi x{:}A.\ F \qquad \Gamma; \cdot \vdash M : A}{\Gamma; \Omega \vdash D\, M : F[M/x]}$$

and a rule for type conversion:

$$\frac{\Gamma; \Omega \vdash D : F \qquad \Gamma; \Omega \vdash F \equiv_{\beta\eta} F'}{\Gamma; \Omega \vdash D : F'}$$

Note that equivalence of level-2 types, $\equiv_{\beta\eta}$, must be decided in context due to the presence of $\top$.

Since we stratify the type theory into two syntactically distinct levels, $\beta\eta$-equality for level-2 types immediately reduces to $\beta\eta$-equality for propositional objects. Since propositional objects possess canonical (= long $\beta\eta$-normal) forms, this equality is easy to decide, and type-checking in the fragment presented above can easily be seen to be decidable. Furthermore, canonical forms for level-2 objects likewise come as a consequence of level-1 objects having canonical forms. We will use the judgement $\Gamma; \Omega \vdash D \Uparrow F$ to denote that object D is canonical at well-formed type F.

3 Terms & Transforms

This section introduces the direct-style language with exception raise and handle expressions, its CPS counterpart, and the transformation between them. We use underlined constants (e.g. $\underline{\mathsf{handle}}$) and lambdas ($\underline{\lambda}$) to distinguish these objects from their OLF representations which are given in section 4.

3.1 Direct Terms

We use the following syntax for direct-style (DS) terms:

DS Terms	$r ::= e$
DS Expressions	$e ::= e_0\, e_1 \mid \underline{\mathsf{handle}}\, e_0\, (\underline{\lambda} x.\ e_1) \mid \underline{\mathsf{raise}}\, e \mid t$
DS Trivial Expressions	$t ::= \underline{\lambda} x.\ r \mid x$

Evaluating the expression $\underline{\mathsf{raise}}\, e$ first evaluates e. It then aborts the normal execution and locates a handler by going up the current evaluation chain. The e's value is passed to the handler. The handle expression $\underline{\mathsf{handle}}\, e_0\, (\underline{\lambda} x.e_1)$ evaluates e_0. If e_0 raises an exception with value v and there are no other handle expressions between the current one and the raise expression, then the current handler function $\underline{\lambda} x.e_1$ handles it: the v is bound to x in e_1. Otherwise, the value of the handle expression is the value of e_0.

We define the formal semantics of DS terms with a structural operational semantics [Plo81] using Felleisen's evaluation contexts [Fel87]. In doing so, we need to extend the expressions to contain a set of raised values $\bar{t}$ that are thrown from raise expressions: $e \; ::= \; \cdots \mid \bar{t}$. An evaluation context C is defined by the following grammar:

$$C \; ::= \; [\,] \mid C\, e \mid (\underline{\lambda} x.\; r)\; C \mid \underline{\mathsf{handle}}\, C\; \underline{\lambda} x.\; e \mid \underline{\mathsf{raise}}\, C$$

This context defines a left-to-right, call-by-value reduction. As usual, we write $C[e]$ if the hole in context C is filled with e. We use this context to define the reduction rule for arbitrary expressions:

$$\frac{e \mapsto e'}{C[e] \mapsto C[e']}$$

The single reduction step $e \mapsto e'$ for a redex e consists of normal and exceptional reduction steps:

Normal reduction steps	Exceptional reduction steps
$(\underline{\lambda} x.\; r)\; t \mapsto [t/x]r$	$\underline{\mathsf{raise}}\, t \mapsto \bar{t}$
$\underline{\mathsf{handle}}\, t\; (\underline{\lambda} x.\; e) \mapsto t$	$\underline{\mathsf{raise}}\, \bar{t} \mapsto \bar{t}$
	$\underline{\mathsf{handle}}\, \bar{t}\; (\underline{\lambda} x.\; e) \mapsto [t/x]e$
	$\bar{t}\; e \mapsto \bar{t}$
	$(\underline{\lambda} x.\; r)\; \bar{t} \mapsto \bar{t}$

Normal reduction steps are not concerned with exceptions. Exceptional reduction steps specify the generation, propagation and handling of exceptions.

3.2 CPS Terms

Rather than working directly with DS terms, we transform them into CPS terms where the exception mechanism is captured by having a second (handler) continuation in addition to the regular (success) continuation. This transformation exposes the semantics of exceptions in the program text.

We use the following grammar for CPS terms:

Root Terms	$r ::= \underline{\lambda} k.\; e$
Serious Terms	$e ::= t_0\, t_1\, p \mid c\, t$
Trivial Terms	$t ::= \underline{\lambda} x.\; r \mid x \mid v$
Continuation Pairs	$p ::= \underline{\mathsf{pair}}(c_0\, ,\, c_1) \mid k$
Continuation Terms	$c ::= \underline{\lambda} x.\; e \mid \underline{\lambda} v.\; e \mid \underline{\mathsf{nrml}}\, p \mid \underline{\mathsf{hnd}}\, p$

Note that in the CPS syntax, we are distinguishing variables x which are parameters of functions or continuations from variables v which are only parameters to continuations. This distinction will be used to differentiate abstractions introduced by the transform from those already present in the DS term. $\underline{\mathsf{nrml}}$ and $\underline{\mathsf{hnd}}$ are essentially the projections for the continuation pairs.

The formal semantics are defined similarly to that for DS terms. However, rather than using special exception values ($\bar{t}$); exceptional flows ($\underline{\mathsf{raise}}$ and $\underline{\mathsf{handle}}$ expressions) are simulated by continuation functions. Let γ be the set of continuation functions: $\gamma ::= \underline{\lambda}x.e \mid \underline{\lambda}v.e$. An evaluation context C is extended for the cases of continuation pairs:

$$C \;::=\; [\,] \mid C\,p \mid C\,t \mid r\,C \mid \underline{\mathsf{pair}}(C\,,\,c) \mid \underline{\mathsf{pair}}(\gamma\,,\,C) \mid \underline{\mathsf{nrml}}\,C \mid \underline{\mathsf{hnd}}\,C$$

The single reduction step $e \mapsto e'$ for a redex e is:

Reduction steps

$$\begin{aligned} (\underline{\lambda}x.\ r)t &\mapsto [t/x]r \\ (\underline{\lambda}x.\ e)t &\mapsto [t/x]e \\ (\underline{\lambda}v.\ e)t &\mapsto [t/v]e \\ (\underline{\lambda}k.\ e)\underline{\mathsf{pair}}(\gamma_0\,,\,\gamma_1) &\mapsto [\underline{\mathsf{pair}}(\gamma_0\,,\,\gamma_1)/k]e \end{aligned} \qquad \begin{aligned} \underline{\mathsf{nrml}}\,\underline{\mathsf{pair}}(\gamma_0\,,\,\gamma_1) &\mapsto \gamma_0 \\ \underline{\mathsf{hnd}}\,\underline{\mathsf{pair}}(\gamma_0\,,\,\gamma_1) &\mapsto \gamma_1 \end{aligned}$$

3.3 Continuation-passing-style (CPS) Transformation

We use an extension of the conventional continuation-passing-style (CPS) transformation [DF92,Plo75,Ste78] to get from a DS term to a CPS term. We remove the $\underline{\mathsf{raise}}$ and $\underline{\mathsf{handle}}$ expressions by passing two continuations to each expression: one for the normal course of execution, and a second one (the handler continuation) for exceptions.

Only $\underline{\mathsf{raise}}$ and $\underline{\mathsf{handle}}$ expressions use the handler continuation. A $\underline{\mathsf{raise}}$ expression is transformed to call the current handler continuation. A $\underline{\mathsf{handle}}$ expression is transformed to extend the handler function with the current handler continuation. For other expressions, the handler continuation is simply passed along, reflecting the dynamic scope of exceptions.

We show the extended CPS transform in a conventional functional notation.

$$\begin{aligned} &[\![-]\!]^R : \textit{DS Terms} \to \textit{Root Terms} \\ &[\![-]\!]^E : \textit{DS Expressions} \to \textit{Continuation Pairs} \to \textit{Serious Terms} \\ &[\![-]\!]^T : \textit{DS Trivial Expressions} \to \textit{Trivial Terms} \end{aligned}$$

$$\begin{aligned} [\![e]\!]^R &= \underline{\lambda}\langle n,h\rangle.\ [\![e]\!]^E\,\langle n,h\rangle \\ [\![e_0\,e_1]\!]^E\,\langle n,h\rangle &= [\![e_0]\!]^E\,\langle \underline{\lambda}v_0.\ [\![e_1]\!]^E\,\langle \underline{\lambda}v_1.\ v_0\,v_1\,\langle n,h\rangle,h\rangle,h\rangle \\ [\![\underline{\mathsf{handle}}\,e_0\,(\underline{\lambda}x.\ e_1)]\!]^E\,\langle n,h\rangle &= [\![e_0]\!]^E\,\langle n,\underline{\lambda}x.\ [\![e_1]\!]^E\,\langle n,h\rangle\rangle \\ [\![\underline{\mathsf{raise}}\,e]\!]^E\,\langle n,h\rangle &= [\![e]\!]^E\,\langle h,h\rangle \\ [\![t]\!]^E\,\langle n,h\rangle &= n\,[\![t]\!]^T \\ [\![x]\!]^T &= x \\ [\![\underline{\lambda}x.\ r]\!]^T &= \underline{\lambda}x.[\![r]\!]^R \end{aligned}$$

Consider the transformation of an application, $e_0\,e_1$. If an uncaught exception occurs during the evaluation of e_0, the handler h is invoked and the evaluation of $e_0\,e_1$ is aborted. If an uncaught exception occurs during the evaluation of e_1, after an intermediate value v_0 has been computed for e_0, the intermediate value v_0 must be ignored by the handler h. Thus, however evaluation is implemented, invoking the middle occurence of h must be different from invoking the other occurrences of h, where there is no intermediate value to ignore.

In order to reflect this distinction, and show that intermediate values really are stackable, we extend our CPS term syntax as follows:

$$\textit{Continuation Terms} \quad c \ ::= \ \ldots \mid \underline{\mathsf{hnd'}}\, v\, p$$

where v is the intermediate value which must be ignored. We also extend the evaluation contexts to include $\underline{\mathsf{hnd'}}$: $\quad C \ ::= \ \ldots \mid \underline{\mathsf{hnd'}}\, v\, C$
and add a reduction step for $\underline{\mathsf{hnd'}}$: $\quad \underline{\mathsf{hnd'}}\, v\, \underline{\mathsf{pair}}(\gamma_0\,,\,\gamma_1) \ \mapsto\ \gamma_1$.

Here is the extended CPS translation we will use, written in our exact CPS term syntax.

$$\begin{aligned}
[\![e]\!]^R &= \underline{\lambda} k.\ [\![e]\!]^E\, k\\
[\![e_0\ e_1]\!]^E\, p &= [\![e_0]\!]^E\, \underline{\mathsf{pair}}(\underline{\lambda} v_0.\ [\![e_1]\!]^E\, \underline{\mathsf{pair}}(\underline{\lambda} v_1.\ v_0\, v_1\, p\,,\, \underline{\mathsf{hnd'}}\, v_0\, p)\,,\, \underline{\mathsf{hnd}}\, p)\\
[\![\underline{\mathsf{handle}}\, e_0\ (\underline{\lambda} x.\ e_1)]\!]^E\, p &= [\![e_0]\!]^E\, \underline{\mathsf{pair}}(\underline{\mathsf{nrml}}\, p\,,\, \underline{\lambda} x.\ [\![e_1]\!]^E\, p)\\
[\![\underline{\mathsf{raise}}\, e]\!]^E\, p &= [\![e]\!]^E\, \underline{\mathsf{pair}}(\underline{\mathsf{hnd}}\, p\,,\, \underline{\mathsf{hnd}}\, p)\\
[\![t]\!]^E\, p &= (\underline{\mathsf{nrml}}\, p)\ [\![t]\!]^T\\
[\![x]\!]^T &= x\\
[\![\underline{\lambda} x.\ r]\!]^T &= \underline{\lambda} x. [\![r]\!]^R
\end{aligned}$$

Note the use of $\underline{\mathsf{hnd'}}$ in the inner handler continuation of the application translation.

The correctness of this CPS transformation can be proven[KYD98] analogously to the proof of Plotkin's simulation theorem [HD97,Plo75].

3.4 CPS Transformation as a Judgement

In order to represent the transform in OLF, we reformulate it as three mutually recursive judgements corresponding to $[\![-]\!]^R$, $[\![-]\!]^E$, and $[\![-]\!]^T$ in section 3.3. A direct-style term r is transformed into a CPS term r' whenever the judgement $\vdash r \overset{DR}{\longrightarrow} r'$ is satisfied. Given a continuation pair p , a direct-style expression e is transformed into a CPS expression e' whenever the judgement $\vdash e\,;\,p \overset{DE}{\longrightarrow} e'$ is satisfied. Finally, a direct-style trivial expression t is transformed into a CPS trivial expression t' whenever the judgement $\vdash t \overset{DT}{\longrightarrow} t'$ is satisfied.

The derivation rules for the transform are as follows:

$$\frac{\vdash e\,;\,k \overset{DE}{\longrightarrow} e'}{\vdash e \overset{DR}{\longrightarrow} \underline{\lambda} k.\ e'} \qquad \frac{\vdash r \overset{DR}{\longrightarrow} r'}{\vdash \underline{\lambda} x.\ r \overset{DT}{\longrightarrow} \underline{\lambda} x.\ r'}$$

$$\frac{}{\vdash x \overset{DT}{\longrightarrow} x} \qquad \frac{\vdash t \overset{DT}{\longrightarrow} t'}{\vdash t\,;\,p \overset{DE}{\longrightarrow} (\underline{\mathsf{nrml}}\, p)\, t'} \qquad \frac{\vdash e\,;\, \underline{\mathsf{pair}}(\underline{\mathsf{hnd}}\, p\,,\, \underline{\mathsf{hnd}}\, p) \overset{DE}{\longrightarrow} e'}{\vdash \underline{\mathsf{raise}}\, e\,;\, p \overset{DE}{\longrightarrow} e'}$$

$$\frac{\vdash e_1 \;;\; \underline{\mathsf{pair}}(\underline{\lambda} v_1.\, v_0\, v_1\, p \,,\, \underline{\mathsf{hnd'}}\, v_0\, p) \xrightarrow{DE} e_1' \qquad \vdash e_0 \;;\; \underline{\mathsf{pair}}(\underline{\lambda} v_0.\, e_1' \,,\, \underline{\mathsf{hnd}}\, p) \xrightarrow{DE} e'}{\vdash e_0\, e_1 \;;\; p \xrightarrow{DE} e'}$$

$$\frac{\vdash e_1 \;;\; p \xrightarrow{DE} e_1' \qquad \vdash e_0 \;;\; \underline{\mathsf{pair}}(\underline{\mathsf{nrml}}\, p \,,\, \underline{\lambda} x.\, e_1') \xrightarrow{DE} e'}{\vdash \underline{\mathsf{handle}}\, e_0\, (\underline{\lambda} x.\, e_1) \;;\; p \xrightarrow{DE} e'}$$

Note that the v_0 in the application rule is parametric in the left premise and cannot appear free in the right premise.

3.5 Invariants for Results of CPS Transform

Terms resulting from a left-to-right call-by-value CPS translation of direct-style terms satisfy an invariant on occurrences of continuation identifiers k and parameters v. We shall formalize this property with five mutually recursive judgements:

$$\models^{\mathbf{Root}} r \qquad \Phi \models^{\mathbf{Exp}} e \qquad \Phi \models^{\mathbf{Triv}} t; \Phi' \qquad \Phi \models^{\mathbf{CPair}} p \qquad \Phi \models^{\mathbf{Cont}} c$$

where Φ is a stack of both continuation identifiers and parameters:

$$\Phi ::= \cdot \mid \Phi, k \mid \Phi, v$$

When Φ' is a prefix of Φ, we define $\Phi - \Phi'$ as the remainder of Φ.

The derivation rules for these judgements are as follows:

$$\frac{k \models^{\mathbf{Exp}} e}{\models^{\mathbf{Root}} \underline{\lambda} k.\, e}$$

$$\frac{\Phi \models^{\mathbf{Triv}} t; \Phi' \qquad \Phi' \models^{\mathbf{Cont}} c}{\Phi \models^{\mathbf{Exp}} c\, t} \qquad \frac{\Phi \models^{\mathbf{Triv}} t_1; \Phi' \qquad \Phi' \models^{\mathbf{Triv}} t_0; \Phi'' \qquad \Phi'' \models^{\mathbf{CPair}} p}{\Phi \models^{\mathbf{Exp}} t_0\, t_1\, p}$$

$$\frac{}{\Phi \models^{\mathbf{Triv}} x; \Phi} \qquad \frac{\models^{\mathbf{Root}} r}{\Phi \models^{\mathbf{Triv}} \underline{\lambda} x.\, r; \Phi} \qquad \frac{}{\Phi, v \models^{\mathbf{Triv}} v; \Phi}$$

$$\frac{}{k \models^{\mathbf{CPair}} k} \qquad \frac{\Phi \models^{\mathbf{Cont}} c_0 \qquad \Phi \models^{\mathbf{Cont}} c_1}{\Phi \models^{\mathbf{CPair}} \underline{\mathsf{pair}}(c_0 \,,\, c_1)} \qquad \frac{\Phi \models^{\mathbf{Exp}} e}{\Phi \models^{\mathbf{Cont}} \underline{\lambda} x.\, e} \qquad \frac{\Phi, v \models^{\mathbf{Exp}} e}{\Phi \models^{\mathbf{Cont}} \underline{\lambda} v.\, e}$$

$$\frac{\Phi \models^{\mathbf{CPair}} p}{\Phi \models^{\mathbf{Cont}} \underline{\mathsf{nrml}}\, p} \qquad \frac{\Phi \models^{\mathbf{CPair}} p}{\Phi \models^{\mathbf{Cont}} \underline{\mathsf{hnd}}\, p} \qquad \frac{\Phi \models^{\mathbf{CPair}} p}{\Phi, v \models^{\mathbf{Cont}} \underline{\mathsf{hnd'}}\, v\, p}$$

From the judgement rules, it is easy to see that continuation-pair identifiers, k, are used linearly in each root term, and that continuation parameters v (which were introduced by the CPS transform) form a stack in each serious term. In fact, the judgement actually implies the stronger property that continuation-pair identifiers and parameters are used together in a stack-like fashion. Each root term adds a new stack-frame, an identifier followed by parameters, which is fully consumed within that root term. This is apparent from the judgement on $\underline{\lambda}x.r$ which requires that r not depend upon anything currently in the stack.

We would like to prove that $\vdash r \stackrel{DR}{\longrightarrow} r'$ implies $\models^{\mathbf{Root}} r'$. Proving this directly with the above definitions requires a logical relations style argument [DDP99,DP95]. However, by using an ordered logical framework, this may be proved directly.

4 Ordered Logical Framework Representation

In this section, we show how to represent the terms and transform of section 3 in OLF; and how these representations immediately give our desired proof. Following standard practice for LF-style logical frameworks, we shall represent judgements as types and derivations as terms [HHP93] [2]. Furthermore, we will take care that all of our representations are compositional bijections— 1) for every actual object represented there is a corresponding OLF object (and vice-versa); and 2) the representation function and its inverse both commute with substitution. These two properties allow us to transfer results for the representations back to the actual objects and vice-versa. Representations which are compositional bijections are sometimes referred to as adequate.

Our proof proceeds in the following manner.

1. We give a representation for DS terms which is in compositional bijection with all actual DS terms.
2. We give a representation for CPS terms which is in compositional bijection with *only* actual CPS terms satisfying the invariants; our representation does not capture all terms within the CPS grammar of section 3.2.
3. We give a representation for the CPS transform of section 3.4. This representation relates represented DS terms to represented CPS terms. Furthermore it is in compositional bijection with *all* possible CPS transformations (i.e. derivations of section 3.4).
4. By using the preceding compositional bijections, we conclude that $\vdash r \stackrel{DR}{\longrightarrow} r'$ implies $\models^{\mathbf{Root}} r'$.

4.1 DS Terms

Our representation of DS terms will use three basic types corresponding to the three kinds of DS terms.

$$\mathsf{droot} : \mathsf{type}. \qquad \mathsf{dexp} : \mathsf{type}. \qquad \mathsf{dtriv} : \mathsf{type}.$$

We will then build our representations from term constructors corresponding to DS terms. Note that representation uses higher-order abstract syntax, so object-level functions are represented by meta-level functions and likewise object-level

[2] For representing abstract syntax (e.g. DS terms) we may view each syntactic category as a judgement and the constructors for terms of the category as derivation rules for the judgement.

variables are represented (implicitly) by meta-level variables.

$$\begin{array}{rlrl} \mathsf{e2r} : & \mathsf{dexp} \to \mathsf{droot} & \mathsf{t2e} : & \mathsf{dtriv} \to \mathsf{dexp} \\ \mathsf{dapp} : & \mathsf{dexp} \to \mathsf{dexp} \to \mathsf{dexp} & \mathsf{dabort} : & \mathsf{dtriv} \\ \mathsf{handle} : & \mathsf{dexp} \to (\mathsf{dexp} \to \mathsf{dexp}) \to \mathsf{dexp} & \mathsf{dlam} : & (\mathsf{triv} \to \mathsf{droot}) \to \mathsf{dtriv} \\ \mathsf{raise} : & \mathsf{dexp} \to \mathsf{dexp} & & \end{array}$$

Given the previous signature, there is an obvious compositional bijection between DS terms and canonical objects in the above signature. This bijection is established by the following mutually recursive representation functions, $\ulcorner - \urcorner^R$,$\ulcorner - \urcorner^E$,$\ulcorner - \urcorner^T$, and their inverses $\llcorner - \lrcorner^R$,$\llcorner - \lrcorner^E$,$\llcorner - \lrcorner^T$.

$$\begin{array}{rlrl} \ulcorner e \urcorner^R & = \mathsf{e2r} \ulcorner e \urcorner^E & \llcorner \mathsf{e2r}\, E \lrcorner_R & = \llcorner E \lrcorner_E \\ \ulcorner e_0\, e_1 \urcorner^E & = \mathsf{dapp}\ \ulcorner e_0 \urcorner^E \ulcorner e_1 \urcorner^E & \llcorner \mathsf{dapp}\, E_0\, E_1 \lrcorner_E & = \llcorner E_0 \lrcorner_E \llcorner E_1 \lrcorner_E \end{array}$$

$$\begin{array}{rl} \ulcorner \underline{\mathsf{handle}}\, e_0\, (\underline{\lambda} x.\ e_1) \urcorner^E & = \mathsf{handle} \ulcorner e_0 \urcorner^E (\lambda x{:}\mathsf{dtriv}.\ \ulcorner e_1 \urcorner^E) \\ \llcorner \mathsf{handle}\, E_0\, (\lambda x{:}\mathsf{dtriv}.\ E_1) \lrcorner_E = & \underline{\mathsf{handle}} \llcorner E_0 \lrcorner_E (\underline{\lambda} x.\ \llcorner E_1 \lrcorner_E) \end{array}$$

$$\begin{array}{rlrl} \ulcorner \underline{\mathsf{raise}}\, e \urcorner^E & = \mathsf{raise} \ulcorner e \urcorner^E & \llcorner \mathsf{raise}\, E \lrcorner_E & = \underline{\mathsf{raise}} \llcorner E \lrcorner_E \\ \ulcorner t \urcorner^E & = \mathsf{d2e} \ulcorner t \urcorner^T & \llcorner \mathsf{d2e}\, T \lrcorner_E & = \llcorner T \lrcorner_T \\ \ulcorner \underline{\lambda} x.\ r \urcorner^T & = \mathsf{dlam}\, (\lambda x{:}\mathsf{dtriv}.\ \ulcorner r \urcorner^R) & \llcorner \mathsf{dlam}\, (\lambda x{:}\mathsf{dtriv}.\ R) \lrcorner_T & = \underline{\lambda} x.\ \llcorner R \lrcorner_R \\ \ulcorner x \urcorner^T & = x & \llcorner x \lrcorner_T & = x \end{array}$$

4.2 CPS Terms

Next, we give a representation of CPS terms satisfying the invariants of section 3.5. The key idea behind this representation is that ordered types implicitly capture the invariants. Thus, we can directly represent CPS terms which satisfy the invariants, without explicitly representing the invariants. Our representation will use five basic types corresponding to the five basic kinds of CPS terms.

$$\mathsf{root} : \mathsf{type}. \qquad \mathsf{exp} : \mathsf{type}. \qquad \mathsf{triv} : \mathsf{type}. \qquad \mathsf{cont} : \mathsf{type}. \qquad \mathsf{cpair} : \mathsf{type}.$$

We will then build our representations from term constructors corresponding to CPS terms. The use of ordered types forces the CPS term representations to satisfy the invariants.

$$\begin{array}{rlrl} \mathsf{klam} : & (\mathsf{cpair} \twoheadrightarrow \mathsf{exp}) \to \mathsf{root} & \mathsf{vlam} : & (\mathsf{triv} \twoheadrightarrow \mathsf{exp}) \twoheadrightarrow \mathsf{cont} \\ \mathsf{app} : & \mathsf{cpair} \twoheadrightarrow \mathsf{triv} \twoheadrightarrow \mathsf{triv} \twoheadrightarrow \mathsf{exp} & \mathsf{nrml} : & \mathsf{cpair} \twoheadrightarrow \mathsf{cont} \\ \mathsf{kapp} : & \mathsf{cont} \twoheadrightarrow \mathsf{triv} \twoheadrightarrow \mathsf{exp} & \mathsf{hnd} : & \mathsf{cpair} \twoheadrightarrow \mathsf{cont} \\ \mathsf{lam} : & (\mathsf{triv} \to \mathsf{root}) \to \mathsf{triv} & \mathsf{hnd'} : & \mathsf{cpair} \twoheadrightarrow \mathsf{triv} \twoheadrightarrow \mathsf{cont} \\ \mathsf{xlam} : & (\mathsf{triv} \to \mathsf{exp}) \twoheadrightarrow \mathsf{cont} & \mathsf{pair} : & (\mathsf{cont} \,\&\, \mathsf{cont}) \twoheadrightarrow \mathsf{cpair} \end{array}$$

Note that a positive occurrence of an unrestricted function $\to$ as in the type of klam imposes a restriction on the corresponding argument: it may not depend upon continuation-pairs k nor parameters v which are always ordered variables. On the other hand, a negative occurrence of $\to$ as in the type of lam licenses the unrestricted use of the corresponding bound variable x. The right ordered functions $\twoheadrightarrow$ impose the stack-like discipline on parameters of continuations and the continuation-pairs themselves.

Given the previous signature, there is a compositional bijection between CPS terms satisfying the occurrence conditions and canonical objects in the above signature. This bijection is established by the following representation function, $\ulcorner - \urcorner$ and its inverse $\llcorner - \lrcorner$.

$$\begin{array}{rcl@{\qquad}rcl}
\ulcorner \underline{\lambda} k.\ e \urcorner &=& \mathsf{klam}\,(\stackrel{>}{\lambda} k{:}\mathsf{cpair}.\ \ulcorner e \urcorner) & \llcorner \mathsf{klam}\,(\stackrel{>}{\lambda} k{:}\mathsf{cpair}.\ E) \lrcorner &=& \underline{\lambda} k.\ \llcorner E \lrcorner \\
\ulcorner t_0\, t_1\, p \urcorner &=& \mathsf{app}\,{}^{>}\ulcorner p \urcorner\,{}^{>}\ulcorner t_0 \urcorner\,{}^{>}\ulcorner t_1 \urcorner & \llcorner \mathsf{app}\,{}^{>}P\,{}^{>}T_0\,{}^{>}T_1 \lrcorner &=& \llcorner T_0 \lrcorner \llcorner T_1 \lrcorner \llcorner P \lrcorner \\
\ulcorner c\, t \urcorner &=& \mathsf{kapp}\,{}^{>}\ulcorner c \urcorner\,{}^{>}\ulcorner t \urcorner & \llcorner \mathsf{kapp}\,{}^{>}C\,{}^{>}T \lrcorner &=& \llcorner C \lrcorner \llcorner T \lrcorner \\
\ulcorner \underline{\lambda} x.\ r \urcorner &=& \mathsf{lam}\,(\lambda x{:}\mathsf{triv}.\ \ulcorner r \urcorner) & \llcorner \mathsf{lam}\,(\lambda x{:}\mathsf{triv}.\ R) \lrcorner &=& \underline{\lambda} x.\ \llcorner R \lrcorner \\
\ulcorner x \urcorner &=& x & \llcorner x \lrcorner &=& x \\
\ulcorner v \urcorner &=& v & \llcorner v \lrcorner &=& v \\
\ulcorner \underline{\lambda} x.\ e \urcorner &=& \mathsf{xlam}\,{}^{>}(\underline{\lambda} x{:}\mathsf{triv}.\ \ulcorner e \urcorner) & \llcorner \mathsf{xlam}\,{}^{>}(\underline{\lambda} x{:}\mathsf{triv}.\ E) \lrcorner &=& \underline{\lambda} x.\ \llcorner E \lrcorner \\
\ulcorner \underline{\lambda} v.\ e \urcorner &=& \mathsf{vlam}\,{}^{>}(\stackrel{>}{\lambda} v{:}\mathsf{triv}.\ \ulcorner e \urcorner) & \llcorner \mathsf{vlam}\,{}^{>}(\stackrel{>}{\lambda} v{:}\mathsf{triv}.\ E) \lrcorner &=& \underline{\lambda} v.\ \llcorner E \lrcorner \\
\ulcorner \underline{\mathsf{nrml}}\, p \urcorner &=& (\mathsf{nrml}\,{}^{>}\ulcorner p \urcorner) & \llcorner \mathsf{nrml}\,{}^{>}P \lrcorner &=& \underline{\mathsf{nrml}}\, \llcorner P \lrcorner \\
\ulcorner \underline{\mathsf{hnd}}\, p \urcorner &=& (\mathsf{hnd}\,{}^{>}\ulcorner p \urcorner) & \llcorner \mathsf{hnd}\,{}^{>}P \lrcorner &=& \underline{\mathsf{hnd}}\, \llcorner P \lrcorner \\
\ulcorner \underline{\mathsf{hnd'}}\, t\, p \urcorner &=& (\mathsf{hnd'}\,{}^{>}\ulcorner p \urcorner\,{}^{>}\ulcorner t \urcorner) & \llcorner \mathsf{hnd'}\,{}^{>}P\,{}^{>}T \lrcorner &=& \underline{\mathsf{hnd'}}\, \llcorner T \lrcorner \llcorner P \lrcorner \\
\ulcorner k \urcorner &=& k & \llcorner k \lrcorner &=& k \\
\ulcorner \underline{\mathsf{pair}}(c_0\, ,\, c_1) \urcorner &=& \mathsf{pair}\,{}^{>}\langle \ulcorner c_0 \urcorner\, ,\, \ulcorner c_1 \urcorner \rangle & \llcorner \mathsf{pair}\,{}^{>}\langle C_0\, ,\, C_1 \rangle \lrcorner &=& \underline{\mathsf{pair}}(\llcorner C_0 \lrcorner\, ,\, \llcorner C_1 \lrcorner)
\end{array}$$

Note that and $\llcorner \ulcorner u \urcorner \lrcorner = u$ for any term u. Additionally, since variables are mapped to variables, the representation function and its inverse are compositional (i.e., commute with substitution).

Finally we extend $\ulcorner - \urcorner$ and $\llcorner - \lrcorner$ to stacks and contexts as follows:

$$\ulcorner . \urcorner = \cdot \qquad \ulcorner \Phi, k \urcorner = \ulcorner \Phi \urcorner, k{:}\mathsf{cpair} \qquad \ulcorner \Phi, v \urcorner = \ulcorner \Phi \urcorner, v{:}\mathsf{triv}$$

$$\llcorner \cdot \lrcorner = \cdot \qquad \llcorner \Omega, k{:}\mathsf{cpair} \lrcorner = \llcorner \Omega \lrcorner, k \qquad \llcorner \Omega, v{:}\mathsf{triv} \lrcorner = \llcorner \Omega \lrcorner, v$$

We formally prove the correspondence in two parts.

Theorem 2 (Representations are Canonical Forms).
Consider CPS terms r, e, t, c and p with free ordinary variables among $x_1, \ldots, x_n$. Let $\Gamma = x_1{:}\mathsf{triv} \ldots x_n{:}\mathsf{triv}$.

1. *If* $\models^{\mathbf{Root}} r$ *then* $\Gamma; \cdot \vdash \ulcorner r \urcorner \Uparrow \mathsf{root}$.
2. *If* $\Phi \models^{\mathbf{Exp}} e$ *then* $\Gamma; \ulcorner \Phi \urcorner \vdash \ulcorner e \urcorner \Uparrow \mathsf{exp}$.
3. *If* $\Phi \models^{\mathbf{Triv}} t; \Phi'$ *then* $\Gamma; \ulcorner \Phi - \Phi' \urcorner \vdash \ulcorner t \urcorner \Uparrow \mathsf{triv}$.
4. *If* $\Phi \models^{\mathbf{Cont}} c$ *then* $\Gamma; \ulcorner \Phi \urcorner \vdash \ulcorner c \urcorner \Uparrow \mathsf{cont}$.
5. *If* $\Phi \models^{\mathbf{CPair}} p$ *then* $\Gamma; \ulcorner \Phi \urcorner \vdash \ulcorner p \urcorner \Uparrow \mathsf{cpair}$.

Proof: By induction on the structure of the given derivations. □

Theorem 3 (Canonical Forms are Representations).
Let $\Gamma = x_1{:}\mathsf{triv}, \ldots, x_n{:}\mathsf{triv}$ be given.

1. *For any M such that $\Gamma; \cdot \vdash M \Uparrow \mathsf{root}$, $\llcorner M \lrcorner$ is defined and $\models^{\mathbf{Root}} \llcorner M \lrcorner$.*
2. *For any $\Omega = v_1{:}\mathsf{triv}, \ldots, v_m{:}\mathsf{triv}$ and M such that $\Gamma; k{:}\mathsf{cpair}, \Omega \vdash M \Uparrow \mathsf{exp}$, $\llcorner M \lrcorner$ is defined and $\llcorner \Omega \lrcorner \models^{\mathbf{Exp}} \llcorner M \lrcorner$.*

3. *For any* $\Omega = v_1$:triv$, \ldots, v_m$:triv *and* M *such that* $\Gamma; \Omega \vdash M \Uparrow$ triv, $\llcorner M \lrcorner$ *is defined and* $\Phi, \llcorner \Omega \lrcorner \models^{\mathbf{Triv}} \llcorner M \lrcorner; \Phi$ *for any* Φ.
4. *For any* $\Omega = v_1$:triv$, \ldots, v_m$:triv *and* M *such that* $\Gamma; k$:cpair$, \Omega \vdash M \Uparrow$ cont, $\llcorner M \lrcorner$ *is defined and* $\llcorner \Omega \lrcorner \models^{\mathbf{Cont}} \llcorner M \lrcorner$.
5. *For any* $\Omega = v_1$:triv$, \ldots, v_m$:triv *and* M *such that* $\Gamma; k$:cpair$, \Omega \vdash M \Uparrow$ cpair, $\llcorner M \lrcorner$ *is defined and* $\llcorner \Omega \lrcorner \models^{\mathbf{CPair}} \llcorner M \lrcorner$.

Proof: By induction on the structure of the given canonical derivations. For the cases when $M =$ lam $(\lambda x$:triv. $r)$, and $M =$ klam $(\overset{>}{\lambda} k$:(triv $\to$ exp). $e)$ note that the ordered context Ω must be empty since no ordered variables can occur in the argument to an intuitionistic application. □

5 CPS Transform

We represent CPS transform with three basic types corresponding to the three judgements of the transform.

cps_r : droot→root→type. cps_e : dexp→cpair→exp→type. cps_t : dtriv→triv→type.

We then use the following terms to construct representations of the CPS transform.

$$\begin{aligned}
\text{cps_root} : \;& \Pi E{:}\text{dexp}.\ \Pi E'{:}\text{cpair} \twoheadrightarrow \text{exp}.\\
& (\Pi k{:}\text{cpair}.\ \text{cps_e}\, E\, k\, (E' \,{}^{>}\, k)) \to \text{cps_r}\, (\text{e2r}\, E)\, (\text{klam}\, E').
\end{aligned}$$

$$\begin{aligned}
\text{cps_triv} : \;& \Pi T{:}\text{dtriv}.\ \Pi P{:}\text{cpair}.\ \Pi T'{:}\text{triv}.\\
& \text{cps_t}\, T\, T' \to \text{cps_e}\, (\text{t2e}\, T)\, P\, (\text{kapp} \,{}^{>}\, (\text{nrml} \,{}^{>}\, P) \,{}^{>}\, T').
\end{aligned}$$

$$\begin{aligned}
\text{cps_raise} : \;& \Pi E{:}\text{dexp}.\ \Pi E'{:}\text{exp}.\ \Pi P{:}\text{cpair}.\\
& \text{cps_e}\, E\, (\text{pair} \,{}^{>}\, \langle \text{hnd} \,{}^{>}\, P\, ,\ \text{hnd} \,{}^{>}\, P \rangle)\, E' \to\\
& \text{cps_e}\, (\text{raise}\, E)\, P\, E'.
\end{aligned}$$

$$\begin{aligned}
\text{cps_app} : \;& \Pi E_0{:}\text{dexp}.\ \Pi E_1{:}\text{dexp}.\ \Pi P{:}\text{cpair}.\ \Pi E_1'{:}\text{triv} \twoheadrightarrow \text{exp}.\ \Pi E'{:}\text{exp}.\\
& \text{cps_e}\, E_0\, (\text{pair} \,{}^{>}\, \langle \text{vlam} \,{}^{>}\, E_1'\, ,\ \text{hnd} \,{}^{>}\, P \rangle)\, E' \to\\
& (\Pi v_0{:}\text{triv}.\ \text{cps_e}\, E_1\\
& \quad (\text{pair} \,{}^{>}\, \langle \text{vlam} \,{}^{>}\, \overset{>}{\lambda} v_1{:}\text{triv}.\ \text{app} \,{}^{>}\, P \,{}^{>}\, v_0 \,{}^{>}\, v_1\, ,\ \text{hnd}' \,{}^{>}\, P \,{}^{>}\, v_0 \rangle)\, (E_1' \,{}^{>}\, v_0)) \to\\
& \text{cps_e}\, (\text{dapp}\, E_0\, E_1)\, P\, E'.
\end{aligned}$$

$$\begin{aligned}
\text{cps_handle} : \;& \Pi E_0{:}\text{dexp}.\ \Pi E_1{:}\text{dtriv} \to \text{droot}.\ \Pi E_1'{:}\text{dtriv} \to \text{droot}.\ \Pi P{:}\text{cpair}.\ \Pi E'{:}\text{exp}.\\
& \text{cps_e}\, E_0\, (\text{pair} \,{}^{>}\, \langle \text{nrml} \,{}^{>}\, P\, ,\ \text{xlam} \,{}^{>}\, E_1' \rangle)\, E' \to\\
& (\Pi x{:}\text{dtriv}.\ \Pi x'{:}\text{triv}.\ \text{cps_t}\, x\, x' \to \text{cps_e}\, (E_1\, x)\, P\, (E_1'\, x')) \to\\
& \text{cps_e}\, (\text{handle}\, E_0\, E_1)\, P\, E'.
\end{aligned}$$

$$\begin{aligned}
\text{cps_lam} : \;& \Pi R{:}\text{dtriv} \to \text{droot}.\ \Pi R'{:}\text{triv} \to \text{root}.\\
& (\Pi x{:}\text{dtriv}.\ \Pi x'{:}\text{triv}.\ \text{cps_t}\, x\, x' \to \text{cps_r}\, (R\, x)\, (R'\, x')) \to\\
& \text{cps_t}\, (\text{dlam}\, R)\, (\text{lam}\, R').
\end{aligned}$$

We may now show the adequacy of the above representation in two parts.

In the actual transformation we map variables x to themselves; in the representation we map each variable x from a DS term to a corresponding variable x' in a CPS term[3]. These variables and their relationship are captured in contexts

$$\begin{aligned} \Gamma &= x_1{:}\mathsf{dtriv} \ldots x_n{:}\mathsf{dtriv} \\ \Gamma' &= x'_1{:}\mathsf{triv} \ldots x'_n{:}\mathsf{triv} \\ \Gamma_m &= m_1{:}\mathsf{cps\_t}\, x_1\, x'_1 \ldots m_n{:}\mathsf{cps\_t}\, x_n\, x'_n \end{aligned}$$

which always occur together in this manner. In addition we have contexts

$$\begin{aligned} \Gamma_k &= k_1{:}\mathsf{cpair} \ldots k_m{:}\mathsf{cpair} \\ \Gamma_v &= v_1{:}\mathsf{triv} \ldots v_l{:}\mathsf{triv} \end{aligned}$$

which include all the continuation-pair identifiers k and temporary variables v which may occur in the continuation-pair p and CPS terms resulting from the translation. Note that ordering constraints are ignored during the translation, but will be nonetheless be satisfied by the resulting terms.

Theorem 4 (Representations are Canonical Forms).
Let $\Gamma^* = \Gamma, \Gamma', \Gamma_m, \Gamma_k, \Gamma_v$ be a context of the form explained above which contains all free variables occurring in the relevant judgement. Then

1. $\vdash r \xrightarrow{DR} r'$ *implies* $\exists M.\ \Gamma^*; \cdot \vdash M \Uparrow \mathsf{cps\_r} \ulcorner r \urcorner^R \ulcorner r' \urcorner$
2. $\vdash e\ ; p \xrightarrow{DE} e'$ *and* $\Phi \models^{\mathbf{CPair}} p$ *implies* $\exists M.\ \Gamma^*; \cdot \vdash M \Uparrow \mathsf{cps\_e} \ulcorner e \urcorner^E \ulcorner p \urcorner \ulcorner e' \urcorner$
3. $\vdash t \xrightarrow{DT} t'$ *implies* $\exists M.\ \Gamma^*; \cdot \vdash M \Uparrow \mathsf{cps\_t} \ulcorner t \urcorner^T \ulcorner t' \urcorner$

Proof: By structural induction on the given derivation. For part 2, note that $\ulcorner \Phi \urcorner$ will be part of Γ^*. □

Theorem 5 (Canonical Forms are Representations). *Let $\Gamma^* = \Gamma, \Gamma', \Gamma_m, \Gamma_k, \Gamma_v$ a context of the form explained above and assume the types below are canonical.*

1. $\Gamma^*; \cdot \vdash M \Uparrow \mathsf{cps\_r}\, R\, R'$ *implies* $\vdash \llcorner R \lrcorner_R \xrightarrow{DR} \llcorner R' \lrcorner$.
2. $\Gamma^*; \cdot \vdash M \Uparrow \mathsf{cps\_e}\, E\, P\, E'$ *implies* $\vdash \llcorner E \lrcorner_E\ ; \llcorner P \lrcorner \xrightarrow{DE} \llcorner E' \lrcorner$.
3. $\Gamma^*; \cdot \vdash M \Uparrow \mathsf{cps\_t}\, T\, T'$ *implies* $\vdash \llcorner T \lrcorner_T \xrightarrow{DR} \llcorner T' \lrcorner$.

Proof: By structural induction on the given canonical derivation. □

The adequacy of our representation gives us a simple proof that the terms resulting from a CPS transformation satisfy the occurrence conditions of section 3.2.

Theorem 6. $\vdash r \xrightarrow{DR} r'$ *implies* $\models^{\mathbf{Root}} r'$.

Proof: Suppose r is closed.
By theorem 4 we know $\exists M. \cdot; \cdot \vdash M \Uparrow \mathsf{cps\_r} \ulcorner r \urcorner^R \ulcorner r' \urcorner$.
Then we know $\cdot; \cdot \vdash \ulcorner r' \urcorner \Uparrow \mathsf{root}$ from inversion on canonical typing rules.
Then by theorem 3 we know $\models^{\mathbf{Root}} \llcorner \ulcorner r' \urcorner \lrcorner$.
Then we are done since $\llcorner \ulcorner r' \urcorner \lrcorner = r'$.

Same reasoning applies for open r except that we will have to strengthen away unnecessary hypotheses from the unrestricted context before going from 2nd to 3rd step. □

[3] This is accomplished by the cps_lam rule.

The simplicity of the proof above may be surprising. It is so direct, because the work has been distributed to the proof of the adequacy theorems (which are clearly not trivial), combined with some deep properties of the logical framework such as the existence of canonical forms. This factoring of effort is typical in the use of logical frameworks.

6 Related Work

Berdine, O'Hearn, Reddy and Thielecke have shown that the CPS transform with exceptions produces CPS terms which use their continuation-pair argument linearly [BORT01]. This work refines that analysis and shows that the immediate result of the transform actually uses the continuation-pair argument in an ordered fashion. However, our results are brittle in the sense that the ordering property is not preserved by arbitrary β reduction— β reducing underneath a lambda could result in a term which doesn't satisfy the ordering invariants.

In [PP00], Polakow and Pfenning show how OLF provides a convenient setting for reasoning about the CPS transform which doesn't treat exceptions. This work shows how those representation techniques easily extend to treat the CPS transform which removes exceptions.

In [Dan00], Danvy shows how to implement evaluation for a language with first-class continuations while still leveraging the stackability properties of second-class continuations. His analysis is quite similar in spirit to this work. Where we keep the distinction between (second-class) continuations introduced by the transform and handlers provided by the user, Danvy distinguishes between second-class and first-class continuations. Furthermore, we speculate that Danvy's analysis could be naturally re-cast in OLF.

7 Conclusion & Future Work

We formally proved the stackability and linearity of exception handlers with ML-style semantics using the help of an ordered logical framework (OLF) [PP00]. We transformed exceptions into continuation-passing-style (CPS) terms and formalizeed the exception properties as a judgement on the CPS terms. Then, rather than directly proving that the properties hold for terms, we proved our theorem for OLF representations of the CPS terms and transform. We used the correctness of our representations to transfer the results back to the actual CPS terms and transform. We further showed that the results in [DP95,DDP99] carry-over to the extended CPS transform which removes exceptions. Working with OLF representations allowed for a relatively simple proof in which we could directly use known properties of OLF terms (e.g. substitution properties) rather than re-proving similar properties for actual CPS terms satisfying our invariants.

We can also extend our analysis to cover evaluation of CPS terms. The invariants satisfied by CPS-transformed terms clearly suggest a stack-like evaluation mechanism. In fact, we can show (though space doesn't permit it in this paper) that a stack-like evaluation machine for CPS terms, which takes advantage of the ordering invariants, behaves the same as a regular evaluation machine which always uses substitution.

Our work can be seen as two-fold: it is a theoretical justification of existing compilers that use the stack mechanism to implement exceptions; and it demonstrates the value of a (ordered) logical framework as a conceptual tool in the theoretical study of programming languages. We conjecture that many systems with constrained resource access will have a natural representation in an ordered logical framework.

8 Acknowledgements

We would like to acknowledge insightful discussions with Peter O'Hearn and Frank Pfenning.

References

[App97] Andrew W. Appel. *Modern Compiler Implementation in ML/C/Java: Basic Techniques.* Cambridge University Press, 1997.

[BORT01] Josh Berdine, Peter O'Hearn, Uday S. Reddy, and Hayo Thielecke. Linearly used continuations. In *Informal Proceedings of The Third ACM SIGPLAN Workshop on Continuations (CW '01)*, January 2001. To appear.

[CP99] Iliano Cervesato and Frank Pfenning. A linear logical framework. *Information and Computation*, 1999. To appear in the special issue with invited papers from LICS'96, E. Clarke, editor.

[Dan00] Olivier Danvy. Formalizing implementation strategies for first-class continuations. In *Programming Languages and Systems, The Proceedings of the 9th European Symposium On Programming*, volume 1782 of *Lecture Notes in Computer Science*, pages 88–103, 2000.

[DDP99] Olivier Danvy, Belmina Dzafic, and Frank Pfenning. On proving syntactic properties of cps programs. In *Third International Workshop on Higher Order Operational Techniques in Semantics (HOOTS'99)*, Paris, France, September 1999.

[DF92] Olivier Danvy and Andrzej Filinski. Representing control: a study of the CPS transformation. *Mathematical Structures in Computer Science*, 2(4):361–391, December 1992.

[DP95] Olivier Danvy and Frank Pfenning. The occurrence of continuation parameters in CPS terms. Technical Report CMU-CS-95-121, Department of Computer Science, Carnegie Mellon University, February 1995.

[Fel87] Matthias Felleisen. *The Calculi of λ-v-CS Conversion: A Syntactic Theory of Control and State in Imperative Higher-Order Programming Languages.* PhD thesis, Department of Computer Science, Indiana University, Bloomington, Indiana, August 1987.

[HD97] John Hatcliff and Olivier Danvy. Thunks and the λ-calculus. *Journal of Functional Programming*, 7(3):303–320, 1997.

[HHP93] Robert Harper, Furio Honsell, and Gordon Plotkin. A framework for defining logics. *Journal of the Association for Computing Machinery*, 40(1):143–184, January 1993.

[KYD98] Jungtaek Kim, Kwangkeun Yi, and Olivier Danvy. Assessing the overhead of ml exceptions by selective cps transformation. In *The Proceedings of the ACM SIGPLAN Workshop on ML*, pages 103–114, September 1998.

[Pfe96] Frank Pfenning. The practice of logical frameworks. In Hélène Kirchner, editor, *Proceedings of the Colloquium on Trees in Algebra and Programming*, pages 119–134, Linköping, Sweden, April 1996. Springer-Verlag LNCS 1059. Invited talk.

[Plo75] Gordon D. Plotkin. Call-by-name, call-by-value and the λ-calculus. *Theoretical Computer Science*, 1:125–159, 1975.

[Plo81] Gordon D. Plotkin. A structural approach to operational semantics. Technical report, Aarhus University, September 1981.

[PP99a] Jeff Polakow and Frank Pfenning. Natural deduction for intuitionistic non-commutative linear logic. In J.-Y. Girard, editor, *Proceedings of the Fourth International Conference on Typed Lambda Calculi and Applications (TLCA'99)*, pages 295–309, l'Aquila, Italy, April 1999. Springer-Verlag LNCS 1581.

[PP99b] Jeff Polakow and Frank Pfenning. Relating natural deduction and sequent calculus for intuitionistic non-commutative linear logic. In Andre Scedrov and Achim Jung, editors, *Proceedings of the 15th Conference on Mathematical Foundations of Programming Semantics*, pages 311–328, New Orleans, Louisiana, April 1999. Electronic Notes in Theoretical Computer Science, Volume 20.

[PP00] Jeff Polakow and Frank Pfenning. Properties of terms in continuation passing style in an ordered logical framework. In *Workshop on Logical Frameworks and Meta-Languages (LFM 2000)*, Santa Barbara, California, June 2000.

[Ste78] Guy L. Steele Jr. Rabbit: A compiler for Scheme. Technical Report AI-TR-474, Artificial Intelligence Laboratory, Massachusetts Institute of Technology, Cambridge, Massachusetts, May 1978.

A Higher-Order Colon Translation *

Olivier Danvy and Lasse R. Nielsen

BRICS**
Department of Computer Science
University of Aarhus
Ny Munkegade, Building 540, DK-8000 Aarhus C, Denmark
E-mail: {danvy,lrn}@brics.dk
Home pages: http://www.brics.dk/~{danvy,lrn}

Abstract. A lambda-encoding such as the CPS transformation gives rise to administrative redexes. In his seminal article "Call-by-name, call-by-value and the lambda-calculus", 25 years ago, Plotkin tackled administrative reductions using a so-called colon translation. In "Representing control, a study of the CPS transformation", 15 years later, Danvy and Filinski integrated administrative reductions in the CPS transformation, making it operate in one pass. This one-pass transformation is higher-order, and can be used for other lambda-encodings, but we do not see its associated proof technique used in practice—instead, Plotkin's colon translation appears to be favored. Therefore, in an attempt to link the higher-order transformation and Plotkin's proof technique, we recast Plotkin's proof of Indifference and Simulation in a higher-order setting. To this end, we extend the colon translation from first order to higher order.

Keywords. Call by name, call by value, λ-calculus, continuation-passing style (CPS), CPS transformation, administrative reductions, colon translation, one-pass CPS transformation, Indifference, Simulation.

1   Introduction

In "Call-by-name, call-by-value and the λ-calculus" [9], Plotkin provided the first formalization of the transformation into continuation-passing style (CPS) [10, 11]. Plotkin's CPS transformation is first-order. As most λ-encodings, it is plagued with so-called *administrative redexes*, i.e., redexes that are only artefacts of the λ-encoding. Their reduction steps are interspersed with the reduction steps corresponding to actual reduction steps in the original direct-style program. In the early 90s, a higher-order version of the CPS transformation was developed that eliminates all administrative redexes at transformation time, in one pass [1, 3, 12]. This higher-order version has been formalized in several ways: using a notion of 'schematic' continuations [3], using higher-order rewriting [4], and using logical relations [2]. None of these various ways of formalizing a one-pass CPS transformation, however, match Plotkin's original proof technique.

---

* Extended version available as the technical report BRICS RS-00-33.
** Basic Research in Computer Science (http://www.brics.dk/),
Centre of the Danish National Research Foundation.

H. Kuchen and K. Ueda (Eds.): FLOPS 2001, LNCS 2024, pp. 78–91, 2001.
© Springer-Verlag Berlin Heidelberg 2001

Does it mean that Plotkin's proof technique is inherently first-order? In this article, we answer this question negatively. We adapt his proof technique to the higher-order setting of one-pass CPS transformations.

To tackle administrative reductions, in his formalization, Plotkin introduced a so-called *colon translation* that eliminates administrative redexes until a redex is reached that corresponds to an actual redex in the original program. Our goal here is to present a higher-order colon translation that yields the same effect for a one-pass CPS transformation, thus adapting Plotkin's original proof technique to a higher-order operational setting.

Prerequisites: We assume a basic familiarity with Plotkin's work, as can be gathered from his original article [9] or from Hatcliff and Danvy's revisitation [7]. The one-pass CPS transformation is presented in Danvy and Filinski's article [3] (Section 3 of that article reviews administrative redexes and the colon translation). A pictorial presentation of actual and administrative reductions can be found in Section 3 of Danvy, Dzafic, and Pfenning's 1999 article [2]. Nevertheless, we have tried to make the present article stand alone.

Overview: Section 2 reviews call by name and call by value in the untyped λ-calculus. Sections 3 and 4 present the one-pass CPS transformation and its meta-language. Section 5 states our goal (proving Plotkin's Indifference and Simulation theorems) and our means (a higher-order colon translation). Section 6 recasts Plotkin's four lemmas and Section 7 restates his proof. Section 8 concludes.

2 Call-by-name and call-by-value λ-calculi

We define the untyped λ-calculus by giving its syntax and two semantics, one for call by value (CBV) and the other for call by name (CBN).

Definition 1 (Syntax of the λ-calculus with uninterpreted constants).

$$e ::= x \mid \lambda x.e \mid e \,@\, e \mid c$$

We only distinguish expressions up to renaming of bound variables. So for example, $\lambda x.x$ and $\lambda y.y$ are considered equal.

2.1 Call by value

The CBV semantics of closed expressions is given using evaluation contexts in the style of Felleisen [5].

The evaluation contexts are as follows.

$$\mathrm{C_v}[\,] ::= [\,] \mid \mathrm{C_v}[\,] \,@\, e \mid v_\mathrm{v} \,@\, \mathrm{C_v}[\,]$$

where v_v is a value.

Values form a subset of expressions and are defined as follows.

$$v_{\mathrm{v}} ::= \lambda x.e \mid c$$

The reduction rule is defined as follows.

$$\mathrm{C}_{\mathrm{v}}[(\lambda x.e) @ v_{\mathrm{v}}] \longmapsto_{\mathrm{v}} \mathrm{C}_{\mathrm{v}}[e[v_{\mathrm{v}}/x]]$$

where $e[v/x]$ is the standard capture-avoiding substitution.

$\textsc{Eval}_{\mathrm{v}}$ is the following partial function:

$$\begin{cases} \textsc{Eval}_{\mathrm{v}}(e) = v_{\mathrm{v}} & \text{iff } e \longmapsto_{\mathrm{v}}^{i} v_{\mathrm{v}} \text{ for some value } v_{\mathrm{v}} \text{ and integer } i \\ \textsc{Eval}_{\mathrm{v}}(e) \text{ is undefined otherwise} \end{cases}$$

where $\longmapsto_{\mathrm{v}}^{i}$ denotes i iterations of $\longmapsto_{\mathrm{v}}$.

2.2 Call by name

We give the CBN semantics for closed expressions as in Section 2.1.

The evaluation contexts are:

$$\mathrm{C}_{\mathrm{n}}[\,] ::= [\,] \mid \mathrm{C}_{\mathrm{n}}[\,] @ e$$

The values are:

$$v_{\mathrm{n}} ::= \lambda x.e \mid c$$

The reduction rule is:

$$\mathrm{C}_{\mathrm{n}}[(\lambda x.e) @ e'] \longmapsto_{\mathrm{n}} \mathrm{C}_{\mathrm{n}}[e[e'/x]]$$

$\textsc{Eval}_{\mathrm{n}}$ is the following partial function:

$$\begin{cases} \textsc{Eval}_{\mathrm{n}}(e) = v_{\mathrm{n}} & \text{iff } e \longmapsto_{\mathrm{n}}^{i} v_{\mathrm{n}} \text{ for some value } v_{\mathrm{n}} \text{ and integer } i \\ \textsc{Eval}_{\mathrm{n}}(e) \text{ is undefined otherwise} \end{cases}$$

2.3 Evaluation-order independent reduction

In the remainder of this article, the arrow $\longmapsto$ (without annotation) corresponds to a reduction that is legal in both call by value and call by name. In other words, the $\longmapsto$ relation is the intersection of the $\longmapsto_{\mathrm{v}}$ and $\longmapsto_{\mathrm{n}}$ relations.

2.4 Stuck terms

In both the call-by-value and the call-by-name semantics, we can write closed expressions that are not values, but for which there are no legal reductions. Plotkin said that such expressions "stick".

The stuck closed expressions w.r.t. the CBV semantics are:

$$\mathrm{Sticks}_{\mathrm{v}} ::= c @ v_{\mathrm{v}} \mid \mathrm{Sticks}_{\mathrm{v}} @ e \mid v_{\mathrm{v}} @ \mathrm{Sticks}_{\mathrm{v}}$$

or simply $\mathrm{C}_{\mathrm{v}}[c @ v_{\mathrm{v}}]$.

The stuck expressions are disjoint from the values. All closed expressions are either values, stuck, or there is a possible reduction.

The stuck closed expressions w.r.t. the CBN semantics are:

$$\mathrm{Sticks_n} ::= \mathrm{Sticks_n} \,@\, e \mid c \,@\, e$$

or simply $\mathrm{C_n}[c \,@\, e]$.

Again the stuck expressions are disjoint from the values, and all closed expressions are either values, stuck, or allow a reduction.

3 The meta language of the one-pass CPS transformation

The one-pass CPS transformation maps direct-style λ-expressions into λ-expressions that can be reduced at transformation time, yielding λ-expressions in CPS. Therefore, the implementation language for the transformation contains two kinds of applications, two kinds of λ-abstractions, and two kinds of variables:

$$E ::= c \mid x \mid \lambda x.E \mid E \,@\, E \mid X \mid \overline{\lambda} X.E \mid E \,\overline{@}\, E$$

Following tradition we refer to overlined constructs as static and non-overlined ones as dynamic. The identifiers ranged over by X and x are called static and dynamic variables, respectively. Substituting an expression for a static variable is a static substitution, and substituting an expression for a dynamic variable is a dynamic substitution. As in Section 2, we only distinguish expressions up to renaming of bound variables, both for static and dynamic variables.

We define the following typing system for the meta language:

$$\tau ::= \textsc{Syntax} \mid \tau \rightarrow \tau$$

$$\frac{}{\Gamma \vdash c : \textsc{Syntax}} \qquad \frac{}{\Gamma \vdash x : \textsc{Syntax}} \qquad \frac{\Gamma \vdash E : \textsc{Syntax}}{\Gamma \vdash \lambda x.E : \textsc{Syntax}}$$

$$\frac{\Gamma \vdash E_0 : \textsc{Syntax} \qquad \Gamma \vdash E_1 : \textsc{Syntax}}{\Gamma \vdash E_0 \,@\, E_1 : \textsc{Syntax}} \qquad \frac{\Gamma(X) = \tau}{\Gamma \vdash X : \tau}$$

$$\frac{\Gamma, X : \tau_1 \vdash E : \tau_2}{\Gamma \vdash \overline{\lambda} X.E : \tau_1 \rightarrow \tau_2} \qquad \frac{\Gamma \vdash E_0 : \tau_1 \rightarrow \tau_2 \qquad \Gamma \vdash E_1 : \tau_1}{\Gamma \vdash E_0 \,\overline{@}\, E_1 : \tau_2}$$

Any expression typeable in this typing system is simply typed and hence its reduction terminates and any evaluation strategy leads to the same normal form. We choose to use call by value, arbitrarily.

The meta-language values are:

$$v_{\mathrm{V}} ::= c \mid x \mid \lambda x.v_{\mathrm{V}} \mid v_{\mathrm{V}} \,@\, v_{\mathrm{V}} \mid \overline{\lambda} X.E$$

N.B. If a meta-language value v_{V} has type $\textsc{Syntax}$, it is an expression in the λ-calculus as defined in Section 2. In particular, v_{V} is free of static variables.

The evaluation contexts are:

$$C_V[\,] ::= [\,] \mid \lambda x.C_V[\,] \mid C_V[\,] @ E \mid v_V @ C_V[\,] \mid C_V[\,] \overline{@} E \mid v_V \overline{@} C_V[\,]$$

The reduction rule only allows us to reduce static β-redexes:

$$C_V[(\overline{\lambda} X.E) \overline{@} v_V] \longmapsto_V C_V[E[v_V/X]]$$

Proposition 1 (Context nesting). *Since nested contexts are themselves contexts, the reduction rule satisfies the following property.*

$$E \longmapsto_V E' \iff C_V[E] \longmapsto_V C_V[E']$$

Proof. Omitted. □

We define the static evaluation function, EVAL_V, by

$$\text{EVAL}_V(E) = v_V \iff E \longmapsto_V^* v_V$$

where $\longmapsto_V^*$ denotes zero or more iterations of $\longmapsto_V$. By definition reductions on well-typed expressions are strongly normalizing, so EVAL_V is total on these.

We treat the meta language as a higher-order language in the sense that we equate expressions up to β-equivalence (written $\equiv_V$). We only use simply typed and thus strongly normalizing expressions, so we can equate any expression to the value it reduces to.

The dynamic substitution of a *closed* value, as used for λ-expressions in Section 2, can be extended directly to meta-language terms. The interaction between static and dynamic substitutions satisfies the following property.

Proposition 2 (Substitution). *If E is a meta-language expression, v_V is a meta-language value, and e is a closed λ-expression, then*

$$E[v_V/X][e/x] = E[e/x][v_V[e/x]/X].$$

Proof. By structural induction on E.

Cases $E = c$, x, and Y $(Y \neq X)$**:** In these cases X is not free in E, and hence X is not free in $E[e/x]$. It follows that

$$E[v_V/X][e/x] = E[e/x] = E[e/x][v_V[e/x]/X].$$

Cases $E = E_1 @ E_2$ and $E_1 \overline{@} E_2$**:** These cases both follow directly from the induction hypothesis and the definition of substitution.

Case $E = X$**:** $X[v_V/X][e/x] = v_V[e/x] = X[e/x][v_V[e/x]/X]$

Case $E = \lambda y.E_1$ and $\overline{\lambda} Y.E_1$**:** Since we equate expressions up to alpha-renaming of bound variables, we can assume that y is not free in v_V and $y \neq x$ as well as $Y \neq X$. These cases are thus similar to the $E_1 @ E_2$ case.

□

Corollary 1 (Dynamic substitution respects static β-equivalence). *If E and E' are meta-language expressions, v is a value, and x is a dynamic variable, then*

$$E \longmapsto^*_{\mathrm{V}} E' \Longrightarrow E[v/x] \longmapsto^*_{\mathrm{V}} E'[v/x].$$

I.e., if $E \equiv_{\mathrm{V}} E'$ then $E[v/x] \equiv_{\mathrm{V}} E'[v/x]$.

Proof. It suffices to show that if $E \longmapsto_{\mathrm{V}} E'$ then $E[v/x] \longmapsto_{\mathrm{V}} E'[v/x]$. Since $E \longmapsto_{\mathrm{V}} E$ only if there exists a context $\mathrm{C_V}[\,]$ such that $E = \mathrm{C_V}[(\overline{\lambda} X.E_1)\,\overline{@}\,V]$ $\longmapsto_{\mathrm{V}} \mathrm{C_V}[E_1[V/X]] = E'$, the proof is by induction on the structure of the context.

Case $\mathrm{C_V}[\,] = [\,]$**:** In this case $E = (\overline{\lambda} X.E_1)\,\overline{@}\,V$ and $E' = E_1[V/X]$.

$$\begin{array}{rcll} ((\overline{\lambda} X.E_1)\,\overline{@}\,V)[v/x] & = & (\overline{\lambda} X.E_1[v/x])\,\overline{@}\,V[v/x] & \\ & \longmapsto_{\mathrm{V}} & E_1[v/x][V[v/x]/X] & \\ & = & E_1[V/X][v/x] & \text{by Proposition 2} \end{array}$$

Case $\mathrm{C_V}[\,] = \mathrm{C_1}[\,]\,\overline{@}\,E_2$**:**

$$\begin{array}{rcll} E[v/x] & = & \mathrm{C_1}[(\overline{\lambda} X.E_1)\,\overline{@}\,V][v/x] & \\ & = & (\mathrm{C_1}[(\overline{\lambda} X.E_1)\,\overline{@}\,V]\,\overline{@}\,E_2)[v/x] & \\ & = & \mathrm{C_1}[(\overline{\lambda} X.E_1)\,\overline{@}\,V][v/x]\,\overline{@}\,E_2[v/x] & \\ & \longmapsto_{\mathrm{V}} & \mathrm{C_1}[E_1[V/X]][v/x]\,\overline{@}\,E_2[v/x] & \text{by I.H. and Proposition 1} \\ & = & (\mathrm{C_1}[E_1[V/X]]\,\overline{@}\,E_2)[v/x] & \\ & = & \mathrm{C_V}[E_1[V/X]][v/x] & \\ & = & E'[v/x] & \end{array}$$

Cases $\mathrm{C_V}[\,] = \mathrm{C_1}[\,]\,@\,E_2$, $V\,\overline{@}\,\mathrm{C_1}[\,]$, $V\,@\,\mathrm{C_1}[\,]$, and $\lambda y.\mathrm{C_1}[\,]$**:** Similar to the previous case.

□

This corollary shows that we can use an arbitrary representative for the equivalence classes up to $\equiv_{\mathrm{V}}$ when performing dynamic reductions. Therefore, in the remainder of this article, we will use $=$ instead of $\equiv_{\mathrm{V}}$.

4 The one-pass CPS transformation

We consider the one-pass version of Plotkin's (left-to-right) call-by-value CPS transformation [3]. (Many others exist, depending, e.g., on the evaluation order of the source language [6].)

The one-pass CPS transformation is defined inductively with the two functions $[\![\cdot]\!]$ and $[\![\cdot]\!]'$ displayed in Figure 1. Whereas Plotkin's CPS transformation uses only one function, the one-pass transformation uses two, depending on whether the continuation is known statically ($[\![\cdot]\!]$) or not ($[\![\cdot]\!]'$). These two functions map λ-expressions as defined in Section 2 to expressions in the meta

$$
\begin{aligned}
\llbracket\cdot\rrbracket &: \textsc{Syntax} \rightarrow (\textsc{Syntax} \rightarrow \textsc{Syntax}) \rightarrow \textsc{Syntax} \\
\llbracket c\rrbracket &= \overline{\lambda}\mathrm{K}.\mathrm{K}\,\overline{@}\,c \\
\llbracket x\rrbracket &= \overline{\lambda}\mathrm{K}.\mathrm{K}\,\overline{@}\,x \\
\llbracket \lambda x.e\rrbracket &= \overline{\lambda}\mathrm{K}.\mathrm{K}\,\overline{@}\,\lambda x.\lambda \mathrm{k}.\llbracket e\rrbracket'\,\overline{@}\,\mathrm{k} \\
\llbracket e_1 \,@\, e_2\rrbracket &= \overline{\lambda}\mathrm{K}.\llbracket e_1\rrbracket\,\overline{@}\,\overline{\lambda}\mathrm{V}_1.\llbracket e_2\rrbracket\,\overline{@}\,\overline{\lambda}\mathrm{V}_2.\mathrm{V}_1 \,@\, \mathrm{V}_2 \,@\, \lambda \mathrm{v}.\mathrm{K}\,\overline{@}\,\mathrm{v}
\end{aligned}
$$

$$
\begin{aligned}
\llbracket\cdot\rrbracket' &: \textsc{Syntax} \rightarrow \textsc{Syntax} \rightarrow \textsc{Syntax} \\
\llbracket c\rrbracket' &= \overline{\lambda}\mathrm{K}.\mathrm{K} \,@\, c \\
\llbracket x\rrbracket' &= \overline{\lambda}\mathrm{K}.\mathrm{K} \,@\, x \\
\llbracket \lambda x.e\rrbracket' &= \overline{\lambda}\mathrm{K}.\mathrm{K} \,@\, \lambda x.\lambda \mathrm{k}.\llbracket e\rrbracket'\,\overline{@}\,\mathrm{k} \\
\llbracket e_1 \,@\, e_2\rrbracket' &= \overline{\lambda}\mathrm{K}.\llbracket e_1\rrbracket\,\overline{@}\,\overline{\lambda}\mathrm{V}_1.\llbracket e_2\rrbracket\,\overline{@}\,\overline{\lambda}\mathrm{V}_2.\mathrm{V}_1 \,@\, \mathrm{V}_2 \,@\, \mathrm{K}
\end{aligned}
$$

The transformation uses some fixed variables that are assumed to be "fresh", i.e., that do not occur in the program to be transformed. These variables are denoted by 'k' and 'v', which are dynamic variables. We also fix the static variables K, V_1, and V_2. The static variables cannot clash with variables in the original program, but they must be distinct. All these fresh variables are written in Roman font.

Fig. 1. The left-to-right, call-by-value CPS transformation in one pass

language defined in Section 3. Their type are easily inferred using the rules of Section 3.

We define the function Ψ to map direct-style values to CPS values:

$$
\begin{aligned}
\Psi(c) &= c \\
\Psi(\lambda x.e) &= \lambda x.\lambda \mathrm{k}.\llbracket e\rrbracket'\,\overline{@}\,\mathrm{k}
\end{aligned}
$$

N.B. $\llbracket v_{\mathrm{v}}\rrbracket = \overline{\lambda}\mathrm{K}.\mathrm{K}\,\overline{@}\,\Psi(v_{\mathrm{v}})$ and $\llbracket v_{\mathrm{v}}\rrbracket' = \overline{\lambda}\mathrm{K}.\mathrm{K} \,@\, \Psi(v_{\mathrm{v}})$.

The two-level η-redex $\lambda \mathrm{v}.\kappa\,\overline{@}\,\mathrm{v}$ coerces a meta-language expression of type $\textsc{Syntax} \rightarrow \textsc{Syntax}$ into a meta-language expression of type $\textsc{Syntax}$, and therefore, the two CPS-transformation functions are related as follows.

Proposition 3. *If* e *is a* λ*-expression and* κ *is a meta-language expression of type* $\textsc{Syntax} \rightarrow \textsc{Syntax}$ *then*

$$
\llbracket e\rrbracket'\,\overline{@}\,\lambda \mathrm{v}.\kappa\,\overline{@}\,\mathrm{v} \longmapsto^{*} \llbracket e\rrbracket\,\overline{@}\,\kappa
$$

remembering that we equate expressions up to static β*-equivalence and that the identifier* v *is fresh, so it is not free in* κ*.*

Proof. By structural induction on e.

Case $e = x$:

$$\begin{aligned}
[\![x]\!]' \mathbin{\overline{@}} \lambda \mathrm{v}.\kappa \mathbin{\overline{@}} \mathrm{v} &= (\lambda \mathrm{v}.\kappa \mathbin{\overline{@}} \mathrm{v}) @ x \\
&\longmapsto \kappa \mathbin{\overline{@}} \mathrm{v}[x/\mathrm{v}] \\
&= \kappa \mathbin{\overline{@}} x \qquad \text{by Corollary 1} \\
&= [\![x]\!] \mathbin{\overline{@}} \kappa
\end{aligned}$$

Case $e = \lambda x.e_1$:

$$\begin{aligned}
[\![\lambda x.e_1]\!]' \mathbin{\overline{@}} \lambda \mathrm{v}.\kappa \mathbin{\overline{@}} \mathrm{v} &= (\lambda \mathrm{v}.\kappa \mathbin{\overline{@}} \mathrm{v}) @ \Psi(\lambda x.e_1) \\
&\longmapsto \kappa \mathbin{\overline{@}} \mathrm{v}[\Psi(\lambda x.e_1)/\mathrm{v}] \\
&= \kappa \mathbin{\overline{@}} \Psi(\lambda x.e_1) \\
&= [\![\lambda x.e_1]\!] \mathbin{\overline{@}} \kappa
\end{aligned}$$

Case $e = e_1 @ e_2$:

$$\begin{aligned}
[\![e_1 @ e_2]\!]' \mathbin{\overline{@}} \lambda \mathrm{v}.\kappa \mathbin{\overline{@}} \mathrm{v} &= [\![e_1]\!] \mathbin{\overline{@}} \overline{\lambda} \mathrm{V}_1.[\![e_2]\!] \mathbin{\overline{@}} \overline{\lambda} \mathrm{V}_2.\mathrm{V}_1 @ \mathrm{V}_2 @ \lambda \mathrm{v}.\kappa \mathbin{\overline{@}} \mathrm{v} \\
&= [\![e_1 @ e_2]\!] \mathbin{\overline{@}} \kappa
\end{aligned}$$

□

5 The goal

Plotkin proved three properties of the CPS transformation: Indifference, Simulation, and Translation. We prove the first two for the one-pass CPS transformation.

Theorem 1 (Indifference). $\textsc{Eval}_{\mathrm{v}}([\![e]\!] \mathbin{\overline{@}} \overline{\lambda}\mathrm{V}.\mathrm{V}) = \textsc{Eval}_{\mathrm{n}}([\![e]\!] \mathbin{\overline{@}} \overline{\lambda}\mathrm{V}.\mathrm{V})$.

The Indifference theorem formalizes a key property of CPS, namely that CPS programs are evaluation-order independent.

Theorem 2 (Simulation). $\textsc{Eval}_{\mathrm{v}}([\![e]\!] \mathbin{\overline{@}} \overline{\lambda}\mathrm{V}.\mathrm{V}) = \Psi(\textsc{Eval}_{\mathrm{v}}(e))$.

where Ψ was defined in Section 4, just before Proposition 3.

The Simulation theorem formalizes the correctness of the call-by-value CPS transformation. For one point, the theorem shows that termination is preserved, but more essentially, it says that evaluating a CPS-transformed program yields the CPS counterpart of the result of evaluating the original program.

To prove Indifference and Simulation, Plotkin used four lemmas. We prove the same four lemmas for the one-pass CPS transformation. Plotkin's proof then applies as is (see Section 7).

To handle administrative redexes, Plotkin introduced a colon translation. This translation is an infix operation mapping an expression and a continuation to the CPS counterpart of that expression applied to the continuation, but bypassing the initial administrative redexes introduced by the CPS transformation. To account for meta-level reductions at CPS-transformation time, we define a higher-order version of Plotkin's colon translation.

Definition 2 (Higher-order colon translation).

$$
\begin{array}{rcll}
c : \kappa & = & \kappa \,\overline{@}\, \Psi(c) & \\
\lambda x.e : \kappa & = & \kappa \,\overline{@}\, \Psi(\lambda x.e) & \\
v_1 @ v_2 : \kappa & = & \Psi(v_1) @ \Psi(v_2) @ \lambda v.\kappa \,\overline{@}\, v & \\
v_1 @ e_2 : \kappa & = & e_2 : \overline{\lambda} V_2.\Psi(v_1) @ V_2 @ \lambda v.\kappa \,\overline{@}\, v & e_2 \textit{ not a value} \\
e_1 @ e_2 : \kappa & = & e_1 : \overline{\lambda} V_1.\llbracket e_2 \rrbracket \,\overline{@}\, \overline{\lambda} V_2.\, V_1 @ V_2 @ \lambda v.\kappa \,\overline{@}\, v & e_1 \textit{ not a value}
\end{array}
$$

Unlike Plotkin's colon translation, which is first order and interspersed with the actual reductions, this colon translation is higher order (as indicated by the overlines) and its static, administrative reductions occur before the actual, dynamic reductions.

6 Plotkin's four lemmas

Lemma 1 (Substitution lemma).
For all λ-expressions e and all closed values v and variables x,

$$
\begin{aligned}
\llbracket e \rrbracket [\Psi(v)/x] &= \llbracket e[v/x] \rrbracket \\
\llbracket e \rrbracket' [\Psi(v)/x] &= \llbracket e[v/x] \rrbracket'
\end{aligned}
$$

Proof. By structural induction on e.

Case $e = x$:

$$
\begin{aligned}
\llbracket x \rrbracket [\Psi(v)/x] &= (\overline{\lambda}\mathrm{K}.\mathrm{K} \,\overline{@}\, x)[\Psi(v)/x] \\
&= \overline{\lambda}\mathrm{K}.\mathrm{K} \,\overline{@}\, \Psi(v) \\
&= \llbracket v \rrbracket \\
&= \llbracket x[v/x] \rrbracket
\end{aligned}
$$

Case $e = y$:

$$
\begin{aligned}
\llbracket y \rrbracket [\Psi(v)/x] &= (\overline{\lambda}\mathrm{K}.\mathrm{K} \,\overline{@}\, y)[\Psi(v)/x] \\
&= \overline{\lambda}\mathrm{K}.\mathrm{K} \,\overline{@}\, y \\
&= \llbracket y[v/x] \rrbracket
\end{aligned}
$$

Case $e = \lambda y.e_1$, where $y \neq x$

$$
\begin{aligned}
\llbracket \lambda y.e_1 \rrbracket [\Psi(v)/x] &= (\overline{\lambda}\mathrm{K}.\mathrm{K} \,\overline{@}\, \lambda y.\lambda \mathrm{k}.\llbracket e_1 \rrbracket' \,\overline{@}\, \mathrm{k})[\Psi(v)/x] \\
&= \overline{\lambda}\mathrm{K}.\mathrm{K} \,\overline{@}\, ((\lambda y.\lambda \mathrm{k}.\llbracket e_1 \rrbracket' \,\overline{@}\, \mathrm{k})[\Psi(v)/x]) \\
&= \overline{\lambda}\mathrm{K}.\mathrm{K} \,\overline{@}\, (\lambda y.\lambda \mathrm{k}.\llbracket e_1 \rrbracket' [\Psi(v)/x] \,\overline{@}\, \mathrm{k}) \\
&= \overline{\lambda}\mathrm{K}.\mathrm{K} \,\overline{@}\, (\lambda y.\lambda \mathrm{k}.\llbracket e_1[v/x] \rrbracket' \,\overline{@}\, \mathrm{k}) \qquad \text{by I.H.} \\
&= \llbracket \lambda y.e_1[v/x] \rrbracket
\end{aligned}
$$

Case $e = e_1 @ e_2$:

$$
\begin{aligned}
&\llbracket e_1 @ e_2 \rrbracket [\Psi(v)/x] \\
&= \overline{\lambda}\mathrm{K}.(\llbracket e_1 \rrbracket \,\overline{@}\, \overline{\lambda}\mathrm{V}_1.\llbracket e_2 \rrbracket \,\overline{@}\, \overline{\lambda}\mathrm{V}_2.\mathrm{V}_1 @ \mathrm{V}_2 @ \lambda \mathrm{v}.\mathrm{K} \,\overline{@}\, \mathrm{v})[\Psi(v)/x] \\
&= \overline{\lambda}\mathrm{K}.(\llbracket e_1 \rrbracket [\Psi(v)/x]) \,\overline{@}\, \overline{\lambda}\mathrm{V}_1.(\llbracket e_2 \rrbracket [\Psi(v)/x]) \,\overline{@}\, \overline{\lambda}\mathrm{V}_2.\mathrm{V}_1 @ \mathrm{V}_2 @ \lambda \mathrm{v}.\mathrm{K} \,\overline{@}\, \mathrm{v} \\
&= \overline{\lambda}\mathrm{K}.\llbracket e_1[v/x] \rrbracket \,\overline{@}\, \overline{\lambda}\mathrm{V}_1.\llbracket e_2[v/x] \rrbracket \,\overline{@}\, \overline{\lambda}\mathrm{V}_2.\mathrm{V}_1 @ \mathrm{V}_2 @ \lambda \mathrm{v}.\kappa \,\overline{@}\, \mathrm{v} \quad \text{by I.H.} \\
&= \llbracket e_1[v/x] @ e_2[v/x] \rrbracket \\
&= \llbracket (e_1 @ e_2)[v/x] \rrbracket
\end{aligned}
$$

The cases for $[\![\cdot]\!]'$ are similar. □

Lemma 2 (Administrative reductions).
If e is a closed λ-expression and κ is a closed meta-language expression of type $\text{Syntax} \rightarrow \text{Syntax}$ *then* $[\![e]\!]\,\overline{@}\,\kappa \longmapsto_{\mathrm{V}}^{+} e : \kappa$ *(i.e., they are equal modulo $\equiv_{\mathrm{V}}$).*

Proof. By structural induction on e.

Case $e = c$:

$$\begin{array}{rcl} [\![c]\!]\,\overline{@}\,\kappa & = & (\overline{\lambda}\mathrm{K}.\mathrm{K}\,\overline{@}\,c)\,\overline{@}\,\kappa \\ & \longmapsto_{\mathrm{V}} & \kappa\,\overline{@}\,c \\ & = & c : \kappa \end{array}$$

Case $e = \lambda x.e_1$:

$$\begin{array}{rcl} [\![\lambda x.e_1]\!]\,\overline{@}\,\kappa & = & (\overline{\lambda}\mathrm{K}.\mathrm{K}\,\overline{@}\,\Psi(\lambda x.e_1))\,\overline{@}\,\kappa \\ & \longmapsto_{\mathrm{V}} & \kappa\,\overline{@}\,\Psi(\lambda x.e_1) \\ & = & \lambda x.e_1 : \kappa \end{array}$$

Case $e = v_1 \,@\, v_2$:

$$\begin{array}{rcl} [\![v_1 \,@\, v_2]\!]\,\overline{@}\,\kappa & = & (\overline{\lambda}\mathrm{K}.[\![v_1]\!]\,\overline{@}\,\overline{\lambda}\mathrm{V}_1.[\![v_2]\!]\,\overline{@}\,\overline{\lambda}\mathrm{V}_2.\mathrm{V}_1\,@\,\mathrm{V}_2\,@\,\lambda\mathrm{v}.\mathrm{K}\,\overline{@}\,\mathrm{v})\,\overline{@}\,\kappa \\ & = & (\overline{\lambda}\mathrm{K}.(\overline{\lambda}\mathrm{K}.\mathrm{K}\,\overline{@}\,\Psi(v_1))\overline{@} \\ & & \quad \overline{\lambda}\mathrm{V}_1.(\overline{\lambda}\mathrm{K}.\mathrm{K}\,\overline{@}\,\Psi(v_2))\,\overline{@}\,\overline{\lambda}\mathrm{V}_2.\mathrm{V}_1\,@\,\mathrm{V}_2\,@\,\lambda\mathrm{v}.\mathrm{K}\,\overline{@}\,\mathrm{v})\overline{@}\kappa \\ & \longmapsto_{\mathrm{V}}^{5} & \Psi(v_1)\,@\,\Psi(v_2)\,@\,\lambda\mathrm{v}.\kappa\,\overline{@}\,\mathrm{v} \\ & = & v_1\,@\,v_2 : \kappa \end{array}$$

Case $e = v_1 \,@\, e_2$:

$$\begin{array}{rcll} [\![v_1 \,@\, e_2]\!]\,\overline{@}\,\kappa & = & (\overline{\lambda}\mathrm{K}.[\![v_1]\!]\,\overline{@}\,\overline{\lambda}\mathrm{V}_1.[\![e_2]\!]\,\overline{@}\,\overline{\lambda}\mathrm{V}_2.\mathrm{V}_1\,@\,\mathrm{V}_2\,@\,\lambda\mathrm{v}.\mathrm{K}\,\overline{@}\,\mathrm{v})\,\overline{@}\,\kappa & \\ & = & (\overline{\lambda}\mathrm{K}.(\overline{\lambda}\mathrm{K}.\mathrm{K}\,\overline{@}\,\Psi(v_1))\,\overline{@}\,\overline{\lambda}\mathrm{V}_1.[\![e_2]\!]\,\overline{@}\,\overline{\lambda}\mathrm{V}_2.\mathrm{V}_1\,@\,\mathrm{V}_2\,@\,\lambda\mathrm{v}.\mathrm{K}\,\overline{@}\,\mathrm{v})\,\overline{@}\,\kappa & \\ & \longmapsto_{\mathrm{V}}^{3} & [\![e_2]\!]\,\overline{@}\,\overline{\lambda}\mathrm{V}_2.\Psi(v_1)\,@\,\mathrm{V}_2\,@\,\lambda\mathrm{v}.\kappa\,\overline{@}\,\mathrm{v} & \\ & \longmapsto_{\mathrm{V}}^{*} & e_2 : \overline{\lambda}\mathrm{V}_2.\Psi(v_1)\,@\,\mathrm{V}_2\,@\,\lambda\mathrm{v}.\kappa\,\overline{@}\,\mathrm{v} & \text{by I.H.} \\ & = & v_1\,@\,e_2 : \kappa & \end{array}$$

Case $e = e_1 \,@\, e_2$:

$$\begin{array}{rcll} [\![e_1 \,@\, e_2]\!]\,\overline{@}\,\kappa & = & (\overline{\lambda}\mathrm{K}.[\![e_1]\!]\,\overline{@}\,\overline{\lambda}\mathrm{V}_1.[\![e_2]\!]\,\overline{@}\,\overline{\lambda}\mathrm{V}_2.\mathrm{V}_1\,@\,\mathrm{V}_2\,@\,\lambda\mathrm{v}.\mathrm{K}\,\overline{@}\,\mathrm{v})\,\overline{@}\,\kappa & \\ & \longmapsto_{\mathrm{V}} & [\![e_1]\!]\,\overline{@}\,\overline{\lambda}\mathrm{V}_1.[\![e_2]\!]\,\overline{@}\,\overline{\lambda}\mathrm{V}_2.\mathrm{V}_1\,@\,\mathrm{V}_2\,@\,\lambda\mathrm{v}.\kappa\,\overline{@}\,\mathrm{v} & \\ & \longmapsto_{\mathrm{V}}^{*} & e_1 : \overline{\lambda}\mathrm{V}_1.[\![e_2]\!]\,\overline{@}\,\overline{\lambda}\mathrm{V}_2.\mathrm{V}_1\,@\,\mathrm{V}_2\,@\,\lambda\mathrm{v}.\kappa\,\overline{@}\,\mathrm{v} & \text{by I.H.} \\ & = & e_1\,@\,e_2 : \kappa & \end{array}$$

This enumeration accounts for all expressions e. □

Lemma 3 (Single-step simulation).
If e is a closed λ-expression, κ is a closed meta-language expression of type $\text{Syntax} \rightarrow \text{Syntax}$, *and* $e \longmapsto_{\mathrm{v}} e'$ *then* $e : \kappa \longmapsto^{+} e' : \kappa$.

Proof. By structural induction on the evaluation context in the derivation of $e \longmapsto_{\mathrm{v}} e'$.

Case $\mathrm{C}[\,] = [\,]$, i.e., $(\lambda x.e) @ v \longmapsto_{\mathrm{v}} e[v/x]$:

$$\begin{array}{rcll}
(\lambda x.e) @ v : \kappa & = & \Psi(\lambda x.e) @ \Psi(v) @ \lambda \mathrm{v}.\kappa \overline{@} \mathrm{v} & \\
& = & (\lambda x.\lambda \mathrm{k}.[\![e]\!]' \overline{@} \mathrm{k}) @ \Psi(v) @ \lambda \mathrm{v}.\kappa \overline{@} \mathrm{v} & \\
& \longmapsto & ((\lambda \mathrm{k}.[\![e]\!]' \overline{@} \mathrm{k})[\Psi(v)/x]) @ \lambda \mathrm{v}.\kappa \overline{@} \mathrm{v} & \\
& = & (\lambda \mathrm{k}.[\![e]\!]'[\Psi(v)/x] \overline{@} \mathrm{k}) @ \lambda \mathrm{v}.\kappa \overline{@} \mathrm{v} & \text{by Corollary 1} \\
& = & (\lambda \mathrm{k}.[\![e[v/x]]\!]' \overline{@} \mathrm{k}) @ \lambda \mathrm{v}.\kappa \overline{@} \mathrm{v} & \text{by Lemma 1} \\
& \longmapsto & [\![e[v/x]]\!]' \overline{@} (\lambda \mathrm{v}.\kappa \overline{@} \mathrm{v}) & \\
& \longmapsto^{*} & [\![e[v/x]]\!] \overline{@} \kappa & \text{by Proposition 3} \\
& = & e[v/x] : \kappa & \text{by Lemma 2}
\end{array}$$

Case $\mathrm{C}[\,] = \mathrm{C}_1[\,] @ e_2$, i.e., $\mathrm{C}_1[e_1] @ e_2 \longmapsto_{\mathrm{v}} \mathrm{C}_1[e_1'] @ e_2$ derived from $e_1 \longmapsto_{\mathrm{v}} e_1'$:

$$\begin{array}{rcll}
\mathrm{C}_1[e_1] @ e_2 : \kappa & = & \mathrm{C}_1[e_1] : \overline{\lambda} \mathrm{V}_1.[\![e_2]\!] \overline{@} \overline{\lambda} \mathrm{V}_2.\mathrm{V}_1 @ \mathrm{V}_2 @ \lambda \mathrm{v}.\kappa \overline{@} \mathrm{v} & \\
& \longmapsto^{+} & \mathrm{C}_1[e_1'] : \overline{\lambda} \mathrm{V}_1.[\![e_2]\!] \overline{@} \overline{\lambda} \mathrm{V}_2.\mathrm{V}_1 @ \mathrm{V}_2 @ \lambda \mathrm{v}.\kappa \overline{@} \mathrm{v} & \text{by I.H.} \\
& = & e' \qquad \text{to give it a name} &
\end{array}$$

- If $\mathrm{C}_1[e_1']$ is not a value, then $\mathrm{C}_1[e_1'] @ e_2 : \kappa = e'$
- If $\mathrm{C}_1[e_1']$ is a value then

$$\begin{array}{ll}
e' = [\![e_2]\!] \overline{@} \overline{\lambda} \mathrm{V}_2.(\Psi(\mathrm{C}_1[e_1']) @ \mathrm{V}_2) @ \lambda \mathrm{v}.\kappa \overline{@} \mathrm{v} & \\
\;\;\, = e_2 : \overline{\lambda} \mathrm{V}_2.\Psi(\mathrm{C}_1[e_1']) @ \mathrm{V}_2 @ (\lambda \mathrm{v}.\kappa \overline{@} \mathrm{v}) & \text{by Lemma 2} \\
\;\;\, = e'' &
\end{array}$$

  - If e_2 is not a value, then $\mathrm{C}_1[e_1'] @ e_2 : \kappa = e''$.
  - If e_2 is a value, then

$$\begin{array}{l}
e'' = \Psi(\mathrm{C}_1[e_1']) @ \Psi(e_2) @ \lambda \mathrm{v}.\kappa \overline{@} \mathrm{v} \\
\;\;\;\, = \mathrm{C}_1[e_1'] @ e_2 : \kappa
\end{array}$$

Case $\mathrm{C}[\,] = v_1 @ \mathrm{C}_1[\,]$, i.e., $v_1 @ \mathrm{C}_1[e_2] \longmapsto_{\mathrm{v}} v_1 @ \mathrm{C}_1[e_2']$ derived from $e_2 \longmapsto_{\mathrm{v}} e_2'$:

$$\begin{array}{rcll}
v_1 @ \mathrm{C}_1[e_2] : \kappa & = & \mathrm{C}_1[e_2] : \overline{\lambda} \mathrm{V}_2.\Psi(v_1) @ \mathrm{V}_2 @ \lambda \mathrm{v}.\kappa \overline{@} \mathrm{v} & \\
& \longmapsto^{+} & \mathrm{C}_1[e_2'] : \overline{\lambda} \mathrm{V}_2.\Psi(v_1) @ \mathrm{V}_2 @ \lambda \mathrm{v}.\kappa \overline{@} \mathrm{v} & \text{by I.H.} \\
& = & e' &
\end{array}$$

- If $\mathrm{C}_1[e_2']$ is a not value then $v_1 @ \mathrm{C}_1[e_2'] : \kappa = e'$.
- If $\mathrm{C}_1[e_2']$ is a value then

$$\begin{array}{l}
e' = \Psi(v_1) @ \Psi(\mathrm{C}_1[e_2']) @ \lambda \mathrm{v}.\kappa \overline{@} \mathrm{v} \\
\;\;\, = v_1 @ e_2' : \kappa
\end{array}$$

□

Lemma 4 (Coincidence of stuck expressions).
If $e \in \mathrm{Sticks_v}$ *and* κ *is a closed meta language expression with type* SYNTAX → SYNTAX, *then* $e : \kappa \in \mathrm{Sticks_n} \cap \mathrm{Sticks_v}$.

Proof. By induction on the structure of the stuck expression e.

Case $e = c \mathbin{@} v$:

$$\begin{aligned}(c \mathbin{@} v) : \kappa &= \Psi(c) \mathbin{@} \Psi(v) \mathbin{@} \lambda \mathrm{v}.\kappa \mathbin{\overline{@}} \mathrm{v} \\ &= c \mathbin{@} \Psi(v) \mathbin{@} \lambda \mathrm{v}.\kappa \mathbin{\overline{@}} \mathrm{v}\end{aligned}$$

which is stuck since $c \mathbin{@} \Psi(v)$ is stuck both in call-by-name and call-by-value.

Case $e = v_1 \mathbin{@} e_2$ where $e_2 \in \mathrm{Sticks_v}$:

$$(v_1 \mathbin{@} e_2) : \kappa = e_2 : \overline{\lambda} \mathrm{V}_2.\Psi(v_1) \mathbin{@} \mathrm{V}_2 \mathbin{@} \lambda \mathrm{v}.\kappa \mathbin{\overline{@}} \mathrm{v}$$

which is stuck by induction hypothesis, e_2 being closed and structurally smaller that e.

Case $e = e_1 \mathbin{@} e_2$ where $e_1 \in \mathrm{Sticks_v}$:

$$(e_1 \mathbin{@} e_2) : \kappa = e_1 : \overline{\lambda} \mathrm{V}_1.[\![e_2]\!] \mathbin{\overline{@}} \overline{\lambda} \mathrm{V}_2.\mathrm{V}_1 \mathbin{@} \mathrm{V}_2 \mathbin{@} \lambda \mathrm{v}.\kappa \mathbin{\overline{@}} \mathrm{v}$$

which is stuck by induction hypothesis, e_1 being closed and structurally smaller that e.

□

7 Plotkin's double proof

Plotkin proved both Indifference and Simulation using four lemmas similar to the ones in the previous section. Let us restate his proof.

Proof. We need to show that for any e, $\mathrm{EVAL_v}([\![e]\!] \mathbin{\overline{@}} \overline{\lambda}\mathrm{V.V})$ and $\mathrm{EVAL_n}([\![e]\!] \mathbin{\overline{@}} \overline{\lambda}\mathrm{V.V})$ either are both defined and yield the same result, which is $\Psi(\mathrm{EVAL_v}(e))$, or they are both undefined.

1. If $\mathrm{EVAL_v}(e) = v_\mathrm{v}$ (i.e., if $e \longmapsto_\mathrm{v}^i v_\mathrm{v}$ for some i, by the definition of $\mathrm{EVAL_v}(\cdot)$ in Section 2.1) then

$$\begin{aligned}[\![e]\!] \mathbin{\overline{@}} \overline{\lambda}\mathrm{V.V} &= e : \overline{\lambda}\mathrm{V.V} && \text{by Lemma 2}\\ &\longmapsto^* v_\mathrm{v} : \overline{\lambda}\mathrm{V.V} && \text{by repeated use of Lemma 3}\\ &= (\overline{\lambda}\mathrm{V.V}) \mathbin{\overline{@}} \Psi(v_\mathrm{v}) && \text{since } v_\mathrm{v} \text{ is a value}\\ &= \Psi(v_\mathrm{v}) \\ &= \Psi(\mathrm{EVAL_v}(e))\end{aligned}$$

   Therefore $\mathrm{EVAL_v}([\![e]\!] \mathbin{\overline{@}} \overline{\lambda}\mathrm{V.V}) = \Psi(\mathrm{EVAL_v}(e))$. Furthermore, Lemma 3 only uses reductions in $\longmapsto$, and this relation is the intersection of the $\longmapsto_\mathrm{v}$ and $\longmapsto_\mathrm{n}$ relations. Therefore $\mathrm{EVAL_v}([\![e]\!] \mathbin{\overline{@}} \overline{\lambda}\mathrm{V.V}) = \mathrm{EVAL_n}([\![e]\!] \mathbin{\overline{@}} \overline{\lambda}\mathrm{V.V})$.
2. If $\mathrm{EVAL_v}(e)$ is undefined then it is either because e reduces to a stuck term, or because e has an infinite reduction sequence.
   (a) In the first case there exists an $e' \in \mathrm{Sticks_v}$ such that $e \longmapsto_\mathrm{v}^* e'$. In that case

$$\begin{aligned}[\![e]\!] \mathbin{\overline{@}} \overline{\lambda}\mathrm{V.V} &= e : \overline{\lambda}\mathrm{V.V} && \text{by Lemma 2}\\ &\longmapsto^* e' : \overline{\lambda}\mathrm{V.V} && \text{by repeated use of Lemma 3}\\ &\in \mathrm{Sticks_n} \cap \mathrm{Sticks_v} && \text{by Lemma 4}\end{aligned}$$

   In words, whether one uses call by name or call by value, $[\![e]\!] \mathbin{\overline{@}} \overline{\lambda}\mathrm{V.V}$ reduces to a stuck term.

(b) In the second case there exists a sequence of expressions

$$e \longmapsto_{\mathrm{v}} e_1 \longmapsto_{\mathrm{v}} e_2 \longmapsto_{\mathrm{v}} \cdots \longmapsto_{\mathrm{v}} e_n \longmapsto_{\mathrm{v}} \cdots$$

In that case

$$\begin{array}{rcll} [\![e]\!] \,\overline{@}\, \overline{\lambda}\mathrm{V}.\mathrm{V} & = & e : \overline{\lambda}\mathrm{V}.\mathrm{V} & \text{by Lemma 2} \\ & \longmapsto^{+} & e_1 : \overline{\lambda}\mathrm{V}.\mathrm{V} & \text{by Lemma 3} \\ & \longmapsto^{+} & e_2 : \overline{\lambda}\mathrm{V}.\mathrm{V} & \text{by Lemma 3} \\ & \longmapsto^{+} & \ldots & \\ & \longmapsto^{+} & e_n : \overline{\lambda}\mathrm{V}.\mathrm{V} & \text{by Lemma 3} \\ & \longmapsto^{+} & \ldots & \end{array}$$

In words, $[\![e]\!] \,\overline{@}\, \overline{\lambda}\mathrm{V}.\mathrm{V}$ has an infinite reduction sequence too, both in call by name and in call by value.

Together these two cases prove the Simulation and Indifference theorems. □

8 Conclusion

We have adapted Plotkin's four lemmas to the one-pass CPS transformation, which required us to introduce a higher-order colon translation. Given these four lemmas, Plotkin's Indifference and Simulation theorems and their proof apply directly to validate the one-pass CPS transformation.

Other λ-encodings exist that give rise to administrative reductions—for example, in denotational semantics, the denotation of a program is obtained by a syntax-directed translation into the λ-calculus. The resulting λ-term contains many administrative redexes that need to be dealt with to reason about programs. A good semantics-directed compiler is expected to eliminate these administrative redexes at compile time. For example, an identifier is typically mapped into an application of the environment, and scope resolution is expected from a compiler, so that variables are looked up in constant time at run time. Factoring out administrative redexes at compile time (a.k.a. staging [8]) is accepted good practice. When the compiler is written in a higher-order functional language (say, ML), administrative reductions can be represented as ML reductions. What we have shown here is a way to prove the correctness of this higher-order representation in the particular case of the CPS transformation.

Acknowledgments: This work is supported by the ESPRIT Working Group APPSEM (`http://www.md.chalmers.se/Cs/Research/Semantics/APPSEM/`). Part of it was carried out while the second author was visiting John Hannan at Penn State, in the fall of 2000. We are grateful to the anonymous reviewers and to Julia Lawall for perceptive comments.

References

1. Andrew W. Appel. *Compiling with Continuations.* Cambridge University Press, New York, 1992.
2. Olivier Danvy, Belmina Dzafic, and Frank Pfenning. On proving syntactic properties of CPS programs. In *Third International Workshop on Higher-Order Operational Techniques in Semantics*, volume 26 of *Electronic Notes in Theoretical Computer Science*, pages 19–31, Paris, France, September 1999. Also available as the technical report BRICS RS-99-23.
3. Olivier Danvy and Andrzej Filinski. Representing control, a study of the CPS transformation. *Mathematical Structures in Computer Science*, 2(4):361–391, December 1992.
4. Olivier Danvy and Kristoffer Høgsbro Rose. Higher-order rewriting and partial evaluation. In Tobias Nipkow, editor, *Rewriting Techniques and Applications*, Lecture Notes in Computer Science, Kyoto, Japan, March 1998. Springer-Verlag. Extended version available as the technical report BRICS-RS-97-46.
5. Matthias Felleisen. *The Calculi of λ-v-CS Conversion: A Syntactic Theory of Control and State in Imperative Higher-Order Programming Languages.* PhD thesis, Department of Computer Science, Indiana University, Bloomington, Indiana, August 1987.
6. John Hatcliff and Olivier Danvy. A generic account of continuation-passing styles. In Hans-J. Boehm, editor, *Proceedings of the Twenty-First Annual ACM Symposium on Principles of Programming Languages*, pages 458–471, Portland, Oregon, January 1994. ACM Press.
7. John Hatcliff and Olivier Danvy. Thunks and the λ-calculus. *Journal of Functional Programming*, 7(2):303–319, 1997. Extended version available as the technical report BRICS RS-97-7.
8. Ulrik Jørring and William L. Scherlis. Compilers and staging transformations. In Mark Scott Johnson and Ravi Sethi, editors, *Proceedings of the Thirteenth Annual ACM Symposium on Principles of Programming Languages*, pages 86–96, St. Petersburg, Florida, January 1986. ACM Press.
9. Gordon D. Plotkin. Call-by-name, call-by-value and the λ-calculus. *Theoretical Computer Science*, 1:125–159, 1975.
10. John C. Reynolds. The discoveries of continuations. *Lisp and Symbolic Computation*, 6(3/4):233–247, December 1993.
11. Guy L. Steele Jr. Rabbit: A compiler for Scheme. Technical Report AI-TR-474, Artificial Intelligence Laboratory, Massachusetts Institute of Technology, Cambridge, Massachusetts, May 1978.
12. Mitchell Wand. Correctness of procedure representations in higher-order assembly language. In Stephen Brookes, Michael Main, Austin Melton, Michael Mislove, and David Schmidt, editors, *Proceedings of the 7th International Conference on Mathematical Foundations of Programming Semantics*, number 598 in Lecture Notes in Computer Science, pages 294–311, Pittsburgh, Pennsylvania, March 1991. Springer-Verlag.

Compiling Lazy Functional Programs Based on the Spineless Tagless G-machine for the Java Virtual Machine

Kwanghoon Choi, Hyun-il Lim, and Taisook Han

Department of Electrical Engineering & Computer Science,
Korea Advanced Institute of Science and Technology, Taejon, Korea
{khchoi,hilim,han}@cs.kaist.ac.kr

Abstract. A systematic method of compiling lazy functional programs based on the Spineless Tagless G-machine (STGM) is presented for the Java Virtual Machine (JVM). A new specification of the STGM, which consists of a compiler and a reduction machine, is presented; the compiler translates a program in the STG language, which is the source language for the STGM, into a program in an intermediate language called L-code, and our reduction machine reduces the L-code program into an answer. With our representation for the reduction machine by the Java language, an L-code program is translated into a Java program simulating the reduction machine.

The translated Java programs also run at a reasonable execution speed. Our experiment shows that execution times of translated benchmarks are competitive compared with those in a traditional Haskell interpreter, Hugs, particularly when Glasgow Haskell compiler's STG-level optimizations are applied.

1 Introduction

The motivation to compile functional languages for the Java Virtual Machine (JVM) [4] comes from the mobility of being able to run the same compiled code on any machine with a JVM, and the potential benefits of interlanguage working with Java. For implementors, the fact that every JVM is equipped with a built-in garbage collector may draw their attention. As a method of functional language implementations, this subject may be an interesting exploration of the strange nexus of functional languages, byte coded virtual machines, and object oriented programming.

Our object is to develop a lazy functional language compiler based on the Spineless Tagless G-Machine (STGM) for the JVM. The reason for using the abstract machine is that it is the state of the art in lazy abstract machine and many optimizations are available for its source language, the Shared Term Graph (STG) [7][8].

There have already been two similar attempts to do this by Tullsen [9] and Vernet [10]. They have tried to translate an STG program directly into a Java

H. Kuchen and K. Ueda (Eds.): FLOPS 2001, LNCS 2024, pp. 92–107, 2001.

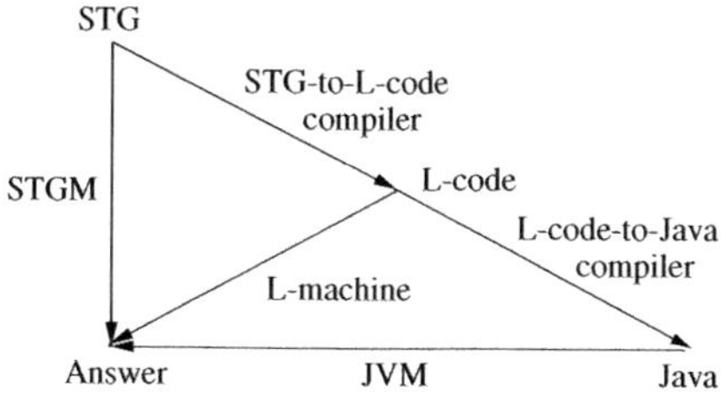

Fig. 1. A Two-Level Translation Scheme

program. Since the STG is simply a functional language, it is the lower level implementation decisions that make the abstract machine spineless and tagless. Hence, in the direct translations, the issues in implementing the STGM are forced to blend with the ones in the representation with Java codes. Besides, both researchers describe their translation methods informally with several examples. For some thing, like tail recursion, it is not clear how they implemented it.

In this study, we develop a two-level translation scheme: the first phase for compiling the STG language into an intermediate language called L-code (lambda code) and the second phase for representing the L-code language with the Java codes, as shown in Figure 1. The L-code is designed to specify precisely the behavior of STG programs with respect to the STGM. Each instruction of the language materializes explicitly the operations on closures, a register file, a stack, or a heap, which may be derived from the intended meaning of the STG language, so it can be directly mapped onto some Java statements. A basic unit of L-code instuctions is clearly identified in the structure of L-code programs, so it can be directly mapped onto exactly one class in Java. Every L-code program will reflect whole aspects necessary for the mapping. With this intermediate language, the translation issues can be separated from the representation ones, and each specific matter can be concentrated on in a modular way. For each level, a *concrete* compilation rule is given, and it is perfectly reproducible. Based on this scheme, we have developed an LFL-to-Java compiler. For five initial benchmarks, performance is very promising.

The contributions of our study are as follows:

- A systematic method of mapping the STGM onto arbitrary machines by the STG-to-L-code compiler and the reduction machine is provided (Section 2).
- The representations necessary for the mapping from L-code to Java are determined, and an L-code-to-Java compiler is presented (Section 3 and 4).
- The performance of the Java programs produced is measured (Section 5).

After surveying related works in Section 6, we conclude in Section 7.

2 The Spineless Tagless G-machine

In this section, the STGM is described by four components: the STG language, the L-code, an STG-to-L-code compiler, and the L-machine.

2.1 Source Language

The STGM treates the STG language as its source language. The syntax of our STG language is as follows:

x, y, z, w			variable
v	$::=$	$\lambda\overline{x}.e \mid c\,\overline{x}$	value
e	$::=$	$x_0\ \overline{x} \mid \text{let}\ \overline{bind}\ \text{in}\ e \mid \text{case}\ e\ \text{of}\ \lambda z.alts$	expression
b	$::=$	$v \mid e$	bound expression
π	$::=$	$u \mid n$	update flag
$bind$	$::=$	$x \overset{\pi}{=} b$	binding
t	$::=$	$\mathsf{c} \mid \lambda \mid \text{default}$	tag
$alts$	$::=$	$\overline{alt}$	alternatives
alt	$::=$	$c\,\overline{x} \rightarrow e \mid \text{default} \rightarrow e$	alternative
$decl$	$::=$	$\mathrm{T}\ \overline{c_i\ n_i}$	type declaration
prg	$::=$	$\overline{decl},\ \text{let}\ \overline{bind}\ \text{in}\ main$	program

The notation $\overline{obj_n}$ denotes $obj_1\ ...\ obj_n$ for $n \geq 0$. All bound expressions are syntactically divided into either weak head normal form (Whnf) v or non-Whnf e. Every binding has a update flag π to determine whether the value of a non-Whnf is shared or not. In case expression, the z is a bound variable that is bound to some resulting value of its case scrutinee e. The symbol λ as a tag over lambda abstractions is distinguished from constructor tags c, and the symbol default is considered as a special tag for convenience. An STG program consists of a let expression and type declarations that define tags and arities of constructors. The full detail can be found in Peyton Jones's paper [7]. An example codelet is as follows:

$$\text{let}\quad s \overset{n}{=} \lambda f\ g\ x.\ \text{let}\ a \overset{u}{=} g\ x\ \text{in}\ f\ x\ a \quad \text{in}\ ...$$

2.2 Target Language

The L-code is determined as the target language. The L-code is a kind of higher-order assembly language in which binding relationships in the source phrase are represented using those in the λ-term, as introduced by Wand [12].

$\mathsf{x,y,z,w,t,s}$	register
l	label
$\mathsf{C} ::= \textbf{let}\ \overline{l = \mathsf{C}}\ \textbf{in}\ \mathsf{C}$	L-code

$\mid$ JMPC x	$\mid$ JMPK x y t	$\mid$ CASE t $\overline{t \rightarrow \langle l, \mathsf{x_0}\,\overline{\mathsf{x}}\rangle}$
$\mid$ GETN (λx.C)	$\mid$ GETNT (λx.λt.C)	$\mid$ GETA ($\lambda\langle l, \mathsf{x_0}\,\overline{\mathsf{x}}\rangle$.C)
$\mid$ PUTARG $\overline{\mathsf{x}}$ C	$\mid$ GETARG ($\lambda\overline{\mathsf{x}}$.C)	$\mid$ ARGCK n C_{mp} C
$\mid$ PUTK $\langle l, \overline{\mathsf{x}}\rangle$ C	$\mid$ GETK ($\lambda\langle l, \overline{\mathsf{x}}\rangle$.C)	$\mid$ REFK (λx.C)
$\mid$ SAVE (λs.C)	$\mid$ DUMP C	$\mid$ RESTORE s C
$\mid$ PUTC $\overline{\mathsf{x} \overset{\pi}{=} \langle l, \overline{\mathsf{x}}\rangle}$ C	$\mid$ GETC x ($\lambda\langle l, \overline{\mathsf{w}}\rangle$.C)	$\mid$ UPDC x $\langle l, \overline{\mathsf{w}}\rangle$
$\mid$ PUTP $\overline{\langle l, \mathsf{x}\rangle}$ (λy.C)	$\mid$ STOP x	

A register is an identifier used in L-code. A label l is uniquely given in **let** blocks for a sequence of L-code instructions. An L-code program for a given STG program will be a nested **let** expression. The meaning of each L-code instruction is precisely defined by the reduction machine shown in the next section.

The purpose for the introduction of L-code is to identify explicitly every operation performed in the STGM by each instruction. This enables us to show our compiler with clearly set out compilation rules as will be shown. The complete specification using L-code for the STGM is also helpful to implement our compiler accurately because it specifies precisely how the STGM is to be implemented. The STG language itself has an operational reading so that it is not impossible to translate the STG language directly into Java, but the language leaves unspecified quite a few things for the implementation of the STGM.

2.3 L-machine

The L-machine is defined as a set of reduction rules for L-code as shown in Figure 2, and it uses runtime structures as follows:

$\langle l, \rho \rangle$		closure
ρ ::=	$\overline{x}$	environment
μ ::=	$\mu_0 \mid \mu[\mathsf{x} \mapsto x] \mid \mu[\mathsf{x} \mapsto l] \mid \mu[\mathsf{t} \mapsto t] \mid \mu[\mathsf{s} \mapsto s]$	register file
s ::=	$s_0 \mid x\ s \mid \langle l, \rho \rangle\ s$	stack
h ::=	$h_0 \mid h[x \mapsto \langle l, \rho \rangle] \mid h[l \mapsto \mathsf{C}]$	heap

The reduction machine is pattern-driven; a reduction rule that matches the pattern of some current state is selected and applied. Usually, a state has the form of $\mathsf{C}\ \mu\ s\ h$. A register file μ is a mapping of registers into addresses, labels, tags, or stacks. Note that an address is represented by a variable. An environment ρ is a sequence of addresses. A closure $\langle l, \rho \rangle$ consists of a label l and an environment ρ. A stack s is a sequence of addresses and closures. A heap h is a mapping of addresses into closures and labels into L-codes. Here, μ_0, s_0, and h_0 are an empty register file, stack, and heap respectively.

In order to give readers intuition, we give a short informal explanation about the behavior of L-machine for each instruction: the JMPC x makes a tail call to the heap-allocated closure at the address stored in x. The JMPK x y t makes a tail call to the stack-allocated closure of the label stored in x, passing the address stored in y and a tag stored in t to the closure. The CASE t $\overline{t_i \rightarrow \langle l_i, \mathsf{x}_0\, \overline{\mathsf{x}}_i \rangle}$ selects a matching alternative of t_i and jumps to the instructions of the label l_i, passing the addresses stored in x_0 and $\overline{\mathsf{x}}_i$. The GETN, GETNT, and GETA receive the addresses passed by JMPC, JMPK, and CASE, respectively. The PUTARG inserts the addresses of some arguments at the top of a stack and the GETARG deletes them. The ARGCK n C_{mp} C checks the availablility of n arguments on stack. Then, it jumps to C if all n arguments are available, otherwise it jumps to C_{mp} in order to make a partial application. The PUTK, GETK, and REFK manipulate stack-allocated closures, while PUTC, GETC, UPDC, and PUTP work with heap-allocated closures. The SAVE, DUMP, and RESTORE control a stack, and the STOP x stops the reduction machine yielding an answer.

$(\mathbf{let}\ \overline{l_i = \mathsf{C}_i}\ \mathbf{in}\ \mathsf{C})\ \mu\ s\ h$	$\Rightarrow \mathsf{C}\ \mu\ s\ h[\overline{l_i \mapsto \mathsf{C}_i}]$	
$(\mathsf{STOP\ x})\ \mu\ s\ h$	$\Rightarrow (\mu(\mathsf{x}), h)$	
$(\mathsf{JMPC\ x})\ \mu\ s\ h$	$\Rightarrow h(l)\ \mu(\mathsf{x})\ s\ h$	$\theta(\mathsf{x}, l, \rho)^1$
$(\mathsf{GETN}\ (\lambda \mathsf{x}.\mathsf{C}))\ x\ s\ h$	$\Rightarrow \mathsf{C}\ \mu_0[\mathsf{x} \mapsto x]\ s\ h$	
$(\mathsf{JMPK\ y\ x\ t})\ \mu\ s\ h$	$\Rightarrow h(\mu(\mathsf{y}))\ \mu(\mathsf{x})\ \mu(\mathsf{t})\ s\ h$	
$(\mathsf{GETNT}\ (\lambda \mathsf{x}.\lambda \mathsf{t}.\mathsf{C})\ x\ t\ s\ h$	$\Rightarrow \mathsf{C}\ \mu_0[\mathsf{x} \mapsto x, \mathsf{t} \mapsto t]\ s\ h$	
$(\mathsf{CASE\ t}\ \overline{t_i \rightarrow \langle l_i, \mathsf{x}_0\, \overline{\mathsf{x}}_i \rangle})\ \mu\ s\ h$	$\Rightarrow h(l_j)\ \langle l_j, \mu(\mathsf{x}_0)\, \overline{\mu(\mathsf{x})}_i \rangle\ s\ h$	if $\exists j.\mu(\mathsf{t}) = t_j$
	$\Rightarrow h(l_d)\ \langle l_d, \mu(\mathsf{x}_0)\, \overline{\mu(\mathsf{x})}_d \rangle\ s\ h$	otherwise^2
$(\mathsf{GETA}\ (\lambda \langle l, \mathsf{x}_0\, \overline{\mathsf{x}} \rangle.\mathsf{C})\ \langle l, x_0\, \overline{x} \rangle\ s\ h$	$\Rightarrow \mathsf{C}\ \mu_0[\mathsf{x}_0 \mapsto x_0, \overline{\mathsf{x} \mapsto x}]\ s\ h$	
$(\mathsf{GETARG}\ (\lambda \overline{\mathsf{x}}_n.\mathsf{C}))\ \mu\ (\overline{x}_n\ s)\ h$	$\Rightarrow \mathsf{C}\ \mu[\overline{\mathsf{x} \mapsto x}]\ s\ h$	
$(\mathsf{PUTARG}\ \overline{\mathsf{x}}\ \mathsf{C})\ \mu\ s\ h$	$\Rightarrow \mathsf{C}\ \mu\ (\overline{\mu(\mathsf{x})}\ s)\ h$	
$(\mathsf{ARGCK}\ n\ \mathsf{C}_{mp}\ \mathsf{C})\ \mu\ (\overline{x}_m\ \langle l, \rho \rangle\ s)\ h$	$\Rightarrow \mathsf{C}\ \mu\ (\overline{x}_m\ \langle l, \rho \rangle\ s)\ h$	if $m \geq n$
	$\Rightarrow \mathsf{C}_{mp}\ \mu\ (\overline{x}_m\ \langle l, \rho \rangle\ s)\ h$	otherwise
$(\mathsf{GETK}\ (\lambda \langle l, \overline{\mathsf{x}} \rangle.\mathsf{C}))\ \mu\ (\langle l, \overline{x} \rangle\ s)\ h$	$\Rightarrow \mathsf{C}\ \mu[\overline{\mathsf{x} \mapsto x}]\ s\ h$	
$(\mathsf{PUTK}\ \langle l, \overline{\mathsf{x}} \rangle\ \mathsf{C})\ \mu\ s\ h$	$\Rightarrow \mathsf{C}\ \mu\ (\langle l, \overline{\mu(\mathsf{x})} \rangle\ s)\ h$	
$(\mathsf{REFK}\ (\lambda \mathsf{x}.\mathsf{C}))\ \mu\ (\langle l, \rho \rangle\ s)\ h$	$\Rightarrow \mathsf{C}\ \mu[\mathsf{x} \mapsto l]\ (\langle l, \rho \rangle\ s)\ h$	
$(\mathsf{SAVE}\ (\lambda \mathsf{s}.\mathsf{C}))\ \mu\ s\ h$	$\Rightarrow \mathsf{C}\ \mu[\mathsf{s} \mapsto s]\ s\ h$	
$(\mathsf{DUMP\ C})\ \mu\ (\langle l, \rho \rangle\ s)\ h$	$\Rightarrow \mathsf{C}\ \mu\ \langle l, \rho \rangle\ h$	
$(\mathsf{RESTORE\ s\ C})\ \mu\ s\ h$	$\Rightarrow \mathsf{C}\ \mu\ \mu(\mathsf{s})\ h$	
$(\mathsf{GETC\ x}\ (\lambda \langle l, \overline{\mathsf{w}} \rangle.\mathsf{C}))\ \mu\ s\ h$	$\Rightarrow \mathsf{C}\ \mu[\overline{\mathsf{w} \mapsto w}]\ s\ h$	$\theta(\mathsf{x}, l, \overline{w})$
$(\mathsf{PUTC\ x} \overset{\pi}{=} \langle l, \overline{\mathsf{w}} \rangle\ \mathsf{C})\ \mu\ s\ h$	$\Rightarrow \mathsf{C}\ \mu'\ s\ h[x^* \mapsto \langle l, \overline{\mu'(\mathsf{w})} \rangle]$	$\mu' = \mu[\mathsf{x} \mapsto x^*]^3$
$(\mathsf{UPDC\ x}\ \langle l, \overline{\mathsf{w}} \rangle\ \mathsf{C})\ \mu\ s\ h$	$\Rightarrow \mathsf{C}\ \mu\ s\ h[\mu(\mathsf{x}) \mapsto \langle l, \overline{\mu(\mathsf{w})} \rangle]$	
$(\mathsf{PUTP}\ \overline{\langle l_i, \mathsf{x}_0 \rangle}_n\ (\lambda \mathsf{y}.\mathsf{C}))\ \mu\ (\overline{x}_m\ \langle l', \rho \rangle\ s)\ h$ $\Rightarrow \mathsf{C}\ \mu[\mathsf{y} \mapsto y^*]\ (\langle l', \rho \rangle\ s)\ h[y^* \mapsto \langle l_{m+1}, \mu(\mathsf{x}_0)\, \overline{x}_m \rangle]$		$n > m$

1. $\theta(\mathsf{x}, l, \rho)$ iff $h(\mu(\mathsf{x})) = \langle l, \rho \rangle$ where μ and h are given on each context
2. default $\rightarrow \langle l_d, \mathsf{x}_0\, \overline{\mathsf{x}}_d \rangle$ is selected
3. x^* means x is a fresh heap address

Fig. 2. Reduction Rules of L-machine

An example of reduction is shown below:

$$
\begin{aligned}
& (\mathsf{GETN}\ (\lambda \mathsf{z}.\mathsf{GETC\ z}\ (\lambda \langle l_s, \rangle.\mathsf{ARGCK}\ 3\ \mathsf{C}_{mp}\ \mathsf{C}_r)))\ z\ (f\ g\ x\ s_0)\ h \\
\Rightarrow\ & (\mathsf{GETC\ z}\ (\lambda \langle l_s, \rangle.\mathsf{ARGCK}\ 3\ \mathsf{C}_{mp}\ \mathsf{C}_r))\ \mu_0[\mathsf{z} \mapsto z]\ (f\ g\ x\ s_0)\ h \\
& \text{where } h(z) = \langle l_s, \rangle \\
\Rightarrow\ & (\mathsf{ARGCK}\ 3\ \mathsf{C}_{mp}\ \mathsf{C}_r)\ \mu_0[\mathsf{z} \mapsto z]\ (f\ g\ x\ s_0)\ h \\
& \text{where } \mathsf{C}_r \equiv \mathsf{GETARG}\ (\lambda \mathsf{f\ g\ x}.(\mathbf{let}\ l_a = \mathsf{C}_a \mathbf{in}\ \mathsf{C}_1)) \\
\Rightarrow\ & (\mathsf{GETARG}\ (\lambda \mathsf{f\ g\ x}.(\mathbf{let}\ l_a = \mathsf{C}_a \mathbf{in}\ \mathsf{C}_1)))\ [\mathsf{z} \mapsto z]\ (f\ g\ x\ s_0)\ h \\
\Rightarrow\ & (\mathbf{let}\ l_a = \mathsf{C}_a \mathbf{in}\ \mathsf{C}_1)\ \mu_0[\mathsf{z} \mapsto z, \mathsf{f} \mapsto f, \mathsf{g} \mapsto g, \mathsf{x} \mapsto x]\ s_0\ h \\
& \text{where } \mathsf{C}_1 \equiv \mathsf{PUTC\ a} \overset{u}{=} \langle l_a, \mathsf{g\,x} \rangle\ (\mathsf{PUTARG\ x\ a\ C_2}),\ \mathsf{C}_2 \equiv \mathsf{JMPC\ f} \\
\Rightarrow\ & (\mathsf{PUTC\ a} \overset{u}{=} \langle l_a, \mathsf{g\,x} \rangle\ (\mathsf{PUTARG\ x\ a\ C_2}))\ \mu_0[\mathsf{z} \mapsto z, ..., \mathsf{x} \mapsto x]\ s_0\ h[l_a \mapsto \mathsf{C}_a] \\
\Rightarrow\ & (\mathsf{PUTARG\ x\ a\ C_2})\ \mu_0[\mathsf{z} \mapsto z, ..., \mathsf{x} \mapsto x, \mathsf{a} \mapsto a]\ s_0\ h[l_a \mapsto \mathsf{C}_a, a \mapsto \langle l_a, g\,x \rangle] \\
& \text{where } a \text{ is a fresh heap address} \\
\Rightarrow\ & (\mathsf{JMPC\ f})\ \mu_0[\mathsf{z} \mapsto z, ..., \mathsf{x} \mapsto x, \mathsf{a} \mapsto a]\ (x\ a\ s_0)\ h[l_a \mapsto \mathsf{C}_a, a \mapsto \langle l_a, g\,x \rangle]
\end{aligned}
$$

Eventually, the L-machine will produce an answer (x, h), if it exists, in which x is an address of some value and h is a final status of the machine's heap.

2.4 Compiling STG Programs

In order to compile STG programs, some auxiliary syntactic elements are needed: the partial applications $(pap\ w_0\ \overline{w})$, the indirection $(ind\ w)$, the standard constructors $(c\ \overline{w})$, selection continuations $(sel\ \lambda z.alts)$, the update continuation $(upd\ w_1\ w_2)$, and the halt continuation $(halt)$.

Our STG compiler is presented in Figure 3. Notice that a set of free variables in some syntactic element is annotated as a prefix of the element, such as $\{\overline{w}\}.\lambda\overline{x}.e$, for convenience; $\{\overline{w}_n\}$ is considered as $\{w_1, ..., w_n\}$. Such annotation is assumed to be calculated on the fly whenever needed. Notice also that symbol tables τ are used in compilation rules. A symbol table τ is a mapping of variables into registers. Similarly, τ_0 is an empty symbol table.

$\tau ::= \tau_0 \mid \tau[x \mapsto \mathsf{x}]$ symbol table

As shown in Figure 3, our compiler is composed of five kinds of compilation rules: B for bound expressions, E for expressions, A for alternatives, C for continuations, and X for some auxiliary expressions. The P rule receives an STG program and produces an L-code program in the form of nested **let** expressions that would be flattened by hoisting transformation.

Note that, according to the compilation rules, all **let**-bound Cs are closed and may be hoisted out to the top level without difficulty. The hoisted version will form a single-level **let** expression, in which any **let**-bound C contains no other **let** expression. An example of compiling an STG program is shown below:

$$
\begin{array}{l}
\quad\textbf{let } l_{upd} = \ ...\ \textbf{in} \\
\quad\textbf{let } l_s = B[\![\{\}.\lambda f\ g\ x.\ \text{let } a \overset{u}{=} g\ x \text{ in } f\ x\ a]\!]\ n\ l_s\ \textbf{in}\ ... \\
= \textbf{let } l_{upd} = \ ...\ \textbf{in} \\
\quad\textbf{let } l_s = \mathsf{GETN}\ (\lambda \mathsf{z}.\mathsf{GETC}\ \mathsf{z}\ (\lambda\langle l_s, \rangle.\mathsf{ARGCK}\ 3\ (...)(\mathsf{GETARG}\ (\lambda \mathsf{f\ g\ x}. \\
\qquad\quad\textbf{let } l_a = \mathsf{GETN}\ (\lambda \mathsf{z}.\mathsf{GETC}\ \mathsf{z}\ (\lambda\langle l_a, \mathsf{g\,x}\rangle.\mathsf{SAVE}\ (\lambda \mathsf{s}.\mathsf{PUTK}\ \langle l_{upd}, \mathsf{z\,s}\rangle \\
\qquad\qquad\qquad(\mathsf{DUMP}\ (\mathsf{PUTARG}\ \mathsf{x}\ (\mathsf{JMPC}\ \mathsf{g})))))) \\
\qquad\quad\textbf{in } \mathsf{PUTC}\ \mathsf{a} \overset{u}{=} \langle l_a, \mathsf{g\,x}\rangle\ (\mathsf{PUTARG}\ \mathsf{x}\ \mathsf{a}\ (\mathsf{JMPC}\ \mathsf{f})))))) \\
\quad\textbf{in}\ ...
\end{array}
$$

From the above example, we get its hosisted version as follows:

$$
\begin{array}{lll}
\textbf{let } l_{upd} & = & ... \\
\quad l_s & = & \mathsf{GETN}\ (\lambda \mathsf{z}.\mathsf{GETC}\ \mathsf{z}\ (\lambda\langle l_s, \rangle).\mathsf{ARGCK}\ 3\ (...)(\mathsf{GETARG}\ (\lambda \mathsf{f\ g\ x}. \\
 & & \ \mathsf{PUTC}\ \mathsf{a} \overset{u}{=} \langle l_a, \mathsf{g\,x}\rangle\ (\mathsf{PUTARG}\ \mathsf{x}\ \mathsf{a}\ (\mathsf{JMPC}\ \mathsf{f})))))) \\
\quad l_a & = & \mathsf{GETN}\ (\lambda \mathsf{z}.\mathsf{GETC}\ \mathsf{z}\ (\lambda\langle l_a, \mathsf{g\,x}\rangle.(\mathsf{SAVE}\ (\lambda \mathsf{s}.\mathsf{PUTK}\ \langle l_{upd}, \mathsf{z\,s}\rangle \\
 & & \ (\mathsf{DUMP}\ (\mathsf{PUTARG}\ \mathsf{x}\ (\mathsf{JMPC}\ \mathsf{g}))))))) \\
\textbf{in}\ ...
\end{array}
$$

Let C be obtained from compiling an STG program. It will be reduced by applying the reduction rule $\Rightarrow$, starting from C $\mu_0\ s_0\ h_0$.

$$
\begin{array}{ll}
B[\![\{\overline{w}\}.\lambda\overline{x}_n.e]\!]\ \pi\ l & = \mathsf{GETN}\ (\lambda \mathsf{z}.\mathsf{GETC}\ \mathsf{z}\ (\lambda\langle l,\overline{\mathsf{w}}\rangle.\mathsf{ARGCK}\ n \\
 & \quad (\mathsf{PUTP}\ \overline{\langle l_{pap,i},\mathsf{z}\rangle}_n\ (\lambda \mathsf{p}.\mathsf{REFK}\ (\lambda \mathsf{y}.\mathsf{JMPK}\ \mathsf{y}\ \mathsf{p}\ \lambda))) \\
 & \quad (\mathsf{GETARG}\ (\lambda\overline{\mathsf{x}}.E[\![e]\!]\ \tau_0[\overline{w\mapsto \mathsf{w}},\overline{x\mapsto \mathsf{x}}])))) \\
B[\![\{\overline{w}\}.c\ \overline{w}]\!]\ \pi\ l & = X[\![\{\overline{w}\}.c\ \overline{w}]\!]\ l \\
B[\![\{\overline{w}\}.e]\!]\ u\ l & = \mathsf{GETN}\ (\lambda \mathsf{z}.\mathsf{GETC}\ \mathsf{z}\ (\lambda\langle l,\overline{\mathsf{w}}\rangle.\mathsf{SAVE}\ (\lambda \mathsf{s}.\mathsf{PUTK}\ \langle l_{upd},\mathsf{z}\,\mathsf{s}\rangle \\
 & \quad (\mathsf{DUMP}\ (E[\![e]\!]\ \tau_0[\overline{w\mapsto \mathsf{w}}]))))) \\
B[\![\{\overline{w}\}.e]\!]\ n\ l & = \mathsf{GETN}\ (\lambda \mathsf{z}.\mathsf{GETC}\ \mathsf{z}\ (\lambda\langle l,\overline{\mathsf{w}}\rangle.E[\![e]\!]\ \tau_0[\overline{w\mapsto \mathsf{w}}]))
\end{array}
$$

$$
\begin{array}{ll}
E[\![x_0\ \overline{x}]\!]\ \tau & = \mathsf{PUTARG}\ \overline{\tau(x)}\ (\mathsf{JMPC}\ \tau(x_0)) \\
E[\![\mathrm{case}\ e\ \mathrm{of}\ \{\overline{w}\}.\lambda x.alts]\!]\ \tau & = \mathbf{let}\ l_{sel} = C[\![\{\overline{w}\}.sel\ \lambda x.alts]\!]\ l_{sel} \\
 & \quad \mathbf{in}\ \mathsf{PUTK}\ \langle l_{sel},\overline{\tau(w)}\rangle\ (E[\![e]\!]\ \tau) \\
 & \quad \mathrm{where}\ l_{sel}\ \mathrm{fresh} \\
E[\![\mathrm{let}\ \overline{x_i \overset{\pi_i}{=} \{\overline{w_i}\}.b_i}\ \mathrm{in}\ e]\!]\ \tau & = \mathbf{let}\ \overline{l_i = B[\![\{\overline{w_i}\}.b_i]\!]\ \pi_i\ l_i}\quad (b_i \not\equiv c\ \overline{y}) \\
 & \quad \mathbf{in}\ \mathsf{PUTC}\ \overline{\mathsf{x}_i \overset{\pi_i}{=} \langle l_i,\overline{\mathsf{w}_i}\rangle}\ (E[\![e]\!]\ \tau[\overline{x_i\mapsto \mathsf{x}_i}]) \\
 & \quad \mathrm{where}\quad l_i \equiv l_c\ \ \mathrm{and}\ \mathsf{w}_i \equiv \tau[\overline{x_i\mapsto \mathsf{x}_i}](y)\qquad \mathrm{if}\ b_i \equiv c\ \overline{y} \\
 & \qquad\qquad\ \ l_i\ \mathrm{fresh\ and}\ \mathsf{w}_i \equiv \tau[\overline{x_i\mapsto \mathsf{x}_i}](w)\qquad \mathrm{otherwise}
\end{array}
$$

$$
\begin{array}{ll}
A[\![\{\overline{w}\}.c\ \overline{x}\rightarrow e]\!]\ l & = \mathsf{GETA}\ (\lambda\langle l,\mathsf{z}\,\overline{\mathsf{w}}\rangle.\mathsf{GETC}\ \mathsf{z}\ (\lambda\langle l_c,\overline{\mathsf{x}}\rangle.E[\![e]\!]\ \tau_0[\overline{w\mapsto \mathsf{w}},\overline{x\mapsto \mathsf{x}}])) \\
A[\![\{\overline{w}\}.\mathrm{default}\rightarrow e]\!]\ l & = \mathsf{GETA}\ (\lambda\langle l,\mathsf{z}\,\overline{\mathsf{w}}\rangle.E[\![e]\!]\ \tau_0[\overline{w\mapsto \mathsf{w}}])
\end{array}
$$

$$
\begin{array}{ll}
C[\![\{w_1,w_2\}.upd\ w_1\ w_2]\!]\ l & = X[\![\{w_1,w_2\}.upd\ w_1\ w_2]\!]\ l \\
C[\![\{\overline{w}\}.sel\ \lambda w_0.\overline{alt_i}]\!]\ l & = \mathbf{let}\ \overline{l_i = A[\![alt_i]\!]\ l_i} \\
 & \quad \mathbf{in}\ \mathsf{GETNT}\ (\lambda \mathsf{w}_0.\lambda \mathsf{t}.\mathsf{GETK}\ (\lambda\langle l,\overline{\mathsf{w}}\rangle.\mathsf{CASE}\ \mathsf{t}\ \overline{t_i\rightarrow\langle l_i,\mathsf{w}_0\,\overline{\mathsf{w}_i}\rangle})) \\
 & \quad \mathrm{where}\quad \overline{l_i}\ \mathrm{fresh},\ alt_i \equiv \{\overline{w_i}\}.t_i\ldots\rightarrow\ldots \\
C[\![\{\}.halt]\!]\ l & = X[\![\{\}.halt]\!]\ l
\end{array}
$$

$$
\begin{array}{ll}
X[\![\{w_0,\overline{w}\}.pap\ w_0\ \overline{w}]\!]\ l & = \mathsf{GETN}\ (\lambda \mathsf{z}.\mathsf{GETC}\ \mathsf{z}\ (\lambda\langle l,\mathsf{w}_0\,\overline{\mathsf{w}}\rangle.\mathsf{PUTARG}\ \overline{\mathsf{w}}\ (\mathsf{JMPC}\ \mathsf{w}_0))) \\
X[\![\{w\}.ind\ w]\!]\ l & = \mathsf{GETN}\ (\lambda \mathsf{z}.\mathsf{GETC}\ \mathsf{z}\ (\lambda\langle l,\mathsf{w}\rangle.\mathsf{JMPC}\ \mathsf{w})) \\
X[\![\{\overline{w}\}.c\ \overline{w}]\!]\ l & = \mathsf{GETN}\ (\lambda \mathsf{z}.\mathsf{REFK}\ (\lambda \mathsf{x}.\mathsf{JMPK}\ \mathsf{x}\ \mathsf{z}\ c)) \\
X[\![\{w_1,w_2\}.upd\ w_1\ w_2]\!]\ l & = \mathsf{GETNT}\ (\lambda \mathsf{z}.\lambda \mathsf{t}.\mathsf{GETK}\ (\lambda\langle l,\mathsf{w}_1\,\mathsf{w}_2\rangle. \\
 & \quad \mathsf{RESTORE}\ \mathsf{w}_2\ (\mathsf{UPDC}\ \mathsf{w}_1\ \langle l_{ind},\mathsf{z}\rangle\ (\mathsf{JMPC}\ \mathsf{z})))) \\
X[\![\{\}.halt]\!]\ l & = \mathsf{GETNT}\ (\lambda \mathsf{z}.\lambda \mathsf{t}.\mathsf{GETK}\ (\lambda\langle l,\rangle.\mathsf{STOP}\ \mathsf{z}))
\end{array}
$$

$$
\begin{array}{ll}
P[\![\overline{decl},e]\!] & = \mathbf{let}\ l_{pap,m} = X[\![\{\overline{w}_m\}.pap\ \overline{w}_m]\!]\ l_{pap,m}\quad (m \geq 1) \\
 & \qquad\ l_{ind} \quad\ = X[\![\{w\}.ind\ w]\!]\ l_{ind} \\
 & \qquad\ l_{upd} \quad = X[\![\{w_1,w_2\}.upd\ w_1\ w_2]\!]\ l_{upd} \\
 & \qquad\ l_{halt} \quad = X[\![\{\}.halt]\!]\ l_{halt} \\
 & \qquad\ l_c \qquad = X[\![\{\overline{w}_n\}.c\ \overline{w}_n]\!]\ l_c\quad (\mathrm{T}\ \overline{c\ n} \in \overline{decl}) \\
 & \quad \mathbf{in}\ \mathsf{PUTK}\ \langle l_{halt},\rangle\ (E[\![e]\!]\ \tau_0)
\end{array}
$$

Fig. 3. Compilation Rules for the STG Language

3 Representation

From now on, we will concentrate on the development of an L-code-to-Java compiler. In this section, the method with which the elements in the L-machine is represented in Java language is explained. In the next section, the compiler is defined, based on the representations.

3.1 Closure

The class *Clo* is a base class that captures common elements among closures. It has a public member variable *ind* that is initialized to itself, and an abstract member function *code*().

```
public abstract class Clo {
    public Clo ind = this;
    public abstract Clo code();
}
```

Every closure, e.g. of label l, is represented by a class that extends the base class by adding some member variables as its free variables and overriding the *code*() of the base class as follows:

```
public class C_l extends Clo {
    public Object f_1, ... , f_n;
    public Clo code() { ... }
}
```

Note that member variables are declared as type *Object*, which is the superclass of all classes in Java. Whenever items specific to some inherited class, such as accessing member variables in the class, are needed, the *Object* class can be cast into an appropriate class in our compilation scheme.

3.2 Runtime System

Our runtime system is a class G that equips static variables *node*, *tag*, *loopflag*, *sp*, *bp*, and *stk*.

```
public class G {
    public static Object node;
    public static int tag;
    public static boolean loopflag;

    public static int sp, bp;
    public static Object[] stk;
        ...
}
```

The node variable $G.node$ and the tag variable $G.tag$ are used for passing the address x of a heap-allocated closure and the tag t respectively, as shown in the reduction rule:

$$(\mathsf{GETNT}\ (\lambda \mathsf{x}.\lambda \mathsf{t}.\mathsf{C}))\ x\ t\ s\ h \Rightarrow \mathsf{C}\ \mu_0[\mathsf{x} \mapsto x, \mathsf{t} \mapsto t]\ s\ h$$

A register file does not require any gadgets. Instead, the mapping by the register file is simply resolved by the scope rule in Java languages. A stack is represented by a big array *G.stk* of type *Object*, and *G.sp* and *G.bp* point to the top and bottom elements of the top portion of the stack respectively. A heap is represented by the internal heap provided by the JVM.

Note that the stack represented by an array has to be carefully handled. First, after an object is deleted from the top of a stack, the deleted entry of the object must be filled with null in order to inform the JVM that the object in the entry may be unnecessary. Second, an array of type *Object* can contain only values of any classes (or reference data type [3]), but the insertion of primitive values of types such as int and boolean will cause type violation at compile-time. This prevents the passing of unboxed arguments that are represented by primitive values. Instead, we pass them through global registers which are represented by static variables of appropriate primitive types.

3.3 Updating

In conventional machines, updating is achieved by directly overwriting a value at a given address. However, the JVM provides no way to construct one object directly on top of another. Therefore, updates must be managed in an alternative way. To do this, a special class *Ind* is introduced.

```
public class Ind extends Clo {
    public Clo code() { return this.ind; }
}
```

Whenever any non-Whnf is allocated, an object of *Ind* class is created together and its *ind* field is set to point to the non-Whnf. Later, at the time the non-Whnf is updated with a value, the *ind* field is given the value. Refer to the compilation rule for PUTC and UPDC in Section 4.

Note that every object representing a thunk is reachable only through an additional indirection object of the class *Ind* in this implementation. This indirection cannot be easily removed if a garbage collector does not treat it specially as in the conventional implementations. Although it is not possible to build up a chain of indirections in this implementation, even one-lengthed chains may cause a space leak. Probably, all the approaches in compiling lazy functional languages for the JVM are expected to suffer from this problem since it is not possible to interact with the built-in garbage collector of the JVM in general.

3.4 Tail Call

The STGM mostly transfers control in tail calls. Every tail call can be implemented by a single jump instruction on conventional machines. Since no tail call instruction is provided in the JVM, they must be simulated by a tiny interpreter as follows:

```
public static void loop (Clo c) { while(loopflag) c=c.ind.code(); }
```

Every sequence of L-code instructions ends with one of JMPK, JMPC, and CASE, according to our compilation rule shown in Figure 3. The three instructions are translated into Java statements that return an object to which control is transferred. After the return, control will reach the assignment statement in the body of the while loop of the above interpreter, and the interpreter will call the object's *code*() if *loopflag* is true. Here, the *loopflag* is a static boolean variable to make the STGM go or stop.

4 Compilation

Our compiler receives a hoisted version of L-code program, and generates Java classes using compilation rules for L-code instructions shown in Figure 4. Basically, our compilation scheme considers each closure as one class, which has member variables as the closure's free variables and has one method that simulates the closure's instructions.

Recall that a hoisted version of L-code program forms a single-level **let** expression containing **let** bindings $\overline{l = \mathsf{C}}$. By hoisting transformation, each C contains no inner **let** expression. Hence, a simple driver is needed to generate a class for each binding.

The driver may introduce member variables of the class from the relevant free variables obtained by analyzing the C. For convenience's sake, the STG-to-L-code compiler is assumed to annotate them to the binding like $l = \{\overline{w}\}.\mathsf{C}$, so the driver will use the annotation to make the member variables. The body of *code*() in the class will be filled with the Java statements generated by applying our L-code-to-Java compiler to the C in the binding.

Our compiler neatly maps registers used in L-code into some variables in Java codes. Each register will be accessed by its name, rather than by some offset as in conventional implementations. Accessing variables by names is much better, as it does not require costly array accesses.

In general, for bound variables $\overline{\mathsf{x}}$ in some L-code ... ($\lambda\overline{\mathsf{x}}$. ...), local variables $\overline{\mathtt{x}}$ of type *Object* are declared in J rules. Sometimes, it is not necessary to declare such local variables, for example, as in the rule for GETA. The reason is that the required local variables are already declared. According to the rule for CASE, Java codes generated from this instruction are combined with those generated from alternatives, though they are not in the same closure in terms of L-code. Since free variables that occur in the alternatives must be declared in the closure in which the CASE resides, the free variables in the alternative can be accessed from the preceding declaration by the scope rule in Java language without any additional declaration as in GETA.

For SAVE and RESTORE, the base pointer $G.bp$ is stored and restored instead of an entire stack, which is a well-known technique explained by Peyton Jones [7]. Note that, in the case of SAVE (λs.C), J declares a variable s of type int as the bound variable s because it will hold the value of $G.bp$.

Due to space limitations, we omit discussion of some details of the L-code-to-Java compiler, including unboxed values and primitives. We also omit discussion

$$
\begin{array}{lll}
J\llbracket \mathsf{JMPC\ x} \rrbracket & = & G.node = x;\ \text{return}\ (Clo)x \\
J\llbracket \mathsf{JMPK\ x\ y\ t} \rrbracket & = & G.node = y;\ G.tag = t;\ \text{return}\ (Clo)x \\
J\llbracket \mathsf{GETN}\ (\lambda \mathsf{x.C}) \rrbracket & = & Object\ x = G.node;\ J\llbracket \mathsf{C} \rrbracket \\
J\llbracket \mathsf{GETNT}\ (\lambda \mathsf{x}.\lambda \mathsf{t.C}) \rrbracket & = & Object\ x = G.node;\ \text{int}\ t = G.tag;\ J\llbracket \mathsf{C} \rrbracket \\
J\llbracket \mathsf{GETA}\ (\lambda \langle l, \mathsf{x}\,\overline{\mathsf{w}} \rangle.\mathsf{C}) \rrbracket & = & J\llbracket \mathsf{C} \rrbracket \\
J\llbracket \mathsf{PUTARG}\ \overline{\mathsf{x}}_n\ \mathsf{C} \rrbracket & = & push\ x_n; \ldots\ push\ x_1;\ J\llbracket \mathsf{C} \rrbracket \\
J\llbracket \mathsf{GETARG}\ (\lambda \overline{\mathsf{x}}_n.\mathsf{C}) \rrbracket & = & Object\ x_1, \ldots, x_n;\ pop\ x_1; \ldots\ pop\ x_n;\ J\llbracket \mathsf{C} \rrbracket \\
J\llbracket \mathsf{PUTK}\ \langle l, \overline{\mathsf{x}}_n \rangle\ \mathsf{C}) \rrbracket & = & C_l\ o = \text{new}\ C_l();\ o.f_1 = x_1; \ldots\ o.f_n = x_n;\ push\ o;\ J\llbracket \mathsf{C} \rrbracket \\
 & & \text{where}\ o\ \text{fresh} \\
J\llbracket \mathsf{GETK}\ \lambda \langle l, \overline{\mathsf{x}}_n \rangle.\mathsf{C}) \rrbracket & = & Object\ o;\ pop\ o; \\
 & & Object\ x_1 = ((C_l)o).f_1,\ \ldots\ , x_n = ((C_l)o).f_n;\ J\llbracket \mathsf{C} \rrbracket \\
 & & \text{where}\ o\ \text{fresh} \\
J\llbracket \mathsf{REFK}\ (\lambda \mathsf{x.C}) \rrbracket & = & Object\ x = G.stk[G.sp];\ J\llbracket \mathsf{C} \rrbracket \\
J\llbracket \mathsf{SAVE}\ (\lambda \mathsf{s.C}) \rrbracket & = & \text{int}\ s = G.bp;\ J\llbracket \mathsf{C} \rrbracket \\
J\llbracket \mathsf{DUMP\ C} \rrbracket & = & G.bp = G.sp;\ J\llbracket \mathsf{C} \rrbracket \\
J\llbracket \mathsf{RESTORE\ s\ C} \rrbracket & = & G.bp = s;\ J\llbracket \mathsf{C} \rrbracket \\
J\llbracket \mathsf{PUTC}\ \overline{\mathsf{x}_i \overset{\pi_i}{=} \langle l_i, \overline{\mathsf{w}^i_j}_{m_i} \rangle}_n\ \mathsf{C} \rrbracket & = & \ldots\ alloc_i;\ \ldots\ assign^i_j; \ldots\ J\llbracket \mathsf{C} \rrbracket \\
 & & \text{where}\ alloc_i \equiv C_{l_i}\ x_i = \text{new}\ C_{l_i}() \qquad \text{if}\ \pi_i = n \\
 & & \qquad\qquad \equiv Ind\ x_i = \text{new}\ Ind(); \qquad \text{if}\ \pi_i = u \\
 & & \qquad\qquad\quad x_i.ind = \text{new}\ C_{l_i}() \\
 & & \qquad assign^i_j \equiv x_i.f_j = w^i_j \qquad \text{if}\ \pi_i = n \\
 & & \qquad\qquad \equiv ((C_{l_i})x_i.ind).f_j = w^i_j \qquad \text{if}\ \pi_i = u \\
J\llbracket \mathsf{GETC\ y}\ (\lambda \langle l, \overline{\mathsf{x}}_n \rangle.\mathsf{C}) \rrbracket & = & Object\ x_1 = ((C_l)y).f_1; \ldots; x_n = ((C_l)y).f_n;\ J\llbracket \mathsf{C} \rrbracket \\
J\llbracket \mathsf{UPDC\ x}\ \langle l, \overline{\mathsf{w}}_n \rangle\ \mathsf{C} \rrbracket & = & C_l\ o = \text{new}\ C_l();\ o.f_1 = w_1;\ \ldots\ o.f_n = w_n; \\
 & & ((Clo)x).ind = o;\ J\llbracket \mathsf{C} \rrbracket \quad \text{where}\ o\ \text{fresh} \\
J\llbracket \mathsf{PUTP}\ \overline{\langle l_i, \mathsf{y} \rangle}_n \rangle\ (\lambda \mathsf{x.C}) \rrbracket & = & \text{switch}(G.sp - G.bp)\ \{ \\
 & & \quad \text{case}\ 0: C_{l_1}\ x = \text{new}\ C_{l_1}();\ x.f_1 = y;\ \text{break};\ \ldots \\
 & & \quad \text{case}\ n-1: C_{l_n}\ x = \text{new}\ C_{l_n}();\ x.f_1 = y; \\
 & & \qquad\qquad pop\ x.f_2; \ldots\ pop\ x.f_n;\ \text{break}; \\
 & & \}\ J\llbracket \mathsf{C} \rrbracket \\
\multicolumn{3}{l}{J\llbracket \mathsf{CASE\ t}\ \overline{c_i \rightarrow \langle l_i, \mathsf{x}_0\, \overline{\mathsf{x}}_i \rangle}\ \text{default} \rightarrow \langle l_d, \mathsf{x}_0\, \overline{\mathsf{x}}_d \rangle \rrbracket} \\
 & = & \text{switch}(t)\ \{ \ldots\ \text{case}\ c_i : J\llbracket \mathsf{C}_{l_i} \rrbracket\ \ldots\ \text{default} : J\llbracket \mathsf{C}_{l_d} \rrbracket \} \\
J\llbracket \mathsf{ARGCK}\ n\ \mathsf{C}_1\ \mathsf{C}_2) \rrbracket & = & \text{if}(n > G.sp - G.bp)\ \text{then}\ \{\ J\llbracket \mathsf{C}_1 \rrbracket\ \}\ \text{else}\ \{\ J\llbracket \mathsf{C}_2 \rrbracket\ \} \\
J\llbracket \mathsf{STOP\ y} \rrbracket & = & G.loopflag = \text{false};\ \text{return null}; \\
 & & \\
push\ X & = & G.sp{+}{+};\ G.stk[G.sp] = X \\
pop\ X & = & G.sp{-}{-};\ X = G.stk[G.sp+1];\ G.stk[G.sp+1] = \text{null}
\end{array}
$$

Fig. 4. Compilation Rules for L-code

of the known-call optimization to pass arguments via some agreed static variables rather than via the costly stack.

An example of compiling the L-code instructions bound to l_a presented in Section 2.4 will be shown as follows. This example shows well the relationship that a **let** binding is directly translated into one Java class. Since our STG-to-L-code compiler expresses each closure with a **let** binding, this example also shows the direct relationship between a closure and a class.

```
public class C_{l_a} extends Clo {               // l_a =
    public Object f1, f2;                        // {g, x}.
    public Clo code() {
        Object z = G.node;                       // GETN λz.
        Object g = ((C_{l_a})z).f1;              // GETC λ⟨l_a, g x⟩.
        Object x = ((C_{l_a})z).f2;
        int s = G.bp;                            // SAVE λs.
        C_{l_upd} o = new C_{l_upd}();           // PUTK ⟨l_upd, z s⟩
        o.f1 = z; o.f2 = s;
        G.sp ++; G.stk[G.sp] = o;
        G.bp = G.sp;                             // DUMP
        G.sp ++; G.stk[G.sp] = x;                // PUTARG x
        return (Clo)g;                           // JMPC g
    }
}
```

5 Benchmarking

We experiment with five small Haskell programs that have been used by Meehan and Joy [5]: fib 30, edigits 250, prime 500, soda, and queen 8. A SUN UltraSPARC-II workstation with a 296MHz processor, 768Mbytes of memory and Solaris version 2.5.1 is used. For compilers, GHC 4.04, Hugs98 Feb-2000, and Sun JIT compiler version 1.2.2 are used. To obtain optimized versions of STG programs, GHC are executed with `-O2` option.

5.1 STG-Level Optimizations

One of advantages in using the STGM is that many STG-level optimizations in GHC can be exploited freely. Ideally, our implementation can be imagined as a back end of GHC. In our prototype, our own STG-like functional language is defined, showing that the language is capable of precisely expressing the operational behaviors of the STG language in terms of the STGM. We extracted STG programs by running GHC with the option `-ddump-stg` from our Haskell benchmarks. Then the STG programs are semi-automatically modified according to the syntax of our own STG-like language. The main reason for the modification is that our implementation covers only a part of the libraries implemented in GHC. This translation is quite straightforward. Then, the modified STG programs are compiled into Java programs according to our compilation rules.

5.2 Results

Table 1 compares code sizes in bytes. For GHC, the sizes express the dynamically-linked executables stripped of redundant symbol table information. For Hugs, no

Table 1. Code Sizes in Bytes

Pgms	GHC	JIT:unopt	JIT:opt
fib	268,028	24,830 (037 classes)	18,610 (034 classes)
edigits	283,092	113,913 (135 classes)	64,327 (092 classes)
prime	280,248	74,161 (096 classes)	50,025 (070 classes)
queen	274,816	108,705 (134 classes)	75,619 (101 classes)
soda	302,972	335,873 (388 classes)	185,496 (203 classes)

sizes are given, as compiled codes exist only within the develpment environment. For our compiler, the sizes are obtained by summing up the sizes of class files produced from each program itself and the runtime system. The number in each parenthesis is the number of classes. Note that our runtime system consists of 4 classes with 2972 bytes.

Table 2 compares execution times in seconds. Each entry is the sum of user time and system time. The execution time is measured by UNIX `time` command; each benchmark is run five times and the shortest execution time is chosen. For Hugs, each execution time is calculated by a timer supported in Hugs and it excludes the time on parsing, type checking, and G-code generation.

5.3 Discussion

According to Table 1, each program consists of relatively many classes, since one class is generated for each closure. Particularly, the size of the unoptimized soda program is larger than that of the binary soda program generated by GHC, which stems from generating more updatable expressions by the naive translation of the string lists. As Wakeling did in his JFP paper [11], we can similarly reduce the bytecode size of generated classes by merging classes that have the same types of fields. By modifying only the L-code-to-Java compiler, we can cut the bytecode size by half and the number of classes is reduced to about 20 in all benchmarks.

According to Table 2, the execution times of generated Java programs lie between those of the relevant programs by GHC and Hugs. First, it is not surprising that the generated Java programs are slower than binary executables by GHC. The JVM is known to make memory allocation more costly, it ignores strong typedness of the Haskell programs so that it repeats unnecessary runtime checks, every tail call must be simulated by a return and a call instead of a single jump instruction, and the simulated stack incurs unnecessary cost for checking array out-of-bound index and assigning null after a pop.

Second, the generated Java programs tend to outperform the execution times in Hugs, particularly when GHC's STG-level optimizations are applied; in that case, all programs except soda run faster. In the case of soda, because the warming-up time of the JVM varies from 0.68 to 0.74 seconds, any generated Java program for soda cannot run faster than in Hugs. By refining the way of interaction between a primitive and a case expression in the STG-to-L-code

Table 2. Execution Time in Seconds

Programs	GHC	Hugs	JIT:unopt	JIT:opt
fib	0.18s	106.48s	25.70s	5.72s
edigits	0.16s	3.10s	9.15s	2.42s
prime	0.14s	3.30s	86.38s	1.97s
queen	0.07s	5.79s	5.35s	2.29s
soda	0.03s	0.41s	2.26s	1.59s

compiler, all the above execution times can be cut down to a half, on average. These results show that our systematic compiler also generates Java programs which run at a reasonable execution speed.

The STG-level optimizations by GHC dominantly affect the execution times of all programs. In the case of prime, they are particularly effective. Its explanation may be given in the aspect of total heap allocation since execution time is usually affected by the amount of heap allocation in lazy functional languages. An optimized version of prime allocates 35,061,856 bytes, while unoptimized version allocates 2,603,827,792 bytes. The unoptimized prime allocated 74.3 times more heap objects than in its optimized version. By this observation, we notice that more reduction in heap allocation tends to affect more reduction in execution time. This is a reasonable expectation as in conventional implementations, and we believe this is also true for the implementations on the JVM, particularly because the cost of memory allocation is known to be more expensive in the JVM than in the conventional machines.

6 Related Works

The previous works based on the STGM are Tullsen [9] and Vernet [10]. As done in the original paper regarding the STGM [7], both papers explained their own mapping informally based on examples. With these descriptions, we cannot reproduce their compilers. Furthermore, we cannot compare the performance, since no experimental result for performance is provided.

Other works are based on either G-machine or $\langle \nu, \mathrm{G} \rangle$-machine. Wakeling's compiler [11] has two distinct features. It employs a list of small local stacks instead of one single big stack, which comes from a feature of $\langle \nu, \mathrm{G} \rangle$-machine, and it also generates much smaller number of classes over quite big benchmarks by efficient representations. The generated Java programs run at competitive speed with Hugs. Wakeling explained that the size of class files affects performance. Although we didn't compare our compiler with his in terms of performance, our compiler based on the STGM is believed to be advantageous in that it can exploit STG-level optimizations as well as his idea on the efficient representations to reduce the size of class files. Further work is required.

Meehan and Joy's compiler [5] represents functions by methods in a single class and uses the Java reflection package to access the methods. Their generated Java programs by the compiler runs slower than with Hugs.

Recently, we heard that Erik Meijer, Nigel Perry, and Andy Gill are working on a Java back end for GHC, though no documentation is available for their work [6].

Some research has been done on compiling strict functional languages for the JVM. Benton, Kennedy, and Russel have taken with Standard ML(SML) as their source language, improving performance through extensive optimizations and providing SML with an interface to Java [1][2]. Their approach is similar to ours with Haskell.

7 Conclusion and Further Works

In this study, a systematic specification of the STGM is presented by defining our STG-to-L-code compiler and L-machine. It is a new attempt to describe the mapping accurately by the provision of *concrete* compilation rules. It is compact enough to be presented in a few pages, but exposes every aspect for the mapping of the STGM. Each instruction of L-code is directly mapped onto some Java statements, and each **let** binding identifies all the instructions within one closure so that the closure is nicely mapped onto one class in Java.

Based on the specification, a concrete compilation rule for the JVM is defined. In this phase, the goal of implementing the STGM is decomposed into the sub-goals of implementing L-code instructions. We have defined an L-code-to-Java compiler with our representation decisions.

Since our approach is based on the STGM, the generated Java programs are indirectly amenable to the STG-level optimizations in GHC. The initial performance is measured with five small Haskell benchmarks. Combining the optimizations, promising results are obtained for the benchmarks.

As a further work, we hope to devise more ingenious Java representation; our representation scheme is a bit straightforward. Also, it is important to apply our compiler to bigger benchmarks, and this will give more decisive figures for performance of the translated Java programs. Finally, we hope to more fully exploit the features of the two-level translation; one may analyze flow information in terms of L-code to optimize L-code programs, and one may devise Java-related optimizations relevant to our compilation scheme. Each work could be done separately.

Acknowledgment

We thank anonymous referees for their many helpful comments. The first author also thanks Hyeon-Ah Moon for her encouragement. This work is supported by Advanced Information Technology Research Center.

References

1. N. Benton and A. Kennedy. Interlanguage Working Without Tears: Blending SML with Java. In *Proceedings of the 4th ACM SIGPLAN Conference on Functional Prgramming*, pages 126–137, 1999.

2. N. Benton, A. Kennedy, and G. Russell. Compiling Standard ML to Java Bytecodes. In *Proceedings of the 3rd ACM SIGPLAN Conference on Functional Prgramming*, pages 129–140, 1998.
3. M. Campione and K. Walrath. *The Java Tutorial (2nd Ed.)*. Addison Wesley, March 1998.
4. T. Lindholm and F. Yellin. *The Java^{TM} Virtual Machine Specification (2nd Ed.)*. Addison Wesley, 1999.
5. G. Meehan and M. Joy. Compiling Lazy Functional Programs to Java Bytecode. *Software-Practice and Experience*, 29(7):617–645, June 1999.
6. S. L. Peyton Jones. A Java Back End for Glasgow Haskell Compiler. The Haskell Mailing List haskell@haskell.org (http://www.haskell.org/mailinglist.html), May 2000.
7. S. L. Peyton Jones. Implementing Lazy Functional Languages on Stock Hardware: the Spineless Tagless G-machine. *Journal of Functional Programming*, 2(2):127–202, April 1992.
8. S. L. Peyton Jones and A. L. M. Santos. A Transformation-based Optimiser for Haskell. *Science of Computer Programming*, 32(1–3):3–47, 1998.
9. M. Tullsen. Compiling Haskell to Java. 690 Project, Yale University, September 1997.
10. A. Vernet. The Jaskell Project. A Diploma Project, Swiss Federal Institute of Technology, February 1998.
11. D. Wakeling. Compiling Lazy Functional Programs for the Java Virtual Machine. *Journal of Functional Programming*, 9(6):579–603, November 1999.
12. M. Wand. Correctness of Procedure Representations in Higher-Order Assembly Language. In S. Brookes, editor, *Proceedings Mathematical Foundations of Programming Semantics '91*, volume 598 of *Lecture Notes in Computer Science*, pages 294–311. Springer Verlag, 1992.

A Higher-Order Logic Programming Language with Constraints

Javier Leach and Susana Nieva *

Dpto. de Sistemas Informáticos y Programación.
Univ. Complutense de Madrid
{leach,nieva}@sip.ucm.es

Abstract. We present a framework for the combination of Constraint Logic Programming (*CLP*) and higher-order Hereditary Harrop Formulas (*hoHH*). Our aim is to improve the expressiveness of traditional Logic Programming with the benefits of both fields: *CLP* and *hoHH*. The result is denoted higher-order Hereditary Harrop Formulas with Constraints (*hoHH*($\mathcal{C}$)). The syntax of *hoHH* is introduced using lambda-terms and is enriched with a basic constraint system. Then an intuitionistic sequent calculus is defined for this combined logic, that preserves the property of an abstract logic programming language. In addition, a sound and complete procedure for goal solving is presented as a transformation system that explains the operational semantics.

1 Introduction

Expressiveness is a valuable help for the user of a programming language. Constraint Logic Programming (*CLP*) [4] and Hereditary Harrop Formulas (*HH*) [9] are two different extensions of Logic Programming (*LP*) increasing the expressive capacity of this kind of programming in two new significant ways. Namely, *CLP* enriches *LP* with the aptitude to obtain declarative programs over different computation domains in which the constraints are interpreted, while *HH* offers a broader deduction system in which the declarative meaning of a program is operationally interpreted.

On the other way functional programming languages involve a substantial increment of expressiveness permitting the treatment of programs as data. This idea of higher-order programming has been also developed within the logic programming. For instance, Miller et al. [8] elaborated higher-order logic programming by utilizing higher-order horn clauses and *HH*. It is also well known that programming languages based on higher-order logic support some additional abilities like meta-programming, and theorem proving tasks. In particular, there are several examples of the use of λ-Prolog –based on higher-order *HH*– from the perspective of meta-language, [10, 2].

In [5] a framework for the combination of *CLP* and *HH* approaches was introduced, improving the syntax of first-order *HH* with constraints belonging to a given constraint system $\mathcal{C}$, obtaining a scheme *HH*($\mathcal{X}$) with instances *HH*($\mathcal{C}$).

* The authors have been partially supported by the Spanish National Project TIC 98-0445-C03-02 *TREND*.

H. Kuchen and K. Ueda (Eds.): FLOPS 2001, LNCS 2024, pp. 108–122, 2001.

This combination makes it possible for the user to transcend the lack of expressiveness of Horn clauses, limited to the boundaries of the Herbrand universe.

The aim of this paper is to incorporate higher-order to $HH(\mathcal{C})$ in order to improve the capabilities of the language introduced in [5] with the expressiveness and abstraction of higher-order. The higher-order extension presented ($hoHH(\mathcal{C})$) is based on the Church's formulation of Simple Theory of types, which permits the use of λ-terms as a tool for representing and manipulating both functions and predicates as data. An intuitionistic sequent calculus is defined, resulting in a constructive inference mechanism to deduce goals from program clauses. So we obtain a higher-order language with constraints that preserves the property of an *abstract logic programming language* in the sense of [8]. In addition, a sound and complete procedure for goal solving is presented as a transformation system that explains the operational semantics. As in *CLP*, the result of solving a goal using a program will be an *answer constraint*.

The following example (written with a sugared notation) belongs to the instance $hoHH(\mathcal{R})$ given by a constraint system for real numbers in the higher-order context. Let Δ_1 be a program with definitions of geometrical figures of the plane by means of definite clauses:

$$\begin{aligned}\Delta_1 = \{&\forall x \forall y(x^2 + y^2 \approx 1 \Rightarrow \mathit{circle1}(x, y)),\\ &\forall x \forall y(x^2 + y^2 \approx 2 \Rightarrow \mathit{circle2}(x, y)),\\ &\forall x \forall y(x^2 + 6y^2 \approx 2 \Rightarrow \mathit{ellipse}(x, y))\}.\end{aligned}$$

Now we may introduce atoms expressing that *circle1*, *circle2* and *ellipse* are figures:

$$\Delta_2 = \{\mathit{fig}(\mathit{circle1}), \mathit{fig}(\mathit{circle2}), \mathit{fig}(\mathit{ellipse})\}.$$

Suppose we may wish to know, for a provided database of defined geometrical figures of the plane, the intersection points of a pair of figures. For the program $\Delta_1 \cup \Delta_2$, this problem has a higher-order formulation:

$$G \equiv \exists C_1 \exists C_2(\mathit{fig}(C_1) \wedge \mathit{fig}(C_2) \wedge C_1 \not\approx C_2 \wedge C_1(x, y) \wedge C_2(x, y)).$$

Note that, for instance, the constraint $C_1 \not\approx C_2$, expressing that the two predicate variables C_1, C_2 are not equal, can not be expressed in λ-Prolog.

A more general approach could be to define the property *intersection* that is verified by the binary relations which relate x and y if (x, y) is a point in two different figures:

$$\begin{aligned}\Delta_3 = \{&\forall C_1 \forall C_2(\mathit{fig}(C_1) \wedge \mathit{fig}(C_2) \wedge C_1 \not\approx C_2 \Rightarrow\\ &\mathit{intersection}(\lambda x.\lambda y.(C_1(x, y) \wedge C_2(x, y))))\}.\end{aligned}$$

For the program $\Delta = \Delta_1 \cup \Delta_2 \cup \Delta_3$, the preceding goal can be expressed by $G \equiv \exists T(\mathit{intersection}(T) \wedge T(x, y))$. Then one of the possible answers is the constraint: $R \equiv x \approx \frac{2}{\sqrt{5}} \wedge y \approx \frac{1}{\sqrt{5}}$.

If we modify the program Δ_1:

$$\begin{aligned}\Delta_1' = \{&\forall x \forall y(x^2 + y^2 \leq 1 \Rightarrow \mathit{circle1}(x, y)),\\ &\forall x \forall y(x^2 + y^2 \leq 2 \Rightarrow \mathit{circle2}(x, y)),\\ &\forall x \forall y(x^2 + 6y^2 \leq 2 \Rightarrow \mathit{ellipse}(x, y))\},\end{aligned}$$

the goal:

$$G' \equiv \forall x \forall y(x^2 + y^2 \leq 2 \Rightarrow \mathit{fig}(C) \wedge C(x, y))$$

searches figures contained in *circle2*. There are three possible constraint answers:

$R_1 \equiv C \approx \mathit{circle1}$, $R_2 \equiv C \approx \mathit{circle2}$, $R_3 \equiv C \approx \mathit{ellipse}$.

The rest of this paper is organized as follows: In Section 2 we recall the notion of a constraint system and we define the syntax of a general higher-order logic with constraints, for which an intuitionistic sequent calculus is introduced. In Section 3 we restrict the logic to the higher-order Hereditary Harrop Formulas. Then, in Section 4 we present a new calculus that only allows uniform proofs. For the new logic, this proof system is equivalent to that presented in Section 2. Based on this second calculus, a sound and complete procedure for goal solving is presented as a transformation system in Section 5. We finish developing some application examples in Section 6, and summarizing conclusions and possible lines for future research, in Section 7.

2 Higher-Order Formulas with Constraints

The syntax of the higher-order logic we present is based on the typed λ-calculus. The main components of this language are the terms and the types. Types are built up from a set $\mathcal{S}$ of sorts s, that contains a special sort for formulas $\circ$, and a set $\mathcal{TC}$ of type constructors *ct*. The set of *types*, with elements denoted τ, is defined by the following syntactic rules: $\tau := s \mid ct(\tau_1, \ldots, \tau_n) \mid \tau_1 \rightarrow \tau_2$. The functional type $\rightarrow$ associates to the right.

Terms are obtained from a set V of typed variables, $x : \tau$, and a signature Σ that is a set of typed constant symbols, $c : \tau$, by abstraction and application operations of the λ-calculus. V and Σ are implicitly related to $\mathcal{S}$ and $\mathcal{TC}$, but in order to simplify the notation, we do not note this explicitly. The set of *terms* $\mathcal{T}_\Sigma(V)$ (or simply $\mathcal{T}$), with elements denoted t, is defined by the following syntactic rules: $t := x : \tau \mid c : \tau \mid (\lambda x : \tau . t) \mid (t_1 \, t_2)$. We omit parenthesis when they are not necessary, assuming that abstraction and application are right and left associative, respectively, and that application has smaller scope than abstraction.

If t is of type τ_2, then $\lambda x : \tau_1 . t$ is of type $\tau_1 \rightarrow \tau_2$. If t_1 is of type $\tau_1 \rightarrow \tau_2$ and t_2 is of type τ_1 then $t_1 \, t_2$ is of type τ_2. We remove the type mark of variables and constant symbols when it is not relevant. Instead, when it is needed to state explicitly the type of a term, we write $t : \tau$ to express that the type of t is τ. Terms of type $\circ$ are called *formulas*, and they are usually denoted by F.

We will assume that Σ is partitioned into nonlogical constants and logical constants. The latter comprises the following typed symbols $\top : \circ$, $\bot : \circ$ (representing true and false, resp.), $\wedge : \circ \rightarrow \circ \rightarrow \circ$, $\vee : \circ \rightarrow \circ \rightarrow \circ$, $\Rightarrow : \circ \rightarrow \circ \rightarrow \circ$, and for each type τ, $\exists : (\tau \rightarrow \circ) \rightarrow \circ$, $\forall : (\tau \rightarrow \circ) \rightarrow \circ$. We use infix notation for $\wedge$, $\vee$, $\Rightarrow$, and we abbreviate $\exists(\lambda x . F)$, $\forall(\lambda x . F)$ by $\exists x F$ and $\forall x F$, respectively. We simplify $\neg F$ for $F \Rightarrow \bot$. We call a formula whose leftmost non-parenthesis symbol is either a nonlogical constant or a variable *atomic formula*, *rigid* for the former case, and *flexible* for the latter. The symbol is called *predicate symbol* and *predicate variable*, respectively.

The concepts of free and bound variables of a term, and the substitution of a free variable by a term are defined as usual in the λ-calculus. We use the notation *Free(t)* or *Free(S)* to denote the set of free variables in a term t or in a set S, respectively; t is *closed* if *Free(t)* $= \emptyset$. We denote by σ substitutions of the form $[t_1/x_1, \ldots, t_n/x_n]$, and $t\sigma$ or $S\sigma$ the application of a substitution σ to a term t or to every term of a set S, respectively.

We adopt the usual α, β, η-conversion rules of the λ-calculus, that in fact determine an equivalence relation $\equiv_{\alpha\beta\eta}$ between terms. We say that a term is in λ-*normal* form, when it is in both β, η-normal form. We denote by $\Lambda(t)$ the λ-normal form of the term t.

In order to distinguish formulas that are constraints, we assume that the predicate symbols of the nonlogical part of Σ are divided into definite and indefinite predicates. The indefinite predicate symbols are used by the constraint system. We assume also that for every type τ, there is an indefinite predicate symbol $\approx : \tau \rightarrow \tau \rightarrow o$, to represent the equality relation, that we will use in infix notation.

Following [12], we view a constraint system as a pair $\mathcal{C} = (\mathcal{L}_{\mathcal{C}}, \vdash_{\mathcal{C}})$, where $\mathcal{L}_{\mathcal{C}}$ is the set of formulas in λ-normal form allowed as constraints, and $\vdash_{\mathcal{C}} \subseteq \mathcal{P}(\mathcal{L}_{\mathcal{C}}) \times \mathcal{L}_{\mathcal{C}}$ is an *entailment relation*. We use Γ for a finite set of constraints. $\Gamma \vdash_{\mathcal{C}} C$ means that C is entailed by Γ. We write just $\vdash_{\mathcal{C}} C$ if Γ is empty. We will say that a constraint C with $Free(C) = \{x_1, \ldots, x_n\}$ is $\mathcal{C}$-satisfiable when $\vdash_{\mathcal{C}} \exists x_1 \ldots \exists x_n C$. $\mathcal{C}$ is required to satisfy certain minimal assumptions, mainly related to α, β, η-conversion in λ-calculus, the equality relation, and to the logical constant symbols. We assume that:

- Every first-order formula in λ-form built using indefinite predicate symbols, and the logical constants $\wedge, \Rightarrow, \exists$ and $\forall$ is in $\mathcal{L}_{\mathcal{C}}$.
- All equations $t_1 \approx t_2$ are in $\mathcal{L}_{\mathcal{C}}$.
- All the inference rules related to $\wedge, \Rightarrow, \exists, \forall$ and $\approx$ valid in the intuitionistic logic with equality are valid to infer entailments in the sense of $\vdash_{\mathcal{C}}$ (see e.g. [11]).[1]
- $\Gamma \vdash_{\mathcal{C}} C$ implies $\Gamma\sigma \vdash_{\mathcal{C}} C\sigma$ for every substitution σ.
- If $t_1 \equiv_{\alpha\beta\eta} t_2$, then $\vdash_{\mathcal{C}} t_1 \approx t_2$.

Note that these conditions must be considered as sufficient for a system to be a constraint system. In this way, the equality relation is always included, but the system can include other relations like $\leq$ –see the example of the Introduction– or additional connectives like $\vee$. Note also that $\mathcal{L}_{\mathcal{C}}$ is restricted to first-order formulas, except for equations that in general are used to represent substitutions or α, β, η-equivalence. This first-order condition could be eliminated, but then the constraint system will become unjustifiably hard for implementation. In practice, usual constraints (other than equations) belong to a first-order language.

Two examples of valid constraint systems are: $\mathcal{H}$, where $\vdash_{\mathcal{H}}$ is the entailment relation of classical logic modulo Clark's axiomatization of the Herbrand universe [1], with equality and α, β, η-equivalence between terms. $\mathcal{R}$, where the entailment relation $\vdash_{\mathcal{R}}$ is similar to the example before, but modulo Tarski's axiomatization of the real numbers [13]. In these cases, the first-order part of the the constraint system is known to be *effective*, in the sense that the validity of entailments

[1] We note that regarding equality between predicates, the axiom of extensionality is not assumed.

$\Gamma \vdash_{\mathcal{C}} C$, with finite Γ, can be decided by an effective procedure. This procedure should incorporate special tasks to solve equations.

2.1 A Proof System

We present an intuitionistic sequent calculus for higher-order formulas with constraints, called $ho\mathcal{IC}$ that works with sequents of the form $\Theta \mid\!- F$, where Θ is a finite set of formulas in λ-normal form, and F is a formula in λ-normal form. It combines the usual inference rules from intuitionistic logic with the entailment relation $\vdash_{\mathcal{C}}$ of a constraint system $\mathcal{C}$. $ho\mathcal{IC}$ stands for a higher-order Intuitionistic sequent calculus that handles Constraints. $\Theta \vdash_{ho\mathcal{IC}} F$ if and only if the sequent $\Theta \mid\!- F$ has a proof using the rules of the system $ho\mathcal{IC}$ that we introduce in the following. A proof of a sequent is a tree whose root is the sequent and whose leaves match axioms of the calculus. The rules regulate relationship between child and parent nodes. We will simplify $\Theta \cup \{F\}$ by Θ, F, and we will represent by Γ the set of constraints contained in the set Θ.

Rules to deal with (rigid or flexible) atomic formulas or constraints:

$$\frac{}{\Theta, F \mid\!- F'}\ (Atom_r)\ F,\ F' \text{ atomic, } F' \text{ rigid, } \Gamma \vdash_{\mathcal{C}} F \approx F'.$$

$$\frac{\Theta \mid\!- F}{\Theta \mid\!- X t_1 \ldots t_n}\ (Atom_f),\ \text{where } X \text{ a predicate variable, } \Gamma \vdash_{\mathcal{C}} X \approx t,$$
$$\mathit{Free}(t) \subseteq \mathit{Free}(\{t_1, \ldots, t_n\}),\ F \equiv \Lambda((X\, t_1 \ldots t_n)[t/X]).$$

$$\frac{}{\Theta \mid\!- C}\ (C_R),\ \text{if } C \text{ is a constraint and } \Gamma \vdash_{\mathcal{C}} C.$$

Rule concerning contradiction:

$$\frac{\Theta \mid\!- \bot}{\Theta \mid\!- F}\ (\bot)$$

Rules introducing connectives and quantifiers:

$$\frac{\Theta, F_1 \mid\!- F \quad \Theta, F_2 \mid\!- F}{\Theta, F_1 \vee F_2 \mid\!- F}\ (\vee_L) \qquad \frac{\Theta \mid\!- F_i}{\Theta \mid\!- F_1 \vee F_2}\ (\vee_R)\ (i = 1, 2)$$

$$\frac{\Theta, F_1, F_2 \mid\!- F}{\Theta, F_1 \wedge F_2 \mid\!- F}\ (\wedge_L) \qquad \frac{\Theta \mid\!- F_1 \quad \Theta \mid\!- F_2}{\Theta \mid\!- F_1 \wedge F_2}\ (\wedge_R)$$

$$\frac{\Theta \mid\!- F_1 \quad \Theta, F_2 \mid\!- F}{\Theta, F_1 \Rightarrow F_2 \mid\!- F}\ (\Rightarrow_L) \qquad \frac{\Theta, F_1 \mid\!- F_2}{\Theta \mid\!- F_1 \Rightarrow F_2}\ (\Rightarrow_R)$$

$$\frac{\Theta, F_1[y/x] \mid\!- F}{\Theta, \exists x F_1 \mid\!- F}\ (\exists_L) \qquad \frac{\Theta, C \mid\!- F[y/x]}{\Theta \mid\!- \exists x F}\ (\exists_R),\ C \text{ a constraint, } \Gamma \vdash_{\mathcal{C}} \exists y C.$$

In both rules, y does not appear free in the sequent of the conclusion.

$$\frac{\Theta, F_1[y/x], C \models F}{\Theta, \forall x F_1 \models F} (\forall_L),\ C \text{ a constraint},\ \Gamma \vdash_{\mathcal{C}} \exists y C. \qquad \frac{\Theta \models F[y/x]}{\Theta \models \forall x F} (\forall_R)$$

In both rules, y does not appear free in the sequent of the conclusion.

In the rules dealing with atomic formulas, and in those introducing a connective, the involved atomic formulas, and the formulas containing the introduced connectives, respectively, are not a constraint.

The structural rules *contraction* and *interchange*, common in this kind of calculus are not necessary here, because Θ is taken to be a set, not a list. This calculus is similar to those defined for higher-order formulas in the literature (see e.g. [8]), but the presence of constraints induces some modifications. There are not rules for $\neg$, since the notion of negation may be provided replacing $\neg F$ by $F \Rightarrow \bot$. $\bot$ can be considered as a constraint that could be deduced with (C_R) if there are inconsistent premises. The rule (λ), that transforms formulas by λ-conversion, is not defined in $ho\mathcal{IC}$ because assuming that formulas in the initial sequent are in λ-normal form, every formula in a sequent of a proof is also in λ-normal form. Note that no substitution of a term by a variable is made during the application of the rules, except in $(Atom_f)$, where λ-normal form of the consequent is required.

The motivation for rules $(\exists_R)$ and $(\forall_L)$ appears in [5], they include the fact that substitutions can be simulated by equality constraints, and at the same time, they reflect the possibility of finding a proof for an existentially quantified formula, knowing a property (represented as a constraint) of the instance of the existential quantified variable.

The rule $(Atom_r)$ corresponds with the usual definition of initial sequent, but adding the power of the constraint system. For instance:

$$\frac{}{annoyed(john), annoyed \approx irritated \models irritated(john)} (Atom_r)$$

because: $annoyed \approx irritated \vdash_{\mathcal{C}} annoyed(john) \approx irritated(john)$.

The rule $(Atom_f)$ is needed due to the facts that substitutions are not performed in the rules for quantifiers, and that in higher-order logic, replacing a predicate variable by a term not necessarily preserves the atomic structure. Let us see an example using the notation of the Introduction.

$$\cfrac{\cfrac{T \approx \lambda x.\lambda y.(circle1(x,y) \wedge ellipse(x,y)) \models circle1(x,y) \wedge ellipse(x,y)}{T \approx \lambda x.\lambda y.(circle1(x,y) \wedge ellipse(x,y)) \models T(x,y)} (Atom_f)}{\models \exists T(T(x,y))} (\exists_R)$$

because: $\vdash_{\mathcal{C}} \exists T(T \approx \lambda x.\lambda y.(circle1(x,y) \wedge ellipse(x,y)))$, and $\Lambda(T(x,y)[\lambda x.\lambda y.(circle1(x,y) \wedge ellipse(x,y))/T]) \equiv circle1(x,y) \wedge ellipse(x,y)$.

3 Higher-Order Hereditary Harrop Formulas with Constraints

In order to obtain a language that preserves the property of goal-oriented search for solution, common in Logic Programming, we will restrict the logic to *higher-order Hereditary Harrop Formulas* (shortly, *hoHH*). The atomic formulas of *hoHH* use definite predicate symbols, and are limited to be positive in accordance with the following definition.

Definition 1 *Given a signature Σ and a set of variables V, the set of* positive terms *$\mathcal{PT}_\Sigma(V)$ (simplified $\mathcal{PT}$) consists of all the terms in λ-normal form not containing indefinite predicate symbols, nor the logical constants $\bot$ and $\Rightarrow$.*

A positive atomic formula *is an atomic formula concerning only positive terms. We denote positive atomic formulas by A. A_r represents a rigid positive atomic formula.*

A positive constraint *is a constraint such that every equation in it involves only positive terms. C_p represents a positive constraint.*

Definition 2 *The set of* definite clauses, *with elements denoted D, and the set of* goals, *with elements denoted G, are sets of formulas, in λ-normal form, defined by the following syntactic rules:*

$$D := A_r \,|\, G \Rightarrow A_r \,|\, \forall x D$$
$$G := A \,|\, C_p \,|\, G_1 \wedge G_2 \,|\, G_1 \vee G_2 \,|\, D \Rightarrow G \,|\, C_p \Rightarrow G \,|\, \exists x G \,|\, \forall x G$$

A program *is any finite set Δ of closed definite clauses.*

In order to simplify the technicalities, the construction $D_1 \wedge D_2$, usual in the literature for *hoHH* (e.g. [8]), is not considered here, but this restriction does not decrease the expressivity of the language, because a goal of the form $D_1 \wedge D_2 \Rightarrow G$ can be simulated by $(D_1 \Rightarrow G) \vee (D_2 \Rightarrow G)$, and a clause $\forall x(D_1 \wedge D_2)$ in a program can be replaced by two: $\forall x D_1$, $\forall x D_2$. On the other hand, notice that positive constraints can occur in goals, and therefore also in definite clauses.

In the sequel, we assume an arbitrarily fixed effective constraint system $\mathcal{C}$. Moreover, all constructions and results are valid for any constraint system, so we speak of a *scheme hoHH($\mathcal{X}$)* with *instances hoHH($\mathcal{C}$)*. *CLP* and λ-Prolog programs can be considered particular cases. As in *CLP*, the result of solving a goal G using a program Δ will be an *answer constraint* R such that G can be deduced from Δ and R by means of a proof system. But here we are aiming at an *abstract logic programming language* in the sense of [8]. So we need a proof system that guarantees the existence of a uniform proof for every provable sequent. This system will be presented in the next section, and it is a reduction of that presented before for the whole logic.

4 Uniform proofs

The idea of uniform proof in our system consists in breaking down a goal in its components until obtaining an atomic formula or a constraint, before using the rules for introduction of connectives on the left or resorting to constraint entailment. The proof system $ho\mathcal{IC}$ presented in Subsection 2.1 has not yet this property. We will transform $ho\mathcal{IC}$-derivations for $hoHH(\mathcal{C})$ into uniform derivations in two steps. First we will see that, for $hoHH(\mathcal{C})$, the term that substitutes the predicate variable in the rule $(Atom_f)$ can always be positive, and that the auxiliary constraints of the rules $(\forall_L)$ and $(\exists_R)$ can also be positive. In a second step and taking into account the previous consideration, since the syntax of the formulas has been reduced, we show that some rules of the previous calculus can be omitted obtaining only uniform deductions, without reducing derivability, and preserving sequents containing only clauses, positive constraints and goals. In the next subsection the first step is tackled. Some technicalities are needed concerning positive terms.

4.1 Positive terms and positive derivations

The following mapping converts a term into a positive one.

Definition 3 *The function pos on terms t is defined as follows:*

i) If t is a constant or a variable: $pos(t) = \begin{cases} \top, & \text{if } t \text{ is } \bot \\ \lambda x : o.\lambda y : o.\top, & \text{if } t \text{ is } \Rightarrow \\ t & \text{otherwise.} \end{cases}$

ii) $pos(t_1 t_2) = pos(t_1) pos(t_2)$. *iii)* $pos(\lambda x.t) = \lambda x.pos(t)$.
Given a term t, t^+ *denotes* $\Lambda(pos(t))$ *and is called the* positivization *of t.*

We enunciate some known properties of the mapping pos and of the positivization. If $t \in \mathcal{T}$, $t^+ \in \mathcal{PT}$. If $t \in \mathcal{PT}$, $t^+ = t$. For any $t_1, t_2 \in \mathcal{T}$, if t_1 λ-converts to t_2, then $pos(t_1)$ also λ-converts to $pos(t_2)$.

Definition 4 *The calculus* $ho\mathcal{IC}^+$ *is equal to* $ho\mathcal{IC}$, *but replacing the rules* $(Atom_f)$, $(\exists_R)$ *and* $(\forall_L)$ *by the rules* $(Atom_f^+)$, $(\exists_R^+)$ *and* $(\forall_L^+)$, *respectively, defined as follows.* $(Atom_f^+)$ *is defined like* $(Atom_f)$, *replacing the side condition* $\Gamma \vdash_{\mathcal{C}} X \approx t$, *by* $\Gamma \vdash_{\mathcal{C}} X \approx t$, $t \in \mathcal{PT}$. $(\exists_R^+)$ *is defined like* $(\exists_R)$, *replacing the side condition* $\Gamma \vdash_{\mathcal{C}} \exists y C$, *by* $\Gamma \vdash_{\mathcal{C}} \exists y C$, *where C is positive. Analogous for* $(\forall_L^+)$.

Note that if $(X t_1 \ldots t_n)$ is a goal, then $t_1, \ldots, t_n \in \mathcal{PT}$, hence the formula F in the premise of the rule $(Atom_f^+)$ is also a goal, and that a $ho\mathcal{IC}^+$-proof is also a $ho\mathcal{IC}$-proof. We are also interested in derivations that preserve sequents whose left-hand sides contain only clauses or positive constraints, and whose right-hand sides contain only goals. The Positivization Lemma below is the first step to attain this aim. Proving it we use the following notation and Lemma.

If σ is a substitution $[t_1/X_1] \ldots [t_n/X_n]$, where $X_1, \ldots, X_n$ are predicate variables, we denote by σ^+ the substitution $[t_1^+/X_1] \ldots [t_n^+/X_n]$. If F is a formula of the form $\Lambda(F'\sigma)$, replace every subformula of F' that is an equation, $s_1 \approx s_2$, by $s_1^+ \approx s_2^+$ obtaining F'', then $F^* \equiv \Lambda(F''\sigma^+)$. If S is a set of formulas, $S^* = \{F^* | F \in S\}$. The following properties can be proved: if $\Gamma \vdash_{\mathcal{C}} X \approx t$, then $\Gamma^* \vdash_{\mathcal{C}} X \approx t^+$; if $\Gamma \vdash_{\mathcal{C}} \exists y C$, then $\Gamma^* \vdash_{\mathcal{C}} \exists y C^*$; if $\Gamma \vdash_{\mathcal{C}} A'_r \approx A_r$, then $\Gamma^* \vdash_{\mathcal{C}} A'^*_r \approx A^*_r$.

Lemma 1 *Let Θ be any set of formulas of the form $\Theta \equiv \{\Lambda(F'\sigma) | F' \in \Theta'\}$, where Θ' is a set of clauses or positive constraints, and let $F \equiv \Lambda(G'\sigma)$, where G' is a goal. Let σ be any substitution of the form: $[s_1/Y_1]\ldots[s_r/Y_r]$, where $Y_1, \ldots, Y_r$ are the predicate variables free in Θ', G'. If $\Theta \mid\!\!-F$ has a hoIC-derivation, then $\Theta^* \mid\!\!- F^*$ has a $hoIC^+$-derivation.*

Proof By induction on the size of the proof of $\Theta \mid\!\!- F$, analyzing cases depending on the last inference rule applied. The properties verified by the entailment relation, mentioned before, are crucial in the proof. Some technicalities similar to that used in [8] for *hoHH* are also needed. ■

Lemma 2 (Positivization Proof Transformation) *Let Θ be a finite set of clauses and positive constraints, and let G be a goal. $\Theta \mid\!\!- G$ has a hoIC-derivation if and only if $\Theta \mid\!\!- G$ has a $hoIC^+$-derivation.*

Proof The not obvious implication is a direct consequence of Lemma 1, taking σ as the identity, since we are considering only positive constraints and every clause or goal also contains only positive constraints. ■

If G is a goal and Θ is a set of formulas that is divided into a program Δ and a set of positive constraints Γ, we write the sequent $\Theta \mid\!\!- G$ as $\Delta; \Gamma \mid\!\!- G$. Using the Positivization Proof Transformation Lemma, we will show the existence of *uniform proofs* and the possibility of working with sequents of the form $\Delta; \Gamma \mid\!\!- G$.

Lemma 3 (Uniform Proof Transformation) *If G is a goal, Δ a program and Γ a set of positive constraint formulas, such that $\Delta; \Gamma \mid\!\!- G$ has a proof of size l, then we can assure the following:*

1. *If $G \equiv P t_1 \ldots t_m$, P a predicate symbol, then there are n positive constraint $C_1, \ldots, C_n$ ($n \geq 0$) and a formula of the form $\forall x_1 \ldots \forall x_n\ (G' \Rightarrow A'_r)$ or $\forall x_1 \ldots \forall x_n\ A'_r$, that is α-equivalent to a clause in Δ such that $x_1, \ldots, x_n$ are new distinct variables not in Free($\Delta \cup \Gamma \cup \{A_r\}$), where, for $1 < i \leq n$, $x_i \notin$ Free($\{C_1, \ldots, C_{i-1}\}$) , and:*
   (a) $\Gamma \vdash_{\mathcal{C}} \exists x_1 C_1,\quad \Gamma, C_1 \vdash_{\mathcal{C}} \exists x_2 C_2, \ldots, \Gamma, C_1, \ldots, C_{n-1} \vdash_{\mathcal{C}} \exists x_n C_n$.
   (b) $\Gamma, C_1, \ldots, C_n \vdash_{\mathcal{C}} A'_r \approx A_r$.
   (c) For the first case, $\Delta; \Gamma, C_1, \ldots, C_n \mid\!\!- G'$ has a proof of size less than l.
2. *If $G \equiv X t_1 \ldots t_m$, X a predicate variable, there is $t \in \mathcal{PT}$, with Free(t) $\subseteq$ Free($\{t_1, \ldots, t_m\}$), $G' \equiv \Lambda((X t_1 \ldots t_m)[t/X])$ such that:*
   (a) $\Gamma \vdash_{\mathcal{C}} X \approx t$.
   (b) $\Delta; \Gamma \mid\!\!- G'$ has a proof of size less than l.

3. *If* $G \equiv C_p$, *then* $\Gamma \vdash_{\mathcal{C}} C_p$.
4. *If* $G \equiv G_1 \wedge G_2$, *then* $\Delta; \Gamma \mid\!\!- G_1$ *and* $\Delta; \Gamma \mid\!\!- G_2$ *have proofs of size less than* l.
5. *If* $G \equiv G_1 \vee G_2$, *then* $\Delta; \Gamma \mid\!\!- G_i$ *has a proof of size less than* l *for i=1 or 2.*
6. *If* $G \equiv D \Rightarrow G_1$, *then* $\Delta, D; \Gamma \mid\!\!- G_1$ *has a proof of size less than* l.
7. *If* $G \equiv C_p \Rightarrow G_1$, *then* $\Delta; \Gamma, C_p \mid\!\!- G_1$ *has a proof of size less than* l.
8. *For* $G \equiv \exists x G_1$, *if* $y \notin$ *Free*$(\Delta \cup \Gamma \cup \{G\})$, *then there is* C_p *such that:*
   (a) $\Gamma \vdash_{\mathcal{C}} \exists y C_p$.
   (b) $\Delta; \Gamma, C_p \mid\!\!- G_1[y/x]$ *has a proof of size less than* l.
9. *If* $G \equiv \forall x G_1$, *then* $\Delta; \Gamma \mid\!\!- G_1[y/x]$ *has a proof of size less than* l, *where* $y \notin$ *Free*$(\Delta \cup \Gamma \cup \{G\})$.

Proof Since, by Lemma 2, the calculi *hoℐ𝒞* and *hoℐ𝒞*$^+$ are equivalent for *hoHH*($\mathcal{C}$), we can work always with positive constraints, therefore the proof of the lemma is similar to that of first-order [5], but including the case ($Atom_f^+$), because due to the syntax of clauses and goals, some rules like ($\exists_L$) will not be applied. ■

4.2 The calculus *ho𝒰𝒞*

In this subsection we present an alternative proof system *ho𝒰𝒞* for *hoHH*($\mathcal{C}$). Our motivation is the following: *ho𝒰𝒞* builds always Uniform proofs, and it is parameterized by a given Constraint system. $\vdash_{ho\mathcal{UC}}$ replaces the left-introduction rules by a backchaining mechanism.

With the help of Lemma 3 we can show that *ho𝒰𝒞* has the same derivable sequents of the form $\Delta; \Gamma \mid\!\!- C$ as *hoℐ𝒞*.

Intuitively, *ho𝒰𝒞*-derivations are closer to computations. Hence this proof system will be very helpful in the next section for designing a sound and complete goal solving procedure.

Provability in *ho𝒰𝒞* is defined as follows. $\Delta; \Gamma \vdash_{ho\mathcal{UC}} G$ if and only if the sequent $\Delta; \Gamma \mid\!\!- G$ has a proof using the following rules.

Axioms to deal with constraints and flexible atomic goals:
(C_R), ($Atom_f^+$), defined as in the system *hoℐ𝒞*$^+$.

Backchaining rule for rigid atomic goals:

$$\frac{\Delta; \Gamma \mid\!\!- \exists x_1 \ldots \exists x_n ((A'_r \approx A_r) \wedge G)}{\Delta; \Gamma \mid\!\!- A_r} \ (Clause)$$

where $\forall x_1 \ldots \forall x_n (G \Rightarrow A'_r)$ is α-equivalent to a formula of Δ, (or $\forall x_1 \ldots \forall x_n A'_r$ is α-equivalent to a formula of Δ, and $G \equiv \top$), $x_1, \ldots, x_n$ do not appear free in the sequent of the conclusion.

Rules introducing the connectives and quantifiers of the goals:
($\vee_R$), ($\wedge_R$), ($\Rightarrow_R$), ($\exists_R^+$), ($\forall_R$), defined as in the system *hoℐ𝒞*$^+$.

Now we can prove the intended equivalence between *ho𝒰𝒞* and *hoℐ𝒞*.

Theorem 1 *The proof systems $ho\mathcal{IC}$ and $ho\mathcal{UC}$ are equivalent for $hoHH(\mathcal{C})$. That means, for any program Δ, for any set of positive constraints Γ, and for any goal G it holds: $\Delta; \Gamma \vdash_{ho\mathcal{IC}} G$ if and only if $\Delta; \Gamma \vdash_{ho\mathcal{UC}} G$.*

Proof The theorem is a consequence of the Uniform Proof Transformation Lemma 3, and the definition of calculi $ho\mathcal{UC}$, $ho\mathcal{IC}$. Both implications can be proved by induction on the size of the proof, analyzing cases on the structure of G. ■

5 A Goal Solving Procedure

We now turn to the view of $hoHH(\mathcal{C})$ as a logic programming language. Solving a goal G using a program Δ means to find a $\mathcal{C}$-satisfiable constraint R such that $\Delta; R \vdash_{ho\mathcal{UC}} G$. Any constraint R with this property is called a *correct answer constraint.*

We will present a goal solving procedure as a transition system. Goal solving will proceed by transforming an initial state through a sequence of intermediate states, ending in a final state. Each state will conserve the goals that remain to be solved and a partially calculated answer constraint. The final state will not have any goal to be solved.

Definition 5 *A state w.r.t. a finite set of variables V, written $\mathcal{S}$, has the form $\Pi[S \square \mathcal{G}]$ where: $\mathcal{G}$ is a multiset of triples $\langle \Delta, C, G \rangle$ (Δ* local program, *C* local constraint *and G* local goal*). Π is a quantifier prefix $Q_1x_1 \ldots Q_kx_k$ where $x_1, \ldots, x_k$ are distinct variables not belonging to V, and every Q_i, $1 \leq i \leq k$, is the quantifier $\forall$ or $\exists$. S is a* global constraint *formula.*

We say that a *state* $\Pi[S \square \mathcal{G}]$ is *satisfiable* when the associated constraint formula ΠS, also called *partially calculated answer constraint*, is $\mathcal{C}$-satisfiable.

If Π', Π are quantifier prefixes such that Π' coincides with the first k elements of Π, $0 \leq k \leq n$, where n is the number of elements of Π, then $\Pi - \Pi'$ represents the result of eliminating Π' of Π. To represent a multiset $\mathcal{G}$, we will use the notation employed in the sequents for programs and constraints. That means we will use commas to express union and we will omit brackets.

Definition 6 *The* rules for transformation of states, *permitting to pass from a state w.r.t. a set of variables V, $\mathcal{S}$, to another state w.r.t. V, $\mathcal{S}'$, written as $\mathcal{S} \Vdash \mathcal{S}'$, are the following:*

i) Conjunction.
$\Pi[S \square \mathcal{G}, \langle \Delta, C, G_1 \wedge G_2 \rangle] \Vdash \Pi[S \square \mathcal{G}, \langle \Delta, C, G_1 \rangle, \langle \Delta, C, G_2 \rangle]$.

ii) Disjunction.
$\Pi[S \square \mathcal{G}, \langle \Delta, C, G_1 \vee G_2 \rangle] \Vdash \Pi[S \square \mathcal{G}, \langle \Delta, C, G_i \rangle]$, *for $i = 1$ or 2 (don't know choice).*

iii) Implication with local clause.
$\Pi[S \square \mathcal{G}, \langle \Delta, C, D \Rightarrow G \rangle] \Vdash \Pi[S \square \mathcal{G}, \langle \Delta \cup \{D\}, C, G \rangle]$.

iv) Implication with local constraint.
$\Pi[S\Box\mathcal{G},\langle\Delta,C,C'\Rightarrow G\rangle] \Vdash \Pi[S\Box\mathcal{G},\langle\Delta,C\wedge C',G\rangle]$.

v) Existential quantification.
$\Pi[S\Box\mathcal{G},\langle\Delta,C,\exists xG\rangle] \Vdash \Pi\exists w[S\Box\mathcal{G},\langle\Delta,C,G[w/x]\rangle]$, *where w does not appear in Π nor in V.*

vi) Universal quantification.
$\Pi[S\Box\mathcal{G},\langle\Delta,C,\forall xG\rangle] \Vdash \Pi\forall w[S\Box\mathcal{G},\langle\Delta,C,G[w/x]\rangle]$, *where w does not appear in Π nor in V.*

vii) Constraint.
$\Pi[S\Box\mathcal{G},\langle\Delta,C,C'\rangle] \Vdash \Pi[S\wedge(C\Rightarrow C')\Box\mathcal{G}]$. *If $\Pi(S\wedge(C\Rightarrow C'))$ is $\mathcal{C}$-satisfiable.*

viii) Clause of the program.
$\Pi[S\Box\mathcal{G},\langle\Delta,C,A_r\rangle] \Vdash \Pi[S\Box\mathcal{G},\langle\Delta,C,\exists x_1\ldots\exists x_n((A'_r\approx A_r)\wedge G)\rangle]$. *Provided that $x_1,\ldots,x_n\notin\Pi\cup V$, and $\forall x_1\ldots\forall x_n(G\Rightarrow A'_r)$ is α-equivalent to some clause in Δ (or $\forall x_1\ldots\forall x_n A'_r$ is α-equivalent to some clause in Δ, $G\equiv\top$) (don't know choice).*

ix) Flexible atom. $\Pi[S\Box\mathcal{G},\langle\Delta,C,(Xt_1\ldots t_n)\rangle] \Vdash \Pi[S\wedge(C\Rightarrow(X\approx t))\Box\mathcal{G},\langle\Delta,C,G\rangle]$. *Provided that $G\equiv\Lambda((Xt_1\ldots t_n)[t/X])$, $t\in\mathcal{PT}$, $Free(t)\subseteq Free(\{t_1\ldots t_n\})$, and $\Pi(S\wedge(C\Rightarrow(X\approx t)))$ is $\mathcal{C}$-satisfiable.*

The following definition formalizes the setting needed for goal solving.

Definition 7 *The* initial state *for a program Δ and a goal G is a state w.r.t. the set of free variables of Δ and G consisting in $\mathcal{S}_0\equiv[\top\Box\langle\Delta,\top,G\rangle]$.*

A resolution of a goal G from a program Δ *is a finite sequence of states w.r.t. the free variables of Δ and G, $\mathcal{S}_0,\ldots,\mathcal{S}_n$, such that:*

- *$\mathcal{S}_0$ is the initial state for Δ and G.*
- *$\mathcal{S}_{i-1}\Vdash\mathcal{S}_i$, $1\le i\le n$, by means of any of the transformation rules.*
- *The* final state *$\mathcal{S}_n$ has the form $\Pi_n[S_n\Box\emptyset]$.*

The constraint Π_nS_n is called the answer constraint *of this resolution.*

From the definition of the resolution procedure, it follows that every answer constraint is positive. The rule *ix)* corresponds to the rule ($Atom^+_f$) of $ho\mathcal{UC}$-calculus, and transforms a flexible atom in a (simpler) goal that, using the local constraint, can be proved to be equal to the atom. It is essentially the only new rule with respect to the goal solving procedure given in [5] for the first-order version of this language. Nevertheless as we will see in section 6, in the context of higher-order, these rules are more powerful in the sense that they solve more complex goals. This implies the incorporation of a system able to determine the satisfiability of constraints in which higher-order equations may appear.

This procedure is sound and complete in the following sense:

Theorem 2 (Soundness) *Let Δ be any program. If G is a goal such that there is a resolution $\mathcal{S}_0,\ldots,\mathcal{S}_n$ of G from Δ with answer constraint $R\equiv\Pi_nS_n$, then R is $\mathcal{C}$-satisfiable and $\Delta;R\vdash_{ho\mathcal{UC}}G$.*

Theorem 3 (Completeness) *Let Δ be a program, G a goal and R_0 a positive $\mathcal{C}$-satisfiable constraint such that $\Delta; R_0 \vdash_{h\mathcal{UC}} G$. Then there is a resolution of G from Δ with answer constraint R such that $R_0 \vdash_{\mathcal{C}} R$.*

The proofs of this theorems are equivalent of the corresponding ones included in [5] for first-order, but adding the case for the rule *ix)*.

In the next section we will see an example of the application of the state transformation rules *i)* to *ix)*.

6 Examples

We begin referring to the example of the Introduction, that we have used to illustrate the expressivity of the language.

Example 1 Let the program:

$$\begin{aligned}\Delta = \{&\forall x \forall y(x^2 + y^2 \approx 1 \Rightarrow \mathit{ci1}(x,y)),\\ &\forall x \forall y(x^2 + y^2 \approx 2 \Rightarrow \mathit{ci2}(x,y)),\\ &\forall x \forall y(x^2 + 6y^2 \approx 2 \Rightarrow \mathit{el}(x,y)),\\ &\mathit{fig}(\mathit{ci1}), \mathit{fig}(\mathit{ci2}), \mathit{fig}(\mathit{el}),\\ &\forall C_1 \forall C_2(\mathit{fig}(C_1) \wedge \mathit{fig}(C_2) \wedge C_1 \not\approx C_2 \Rightarrow \mathit{in}(\lambda x.\lambda y.(C_1(x,y) \wedge C_2(x,y))))\}.\end{aligned}$$

And let:

$$G \equiv \exists T(\mathit{in}(T) \wedge T(x,y)).$$

We present a resolution of G from Δ:

$$[\top \Box \langle \Delta, \top, \exists T(\mathit{in}(T) \wedge T(x,y))\rangle] \Vdash_{v),i)}$$

$$\exists T'[\top \Box \langle \Delta, \top, \mathit{in}(T')\rangle, \langle \Delta, \top, T'(x,y)\rangle] \Vdash_{viii),v),v),i),i),i)}$$

$$\begin{aligned}&\exists T' \exists C_1' \exists C_2'[\top \Box \langle \Delta, \top, T' \approx \lambda u.\lambda v.(C_1'(u,v) \wedge C_2'(u,v))\rangle, \langle \Delta, \top, \mathit{fig}(C_1')\rangle,\\ &\quad \langle \Delta, \top, \mathit{fig}(C_2')\rangle, \langle \Delta, \top, C_1' \not\approx C_2'\rangle, \langle \Delta, \top, T'(x,y)\rangle] \Vdash_{vii),viii),viii)}\end{aligned}$$

$$\begin{aligned}&\exists T' \exists C_1' \exists C_2'[T' \approx \lambda u.\lambda v.(C_1'(u,v) \wedge C_2'(u,v)) \Box \langle \Delta, \top, C_1' \approx \mathit{ci1}\rangle,\\ &\quad \langle \Delta, \top, C_2' \approx \mathit{el}\rangle, \langle \Delta, \top, C_1' \not\approx C_2'\rangle, \langle \Delta, \top, T'(x,y)\rangle] \Vdash_{vii),vii),vii)}\end{aligned}$$

$$\begin{aligned}&\exists T' \exists C_1' \exists C_2'[T' \approx \lambda u.\lambda v.(C_1'(u,v) \wedge C_2'(u,v)) \wedge C_1' \approx \mathit{ci1} \wedge C_2' \approx \mathit{el} \wedge\\ &\quad C_1' \not\approx C_2' \Box \langle \Delta, \top, T'(x,y)\rangle] \Vdash_{ix),i)}\end{aligned}$$

$$\begin{aligned}&\exists T' \exists C_1' \exists C_2'[T' \approx \lambda u.\lambda v.(C_1'(u,v) \wedge C_2'(u,v)) \wedge C_1' \approx \mathit{ci1} \wedge C_2' \approx \mathit{el} \wedge\\ &\quad C_1' \not\approx C_2' \Box\ \langle \Delta, \top, \mathit{ci1}(x,y)\rangle, \langle \Delta, \top, \mathit{el}(x,y)\rangle] \Vdash_{viii),v),v),i),viii),v),v)i)}\end{aligned}$$

$$\begin{aligned}&\exists T' \exists C_1' \exists C_2' \exists x' \exists y' \exists x'' \exists y''[T' \approx \lambda u.\lambda v.(C_1'(u,v) \wedge C_2'(u,v)) \wedge C_1' \approx \mathit{ci1} \wedge\\ &\quad C_2' \approx \mathit{el} \wedge C_1' \not\approx C_2' \Box \langle \Delta, \top, x' \approx x \wedge y' \approx y\rangle, \langle \Delta, \top, x'^2 + y'^2 \approx 1\rangle,\\ &\quad \langle \Delta, \top, x'' \approx x \wedge y'' \approx y\rangle, \langle \Delta, \top, x''^2 + 6y''^2 \approx 2\rangle] \Vdash_{i),vii),i),vii),vii),vii)}\end{aligned}$$

$$\begin{aligned}&\exists T' \exists C_1' \exists C_2' \exists x' \exists y' \exists x'' \exists y''[T' \approx \lambda u.\lambda v.(C_1'(u,v) \wedge C_2'(u,v)) \wedge C_1' \approx \mathit{ci1} \wedge\\ &\quad C_2' \approx \mathit{el} \wedge C_1' \not\approx C_2' \wedge x' \approx x \wedge y' \approx y \wedge x'^2 + y'^2 \approx 1 \wedge\\ &\quad x'' \approx x \wedge y'' \approx y \wedge x''^2 + 6y''^2 \approx 2 \Box]\end{aligned}$$

The answer is equivalent (in the constraint system $\mathcal{R}$) to $x^2 + y^2 \approx 1 \wedge x^2 + 6y^2 \approx 2$. That has two solutions: $x \approx \frac{2}{\sqrt{5}} \wedge y \approx \frac{1}{\sqrt{5}}$ and $x \approx \sqrt{2} \wedge y \approx 0$.

The next simple example adds more explanation about the treatment of $\approx$.

Example 2 Given the database:
$\Delta = \{$ *annoyed(john)*, *annoyed(jane)*, *irritated(louise)* $\}$,
if we formulate the query: $G \equiv$ *annoyed* $\approx$ *irritated* $\Rightarrow$ *irritated(x)*, the local constraint *annoyed* $\approx$ *irritated* is added to the database (rule *iv)*), then in accordance with the rules *viii)* and *vii)*, the constraint solver should deduce, for instance, the satisfiability of *annoyed* $\approx$ *irritated* $\Rightarrow$ *(annoyed(john)* $\approx$ *irritated(x))*. We conclude that the goal G has the following possible answers: $x \approx$ *john*, $x \approx$ *jane*, $x \approx$ *louise*.

We finish with an example in which we show how the benefits of *HH* based languages implementing modules ([7]) are improved with the use of constraints.

Example 3 We follow the idea of identify a class of objects with a module of clauses. Then if a goal is used to send a message to an object, it will be solved in the presence of the corresponding module. In the example we define a module to represent the object class of employees[2].
`MODULE` *staff*
`LOCAL` *Emp*
$D_1 \equiv \forall l \forall s \forall c(dataemp(Emp(l,s,c),l,s,c).$
$D_2 \equiv \forall l \forall s \forall c(level(Emp(l,s,c),l).$
$D_3 \equiv \forall l \forall s \forall c(basesalary(Emp(l,s,c),s).$
$D_4 \equiv \forall l \forall s \forall c(complement(Emp(l,s,c),c).$
$D_5 \equiv \forall E \forall l \forall s \forall c \forall pay((level(E,l) \wedge basesalary(E,s) \wedge complement(E,c) \wedge$
$(0 < l < 3 \Rightarrow pay \approx ((s/12)+c)*0.8) \wedge$
$(3 \leq l < 5 \Rightarrow pay \approx ((s/12)+c)*0.7)) \Rightarrow monthsalary(E,pay)).$
If we want to know which is the level of an employee, whose pay in a month is \$400, has a base salary of \$4800 and a complement of \$100, we send the message *staff* ==> $\exists E'(dataemp(E',l,4800,100) \wedge monthsalary(E',400))$, that means $\forall Emp(D_1 \Rightarrow D_2 \Rightarrow D_3 \Rightarrow D_4 \Rightarrow D_5 \Rightarrow (\exists E'(dataemp(E',l,4800,100) \wedge monthsalary(E',400)))$. The expected answer will be $0 < l < 3$.

7 Conclusions and Future Work

The applications of *CLP*, and higher-order logic programming are well known. We have proposed a novel combination of *CLP* with higher-order *HH* with the purpose of summing up the advantages of higher-order programming, *CLP* and *HH*. For the amalgamated logic we present, a proof system and a goal solving procedure are included, showing the existence of uniform proofs as well as soundness and completeness of the resolution procedure w.r.t. the proof system.

A related, but more limited approach, can be found in [6]. where it is shown how to manage hard constraints in a higher-order logic programming language like λ-Prolog or Elf. But there, constraints are reduced to be equations over

[2] We use the reserved words that λ-Prolog uses for modules.

terms, and higher-order unification is the constraint solving mechanism. Our results are parametric for more general constraint systems.

In relation with functional logic programming languages with constraints, as Curry [3], our language does not have the benefits of the evaluation of functions by rewriting rules. However, the advantages of *hoHH($\mathcal{C}$)* w.r.t. Curry are manifest in expressiveness.

An interesting issue that remains for future research concerns implementation techniques. For instance, the goal solving procedure is open to use incremental checkers that reuse the work previously done to stablish the satisfiability of a partially calculated answer constraint, to check the satisfiability of the next. The term t, that appears new in the rule *ix)*, can be guess as a solution for X, solving the system $\Pi(S \wedge C)$. In order to solve equations, it should be appropriate to define higher-order E-unification algorithms under a mixed prefix. We are also investigating decidable theories that can be useful as constraint systems.

References

1. Clark, K.L., Negation as Failure, in: H. Gallaire and J. Minker (eds.), *Logic and Databases* 293-322, Plenum Press, 1978.
2. Felty, A., Implementing Tactics and Tacticals in a Higher-Order Logic Programming Language, *Journal of Automated Reasoning* 11(1):43-81 (1993).
3. Hanus, M. (ed.), *Curry: an Integrated Functional Logic Language*, Version 0.7, February 2, 2000. Available at http://www.informatik.uni-kiel.de/~curry/.
4. Jaffar, J. and Maher, M.J., Constraint Logic Programming: A Survey, *Journal of Logic Programming* 19(20):503-581 (1994).
5. Leach, J., Nieva, S. and Rodríguez-Artalejo, M., Constraint Logic Programming with Hereditary Harrop Formulas in: J. Małuszyński (ed.), *ILPS'97* 307–321, MIT Press, 1997.
6. Michaylov, S., Pfenning, F., Higher-Order Logic Programming as Constraint Logic Programming, in: Proc. of First *Workshop on Principles and Practice of Constraint Programming*, 221-229, Brown University, 1993.
7. Miller, D., A Logical Analysis of Modules in Logic Programming, *Journal of Logic Programming* 6(1,2):79-108 (1989).
8. Miller, D., Nadathur, G., Pfenning, F. and Scedrov, A., Uniform Proofs as a Foundation for Logic Programming, *Annals of Pure and Applied Logic* 51:125-157 (1991).
9. Miller, D., Nadathur, G. and Scedrov, A., Hereditary Harrop Formulas and Uniform Proof Systems, in: D. Gries (ed.), *LICS'87* 98-105, IEEE Comp. Soc. Press, 1987.
10. Nadathur, G. and Miller, D., An Overview of λ-Prolog, in: K.A. Bowen and R. A. Kowalski (eds.), *ICLP'88* 810-827, MIT Press, 1988.
11. Nerode, A., Some Lectures on Intuitionistic Logic, in: S. Homer, A. Nerode, R.A. Platek, G.E. Sacks, A. Scedrov (eds.), *LCS'88* 12-59, Springer LNM 1429, 1988.
12. Saraswat, V., The Category of Constraint Systems is Cartesian Closed, in: *LICS'92* 341-345, IEEE Comp. Soc. Press, 1992.
13. Tarski, A., *A Decision Method for Elementary Algebra and Geometry* , University of California Press, 1951.

Specifying and Debugging Security Protocols via Hereditary Harrop Formulas and λProlog - A Case-study -

Giorgio Delzanno

Dipartimento di Informatica e Scienze dell'Informazione
via Dodecaneso 35, I-16146 Genova
giorgio@disi.unige.it

Abstract. We investigate the fragment of intuitionistic logic consisting of hereditary Harrop formulas [MNPS91] as a specification language for security protocols. In this setting, embedded implications and universal quantification provide a natural built-in mechanism to model the dynamics in the knowledge of the agents involved in a protocol. We take advantage of the system λProlog [NM88,NM99] in order to turn specifications in hereditary Harrop formulas into executable prototypes, ready to be debugged. To exploit these features, we select as main case-study the well-known Needham-Schroeder protocol [NS78]. In this paper we report on the results of our experiments and we discuss potentially interesting directions of future research.

1 Introduction

Security protocols are often specified in a very informal way. As an example, let us consider the following rule of the well-known Needham-Schroeder protocol [NS78] (we will describe later in more detail):

$$A \rightarrow B : \{A, N_a\}_{K_b}$$

The rule specifies a message sent from agent A to agent B. The message contains the identification of A, a fresh name (called *nonce*) N_a, and it is encrypted with the public-key K_b of B. This example shows that the language used to specify the protocol gives only a partial view of the knowledge that agents acquire while talking each other. Furthermore, side-conditions like 'N_a is a fresh nonce' are stated only at the meta-level. The use of informal specification may lead to ambiguous interpretations of the rules, and makes difficult the validation phase of the protocols.

In this paper we present an *experimental* evaluation of intuitionic logic and more precisely of the fragment of hereditary Harrop formulas [MNPS91], *hhf* for short, as a potential specification language for security protocols involving a fixed number of principals. The features that make hereditary Harrop formulas appealing for the specification of security protocols are described below.

H. Kuchen and K. Ueda (Eds.): FLOPS 2001, LNCS 2024, pp. 123–137, 2001.

Dynamic Augmentation of Knowledge. Typically, at the initial stage of a protocol agents have very few information about the environment. The knowledge augments when messages are exchanged during the protocol. Via the use of embedded implications, the logic *hhf* provides a clean mechanism to model dynamic augmentation of knowledge. For this purpose, we can in fact use implicational goals of the form $D \supset G$. When excuted, such a goal enriches the current program with the clause D. The augmented program can be used then to refute the continuation goal G.

Creation of New Names. As mentioned before, side conditions like 'N_a is a fresh name' are frequently used in the specification of security protocols. The logic *hhf* provides a built-in mechanism to ensure the *freshness* of nonces created by the agents involved in the protocol via the use of *universal quantification.* For this purpose, in *hhf* we can use goals with universal quantification of the form $\forall x.G$. When excuted, such a goal enriches the *signature* of the current program with a *new* name c. The new environment can then be used to refute the continuation goal $G[c/x]$.

Executable Specifications. Being an Abstract Logic Programming Language [MNPS91], *hhf* programs enjoy a natural procedural reading that makes them executable specifications. The language λProlog provides in fact an interpreter [NM88] and a compiler [NM99] that can be used to run programs written in *hhf*. This is a crucial aspect in order to use a protocol specification as a prototype for *debugging* and *testing*.

On the basis of the previous observations, our technical contributions are as follows. We present a general program scheme that can be used to model the main features of security protocols in the fragment *hhf* of intuitionistic logic. In this setting, we use *hhf* program clauses to describe the *actions* of individual agents, the *dynamics* in their knowledge, and *initial* and *final* configurations for a successful execution of the protocol. Furthermore, we describe the potential moves of an *intruder*, and conditions under which the security of the protocol is broken by the intruder. As case-study, we present a detailed encoding of the well-know Needham-Schroeder public-key cryptography protocol. For this case-study, we have used the logic programming system λProlog as an automatic debugging tool. The results of this experiment are reported in the last section of the paper. Despite of the several proposed logics for reasononing about security (see e.g. [BAN90,Mas99]), the problem of finding a *general* formal model for the specification and verification of security protocols is still an open problem. For this reason, we believe in the importance of investigating existing techniques and tools like λProlog in order to find new insights into the problem. Also, we hope that our experiment will attract the curiosity of other researchers looking for non-standard applications of logic programming tools.

Plan of the paper. In Section 2, we introduce the logic of hereditary Harrop formulas focusing on the operational reading of the corresponding logic programs. In Section 3, we present the case-study, i.e., the Needham-Schroeder Protocol. In Section 4, we define a general schema for specifying security protocols in *hhf*. In Section 4.2, we present the *hhf* specification of the Needham-Schroeder protocol. In Section 5, we specify a generic *hhf* theory for intruders of public-key cryptography protocols. In Section 6, we briefly comment on the experiments we perform with the resulting *hhf* specification. In the experiments we specialize the intruder theory to the case-study taken into consideration. Finally, we discuss related works and future directions of research in Section 7 and Section 8, respectively.

2 An Operational View of Intuitionistic Logic

The notion of *Abstract Logic Programming* (ALP) language [MNPS91] characterizes in a rigourous way fragments of intuitionistic logic that can be used as a platform to define logic programming languages. An ALP language is defined as a triple $\langle \mathcal{D}, \mathcal{G}, \vdash \rangle$ where $\mathcal{D}$ is the set of program clauses, $\mathcal{G}$ is a set of goal formulas, and $\vdash$ is a provability relation such that $P \vdash G$ is true if and only if there exists a uniform (i.e. goal driven) intuitionistic proof for the sequent $P \rightarrow G$. Hereditary harrop formulas form one of the most interesting examples of ALP language. In the first-order case, program and goal formulas are defined as follows:

$$G ::= \top \mid A \mid G_1 \wedge G_2 \mid G_1 \vee G_2 \mid \forall x.G \mid \exists x.G \mid D \supset G,$$
$$D ::= A \mid G \supset A \mid \forall x.D.$$

Let P be a set of D-formula, and G a goal formula. The provability relation $P \vdash G$ is defined via the following *meta-interpreter*:

$\top$-R: $P \vdash \top$.
$\wedge$-R: $P \vdash G_1 \wedge G_1$, if $P \vdash G_1$ AND $P \vdash G_2$.
$\vee$-R: $P \vdash G_1 \vee G_1$, if $P \vdash G_1$ OR $P \vdash G_2$.
$\supset$-R: $P \vdash D \supset G$, if $P, D \vdash G$.
$\forall$-R: $P \vdash \forall x.G$, if $P \vdash G[c/x]$, where c does not occur free in G.
Backchain: $P \vdash A$, if there is a ground instance $G \supset A$ of a clause in P such that $P \vdash G$.

Clearly, Horn programs form a special class of *hhf* programs. Universal quantification and embedded implications add new interesting *programming constructs* to Horn programs. Specifically, implication in the goals gives us the possibility of performing *hypothetical* reasoning. In fact, note that to prove $D \supset G$ we first have to load D into the program, and then prove G. Also, note the difference between the goal $D \supset (G_1 \wedge G_2)$ and the goal $(D \supset G_1) \wedge G_2$. In the first case D is loaded into the program to prove $G_1 \wedge G_2$, whereas in the second one D is loaded into the program only to prove G_1. In [Mil89], Miller has shown how implications can be used to give a modular structure to logic programs. Universal quantification allows the creation of *fresh* names during the execution of a goal. This idea has been used, e.g., to implement *hiding* mechanism for module systems [Mil89,Mil89b].

To sum up, proving that a formula G is a logical consequence of a program P in intuitionistic logic, amounts to search for a goal-driven proof of $P \vdash G$. This can be done automatically in the *incomplete* theorem prover λProlog [NM88]. As Prolog, λProlog combines in fact a left-to-right selection rule with a depth-first search of successful derivations.

3 The Needham-Schroeder Protocol

In this paper we will mainly focus our attention on *public-key cryptography* protocols. In this setting, any agent (*principal*) involved in the protocol has a pair of keys: a *public* key, and a *secret* key. Typically, the secret key of agent A is used to decipher messages (encrypted with A's public key) that other agents send to A. To give a concrete example, in the rest of the section we will briefly describe the security protocol based on *public-key cryptography* proposed by Needham and Schroeder in [NS78]. The protocol allows two *principals*, say Alice and Bob, to exchange two *secret numbers*. The secret numbers will be used later for *signing* messages. The core of the protocol is defined as follows. Assume that Alice knows the public key of Bob (e.g. it asks for it to a *certification authority*). As a first step, Alice creates a *nonce* N_a and sends it to Bob, together with its identity. A nonce is a randomly generated value used to defeat 'playback' attacks. The message is encrypted with Bob's public key, so that only Bob will be able to decipher the message. When Bob receives the message, he creates a new nonce N_b. Then, he sends the message $\langle N_a, N_b\rangle$ encrypted with the public key of Alice. Alice decrypts the message, and sends back the nonce N_b encrypted with the public key of Bob. At this point, Alice and Bob know the two secret numbers N_a and N_b. In synthesis, the protocol has the following rules

$$\begin{array}{l} 1.\ A \rightarrow B : \{A, N_a\}_{K_b} \\ 2.\ B \rightarrow A : \{N_a, N_b\}_{K_a} \\ 3.\ A \rightarrow B : \{N_b\}_{K_b} \end{array}$$

The previous specification does not take into account the presence of potential *intruders*. Intruders might intercept messages, and use them to cheat the two principals. In order to validate security protocols it is fundamental to model the knowledge of each participant during the execution of the protocol, and to model the possible actions that an intruder can take in order to break the security of the communication. In the following sections we will show how to exploit the features of the fragment *hhf* of intuitionistic logic in order to achieve the previous goals.

4 Specifying Security Protocols in *hhf*

Before focusing on our case-study, we will describe some general ideas that can be used to specify a security protocol using intuitionistic logic. For simplicity, we will focus on protocols involving two agents, we call A and B in order to distinguish the general case from the case-study. As illustrated in Section 3, security protocols are typically specified via a sequence of rules having the following form

$$Agent_1 \rightarrow Agent_2 : Msg.$$

Here $Agent_1$ and $Agent_2$ are the agent names, Exp is an expression represing encrypted messages, that in turn may include the agent names, nonces, time-stamps, and other encrypted messages. The rules represent the sequence of steps the two agents must perform to successfully terminate the protocol. In order to transform these rules into non ambiguous specifications it is necessary to formally represent the change of the knowledge of A and B when a message is successfully delivered to one of them. To achieve this goal using *hhf*, we first need to symbolically represent the *current state* and *knowledge* of the agents, and the *global information* available on the network. Specifically, in order to model the state of the network during the execution of the protocol we use the atomic formula

$$(state\ State_A\ State_B\ State_N),$$

where $State_A$, $State_B$, and $State_N$ represent the current state of A, B and of the communication channel N between A and B, respectively. We assume that each principal has a finite set of possible states (that correspond to the steps of the protocol) denoted as non-logical constants (e.g. $alice_0, alice_1, \ldots$ if $alice$ is Alice's identifier). N will represent the messages sent by the agents. In this paper we will consider communication via a one-place buffer, `no_msg` being the empty buffer (other possible communication models like FIFO channels can be easily modeled using appropriate data structures). Encrypted messages we will be represented via *terms* having the following form

$$(enc\ Key\ Message),$$

where *Message* can be either a non-logical symbol, a pair of messages $\langle M_1, M_2\rangle$, and so on. We will discuss later how to represent *nonces*. Global information can be represented via a collection of unit clauses (*facts*). For instance, a fact like

$$(keypair\ Agent\ PrivateKey\ PublicKey)$$

can be used to represent the initial knowledge of an agent in a *public-key cryptography* protocol. Furthermore, we can use the fact

$$(announce\ PublicKey),$$

if we assume that a *trusted* entity makes the *public* keys of all the principals available on the network (we assume that agents contacts other agents selecting their public keys). Alternatively, in a protocol based on secret-key cryptography the fact

$$(secretkey\ Agent\ SecretKey)$$

will represent the initial knowledge of an agent. We are ready now to describe the mechanisms needed to model protocol rules.

4.1 The Dynamics of the Network

Protocol rules specify how the knowledge of agents must be updated. More precisely, suppose that during the k-step of the protocol an agent B first receives the message M_1 from B (i.e., $A \rightarrow B : M_1$), and then it replies with message M_2 (i.e, $B \rightarrow A : M_2$). Also, suppose that the current state of B will change from $State_B$ to $State'_B$ (e.g. from $alice_{k-1}$ to $alice_k$). Then, the current knowledge of B must be updated with all the information that B is able to extract from M_1. Furthermore, we have to ensure the freshness of all *nonces* created by B and included in M_2. We model all of these aspects in *hhf* as follows. We first represent the *current* knowledge of an agent A using a collection (i.e. conjunctions) of facts having the form

$$(knows\ Agent\ M),$$

where M can be any kind of information (messages, keys, time-stamps, nonces, and so on). Then, we consider *hhf* clauses having the following:

$$(\forall N_1. \ldots . \forall N_m. \ (\mathbf{G}\ \wedge\ (\mathbf{U} \supset \mathbf{S}'))) \supset \mathbf{S},$$

where

$$\cfrac{P \vdash \mathbf{G} \qquad \cfrac{P, \mathbf{U}[c/x] \vdash \mathbf{S}'}{P \vdash \mathbf{U}[c/N] \supset \mathbf{S}'[c/N]}}{\cfrac{P \vdash \mathbf{G}[c/N] \wedge (\mathbf{U} \supset \mathbf{S}')[c/N]}{\cfrac{P \vdash \forall N.(\mathbf{G} \wedge (\mathbf{U} \supset \mathbf{S}'))}{P \vdash \mathbf{S}}}}$$

where $\forall N.\ (\mathbf{G} \wedge (\mathbf{U} \supset \mathbf{S}')) \supset \mathbf{S} \in P$, and c is a new name.

Fig. 1. Proof scheme for the protocol theory.

- $\mathbf{S} = (state\ State_A\ State_B\ M_1)$ is the current network state,
- $\mathbf{S}' = (state\ State_A\ State'_B\ M_2)$ is the new state of the network,
- $\mathbf{U} = (knows\ B\ m_1) \wedge \ldots \wedge (knows\ B\ m_q)$ is the update of B's knowledge ($m_1, \ldots, m_q$ being the pieces of information that B manages to extract from M_1),
- $\mathbf{G}$ (the guard) is a goal formulas used to extract information from M_1, and to build the message M_2,
- $N_1, \ldots, N_m$ are the new nonces created by B (as explained before, modeled via universally quantified variables), with the proviso that they do not occur free in $\mathbf{G}$.

The effect of applying this kind of rules in a backchaining step is described by the proof scheme in Fig. 1. Note that, the left branch of the scheme in Fig. 1 is used to check the 'guard' $\mathbf{G}$ against the current global information, whereas the right branch is used to update the agent knowledge and to create the new names.

Setting up the Initial Scenario. As an example, the *hhf* rule we can use to set up the initial scenario of a security protocol based on *public-key cryptography* with two principals is as follows

$$\begin{array}{l}\forall PK_a, PK_b, SK_a, SK_b. \\ \quad (((keypair\ A\ SK_a\ PK_a) \wedge (keypair\ B\ SK_b\ PK_b) \wedge (announce\ PK_a) \\ \qquad \wedge (announce\ PK_b)) \supset (state\ Init_A\ Init_B\ no\_msg)) \\ \qquad\qquad \supset (initialize\ A\ Init_A\ B\ Init_B).\end{array}$$

Note that, in the previous formula there is no $\mathbf{G}$-component (its use will be illustrated in Section 4.2); the body of the clause consists of a universally quantified G-formula containing an implicational subgoal. The universal quantification in the body ensures that all the keys will be *fresh* and *distinct* from each other.

Termination of the protocol. Following the ideas presented in the previous sections, the execution of a protocol can be viewed as a derivation that leads from (*initialize* ...) to a state in which the agents have achieved their *goals* (e.g. Alice and Bob receive the nonces). The successful termination of the protocol can be expressed then via clauses like

$$\mathbf{G} \supset (state\ Final_A\ Final_B\ Network),$$

where **G** is used to check that the requirements of A and B are satisfied in the final global state. In other words, (*initialize* ...) will have a refutation in the *hhf* theory obtained merging rules and agents goals if and only if there exists a successful execution of the protocol. Let us apply these ideas to our case-study.

4.2 The *hhf* Theory for Needham-Schroeder

Let *alice* and *bob* be the symbolic names for the two principals.

Initial States. Invoking the goal ($initialize\ alice\ alice_0\ bob\ bob_0$) (see previous Section) will create the initial scenario for our protocol.

Protocol Rules. The rules of Alice and Bob's are defined using the general schema of Section 4. As an example, when in state $alice_0$ Alice must create a new nonce N_a, and send it to Bob. As a side-effect, her knowledge should be augmented with the information 'Alice knows N_a'. Formally, we encode the first rule of the protocol as follows:

$$\begin{array}{l} \forall\ N_a. \\ \quad ((keypair\ alice\ SK_a\ PK_a) \wedge (announce\ K_b) \wedge \\ \quad\quad ((knows\ alice_0\ N_a) \supset (state\ alice_1\ Bob\ (enc\ K_b\ \langle N_a, PK_a \rangle)))) \\ \quad\quad\quad \supset (state\ alice_0\ Bob\ no\_msg). \end{array}$$

Here the G-formula $(keypair\ alice\ SK_a\ PK_a) \wedge (announce\ K_b)$ is used as a guard (i.e. **G**-component) to retrieve Bob's public key and to build the initial message. Similarly, the reply from Bob is defined as follows:

$$\begin{array}{l} \forall N_b. \\ \quad ((keypair\ bob\ SK_b\ PK_b) \wedge \\ \quad\quad (((knows\ bob_0\ N_a) \wedge (knows\ bob_0\ K_a) \wedge (knows\ bob_1\ N_b)) \\ \quad\quad\quad \supset (state\ Alice\ bob_1\ (enc\ K_a\ \langle N_a, N_b \rangle)))) \\ \quad \supset (state\ Alice\ bob_0\ (enc\ PK_b\ \langle N_a, K_a \rangle)). \end{array}$$

Finally, the second rule for Alice is defined as follows:

$$\begin{array}{l} ((keypair\ alice\ SK_a\ PK_a) \wedge (knows\ alice_0\ N_a) \wedge (knows\ alice_0\ K_b) \wedge \\ \quad ((knows\ alice_1\ N_b) \supset (state\ alice_2\ Bob\ (enc\ K_b\ N_b)))) \\ \supset (state\ alice_1\ Bob\ (enc\ PK_a\ \langle N_a, N_b \rangle)). \end{array}$$

Termination. The protocol terminates successfully if Bob receives the nonce N_b he created. We can specify this requirement as the following clause.

$$((keypair\ bob\ SK_b\ PK_b) \wedge (knows\ bob_1\ N_b))$$
$$\supset\ (state\ Alice\ bob_1\ (enc\ PK_b\ N_b)).$$

In the ideal setting where only Alice and Bob are connected on the network the goal $(initialize\ alice\ alice_0\ bob\ bob_0)$ will have a refutation in the *hhf* theory consisting of the previous clauses, called $\mathcal{P}$, if and only if the protocol is safe (e.g. it has no deadlocks). We discuss next the problem due to the presence of malicious agents.

5 The Intruder Theory

In order to test a protocol it is necessary to specify the actions of potential intruders. Following [CDKS00,Mas99], an intruder can be viewed as an agent with public and privat keys who has the capability of decomposing and storing all messages he receives. Furthermore, intruders can create new nonces and compose new messages using the information they stored (e.g. composing a new messages using old nonces). To formalize this idea, we consider one possible intruder, called Trudy, and we incorporate her state into the global state as follows

$$(state\ A\ B\ Trudy\ Network).$$

Trudy must be considered as just another *user*, she will intervene only if some agent contacts her. The capabilities of Trudy in a generic *public-key* cryptographic protocol can be specified via the following rule (where we use *trudy* as identifier).

$$\begin{array}{l}\forall N_t.\forall N_s.\\ \quad ((keypair\ trudy\ SK_t\ PK_t) \wedge (announce\ K_b) \wedge\\ \quad\ (((knows\ trudy\ N_t) \wedge (knows\ trudy\ N_s) \wedge (knows\ trudy\ M_1)\\ \qquad\quad \wedge\ (knows\ trudy\ M_2))\\ \qquad \supset ((compose\_msg\ M) \wedge (state\ A\ B\ trudy_{i+1}\ (enc\ K_b\ M)))))\\ \quad \supset (state\ A\ B\ trudy_i\ (enc\ PK_t\ \langle M_1, M_2\rangle)).\end{array}$$

Note that, the subgoal in the body of the previous clause has the following form $\mathbf{G} \wedge (\mathbf{U} \supset (\mathbf{G}' \wedge \mathbf{S}'))$, where $\mathbf{G}'$ is used to check conditions after the update of Trudy's knowledge. The predicate *compose_msg* nondeterministically generates all possible messages starting from the current knowledge of the intruder. Formally,

$$(compose\_msg\ M) \wedge (compose\_msg\ N) \supset (compose\_msg\ \langle M, N\rangle).$$
$$(knows\ trudy_i\ M) \supset (compose\_msg\ M).$$

Trudy also has the capability of sending messages to all agents she knows:

$$\begin{array}{l}
\forall N_t.\forall N_s.\\
\quad ((\mathit{keypair}\ \mathit{trudy}\ SK_t\ PK_t) \wedge (\mathit{knows}\ \mathit{trudy}_{\mathit{any_step}}\ PK) \wedge\\
\quad\ (((\mathit{knows}\ \mathit{trudy}\ N_t) \wedge (\mathit{knows}\ \mathit{trudy}\ N_s) \wedge\\
\qquad\quad (\mathit{knows}\ \mathit{trudy}\ M_1) \wedge (\mathit{knows}\ \mathit{trudy}\ M_2))\\
\qquad \supset ((\mathit{compose_msg}\ M) \wedge (\mathit{state}\ A\ B\ \mathit{trudy}_{i+1}\ (\mathit{enc}\ PK\ M)))))\\
\quad\ \supset (\mathit{state}\ A\ B\ \mathit{trudy}_i\ (\mathit{enc}\ PK_t\ \langle M_1, M_2\rangle)).
\end{array}$$

Similar rules can be given for atomic messages. We will call $\mathcal{I}$ the theory consisting of the previously described clauses. In order to test a protocol it also necessary to identify potential *violations*. Clearly, violations depend on the protocol taken into consideration. We will discuss how to specify them in *hhf* for our example.

5.1 Specifying the Attacks for Needham-Schroeder

As mentioned in Section 3, the goal of Alice and Bob is to learn the nonces N_a and N_b. What is the goal of Trudy the intruder? She would like to learn the nonces N_a and N_b without affecting the termination of the protocol, i.e., Alice and Bob should not realize that the intruder has intercepted their messages. Since the attack is valid only if the protocol succeeds for Bob, we proceed as follows. Let $\mathcal{PA}$ be the *hhf* theory obtained from the theory $\mathcal{P}$ of Section 4.2 extending the predicate *state* with the parameter Trudy (never modified). Then, we turn the termination clause of $\mathcal{P}$ into the following new one:

$$\begin{array}{l}
(\mathit{keypair}\ \mathit{bob}\ SK_b\ PK_b) \wedge (\mathit{knows}\ \mathit{bob}_0\ N_a) \wedge (\mathit{knows}\ \mathit{bob}_1\ N_b) \wedge\\
\quad (\mathit{knows}\ \mathit{alice}_0\ N_a) \wedge (\mathit{knows}\ \mathit{alice}_1\ N_b) \wedge\\
\qquad (\mathit{knows}\ \mathit{trudy}\ N_a) \wedge (\mathit{knows}\ \mathit{trudy}\ N_b)\\
\qquad\quad \supset (\mathit{state}\ \mathit{Alice}\ \mathit{bob}_1\ \mathit{Trudy}\ (\mathit{enc}\ PK_b\ N_b)).
\end{array}$$

Now, let $\mathcal{T} = \mathcal{PA} \cup \mathcal{I}$ ($\mathcal{I}$ is the intruder theory of Section 5). All derivations of the goal ($\mathit{initialize}\ \mathit{alice}\ \mathit{alice}_0\ \mathit{bob}\ \mathit{bob}_0\ \mathit{trudy}\ \mathit{trudy}_0$) (the natural extension of the initialization theory to the 3 agents case) correspond to all interleaving executions of the protocol and of the attacks of the intruder. Formally, if $\mathcal{T} \vdash (\mathit{initialize}\ \mathit{alice}\ \mathit{alice}_0\ \mathit{bob}\ \mathit{bob}_0\ \mathit{trudy}\ \mathit{trudy}_0)$ holds, then the intruder has a strategy to learn the nonces exchanged by Alice and Bob without influencing the termination of the Needham-Schroeder protocol. Since a priori we do not know how many actions are needed for the intruder to find the attack, we can fix a bound on the depth of the search (i.e. number of states) of the intruder, and iterate the execution of the goal *initialize* for increasing bounds. Clearly, this way we can only debug the protocol (if an attack exists we will find it).

$$((knows\_key\ trudy_0\ K) \wedge (knows\ trudy_0\ M) \wedge$$
$$(state\ Alice\ Bob\ (enc\ PK\ \langle M, K\rangle)\ Trudy))$$
$$\supset\ (chooseMsgKey\ Alice\ Bob\ Trudy\ PK).$$

$$((knows\ trudy_0\ M_1) \wedge (knows\ trudy_0\ M_2) \wedge$$
$$(state\ Alice\ Bob\ Trudy\ (enc\ PK\ \langle M_1, M_2\rangle)))$$
$$\supset\ (chooseMsgMsg\ Alice\ Bob\ Trudy\ PK).$$

Fig. 2. Generation of Trudy's messages.

6 Practical Experiments using λProlog

The *hhf* specification $\mathcal{T}$ we introduce in the previous sections can be directly turned into a λProlog program. Since the interpreter of λProlog uses an incomplete strategy to find refutations, in our experiments we avoid possible infinite derivations by considering intruders with four possible states ($trudy_0$ through $trudy_3$) and messages encoded by terms of depth one. Furthermore, to reduce the non-determinism of the intruder, we specialize the intruder theory in order to take into account the structure of messages exchanged by Alice and Bob in the protocol taken into consideration. For this purpose, we introduce a new predicate *knows_key* to store information about public keys. The specialization of the intruder theory is based on the following assumptions. Alice's first message contains a public-key. Trudy will probably try to susbtitute Alice's public-key with a key she has stored in a previous step. To create Trudy's messages we use two predicates *chooseMsgKey* and *chooseMsgMsg* defined in Fig. 2. The first predicate generates all possible pairs message-key whose components are known by the intruder. The second one generates all possible pairs message-message. The two predicates described above are incorporated into Trudy's theory as shown in Fig. 3. In order to debug the Needham-Schroeder protocol, we execute the goal

$$(initialize\ alice\ alice_0\ bob\ bob_0\ trudy\ trudy_0) \wedge fail,$$

where $fail$ is used to explore all alternatives in *backtracking*. All possible refutations of the first subgoal will result in strategies for Trudy to reach her goal. By including an auxiliary 'history' parameter, we automatically found two strategies for Trudy. The first strategy consists of the following

$$
\begin{array}{l}
\forall Nt.\\
\quad ((keypair\ trudy\ SK\ PK) \wedge (announce\ PK_B)\\
\quad\ (((knows\_key\ trudy_0\ PK) \wedge (knows\_key\ trudy_0\ PK_B) \wedge\\
\qquad (knows\_key\ trudy_0\ M_1) \wedge (knows\ trudy_0\ M_2) \wedge (knows\ trudy_0\ Nt))\\
\qquad\quad \supset (chooseMsgKey\ Alice\ Bob\ trudy_1\ PK_B)))\\
\qquad\qquad \supset\ (state\ Alice\ Bob\ trudy_0\ (enc\ PK\ \langle M1, M2\rangle)).
\end{array}
$$

$$
\begin{array}{l}
((keypair\ trudy\ SK\ PK) \wedge (knows\_key\ trudy_0\ PK_A) \wedge\\
\ (((knows\ trudy_0\ M_1) \wedge (knows\ trudy_0\ M_2))\\
\qquad \supset (chooseMsgMsg\ Alice\ Bob\ trudy_2\ PK_A)))\\
\qquad\quad \supset\ (state\ Alice\ Bob\ trudy_1\ (enc\ PK\ \langle M_1, M_2\rangle))).
\end{array}
$$

$$
\begin{array}{l}
((keypair\ trudy\ SK\ PK) \wedge (knows\_key\ trudy_0\ PK_B) \wedge\\
\quad ((knows\ trudy_0\ M)\ \ \supset\ \ (state\ Alice\ Bob\ trudy_3\ (enc\ PK_B\ M))))\\
\qquad\quad \supset\ (state\ Alice\ Bob\ trudy_2\ (enc\ PK\ M)).
\end{array}
$$

Fig. 3. Specialized Trudy's theory.

steps.

$$
\begin{array}{lll}
1.\ Alice & \rightarrow Trudy : & \{N_a, K_a\}_{K_t}\\
2.\ Trudy & \rightarrow Bob : & \{N_t, K_t\}_{K_b}\\
3.\ Bob & \rightarrow Trudy : & \{N_t, N_b\}_{K_t}\\
4.\ Trudy & \rightarrow Alice : & \{N_a, N_b\}_{K_a}\\
5.\ Alice & \rightarrow Trudy : & \{N_b\}_{K_t}\\
6.\ Trudy & \rightarrow Bob : & \{N_b\}_{K_b}
\end{array}
$$

This strategy corresponds to the one found by Lowe in [Low96]. Here Alice first contacts Trudy instead of Bob. At this point, Trudy opens a new session with Bob. Alice and Bob exchange the secret numbers and conclude the protocol successfully. However, Trudy learns all the secret information. In the second strategy we found, Trudy does not open a connection as a 'normal' agent (i.e. creating a new nonce etc). It simply passes the nonce he got from Alice to Bob. More precisely, the second strategy consists of the following steps.

$$
\begin{array}{lll}
1.\ Alice & \rightarrow Trudy : & \{N_a, K_a\}_{K_t}\\
2.\ Trudy & \rightarrow Bob : & \{N_a, K_t\}_{K_b}\\
3.\ Bob & \rightarrow Trudy : & \{N_a, N_b\}_{K_t}\\
4.\ Trudy & \rightarrow Alice : & \{N_a, N_b\}_{K_a}\\
5.\ Alice & \rightarrow Trudy : & \{N_b\}_{K_t}\\
6.\ Trudy & \rightarrow Bob : & \{N_b\}_{K_b}
\end{array}
$$

The λProlog code of the protocol specification is available at the following URL: http://www.disi.unige.it/person/DelzannoG/.

7 Related Works

In the last years many works have been devoted to the analysis of security protocols. Besides case-studies like [Low96], many efforts have been spent in order to find appropriate logics [BAN90,Mas99], languages [CDL+99,DY83], and tools [CJM98,CJM00,Mea96], to face the problem of protocol validation in a general way. In the seminal work [BAN90], Burrows, Abadi and Needham invented the logic BAN to reason about security. The logic provides constructs to specify beliefs of agents and to describe their modification as an effect of the interaction with the environment. Being a specialized logic, BAN is a very rich specification language, that however does not have an immediate operational reading. Recently, Cervesato et al. [CDL+99,CDKS00,CDL+00] have studied and compared several models (including Dolev-Yao [DY83]) with specification languages closer to the logic programming perspective, i.e., enjoying a simple procedural view. In [CDL+99] (an important inspiration for our experiments) Cervesato et al. showed that *multiset rewriting systems* enriched with a mechanism for handling the generation of new names (universal quantification) is a suitable formalism to model several security protocols in a uniform way. The logic underlying the language is Girard's linear logic [Gir87]. Differently from our encoding, in [CDL+99] the information of an individual agent is encoded *inside* atomic predicates (like $bob(key_{pr}, key_{pb}, key_{alice}, \ldots)$), and updated via rewriting steps. With our work, we have tried to show that ideas coming from intuitionistic logic could be useful as well in this setting. In particular, we have used embedded implications in order to model in an elegant way the update of knowledge. This way, implications in goal formulas can be viewed as a built-in operator whose semantics is described by the underlying logical system.

8 Conclusions and Future Work

The more important restriction we had to face while experimenting the specification of the Needham-Schroeder protocol in λProlog was on the number of *players* involved in the game. (In many practical cases it is in fact possible to put bounds on the depth of messages [BAN90,CDL+99]). While it is relatively simple to handle a finite number of agents, it is not clear yet if the same ideas could be applied to the general case of a multi-agent communication protocol. An interesting direction could be the use of a combination of aspects of linear and intuitionistic logic, achieved in languages like Forum [Mil96]. In this setting it could be possible to specify *locally* the actions of single agents (as in [CDL+99]), whereas the knowledge common to all agents could still be modeled using the 'intuitionistic component' of Forum. Without fixing the number of principals in the initial stage of the protocol, it could still be very difficult to use the resulting specification for debugging. To attack this problem, in our opinion there are at least two interesting directions to investigate.

The first one is the use of a meta-logic to reason about specifications in languages like *hhf* and Forum. Embedding the logic specification within a meta-logic like the one described in [MM97] could give in fact a further tool in order to study intensional properties (i.e., that do not require an explicit state exploration [CJM98]) of security protocols.

The other direction concerns alternative execution models for (linear logic and/or intuitionistic-based) specifications that do not require to fix an initial state (i.e. that work independently by the number of agents in the system). Bottom-up evaluation of logic programs and linear logic programs (see e.g. [BDM00,BDM01,Hui92]) could be a potentially interesting tool for achieving this goal.

Acknoledgements. The author would like to thank the anonymous referees for their usefule suggestions that helped us to improve the presentation.

References

[BDM00] M. Bozzano, G. Delzanno, and M. Martelli. A Bottom-up semantics for Linear Logic Programs. In *Proc. PPDP'00*, page 92-102, 2000.

[BDM01] M. Bozzano, G. Delzanno, and M. Martelli. An Effective Bottom-up Semantics for First-Order Linear Logic Programs. To appear in *Proc. FLOPS 2001*, March 2001.

[BAN90] M. Burrows, M. Abadi, R. M. Needham. A Logic of Authentication. TOCS 8(1): 18-36, 1990.

[CDL+99] I. Cervesato, N. Durgin, P. Lincoln, J. Mitchell, and A. Scedrov. A Meta-Notation for Protocol Analysis. In *Proc. Computer Security Foundations Workshop CSFW'99*, pages 28-30, 1999.

[CDKS00] I. Cervesato, N. Durgin, M. Kanovich, and A. Scedrov. Interpreting Strands in Linear Logic In *Proc. of Formal Methods and Computer Security FMCS'00*, 2000.

[CDL+00] I. Cervesato, N. Durgin, P. Lincoln, J. Mitchell, and A. Scedrov. Relating Strands and Multiset Rewriting for Security Protocol Analysis. In *Proc. of Computer Security Foundations Workshop CSFW'00*, pages 35-51, 2000.

[CJM98] E. Clarke, S. Jha, W. Marrero. Using State Space Exploration and a Natural Deduction Style Message Derivation Engine to Verify Security Protocols. In *Proc. of PRO-COMET'98*, 1998.

[CJM00] E. Clarke, S. Jha, W. Marrero. Partial Order Reductions for Security Protocol Verification. In *Proc. of TACAS 2000*, pages 503-518, LNCS 1785, 2000.

[DY83] D. Dolev and A. Yao. On the Security pf Public-key Protocols. IEEE Transactions on Information Theory, 2(29), 1983.

[Gir87] J.Y. Girard. Linear logic. *Theoretical Computer Science*, 50:1–102, 1987.

[HM94] J. Hodas and D. Miller. Logic Programming in a Fragment of Intuitionistic Linear Logic. *Information and Computation*, 110(2):327–365, 1994.

[Hui92] A. Hui Bon Hoa. A Bottom-Up Interpreter for a Higher-Order Logic Programming Language. In *Proc. PLILP 1992*, pages 326-340, LNCS 631, 1992.

[Low96] G. Lowe. Breaking and Fixing the Needham-Schroeder Public-key Protocol usinmg CSP and FDR. In *Proc. TACAS'96*, page 147-166, LNCS 1055, 1996.

[Mas99] F. Massacci. Automated Reasoning and the Verification of Security Protocols In *Proc. of TABLEAUX '99*, pages 32-33, LNAI 1617, 1999.

[Mea96] C. Meadows. The NRL Protocol Analyzer: An Overview. JLP 26(2): 113-131, 1996.

[MM97] R. McDowell, D. Miller. A Logic for Reasoning with Higher-Order Abstract Syntax. In *Proc. LICS '97*, pages 434-445, 1997.

[Mil89] D. Miller. Lexical Scoping as Universal Quantification. In *Proc. ICLP '89*, pages 268-283, 1989.

[Mil89b] D. Miller. A Logical Analysis of Modules in Logic Programming. JLP 6(1&2): 79-108, 1989.

[Mil96] D. Miller. Forum: A Multiple-Conclusion Specification Logic. *Theoretical Computer Science*, 165(1):201–232, 1996.

[MNPS91] D. Miller, G. Nadathur, F. Pfenning, and A. Scedrov. Uniform Proofs as a Foundation for Logic Programming. *Annals of Pure and Applied Logic*, 51:125–157, 1991.

[NM88] G. Nadathur and D. Miller. An Overview of λ-Prolog. In *Proc. of ILPS/SLP '88*, pages 810-827, 1988.

[NM99] G. Nadathur, D. J. Mitchell. System Description: Teyjus - A Compiler and Abstract Machine Based Implementation of lambda-Prolog. In *Proc CADE'99*, LNCS 1632, pages 287-291, 1999.

[NS78] R. M. Needham and M. D. Schroeder. Using Encryption for Authentication in Large Networks of Computers. CACM 21(12): 993-999, 1978.

An Effective Bottom-Up Semantics for First-Order Linear Logic Programs

Marco Bozzano, Giorgio Delzanno, and Maurizio Martelli

Dipartimento di Informatica e Scienze dell'Informazione
Università di Genova
Via Dodecaneso 35, 16146 Genova - Italy
{bozzano,giorgio,martelli}@disi.unige.it

Abstract. We study the connection between algorithmic techniques for symbolic model checking [ACJT96,FS98,AJ99], and declarative and operational aspects of linear logic programming [And92,AP90]. Specifically, we show that the construction used to decide verification problems for Timed Petri Nets [AJ99] can be used to define a new fixpoint semantics for the fragment of linear logic called LO [AP90]. The fixpoint semantics is based on an effective T_P operator. As an alternative to traditional top-down approaches [And92,AP90,APC93], the effective fixpoint operator can be used to define a bottom-up evaluation procedure for first-order linear logic programs.

1 Introduction

Since its introduction in [Gir87], linear logic has been understood as a framework to reason about concurrent computations. Several researcher have in fact observed the existence of natural connections between linear logic and the theory of Petri Nets, see e.g., [Cer95,Kan94,MM91]. In this work we will investigate this connection focusing on the relations between algorithmic techniques used for the analysis of Petri Nets and provability in fragments of linear logic. The fragment we consider in this paper is called LO [AP90]. LO was originally introduced as a theoretical foundation for extensions of *logic programming* languages [And92]. As we will show next, LO programs enjoy a simple operational reading that makes clear the connection between provability in linear logic and verification methods in Petri Nets. Let us illustrate these ideas with the help of some examples.

Petri Nets in Propositional Linear Logic. Following [MM91], a Petri Net can be represented as a multiset-rewriting system over a finite alphabet $p, q, r, \ldots$ of *place* names. Among several possible ways, multiset rewrite rules can be expressed in linear logic using the connectives $\parr$ (multiplicative disjunction), and $\multimapinv$ (reversed linear implication). Multiplicative disjunction plays the role of multiset constructor, whereas linear implication can be used to define rewriting rules. Both connectives are allowed in the fragment LO. For instance, as shown in [Cer95] the LO clause

$$p \parr q \multimapinv p \parr p \parr q \parr t$$

H. Kuchen and K. Ueda (Eds.): FLOPS 2001, LNCS 2024, pp. 138–152, 2001.

can be viewed as a Petri Net *transition* that removes a token from places p and q and puts two tokens in place p, one in q, and one in t. Being a first-order language and thanks to the presence of other connectives, LO supports more sophisticated specifications than Petri Nets. For instance, Andreoli and Pareschi used LO clauses with occurrences of $\parr$ and & (additive conjunction) in their *body* to express what they called *external* and *internal* concurrency [AP90].

In our previous work [BDM00], we have defined an effective procedure to evaluate bottom-up LO propositional programs. Our construction is based on the *backward reachability* algorithm of [ACJT96] used to decide the so called *control state reachability problem* of Petri Nets (i.e. the problem of deciding if a given set of configurations are reachable from an initial one). The algorithm of [ACJT96] works as follows. Starting from a set of *target states*, the algorithm computes symbolically the transitive closure of the *predecessor* relation of the Petri Net taken into consideration (predecessor relation=transition relation read backwards). The algorithm is used to check safety properties: if the algorithm is executed starting from the set of *unsafe states*, the corresponding safety property holds if and only if the initial marking is not in the resulting fixpoint.

In order to illustrate the connection between backward reachability for Petri Nets and provability in LO, we first observe that LO clauses like

$$A_1 \parr \ldots \parr A_n \multimapinv \top$$

plays the same role that *facts* (unit clauses) do in logic programming. In fact, when applied in a resolution step, they generate instances of the LO axiom associated to the connective $\top$ (one of the logic constants of linear logic). Now, suppose we represent a Petri Net via an LO program P and the set of *target states* using a collection of LO facts T. Then, the set of *logical consequences* of the LO program $P \cup T$ will represent the set markings that are backward reachable from the target states. The algorithm we presented in [BDM00] is based on this idea, and it extends the backward reachability algorithm for Petri Nets of [ACJT96] to the more general case of propositional LO programs. This connection can be extended to more sophisticated classes of Petri Nets, as we discuss next.

Timed Petri Nets in First-Order Linear Logic. In Timed Petri Nets [AJ99], each token carries along its age. Furthermore, transitions are guarded by conditions over the age of tokens. To model the age of each token we can lift the specification in linear logic from the propositional to the first-order case. Basically, we can use an atomic formula $p(n)$ to model a token in place p with age n. For instance, the first-order linear logic rule (where for convenience, we use $\ldots \,\Box\, c$ to denote a *constrained* formula in the style of Constraint Logic Programming [JM94])

$$p(X) \parr p(Y) \multimapinv r(Z) \,\Box\, X \leq 1,\ Y \geq 2,\ Z \geq 1$$

can be read as a *discrete transition* of the Timed Petri Nets of [AJ99] that removes a token from place p if its *age* is less equal than 1, a token from place p

if and only if its *age* is greater or equal than 2, and adds a token with age greater or equal than 1 to place r. The previous clause can be seen as a compact way for expressing an infinite set of clauses (one for every evaluation of the variables which satisfies the constraints).

Recent results [ACJT96,AJ99] show that the *control state reachability problem*, under suitable hypothesis, is still decidable for Timed Petri Nets. The problem can be solved using the *backward reachability algorithm* of [ACJT96] in combination with a symbolic representation of sets of global states of Timed Petri Net via the so called *existential regions* [AJ99]. Now, can we exploit the results of [AJ99] for first-order (or even better, constrained) LO programs?

Our Contribution. In this paper we will show that it is possible to extend the parallel between the results on Petri Nets and provability in propositional LO, to new results relating Timed Petri Nets and provability in first-order LO. Specifically, we define a bottom-up fixpoint semantics for first-order LO programs (actually, we will consider the more general case of LO programs with constraints) using a *generalization* of the backward reachability algorithm for Timed Petri Nets of [AJ99]. Our procedure is a generalization in the following sense: we abstract away from the specific domain of Timed Petri Nets (e.g. where constraints are the *clock constraint* of [AJ99]); we handle the entire class of first-order LO programs (i.e. with nested occurrences of $\parr$ and & in the body of clauses). The resulting fixpoint semantics is based on an *effective* fixpoint operator and on a *symbolic* and *finite* representation of potentially infinite collections of first-order provable LO (atomic) goals. The termination of the fixpoint computation cannot be guaranteed in general, first-order LO programs are in fact Turing complete. As a consequence of the results in [AJ99,AN00], for a class of first-order LO programs that includes the *discrete component* of the Timed Petri Nets of [AJ99] the fixpoint semantics can be computed in finitely many steps.

Besides the relationships with Petri Nets, the new fixpoint semantics for first-order LO programs represents an interesting alternative to the traditional top-down semantics for linear logic programs studied in the literature [And92,AP90]. Our construction gives in fact an effective (though not complete) algorithm for the bottom-up evaluation of LO programs. Thus, also from the point-of-view of logic programming, we extend the applicability of our previous work [BDM00] (that was restricted to the propositional case) towards more interesting classes of linear logic programs.

Plan of the paper. After introducing some notations in Section 2, in Section 3 we present the language LO [AP90] enriched with constraints. In Section 4, we briefly review the approach we followed in [BDM00], and we extend it to the first-order case. In Section 5 we discuss the connection between LO fixpoint semantics and the reachability algorithm for Timed Petri Nets presented in [AJ99]. Finally, we discuss related work and conclusions in Sections 6 and 7. The proofs of all results are in the extended version of the paper [BDM00a].

2 Preliminaries and Notation

In this paper we will consider first-order linear logic languages built upon a signature Σ comprising a finite set of term constructors, a finite set of predicate symbols, and a denumerable set of variable symbols. We will denote term constructors by $a, b, \ldots, f, g, \ldots$, predicate symbols by $p, q, r, \ldots$, and variables by $X, Y, Z, \ldots$. The set of (possibly non ground) atoms over Σ will be denoted A_Σ. We will use $\mathcal{A}, \mathcal{B}, \mathcal{C}, \ldots$ to denote multisets of (possibly non ground) atoms. We denote a multiset $\mathcal{A}$ with (possibly duplicated) elements $A_1, \ldots, A_n$ by $\{A_1, \ldots, A_n\}$ or simply $A_1, \ldots, A_n$ if this notation is not ambiguous. A multiset $\mathcal{A}$ is uniquely determined by a finite map Occ from A_Σ to the set of natural numbers, such that $Occ_{\mathcal{A}}(A)$ is the number of occurrences of A in $\mathcal{A}$. The *multiset inclusion* relation $\preccurlyeq$ is defined as follows: $\mathcal{A} \preccurlyeq \mathcal{B}$ iff $Occ_{\mathcal{A}}(A) \leq Occ_{\mathcal{B}}(A)$ for every A. The *empty* multiset is denoted ϵ and is such that $Occ_\epsilon(A) = 0$ for every A (clearly, $\epsilon \preccurlyeq \mathcal{A}$ for any $\mathcal{A}$). The *multiset union* $\mathcal{A}, \mathcal{B}$ (written $\mathcal{A} + \mathcal{B}$ when ',' is ambiguous) of $\mathcal{A}$ and $\mathcal{B}$ is such that $Occ_{\mathcal{A},\mathcal{B}}(A) = Occ_{\mathcal{A}}(A) + Occ_{\mathcal{B}}(A)$ for every A. The *multiset difference* $\mathcal{A} \setminus \mathcal{B}$ is such that $Occ_{\mathcal{A}\setminus\mathcal{B}}(A) = max(0, Occ_{\mathcal{A}}(A) - Occ_{\mathcal{B}}(A))$ for every A. Finally, we define an operation $\bullet$ to compute the *least upper bound* of two multisets with respect to $\preccurlyeq$. Namely, $\mathcal{A} \bullet \mathcal{B}$ is such that $Occ_{\mathcal{A}\bullet\mathcal{B}}(A) = max(Occ_{\mathcal{A}}(A), Occ_{\mathcal{B}}(A))$ for every A.

In the rest of the paper we will use $\Delta, \Theta, \ldots$ to denote multisets of possibly compound formulas. Given two multisets Δ and Θ, $\Delta \preccurlyeq \Theta$ indicates multiset inclusion and Δ, Θ multiset union, as before, and $\Delta, \{G\}$ is written simply Δ, G. In the following, we will refer to a multiset of goal-formulas as a *context*. Given a linear disjunction of atomic formulas $H = A_1 \parr \ldots \parr A_n$, we also introduce the notation $\widehat{H}$ to denote the multiset $A_1, \ldots, A_n$.

3 The Language LO Enriched with Constraints

LO [AP90] is a logic programming language based on a fragment of linear logic defined over the linear connectives $\multimapinv$, $\&$, $\parr$, and $\top$. In this paper we will present a first-order formulation of LO using *constraints*. We will use constraints as a means to *represent concisely collections of ground program clauses* defined over a parametric interpretation domain.

Constraints. Let $\mathcal{V}$ be a denumerable set of variables. In this paper a *constraint* is a conjunction (in the 'classical' sense) of atomic predicates $c_1 \wedge \ldots \wedge c_n$, where c_i has variables from $\mathcal{V}$. The interpretation domain $\mathcal{D}$ of the constraints is fixed a priori. As an example, linear arithmetic constraints are conjunctions of inequalities of the form $k_1X_1 + \ldots + k_nX_n$ op k, where k_i is an integer constant, X_i is a variable that ranges over integer (real) numbers for all $i : 1, \ldots, n$, op is one operator taken from $\leq, \geq, <, >, =$, and k is an integer constant (e.g., $2X + 3X \geq 1 \wedge X \geq 0 \wedge Y \geq 0$). An *evaluation* is an assignment σ which maps variables in $\mathcal{V}$ to values in $\mathcal{D}$. We denote the result of applying an evaluation σ to a constraint c by $\sigma(c)$. A *solution* for a constraint c is an evaluation σ such that $\sigma(c)$ is true. Note that values assigned to variables which do not appear in c can be disregarded. For instance, any evaluation which maps X to 0.5, Y to 2 and Z to 1.7 is a solution for the constraint (over the real numbers) $X \leq 1 \wedge Y \geq 2 \wedge Z \geq 1$. We call $Sol(c)$ the set of solutions of c. In this paper we will always consider a constraint language with equality, so that $t_1 = t_2$ is always defined for any expression t_1, t_2. This property ensures that it is always possible to express *unification constraints*. Given two constraints c_1 and c_2, we define

$$c_1 \textbf{ entails } c_2 \text{ if and only if } Sol(c_1) \subseteq Sol(c_2)$$

(e.g. $X = 2$ **entails** $X \geq 2$). In this paper we will limit ourselves to consider domains in which the relation **entails** is *decidable*, and there are two constraints *true* and *false* such that c **entails** *true*, and *false* **entails** c for any c.

Multisets Unifiers. Let $\mathcal{A} = p_1(\mathbf{x_1}), \ldots, p_n(\mathbf{x_n})$ and $\mathcal{B} = q_1(\mathbf{y_1}), \ldots, q_n(\mathbf{y_n})$ be two multisets of atomic formulas such that $\mathbf{x_i}$ and $\mathbf{y_i}$ are vectors of variables (distinct from each other) for $i : 1, \ldots, n$. If $p_i = q_i$ (and they have the same arity) for $i : 1, \ldots, n$, then the two multisets are *unifiable*. The resulting unifier will be the constraint $\mathbf{x_1} = \mathbf{y_1} \wedge \ldots \wedge \mathbf{x_n} = \mathbf{y_n}$. Since the order of atoms inside a multiset does not count, there can be more than one way for two multisets to be unified. In the following, we will use the notation $\mathcal{A} = \mathcal{B}$ to denote one constraint which is *non-deterministically* selected from the set of unifiers of $\mathcal{A}$ and $\mathcal{B}$. If there are no permutations of one of the two multisets such that the previous conditions are satisfied, then $\mathcal{A} = \mathcal{B}$ will denote the constraint *false*. Finally, in case $n = 0$ we have the constraint $\epsilon = \epsilon$ which stands for *true*.

LO Programs. We first define a *goal* formula via the following grammar.

$$G ::= G \invamp G \mid G \,\&\, G \mid p(\mathbf{x}) \mid \top.$$

Here $\mathbf{x}$ is a vector of variables from the set $\mathcal{V}$. An LO program with constraints consists of a set of universally quantified formulas having the following form:

$$A_1 \invamp \ldots \invamp A_n \multimapinv G \,\Box\, c,$$

where $n \geq 1$, $A_i = p_i(\mathbf{x_i})$ for $i : 1, \ldots, n$, and $\mathbf{x_i}$ is a vector of variables in $\mathcal{V}$, G is a goal formula, and c is a constraint whose *scope* extends over the whole implication $A_1 \invamp \ldots \invamp A_n \multimapinv G$. Note that we assume that all compound terms occur in c. For instance, using constraints we would write the first-order LO clause $p(f(X)) \multimapinv q(X)$ as $p(Y) \multimapinv q(X) \,\Box\, Y = f(X)$. Given a constrained expression $F \,\Box\, c$ (F can be a clause, a goal, a multiset of atoms, etc.) we define

$$Gnd(F \,\Box\, c) = \{\sigma(F) \mid \sigma \in Sol(c)\}.$$

We say that $A \in Gnd(F \,\Box\, c)$ is an *instance* of $F \,\Box\, c$. The definition can be extended to sets of expressions in the canonical way. Thus, given a program P, $Gnd(P)$ denotes the set of all instances of clauses in P. Furthermore, note that a G-formula by itself is not very interesting, whereas *constrained goals* like $p(X) \,\&\, q(Y) \,\Box\, X - Y \geq 1$ are the counterpart of the goals of Constraint Logic Programming [JM94].

$$\frac{}{P \Rightarrow \top, \Delta}\ \top_r \qquad \frac{P \Rightarrow G_1, G_2, \Delta}{P \Rightarrow G_1 \parr G_2, \Delta}\ \parr_r \qquad \frac{P \Rightarrow G_1, \Delta \quad P \Rightarrow G_2, \Delta}{P \Rightarrow G_1 \,\&\, G_2, \Delta}\ \&_r$$

$$\frac{P \Rightarrow G, \mathcal{A}}{P \Rightarrow \widehat{H}, \mathcal{A}}\ bc \text{ provided } H \multimapinv G \in Gnd(P)$$

Fig. 1. Proof system for LO.

Example 1. Let $C = p(X,Y) \parr q(Z) \multimapinv t(Z,Y) \,\Box\, X = f(Z)$. If we interpret constraints over the term algebra $\{a, f(a), \ldots\}$, then $p(f(a), a) \parr q(a) \multimapinv t(a,a) \in Gnd(C)$.

Top-down Ground Semantics. We define the *top-down* operational semantics of LO with constraints using the *uniform* (goal-driven) proof system of [AP90], presented in Fig. 1. As said at the beginning of this section, we introduce constraints just as a convenient means to represent sets of ground clauses, therefore the proof system of [AP90] is sufficient for our purposes. In Fig.1, P is a set of implicational clauses, $\mathcal{A}$ denotes a multiset of atomic formulas, whereas Δ denotes a multiset of G-formulas. A sequent is provable if all branches of its proof tree terminate with instances of the $\top_r$ axiom. The proof system of Fig. 1 is a specialization of more general uniform proof systems for linear logic like Andreoli's focusing proofs [And92], and Forum [Mil96]. The rule bc denotes a backchaining (resolution) step. Note that bc can be executed only if the right-hand side of the current LO sequent consists of atomic formulas. Thus, LO clauses behave like *multiset* rewriting rules. LO clauses having the form $H \multimapinv \top \,\Box\, c$, where c is a satisfiable constraint, play the same role as the unit clauses of Horn programs. In fact, a backchaining step over these clauses *succeeds* independently of the current context. This observation shows that the *weakening* rule is *admissible* in LO, i.e., if $P \Rightarrow \Delta$ is provable, then $P \Rightarrow \Delta'$ is provable for any $\Delta \preccurlyeq \Delta'$. Finally, the *success set* or *operational semantics* of a (ground) LO program P is defined as

$$O(P) = \{\mathcal{A} \mid \mathcal{A} \textit{ is a ground multiset and } P \Rightarrow \mathcal{A} \textit{ is provable}\}.$$

Remark 1 (Interpretation of constraints and $\Box$ in Linear Logic.). At least in principle, it seems possible to model constrained LO clauses inside linear logic itself. For this purpose, however, we need fragments larger than LO. In presence of the connective $\otimes$, the constrained LO formula

$$H \multimapinv G \,\Box\, c_1 \wedge \ldots \wedge c_n$$

could be represented as the linear logic formula

$$H \multimapinv (G \otimes (c_1 \otimes \ldots \otimes c_n)),$$

while provability of constraint formulas could be expressed using a specialized (linear logic) theory.

Bottom-Up Ground Semantics. In [BDM00], we have defined a ground fixpoint semantics based on a new fixpoint operator T_P for LO programs. We recall here the main ideas (see [BDM00] for the details). Given a finite alphabet of propositional atoms (symbols), the (ground) Herbrand base B_P is defined as

$$B_P = \{\mathcal{A} \mid \mathcal{A} \text{ is a ground multiset of atoms in P}\}.$$

We say that $I \subseteq B_P$ is a Herbrand interpretation. Herbrand interpretations form a complete lattice wrt set inclusion. Satisfiability of a context (i.e. a multiset of goals) Δ in a given interpretation I, is defined via the judgment $I \models \Delta[\mathcal{A}]$. Let us assume that I is a set of provable multisets. Then, the *output* $\mathcal{A}$ of the judgment $I \models \Delta[\mathcal{A}]$ is any multiset of *resources* such that $\Delta + \mathcal{A}$ is provable.

Definition 1 (Ground Satisfiability). *Let $I \subseteq B_P$, then $\models$ is defined as follows:*

$$I \models \top, \mathcal{A}[\mathcal{A}'] \textit{ for any ground multiset } \mathcal{A}';$$

$$I \models \mathcal{A}[\mathcal{A}'] \textit{ if } \mathcal{A} + \mathcal{A}' \in I;$$

$$I \models G_1 \mathbin{⅋} G_2, \Delta[\mathcal{A}] \textit{ if } I \models G_1, G_2, \Delta[\mathcal{A}];$$

$$I \models G_1 \,\&\, G_2, \Delta[\mathcal{A}] \textit{ if } I \models G_1, \Delta[\mathcal{A}] \textit{ and } I \models G_2, \Delta[\mathcal{A}].$$

Given a program P, the operator T_P for constrained LO programs is defined as follows:

$$T_P(I) = \{\widehat{H} + \mathcal{A} \mid H \mathrel{\circ\!-} G \in Gnd(P),\ I \models G[\mathcal{A}]\}.$$

The fixpoint semantics, defined as the least fixpoint of T_P, is sound and complete with respect to the operational semantics, as stated in the following theorem.

Theorem 1 ([BDM00]). *For every LO program P, $O(P) = lfp(T_P)$.*

4 Towards an Effective Non-ground Semantics

The bottom-up ground semantics for first-order LO is not effective for two different reasons: there might be possibly infinite instantiations of a constrained LO clause (this makes the condition $H \mathrel{\circ\!-} G \in Gnd(P)$ not effective); there are infinitely many *output* contexts in a satisfiability judgment (this makes the computation of $I \models \Delta\ [\mathcal{A}]$ not effective). In [BDM00], we have shown how to circumvent the second problem in the propositional case.

Propositional Case. By exploiting the fact that *weakening* is admissible in LO, in [BDM00] we noted that a provable multiset $\mathcal{A}$ can be used to implicitly represent the set of provable multisets $Up(\mathcal{A}) = \{\mathcal{B} \mid \mathcal{A} \preccurlyeq \mathcal{B}\}$ where $\preccurlyeq$ is multiset inclusion, i.e., $Up(\mathcal{A})$ is the *ideal* generated by $\mathcal{A}$ wrt $\preccurlyeq$. As in the ground semantics, interpretations are still collections of multisets, however the denotation of an interpretation I becomes now $[\![I]\!] = \bigcup_{\mathcal{A}\in I} Up(\mathcal{A})$. Since multiset inclusion is a well-quasi ordering [ACJT96], the termination of the fixpoint computation is guaranteed by choosing the following *pointwise* ordering of interpretations:

$$I \sqsubseteq J \text{ iff } \forall\ \mathcal{A} \in I\ \exists\ \mathcal{B} \in J\ \mathcal{B} \preccurlyeq \mathcal{A}.$$

Note that, $\mathcal{A} \preccurlyeq \mathcal{B}$ implies $Up(\mathcal{B}) \subseteq Up(\mathcal{A})$, whereas $I \sqsubseteq J$ implies $[\![I]\!] \subseteq [\![J]\!]$. The property of being a well-quasi order can be lifted from $\preccurlyeq$ to $\sqsubseteq$. Based on this observation, it is possible to define an *effective* operator whose fixpoint is computable in finitely many steps (see [BDM00] for its definition). In the following section we will lift these ideas to first-order programs.

First-Order Case. In view of our main goal (the definition of an effective fixpoint semantics for first order LO), we first define a new notion of Herbrand interpretation based on the notion of *constrained multiset.* Constrained multisets will be our *symbolic representation* of sets of ground multisets. A constrained multiset $\mathcal{A} \;\Box\; c$ is a multiset of atomic formulas $\mathcal{A}$ whose free variables are constrained by c, e.g., like $p(X), q(Y) \;\Box\; X \geq Y$ (Note that the whole multiset is in the scope of the constraint). Variables which appear in c but not in $\mathcal{A}$ are *implicitly* considered *existentially* quantified, i.e. for instance $p(X), q(Y) \;\Box\; X \geq Y \wedge Y = Z$ is logically equivalent to $p(X), q(Y) \;\Box\; \exists Z.(X \geq Y \wedge Y = Z)$. In the following. we will use $\mathbf{M}, \mathbf{N}, \ldots$ to denote constrained multisets. Now, we extend the ideas used in the propositional case as follows. A constrained multiset $\mathbf{M}$ defined as $\mathcal{A} \;\Box\; c$ will represent the collection of provable goals that satisfy *at least* the constraint (wrt the multiset component $\mathcal{A}$ and the constraint part c) imposed by $\mathbf{M}$. Formally,

$$[\![\mathcal{A} \;\Box\; c]\!] = Up(Gnd(\mathcal{A} \;\Box\; c)),$$

the denotations are defined by taking first all instances of $\mathcal{A} \;\Box\; c$, and then (as in the propositional case) taking their upward closure wrt $\preccurlyeq$. As an example, the denotation (over the real numbers) of $\mathbf{M} = (p(X), q(Y) \Box X \geq Y)$ contains both $\{p(1), q(0)\}$ and $\{p(1), q(0), q(9)\}$, since they both satisfy *at least* the constraint in $\mathbf{M}$. We are now ready to define the new notion of interpretation.

Definition 2 (Extended Herbrand Base and Interpretations). *The extended base is defined as* $B_P = \{\ \mathcal{A} \;\Box\; c \mid \mathcal{A}$ *is a multiset of atoms* $p(\mathbf{x})$, c *is a constraint* $\}$. $I \subseteq B_P$ *is called extended Herbrand interpretation and*

$$[\![I]\!] = \bigcup_{(\mathcal{A} \;\Box\; c) \in I} [\![\mathcal{A} \;\Box\; c]\!].$$

Definition 3 (Lattice of Interpretations). *The lattice* $\langle \mathcal{I}, \sqsubseteq \rangle$ *of extended Herbrand interpretations is defined as follows:*

- $\mathcal{I} = \mathcal{P}(B_P)/\simeq$ *where* $I \simeq J$ *if and only if* $[\![I]\!] = [\![J]\!]$;
- $[I]_{\simeq} \sqsubseteq [J]_{\simeq}$ *if and only if* $[\![I]\!] \subseteq [\![J]\!]$;
- *the bottom element is the empty set* $\emptyset$, *the top element is the* $\simeq$*-equivalence class of the singleton* $\{(\epsilon \;\Box\; true)\}$;
- *the least upper bound* $I \sqcup J$ *is the* $\simeq$*-equivalence class of* $I \cup J$.

The equivalence $\simeq$ allows us to reason modulo *redundancies.* For the sake of simplicity, in the rest of the paper we will identify an interpretation I with its class $[I]_{\simeq}$. In the following, we will lift the fixpoint semantics from the propositional to the first-order case using the new notion of interpretation. To this aim, we will first need an effective notion of satisfiability wrt an interpretation.

4.1 Effective Satisfiability Test

To decide if a given constrained goal $G \,\Box\, c$ is satisfiable in the extended interpretation I, we must extend the judgments used in the propositional case in order to handle the constraint components. Since G may contain nested occurrences of connectives, it might be necessary to decompose G into a multiset of atoms $\mathcal{A}$ and then match $\mathcal{A}$ against I. The last step may introduce new *bindings* for the variables in G. We must return these bindings in form of constraints, since they will be used when incorporated in the backward application of a clause $H \multimapinv G$ (e.g., whenever H and G share common variables). For this purpose, we introduce the new judgment

$$I \Vdash \mathbf{G}\ [\mathcal{C}\ ;\ c]$$

where $\mathbf{G}$ is a constrained goal (later extended to a constrained multiset of goals), $\mathcal{C}$ is the output multiset (as in the propositional case) and c is the output constraint. The judgment $I \Vdash \mathbf{G}\ [\mathcal{C}\ ;\ c]$ should return in $\mathcal{C}$ a representation of all possible multisets which, added to $\mathbf{G}$, make it provable (under the constraint c). Based on the previous intuition, we will formally define the satisfiability relation as follows. In the following the notation $G, \Delta \,\Box\, c$ must be read as $(G, \Delta) \,\Box\, c$.

Definition 4 (Non-ground Satisfiability Relation $\Vdash$). *Let $I \in \mathcal{I}$, then $\Vdash$ is defined as follows:*

ALL $\quad I \Vdash \top, \mathcal{A} \,\Box\, c\ [\epsilon\ ;\ c]$;

PAR $\quad I \Vdash G_1 \invamp G_2, \Delta \,\Box\, c\ [\mathcal{C}\ ;\ c']$ *if and only if* $I \Vdash G_1, G_2, \Delta \,\Box\, c\ [\mathcal{C}\ ;\ c']$;

MULT $\quad I \Vdash \mathcal{A} \,\Box\, c\ [\mathcal{C}\ ;\ c']$ *if and only if there exists a renamed copy* $\mathcal{B} \,\Box\, d$ *of an element of* I, $\mathcal{B}' \preccurlyeq \mathcal{B}$, *and* $\mathcal{A}' \preccurlyeq \mathcal{A}$ *such that* $c' \equiv \mathcal{B}' = \mathcal{A}' \wedge c \wedge d$ *is satisfiable, and* $\mathcal{C} = \mathcal{B} \setminus \mathcal{B}'$;

WITH $\quad I \Vdash G_1 \,\&\, G_2, \Delta \,\Box\, c\ [\ \mathcal{C}\ ;\ c']$ *if and only if* $I \Vdash G_1, \Delta \,\Box\, c\ [\ \mathcal{C}_1\ ;\ c_1]$, $I \Vdash G_2, \Delta \,\Box\, c\ [\ \mathcal{C}_2\ ;\ c_2]$, *and there exist* $\mathcal{C}_1' \preccurlyeq \mathcal{C}_1$, $\mathcal{C}_2' \preccurlyeq \mathcal{C}_2$, *such that* $c' \equiv \mathcal{C}_1' = \mathcal{C}_2' \wedge c_1 \wedge c_2$ *is satisfiable, and* $\mathcal{C} = \mathcal{C}_1 + (\mathcal{C}_2 \setminus \mathcal{C}_2')$.

The above definition is entirely algorithmic. Given an interpretation and a constrained goal G (a multiset of goals, in general), the set $\{\langle \mathcal{C}, c\rangle \mid I \Vdash \mathbf{G}\ [\mathcal{C}\ ;\ c]\}$ is always finite. Rules PAR and ALL should be clear. In rule WITH, given the output context $\mathcal{C}_1 \,\Box\, c_1$ and $\mathcal{C}_2 \,\Box\, c_2$ for the two conjuncts, the output context for $G_1 \,\&\, G_2$ is obtained by merging in all possible ways sub-multisets of $\mathcal{C}_1$ and $\mathcal{C}_2$ that are unifiable. Rule MULT is for goals consisting of a constrained multiset $\mathcal{A} \,\Box\, c$ of atomic formulas. If $\mathcal{A}$ contains a sub-multiset unifiable with a sub-multiset $\mathcal{B}'$ of an element $\mathcal{B}$ of I, $\mathcal{B} \setminus \mathcal{B}'$ is the minimal context to be added to $\mathcal{A}$.

Example 2. Consider a language over the term universe $\{a, f(a), \ldots\}$, let $\mathbf{G}$ be the goal $(q(X) \invamp r(Y)) \,\&\, s(Z) \,\Box\, Z = a$, and I be the interpretation consisting of the two constrained multisets

$$\mathbf{M}_1 \equiv t(U_1, V_1), q(W_1) \,\Box\, U_1 = f(Q_1) \wedge W_1 = a,$$
$$\mathbf{M}_2 \equiv t(U_2, V_2), s(W_2) \,\Box\, V_2 = f(Q_2) \wedge W_2 = a.$$

Using the WITH rule, we have to compute $\mathcal{C}_1, \mathcal{C}_2, c_1, c_2$ such that $I \Vdash q(X) \parr r(Y) \;\square\; Z = a\ [\mathcal{C}_1\ ;\ c_1]$ and $I \Vdash s(Z) \;\square\; Z = a\ [\mathcal{C}_2\ ;\ c_2]$. For the first conjunct and using the PAR rule, we have that $I \Vdash q(X) \parr r(Y) \;\square\; Z = a\ [\mathcal{C}_1\ ;\ c_1]$ iff $I \Vdash q(X), r(Y) \;\square\; Z = a\ [\mathcal{C}_1\ ;\ c_1]$. By MULT rule, applied to $\mathbf{M}_1 \in I$, we have that $\mathcal{C}_1 = t(U_1, V_1)$ and $c_1 \equiv X = W_1 \wedge W_1 = a \wedge Z = a \wedge U_1 = f(Q_1)$. For the second conjunct and using the MULT rule applied to $\mathbf{M}_2 \in I$, we have that $\mathcal{C}_2 = t(U_2, V_2)$ and $c_2 \equiv Z = W_2 \wedge Z = a \wedge W_2 = a \wedge V_2 = f(Q_2)$. Therefore by definition of the WITH rule, if we unify $t(U_1, V_1)$ and $t(U_2, V_2)$, we have that

$$I \Vdash \mathbf{G}\ [t(U_1, V_1)\ ;\ U_1 = U_2 \wedge V_1 = V_2 \wedge c_1 \wedge c_2].$$

More concisely, by renaming the variables, we get $I \Vdash \mathbf{G}\ [t(U, V)\ ;\ X = a \wedge Z = a \wedge U = f(Q) \wedge V = f(Q')]$. We also have, by choosing empty sub-multisets in WITH rule, that

$$I \Vdash \mathbf{G}\ [t(U_1, V_1), t(U_2, V_2)\ ;\ c_1 \wedge c_2].$$

More concisely, by renaming the variables, we get $I \Vdash \mathbf{G}\ [t(U, V), t(U', V')\ ;\ X = a \wedge Z = a \wedge U = f(Q) \wedge V' = f(Q')]$.

4.2 Effective Fixpoint Semantics

Based on the previous definitions, we can define a fully symbolic fixpoint operator S_P for LO programs with constraints. The operator S_P transforms extended interpretations in extended interpretations as follows.

Definition 5 (Fixpoint Operator S_P). *Given an LO program P, and $I \in \mathcal{I}$,*

$$S_P(I) = \{\ \widehat{H} + \mathcal{C} \;\square\; c')\ |\ \exists\ (H \multimap G \;\square\; c)\ \textit{variant of a clause in } P \textit{ s.t. } I \Vdash\ G \;\square\; c\ [\mathcal{C}\ ;\ c']\ \}$$

Proposition 1. *S_P is monotonic and continuous over the lattice $\langle \mathcal{I}, \sqsubseteq \rangle$.*

Then, we have the following results.

Proposition 2. *Let P be a constrained LO program, and $I \in \mathcal{I}$. Then, $[\![S_P(I)]\!] = T_{Gnd(P)}([\![I]\!])$.*

Corollary 1. $[\![\mathit{lfp}(S_P)]\!] = \mathit{lfp}(T_{Gnd(P)})$.

Let $SymbF(P) = \mathit{lfp}(S_P)$. Then, we have the following main Theorem.

Theorem 2 (Soundness and Completeness). *Given a constrained LO program P, $O_{Gnd(P)} = [\![SymbF(P)]\!]$.*

Though a single application of the operator S_P is effective, in general it might be impossible to compute the fixpoint of S_P (first-order LO programs are Turing complete). We can make a similar observation for the non-ground operator S_P of Constraint Logic Programming [JM94].

Example 3. Consider the clause $p(X) \parr p(Z) \multimap (q(X) \parr r(Y))\ \&\ s(Z) \,\Box\, Z = a$, and the interpretation I of Example 2. Let $\mathbf{G} = (q(X) \parr r(Y))\ \&\ s(Z) \,\Box\, Z = a$. From Example 2, we know that $I \Vdash \mathbf{G}\ [t(U,V)\ ;\ X = a \wedge Z = a \wedge U = f(Q) \wedge V = f(Q')]$ and $I \Vdash G\ [t(U,V), t(U',V')\ ;\ X = a \wedge Z = a \wedge U = f(Q) \wedge V' = f(Q')]$. Thus, we get that $S_P(I)$ contains

$$p(X), p(Z), t(U,V) \,\Box\, X = a \wedge Z = a \wedge U = f(Q) \wedge V = f(Q'),$$
$$p(X), p(Z), t(U,V), t(U',V') \,\Box\, X = a \wedge Z = a \wedge U = f(Q) \wedge V' = f(Q').$$

As particular instances, we have that $S_P(I)$ includes (representations of) the multisets $p(a), p(a), t(f(a), f(a))$ and $p(a), p(a), t(f(a), a), t(a, f(a))$. This example shows the importance of maintaining all constraints generated during an evaluation of a judgment (e.g. $X = a$ in the first case). In fact, the scope of these constraints extends over the atoms in the *head* of clauses (e.g. $p(X)$).

5 Relationship with Timed Petri Nets

We will illustrate the main ideas of the connection between our fixpoint semantics and the framework of [AJ99] to decide reachability problems for Timed Petri Nets. As explained in the introduction, Timed Petri Nets (TPNs) are infinite-state networks where tokens move from place to place (place=node of the net) carrying along their age. TPN transitions have two possible forms. Discrete transitions specify how tokens move around the network, whereas timed transitions simply increase the age of every token in the network. The results of [AJ99] are based on a *symbolic* representation of potentially infinite sets of TPN configurations (i.e. tokens with their age) via *existential regions*. An existential region is a formula having the following form

$$\exists x_1 \ldots \exists x_n.\ P(x_1, ..., x_n)\ \mathit{and}\ c(x_1, ..., x_n)$$

whose meaning is as follows: *there exist* at least n distinct *tokens distributed in the network as described by formula P and whose ages satisfy the constraint c.* The formula P is a conjunction of constraints of the form $x_j \in p_i$, whose meaning is *the token x_j is in place p_i*. In the interpretation domain existentially quantified variables are required to denote *distinct* values. The constraint c is a *clock constraint* [AJ99], i.e., a conjunction of atomic predicates like $x_i - x_j \leq k$ (where k is an integer constant), which expresses a bound on the difference between the clock values of different tokens. More simple constraints like $x_i \leq k$ or $x_i \geq k$, which limit the clock value of a single token, can be seen as subcases of the previous class of constraints. An existential region Φ denotes an *upward closed* set of TPN configurations (i.e. those satisfying *at least* the constraints in Φ). Based on this construction, the algorithm of [AJ99] solves the following type of reachability problems.

Control state reachability: given an initial configuration I_0 and an existential region Φ, is it possible to *reach* a configuration in (the denotation of) Φ starting from (an instance of) I_0?

The algorithm works as follows. It computes the effect of applying *backwards* the transitions of the TPN starting from Φ, until it reaches a fixpoint F. As a last step, it checks if $[\![I_0]\!] \cap [\![F]\!] = \emptyset$. The termination of the algorithm is guaranteed by the following properties: existential regions are *well-quasi ordered* [AJ99,AN00]; the class of existential regions is closed under backward applications of TPN transitions, i.e., if we apply backwards TPN transitions to a set of existential regions we still obtain a set of existential regions. Instead of entering in more details in the TPN formalism, we immediately show how the discrete components of TPNs can be modeled via LO programs.

TPNs as First-Order Linear Logic Theories. First of all, a token in place p and age n can be represented as the atomic predicate $p(n)$. Thus, discrete transitions can be represented via LO clauses of the form:

$$p_1(X_1) \mathbin{\wp} \ldots \mathbin{\wp} p_n(X_n) \multimapinv q_1(Y_1) \mathbin{\wp} \ldots \mathbin{\wp} q_m(Y_m) \,\Box\, c$$

where p_i, q_j are place names and X_i, Y_j are variables associated to the ages, and c is a constraint over the age of tokens. Specifically, c specifies the constraint under which the tokens can be removed from $p_1, \ldots, p_n$, and the new constraint on the ages of the tokens added to $q_1, \ldots, q_m$. Timed transitions cannot be represented directly in LO. This encoding can be done via a meta-rule

$$\frac{P \Rightarrow p_1(X_1 + \delta), \ldots, p_n(X_n + \delta)}{P \Rightarrow p_1(X_1), \ldots, p_n(X_n)} \quad Time \;\; (\delta \geq 0)$$

whose definition in Linear Logic (e.g. in Forum [Mil96]) requires giving a *family* of clauses, using the constant **1** to ensure that the age of *every* token in the network is incremented as a result of a timed transition. In contrast with $\top$, **1** succeeds only in the empty context. The semantics for LO presented here could be extended, similarly to what done in the propositional case [BDM00], to include the constant **1**. Anyway, as far as the application to TPNs is concerned, in [AJ99] the authors show how to compute effectively the backward application of timed transitions (i.e. our meta-rule) on a given existential region. We skip therefore a detailed discussion about encoding timed transitions in LO. We can use the ideas of [AJ99] provided we find a counterpart of existential regions in the LO setting, and provided we can find a way to connect a *backward reachability step* with the LO operational semantics.

Existential Regions as Constrained Multisets. Existential regions can be naturally represented as *constrained* multisets having the following form:

$$p_1(X_1), \ldots, p_n(X_n) \,\Box\, c$$

where c is a constraint. In fact, the denotation $[\![\mathcal{A} \,\Box\, c]\!]$ of a constrained multiset $\mathcal{A} \,\Box\, c$, captures precisely the intended meaning of the existential regions of [AJ99]. As an example, $[\![p(X), q(Y) \,\Box\, 0 \leq X - Y \leq 1]\!] = \{\{p(1), q(0)\}, \{p(1), q(0), q(3.6)\}, \ldots\}$.

Backward Reachability = Bottom-Up Evaluation. At this point, it should be clear that computing the effect of a backward application of the transitions of a TPN N coincides with computing an application of the S_{P_N} operator associated to the LO program P_N encoding N. In order to *start up* the bottom-up evaluation from the set of configurations represented by the target existential region Φ, we simply have to add the clause: $p_1(X_1) \parr \ldots \parr p_m(X_m) \multimapinv \top \,\Box\, c$ where $\Phi = \exists x_1, \ldots x_m.\ x_1 \in p_1$ *and* $\ldots$ *and* $x_m \in p_m$ *and* c. Through this encoding, we automatically inherit from [AJ99] the following property.

Theorem 3. *Let N be a TPN, Φ an existential region, and P_N be their encoding in LO enriched with the meta-rule for timed transitions. Then, $SymbF(P_N)$ is computable in finitely many steps.*

Besides the basic multiset rewriting mechanism, the linear logic language LO provides other connectives that add further expressiveness to the operational reading of specifications. For instance, we give some hints about using the additive conjunction & to specify an operation to hierarchically compose TPNs. If we think about TPNs as representing the execution of some kind of *protocol*, the rule $p(X) \multimapinv p_1(X_1)\ \&\ p_2(X_2) \,\Box\, c$ could be seen as the specification that the protocol p will start (at the time specified by c) two sub-protocols that must succeed in order for p to succeed. The subsystems p_1 and p_2 will run independently. Since clock constraints are closed under conjunctions, the result of Theorem 3 can be extended in order to include LO programs with conjunction as the one in the previous example.

6 Related Works

To our knowledge, our work is the first attempt to connect algorithmic techniques used in symbolic model checking with declarative and operational aspects of linear logic programming. In [BDM00], we have considered the relation between *propositional* LO and Petri Nets. In this paper we have extended the connection to first-order LO programs and more general notions of Petri Nets.

In [HW98], Harland and Winikoff present an abstract deductive system for bottom-up evaluation of linear logic programs. The left introduction plus weakening and cut rules are used to compute the logical consequences of a given formula. Though the framework is given for a more general fragment than LO, it does not provide for an *effective* procedure to evaluate programs.

Finally, in [Cer95] Cervesato shows how to encode Petri Nets in LO, Lolli and Forum exploiting the different features of these languages; whereas in [APC93], Andreoli, Pareschi and Castagnetti define an improved *top-down* strategy for *propositional* LO based on the Karp-Miller's coverability tree of Petri Nets, i.e., a *forward* exploration with accelerations.

7 Conclusions and Future Work

In this paper we have investigated the connections between techniques used for symbolic model checking of infinite-state systems [ACJT96,AJ99,FS98] and provability for first-order linear logic programs [AP90]. We have generalized the construction used in [AJ99] to decide verification problems for Timed Petri Nets in order to build an effective *fixpoint* semantics for first-order LO programs. Ad hoc notions like the existential regions of [AJ99] find a natural counterpart as elements of the non-ground interpretations of LO programs, a notion inspired by the more advanced semantics of Constraint Logic Programming [GDL95,JM94]. Furthermore, we have shown that the algorithms used for (Timed) Petri Nets can be extended in order to capture the richer specification language LO.

The main interest of the new semantics is that it gives us a way to evaluate bottom-up first-order LO programs, i.e., an alternative operational semantics that could be useful to study new applications of linear logic programming (as discussed in [HW98]). For this reason, we think it would be important to extend our method to other linear logic languages like Lolli [HM94] and Forum [Mil96].

The work presented in this paper can also be a source of further investigations concerning the analysis of programs and the development of new observable semantics. In particular, the semantics could be extended in order to cope with observables like the *non ground success set* and *computed answer substitutions* [FLMP93] of LO programs. To this aim, we plan to formulate the constraint-based semantics presented here using a more traditional approach based on substitutions and most general unifiers. While the constraint-based formulation was particularly suitable to study the connection with TPNs, a formulation based on substitutions could be useful for extending traditional program analysis techniques to linear logic programs.

Acknowledgments. The authors would like to thank Iliano Cervesato and the anonymous reviewers for their useful comments and suggestions.

References

[ACJT96] P. A. Abdulla, K. Cerāns, B. Jonsson and Y.-K. Tsay. General Decidability Theorems for Infinite-State Systems. In *Proc. of LICS 96*, pages 313–321, 1996.

[AJ99] P. A. Abdulla, and B. Jonsson. Ensuring Completeness of Symbolic Verification Methods for Infinite-State Systems. To appear in *Theoretical Computer Science*, 1999.

[AN00] P. A. Abdulla, and A. Nylen. Better is Better than Well: On Efficient Verification of Infinite-State Systems. In *Proc. LICS'2000*, pages 132-140, 2000.

[And92] J. M. Andreoli. Logic Programming with Focusing proofs in Linear Logic. *Journal of Logic and Computation*, 2(3):297–347, 1992.

[AP90] J. M. Andreoli and R. Pareschi. Linear Objects: Logical Processes with Built-In Inheritance. In *Proc. of ICLP'90*, pages 495–510, 1990.

[APC93] J. M. Andreoli, R. Pareschi and T. Castagnetti. Abstract Interpretation of Linear Logic Programming. In *Proc. of ILPS'93*, pages 295–314, 1993.

[BDM00] M. Bozzano, G. Delzanno, and M. Martelli. A Bottom-up semantics for Linear Logic Programs. In *Proc. of PPDP 2000*, pages 92-102, 2000.

[BDM00a] M. Bozzano, G. Delzanno, and M. Martelli. An Effective Bottom-Up Semantics for First-Order Linear Logic Programs and its Relationship with Decidability Results for Timed Petri Nets. Technical Report, DISI, Università di Genova, Decemeber 2000.

[Cer95] I. Cervesato. Petri Nets and Linear Logic: a Case Study for Logic Programming. In *Proc. of GULP-PRODE'95*, pages 313–318, 1995.

[DP99] G. Delzanno and A. Podelski. Model Checking in CLP. In *Proc. of TACAS'99*, LNCS 1579, pages 223–239, 1999.

[FLMP93] M. Falaschi and G. Levi and M. Martelli and C. Palamidessi. A Model-Theoretic Reconstruction of the Operational Semantics of Logic Programs. *Information and Computation*, 102(1):86-113, 1993.

[FS98] A. Finkel and P. Schnoebelen. Well-structured Transition Systems Everywhere! Technical Report LSV-98-4, Laboratoire Spécification et Vérification, ENS Cachan, 1998. To appear in *Theoretical Computer Science*, 1999.

[Fri00] L. Fribourg. Constraint logic programming applied to model checking. In *Proc. LOPSTR'99*, pages 31-42, 2000.

[GDL95] M. Gabbrielli, M. G. Dore and G. Levi. Observable Semantics for Constraint Logic Programs. *Journal of Logic and Computation*, 5(2): 133–171, 1995.

[Gir87] J. Y. Girard. Linear Logic. *Theoretical Computer Science*, 50:1–102, 1987.

[HM94] J. S. Hodas and D. Miller. Logic Programming in a Fragment of Intuitionistic Linear Logic. *Information and Computation*, 110(2):327–365, 1994.

[HW98] J. Harland and M. Winikoff. Making Logic Programs Reactive. In *Proc. of JICSLP'98 Workshop Dynamics'98*, pages 43–58, 1998.

[JM94] J. Jaffar and M. J. Maher. Constraint Logic Programming: A Survey. *Journal of Logic Programming*, 19-20:503–582, 1994.

[Kan94] M. I. Kanovich. Petri Nets, Horn Programs, Linear Logic, and Vector Games. In *Proc TACS. '94*, pages 642–666, 1994.

[KMM+97] Y. Kesten, O. Maler, M. Marcus, A. Pnueli, E. Shahar. Symbolic Model Checking with Rich Assertional Languages. In *Proc. CAV '97*, pages 424–435, 1997.

[Kop95] A. P. Kopylov. Propositional Linear Logic with Weakening is Decidable. In *Proc. LICS 95*, pages 496-504, 1995.

[Llo87] J. W. Lloyd. Foundations of Logic Programming. Springer-Verlag, 1987.

[MM91] N. Martí-Oliet, J. Meseguer. From Petri Nets to Linear Logic. Mathematical Structures in Computer Science 1(1):69–101, 1991.

[Mil96] D. Miller. Forum: A Multiple-Conclusion Specification Logic. *Theoretical Computer Science*, 165(1):201–232, 1996.

A Framework for Goal-Directed Bottom-Up Evaluation of Functional Logic Programs

Jesús M. Almendros-Jiménez* and Antonio Becerra-Terón
Dpto. de Lenguajes y Computación. Universidad de Almería.
04120-Almería. Spain. email: {jalmen,abecerra}@ual.es

Abstract. In this paper we start the design of a functional-logic deductive database language. Given that most logic deductive languages consider bottom-up evaluation as operational mechanism, here we will focus on the development of an operational semantics based on bottom-up evaluation for functional logic languages. As in the logic paradigm, the bottom-up evaluation will consist in a magic transformation for a given program-query into a magic program-query for which the bottom-up evaluation will simulate the top-down one of the original program.

1 Introduction

Deductive databases are database management systems whose query language and, usually, storage structure are designed around a logical data model. It is easy to see deductive database systems as an advanced form of relational systems, and they are best suited for applications in which a large amount of data must be accessed and complex queries must be supported. Deductive databases languages [21] have been influenced by work in logic programming and offer a rich query language, which extends *SQL* in many important directions (including support for *aggregation*, *negation*, and *recursion*). Deductive databases languages use logic programming concepts but do not share in most cases the evaluation mechanism of traditional logic programming languages as Prolog. There are three main reasons for it:

- Prolog's *depth-first* evaluation strategy leads to *infinite loops*, even for definite programs and even in the absence of function symbols or arithmetic. In the presence of large volumes of data, operational reasoning is not desirable, and a higher premium is placed upon *completeness* and *termination* of the evaluation method.
- In a typical database application, the amount of data is sufficiently large that much of it is on *secondary storage*. Prolog systems evaluate logic programs efficiently in *main-memory*, but are *tuple-at-a-time*; that is, they process one (sub) goal at a time, and thus inefficiently w.r.t. disk accesses. Efficient access to these data is crucial to good performance.
- When evaluating a database query, it is customary to want to compute *all of the answers* to the query. When writing a program for computation purposes, such as a typical Prolog program, it is common to only need *one answer* to the query.

* The author has been partially supported by the Spanish CICYT (project TIC 98-0445-C03-02 TREND)

H. Kuchen and K. Ueda (Eds.): FLOPS 2001, LNCS 2024, pp. 153–169, 2001.

One consequence of this is that most deductive database systems (for instance, DATALOG [25], CORAL [20], ADITI [26]) use *bottom-up* evaluation methods instead of *top-down* one. Bottom-up approach allows us to use *set-at-a-time* evaluation, i.e. it processes sets of goals, rather than proceeding one (sub) goal at a time, where operations like relational joins can be made for disk-resident data efficiently. In this sense, deductive systems are an attempt to adapt Prolog, which has a "small-data" view of the world, to a "large-data" world. On the other hand, the bottom-up evaluation avoids infinite loops over programs under certain conditions.

An important problem is that a query asks not for the entire relation corresponding to an intensional predicate but for a small subset. It is important that we answer a query by examining only the part of database that involves the predicates relevant to the instantiated or partially instantiated arguments in the query. The goal-directed bottom-up evaluation generates the subset of the *Herbrand model* of the program relevant to the query. With this aim, the bottom-up evaluation in such languages involves a query-program transformation termed *Magic Sets* [5].

The basic idea of this technique is that a logic program-query is transformed into a *magic* logic program-query whose bottom-up *fixed point evaluation* [3] is devised to simulate top-down evaluation of the original program and query. The program is evaluated using bottom-up evaluation until no new facts are generated or the answer to the query is found. The transformed program adds new predicates, called *magic predicates*, whose role is to pass information (instantiated and partially instantiated arguments in the predicates of the query) to the program in order to consider only those instances of the program rules relevant to the query solving.

Example 1. Given a set of facts for a relation par and the following logic rules:

```
anc(X,Y):-par(X,Y).
anc(X,Y):-par(X,Z),anc(Z,Y).
```

and a query anc(john,X), the magic-sets transformation rewrites this program into the following logic program:

```
anc(X,Y):-mg_anc(X),par(X,Y).
anc(X,Y):-mg_anc(X),par(X,Z),anc(Z,Y).
mg_anc(Z):-mg_anc(X),par(X,Z).
mg_anc(john).
```

together with par(α,β):-mg_par(α,β) for each pair α, β in the relation par. The fixed point evaluation computes only the ancestors of john (and those intermediate results needed for it).

Several transformation magic methods have been widely studied in the past with the aim to deal with *recursive queries*, *non-ground facts*, *function symbols*, *partially instantiated terms*, *negation* and to provide optimizations such as avoiding the computation of *duplicated facts*, and the memoization of *intermediate results*.

As examples, we have the transformations called *Generalized Magis Sets* [5, 12], *Generalized Supplementary Magic Sets* [5], *Magic Templates* [19], *Alexander Templates* [24], *Counting Methods* [23] and recently *Induced Magic Sets* [6].

Although bottom-up evaluation based on magic-sets has been studied in the context of logic programming, there are some approaches (for instance [13]) which consider bottom-up evaluation of *constraint logic programs*, showing a new research area in the application of the CLP scheme for databases in the framework of *constraint query languages* [11]. Moreover, the bottom-up evaluation has been used in the context of semantic-based program analysis (for instance [4]).

Deductive databases have also been studied in a functional programming context (PFL [22], FDL [18]), enjoying the three following advantages, *ease of reasoning*: the reasoning can be used to transform queries into a more efficient form or to prove that transactions preserve consistency constraints; *freedom from a detailed execution order*: this freedom has been used to improve query evaluation by selecting an appropriate execution order for subqueries, in such a way that this freedom makes parallel execution natural in functional database query languages; and *freedom from side-effects*: because side-effects may not be anticipated by the programmer, they complicate the programmer's task, especially in large database applications.

On the other hand, the integration of functional and logic programming has been widely investigated during the last years, see [8] for a survey. It has leaded to the recent design of modern programming languages such as CURRY [9] and $\mathcal{TOY}$ [16] following the ideas of the predecessors BABEL and K-LEAF. The aim of such integration is to include features from functional (cfr. determinism, higher order functions, partial, non strict and lazy functions, possibly infinite data structures) and logic languages (cfr. logic variables, function inversion, non-determinism, built-in search). The basic ideas in functional-logic programming consist in *lazy narrowing* as operational mechanism, following some class of *narrowing strategy* [2, 14] combined with some kind of *constraints solving* [15] and *higher order* features [10].

The aim of this paper is to study a functional-logic deductive database language. Given that most logic deductive languages consider bottom-up evaluation as operational mechanism, here we focus on the development of an operational semantics based on bottom-up evaluation for functional logic languages. As in the logic paradigm, the bottom-up evaluation will consist in a magic transformation for a given program-query into a magic program-query for which the bottom-up evaluation will simulate the top-down one of the original program.

With respect to logic programming paradigm, we have to solve the old and new problems. In the earliest logic deductive databases, logic programs were constrained to be free of function-symbols, facts were grounds and deduction rules were well-formed, i.e. each variable that appears in the head of the rule also appears in its body [5]. These conditions ensure termination of the bottom-up evaluation based on magic-sets given that the least Herbrand model [3] is finite in the original and magic program, and thus bottom-up is a complete deduction procedure whereas Prolog is not.

Example 2. In the following logic program:

```
p(X):-p(X).
p(0).
```

the Prolog solving of the goal p(0) loops and no answer is found, however the bottom-up does not; the evaluation of the transformed magic program:

```
p(X):-mg_p(X),p(X).
p(0):-mg_p(0).
mg_p(0).
```

where mg_p is the magic predicate associated to p, ends and obtains p(0) as fact.

Later [19], the well-formed condition was removed but no general result of termination for bottom-up evaluation was presented by allowing function-symbols (and therefore for general Horn-logic programs), although some attempts were done [24, 19]. In the presence of function symbols, the Herbrand model of a logic program can be infinite and thus, in the general case, the bottom-up evaluation of the original and transformed program cannot end. Therefore, the introduction of function symbols causes uncompleteness for negative information.

In summary, the main aims of such works were to find a bottom-up evaluation method for restricted or general Horn-logic programs which simulates top-down evaluation, that is, a goal-directed and efficient evaluation method (in terms of intermediates facts (subgoals) that are generated [24, 6]) which retains the advantages of avoiding infinite loops and set-at-a-time computations. They also study semantic models and magic transformations for deductive database languages with negation [12]. Thus, we may say that the bottom-up evaluation is better than top-down one w.r.t. positive goals: bottom-up evaluation is a complete deduction procedure when top-down is not. In the presence of function symbols and negative goals, both bottom-up and top-down evaluation with negative goals are, in general, uncomplete procedures.

In our case, we will consider a functional logic language like $\mathcal{TOY}$ [7], that is, our programs will be conditional constructor-based rewriting rules in which no additional restrictions in the form of program rules will be required. Therefore, Horn-logic programs will be considered as particular cases of our functional-logic programs. It means that we will have the same problems due to the introduction of function symbols in deductive logic programs (called constructors in a functional-logic context). Given that in this paper we do not deal with negation, we will now not care about it. We are interested in the definition of an operational semantics for $\mathcal{TOY}$ programs based on bottom-up evaluation which simulates the top-down one of a $\mathcal{TOY}$ program. This bottom-up evaluation will be as goal-directed as top-down evaluation, that is, it generates the same intermediate results than the top-down evaluation, retaining the advantages of bottom-up evaluation. We will consider the standard magic transformation with left-to-right information passing strategy [5].

As new contributions of this paper, we have the dealing with functions instead of logic predicates, which can be lazy, partial and non-strict, and the dealing with possible infinite data, which introduces new problems in the bottom-up evaluation once we have to apply program rules lazily in every step of the fixed point operator application. The laziness of the evaluation will be driven by the goal evaluating program rules (arguments and conditions) as far as the goal requires. In this sense, our bottom-up evaluation is similar to the demand-driven [14] top-down evaluation of functional logic programs. As far as we know, this is the first time that such kind of evaluation method for functional logic languages has been presented. To put an end to the comparison of bottom-up and top-down evaluations in our framework, we will establish the equivalence results of our bottom-up evaluation and the conditional rewriting logic (CRWL) [7] which provides logic foundations to the $\mathcal{TOY}$ language, and therefore ensuring soundness and completeness of our bottom-up evaluation. Moreover, we will establish correspondences among proofs of a given goal in the cited logic and the "facts" computed by means of the bottom-up evaluation showing the optimality of our evaluation method.

The rest of the paper will be organized as follows. In section 2 we will introduce basic notions that will be used in the rest of the paper; in section 3 we present the language; the section 4 will define Herbrand models for our language; section 5 will present the magic transformation; section 6 will show the results of soundness, completeness and optimality and finally in section 7 we will describe the future work and conclusions. Due to the lack of space, the proofs of our results have not been included in this version but the full proofs can be found in [1].

2 Basic Notions

We assume the reader has familiarity with basic concepts of model theory on logic programming and functional-logic programming (see [3, 17, 7] for more details). We now point up some of the notions used in this paper.

Given S, a *partially ordered set* (in short, *poset*) with *bottom* $\perp$ (equipped with a partial order $\leq$ and a least element $\perp$), the set of all totally defined elements of S will be noted *Def(S)*. We write $\mathcal{C}(S)$, $\mathcal{I}(S)$ for the sets of cones and ideals of S respectively. The set $\bar{S} =_{def} \mathcal{I}(S)$ denotes the *ideal completion* of S, which is also a *poset* under the *set-inclusion* ordering $\subseteq$, and there is a natural order which maps each $x \in S$ into the principal ideal generated by x, $< x >=_{def} \{y \in S : y \leq x\} \in \bar{S}$. Furthermore, $\bar{S}$ is an algebraic *cpo* whose finite elements are precisely the principal ideals $< x >,\ x \in S$.

A *signature* is a set $\sum = \mathcal{C} \cup \mathcal{F}$, where $\mathcal{C} = \bigcup_{n \in I\!N} \mathcal{C}^n$ and $\mathcal{F} = \bigcup_{n \in I\!N} \mathcal{F}^n$ are disjoint sets of constructor and function symbols respectively, each of them with associated *arity*. $Expr_\Sigma$ and $Term_\Sigma$ denote the set of expressions built up from $\sum$ and a set of variables $\mathcal{V}$, and the subset of terms making only use of $\mathcal{C}$ and $\mathcal{V}$, respectively. We distinguish partial $Expr_{\Sigma_\perp}$ (resp. $Term_{\Sigma_\perp}$) and total expressions (resp. terms) depending whether they include $\perp$ or not. The *approximation ordering* $\leq$ for $Term_{\Sigma_\perp}$ can be defined as the least partial ordering satisfying the following properties: $\perp \leq t$, for every t, and if $t_1 \leq s_1, ..., t_n \leq s_n$ then $c(t_1, ..., t_n) \leq c(s_1, ..., s_n)$, for every $c \in \mathcal{C}^n$.

Substitutions are mappings $\theta : \mathcal{V} \to Term_{\Sigma_\perp}$ which have $\theta : Term_{\Sigma_\perp} \to Term_{\Sigma_\perp}$ as unique natural extension, also noted as θ. $Subst_\Sigma$ (resp. $Subst_{\Sigma_\perp}$) denotes the set of substitutions in total (resp. possibly partial) terms. We note as $t\theta$ the result of applying the substitutions θ to the term t.

3 A Functional Logic Language

A *program* $\mathcal{P}$ is a signature Σ together with a set of conditional constructor-based rewrite rules of the form: $f(t_1, \ldots, t_n) := r \Leftarrow C$ where $f \in \mathcal{F}$ of arity n,

$\bar{t}$ must be a linear tuple of terms $t_i \in Term_\Sigma$, and the condition C must consist of finitely many (possibly zero) of strict equalities $e == e'$ with $e,\ e' \in Expr_\Sigma$. $[\mathcal{P}] = \{(l := r \Leftarrow C)\ \theta \mid (l := r \Leftarrow C) \in \mathcal{P},\ \theta \in Subst_{\Sigma_\perp}\}$ denotes the set of (possibly partial) instances of the program rules of $\mathcal{P}$. We allow extra variables in the body and the condition. In fact, our rules can be used to define non-deterministic functions. A goal $\mathcal{G}$ is like the conditional part of a program rule.

Now we present the semantics of a language through a conditional rewriting logic (CRWL) as in [7]. This logic allows us to prove statements of the form $\mathcal{P} \vdash_{\mathcal{CRWL}} e \rightarrow t$, with $e \in Expr_{\Sigma_\perp}, t \in Term_{\Sigma_\perp}$, called *non-strict equalities*, whose meaning is that term t approximates the value of the expression e, and *strict equalities* $\mathcal{P} \vdash_{\mathcal{CRWL}} e == e'$, $e, e' \in Expr_{\Sigma_\perp}$ whose meaning is that e and e' represent the same totally defined value. A *solution* for a goal $\mathcal{G}$ w.r.t. a program $\mathcal{P}$ is a substitution $\theta \in Subst_{\Sigma_\perp}$ such that $\mathcal{P} \vdash_{\mathcal{CRWL}} \mathcal{G}\theta$. The formal presentation of CRWL is as follows:

Definition 1 (Conditional Rewriting Logic (CRWL)).

(B) $\dfrac{}{e \rightarrow \perp}$

(R) $\dfrac{}{X \rightarrow X}\ X \in \mathcal{V}$ **(DC)** $\dfrac{e_1 \rightarrow t_1\ \ldots\ e_n \rightarrow t_n}{c(e_1,\ \ldots\ , e_n) \rightarrow c(t_1,\ \ldots\ , t_n)}\ c \in \mathcal{C}^n$

(O) $\dfrac{e_1 \rightarrow t_1\ \ldots\ e_n \rightarrow t_n \quad C \quad r \rightarrow t}{f(e_1,\ \ldots\ , e_n) \rightarrow t}$ **(S)** $\dfrac{e \rightarrow t \quad e' \rightarrow t}{e == e'}\ t \in Term_\Sigma$

$t \not\equiv \perp,\ f(t_1,\ \ldots\ , t_n) := r \Leftarrow C \in [\mathcal{P}]$

4 Herbrand Models

4.1 CRWL-Algebras

In this section we present Herbrand algebras and models as a particular case of CRWL-algebras. Firstly, we need the following definitions.

Definition 2 (Non-deterministic and Deterministic Functions). *Given two posets D and E with $\perp$ we define:*

- *The set of all non-deterministic functions from D to E as:*
  $[D \rightarrow_n E] =_{def} \{f : D \rightarrow \mathcal{C}(E) \mid \forall\ u, u' \in D : (u \leq u' \Rightarrow f(u) \subseteq f(u'))\}$
- *The set of all deterministic functions from D to E as:*
  $[D \rightarrow_d E] =_{def} \{f \in [D \rightarrow_n E] \mid \forall\ u \in D : f(u) \in \mathcal{I}(E)\}$

Now we can define the class of algebras which will be used as models for CRWL:

Definition 3 (CRWL-Algebras). *For any given signature, CRWL-algebras are algebraic structures of the form: $\mathcal{A} = (D_\mathcal{A}, \{c^\mathcal{A}\}_{c \in \mathcal{C}}, \{f^\mathcal{A}\}_{f \in \mathcal{F}})$ where $D_\mathcal{A}$ is a poset, $c^\mathcal{A} \in [D^n_\mathcal{A} \rightarrow_d D_\mathcal{A}]$ for $c \in \mathcal{C}^n$, and $f^\mathcal{A} \in [D^n_\mathcal{A} \rightarrow_n D_\mathcal{A}]$ for $f \in \mathcal{F}^n$. For $c_\mathcal{A}$ we still require the following additional condition: for all $u_1, \ldots, u_n \in D_\mathcal{A}$ there is $v \in D_\mathcal{A}$ such that $c^\mathcal{A}(u_1, \ldots, u_n) =< v >$. Moreover, $v \in Def(D_\mathcal{A})$ in case that all $u_i \in Def(D_\mathcal{A})$*

The next definition shows how to evaluate expressions in CRWL-algebras:

Definition 4 (Expression evaluation). *Let $\mathcal{A}$ be a CRWL-algebra of signature $\sum$. A evaluation over $\mathcal{A}$ is any mapping $\eta : \mathcal{V} \rightarrow \mathcal{D}_\mathcal{A}$, and we say that η is totally defined iff $\eta(X) \in Def(D_\mathcal{A})$ for all $X \in \mathcal{V}$. We denote by $Val(\mathcal{A})$ the set of all valuations, and by $DefVal(\mathcal{A})$ the set of all totally defined valuations. The evaluation of $e \in Expr_{\Sigma_\perp}$ in $\mathcal{A}$ under η yields $\|e\|^\mathcal{A}\eta \in \mathcal{C}(D_\mathcal{A})$ which is defined recursively as follows:*

– $\|\bot\|^{\mathcal{A}}\eta =_{def} <\bot_{\mathcal{A}}>$.
– $\|X\|^{\mathcal{A}}\eta =_{def} <\eta(X)>$, *for* $X \in \mathcal{V}$.
– $\|h(e_1, \ldots, e_n)\|^{\mathcal{A}}\eta =_{def} h^{\mathcal{A}}(\|e_1\|^{\mathcal{A}}\eta, \ldots, \|e_n\|^{\mathcal{A}}\eta)$, *for all* $h \in \mathcal{C}^n \cup \mathcal{F}^n$.

Due to non-determinism, the evaluation of an expression yields a cone rather than an element. However, this cone can still represent an element (in the ideal completion) in the case that it is an ideal. It can be proved that given a CRWL-algebra $\mathcal{A}$, for any $e \in Expr_{\Sigma_\bot}$ and any $\eta \in Val(\mathcal{A})$ then $\|e\|^{\mathcal{A}}\eta \in \mathcal{C}(D_{\mathcal{A}})$, $\|e\|^{\mathcal{A}}\eta \in \mathcal{I}(D_{\mathcal{A}})$ if $f^{\mathcal{A}}$ is deterministic for every defined function symbol f occurring in e, and $\|e\|^{\mathcal{A}}\eta =< v >$ for some $v \in D_{\mathcal{A}}$, if $e \in Term_{\Sigma_\bot}$ and $v \in Def(D_{\mathcal{A}})$ if $e \in Term_{\Sigma}$ and $\eta \in DefVal(\mathcal{A})$. Moreover, given a valuation over a CRWL-algebra $\mathcal{A}$, for any $e \in Expr$ and any $\theta \in Subst$ we have $\|e\theta\|^{\mathcal{A}}\eta = \|e\|^{\mathcal{A}}\eta\theta$, where $\eta\theta$ is the uniquely determined valuation that satisfies $<\eta\theta(X)>= \|X\theta\|^{\mathcal{A}}\eta$ *for all* $X \in \mathcal{V}$.

4.2 Herbrand Models

Now we can introduce Herbrand models. The main ideas are to interpret non-strict equalities in $\mathcal{A}$ as inclusions among cones and to interpret strict equalities as asserting the existence of some common, totally defined approximation.

Definition 5 (Models). *Assume a program $\mathcal{P}$ and a CRWL-algebra $\mathcal{A}$. We define:*

– *$\mathcal{A}$ satisfies a non-strict equality $e \rightarrow e'$ under a valuation η (in symbols, $(\mathcal{A}, \eta) \models e \rightarrow e'$) iff $\|e\|^{\mathcal{A}}\eta \supseteq \|e'\|^{\mathcal{A}}\eta$.*
– *$\mathcal{A}$ satisfies a strict equality $e == e'$ under a valuation η (in symbols, $(\mathcal{A}, \eta) \models e == e'$) iff $\|e\|^{\mathcal{A}}\eta \bigcap \|e'\|^{\mathcal{A}}\eta \bigcap Def(D_{\mathcal{A}}) \neq \emptyset$.*
– *$\mathcal{A}$ satisfies a rule $l := r \Leftarrow C$ iff every valuation η such that $(\mathcal{A}, \eta) \models C$ verifies: $(\mathcal{A}, \eta) \models l \rightarrow r$.*
– *$\mathcal{A}$ is a model of $\mathcal{P}$ (in symbols, $\mathcal{A} \models \mathcal{P}$) iff $\mathcal{A}$ satisfies all the rules in $\mathcal{P}$.*

Theorem 1 (Soundness). *For any program $\mathcal{P}$ and any non-strict or strict equality φ: $\mathcal{P} \vdash_{\mathcal{CRWL}} \varphi \Rightarrow (\mathcal{A}, \eta) \models \varphi$, for all $\mathcal{A} \models \mathcal{P}$ and all $\eta \in DefVal(\mathcal{A})$.*

Now we define Herbrand algebras as a particular case of CRWL-algebras in which the poset is the set of terms partially ordered by $\leq$ and the interpretation of the constructors consists of the ideal generated for the represented term.

Definition 6 (Herbrand Algebras). *Given a program $\mathcal{P}$, a Herbrand Algebra $\mathcal{A}$ is defined as follows. $D_{\mathcal{A}}$ is the poset $Term_{\Sigma_\bot}$ with the approximation ordering $\leq$ and $c^{\mathcal{A}}(t_1, \ldots, t_n) =_{def} < c(t_1, \ldots, t_n) >$ (principal ideal), for all $t_i \in Term_{\Sigma_\bot}$.*

From now on Val_H denotes the valuations in Herbrand algebras.

Definition 7 (Poset of Herbrand Algebras). *Given a program $\mathcal{P}$ we define the poset CRWLH of Herbrand algebras as follows: $\mathcal{A} \leq \mathcal{B}$ iff $f^{\mathcal{A}}(t_1, \ldots, t_n) \subseteq f^{\mathcal{B}}(t_1, \ldots, t_n)$ for every $f \in \mathcal{F}$ and $t_i \in Term_{\Sigma_\bot}, 1 \leq i \leq n$.*

Moreover, we can prove that the ideal completion of *CRWLH* is a cpo, and $\| \ \|$ is continuous w.r.t. the ideal completion of *CRWLH* and Val_H.

Definition 8 (Fix Point Operator). *Given $\mathcal{A} \in CRWLH$, $f \in \mathcal{F}$, we define the fix point operator as:*

$$T_{\mathcal{P}}(\mathcal{A}, f)(s_1, \ldots, s_n) =_{def} \{\|r\|^{\mathcal{A}}_{\eta} \mid \text{there exists } f(\bar{t}) := r \Leftarrow C \in \mathcal{P}, \text{ and } \eta \in Val(\mathcal{A}) \text{ such that } \|t_i\|^{\mathcal{A}}_{\eta} = s_i, (\mathcal{A}, \eta) \models C\}$$

Proposition 1. *Given $\mathcal{A} \in CRWLH$ there exists a unique $\mathcal{B} \in CRWLH$ denoted by $T_\mathcal{P}(\mathcal{A})$ such that $f^\mathcal{B}(t_1, \ldots, t_n) = T_\mathcal{P}(\mathcal{A}, f)(t_1, \ldots, t_n)$ for every $f \in \mathcal{F}$ and $t_i \in Term_{\Sigma_\perp}, 1 \leq i \leq n$.*

With these definitions, we can ensure the following result which characterizes the least Herbrand model.

Theorem 2. *The fix point operator $T_\mathcal{P}$ is continuous and satisfies:*

1. *For every $\mathcal{A} \in CRWLH$: $\mathcal{A} \models \mathcal{P}$ iff $T_\mathcal{P}(\mathcal{A}) \leq \mathcal{A}$.*
2. *$T_\mathcal{P}$ has a least fix point $\mathcal{M}_\mathcal{P} = \sqcup_{k\geq 0}{\mathcal{H}_\mathcal{P}}^k$ where ${\mathcal{H}_\mathcal{P}}^0$ is the bottom in CRWLH and ${\mathcal{H}_\mathcal{P}}^{k+1} = T_\mathcal{P}({\mathcal{H}_\mathcal{P}}^k)$*
3. *$\mathcal{M}_\mathcal{P}$ is the least Herbrand model of $\mathcal{P}$.*

Moreover we can see that satisfaction in $\mathcal{M}_\mathcal{P}$ can be characterized in terms of $\vdash_{\mathcal{CRWL}}$ provability.

Lemma 1 (Characterization Lemma). *Let* id *be the identity valuation over $\mathcal{M}_\mathcal{P}$, defined by $\mathsf{id}(X) = X$ for all $X \in \mathcal{V}$. For any non-strict or strict equality φ, we have $(\mathcal{M}_\mathcal{P}, \mathsf{id}) \models \varphi \Leftrightarrow \mathcal{P} \vdash_{\mathcal{CRWL}} \varphi$.*

As a consequence of the Characterization Lemma, we also get that for any substitution $\theta \in Subst_{\Sigma_\perp}$ (which is also a valuation over $\mathcal{M}_\mathcal{P}$) and any non-strict or strict equality φ, we have $(\mathcal{M}_\mathcal{P}, \theta) \models \varphi \Leftrightarrow \mathcal{P} \vdash_{\mathcal{CRWL}} \varphi\theta$.

Theorem 3 (Adequateness of $\mathcal{M}_\mathcal{P}$). *$\mathcal{M}_\mathcal{P}$ is a model of $\mathcal{P}$, for any non-strict or strict equality φ, the following conditions are equivalent:*

a) $\mathcal{P} \vdash_{\mathcal{CRWL}} \varphi$.
b) $(\mathcal{A}, \eta) \models \varphi$ for every $\mathcal{A} \models \mathcal{P}$, and every $\eta \in DefVal(\mathcal{A})$.
c) $(\mathcal{M}_\mathcal{P}, \mathsf{id}) \models \varphi$, where id *is the identity valuation.*

Note that the completeness of $\vdash_{\mathcal{CRWL}}$ also follows from Theorem 3. According to this result, $\mathcal{M}_\mathcal{P}$ can be regarded as the intended *(canonical) model of program $\mathcal{P}$*. In particular, a given $f \in \mathcal{F}$ will denote a deterministic function iff $f^{\mathcal{M}_\mathcal{P}}(t_1, \ldots, t_n)$ is an ideal for all $t_i \in Term_{\Sigma_\perp}$.

5 On the Power of Magic

In this section we will present the basic ideas of the bottom-up evaluation method for our functional logic language. The main idea in the goal solving of a lazy functional logic language under a top-down evaluation, is to select a subgoal (strict equation) at a time and to reduce, by applying narrowing steps, every side of the equation as far as needed until terms in both sides are found. The narrowing steps involve, as it is expressed in CRWL, to select a program rule for the outermost function symbol, to solve lazily non-strict equations as parameter passing in the function's calling and to solve the subgoals of the conditions of the applied rule.

Bottom-up evaluation will solve goals obtaining by means of the fix point operator a Herbrand algebra in which every strict equality in the goal is satisfied. Like logic programming, the so-called *passing magic (boolean) functions* will activate the evaluation of the functions through the fix point operator, whenever there exists a call, passing the arguments from the head to the body and conditions of every program rule for them. In every step of the fix-point operator application, new approximations to the value (or values, due to the non-determinism) of every function are computed.

Table 1. Example 1

(1) $\mathtt{f(s(s(A)),B)} := \mathtt{B} \Leftarrow \mathtt{h(A,C)} == \mathtt{0}, \mathtt{p(C)} == \mathtt{s(0)}, \mathtt{t(0)} == \mathtt{0}.$
(2) $\mathtt{g(s(D))} := \mathtt{s(g(D))}.$
(3) $\mathtt{h(s(E),s(0))} := \mathtt{0}.$
(4) $\mathtt{p(s(I))} := \mathtt{s(p(I))}.$
(5) $\mathtt{p(0)} := \mathtt{0}.$
(6) $\mathtt{t(0)} := \mathtt{0}.$
(7) $\mathtt{t(s(0))} := \mathtt{0}.$
(8) $\mathtt{k} := \mathtt{0}.$
(9) $\mathtt{k} := \mathtt{s(0)}.$
(10) $\mathtt{k} := \mathtt{s(s(0))}.$

Let the program example in table 1[1] and the goal `f(g(X),Y)==t(k)` be, wherein program rules with conditions, terminating and non-terminating recursion, non-strictness, and non-determinism are mixed.

In a top-down evaluation, f(g(X), Y) is narrowed by applying a program rule for f like **(1)** shown in table 1. However, g(X) must be lazily unified previously with s(s(A)), and Y with B respectively. Once unified, the bindings for A and B instantiate the conditions $\Leftarrow$ h(A, C) == 0, p(C) == s(0), t(0) == 0 which became subgoals; similarly with t(k).

In functional-logic bottom-up evaluation the passing magic function for f, named $\mathtt{mg\_f}^{\mathtt{P}}$, activates the evaluation of the body and the conditions for the binding obtained by the lazy unification of g(X) with s(s(A)) and Y with B, and therefore obtaining approximations for (instances of) f(g(X), Y) by means of the fix-point operator. Similarly with t(k). The approximations computed for (instances of) f(g(X), Y) and t(k) are compared in every step of the fix-point operator application and the goal solving successes every time that some (due to non-determinism) of the approximations agrees, for a particular case of the goal, in a total term.

The magic transformation transforms every pair ($\mathcal{P}$,$\mathcal{G}$), where $\mathcal{P}$ is a program and $\mathcal{G}$ is a goal, into a pair ($\mathcal{P}^{\mathcal{MG}}$,$\mathcal{G}^{\mathcal{MG}}$) in such a way that the transformed program, evaluated by means of the fix point operator, computes the same solutions θ of the goal $\mathcal{G}$ w.r.t. the program $\mathcal{P}$.

The transformation process needs the use, in some cases like in our running example, of auxiliary intermediate functions whenever there exist nested constructors occurring in the head of the rules; for instance, `f(s(s(A)),B)` forces to use an auxiliary intermediate function, called $\mathtt{f_1}$, and to add the rules $\mathtt{f(s(A),B)} := \mathtt{f_1(A,B)}$ and $\mathtt{f_1(s(C),D)} := \mathtt{D}$ replacing **(1)** shown in the table 1 which preserves the semantics of f in the original program.

Once the quoted intermediate functions have been introduced, the magic transformation transforms the program, aided by the passing magic boolean functions $\mathtt{mg\_f}^{\mathtt{P}}$, $\mathtt{mg\_f_1}^{\mathtt{P}}$, $\mathtt{mg\_g}^{\mathtt{P}}$, etc., into a filtered program (rules **(1)**-**(11)** shown in table 2) where passing magic functions $mg\_f^P(\bar{t}) == true$ will filter the fix point evaluation for those functions needed by the goal solving. The passing magic functions have its own program rules (see rules **(12)**-**(16)** shown in table 2) activating the evaluation of the body and the left-to-right evaluation of the conditions. In our example, the passing magic function for f will activate the evaluation of $\mathtt{f_1}$ by rule **(1)**, the magic function for $\mathtt{f_1}$ will activate the evaluation

[1] We rename program rules in our examples.

Table 2. Example 1

Filtered Rules

(1) $\mathtt{f(s(A),B)} := \mathtt{f_1(A,B)} \Leftarrow \mathtt{mg\_f^P(s(A),B)} == \mathtt{true}.$
(2) $\mathtt{f_1(s(C),D)} := \mathtt{D} \Leftarrow \mathtt{mg\_f_1^P(s(C),D)} == \mathtt{true}, \mathtt{h(C,E)} == \mathtt{0},$
$\mathtt{p(E)} == \mathtt{s(0)}, \mathtt{t(0)} == \mathtt{0}.$
(3) $\mathtt{g(s(F))} := \mathtt{s(g(F))} \Leftarrow \mathtt{mg\_g^P(s(F))} == \mathtt{true}.$
(4) $\mathtt{h(s(G),s(0))} := \mathtt{0} \Leftarrow \mathtt{mg\_h^P(s(G),s(0))} == \mathtt{true}.$
(5) $\mathtt{p(s(H))} := \mathtt{s(p(H))} \Leftarrow \mathtt{mg\_p^P(s(H))} = \mathtt{true}.$
(6) $\mathtt{p(0)} := \mathtt{0} \Leftarrow \mathtt{mg\_p^P(0)} == \mathtt{true}.$
(7) $\mathtt{t(0)} := \mathtt{0} \Leftarrow \mathtt{mg\_t^P(0)} == \mathtt{true}.$
(8) $\mathtt{t(s(0))} := \mathtt{0} \Leftarrow \mathtt{mg\_t^P(s(0))} == \mathtt{true}.$
(9) $\mathtt{k} := \mathtt{0} \Leftarrow \mathtt{mg\_k^P} == \mathtt{true}.$
(10) $\mathtt{k} := \mathtt{s(0)} \Leftarrow \mathtt{mg\_k^P} == \mathtt{true}.$
(11) $\mathtt{k} := \mathtt{s(s(0))} \Leftarrow \mathtt{mg\_k^P} == \mathtt{true}.$

Magic Rules

(12) $\mathtt{mg\_f_1^P(I,J)} := \mathtt{mg\_f^P(s(I),J)}.$
(13) $\mathtt{mg\_h^P(K,L)} := \mathtt{mg\_f_1^P(s(K),L_1)}.$
(14) $\mathtt{mg\_p^P(M)} := \mathtt{mg\_f_1^P(s(N),P)} \Leftarrow \mathtt{h(N,M)} == \mathtt{0}.$
(15) $\mathtt{mg\_t^P(0)} := \mathtt{mg\_f_1^P(s(R),S)} \Leftarrow \mathtt{h(R,T)} == \mathtt{0}, \mathtt{p(T)} == \mathtt{s(0)}.$
(16) $\mathtt{mg\_p^P(U)} := \mathtt{mg\_p^P(s(U))}.$
(17) $\mathtt{mg\_f_1^P(s(mg\_g^N(V)),X_1)} := \mathtt{mg\_f_1^P(mg\_g^N(s(V)),X_1)}.$
(18) $\mathtt{mg\_f^P(s(mg\_g^N(Y_1)),Z)} := \mathtt{mg\_f^P(mg\_g^N(s(Y_1)),Z)}.$
(19) $\mathtt{mg\_t^P(0)} := \mathtt{mg\_t^P(mg\_k^N)}.$
(20) $\mathtt{mg\_t^P(s(0))} := \mathtt{mg\_t^P(mg\_k^N)}.$
(21) $\mathtt{mg\_t^P(s(s(0)))} := \mathtt{mg\_t^P(mg\_k^N)}.$
(22) $\mathtt{mg\_h^P(s(mg\_g^N(A_1)),B_1)} := \mathtt{mg\_h^P(mg\_g^N(s(A_1)),B_1)}.$
(23) $\mathtt{mg\_f^P(mg\_g^N(X),Y)} := \mathtt{true}.$
(24) $\mathtt{mg\_t^P(mg\_k^N)} := \mathtt{true}.$

Goal Solving Rules

(25) $\mathtt{f(mg\_g^N(s(C_1)),D_1)} := \mathtt{f(s(mg\_g^N(C_1)),D_1)} \Leftarrow \mathtt{mg\_f^P(mg\_g^N(s(C_1)),D_1)} == \mathtt{true}.$
(26) $\mathtt{f_1(mg\_g^N(s(E_1)),F_1)} := \mathtt{f_1(s(mg\_g^N(E_1)),F_1)} \Leftarrow \mathtt{mg\_f_1^P(mg\_g^N(s(E_1)),F_1)} == \mathtt{true}.$
(27) $\mathtt{h(mg\_g^N(s(G_1)),H_1)} := \mathtt{h(s(mg\_g^N(G_1)),H_1)} \Leftarrow \mathtt{mg\_h^P(mg\_g^N(s(G_1)),H_1)} == \mathtt{true}.$
(28) $\mathtt{t(mg\_k^N)} := \mathtt{t(0)} \Leftarrow \mathtt{mg\_t^P(mg\_k^N)} == \mathtt{true}.$
(29) $\mathtt{t(mg\_k^N)} := \mathtt{t(s(0))} \Leftarrow \mathtt{mg\_t^P(mg\_k^N)} == \mathtt{true}.$
(30) $\mathtt{t(mg\_k^N)} := \mathtt{t(s(s(0)))} \Leftarrow \mathtt{mg\_t^P(mg\_k^N)} == \mathtt{true}.$

of h, p and t, as they appear as outermost function symbols of the conditions of the rule **(2)** for $\mathtt{f_1}$ and finally, the magic function for p will trigger the recursion in p by rule **(5)**. In the general case, the transformation process adds only magic rules for the *outermost function symbols* (set denoted by $outer(\mathcal{P},\mathcal{G})$), which are defined as those ones occurring either in the goal, or in the body and conditions of some program rule of the outermost function symbols, or in the conditions of some program rule of function symbols occurring in the scope of an outermost function symbol.

Secondly, the idea is that whenever a function symbol is in the scope of an outermost function symbol, every program rule for the *inner function symbol* generates a rule for the passing magic function of the outermost one. In our example $\mathtt{g(s(D))} := \mathtt{s(g(D))}$, and $\mathtt{k} := \mathtt{0}, \mathtt{k} := \mathtt{s(0)}, \mathtt{k} := \mathtt{s(s(0))}$, generate the rules **(17)-(21)** shown in table 2 for $\mathtt{f_1}$, f, and t, respectively. The head and the body of every program rule of each inner function symbol are "turned around" and introduced as arguments of the head and the body, respectively, of the magic rule for the outermost function symbol, occurring at the same position where they appear in the goal, and filling the rest of arguments with fresh variables. The conditions of the program rules for the inner function symbol, if any, are added as conditions of the magic rule for the outermost one. The inner function symbols are substituted in the magic rules by the so-called *nesting magic constructors*, given that patterns in program rules must be terms.

Moreover, like in our running example, given that g becomes an inner function symbol for h due to the information passing from the first argument of $\mathtt{f_1}$ to h in the rule **(2)**, then the rule **(22)** shown in table 2 is also included. In the general case, for every information passing from the head to an outermost function symbol in the body and conditions, a magic rule of this kind for the outermost symbol is added.

Furthermore, the facts **(23)** and **(24)** shown in table 2 are introduced for the given goal, which activate the evaluation of the outermost symbols f and t in the goal. Therefore, the evaluation of the outermost function symbols, which appear in the bodies and conditions of every program rule for f and t, is activated by means of the corresponding magic rules. This is the same class of transformation of a program rule in the particular case of a goal.

Thirdly, the goal f(g(X),Y)==t(k) is transformed into a new magic goal $\mathtt{f(mg\_g^N(X), Y) == t(mg\_k^N)}$. In the general case, given a goal $\mathcal{G}$, every equation $e == e' \in \mathcal{G}$ is transformed into a new equation wherein each inner function symbol is replaced by nesting magic constructors.

Finally, the rules **(25)-(30)** shown in table 2 must be added. These rules, also named "goal solving rules", allow us to solve the new magic goal whenever the original one has been modified. In our case, the goal solving rules just are the corresponding ones for the magic rules **(17)-(22)**.

Once the program has been transformed, the operational mechanism of the bottom-up evaluation simulates the lazy unification, and the passing of the binding obtained by the unification up to the body and conditions of the program rules. With respect to lazy unification, and starting with the fact **(23)**, the rules **(18)**, **(12)** and **(17)** simulate the evaluation of g for unifying with the first argument of f. The magic rules **(13)**, **(14)** and **(15)** make the information passing up to the conditions of $\mathtt{f_1}$. The rule **(22)** allows to evaluate lazily g for unifying with the first argument of h. Therefore g is evaluated three times in order to apply the rule of f. In general, the magic rules allow to pass the (partial) evaluation of the inner function to evaluate the outermost one for the given (partial) result.

Let remark us that given that our transformation cannot bring forward the required narrowing steps, some magic rules are introduced but not used. For instance, let the program $\mathtt{f(s(X)) := X \Leftarrow h(X) == X}$, $\mathtt{h(s(X)) := X}$ and $\mathtt{g(0) := s(s(0))}$ and the goal $\mathtt{f(g(0)) == 0}$ be, the transformation generates $\mathtt{mg\_h^P(X) := mg\_f^P(s(X))}$, $\mathtt{mg\_f^P(s(s(0))) := mg\_f^P(mg\_g^N(0))}$, $\mathtt{mg\_h^P(s(s(0))) := mg\_h^P(mg\_g^N(0))}$, but given that g only needs to be evaluated once, the last magic rule is never applied, corresponding to lazy evaluation of g.

Note that the fact that every program rule of the inner functions is introduced as argument of the magic rule for the outermost function, is justified as a mechanism of a *demanded driven evaluation* of the outermost function symbol; that is, the inner symbol is evaluated as far as needed to unify lazily with the patterns of every rule of the outermost symbol. The magic transformation passes the inner symbols up to the conditions in order to check if the conditions demand the evaluation of some of the arguments. For instance, let the program $\mathtt{h(Y) := 0 \Leftarrow s(Y) == s(0)}$, $\mathtt{g(0) := s(f(0))}$ and $\mathtt{f(0) := 0}$ and the goal $\mathtt{h(g(0)) == 0}$ be,

Table 3. Bottom-Up Evaluation

$\odot\ \mathcal{H}^{0}_{\mathcal{PMG}} = \bot$
$\odot\ \mathcal{H}^{1}_{\mathcal{PMG}} = \mathcal{H}^{0}_{\mathcal{PMG}} \cup \{\mathtt{mg\_f}^{P}(\mathtt{mg\_g}^{N}(\mathtt{X}),\mathtt{Y}) = \mathtt{true}, \mathtt{mg\_t}^{P}(\mathtt{mg\_k}^{N}) = \mathtt{true}\}$
$\odot\ \theta_1 = \{\mathtt{X/s(Y_1)}, \mathtt{Y/Z}\}\ \mathcal{H}^{2}_{\mathcal{PMG}} = \mathcal{H}^{1}_{\mathcal{PMG}} \cup \{\mathtt{mg\_f}^{P}(\mathtt{s}(\mathtt{mg\_g}^{N}(\mathtt{Y_1})),\mathtt{Z}) = \mathtt{true},$
$\mathtt{mg\_t}^{P}(0) = \mathtt{true}, \mathtt{mg\_t}^{P}(\mathtt{s}(0)) = \mathtt{true}, \mathtt{mg\_t}^{P}(\mathtt{s}(\mathtt{s}(0))) = \mathtt{true}\}$
$\odot\ \theta_2 = \theta_1 \circ \{\mathtt{I}/\mathtt{mg\_g}^{N}(\mathtt{Y_1}), \mathtt{J/Z}\}\ \mathcal{H}^{3}_{\mathcal{PMG}} = \mathcal{H}^{2}_{\mathcal{PMG}} \cup \{\mathtt{t}(\mathtt{s}(0)) = 0, \mathtt{t}(0) = 0,$
$\mathtt{mg\_f}^{P}_{1}(\mathtt{mg\_g}^{N}(\mathtt{Y_1}),\mathtt{Z}) = \mathtt{true}\}$
$\odot\ \theta_3 = \theta_2 \circ \{\mathtt{Y_1/s(V)}, \mathtt{Z/X_1}\}\ \mathcal{H}^{4}_{\mathcal{PMG}} = \mathcal{H}^{3}_{\mathcal{PMG}} \cup \{\mathtt{mg\_f}^{P}_{1}(\mathtt{s}(\mathtt{mg\_g}^{N}(\mathtt{V})),\mathtt{X_1}) = \mathtt{true}, \mathtt{t}(\mathtt{mg\_k}^{N}) = 0\}$
$\odot\ \theta_4 = \theta_3 \circ \{\mathtt{K}/\mathtt{mg\_g}^{N}(\mathtt{V}), \mathtt{L_1/X_1}\}\ \mathcal{H}^{5}_{\mathcal{PMG}} = \mathcal{H}^{4}_{\mathcal{PMG}} \cup \{\mathtt{mg\_h}^{P}(\mathtt{mg\_g}^{N}(\mathtt{V}),\mathtt{L}) = \mathtt{true}\}$
$\odot\ \theta_5 = \theta_4 \circ \{\mathtt{V/s(A_1)}, \mathtt{L/B_1}\}\mathcal{H}^{6}_{\mathcal{PMG}} = \mathcal{H}^{5}_{\mathcal{PMG}} \cup \{\mathtt{mg\_h}^{P}(\mathtt{s}(\mathtt{mg\_g}^{N}(\mathtt{A_1})),\mathtt{B_1}) = \mathtt{true}\}$
$\odot\ \theta_6 = \theta_5 \circ \{\mathtt{G}/\mathtt{mg\_g}^{N}(\mathtt{A_1}), \mathtt{B_1/s(0)}\}\ \mathcal{H}^{7}_{\mathcal{PMG}} = \mathcal{H}^{6}_{\mathcal{PMG}} \cup \{\mathtt{h}(\mathtt{s}(\mathtt{mg\_g}^{N}(\mathtt{A_1})),\mathtt{s}(0)) = 0\}$
$\odot\ \theta_7 = \theta_6 \circ \{\mathtt{G_1/A_1}, \mathtt{H_1/s(0)}\}\mathcal{H}^{8}_{\mathcal{PMG}} = \mathcal{H}^{7}_{\mathcal{PMG}} \cup \{\mathtt{h}(\mathtt{mg\_g}^{N}(\mathtt{s}(\mathtt{A_1})),\mathtt{s}(0)) = 0\}$
$\odot\ \theta_8 = \theta_7 \circ \{\mathtt{N}/\mathtt{mg\_g}^{N}(\mathtt{s}(\mathtt{A_1})), \mathtt{M/s(0)}, \mathtt{P/X_1}\}\ \mathcal{H}^{9}_{\mathcal{PMG}} = \mathcal{H}^{8}_{\mathcal{PMG}} \cup \{\mathtt{mg\_p}^{P}(\mathtt{s}(0)) = \mathtt{true}\}$
$\odot\ \theta_9 = \theta_8 \circ \{\mathtt{U/0}\}\ \mathcal{H}^{10}_{\mathcal{PMG}} = \mathcal{H}^{9}_{\mathcal{PMG}} \cup \{\mathtt{mg\_p}^{P}(0) = \mathtt{true}\}$
$\odot\ \mathcal{H}^{11}_{\mathcal{PMG}} = \mathcal{H}^{10}_{\mathcal{PMG}} \cup \{\mathtt{p}(0) = 0\}$
$\odot\ \theta_{10} = \theta_9 \circ \{\mathtt{H/0}\}\ \mathcal{H}^{12}_{\mathcal{PMG}} = \mathcal{H}^{11}_{\mathcal{PMG}} \cup \{\mathtt{p}(\mathtt{s}(0)) = \mathtt{s}(0)\}$
$\odot\ \theta_{11} = \theta_{10} \circ \{\mathtt{T/s(0)}, \mathtt{R}/\mathtt{mg\_g}^{N}(\mathtt{s}(\mathtt{A_1})), \mathtt{S/X_1}\}\ \mathcal{H}^{13}_{\mathcal{PMG}} = \mathcal{H}^{12}_{\mathcal{PMG}} \cup \{\mathtt{mg\_t}^{P}(0) = 0\}$
$\odot\ \theta_{12} = \theta_{11} \circ \{\mathtt{C}/\mathtt{mg\_g}^{N}(\mathtt{s}(\mathtt{A_1})), \mathtt{D/X_1}, \mathtt{E/s(0)}\}\ \mathcal{H}^{14}_{\mathcal{PMG}} = \mathcal{H}^{13}_{\mathcal{PMG}} \cup \{\mathtt{f_1}(\mathtt{s}(\mathtt{mg\_g}^{N}(\mathtt{s}(\mathtt{A_1}))),\mathtt{X_1}) = \mathtt{X_1}\}$
$\odot\ \theta_{13} = \theta_{12} \circ \{\mathtt{E_1}/\mathtt{mg\_g}^{N}(\mathtt{s}(\mathtt{A_1})), \mathtt{F_1/X_1}\}\ \mathcal{H}^{15}_{\mathcal{PMG}} = \mathcal{H}^{14}_{\mathcal{PMG}} \cup \{\mathtt{f_1}(\mathtt{mg\_g}^{N}(\mathtt{s}(\mathtt{s}(\mathtt{A_1}))),\mathtt{X_1}) = \mathtt{X_1}\}$
$\odot\ \theta_{14} = \theta_{13} \circ \{\mathtt{A}/\mathtt{mg\_g}^{N}(\mathtt{s}(\mathtt{s}(\mathtt{A_1}))), \mathtt{B/X_1}\}\ \mathcal{H}^{16}_{\mathcal{PMG}} = \mathcal{H}^{15}_{\mathcal{PMG}} \cup \{\mathtt{f}(\mathtt{s}(\mathtt{mg\_g}^{N}(\mathtt{s}(\mathtt{s}(\mathtt{A_1})))),\mathtt{X_1}) = \mathtt{X_1}\}$
$\odot\ \theta_{15} = \theta_{14} \circ \{\mathtt{C_1}/\mathtt{s}(\mathtt{s}(\mathtt{A_1})), \mathtt{D_1/X_1}\}\ \mathcal{H}^{17}_{\mathcal{PMG}} = \mathcal{H}^{16}_{\mathcal{PMG}} \cup \{\mathtt{f}(\mathtt{mg\_g}^{N}(\mathtt{s}(\mathtt{s}(\mathtt{s}(\mathtt{A_1})))),\mathtt{X_1})) = \mathtt{X_1},$
$\mathtt{t}(\mathtt{mg\_k}^{N}) = 0\}$

then the magic transformation generates $\mathtt{mg\_h}^{P}(\mathtt{s}(\mathtt{mg\_f}^{N}(0))) := \mathtt{mg\_h}^{P}(\mathtt{mg\_g}^{N}(0))$, $\mathtt{mg\_h}^{P}_{1}(\mathtt{Y}) := \mathtt{mg\_h}^{P}(\mathtt{s}(\mathtt{Y}))$, and $\mathtt{mg\_h}^{P}_{1}(0) := \mathtt{mg\_h}^{P}_{1}(\mathtt{mg\_f}^{N}(0))$. Therefore g(0) is demanded for satisfying the condition $\mathtt{s(Y)} == \mathtt{s}(0)$.

In summary, in order to get laziness, there is an imposed condition to pass program rules (for inner symbols) as arguments of magic rules for outermost symbols: either the corresponding pattern of the outermost function is a constructor term or it is a variable occurring in a safe position (i.e. out of the scope of a function symbol) in the body or condition. Both cases ensure the laziness of the evaluation process. Otherwise, that is, if the variable occurs in the scope of a function symbol f then there could exist the corresponding magic rule for f.

For instance, let $\mathtt{f}(\mathtt{g}(0)) == 0$ the goal and the program $\mathtt{f}(\mathtt{s}(\mathtt{X})) := \mathtt{X}$, $\mathtt{g}(0) := \mathtt{s}(0)$ be, then there is a passing magic rule $\mathtt{mg\_f}^{P}(\mathtt{s}(0)) := \mathtt{mg\_f}^{P}(\mathtt{mg\_g}^{N}(0))$, expressing that f demands the evaluation of g for lazily unifying with the pattern s(X). Now, let $\mathtt{f}(\mathtt{g}(0)) == \mathtt{s}(0)$ the goal and the program $\mathtt{f}(\mathtt{Y}) := \mathtt{s}(\mathtt{Y})$, $\mathtt{g}(0) := 0$ be, then there exists the same passing magic rule $\mathtt{mg\_f}^{P}(0) := \mathtt{mg\_f}^{P}(\mathtt{mg\_g}^{N}(0))$, since f is an outermost symbol (thus occurring in the goal or in a subgoal), and for complying with the strict semantics, Y must be necessarily evaluated. However, there are no passing rules of this class whenever $\mathtt{f}(\mathtt{T}) := \mathtt{h}(\mathtt{T})$ and $\mathtt{h}(\mathtt{Y}) := 0$, given that both f and h are non-strict in T and Y, respectively.

The bottom-up evaluation (shown in table 3) of the magic program in table 2 with the fix point operator of the definition 8 ends (that is, the Herbrand model for the magic program is computed in a finite number of steps) computing $\theta = \{\mathtt{X}/\mathtt{s}(\mathtt{s}(\mathtt{s}(\mathtt{A_1}))), \mathtt{Y/0}\}$ as answer; that is, the instance $\mathtt{f}(\mathtt{mg\_g}^{N}(\mathtt{s}(\mathtt{s}(\mathtt{s}(\mathtt{A_1})))), 0) == \mathtt{t}(\mathtt{mg\_k}^{N})$ is satisfied in the computed Herbrand model.

The algorithm for the magic transformation is shown in tables 4 and 5, where

– $\bar{t}|_i$ represents the subterm of $\bar{t}$ at position i
– $\bar{e}[e']_i$ represents $\bar{e}$ replacing the subexpression at position i by e'

- safe(φ) represents the sub-expression of φ out of the scope of a function symbol
- e^N is defined as $X^N =_{def} X, c(\bar{e})^N =_{def} c(\overline{e^N})$ and $f(\bar{e})^N =_{def} f(\overline{e^{mg^N}})$ and $X^{mg^N} =_{def} X$, $c(\bar{e})^{mg^N} =_{def} c(\overline{e^{mg^N}})$ and $f(\bar{e})^{mg^N} =_{def} mg\_f^N(\overline{e^{mg^N}})$; that is, the inner function symbols are replaced by nesting magic constructors
- e^P is defined as $X^P =_{def} X, c(\bar{e})^P =_{def} c(\overline{e^P})$ and $f(\bar{e})^P =_{def} mg\_f^P(\overline{e^{mg^N}})$; that is, the outermost function symbols are replaced by passing magic functions and the inner function symbols by nesting magic constructors.
- The meaning of the algorithm parameters is as follows: $\bar{e}$ represents the expression or sequence of expressions to be considered (there can be subexpressions occurring in the goal or in some program rule); $h(\bar{t})$ is the head of a program rule; the boolean *Rule?* is true whenever the parameter $h(\bar{t})$ has been input; f is a function symbol representing that $\bar{e}$ is in the scope of the outermost symbol f; the boolean *Nested?* is true whenever the parameter f has been input; C represents conditions of some program rule or goal; M_g represents the computed set of magic rules; P_g represents the computed set of program rules; *ind* indicates the position of $\bar{e}$ in the scope of the outermost symbol f and G represents a set of triples (f, g, i) where each triple means that the function g is nested by f at position i.

The algorithm transforms every pair ($\mathcal{P}$,$\mathcal{G}$), where $\mathcal{P}$ is a program and $\mathcal{G}$ is a goal, into a pair ($\mathcal{P}^{\mathcal{MG}}$,$\mathcal{G}^{\mathcal{MG}}$) in such a way that the transformed program, evaluated by means of the fix point operator, computes the same solutions θ of the goal $\mathcal{G}$ w.r.t. the program $\mathcal{P}$. It is applied as follows:

$C := \emptyset$; $Mg := \emptyset$; $Pg := \mathcal{P}$; $G := \emptyset$; $ind := 0$;
for every $e == e' \in \mathcal{G}$ **do**
Magic_Alg$(e, \_, false, \_false, C, M_g, P_g, ind, G)$;
Magic_Alg$(e', \_, false, \_, false, C, M_g, P_g, ind, G)$;
$C := C \cup \{e == e'\}$
endfor

where "_" denotes arguments not needed for the calling.

Once the algorithm has been applied, $\mathcal{P}^{\mathcal{MG}}$ consists of $P_g^P \cup M_g$, where $(f(\bar{t}) := r \Leftarrow C)^P$ is of the form $f(\bar{t}) := r \Leftarrow mg\_f^P(\bar{t}) == true, C$, and $\Sigma^{\mathcal{MG}}$ consists of $\mathcal{C} \cup \mathcal{C}^{\mathcal{MG}}$ and $\mathcal{F} \cup \mathcal{F}^{\mathcal{MG}}$ where $\mathcal{C}^{\mathcal{MG}}$ and $\mathcal{F}^{\mathcal{MG}}$ denote the set of nesting magic constructors, and passing magic functions, respectively. $\mathcal{G}^{\mathcal{MG}}$ consists of the set $e^N == e'^N$ for each $e == e' \in \mathcal{G}$.

The basic idea of this algorithm is starting from the goal to traverse the program rules of the outermost function symbols in the goal. For every traversed program rule the algorithm includes in Mg the magic rules of the information passing from the outermost symbols to the body and conditions in its rules; and in Pg the new rules for the outermost symbols.

The parameter G includes the collection of occurrences of inner function symbols in outermost function symbols in order to use it in each information passing.

The main algorithm **Magic_Alg** uses an auxiliary algorithm **Nesting** which introduces the rules of inner function symbols as arguments of the outermost ones in both new and magic rules.

Table 4. Magic Algorithm

```
Magic_Alg(in ē : tuple(Expression); in h(t̄) : Expression; in Rule? : Bool;
 in f : FunctionSymbol; in Nested? : Bool; in C : Goal; in/out M_g : Program;
 in/out P_g : Program; in/out ind : Index; in/out G : set(tuple(FunctionSymbol,
FunctionSymbol, Index)))
var C'' : Goal;
if Nested? then
   if Rule? then M_g := M_g ∪ {f_ind(ē)^P := mg_h^P(t̄) ⇐ C}
            else M_g := M_g ∪ {f_ind(ē)^P := true}
   endif;
   for every e_1, ..., e_n do
   case e_i of
     X, X ∈ V  :
      if Rule? then
        if ((h, k, j) ∈ G) and (t̄|_j ≡ X) then
          G := G ∪ {(f_ind, k, i)}; Nesting(k, f, M_g, P_g, ind, i, G);
        endif;
      endif;
     c(ē'), c ∈ C^{MG}  :
      for every f_ind(t̄) := r ⇐ C' ∈ P_g do
        if (t_i ≡ c(t̄') and not (t̄' ≡ X̄ and X̄ ∩ (safe(r) ∪ safe(C')) = ∅)) then
         P_g := P_g ∪ {f_ind+1(t̄[t̄']_i) := r ⇐ C', f_ind(X̄[c(V̄)]_i)^N := f_ind+1(X̄[V̄]_i)^N};
         M_g := M_g ∪ {f_ind+1(X̄[V̄]_i)^P := f_ind(X̄[c(V̄)]_i)^P};
         endif;
         if (t_i ∈ V and t_i ∈ safe(r) ∪ safe(C')) then
         P_g := P_g ∪ {f_ind+1(t̄) := r ⇐ C', f_ind(X̄[c(V̄)]_i)^N := f_ind+1(X̄[V̄]_i)^N};
         M_g := M_g ∪ {f_ind+1(X̄[V̄]_i)^P := f_ind(X̄[c(V̄)]_i)^P};
        endif;
      endfor;
      ind := ind + 1; Magic_Alg(ē', h(t̄), Rule?, f, true, C, M_g, P_g, ind, G);
     k(ē'), k ∈ F :
      if ((f_ind, k, i) ∉ G) then
        G := G ∪ {(f_ind, k, i)}; Nesting(k, f, M_g, P_g, ind, i, G);
        Magic_Alg(mg_k^N(ē'), h(t̄), Rule?, f, true, C, M_g, P_g, ind, G);
      endif;
   endcase;
   endfor;
else
   for every e_1, ..., e_n do
    case e_i of
     c(ē'), c ∈ C :
      Magic_Alg(ē', h(t̄), Rule?, −, false, C, M_g, P_g, ind, G);
     k(ē'), k ∈ F :
      Magic_Alg(ē', h(t̄), Rule?, k, true, C, M_g, P_g, ind, G);
      for every k(s̄) := r ⇐ C' ∈ P_g do
        Magic_Alg(r, k(s̄), true, −, false, C', M_g, P_g, ind, G);
        C'' := ∅;
        for every e == e' ∈ C' do
          Magic_Alg(e, k(s̄), true, −, false, C'', M_g, P_g, ind, G);
          Magic_Alg(e', k(s̄), true, −, false, C'', M_g, P_g, ind, G);
          C'' := C'' ∪ {e == e'}
        endfor;
      endfor;
    endcase;
   endfor;
endif;
```

In the magic algorithm, we can distinguish the following main cases: (a) nested expressions (in the scope of an outermost function symbol) and (b) non-nested expressions (out of the scope of an outermost function symbol):

(a) in this case, let f the outermost function symbol and e the expression nested by f be, then a passing magic rule from the head of the rule to the nesting expression is included. In the particular case of the goal, the passing magic rule is a fact (see rules **(12)**-**(16)** and **(23)**-**(24)**).

Table 5. Nesting Transformation

Nesting(**in** k : *FunctionSymbol*; **in** f : *FunctionSymbol*; **in/out** M_g : *Program*; **in/out** P_g : *Program*; **in** *ind* : *Index*; **in** i : *Index*; **in** G : *set*(*tuple*(*FunctionSymbol*, *FunctionSymbol*, *Index*)));
var C'' : *Goal*;
for every $f_{ind}(\bar{t}) := r \Leftarrow C \in P_g$ **do**
    if $(t_i \notin \mathcal{V})$ **or** $((t_i \in \mathcal{V})$ **and** $(t_i \in safe(r) \cup safe(C)))$ **then**
      for every $k(\bar{s}) := r' \Leftarrow C' \in P_g$ **do**
        $M_g := M_g \cup \{f_{ind}(\bar{X}[r']_i)^P := f_{ind}(\bar{X}[k(\bar{s})]_i)^P \Leftarrow C'\}$;
        $P_g := P_g \cup \{f_{ind}(\bar{X}[k(\bar{s})]_i)^N := f_{ind}(\bar{X}[r']_i)^N \Leftarrow C'\}$;
        Magic_Alg($r', k(\bar{s})$, *true*, f, *true*, C', M_g, P_g, *ind*, G);
        $C'' := \emptyset$;
        for every $e == e' \in C'$ **do**
            Magic_Alg($e, f_{ind}(\bar{X}[k(\bar{s})]_i)^P$, *true*, $-$, *false*, C'', M_g, P_g, *ind*, G);
            Magic_Alg($e', f_{ind}(\bar{X}[k(\bar{s})]_i)^P$, *true*, $-$, *false*, C'', M_g, P_g, *ind*, G);
            $C'' := C'' \cup \{e == e'\}$;
            $Mg := Mg \cup \{f_{ind}(\bar{X}[e]_i)^P := f_{ind}(\bar{X}[k(\bar{s})]_i)^P,$
                $f_{ind}(\bar{X}[e']_i)^P := f_{ind}(\bar{X}[k(\bar{s})]_i)^P\}$;
        endfor;
      endfor;
    endif;
endfor;

- If e is a variable occurring in a program rule for h, and it occurs in the head, then the algorithm checks using G if h nests some function in the position of the variable in the head; if any, the algorithm passes the nested function as argument of f (see rule **(22)**).
- If e is a constructor expression, the algorithm introduces the quoted auxiliary functions (see rules **(1)**-**(2)**).
- Finally, if e is a functional expression $k(\bar{e})$, the algorithm passes every rule of k as argument of the outermost symbol f in each rule of f, whenever the nested expression $k(\bar{e})$ is demanded by the rule; that is, the pattern of the rule is a constructor term or it is a variable occurring in a safe position of the body or conditions (see rules **(17)**-**(22)** and **(25)**-**(30)**).

(b) In the case of non-nested expression, the algorithm has only to decompose the arguments, so that if the expression is a functional one (there exists an outermost function symbol), then each rule for it must be analyzed.

6 Soundness, Completeness and Optimality

In this section we present our soundness, completeness and optimality results of our evaluation method based on the magic transformation proposed. From now on, we suppose there is a program $\mathcal{P}$, a goal $\mathcal{G}$ and $\mathcal{P}^{\mathcal{MG}}$, $\mathcal{G}^{\mathcal{MG}}$ represents the program and goal obtained by following the magic transformation. Our first result establishes the equivalence among both the original and transformed program w.r.t. the given goal.

Theorem 4 (Soundness and Completeness). *$\mathcal{P} \vdash_{\mathcal{CRWL}} \mathcal{G}\theta \Leftrightarrow \mathcal{P}^{\mathcal{MG}} \vdash_{\mathcal{CRWL}} \mathcal{G}^N\theta$.*

The second result ensures optimality of our bottom-up evaluation method, in the sense of, every value computed for a function symbol corresponds either with a subproof of a proof of some solution for the goal, or with a subproof for a non-strict equation involved in the lazy unification of an expression with the pattern of a rule of an outermost function symbol. Moreover, the result assures that each computed magic fact corresponds with one of the evaluated functions.

Theorem 5 (Optimality).

– *If* $\mathcal{P}^{\mathcal{MG}} \vdash_{\mathcal{CRWL}} f(\bar{e})^N \rightarrow t$, $t \neq \bot$, *then* $f \in outer(\mathcal{P}, \mathcal{G})$ *and either:*
  - *there exist* θ, *a proof* $\mathcal{P} \vdash_{\mathcal{CRWL}} \mathcal{G}\theta$ *of minimal size and a subproof of the form* $\mathcal{P} \vdash_{\mathcal{CRWL}} f(\bar{e}) \rightarrow t$
  - *or there exists* $f(\bar{t}) := r \Leftarrow C \in [\mathcal{P}]$ *such that* $\mathcal{P} \vdash_{\mathcal{CRWL}} e_i \rightarrow t_i$ *is a proof of minimal size.*

– *If* $\mathcal{P}^{\mathcal{MG}} \vdash_{\mathcal{CRWL}} f_k(\bar{e})^N \rightarrow t, t \neq \bot$ *then* $f \in outer(\mathcal{P}, \mathcal{G})$ *and either:*
  - *there exist* θ, *a proof* $\mathcal{P} \vdash_{\mathcal{CRWL}} \mathcal{G}\theta$ *of minimal size and a subproof of the form* $\mathcal{P} \vdash_{\mathcal{CRWL}} f(\bar{e'}) \rightarrow t$ *containing subproofs* $\mathcal{P} \vdash_{\mathcal{CRWL}} e_i \rightarrow t_i$ *for some* $f(\bar{t}) := r \Leftarrow C \in [\mathcal{P}]$
  - *or there exists* $f(\bar{t}) := r \Leftarrow C \in [\mathcal{P}]$ *such that* $\mathcal{P} \vdash_{\mathcal{CRWL}} e_i \rightarrow t_i$ *is a proof of minimal size.*

– *If* $\mathcal{P}^{\mathcal{MG}} \vdash_{\mathcal{CRWL}} f(\bar{e})^P \rightarrow true$ *then there exists a proof* $\mathcal{P}^{\mathcal{MG}} \vdash_{\mathcal{CRWL}} f(\bar{e})^N \rightarrow t$ *for some* t.

7 Conclusions and Future Work

In this paper, we have presented a framework for goal-directed bottom-up evaluation of functional logic programs. We have shown that our evaluation method is sound and complete w.r.t. a conditional rewriting logic which provides logic foundations to our functional logic language. We have also proved that our method is optimal, that is, the computed "facts" can be mapped with subproofs of a proof for some solution of the goal. We want to remark that our magic algorithm also provides a transformation for functional logic programs which can be used under a top-down evaluation; in fact a Prolog interpreter as:

$\mathtt{X} == \mathtt{X} : -\mathtt{var(X)}.$
$\mathtt{c(X_1, \ldots, X_n)} == \mathtt{c(Y_1, \ldots, Y_n)} : -\mathtt{X_1} == \mathtt{Y_1}, \ldots, \mathtt{X_n} == \mathtt{Y_n}.$ % for every $\mathtt{c} \in C$
$\mathtt{X} == \mathtt{Y} : -\mathtt{X} := \mathtt{Z}, \mathtt{Z} == \mathtt{Y}.$
$\mathtt{X} == \mathtt{Y} : -\mathtt{Y} := \mathtt{Z}, \mathtt{X} == \mathtt{Z}.$

where every rule is defined as a Prolog rule of the form: $\mathtt{f(\bar{t})} := \mathtt{r} : -\mathtt{C}.$, evaluates goals with a top-down lazy narrowing strategy. Similarly, we could write a bottom-up interpreter in the line of the presented for logic programming in [6]. We expect that other magic transformations presented in the literature can be successfully applied in our framework. As future work, we will study how to consider, like the most deductive query languages, the dealing with negative goals in our language. Moreover, we would like to provide an implementation of our framework based on the indexation of the original and magic rules as well as the management of the secondary memory.

Acknowledgements: We would like to thank anonymous referees for their useful comments.

References

1. J. M. Almendros-Jiménez and A. Becerra-Terón. A Framework for Goal-Directed Bottom-Up Evaluation of Functional Logic Programs, available in `http://www.ual.es/~jalmen`. Technical report, Universidad de Almería, 2000.
2. S. Antoy, R. Echahed, and M. Hanus. A Needed Narrowing Strategy. In *Proc. of POPL'94*. pp. 268–279. ACM Press.

3. K. R. Apt. Logic programming. In *Handbook of Theoretical Computer Science*. vol B: Formal Models and Semantics, chapter 10, pp. 493–574. MIT Press, 1990.
4. R. Barbuti, R. Giacobazzi, and G. Levi. A General Framework for Semantics-based Bottom-up Abstract Interpretation of Logic Programs. *TOPLAS*, 15(1):133–181, 1993.
5. C. Beeri and R. Ramakrishnan. On the Power of Magic. *JLP*, 10(3,4):255–299, 1991.
6. M. Codish. Efficient Goal Directed Bottom-up Evaluation of Logic Programs. In *Proc. of ICLP'97*. pp. 422–439. MIT Press.
7. J. C. González-Moreno, M. T. Hortalá-González, F. López-Fraguas, and M. Rodríguez-Artalejo. An Approach to Declarative Programming Based on a Rewriting Logic. *JLP*, 1(40):47–87, 1999.
8. M. Hanus. The Integration of Functions into Logic Programming: From Theory to Practice. *JLP*, 19,20:583–628, 1994.
9. M. Hanus. Curry, An Integrated Functional Logic Language, Version 0.7.1. Technical report, University of Kiel, Germany, June 2000.
10. M. Hanus and C. Prehofer. Higher-order Narrowing with Definitional Trees. *JFP*, 9(1):33–75, 1999.
11. P. Kanellakis, G. Kuper, and P. Revesz. Constraint Query Languages. *JCSS*, 51(1):26–52, 1995.
12. D. Kemp, D. Srivastava, and P. Stuckey. Bottom-up Evaluation and Query Optimization of Well-founded Models. *TCS*, 146(1–2):145–184, 1995.
13. D. Kemp and P. Stuckey. Optimizing Bottom-up Evaluation of Constraint Queries. *JLP*, 26(1):1–30, 1996.
14. R. Loogen, F. J. López-Fraguas, and M. Rodríguez-Artalejo. A Demand Driven Computation Strategy for Lazy Narrowing. In *Proc. of PLILP'93*. pp. 184–200. LNCS 714.
15. F. J. Lopez-Fraguas. A General Scheme for Constraint Functional Logic Programming. In *Proc. of ALP'92*. pp. 213–227. LNCS 632.
16. F. J. López-Fraguas and J. Sánchez-Hernández. $\mathcal{TOY}$: A Multiparadigm Declarative System. In *Proc. of the RTA'99*. pp. 244–247. LNCS 1631.
17. J. J. Moreno-Navarro and M. Rodríguez-Artalejo. Logic Programming with Functions and Predicates: The Language BABEL. *JLP*, 12(3):191–223, 1992.
18. A. Poulovasslis and C. Small. A Domain-theoretic Approach to Integrating Functional and Logic Database Languages. In *Proc. of VLDB'93*. pp. 416–428. Morgan Kaufmann.
19. R. Ramakrishnan. Magic Templates: A Spellbinding Approach to Logic Programs. *JLP*, 11(3,4):189–216, 1991.
20. R. Ramakrishnan, D. Srivastava, S. Sudarshan, and P. Seshadri. The CORAL Deductive System. In *VLDB Journal*, 3(2):161–210, 1994.
21. R. Ramakrishnan and J. Ullman. A Survey of Deductive Database Systems. *JLP*, 23(2):125–149, 1995.
22. S. Reddi, A. Poulovassilis, and C. Small. PFL: An Active Functional DBPL. In *Active Rules in Database Systems*. chapter 16, pp. 297–308. Springer, 1999.
23. D. Sacca and C. Zaniolo. The Generalized Counting Method for Recursive Logic Queries. *TCS*, 62(1-2):187–220, 1988.
24. H. Seki. On the Power of Alexander Templates. In *Proc. of PODS'89*. pp. 150–159. ACM Press.
25. J. D. Ullman. Bottom-up Beats Top-down for Datalog. In *Procs. of PODS'89*. pp. 140–149. ACM Press.
26. J. Vaghani, K. Ramamohanarao, D. B. Kemp, Z. Somogyi, P. J. Stuckey, T. S. Leask, and J. Harland. The Aditi Deductive Database System. *VLDB*, 3(2):245–288, 1994.

Theoretical Foundations for the Declarative Debugging of Lazy Functional Logic Programs

Rafael Caballero, Francisco J. López-Fraguas, and Mario Rodríguez-Artalejo *
E-mail: {rafa,paco,mario}@sip.ucm.es

Departamento de Sistemas Informáticos y Programación,
Universidad Complutense de Madrid

Abstract. The aim of this paper is to provide theoretical foundations for the declarative debugging of wrong answers in lazy functional logic programming. We rely on a logical framework which formalizes both the intended meaning and the execution model of programs in a simple language which combines the expressivity of pure Prolog and a significant subset of Haskell. As novelties w.r.t. to previous related approaches, we deal with functional values both as arguments and as results of higher order functions, we obtain a completely formal specification of the debugging method, and we extend known soundness and completeness results for the debugging of wrong answers in logic programming to a substantially more difficult context. A prototype implementation of a working debugger is planned as future work.

1 Introduction

Traditional debugging techniques are not well suited for declarative programming languages, because of the difficult-to-predict evaluation order. In the field of logic programming, Shapiro [19] proposed *declarative debugging* (also called *algorithmic debugging*), a semi-automatic technique which allows to detect bugs on the basis of the intended meaning of the source program, disregarding operational concerns. Declarative debugging of logic programs can diagnose both *wrong* and *missing* computed answers, and it has been proved logically sound and complete [2, 8]. Later on, declarative debugging has been adapted to other programming paradigms, including lazy functional programming [15–17, 11, 14] and combined functional logic programming [13, 12]. A common feature of all these approaches is the use of a *computation tree* whose structure reflects the functional dependencies of a particular computation, abstracting away the evaluation order. In [12], Lee Naish has formulated a generic debugging scheme, based on computation trees, which covers all the declarative debugging methods cited above as particular instances. In the case of logic programming, [12] shows that the computation trees have a clear interpretation w.r.t. the declarative semantics of programs. On the other hand, the computation trees proposed up to now for the declarative debugging of lazy functional programs (or combined functional logic programs) do not yet have a clear logical foundation.

* Work partially supported by the Spanish CICYT (project CICYT-TIC98-0445-C03-02/97 "TREND")

H. Kuchen and K. Ueda (Eds.): FLOPS 2001, LNCS 2024, pp. 170–184, 2001.

The aim of this paper is to provide firm theoretical foundations for the declarative debugging of wrong answers in lazy functional logic programming. Adapting a logical framework borrowed from [5,4], we formalize both the declarative and the operational semantics of programs in a simple language which combines the expressivity of pure Prolog [20] and a significant subset of Haskell [18]. Our approach supports a simple syntactical representation of functions as values. Following the generic scheme from [12], we define a declarative debugging method, giving a formal characterization of computation trees as *proof trees* that relate computed answers to the declarative semantics of programs. More precisely, we formalize a procedure for building proof trees from successful computations. This allows us to prove the logical correctness of the debugger, extending older results from the field of logic programming [2,8] to a substantially more difficult context. Our work is intended as a foundation for the implementation of declarative debuggers for languages such as $\mathcal{TOY}$ [10] and Curry [7], whose execution mechanism is based on *lazy narrowing*.

The paper is organized as follows. Sect. 2 presents the general debugging scheme from [12], recalls some of the known approaches to the declarative debugging of lazy functional and logic programs, and gives an informal motivation of our own proposal. Sect. 3 introduces the simple functional logic language used in the rest of the paper. In Sect. 4 the logical framework which gives a formal semantics to this language is presented. Sect. 5 specifies the debugging method, as well as the formal procedure to build proof trees from successful computations. Sect. 6 concludes and points to future work.

2 Debugging with Computation Trees

The debugging scheme proposed in [12] assumes that any terminated computation can be represented as a finite tree, called *computation tree*. The root of this tree corresponds to the result of the main computation, and each node corresponds to the result of some intermediate subcomputation. Moreover, it is assumed that the result at each node is *determined* by the results of the children nodes. Therefore, every node can be seen as the outcome of a single *computation step*. The debugger works by traversing a given computation tree, looking for *erroneous* nodes. Different kinds of programming paradigms and/or errors need different types of trees, as well as different notions of *erroneous*. A debugger is called *sound* if all the bugs it reports do really correspond to wrong computation steps. Notice, however, that an erroneous node which has some erroneous child does not necessarily correspond to a wrong computation step. Following the terminology of [12], an erroneous node with no erroneous children is called a *buggy node*. In order to avoid unsoundness, the debugging scheme looks only for buggy nodes, asking questions to an *oracle* (generally the user) in order to determine which nodes are erroneous. The following relation between buggy and erroneous nodes can be easily proved:

Proposition 1 *A finite computation tree has an erroneous node iff it has a buggy node. In particular, a finite computation tree whose root node is erroneous has some buggy node.*

This result provides a 'weak' notion of *completeness* for the debugging scheme that is satisfactory in practice. Usually, actual debuggers look only for a topmost buggy node in a computation tree whose root is erroneous. Multiple bugs can be found by reiterated application of the debugger.

The known declarative debuggers can be understood as concrete instances of Naish's debugging scheme. The instances of the debugging scheme needed for diagnosing *wrong* and *missing* answers in pure Prolog are described in [12]. In these two cases, computation trees can be formally defined so that they relate answers computed by SLD resolution to the declarative semantics of programs in a precise way. This fact allows to prove logical correctness of the debugger [2, 8]. The existing declarative debuggers for lazy functional [15–17, 11, 14] and functional logic programs [13, 12] have proposed different, but essentially similar notions of computation tree. Each node contains an oriented equation $f a_1 ... a_n = r$ corresponding to a function call which has been evaluated, together with the returned result, and the children nodes (if any) correspond to those function calls whose evaluation became eventually needed in order to obtain $f a_1 ... a_n = r$. Moreover, the result r is displayed in the most evaluated form eventually reached during the computation, and the same happens for each argument a_i, except in the case of the root node [1]. Such a tree structure abstracts away the actual order in which function calls occur under the lazy evaluation strategy. A node is considered erroneous iff its oriented equation is false in the intended interpretation of the program, and the bug indication extracted from a buggy node is the instance of the oriented equation in the program applied at the outermost level to evaluate the function call in that node.

To illustrate these ideas, let us consider the small program shown in Fig. 1, written in Haskell-like, hopefully self-explanatory syntax. The data constructors s and z represent the successor of a natural number and the natural number zero, respectively, while : acts as an infix binary constructor for non-empty lists and [ ] is a nullary constructor for the empty list. Different defining equations for the same function f are labeled as $f.i$, with indices $i \geq 1$.

```
(from.1) from N                 → N : from N
(take.1) take z      Xs         → [ ]
(take.2) take (s N) [ ]         → [ ]
(take.3) take (s N) (X : Xs)    → X : take N Xs
```

Figure 1: A program example

A function call (*take N Xs*) is intended to compute the first N elements of the list Xs, while (*from N*) is intended to compute the infinite list of all numbers greater or equal than N. The definition of *from* is mistaken, because its right-hand side should be (N : *from* ($\underline{s}\, N$)). Due to this bug, the program can compute *take* $(s(s\, z))$ (*from* z) $= z : z : [\,]$, which is false in the intended interpretation. A computation tree (built according to the method suggested in [16, 13] and related

[1] In order to avoid this exception, some actual debuggers assume a call to a nullary function main at the root node.

papers) would look as shown in Fig. 2, where erroneous nodes are displayed in boldface and the leftmost-topmost buggy node is surrounded by a double box.

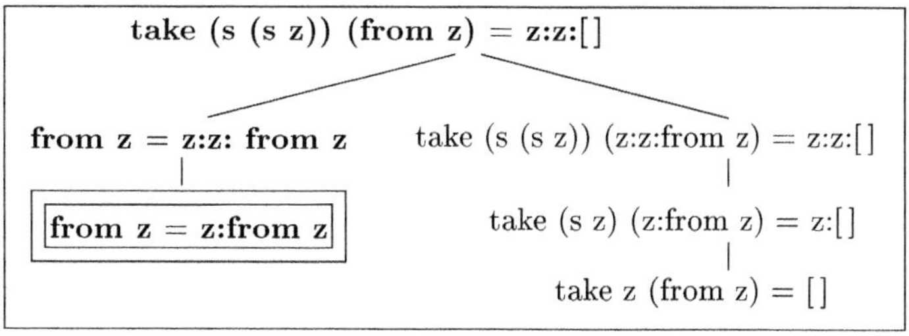

Figure 2: Computation tree with oriented equations

To the best of our knowledge, no formal proofs of correctness exist for the known lazy functional (logic) declarative debuggers, in contrast to the pleasant results shown in [2, 8] for the logic programming case. To achieve such a proof, one needs a sufficiently formal characterization of the relationship between computation trees and a suitable formalization of program semantics. The best attempt we know to formalize computation trees for lazy functional programming has been made in [16], using denotational semantics. However, as the authors acknowledge, their definition only gives an informal characterization of the function calls whose evaluation becomes eventually demanded[2]. A more practical problem with existing debuggers for lazy functional (logic) languages is related to the presentation of the questions asked to the oracle. In principle, such questions should ask whether the oriented equations $f a_1 ... a_n = r$ found at the tree's nodes are valid according to the intended program meaning. In these equations, both the argument expressions a_i and the result expression r can include arbitrarily complex, suspended function calls. Several solutions to this problem have been proposed, trying to ban the offending closures in various ways. In particular, Lee Naish [11] suggests the following simplification procedure: to replace unevaluated closures within the a_i by fresh variables $\overline{X}$; to replace unevaluated closures within r by fresh variables $\overline{Y}$; and to append a quantifier prefix $\forall \overline{X} \, \exists \overline{Y}$ in front of the new oriented equation. Applying this simplification method to Fig. 2, we obtain that the second child of the root node simplifies to $\forall Xs.\ take\ (s(s\,z))(z : z : Xs) = z : z : [\,]$, while the buggy node simplifies to $\exists Ys.\ from\, z = z : Ys$. Note that the simplified question at the older buggy node has become valid in the intended program meaning. Therefore, the older buggy node is not buggy any more in the simplified tree. Its parent becomes buggy instead (and it points to the same program bug).

The example shows that Naish's simplification does not preserve the semantics of oracle questions. Moreover, a simplified oracle question like $\forall \overline{X} \exists \overline{Y}. f a'_1 ... a'_n = r'$ has the same meaning as $f t_1 ... t_n \to t$, where the quantifier prefix has been removed and t_i resp. t are obtained from a'_i resp. r' by substituting the *bottom* symbol $\perp$ (meaning an undefined value) in place of the new variables $\overline{X}$,

[2] Maybe this problem has been better solved in [17], a reference we obtained from the referees upon finishing the paper.

$\overline{Y}$ introduced by simplification. Due to the occurrences of $\bot$ in places where suspended function calls occurred before, the meaning of $\rightarrow$ cannot be understood as oriented equality any more. Instead, $f\,t_1...t_n \rightarrow t$ means that t *approximates* the value of $f\,t_1...t_n$, where each t_i approximates the value of the original argument expression a_i. Coming back to our example, the simplified question $\forall Xs.\ take\ (s(s\,z))\ (z : z : Xs) = z : z : []$ is equivalent to $take\ (s(s\,z))(z : z : \bot) \rightarrow z : z : []$, while $\exists Ys. from\,z = z : Ys$ is equivalent to $from\,z \rightarrow z : \bot$.

We aim at a debugging method based on computation trees whose nodes include statements of the form $f\,t_1...t_n \rightarrow t$, where t_i and t include no function calls, but can include occurrences of the undefined symbol $\bot$. Such statements will be called *basic facts* in the sequel. As we have seen, basic facts have a natural (not equational) meaning, and they help to obtain more simple oracle questions. Moreover, there is a well developed logical framework for functional logic programming [5, 4], based on the idea of viewing basic facts as the analogon of atomic formulas in logic programming. Relying on a variant of this framework, we will obtain a formal characterization of our debugging method.

3 A Simple Functional Logic Programming Language

The functional logic programming (FLP for short) paradigm [6] tries to bridge the gap between the two main streams in declarative programming: functional programming (FP) and logic programming (LP). For the purposes of this paper, we have chosen to work with a simple variant of a known logical framework for FLP [5, 4], which enjoys well-defined proof-theoretic and model-theoretic semantics and has been implemented in the $\mathcal{TOY}$ system [10]. In this section we present the syntax and informal semantics used for programs and goals in the rest of the paper. Pure Prolog [20] programs and Haskell-like programs [18] can be expressed in our language.

3.1 Preliminaries

A *signature with constructors* is a countable set $\Sigma = DC_\Sigma \cup FS_\Sigma$, where $DC_\Sigma = \bigcup_{n \in \mathbb{N}} DC^n_\Sigma$ and $FS_\Sigma = \bigcup_{n \in \mathbb{N}} FS^n_\Sigma$ are disjoint sets of *data constructors* and *defined function symbols* respectively, each one with an associated arity. In the sequel the explicit mention of Σ is omitted. We also assume a countable set $\mathcal{V}$ of variables, disjoint from Σ.

The set of *partial expressions* built up with aid of Σ and $\mathcal{V}$ will be denoted as $Exp_\bot$ and defined as: $Exp_\bot ::= \bot \mid X \mid h \mid (e\,e')$ with $X \in \mathcal{V}$, $h \in \Sigma$, $e, e' \in Exp_\bot$. Expressions of the form $(e\,e')$ stand for the application of e (acting as a function) to e' (acting as an argument). As usual, we assume that application associates to the left and thus $(e_0\,e_1 \ldots e_n)$ abbreviates $((\ldots(e_0\,e_1)\ldots)\,e_n)$. As explained in Sect. 2, the symbol $\bot$ (read *bottom*) represents an undefined value. We distinguish an important kind of partial expressions called *partial patterns*, denoted as $Pat_\bot$ and defined as: $Pat_\bot ::= \bot \mid X \mid c\,t_1 \ldots t_m \mid f\,t_1 \ldots t_m$ where $t_i \in Pat_\bot$, $c \in DC^n$, $0 \le m \le n$ and $f \in FS^n$, $0 \le m < n$. Partial patterns represent *approximations* of the values of expressions. Moreover, partial patterns of the form $f\ t_1 \ldots t_m$ with $f \in FS^n$ and $m < n$ serve as a convenient representation of functions as values; see [4]. Expressions and patterns without any occurrence of $\perp$ are called *total*. We write Exp and Pat for the sets of total expressions and patterns, respectively.

Total substitutions are mappings $\theta : \mathcal{V} \rightarrow Pat$ with a unique extension $\hat{\theta} : Exp \rightarrow Exp$, which will be noted also as θ. The set of all substitutions is denoted as $Subst$. The set $Subst_\perp$ of all the *partial substitutions* $\theta : \mathcal{V} \rightarrow Pat_\perp$ is defined analogously. We write $e\theta$ for the result of applying the substitution θ to the expression e. As usual, $\theta = \{X_1/t_1, \ldots, X_n/t_n\}$ stands for the substitution that satisfies $X_i\theta \equiv t_i$, with $1 \leq i \leq n$ and $Y\theta \equiv Y$ for all $Y \in \mathcal{V} \backslash \{X_1, \ldots, X_n\}$.

3.2 Programs and Goals

In our framework programs are considered as ordered sets of *defining rules* for function symbols. Rule order is not important for the logical meaning of a program. Each rule has a *left-hand side*, a *right-hand side* and an optional *condition*. The general shape of a defining rule for $f \in FS^n$ is:

$$(R) \quad \underbrace{f\ t_1 \ldots t_n}_{\text{left-hand side}} \rightarrow \underbrace{r}_{\text{right-hand side}} \Leftarrow \underbrace{e_1 \rightarrow p_1, \ldots, e_k \rightarrow p_k}_{\text{condition}} \text{ where:}$$

(i) $t_1, \ldots, t_n, p_1, \ldots, p_k$, $(n, k \geq 0)$ is a linear sequence of patterns, where *linear* means that no variable occurs more than once in the sequence.
(ii) $r, e_1, \ldots, e_k$ are expressions. They can contain *extra variables* that don't appear in the left-hand side.
(iii) A variable in p_i can occur in e_j only if $j > i$ (in other words: p_i has no variables in common with $e_1, \ldots, e_i$).
Conditions *(i)*, *(ii)* and *(iii)* above are not too restrictive for programming and technically helpful to obtain well-behaved goal-solving calculi (as the one presented in Subsection 4.3 below). Conditions fulfilling property *(iii)* and such that the sequence $p_1, \ldots, p_k$, is linear will called *admissible* in the sequel. The intended meaning of a rule like (R) is that a call to function f can be reduced to r whenever the actual parameters match the patterns t_i and the conditions $e_j \rightarrow p_j$ are satisfied. In [5, 4], conditions of this kind are called *approximation statements*. They are satisfied whenever e_j can be evaluated to match the pattern p_j. The basic facts $f\ t_1 \ldots t_n \rightarrow t$ mentioned in Sect. 2 are particularly simple approximation statements. Readers familiar with [5, 4] will note that *joinability conditions* $e \bowtie e'$ (written as $e == e'$ in $\mathcal{TOY}$'s concrete syntax) are replaced by *approximation conditions* $e \rightarrow p$ in this paper. This is done in order to simplify the presentation, while keeping expressivity enough for our present purposes.

Fig.1 in Sect.2 shows a program for the signature $DC = \{z/0, s/1, []/0, :/2\}$, $FS = \{from/1, take/2\}$. It will be used as a running example in the rest of this paper. The reader is referred to [5, 4] for more programming examples.

A *goal* in our setting is any admissible condition $e_1 \rightarrow p_1, \ldots, e_k \rightarrow p_k$. Goals with $k = 1$ are called *atomic*. As we will see more formally in the next section, solutions to a goal $e \rightarrow p$ are substitutions θ such that $p\theta$ approximates the value of $e\theta$, according to the semantics of the current program. As in LP, a goal can include *logic variables* that are bound to patterns when the goal is solved.

For instance, considering the goal $take\ N\ (from\ X)) \to Y_s$ for our running example program, and the goal solving calculus presented in Subsection 4.3, the following solutions would be computed in this order: $\theta_1 = \{N/z, Y_s/[\,]\}$; $\theta_2 = \{N/(s\,z), Y_s/X : [\,]\}$; and $\theta_3 = \{N/s\,(s\,z),\ Y_s/X : X : [\,]\}$. Solution θ_3 is incorrect w.r.t. the intended meaning of the program, which calls for debugging. Note that the values for N and X leading to a wrong result can be found by the execution system. In a purely FP setting, the user would have been forced to guess them.

4 A Logical Framework for FLP

We are now ready to formalize a semantics and a goal solving calculus for the simple FLP language described in the previous section. We will follow the approach from [5, 4], with some modifications needed for our present purposes.

4.1 A Semantic Calculus

The *S*emantic *C*alculus *SC* displayed below specifies the meaning of our lazy FLP programs. *SC* is intended to derive an approximation statement $e \to t$ from a given program P just in the case that t approximates the value of e, as computed by the defining rules in P. In the *SC* inference rules, $e, e_i \in Exp_\perp$ are partial expressions, $t_i, t, s \in Pat_\perp$ are partial patterns and $h \in \Sigma$. Moreover, the notation $[P]_\perp$ in rule *RA* stands for the set $\{(l \to r \Leftarrow C)\theta | (l \to r \Leftarrow C) \in P, \theta \in Subst_\perp\}$ of partial instances of the defining rules in P. The *SC* rules are:

BT Bottom: $e \to \perp$

RR Restricted Reflexivity: $X \to X,\ X \in Var$

DC Decomposition: $$\frac{e_1 \to t_1 \ \dots\ e_m \to t_m}{h\,\overline{e}_m \to h\,\overline{t}_m} \quad h\,\overline{t}_m \in Pat_\perp$$

AR Argument Reduction: $$\frac{e_1 \to t_1 \ \dots\ e_n \to t_n \quad \boxed{f\,\overline{t}_n \to s} \quad s\,\overline{a}_k \to t}{f\,\overline{e}_n\,\overline{a}_k \to t}, \quad \begin{array}{l} f \in FS^n \\ t \neq \perp \end{array}$$

RA Rule Application: $$\frac{C \quad r \to s}{\boxed{f\,\overline{t}_n \to s}}, \quad f\,\overline{t}_n \to r \Leftarrow C \in [P]_\perp$$

SC is similar to the rewriting calculus *GORC* from [5, 4]. The main difference is that the *GORC* rule *OR* for *Outer Reduction* has been replaced by *AR* and *RA*. Taken together, these two rules say that a call to a function f is evaluated by computing approximated values for the arguments, and then applying a defining rule for f. This is related to the *strictification* idea in [15, 17], which was intended as an emulation of the innermost evaluation order, but evaluating the arguments only as much as demanded by the rest of the computation.

The conclusion $f\overline{t}_n \to s$ of *RA* is a basic fact that must coincide with the corresponding premise of *AR* when the two rules are combined. The older calculus *GORC* did not explicitly introduce such a basic fact, which is needed for debugging, as we have motivated in Sect. 2. The case $k > 0$ in rule *AR* corresponds to a higher order function f, returning as result another function (represented by the pattern s) which must be applied to some arguments $\overline{a}_k$. Just for convenience, we add to the *SC* calculus the following variant *AR*$'$ of *AR*, to be used only in the case $k = 0$. It can be shown that SC with AR' is equivalent to SC without AR'.

$$\textbf{AR'}\ \frac{e_1 \to t_1 \ \dots \ e_n \to t_n \ \boxed{f\ \bar{t}_n \to t}}{f\ \bar{e}_n \ \to t}\ t \neq \perp, f \in FS^n$$

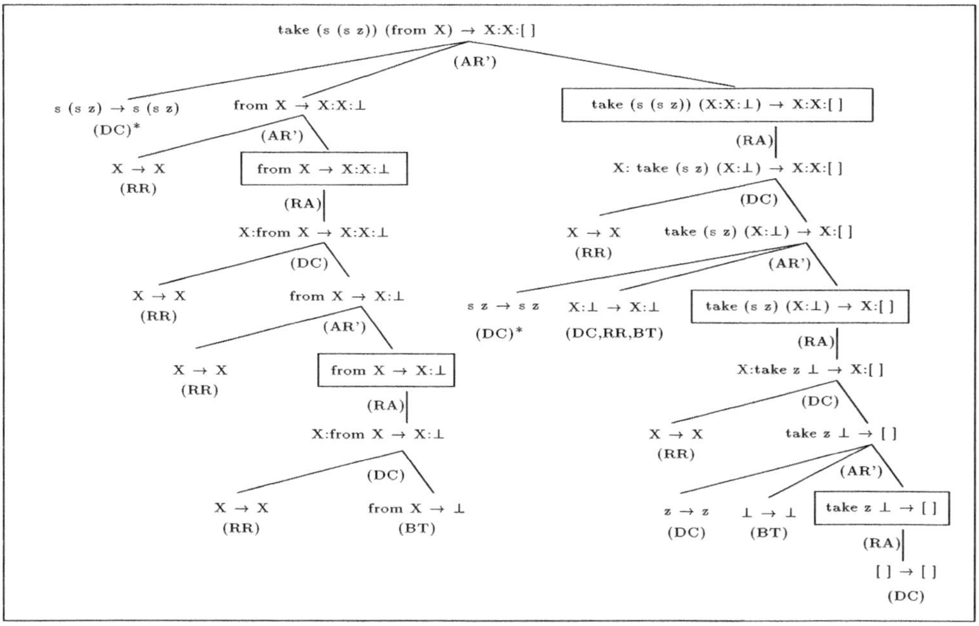

Figure 3: Proof Tree in the semantic calculus SC

We write $P \vdash e \to t$ to indicate that $e \to t$ can be deduced from P using SC. We also define a correct *solution* for a goal $G = e \to t$ w.r.t. program P as any *total substitution* $\theta \in Subst$ such that $P \vdash e\theta \to t\theta$. An SC derivation proving that this is the case can be represented as a tree, which we will call a *proof tree* (PT) for $G\theta$. Each node in a PT corresponds to an approximation statement that follows from its children by means of some SC inference. For instance, the PT from Fig. 3 shows that $\theta = \{N/s\,(s\,z), Ys/X\!:\!X\!:\![\,]\}$ is a solution for the goal $take\,N(from\ X) \to Ys$ w.r.t. our running example program. This is indeed a *bug symptom*. The right solution, according to the program's intended meaning, should be $\theta = \{N/s\,(s\,z), Ys/X\!:\!s\,X\ \!:\![\,]\}$.

4.2 Models

In LP the intended meaning of a program can be formalized as an *intended model*, represented as a set of atomic formulas belonging to the program's Herbrand base [2, 8]. The *open Herbrand universe* (i.e. the set of terms with variables) gives raise to a more informative semantics [3]. In our FLP setting, a natural analogon to the open Herbrand universe is the set $Pat_\perp$ of all the partial patterns, equipped with the approximation ordering: $t \sqsubseteq t' \Longleftrightarrow_{\text{def.}} t' \sqsupseteq t \Longleftrightarrow_{\text{def.}} \emptyset \vdash_{SC} t' \to t$. Similarly, a natural analogon to the open Herbrand base is the collection of all

the basic facts $f\ \bar{t}_n \to t$. Therefore, we define a *Herbrand interpretation* as a set $\mathcal{I}$ of basic facts fulfilling the following three natural requirements, for all $f \in FS^n$ and arbitrary partial patterns $t, \bar{t}_n$:
• $f\,\bar{t}_n \to \perp \in \mathcal{I}$.
• if $f\ \bar{t}_n \to t \in \mathcal{I}$, $t_i \sqsubseteq t'_i, t \sqsupseteq t'$ then $f\,\bar{t}'_n \to t' \in \mathcal{I}$.
• if $f\ \bar{t}_n \to t\ \in \mathcal{I}$, $\theta \in Subst$ then $(f\ \bar{t}_n \to t)\theta \in \mathcal{I}$.

This definition of Herbrand interpretation is simpler than the one in [5, 4], where a more general notion of interpretation (under the name *algebra*) is presented. The trade-off for this simpler presentation is to exclude non-Herbrand interpretations from our consideration. In our debugging scheme we will assume that the intended model of a program is a Herbrand interpretation $\mathcal{I}$. Herbrand interpretations can be ordered by set inclusion. In our running example, the intended interpretation contains basic facts such as $from\ X \to \perp$, $from\ X \to X : \perp$, $from\ X \to X : s\,X : \perp$ or $take\,(s(s\,z))(X|! : s\,X|! : \perp) \to X : s\,X : [\,]$.

By definition, we say that an approximation statement $e \to t$ is *valid* in $\mathcal{I}$ iff $e \to t$ can be proved in the calculus $SC_{\mathcal{I}}$ consisting of the SC rules BT, RR and DC together with the rule $FA_{\mathcal{I}}$ below, whose rôle is similar to the combination of the two SC rules AR and RA:

$$\mathbf{FA}_{\mathcal{I}} \quad \frac{e_1 \to t_1\ \ldots\ e_n \to t_n \quad s\,\bar{a}_k \to t}{f\ \bar{e}_n\,\bar{a}_k \to t} \quad \begin{array}{l} t \text{ pattern},\ t \neq \perp, s \text{ pattern} \\ f\ \bar{t}_n \to s \in \mathcal{I} \end{array}$$

For instance, the approximation statement $take\,(s\,(s\,z))\,(from\,X) \to X : s\,X : [\,]$ is valid in the intended model of our running example program. For any basic fact $f\ \bar{t}_n \to t$ and any Herbrand interpretation $\mathcal{I}$, it can be shown that $f\ \bar{t}_n \to t$ is valid in $\mathcal{I}$ iff $f\ \bar{t}_n \to t \in \mathcal{I}$. The *denotation* of $e \in Exp_\perp$ in $\mathcal{I}$ is defined as the set: $[\![e]\!]^{\mathcal{I}} = \{t \in Pat_\perp \mid e \to t \text{ valid in } \mathcal{I}\}$. Given a program P without bugs, the intended model $\mathcal{I}$ should be a model of P. This relies on the following definition of model, which generalizes the corresponding notion from logic programming:
• $\mathcal{I}$ is a model for P ($\mathcal{I} \models P$) iff $\mathcal{I}$ is a model for every program rule in P.
• $\mathcal{I}$ is a model for a program rule $l \to r \Leftarrow C$ ($\mathcal{I} \models l \to r \Leftarrow C$) iff for any substitution $\theta \in Subst_\perp$, $\mathcal{I}$ satisfies $l\theta \to r\theta \Leftarrow C\theta$.
• $\mathcal{I}$ satisfies a rule instance $l' \to r' \Leftarrow C'$ iff either $\mathcal{I}$ does not satisfy C' or $[\![l']\!]^{\mathcal{I}} \supseteq [\![r']\!]^{\mathcal{I}}$.
• $\mathcal{I}$ satisfies an admissible condition C' iff for any $e' \to p' \in C'$, $[\![e']\!]^{\mathcal{I}} \supseteq [\![p']\!]^{\mathcal{I}}$.
It can be shown that $[\![e']\!]^{\mathcal{I}} \supseteq [\![p']\!]^{\mathcal{I}}$ iff $p' \in [\![e']\!]^{\mathcal{I}}$.
A straightforward consequence of the previous definitions is that $\mathcal{I} \not\models P$ iff there exists a program rule $l \to r \Leftarrow C$, $\theta \in Subst_\perp$ and $t \in Pat_\perp$ such that $e\theta \to p\theta$ is valid in $\mathcal{I}$ for any $e \to p\ \in\ C$, $r\theta \to t$ is valid in $\mathcal{I}$, but $l\theta \to t\ \notin\ \mathcal{I}$. Under these conditions we say that the program rule $l \to r \Leftarrow C$ is *incorrect* w.r.t. the intended model $\mathcal{I}$ and that $(l \to r \Leftarrow C)\theta$ is an *incorrect instance* of the program rule. In our running example, the program rule $from\,X \to X : from\,X$ is incorrect w.r.t. the intended model $\mathcal{I}$, because $X : from\ X \to X : X : \perp$ is valid in $\mathcal{I}$ but $from\ X \to X : X : \perp \notin \mathcal{I}$. By a straightforward adaptation of results given in [5, 4], we can obtain the following relationships between programs and models:

Proposition 2 *Let P be a program and $e \to t$ an approximation statement. Then:*
(a) If $P \vdash e \to t$ then $e \to t$ is valid in any Herbrand model of P.
(b) $M_P = \{f\ \bar{t}_n \to t | P \vdash f\ \bar{t}_n \to t\}$ is the least Herbrand model *of P w.r.t. the inclusion ordering.*
(c) If $e \to t$ is valid in $\mathcal{M}_P$ then $P \vdash e \to t$.

According to these results, the least Herbrand model of a correct program should be a subset of the intended model. This is not the case for our running example, where the approximation statement $take\ (s(s\,z))\ (from\ X) \to X : X : []$ is valid in $\mathcal{M}_P$ but not in the intended model.

4.3 A Goal Solving Calculus

We next present a *Goal Solving Calculus GSC* which formalizes the computation of solutions for a given goal. GSC is inspired by the lazy narrowing calculi from [5, 4], adapted to the modified language in this paper. Since we have no joinability statements here, the rules to deal with them have been omitted. The rules given in [4] to deal with *higher order logic variables* have been also omitted for simplicity; they could be added without any difficulty.

The GSC calculus consists of rules intended to transform a goal step by step. Each step transforms a goal G_{i-1} into a new goal G_i, yielding a substitution σ_i. This is done by selecting an atomic subgoal of G_{i-1} and replacing it by new subgoals according to some GSC rule. Therefore, GSC-rules have the shape $G,\ e \to t,\ G' \Vdash_{\sigma_i} (G, G'', G')\sigma_i$. A GSC computation succeeds when the *empty goal* (represented as $\Box$) is reached. The composition σ of all the substitutions σ_i along a successful computation is called a *GSC computed answer* for the initial goal.

As auxiliary notions, we need to introduce *user-demanded variables* and *demanded variables*. Informally, we say that a variable X is user-demanded if X occurs in t for some atomic subgoal $e \to t$ of the initial goal, or X is introduced by some substitution which binds another user-demanded variable. Formally, let $G_0 = e_1 \to t_1, \ldots e_k \to t_k$ be the initial goal, G_{i-1} any intermediate goal, and $G_{i-1} \Vdash_{\sigma_i} G_i$ any calculus step. Then the sets of user-demanded variables ($udvar$) are defined in the following way:

$$udvar(G_0) = \bigcup_{i=1}^{k} var(t_i) \qquad udvar(G_i) = \bigcup_{x \in udvar(G_{i-1})} var(x\sigma_i),\ i > 0$$

Let $e \to t$ be an atomic subgoal of a goal G. By definition, a variable X in t is demanded if it is either a user-demanded variable or else there is some atomic subgoal in G of the shape: $X\ \bar{e}_k \to t,\ k > 0$, where t must be also demanded if it is a variable. Now we can present the goal solving rules. Note that the symbol $\Vdash$ is used in those rules which compute no substitution.

DC Decomposition: $G,\ h\ \bar{e}_m \to h\,\bar{t}_m,\ G' \Vdash G,\ e_1 \to t_1, \ldots e_m \to t_m,\ G'$.
OB Output Binding: $G,\ X \to t,\ G' \Vdash_{\{X/t\}} (G,\ G')\{X/t\}$, with t not a variable.
IB Input binding: $G,\ t \to X,\ G' \Vdash_{\{X/t\}} (G,\ G')\{X/t\}$, with t a pattern and either X is a demanded variable or X occurs in $(G,\ G')$.

IIM Input Imitation:
$G,\ h\ \overline{e}_m \rightarrow X,\ G' \Vdash_{\{X/h\ \overline{X}_m\}} (G,\ e_1 \rightarrow X_1, \ldots, e_m \rightarrow X_m,\ G')\{X/h\,\overline{X}_m\}$ with $h\ \overline{e}_m$ not a pattern, $\overline{X}_m$ fresh variables, $h\ \overline{X}_m$ a pattern, and either X is a demanded variable or X occurs in (G, G').

EL Elimination: $G, e \rightarrow X,\ G' \Vdash_{\{X/\bot\}} G,\ G'$
if X is not demanded and it does not appear in $(G,\ G')$.

FA Function Application: $G,\ f\ \overline{e}_n\,\overline{a}_k \rightarrow t,\ G' \Vdash G, e_1 \rightarrow t_1, \ldots, e_n \rightarrow t_n,\ C,\ r \rightarrow S,$
$S\ \overline{a}_k \rightarrow t,\ G'$ where S must be a new variable, $f\ \overline{t}_n \rightarrow r \Leftarrow C$ is a variant of a program rule, and t must be demanded if it is a variable.

The GSC rules are intended to be related to the SC rules in a way which will become clear in Subsection 5.1. In particular, the GSC rule FA has been modified w.r.t. the analogous rule in the goal solving calculi from [5, 4], so that it can be related to the combined application of the two SC rules AR and RA. As we did in SC, we introduce an optimized variant FA' of rule FA, for the case $k = 0$:
FA' $G,\ f\ \overline{e}_n \rightarrow t,\ G' \Vdash G,\ e_1 \rightarrow t_1, \ldots, e_n \rightarrow t_n,\ C,\ r \rightarrow t,\ G'$
where $f\ \overline{t}_n \rightarrow r \Leftarrow C$ is a variant of a program rule and t demanded if it is a variable.

As another difference w.r.t. [5, 4], where no particular *selection strategy* was considered, here we view goals as *ordered sequences* of atomic subgoals, and we adopt a *quasi-leftmost selection strategy*. This means to select the leftmost atomic subgoal $e \rightarrow t$ for which some GSC rule can be applied. Note that this is not necessarily the leftmost subgoal. Subgoals $e \rightarrow X$, where X is a non-demanded variable, may be not eligible at some steps. Instead, they are delayed until X becomes demanded or disappears from the rest of the goal. This formalizes the behaviour of shared suspensions in lazy evaluation. In particular, rule EL takes care of detecting undemanded suspensions, whose formal characterization was missing in previous approaches such as [16]. Below we show the first steps of a GSC computation for the goal *take* N (*from* X) $\rightarrow$ *Ys* w.r.t. our running example program. Selected subgoals appear underlined and demanded variables X are marked as $X!$. The composition of all the substitutions yields the computed answer: $\sigma = \{N/s\,(s\,z),\ Y_s/X\!:\!X\!:\![\,]\}$ (wrong in the intended model, as we have seen already).

take N (from X) → Ys! $\Vdash_{(FA')}$ N → s N', from X → X':Xs', X':take N' Xs' → Ys!
$\Vdash_{(OB),\ \{N/sN'\}}$ from X → X':Xs', X':take N' Xs' → Ys! $\Vdash_{(FA')}$
X → M, M:from M → X':Xs', X':take N' Xs' → Ys! $\Vdash_{(IB)\{M/X\}}$ … □

Answers computed by GSC are correct solutions in the sense defined in Subsection 4.1. This *soundness* result is a straightforward corollary of Proposition 3, shown in the next section. Regarding *completeness*, we conjecture that GSC can compute all the answers expected by SC, under the assumption that no application of a free logic variable as a function occurs in the program or in the initial goal. We have not checked this conjecture, which is not important for our present purposes. Completeness results for closely related (but more complex) goal solving calculi are given in [5, 4].

5 Debugging Lazy Narrowing Computations

In this section we introduce an instance of Naish's general scheme [12] for debugging wrong answers in our FLP language. Our computation trees will be called the *abbreviated proof tree* ($APTs$ in short). An APT is obtained in two phases: first a SC proof tree PT is built from a successful GSC computation. Then the PT is simplified obtaining the APT tree. We next explain these two phases and establish the correctness of the resulting debugger.

5.1 Obtaining Proof Trees from Successful Computations

Given any GSC successful computation $G_0 \Vdash_{\sigma_1} G_1 \Vdash_{\sigma_2} \ldots G_{n-1} \Vdash_{\sigma_n} \Box$ with computed answer $\sigma = \sigma_1 \ldots \sigma_n$, we build a sequence of trees $T_0, T_1, \ldots, T_n, T$ as follows:

- The only node in T_0 is G_0.
- For any computation step corresponding to a rule of the GSC different from FA and FA':
$\underbrace{G,\, e \to t,\, G'}_{G_{i-1}} \Vdash_{\sigma_i} \underbrace{(G, G'', G')\sigma_i}_{G_i}$ the tree T_i is built from $T_{i-1}\sigma_i$ by including as children of the leaf $(e \to t)\sigma_i$ in $T_{i-1}\sigma_i$ all the atomic goals in $G''\sigma_i$.
- For any computation step corresponding to rule FA of the GSC:
$G,\, f\ \overline{e}_n\ \overline{a}_k\ \to t,\, G' \Vdash G,\, e_1 \to t_1, \ldots, e_n \to t_n,\ C,\ r \to S,\ S\ \overline{a}_k \to t,\, G'$
the tree T_i is built by 'expanding' the leaf $f\ \overline{e}_n \overline{a}_k \to t$ of T_{i-1} as shown in the diagram below. Analogously for the case of the simplification of FA, i.e. rule FA', a similar diagram can be depicted.

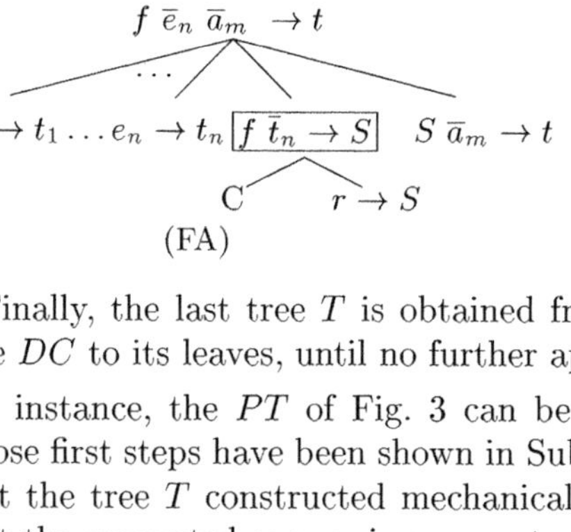

(FA)

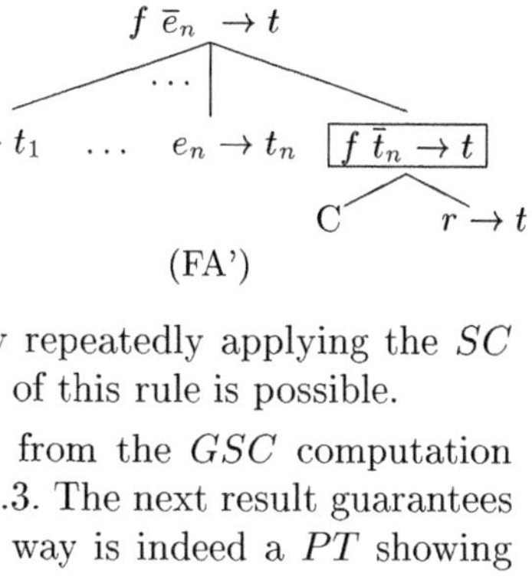

(FA')

- Finally, the last tree T is obtained from T_n by repeatedly applying the SC rule DC to its leaves, until no further application of this rule is possible.

For instance, the PT of Fig. 3 can be obtained from the GSC computation whose first steps have been shown in Subsection 4.3. The next result guarantees that the tree T constructed mechanically in this way is indeed a PT showing that the computed answer is a correct solution.

Proposition 3 *The tree T described above is a PT for goal $G_0\sigma$.*
Proof Sketch. By induction on the number of goal solving steps, showing that the algorithm associates a valid SC step to each GSC rule. This correspondence is:

GSC rule	DC	OB	IB	IIM	EL	FA	FA'
SC rule	DC	-		DC	BT	AR+RA	AR'+RA

Rules IB and OB only apply a substitution and therefore do not correspond to an SC inference step. Therefore, the internal nodes of each tree T_i obtained by the algorithm correspond to valid SC inferences. Moreover, it can be shown that the leaves of each T_i either can be proved by repeatedly applying the SC rules DC, BT and RR or occur in G_i. This means that once the empty goal is reached the tree T_n can be completed as indicated to build the final PT. Note that each boxed node in the final PT corresponds to an application of the SC rule RA with an *associated program rule instance*, which comes from some original program rule variant, affected by the computed answer σ.

5.2 Simplifying Proof Trees

The second phase obtains the APT from the PT by removing all the nodes which do not include non-trivial boxed facts, excepting the root. More precisely, let T be the PT for a given goal G. The APT T' of G can be defined recursively as follows:
• The root of T' is the root of T.
• Given any node N in T' the children of N in T' are the closest descendants of N in T that are boxed basic facts $f\ \bar{t}_n \to t$ with $t \neq \perp$.
• Attached to any boxed fact in the APT, an implicit reference to an associated program rule instance is kept. This information is available in the PT.

The idea behind this simplification is that all the removed nodes correspond either to unevaluated function calls (i.e. undemanded suspensions) or to correct computation steps, as they do not rely on the application of any program rule. To complete an instance of Naish's debugging scheme [12], we still have to define a criterion to determine erroneous nodes, and a method to extract a bug indication from an erroneous node. These definitions are the following:
• Given an APT, we consider as erroneous those nodes which contain an approximation statement not valid in the intended model. Note that, with the possible exception of the root node, all the nodes in an APT include basic facts. This simplifies the questions asked to the oracle (usually the user).
• For any buggy node N in the APT, the debugger will show its associated instance of program rule as incorrect.

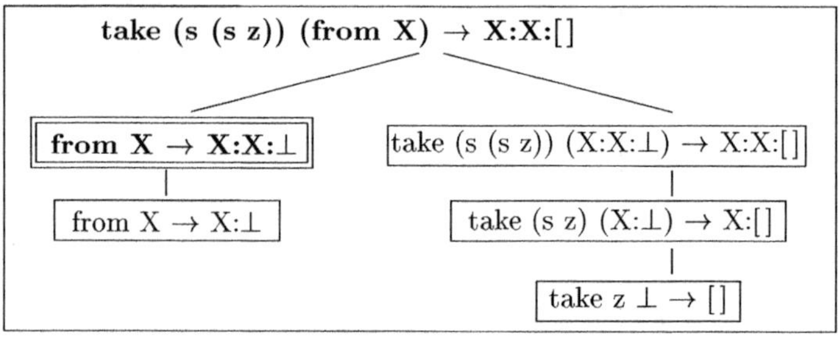

Figure 5: APT corresponding to the PT of Fig. 3

Fig. 5 shows the APT corresponding to the PT of Fig. 3. Erroneous nodes are displayed in bold letters, and the only buggy node appears surrounded by a double box. The relation between this tree and the computation trees used in previous approaches [15–17, 11, 14, 13] has been already discussed in Sect. 2. Assuming a debugger that traverses the tree in preorder looking for a topmost buggy node (see [12] for a discussion about different search strategies when looking for buggy nodes in computation trees), a debugging session could be:

```
from X → X:X:⊥? no
from X → X:⊥? yes
Rule 'from.1' has the incorrect instance 'from X → X:from X'
```

5.3 Soundness and Completeness of the debugger

Now we are in a position to prove the logical correctness of our debugger:

Theorem

(a) Soundness. For every buggy node detected by the debugger, the associated program rule is incorrect w.r.t. the intended model.
(b) Completeness. For every computed answer which is wrong in the intended model, the debugger finds some buggy node.

Proof Sketch

(a) Due to the construction of the *APT*, every buggy node corresponds to the application of some instance of a program rule R. The node (corresponding to R's left hand side) is erroneous, while its children (corresponding to R's right hand side and conditions) are not. Using these facts and the relation between *APT*s and *PT*s, it can be shown that R is incorrect w.r.t. the intended model.
(b) Assuming a wrong computed answer, the root of the *APT* is not valid in the intended model, and a buggy node must exist because of Proposition 1.

6 Conclusions and Future Work

We have proposed theoretical foundations for the declarative debugging of wrong answers in a simple but sufficiently expressive lazy functional logic language. As in other known debuggers for lazy functional [15–17, 11, 14] and functional logic languages [13, 12], we rely on the generic debugging scheme from [12]. As a novelty, we have obtained a formal characterization of computation trees as *abbreviated proof trees* that relate computed answers to the declarative semantics of programs. Our characterization relies on a formal specification of both the declarative and the operational semantics, using *approximation statements* rather than equations. Thanks to this framework, we have obtained a proof of logical correctness for the debugger, extending older results from the logic programming field to a more complex context. To our best knowledge, no previous work in the lazy functional (logic) field has provided a formalization of computation trees precise enough to prove correctness of the debugger. As additional advantages, our framework helps to simplify oracle questions and supports a convenient representation of functions as values.

As future work we plan an extension of our current proposal, supporting the declarative debugging of both *wrong* and *missing* answers. This will require two different kinds of computation trees, as well as suitable extensions of our logical framework to deal with negative information. We also plan to implement the resulting debugging tools within the $\mathcal{TOY}$ system [10], which uses a *demand driven* narrowing strategy [9, 1] for goal solving. To formalize the generation of computation trees for $\mathcal{TOY}$, we plan to modify the goal solving calculus, so that the demand driven strategy and other language features are taken into account. To implement the generation of computation trees, we plan to follow a transformational approach, adapting techniques described in [16, 14].

Acknowledgement

We are grateful to the anonymous referees for their constructive remarks.

References

1. S. Antoy, R. Echahed, M. Hanus. *A Needed Narrowing Strategy.* 21st ACM Symp. on Principles of Programming Languages, Portland, ACM Press, pp. 268–279, 1994.
2. G. Ferrand. *Error Diagnosis in Logic Programming, an Adaptation of E.Y. Shapiro's Method.* The Journal of Logic Programming 4(3), pp. 177–198, 1987.
3. M. Falaschi, G. Levi, M. Martelli, C. Palamidessi. *A Model-theoretic Reconstruction of the Operational Semantics of Logic Programs.* Information and Computation 102(1). pp. 86-113, 1993.
4. J.C. González-Moreno, M.T. Hortalá-González, M. Rodríguez-Artalejo. *A Higher Order Rewriting Logic for Functional Logic Programming.* Procs. of ICLP'97, The MIT Press, pp. 153–167, 1997.
5. J.C. González-Moreno, M.T. Hortalá-González, F.J. López-Fraguas, M. Rodríguez-Artalejo. *An Approach to Declarative Programming Based on a Rewriting Logic,* Journal of Logic Programming 40(1), pp. 47–87, 1999.
6. M. Hanus. *The Integration of Functions into Logic Programming: A Survey.* J. of Logic Programming 19-20, special issue "*Ten Years of Logic Programming*", pp. 583–628, 1994.
7. M. Hanus (ed.), *Curry: an Integrated Functional Logic Language,* Version 0.7, February 2, 2000. Available at `http://www.informatik.uni-kiel.de/~curry/`.
8. J. W. Lloyd. *Declarative Error Diagnosis.* New Generation Computing 5(2), pp. 133–154, 1987.
9. R. Loogen, F.J. López-Fraguas, M. Rodríguez-Artalejo. *A Demand Driven Computation Strategy for Lazy Narrowing.* Procs. of PLILP'93, Springer LNCS 714, pp. 184–200, 1993.
10. F.J. López-Fraguas, J. Sánchez-Hernández. *$\mathcal{TOY}$: A Multiparadigm Declarative System,* in Proc. RTA'99, Springer LNCS 1631, pp 244–247, 1999. Available at `http://titan.sip.ucm.es/toy`.
11. L.Naish. *Declarative dDebugging of Lazy Functional Programs.* Australian Computer Science Communications, 15(1), pp. 287–294, 1993.
12. L. Naish. *A Declarative Debugging Scheme.* J. of Functional and Logic Programming, 1997-3.
13. L. Naish, T. Barbour. *A Declarative Debugger for a Logical-Functional Language.* In Graham Forsyth and Moonis Ali, eds. Eight International Conference on Industrial and Engineering Applications of Artificial Intelligence and Expert Systems - Invited and additional papers, Vol. 2, pp. 91–99, 1995. DSTO General Document 51.
14. L. Naish, T. Barbour. *Towards a Portable Lazy Functional Declarative Debugger.* Australian Computer Science Communications, 18(1), pp. 401–408, 1996.
15. H. Nilsson, P. Fritzson. *Algorithmic Debugging of Lazy Funcional Languages.* The Journal of Functional Programming, 4(3), pp. 337-370, 1994.
16. H. Nilsson, J. Sparud. *The Evaluation Dependence Tree as a Basis for Lazy Functional Debugging.* Automated Software Engineering, 4(2), pp. 121-150, 1997.
17. H. Nilsson. *Declarative Debugging for Lazy Functional Languages.* Ph.D. Thesis. Dissertation No. 530. Univ. Linköping, Sweden. 1998.
18. J. Peterson, K. Hammond (eds.), *Report on the Programming Language Haskell 98, A Non-strict, Purely Functional Language,* 1 February 1999.
19. E.Y. Shapiro. *Algorithmic Program Debugging.* The MIT Press, Cambridge, Mass., 1982.
20. L. Sterling, E. Shapiro. *The Art of Prolog.* The MIT Press, 1986.

Adding Linear Constraints over Real Numbers to Curry

Wolfgang Lux

Universität Münster
wlux@uni-muenster.de

Abstract. Constraint logic programming languages are an extension of logic programming languages where unification has been replaced by constraint solving. Constraint solving techniques allow to reduce the search space of a logic program dramatically and have been shown to be useful in a wide area of application domains.
Functional-logic languages are a different branch in the group of declarative languages, which combine the reduction of expressions with unification. In contrast to purely functional languages, functional-logic languages allow for computations with partially known data and offer built-in search strategies, allowing for a more concise formulation of programs. Compared to purely logic languages, functional-logic languages provide functions and a declarative approach to I/O, thus avoiding the need for non-declarative language constructs (e.g. the ubiquitous cut in Prolog).
In this paper we will consider the integration of constraint programming and functional-logic programming in the context of the language Curry. Curry is a multi-paradigm declarative language, which aims at unifying the different lines of research in functional-logic programming. In particular, we have chosen the domain of linear constraints over real numbers and will describe the semantic and operational issues of this integration.

1 Introduction

Curry [Han00] is a multi-paradigm language that integrates features from functional languages, logic languages, and concurrent programming. The operational model of Curry is based on an optimal reduction strategy [AEH97] which integrates needed narrowing and residuation. Narrowing [Red85] combines unification and reduction, allowing the non-deterministic instantiation of unbound logic variables. The residuation strategy [ALN87], on the other hand, delays the evaluation of expressions containing unbound logic variables until these are sufficiently instantiated by other parts of the program.

Constraint logic programming languages replace unification by the concept of constraint resolution. In a constraint logic calculus, only clauses whose constraints are consistent will be selected in a resolution step. In general, less clauses than in a purely logic program will be selected, reducing the amount of search in the program. This results in a more efficient execution of constraint logic programs compared to purely logic programs.

H. Kuchen and K. Ueda (Eds.): FLOPS 2001, LNCS 2024, pp. 185–200, 2001.

Constraint solving techniques have proven useful in various domains, including equality constraints for infinite terms, boolean constraints, and linear constraints over finite domains, rational numbers and real numbers.

While a lot of research has been devoted to the combination of constraint programming and logic programming in the CLP paradigm, there have been few efforts to integrate constraint programming into functional-logic languages. In this paper we will explore the integration of linear constraints over real numbers into Curry. We have chosen this domain because there is a wide variation of application domains, e.g. financial applications, numerical simulations, or task scheduling. In addition there are well known, efficient algorithms for solving equalities and inequalities between linear expressions, namely Gaussian elimination and the simplex algorithm. One distinguishing feature of our work is the integration of optimization constraints into the language.

This paper is organized as follows. The next section briefly summarizes the computation model of Curry. The third section introduces linear constraints over real numbers. Section 4 outlines the integration of linear constraints in Curry. The fifth section presents the semantics of optimization constraints in Curry. The following section sketches how these constraint solving capabilities can be integrated into our abstract machine for Curry [Lux99]. The final sections present related work and conclude.

2 The computation model of Curry

Curry uses a syntax similar to Haskell [HPW92], but with a few additions.

The basic computational domain of Curry is a set of data terms. A data term t is either a variable or an application of an n-ary data constructor to n argument terms.

$$t ::= x \mid c\, t_1 \cdots t_n$$

The set $vars(t)$ of variables occurring in a term t is defined inductively.

$$vars(x) = \{x\}$$
$$vars(c\, t_1 \cdots t_n) = \bigcup_{i=1}^{n} vars(t_1)$$

A data term t is *ground* if $vars(t) = \emptyset$.

New data constructors can be introduced through data type declarations. E.g., the type `Nat` of natural numbers can be defined by

```
data Nat = Zero | Succ Nat
```

The nullary data constructor `Zero` represents the natural number 0 and the unary data constructor `Succ` applied to some other natural number denotes the successor of that number.

An expression e is either a variable x, a data constructor c, a (defined) function f, or an application of an expression e_1 to an argument expression e_2. New logic variables can be introduced in a `let` expression. The variables $x_1, \ldots, x_n$ are existentially quantified in the body expression e.

$$e ::= x \mid c \mid f \mid e_1\, e_2 \mid \texttt{let}\; x_1, \ldots, x_n\; \texttt{free in}\; e$$

Lambda expressions ($\backslash t_1 \ldots t_n$ `->` e) are supported as syntactic sugar. Lambda lifting [Joh85] is used to translate them into global functions.

The set of free variables of an expression e is given by the following definition.

$$\begin{aligned} fv(x) &= \{x\} \\ fv(c) = fv(f) &= \emptyset \\ fv(e_1\, e_2) &= fv(e_1) \cup fv(e_2) \\ fv(\texttt{let}\; x_1, \ldots, x_n\; \texttt{free in}\; e) &= fv(e) \setminus \{x_1, \ldots, x_n\} \end{aligned}$$

Curry employs a Hindley-Milner type discipline, therefore the expression e_1 in application $e_1\, e_2$ will always be an expression, that accepts an argument of the type of e_2.

Functions are defined by a set of conditional equations of the form

$$f\, t_1 \cdots t_n \mid g = e$$

where the argument patterns t_i are terms and the so-called guard g as well as the body e are expressions. A where clause may added to the right hand side of an equation to provide local definitions and fresh logic variables whose scope is the guard g and the body e of the equation.

The addition function for natural numbers can be defined as follows.

```
add Zero     n = n
add (Succ m) n = Succ (add m n)
```

A conditional equation for the function f is applicable in an expression $f\, e_1 \cdots e_n$ if each argument expression e_i matches the corresponding pattern t_i and the guard g is satisfied (see below). In that case the application is replaced by the body of the function with all variables occurring in the patterns t_i replaced by the expressions in the corresponding positions of the arguments e_i. If an argument expression contains an unbound logic variable at a position where a constructor term occurs in pattern t_i, the variable is either instantiated with the corresponding pattern (narrowing) or the evaluation of the expression is suspended until this variable is instantiated by other parts of the program (residuation).

The evaluation strategy to be used by a function f can be specified with an evaluation annotation f `eval` r, where r is either `flex` or `rigid`. In the former case f uses narrowing, in the latter case f uses residuation. Curry provides reasonable defaults depending on the result type of the function, so that the evaluation strategy rarely needs to be specified explicitly. In particular, functions with result type `Success` (see below) use narrowing, while all other functions use residuation.

2.1 Constraints

Curry has limited support for constraint solving. Expressions of type `Success` are checked for satisfiability. The predefined nullary constraint `success` is an expression that is always satisfied.

Constraints may be composed with the binary operator `(&)`, which denotes the concurrent conjunction of two constraints. An expression e_1 & e_2 is satisfied if both expressions e_1 and e_2 are satisfied. The order of evaluation of the two arguments is unspecified, e_1 may be evaluated before e_2 or vice versa or both expressions may be evaluated in some interleaved order.

Finally, the kernel of Curry provides equational constraints. An equational constraint e_1 =:= e_2 between two arbitrary expressions (of the same type) is satisfied if both arguments can be reduced to the same finite data term. If e_1 or e_2 contain unbound logic variables, an attempt is made to unify both expressions by instantiating variables to terms. If the unification succeeds, the constraint is satisfied.

Note that Curry distinguishes between constraints (of type `Success`) and boolean expressions (of type `Bool`). While the former are checked for satisfiability, the latter reduce to the predefined constant terms `True` or `False`.

Strict equality between terms is implemented by the boolean operator `(==)`. An expression e_1 == e_2 reduces to `True` if both expressions e_1 and e_2 reduce to the same finite data term and `False` otherwise. If the arguments contain unbound variables, the evaluation is delayed until these variables are sufficiently instantiated. In terms of a concurrent constraint language, `(=:=)` corresponds to a *tell* and `(==)` to an *ask* constraint.

Usually, predicates (in the sense of Prolog) are implemented as functions with result type `Success` in Curry. These function use narrowing by default and, thus, may instantiate unbound variables in their arguments.

A predicate that is satisfied for all even natural numbers can be defined as follows in Curry.

```
even Zero              = success
even (Succ (Succ n))  = even n
```

A guard expression in a conditional equation must be either of type `Success` or of type `Bool`. An equation $f\, t_1 \cdots t_n$ | g = e is reduced to e in an application $f\, e_1 \ldots e_n$ only if the arguments $e_1, \ldots, e_n$ can be matched with the terms $t_1, \ldots, t_n$ and if the guard g is satisfied. If the guard expression is of type `Bool`, the expression is satisfied if it reduces to `True`.

2.2 Floating point numbers

In order to implement linear constraints over real numbers, we will assume the existence of a type `Float` representing floating-point numbers.[1] We will also assume the existence of primitive arithmetic operations and relations between floating-point numbers.

[1] Floating-point numbers are not provided by the kernel of Curry

```
(+),(-),(*),(/)     :: Float -> Float -> Float
(<),(>),(<=),(>=) :: Float -> Float -> Bool
```

2.3 Semantics

The operational semantics of Curry can be given by a one-step reduction relation $\mapsto$, between states of a computation. A *state* s is a pair consisting of a constraint ϕ and an expression e. A sequence $s_0 \mapsto \ldots \mapsto s_n$ of zero or more reduction steps with $\forall i \in \{1, \ldots, n\} : s_{i-1} \mapsto s_i$ will be abbreviated as $s_0 \overset{*}{\mapsto} s_n$.

A *constraint* is either the trivial constraint $\top$, an inconsistent constraint $\bot$, a conjunction $\phi_1 \wedge \phi_2$ of two constraints ϕ_1 and ϕ_2, or an equality constraint $x = t$, where x is a variable and t is a data term.

$$\phi ::= \top \mid \bot \mid \phi_1 \wedge \phi_2 \mid x = t$$

The set of constrained variables in a constraint is defined inductively as follows.

$$\begin{aligned} cv(\top) = cv(\bot) &= \emptyset \\ cv(\phi_1 \wedge \phi_2) &= cv(\phi_1) \cup cv(\phi_2) \\ cv(x = t) &= \{x\} \cup vars(t) \end{aligned}$$

A state $s = \langle \phi, e \rangle$ is in *solved form* if e is a data term and $\phi \neq \bot$.

A *derivation* of state s_0 is a sequence of one-step reductions $s_0 \overset{*}{\mapsto} s_n$. A derivation $s_0 \overset{*}{\mapsto} s_n$ is *successful*, if the state s_n is in solved form. A derivation *fails*, if $s_0 \overset{*}{\mapsto} s_n$ such that $s_n = \langle \bot, e \rangle$ for some arbitrary expression e. A derivation $s_0 \overset{*}{\mapsto} s_n$ *flounders*, if $s_n = \langle \phi, e \rangle$ is not in solved form, $\phi \neq \bot$, and s_n is $\mapsto$-irreducible.

3 Linear constraints over Real Numbers

A linear expression is either a real number a, a variable x, the product of a number and a variable, or a sum of linear expressions.

$$l ::= a \mid x \mid a \cdot x \mid l + l$$

A linear constraint is an (in-)equality between two linear expressions. It can always be transformed into the form

$$a_1 x_1 + a_2 x_2 + \cdots + a_n x_n \ \delta \ b$$

where all a_i and b are real numbers, the x_i are pairwise distinct variables and δ is a relation from the set $\{=, \neq, <, >, \leq, \geq\}$. In the case of real numbers, Gaussian elimination can be used to solve linear constraints involving only equalities and the simplex algorithm can be used, if inequalities are included. An algorithm to handle disequalities was presented in [IvH93].

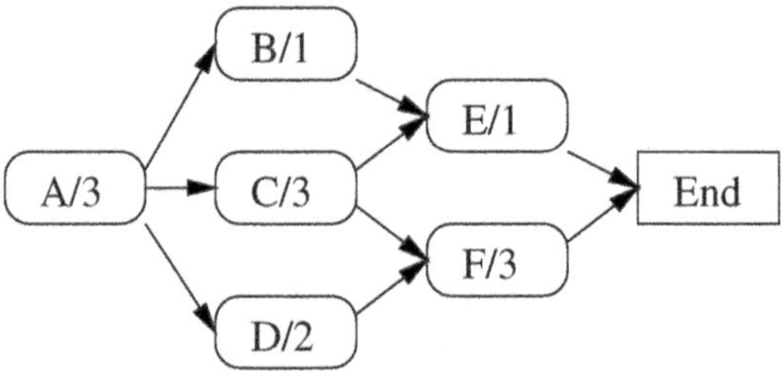

Fig. 1. A simple task graph

As an example for the application of linear constraints we will consider scheduling problems. A scheduling problem can be described by a task graph, where each task is represented by a box containing the name and the duration of the task. Arrows between the tasks impose an order where each task at the base of the arrow must be finished before the task at the tip of the arrow may start. A simple example is shown in Fig. 1. This task graph corresponds to the following set of inequalities, where each variable represents the time at which the corresponding task begins.

$$
\begin{array}{llll}
a+3 \leq b & b+1 \leq e & c+3 \leq f & e+1 \leq \mathit{end} \\
a+3 \leq c & c+3 \leq e & d+2 \leq f & f+3 \leq \mathit{end} \\
a+3 \leq d & & &
\end{array}
$$

4 Linear constraints in Curry

In order to integrate linear constraints over real numbers into Curry we have to allow for linear constraints in computation states.

$$\phi ::= \cdots \mid a_1x_1 + a_2x_2 + \cdots + a_nx_n \ \delta \ b$$

The definition of the set of constrained variables has to be extended by a case for linear (in)equalities, too.

$$cv(a_1x_1 + a_2x_2 + \cdots + a_nx_n \ \delta \ b) = \{x_1, \ldots, x_n\}$$

We assume a constraint solving mechanism $\mapsto^{CS}$ which simplifies the current constraint.

New constraints are added with the binary operators

```
(=:=)                         :: a -> a -> Success
(/:=),(<:),(>:),(<:=),(>:=) :: Float -> Float -> Success
```

$$\langle\phi, a_1\texttt{<:=}a_2\rangle \mapsto \begin{cases}\langle\phi, \texttt{success}\rangle & \text{if } a_1 \le a_2\\ \langle\bot, a_1\texttt{<:=}a_2\rangle & \text{otherwise}\end{cases} \qquad \text{(NUM)}$$

$$\frac{\langle x = a \wedge \phi, a\texttt{<:=}e\rangle \mapsto \langle\phi', e'\rangle}{\langle x = a \wedge \phi, x\texttt{<:=}e\rangle \mapsto \langle\phi', e'\rangle} \quad \frac{\langle x = a \wedge \phi, e\texttt{<:=}a\rangle \mapsto \langle\phi', e'\rangle}{\langle x = a \wedge \phi, e\texttt{<:=}x\rangle \mapsto \langle\phi', e'\rangle} \qquad \text{(VAR)}$$

$$\frac{a_1x_1 + \ldots + a_nx_n - b_1y_1 - \ldots - b_my_m \le b_0 - a_0 \wedge \phi \mapsto^{CS} \bot}{\begin{array}{c}\langle\phi, a_0\texttt{+}a_1\texttt{*}x_1\texttt{+}\ldots\texttt{+}a_n\texttt{*}x_n\texttt{<:=}b_0\texttt{+}b_1\texttt{*}y_1\texttt{+}\ldots\texttt{+}b_m\texttt{*}y_m\rangle \mapsto\\ \langle\bot, a_0\texttt{+}a_1\texttt{*}x_1\texttt{+}\ldots\texttt{+}a_n\texttt{*}x_n\texttt{<:=}b_0\texttt{+}b_1\texttt{*}y_1\texttt{+}\ldots\texttt{+}b_m\texttt{*}y_m\rangle\end{array}} \qquad \text{(LIN1)}$$

$$\frac{a_1x_1 + \ldots + a_nx_n - b_1y_1 - \ldots - b_my_m \le b_0 - a_0 \wedge \phi \mapsto^{CS} \phi'}{\langle\phi, a_0 + a_1\texttt{*}x_1\texttt{+}\ldots\texttt{+}a_n\texttt{*}x_n\texttt{<:=}b_0 + b_1\texttt{*}y_1\texttt{+}\ldots\texttt{+}b_m\texttt{*}y_m\rangle \mapsto \langle\phi', \texttt{success}\rangle} \quad \text{if } \phi' \ne \bot \qquad \text{(LIN2)}$$

$$\frac{\langle\phi, f e_{11}\ldots e_{1j}\rangle \mapsto \langle\phi', e_1'\rangle}{\langle\phi, f e_{11}\ldots e_{1j}\texttt{<:=}e_2\rangle \mapsto \langle\phi', e_1'\texttt{<:=}e_2\rangle} \quad \frac{\langle\phi, f e_{21}\ldots e_{2k}\rangle \mapsto \langle\phi', e_2'\rangle}{\langle\phi, e_1\texttt{<:=}f e_{21}\ldots e_{2k}\rangle \mapsto \langle\phi', e_1\texttt{<:=}e_2'\rangle} \qquad \text{(FUN)}$$

$$\begin{array}{l}\dfrac{\langle\phi, e_1[x_1/y_1, \ldots, x_n/y_n]\texttt{<:=}e_2\rangle \mapsto \langle\phi', e'\rangle}{\langle\phi, (\texttt{let } x_1, \ldots, x_n \texttt{ free in } e_1)\texttt{<:=}e_2\rangle \mapsto \langle\phi', e'\rangle}\\ \dfrac{\langle\phi, e_1\texttt{<:=}e_2[x_1/y_1, \ldots, x_n/y_n]\rangle \mapsto \langle\phi', e'\rangle}{\langle\phi, e_1\texttt{<:=}(\texttt{let } x_1, \ldots, x_n \texttt{ free in } e_2)\rangle \mapsto \langle\phi', e'\rangle}\end{array} \quad \begin{array}{l}\text{where } y_1, \ldots, y_n\\ \text{are fresh variables}\end{array} \qquad \text{(EX)}$$

Fig. 2. Semantics of e_1 `<:=` e_2

Here, `(=:=)` can enter either an equality constraint between terms to the constraint store, e.g. `x =:= Succ y`, or a linear equality, e.g. `x =:= y + 2*z`. The other operators add a disequality or inequality constraint between linear expressions to the constraint store.[2] The semantics for the reduction of an expression $e_1\,\delta\,e_2$ can be defined inductively on the kind of argument expressions which can occur. Fig. 2 shows our semantics for the operator `(<:=)`. The semantics of the other operators is defined analogously.

With the help of these functions, we can now solve scheduling examples in Curry as follows. We use a list of logic variables to hold the time when the corresponding task begins. A dependency between two tasks is represented by a function which imposes a constraint between the two corresponding variables. E.g., the dependency between tasks A and B in Fig. 1 can be implemented by the following (anonymous) function.

```
\[a,b] -> a + 3.0 <:= b
```

A function which represents a schedule can be constructed incrementally from the dependencies between the tasks. E.g., the task graph in Fig. 1 can be implemented by the following function.

[2] We do not consider disequality constraints between terms in this paper.

```
sample [a,b,c,d,e,f,end] =
  mapC (after a 3.0) [b,c,d] & after b 1.0 e &
  mapC (after c 3.0) [e,f]   & after d 2.0 f &
  after e 1.0 end            & after f 3.0 end

mapC f []     = success
mapC f (x:xs) = f x & mapC f xs

after x d y = x + d <:= y
```

If we want to compute a solution which satisfies such a schedule, given some arbitrary start time, it can be computed by instantiating the variables with floating-point numbers. If the head of the list of variables corresponds to the initial task, a naive approach would be to compute valid schedules non-deterministically with the function `schedule`.

```
solution schedule start l =
  schedule l & head l =:= start & mapC (enumerate start) (tail l)

enumerate l x = x =:= l
enumerate l x = enumerate (l + 1.0) x

head (x:xs) = x
tail (x:xs) = xs
```

5 Optimal solutions

Usually the programmer is interested in finding an optimal solution admissible for a variable with respect to a given set of constraints.

A naive approach would be to use Curry's encapsulated search [HS98] for this purpose. Using the predefined function `once` which employs a depth-first strategy and returns only the first solution, a minimal schedule for our sample task graph can be computed as follows.

$$\texttt{once (solution sample 0.0)} \overset{*}{\mapsto} \texttt{(0.0,3.0,3.0,3.0,6.0,6.0,9.0)}$$

However, this approach is problematic. The `enumerate` function generates an infinite number of bindings for its arguments. If the arguments are instantiated in the wrong order, e.g. if we had reversed the list of variables, the above goal would never terminate. Thus, we also have to compute a reasonable upper bound for the schedule in question and pass this upper bound as an additional argument to `solution` and `enumerate`. Even then, the efficiency of the program will depend crucially on the order in which the variables are instantiated.

Another problem with the approach of enumerating solutions is that it works only in the case where the durations of tasks have a common denominator.

These problems are due to the fact, that the program uses the constraints only to check the satisfiability of a generated solution. However, the simplex algorithm, underlying the implementation of linear constraints over real numbers, not only allows to check a set of linear equations for consistency, but also to compute an optimal solution for them. We, therefore, propose to provide also functions `minimize` and `maximize`, which compute the minimum or maximum of an expression with respect to a set of constraints. For the rest of this section we will consider only minimizations, the case of maximizations is analogous to this one.

One has to be careful in the definition of these functions, though. A naive approach would be define `minimize` as a function of type

```
minimize :: Float -> Success
```

with the intention that an expression `minimize` e minimizes the value of the expression e with respect to the current set of constraints. For instance, the expression

```
let x free in x >:= 0.0 & minimize x
```

would bind the variable `x` to the number `0.0`.

Unfortunately, such a definition of `minimize` destroys the declarative reading of the program. Consider the expression

```
let x free in x >:= 0.0 & minimize x & x >:= 1.0
```

If the constraints in the concurrent conjunction are evaluated from left to right, the expression fails, because `x` is first minimized with respect to the constraint `x >:= 0.0` which binds `x` to the value `0.0`. Under this binding the constraint `x >:= 1.0` cannot be satisfied. On the other hand, if the constraints are evaluated from right to left, the expression is satisfiable and binds `x` to `1.0`.[3]

The problem with the naive approach is that the variables occurring in the constraints may be affected by constraints in other expressions of the program. Thus, in order to control which constraints to take into account for the minimization, these constraints must become an explicit argument of the `minimize` function. In addition, the variables over which the minimization should take place have to be abstracted. Thus, `minimize` now becomes a function of type

```
minimize :: (a -> Success) -> (a -> Float) -> a -> Success
```

where `minimize` $g\,f\,x$ succeeds if the constraint $g\,x$ can be satisfied and x is bound to a value for which $f\,x$ becomes minimal. If either f or g are non-deterministic functions, a minimal solution will be computed non-deterministically for each possible solution of $f\,x$ and $g\,x$. In order to give a sound semantics to `minimize` the function must not constrain any of the free variables of $f\,x$ or $g\,x$.

In order to present our semantics of `minimize` $g\,f\,x$, we use an auxiliary function h which does not occur in the program and is defined by the conditional equation

$$h\,x \mid g\,x = f\,x$$

[3] Similar problems are known for $CLP(\Re)$ implementations, e.g. Sicstus Prolog [CWA+95].

For the operational semantics of `minimize` we have to distinguish three cases. First, the evaluation of $h\,y$, where y is a fresh variable, may fail. In that case the minimization will fail as well.

$$\frac{\langle \top, \texttt{let}\ y\ \texttt{free in}\ h\,y\rangle \overset{*}{\mapsto} \langle \bot, e\rangle}{\langle \phi, \texttt{minimize}\,g\,f\,x\rangle \mapsto \langle \bot, \texttt{minimize}\,g\,f\,x\rangle} \qquad \text{(FAIL)}$$

If the evaluation of $h\,y$, where y is a free variable, reduces to a floating-point number, the expression $f\,y$ is obviously independent of the value of y. Therefore, `minimize` $g\,f\,x$ reduces to `success` in this case. Still, the minimization may fail because the constraints imposed by g on its argument may be incompatible with those already present for x.

$$\frac{\langle \top, \texttt{let}\ y\ \texttt{free in}\ h\,y\rangle \overset{*}{\mapsto} \langle \phi', a\rangle \quad \phi \wedge \phi' \wedge (x = y) \mapsto^{CS} \phi'' \quad cv(\phi) \cap cv(\phi') = \emptyset}{\langle \phi, \texttt{minimize}\,g\,f\,x\rangle \mapsto \langle \phi'', \texttt{success}\rangle} \qquad \text{(NUM)}$$

The condition $cv(\phi) \cap cv(\phi') = \emptyset$ will ensure that no constraints for the free variables in $h\,y$ have been added to the constraint store ϕ'.

Finally, if $h\,y$ reduces to a linear expression, `minimize` $g\,f\,x$ succeeds if a minimum exists for $h\,y$.

$$\frac{\begin{array}{c}\langle \top, \texttt{let}\ y\ \texttt{free in}\ h\,y\rangle \overset{*}{\mapsto} \langle \phi', a_0 + a_1x_1 + \ldots + a_jx_j\rangle \\ cv(\phi) \cap cv(\phi') = \emptyset \qquad min(\phi', a_0 + a_1x_1 + \ldots + a_jx_j, y) = \bot\end{array}}{\langle \phi, \texttt{minimize}\,g\,f\,x\rangle \mapsto \langle \bot, \texttt{minimize}\,g\,f\,x\rangle}$$

$$\frac{\begin{array}{c}\langle \top, \texttt{let}\ y\ \texttt{free in}\ h\,y\rangle \overset{*}{\mapsto} \langle \phi', a_0 + a_1x_1 + \ldots + a_jx_j\rangle \\ \phi \wedge \phi' \wedge (x = z) \mapsto^{CS} \phi'' \qquad cv(\phi) \cap cv(\phi') = \emptyset \\ min(\phi', a_0 + a_1x_1 + \ldots + a_jx_j, y) = z\end{array}}{\langle \phi, \texttt{minimize}\,g\,f\,x\rangle \mapsto \langle \phi'', \texttt{success}\rangle} \qquad \text{(LIN)}$$

The auxiliary functions min computes the minimum for the linear expression e under the constraints ϕ

$$min(\phi, e, y) = \begin{cases} z & \text{if } \phi \wedge (y = z) \neq \bot \text{ and} \\ & \nexists : z'(\phi \wedge (y = z') \neq \bot) \wedge e|_{\phi \wedge y = z'} < e|_{\phi \wedge y = z} \\ \bot & \text{otherwise} \end{cases}$$

Here the notation $e|_\phi$ denotes the value of e in the context of the constraint ϕ.

With our new definition of `minimize`, the previous example can be written as follows:

```
minimize (\x -> x >:= 0.0) (\x -> x) x & x >:= 1.0
```

It is now apparent from the code that `x` should be minimized with respect to the constraint `x >:= 0.0`.

If the constraint function has more than one solution, a minimum will be computed non-deterministically for each solution of g. E.g., for

```
p x = x >:= 0.0
p x = x >:= 1.0
```

the expression `minimize p (\x -> x) x` has two solutions which bind `x` to `0.0` and to `1.0`, resp.

In order to find minimal solutions to a non-deterministic constraint function like p above, Curry's encapsulated search can be used. This has the advantage of giving the programmer the chance to use the best suited strategy to prune the function's search space instead of using a fixed strategy. For instance, a simple branch-and-bound strategy with depth first traversal, which is sufficient to find the minimal solution for p, can be coded in a few lines of Curry.

```
min g m = bb m [] (try g)
  where bb m (g:gs) []   = bb m gs (try g)
        bb m gs [g] =
          minimize g id m' &
            bb1 m m' (map (inject (\x -> x <: m')) gs) []
          where m' free
        bb m gs' (g1:g2:gs) = bb m (g2:gs ++ gs') (try g1)
        bb1 m m' [] [] = m =:= m'
        bb1 m m' (g:gs) []   = bb m gs (try g)
        bb1 m _  gs [g] =
          minimize g id m' &
            bb1 m m' (map (inject (\x -> x <: m')) gs) []
          where m' free
        bb1 m m' gs' (g1:g2:gs) = bb m (g2:gs ++ gs') (try g1)

inject p q x = p x & q x
```

The function `min` makes use of the primitive search operator `try`. This function takes a single argument, the *search goal*, which is itself a unary function of type `a -> Success`. The argument of the search goal is normally used to constrain a goal variable the solutions of the goal. The result of `try` is either an empty list, denoting that the reduction of the goal has failed, or it is a singleton list containing a function `\x -> g`, where `g` is a satisfiable constraint (in solved form), or the result is a list with at least two elements if the goal can be reduced only by a non-deterministic computation step. The elements of this list are search goals that represent the different alternatives for the reduction of the goal immediately after this non-deterministic step.

The local functions `bb` and `bb1` perform a pattern matching on the result of evaluating the application `try g`. If an empty list is returned, i.e. `g` has no solution, the goal `g` can simply be discarded and `bb1` proceeds with the next goal or returns the minimum if there are no remaining goals. The function `bb` is undefined in this case because it corresponds to the case where the initial goal to `min` is undefined.

If a single solution is found, `bb` and `bb1` use the minimum value for that solution to prune the search space. This is done by adding the additional constraint to the remaining search goals that their solution must be less than the current minimum.

Due to the lazy evaluation of search spaces, the function `min` will not only compute the minimal solution for `p` but also for a variant of `p` where the second branch leads to an infinite computation:

```
q x = x >:= 0.0
q x = x >:= 1.0 & q x
```

For this function, the evaluation of `min q x` will succeed and bind `x` to `0.0`. Instead of using a simple depth-first traversal more complex functions can be used in order to ensure the termination in all cases if a minimum exists.

6 Implementation

6.1 Interface

For the integration of linear constraints into our abstract machine [Lux99], we assume that the constraint solver implements an interface with the following functions

$$\begin{array}{ll} \mathit{tell}: & \mathit{LinCstrt} \times \mathit{CStore} \rightarrow \mathit{CStore} \cup \{\bot\} \\ \mathit{ask}: & \mathit{LinCstrt} \times \mathit{CStore} \rightarrow \{\mathit{True}, \mathit{False}, \mathit{Unknown}\} \\ \mathit{clone}: & \mathit{CStore} \rightarrow \mathit{CStore} \times \mathit{CStore} \\ \mathit{minimize}: & \mathit{LinExpr} \times \mathit{CStore} \rightarrow \mathit{LinCstrt}^* \cup \{\bot\} \\ \mathit{maximize}: & \mathit{LinExpr} \times \mathit{CStore} \rightarrow \mathit{LinCstrt}^* \cup \{\bot\} \end{array}$$

The *tell* function adds a new linear constraint l to the constraint store cs. If the store remains consistent after adding the constraint l to the store, the new state of the constraint store is returned, otherwise the computation fails. The *ask* function is used to check the entailment of the linear constraint l by the constraint store cs.

The *clone* operation duplicates the current state of the constraint store. This is necessary for the implementation of the encapsulated search, where different solutions may operate on different sets of constraint in parallel. In order to avoid flooding the heap with many identical copies of the constraint store, the actual copying of the store can be delayed until the store is actually modified.

Finally, the *minimize* and *maximize* functions minimize or maximize a linear expression with respect to the constraints in the store. If a minimum exists, the bindings of all variables occurring in the expression are returned as linear constraints. If the linear expression is not bounded by the constraints, this list is empty. If the expression is bounded but no optimum exists, e.g. for the expression `x` and the constraint `x >: 0.0`, the functions fail.

6.2 Representation of linear expressions

The code for the function `(<:=)` and the other floating-point constraints, invokes the *tell* interface function in order to add a new constraint to the constraint store. Unfortunately, the arguments to (<:=) will rarely be linear expressions. Thus, in order to pass a valid constraint to the solver, the code for (<:=) first has to scrutinize the arguments. This may involve the evaluation of suspended applications, e.g. if the body of the following function is evaluated.

```
f = g x y <:= h x
    where x,y free
          g x y = 4.0 * (x + y)
          h x   = 2.0 * x
```

In this example, neither the application g x y nor h x is a linear expression. Both can be reduced to the linear expressions $4x + 4y$ and $2x$, though.

In order to implement this reduction, the abstract machine has to provide a special mode where it reduces a floating-point expression to a linear expression instead to normal form. This mode is turned on when an argument expression to the constraint functions (<:=) etc. is evaluated. In linear expression reduction mode, only the implementation of the primitive functions (+), (-), (*), and (/) has to change, all other functions are left unchanged.

As our machine uses a tagged representation for nodes in the heap, an easy solution would be to add just a new tag to represent linear expressions. However, this would mean that all other functions using floating point numbers would also have to handle this new tag. If such a function expects a floating point number as an argument (e.g. the function sin) and is passed a linear expression as an argument, the evaluation must be suspended until all variables occurring in the expression are instantiated to floating point numbers. Exactly the same will happen if the argument to sin is a suspended application whose evaluation is delayed. Thus we have chosen to represent linear expressions as suspended applications, too.

A suspended application is mostly a closure node which includes information about the function to be evaluated and the arguments to which the function is applied. An additional flag is introduced to signal that this closure is a linear expression. This flag will be set by the arithmetic operations (+), (-), (*), and (/) if they cannot evaluate their arguments to floating point numbers but only to linear expressions and the result of the operation is still a linear expression.

Thus, the evaluation of the suspended application x+y in linear expression reduction, where x or y is an unbound variable, returns the closure node for x+y itself with the linear expression flag set. In order to prevent other functions from repeatedly trying to reduce this suspended application to normal form, the lock bit of the closure is set as well. This bit used to signal that some thread is already evaluating the closure. In fact, (+) also must provide some (delayed) thread capable of continuing the evaluation of x+y once x or y are instantiated to a floating-point number.

The code for (*) is a little bit more involved because it may have to transform its input in order to return a linear expression. E.g. when the application 4.0*(x+y) is evaluated, the corresponding closure is not a linear expression. However, it can be turned into a linear expression by distributing the multiplication into the sum x+y.

Our implementation strategy smoothly fits with non-linear constraints in an expression. The evaluation of a non-linear constraint is automatically delayed until it becomes linear by the instantiation of variables in other parts of the program. For instance, in the expression

```
sin (4.0 * (4.0 * x)) <:= y & x =:= 0
```

the evaluation of the non-linear constraint `sin(4.0*(4.0*x))<:=y` is delayed until the variable `x` is bound to zero by the second constraint.

Note that our strategy incurs no further cost on any function other than the primitive floating-point operations, because these functions must check for a ground result after evaluating a suspended application, anyway.

7 Related work

Constraints over real numbers have been implemented in a logic programming language for the first time in Prolog III [Col87] and CLP($\Re$) [JMSY90]. Many other Prolog implementations since then include a constraint solver for linear constraints over real numbers or for other constraint domains.

Constraint solving has been integrated into functional-logic languages. Oz's evaluation model [Smo95] is based on concurrent constraint solving. Oz does not support linear constraints over real numbers and does not implement optimization constraints. Instead, minimization and maximization have to be implemented with search operators.

The $\mathcal{TOY}$ system [LH99] includes disequality constraints between syntactic terms and linear constraints over real numbers [AHLU96]. However, they consider only arithmetic constraints but not optimizing constraints. The implementation of $\mathcal{TOY}$ is based on a translation into Prolog and uses the constraint solving facilities of the underlying Prolog implementation.

The problem to give a declarative semantics to optimization constraints has been addressed by Marriott and Stuckey [MS93] and Fages [Fag93] in the context of constraint logic programming. Their semantics is not limited to constraints over real numbers and computes an optimal solution for all solutions of a non-deterministic goal. Thus, their implementation must include a general mechanism to prune the search space of a goal. In the context of Curry there is no need to include a search strategy in the implementation of optimization predicates because strategies can be implemented using the encapsulated search. This will allow the user to select a strategy which is best suited to the problem domain, while the approaches of Marriott and Stuckey as well as Fages have to use a fixed strategy. In addition, we think that the use of higher order constraints like `minimum` fits more nicely into the framework of a language which has support for higher-order functions and predicates.

In earlier work [Lux00], we proposed to introduce a constraint solving monad `C` in order to integrate optimization constraints into Curry. While this approach will give a declarative semantics for the optimization constraints, it forces every computation involving minimizations or maximizations to be lifted into the

C-monad. This introduces a dichotomy between the constraints introducing linear inequalities and those computing optimal solutions. In particular, this will complicate the use of optimization predicates in the context of the encapsulated search. With the approach presented in this paper, the optimization constraints have a clean declarative semantics and may be used in all places where other constraints can be used.

8 Conclusion and Future Work

In this paper we have sketched an integration of linear constraints over real numbers into the functional logic language Curry. In particular we have considered optimization predicates which are highly useful in practice because often the user is interested in an optimal solution to a given problem.

The semantics of optimization predicates has been studied in the context of constraint logic programming. However, in the case of Curry an implementation is considerably simpler because in the domain of real numbers there are known efficient algorithms which compute optimal solutions. In general, pruning techniques must be used to find an optimal solution for a given goal. In the context of Curry this is best handled by using search strategies implemented with the encapsulated search, i.e. within the language.

Future work will concern the implementation of optimization constraints within the framework of our abstract machine. In addition, we will study the integration of other constraint domains into our system.

Acknowledgement

I would like to thank the anonymous referees for their useful feedback and comments to the paper.

References

[AEH97] S. Antoy, R. Echahed, and M. Hanus. Parallel evaluation strategies for functional logic languages. In *Proc. ICLP '97*, pages 138–152. MIT Press, 1997.

[AHLU96] P. Arenas-Sánchez, T. Hortalá-González, F.J. López-Fraguas, and E. Ullán-Hernández. Functional logic programming with real numbers. In *Proc. JICSLP'96 Post-Conference Workshop on Multi-Paradigm Logic Programming*. TR 96-28, Technical University Berlin, 1996.

[ALN87] H. Aït-Kaci, P. Lincoln, and R. Nasr. Le Fun: Logic, equations, and functions. In *Proc. ILPS '87*, pages 17–23, 1987.

[Col87] A. Colmerauer. Opening the Prolog III universe. *BYTE*, 12(9):177–182, August 1987.

[CWA+95] M. Carlsson, J. Widén, J. Andersson, S. Andersson, K. Boortz, H. Nilsson, and T. Sjöland. Sicstus prolog user's manual. Technical Report T91:15, SICS, June 1995.

[Fag93] François Fages. On the semantics of optimization predicates in clp languages. In *Proc. FSTTCS 1993*, pages 193–204. Springer LNCS 761, 1993.

[Han00] Curry: An integrated functional logic language, (version 0.7). `http://www-i2.informatik.rwth-aachen.de/~hanus/curry`, 2000.

[HPW92] P. Hudak, S. Peyton Jones, and P. Wadler. Report on the programming language Haskell (version 1.2). *SIGPLAN Notices*, 27(5), 1992.

[HS98] M. Hanus and F. Steiner. Controlling search in functional logic programs. In *Proc. PLILP'98*, 1998.

[IvH93] J.-L. Imbert and P. van Hentenryck. On the handling of disequations in clp over linear rational arithmetic. In F. Benhamou and A. Colmerauer, editors, *Constraint Logic Programming, Selected Research*, pages 49–71. MIT Press, 1993.

[JMSY90] J. Jaffar, S. Michaylov, P.J. Stuckey, and R. Yap. The CLP($\Re$) language and system. Technical report, IBM, 1990.

[Joh85] Thomas Johnsson. Lambda lifting. transforming programs to recursive equations. In *Proc. FPLCA 1985*, pages 190–203. Springer LNCS 201, 1985.

[LH99] F.J. López-Fraguas and T. Hortalá-González. $\mathcal{TOY}$: A multiparadigm declarative system. In *Proc. RTA'99*, pages 244–247. Springer LNCS 1631, 1999.

[Lux99] W. Lux. Implementing encapsulated search for a lazy functional logic language. In *Proc. FLOPS 99*, pages 100–113. Springer LNCS 1722, 1999.

[Lux00] W. Lux. Adding linear constraints over real numbers to curry. In *Proc. WFLP 2000*. TR 2000.2039, Universidad Politecnica de Valencia, 2000.

[MS93] K. Marriott and P. Stuckey. Semantics of constraint logic programs with optimization. *ACM Letters on Programming Languages and Systems*, 2(1–4):197–212, 1993.

[Red85] U. Reddy. Narrowing as the operational semantics of functional languages. In *Proc. ILPS'85*, pages 138–151, 1985.

[Smo95] G. Smolka. The Oz programming model. In J. van Leeuwen, editor, *Current Trends in Computer Science*. Springer LNCS 1000, 1995.

A Complete Selection Function for Lazy Conditional Narrowing

Taro Suzuki[1] and Aart Middeldorp[2]

[1] Research Institute of Electrical Communication
Tohoku University, Sendai 980-8577, Japan
taro@nue.riec.tohoku.ac.jp

[2] Institute of Information Sciences and Electronics
University of Tsukuba, Tsukuba 305-8573, Japan
ami@is.tsukuba.ac.jp

Abstract. This paper is concerned with the lazy conditional narrowing calculus LCNC. In an earlier paper we proved that this calculus is complete with respect to normalizable solutions for the class of confluent but not necessarily terminating conditional rewrite systems without so-called extra variables in the conditional parts of the rewrite rules. Unfortunately, the proof does not provide any useful complete selection function, hence in implementations we need to backtrack over the choice of equations in goals in order to guarantee that all solutions are enumerated. This is in contrast to the unconditional case where completeness with respect to the leftmost selection function is known. In this paper we close the gap by proving the completeness of LCNC with respect to the leftmost selection strategy for the above-mentioned class of conditional rewrite systems.

1 Introduction

Narrowing (Fay [5], Hullot [16]) was originally invented as a general method for solving unification problems in equational theories that are presented by confluent term rewriting systems (TRSs for short). More recently, narrowing was proposed as the computational mechanism of several functional-logic programming languages (Hanus [13]) and several new completeness results concerning the completeness of various narrowing strategies and calculi have been obtained in the past few years. Here completeness means that for every solution to a given goal a solution that is at least as general is computed by the narrowing strategy. Since narrowing is a complicated operation, numerous calculi consisting of a small number of more elementary inference rules that simulate narrowing have been proposed (e.g. [6, 15, 20, 25, 14, 23, 8, 24, 19]).

In this paper we consider the lazy conditional narrowing calculus LCNC of Hamada and Middeldorp [11]. LCNC is the extension of the the lazy narrowing calculus LNC to conditional TRSs (CTRSs for short). Completeness issues of LNC have been extensively studied in [23] and [22]. In [23] Middeldorp *et al.* prove

H. Kuchen and K. Ueda (Eds.): FLOPS 2001, LNCS 2024, pp. 201–215, 2001.

that LNC is *strongly* complete whenever *basic* narrowing (Hullot [16]) is complete. Strong completeness means that the choice of the equation in goals can be made don't care non-deterministic, resulting in a huge reduction of the search space as well as easing implementations. For the completeness of basic narrowing several sufficient conditions are known, including termination. It is also shown in [23] that LNC is complete for arbitrary confluent TRSs and normalized solutions with respect to the selection function $\mathcal{S}_{\text{left}}$ that selects the leftmost equation in every goal. (For this general class of TRSs, LNC is not strongly complete [23, Counterexample 10].) Based on the latter result Middeldorp and Okui [22] present restrictions on the participating TRSs and solutions which guarantee that all non-determinism due to the choice of inference rule of LNC is removed. The resulting deterministic calculus LNC_{d} satisfies the optimality property that different derivations compute incomparable solutions for a class of TRSs that properly includes the class of TRSs for which a similar result was obtained by Antoy *et al.* in the setting of needed narrowing [1].

For the conditional version of LCNC much less is known. Hamada and Middeldorp [11] extended one of the main results of [23] to conditional rewriting: LCNC is strongly complete whenever basic conditional narrowing is complete. The latter is known for decreasing and confluent CTRSs without extra variables (Middeldorp and Hamoen [21]), terminating and level-confluent CTRSs with extra variables in the conditions only (Giovannetti and Moiso [7]), and terminating and shallow-confluent CTRSs with extra variables (Werner [27]). In [12] two further completeness results are presented: (1) for confluent CTRSs without extra variables with respect to normalized solutions and (2) for arbitrary terminating and level-confluent systems. So the only known completeness result for LCNC that does not rely on some kind of termination assumption is (1). However, unlike its unconditional counterpart, the proof in [12] does not give completeness with respect to the leftmost selection function. As a matter of fact, the selection strategy used in the proof is not effective in that it refers to an ordinary conditional narrowing derivation computing the solution that we want to approximate with LCNC. Hence in implementations we need to backtrack over the choice of equations in goals in order to guarantee that all solutions are enumerated. This complicates implementations and, worse, leads to a dramatic increase in the search space, even more so since in conditional narrowing (whether presented as a single inference rule or in the form of a calculus like LCNC) the conditions of the applied rewrite rule are added to the current goal after every narrowing step.

In this paper we strengthen result (1) to completeness with respect to the leftmost selection function. The non-trivial proof is based on a tricky variable condition that is preserved during an inductive transformation process. In order to benefit the reader who is familiar with our earlier completeness proofs (in [11, 22, 23]), the current proof is structured in a similar way. We stress however that the key idea that makes the proof work is original to this paper.

The remainder of the paper is organized as follows. In the next section we recall some definitions pertaining to conditional rewriting and we present the calculus LCNC. In Section 3 we prove our completeness result. We make some concluding remarks in Section 4.

2 Preliminaries

We assume familiarity with the basics of (conditional) term rewriting and narrowing. Surveys can be found in [2, 4, 18, 21].

A conditional term rewriting system (CTRS for short) over a signature $\mathcal{F}$ is a set $\mathcal{R}$ of (conditional) rewrite rules of the form $l \to r \Leftarrow c$ where the conditional part c is a (possibly empty) sequence $s_1 \approx t_1, \ldots, s_n \approx t_n$ of equations. All terms $l, r, s_1, \ldots, s_n, t_1, \ldots, t_n$ must belong to $\mathcal{T}(\mathcal{F}, \mathcal{V})$ and we require that l is not a variable. Here $\mathcal{V}$ denotes a countably infinite set of variables. CTRSs are classified ([21]) according to the distribution of variables in rewrite rules. A 1-CTRS contains no extra variables (i.e., $\mathcal{V}\mathrm{ar}(r, c) \subseteq \mathcal{V}\mathrm{ar}(l)$ for all rewrite rules $l \to r \Leftarrow c$), a 2-CTRS may contain extra variables in the conditions only ($\mathcal{V}\mathrm{ar}(r) \subseteq \mathcal{V}\mathrm{ar}(l)$ for all rewrite rules $l \to r \Leftarrow c$), and a 3-CTRS may also have extra variables in the right-hand sides provided these occur in the corresponding conditions ($\mathcal{V}\mathrm{ar}(r) \subseteq \mathcal{V}\mathrm{ar}(l, c)$ for all rewrite rules $l \to r \Leftarrow c$).

Although extra variables enable a more natural and efficient style of writing specifications or programs, their presence comes with a price. For instance, completeness results for narrowing that hold for arbitrary confluent TRSs and 1-CTRSs typically do not carry over to 2-CTRSs and 3-CTRSs without requiring some kind of termination assumption. In the next section we consider 1-CTRSs.

We assume that every CTRS contains the rewrite rule $x \approx x \to \mathtt{true}$. Here $\approx$ and $\mathtt{true}$ are function symbols that do not occur in the other rewrite rules. These symbols may only occur at the root position of terms. Let $\mathcal{R}$ be a CTRS. We inductively define unconditional TRSs $\mathcal{R}_n$ for $n \geqslant 0$ as follows:

$$\begin{aligned}\mathcal{R}_0 &= \{\, x \approx x \to \mathtt{true} \,\},\\ \mathcal{R}_{n+1} &= \{\, l\theta \to r\theta \mid l \to r \Leftarrow c \in \mathcal{R} \text{ and } c\theta \to^*_{\mathcal{R}_n} \top \,\}.\end{aligned}$$

Here $\top$ stands for any sequence of $\mathtt{true}$s. We define $s \to_{\mathcal{R}} t$ if and only if there exists an $n \geqslant 0$ such that $s \to_{\mathcal{R}_n} t$. Our CTRS are known as *join* CTRSs in the term rewriting literature.

An equation is a term of the form $s \approx t$. The constant $\mathtt{true}$ is also viewed as an equation. A goal is a sequence of equations. A substitution θ is a ($\mathcal{R}$-)solution of a goal G if $s\theta \leftrightarrow^*_{\mathcal{R}} t\theta$. This is equivalent to validity of the equations in $G\theta$ in all models of the underlying conditional equational system of $\mathcal{R}$ (Kaplan [17]) and for confluent $\mathcal{R}$ to $G\theta \to^*_{\mathcal{R}} \top$. We abbreviate the latter to $\mathcal{R} \vdash G\theta$. A *normalized* solution satisfies the additional property that variables are mapped to normal forms with respect to $\mathcal{R}$.

For a substitution θ and a set of variables W, we denote $(W \setminus \mathcal{D}(\theta)) \cup \mathcal{I}(\theta\restriction_W)$ by $\mathcal{V}\mathrm{ar}_W(\theta)$. Here $\mathcal{D}(\theta) = \{x \in \mathcal{V} \mid \theta(x) \neq x\}$ denotes the domain of θ, which is always assumed to be finite, and $\mathcal{I}(\theta\restriction_W) = \bigcup_{x \in \mathcal{D}(\theta) \cap W} \mathcal{V}\mathrm{ar}(x\theta)$ the set of variables introduced by the restriction of θ to W.

The lazy conditional narrowing calculus LCNC (Hamada and Middeldorp [11]) consists of the following five inference rules:

[o] *outermost narrowing*

$$\frac{G', f(s_1, \ldots, s_n) \simeq t, G''}{G', s_1 \approx l_1, \ldots, s_n \approx l_n, r \approx t, c, G''}$$

if there exists a fresh variant $f(l_1, \ldots, l_n) \rightarrow r \Leftarrow c$ of a rewrite rule in $\mathcal{R}$,

[i] *imitation*

$$\frac{G', f(s_1, \ldots, s_n) \simeq x, G''}{(G', s_1 \approx x_1, \ldots, s_n \approx x_n, G'')\theta}$$

if $\theta = \{x \mapsto f(x_1, \ldots, x_n)\}$ with $x_1, \ldots, x_n$ fresh variables,

[d] *decomposition*

$$\frac{G', f(s_1, \ldots, s_n) \approx f(t_1, \ldots, t_n), G''}{G', s_1 \approx t_1, \ldots, s_n \approx t_n, G''},$$

[v] *variable elimination*

$$\frac{G', s \simeq x, G''}{(G', G'')\theta}$$

if $x \notin \mathcal{V}\mathrm{ar}(s)$ and $\theta = \{x \mapsto s\}$,

[t] *removal of trivial equations*

$$\frac{G', x \approx x, G''}{G', G''}.$$

In the rules [o], [i], and [v], $s \simeq t$ stands for $s \approx t$ or $t \approx s$. (Since the inference rules never produce the equation `true`, we assume that LCNC deals only with goals that do not contain `true`.) Note that the outermost narrowing rule is applicable as soon as the root symbol of one side s of an equation equals the root symbol of the left-hand side l of a rewrite rule. The *parameter-passing* equations $s_1 \approx l_1, \ldots, s_n \approx l_n$ code the problem of unifying s and l. Further note that unlike higher-order narrowing calculi (e.g. [24, 19]) we do not permit outermost narrowing at variable positions. This makes the task of proving completeness much more challenging but results in a much smaller search space.

If G and G' are the upper and lower goal in the inference rule $[\alpha]$ ($\alpha \in \{\mathrm{o}, \mathrm{i}, \mathrm{d}, \mathrm{v}, \mathrm{t}\}$), we write $G \Rightarrow_{[\alpha]} G'$. This is called an LCNC-step. The applied rewrite rule or substitution may be supplied as subscript, that is, we write things like $G \Rightarrow_{[\mathrm{o}], l \rightarrow r \Leftarrow c} G'$ and $G \Rightarrow_{[\mathrm{i}], \theta} G'$. A finite LCNC-derivation $G_1 \Rightarrow_{\theta_1} \cdots \Rightarrow_{\theta_{n-1}} G_n$ may be abbreviated to $G_1 \Rightarrow^*_{\theta} G_n$ where θ is the composition $\theta_1 \cdots \theta_{n-1}$ of the substitutions $\theta_1, \ldots, \theta_{n-1}$ computed along its steps. An LCNC-refutation is an LCNC-derivation ending in the empty goal $\square$.

3 Leftmost Selection

This section contains our main result, the completeness of LCNC for arbitrary confluent 1-CTRSs with respect to normalized solutions and the leftmost selection function $\mathcal{S}_{\text{left}}$. So we assume that the sequence G' of equations to the left of the selected equation in the inference rules of LCNC is empty.

In previous results ([11, 12]) we reduced the (strong) completeness of LCNC (for a suitable class of CTRSs and solutions) to either the completeness of conditional narrowing or the completeness of conditional rewriting by means of an inductive transformation process. The advantage of rewriting is that rewrite steps applied to different parts of a goal or equation can be swapped at will, which greatly facilitates a proof of completeness with respect to a particular selection strategy. In the proof below we use the variant of conditional rewriting in which the list of instantiated conditions of the applied rewrite rule is explicitly added to the goal after every rewrite step. Formally, we use the relation $\rightarrowtail$ defined as follows: $G \rightarrowtail G'$ if $G = G_1, e, G_2$, $e \to e'$ by applying the conditional rewrite rule $l \to r \Leftarrow c$ with substitution θ (so $e' = e[r\sigma]_p$ for some position p in e and $\mathcal{R} \vdash c\sigma$), and $G' = G_1, e', c\sigma, G_2$. It is well-known ([3, 21]) that $\mathcal{R} \vdash G$ if and only if $G \rightarrowtail^* \top$. We assume without loss of generality that in a rewrite proof $G \rightarrowtail^* \top$ always the leftmost equation different from `true` is selected.

Similar to previous completeness proofs, we define a couple of basic transformations on rewrite proofs $\Pi\colon G\theta \rightarrowtail^* \top$. In order to make the proof work, we need to keep track of a number of variables along the transformation process. Since these variables cannot be inferred from the current rewrite proof Π, together with G and θ, we need to enrich rewrite proofs. This is the reason why we consider quadruples, called *states*, of the form $\langle G, \theta, \Pi, X\rangle$ where G is a goal, θ a solution of G, $\Pi\colon G\theta \rightarrowtail^* \top$ a rewrite proof of $G\theta$, and X a finite set of variables associated to Π. Variables in X are said to be *of interest* and variables in G but not in X are called *intermediate*. In order to avoid confusion, we occasionally write X-intermediate or even $\underline{\Pi}$-intermediate (when comparing different states with the same X).

We require that the properties defined below are satisfied.

Definition 1. *A state $\underline{\Pi} = \langle G, \theta, \Pi, X\rangle$ is called* normal *if $\theta\restriction_X$ is normalized. We say that $\underline{\Pi}$ satisfies the* variable condition *if for every equation $s \approx t$ in $G = G_1, s \approx t, G_2$ the following three conditions hold:*

VC1 *all intermediate variables in s occur in G_1 or all intermediate variables in t occur in G_1,*
VC2 *if $s\theta$ is rewritten in Π then all intermediate variables in s occur in G_1,*
VC3 *if $t\theta$ is rewritten in Π then all intermediate variables in t occur in G_1.*

A normal state with the variable condition is called admissible.

Example 1. Consider the confluent 1-CTRS consisting of the rewrite rules

$$\begin{array}{rcl} f(x,y) & \to & g(y) \Leftarrow x \approx a \\ a & \to & b \\ g(b) & \to & b \end{array}$$

and the goal $G = f(x, y) \approx g(y), g(g(y)) \approx a$. We determine θ, Π, and X such that $\underline{\Pi} = \langle G, \theta, \Pi, X\rangle$ is admissible. First of all, since the variable y occurs in both sides of the leftmost equation $f(x, y) \approx g(y)$, it must be a variable of interest for otherwise **VC1** is violated. So $y \in X$ and hence, to satisfy normality, $\theta(y)$ should be a normal form. The only normal form that satisfies the second equation of G is b, with associated rewrite proof

$$g(g(b)) \approx a \;\rightarrowtail\; g(b) \approx a \;\rightarrowtail\; b \approx a \;\rightarrowtail\; b \approx b \;\rightarrowtail\; \mathtt{true}.$$

Since $g(g(y)) \approx a$ does not contain intermediate variables, it satisfies **VC1**, **VC2**, and **VC3**. Likewise, since $g(y)$ lacks intermediate variables, $f(x, y) \approx g(y)$ satisfies **VC3**. The only way to solve this equation is by applying the first rewrite rule to its (instantiated) left-hand side. Hence, to satisfy **VC2**, x cannot be an intermediate variable. Consequently, $x \in X$ and thus to conclude that $\underline{\Pi}$ is admissible it only remains to show that we can substitute a normal form for x such that the equation $f(x, b) \approx g(b)$ is solvable. It is easy to see that we should again take the normal form b, with associated rewrite proof

$$f(b, b) \approx g(b) \;\rightarrowtail\; g(b) \approx g(b), b \approx a \;\rightarrowtail\; \mathtt{true}, b \approx a \;\rightarrowtail\; \mathtt{true}, b \approx b \;\rightarrowtail\; \top.$$

An example of a goal without admissible states is $f(x) \approx x$ with respect to the TRS consisting of the rule $a \to f(a)$. Note that $f(x) \approx x$ has no normalized solutions.

Lemma 1. *Let $\underline{\Pi} = \langle G, \theta, \Pi, X\rangle$ be an admissible state with $G = s \approx t, H$.*

1. *If $s\theta$ is rewritten in Π then s is not a variable and does not include intermediate variables.*
2. *If $t\theta$ is rewritten in Π then t is not a variable and does not include intermediate variables.*

Proof. We prove the first statement. Suppose the left-hand side of $s\theta \approx t\theta$ is rewritten in Π. By **VC2** all intermediate variables in s should occur in the equations to the left of $s \approx t$ in G. Since $s \approx t$ is the leftmost equation, there cannot be intermediate variables in s. Hence, if s is a variable then it must be a variable of interest and thus $s\theta$ is a normal form because $\underline{\Pi}$ is normal. This however contradicts the assumption that $s\theta$ is rewritten in Π. The second statement is proved in exactly the same way (with **VC3** instead of **VC2**). □

In the following transformation lemmata $\underline{\Pi}$ denotes an admissible state $\langle G, \theta, \Pi, X\rangle$ such that $G = s \approx t, H$ and, in Lemmata 2, 3, and 5, W denotes a finite set of variables such that $\mathcal{V}\mathrm{ar}(G) \subseteq W$. Recall our earlier assumption that Π respects $\mathcal{S}_{\mathrm{left}}$. In particular, in the first step of Π the equation $s \approx t$ is selected.

Lemma 2. *Let $s = f(s_1, \ldots, s_n)$ and suppose that a reduct of $s\theta \approx t\theta$ in Π is rewritten at position 1. If $l \to r \Leftarrow c$ is the employed rewrite rule in the first such step then there exists an admissible state $\phi_{[o]}(\underline{\Pi}) = \langle G', \theta', \Pi', X\rangle$ with $G' = s \approx l, r \approx t, c, H$ such that $\theta' = \theta$ $[W]$.*

Proof. The given rewrite proof Π is of the form

$$G\theta \;\rightarrowtail^*\; l\tau \approx t', C, H\theta \;\rightarrowtail\; r\tau \approx t', c\tau, C, H\theta \;\rightarrowtail^*\; \top.$$

Here C are the instantiated conditions of the rewrite rules applied in the rewrite sequence from $s\theta \approx t\theta$ to $l\tau \approx t'$. Without loss of generality we assume that $\mathcal{V}\text{ar}(l \to r \Leftarrow c) \cap (X \cup W) = \varnothing$ and $\mathcal{D}(\tau) = \mathcal{V}\text{ar}(l \to r \Leftarrow c)$. Hence the substitution $\theta' = \theta \cup \tau$ is well-defined. Since $\mathcal{D}(\tau) \cap W = \varnothing$, $\theta' = \theta\ [W]$. We have $G'\theta' = s\theta \approx l\tau, r\tau \approx t\theta, c\tau, H\theta$. The first part of Π can be transformed into

$$\begin{aligned} G'\theta' \;&\rightarrowtail^*\; l\tau \approx l\tau, C_1, r\tau \approx t\theta, c\tau, H\theta \\ &\rightarrowtail^*\; l\tau \approx l\tau, C_1, r\tau \approx t', C_2, c\tau, H\theta \\ &\rightarrowtail\; \mathtt{true}, C_1, r\tau \approx t', C_2, c\tau, H\theta. \end{aligned}$$

Here C_1, C_2 and C consist of the same equations in possibly different order. Hence by rearranging the steps in the remaining part of Π we obtain

$$\mathtt{true}, C_1, r\tau \approx t', C_2, c\tau, H\theta \;\rightarrowtail^*\; \top.$$

Concatenating these two derivations yields the rewrite proof Π'. It remains to show that the state $\phi_{[o]}(\underline{\Pi}) = \langle G', \theta', \Pi', X\rangle$ is admissible. Since $\theta'\restriction_X = \theta\restriction_X \cup \tau\restriction_X = \theta\restriction_X$, $\phi_{[o]}(\underline{\Pi})$ inherits normality from $\underline{\Pi}$. For the variable condition we need some more effort. Below we make tacit use of the observation that a variable $x \in \mathcal{V}\text{ar}(s \approx t, H)$ is $\underline{\Pi}$-intermediate in G if and only if x is $\phi_{[o]}(\underline{\Pi})$-intermediate in G'. First consider the equation $s \approx l$. Since $s\theta'$ is rewritten in Π', we obtain from Lemma 1(1) that s does not contain intermediate variables. Hence **VC1** and **VC2** are trivially satisfied. By construction, the right-hand side of $s\theta' \approx l\theta'$ is never rewritten in Π'. Hence **VC3** holds vacuously. Next consider the equations in $r \approx t, c$. Because we deal with CTRSs without extra variables, all variables in r and c occur in l and hence the three variable conditions are true for the equations in c and $r \approx t$ satisfies **VC1** and **VC2**. Suppose the right-hand side of $r\theta' \approx t\theta'$ is rewritten in Π'. By construction of Π', this is only possible if the right-hand side of $s\theta \approx t\theta$ is rewritten in Π. According to Lemma 1(2) t does not contain intermediate variables and thus the equation $r \approx t$ in G' satisfies **VC3**. Finally, consider an equation $s' \approx t'$ in $H = H_1, s' \approx t', H_2$. Let V_1 be the set of intermediate variables in s' and V_2 the set of intermediate variables in t'. Since $\underline{\Pi}$ is admissible, $V_1 \subseteq \mathcal{V}\text{ar}(s \approx t, H_1)$ or $V_2 \subseteq \mathcal{V}\text{ar}(s \approx t, H_1)$. Hence also $V_1 \subseteq \mathcal{V}\text{ar}(s \approx l, r \approx t, H_1)$ or $V_2 \subseteq \mathcal{V}\text{ar}(s \approx l, r \approx t, H_1)$. This proves **VC1**. The proof of **VC2** is just as easy: If $s'\theta'$ is rewritten in Π' then $s'\theta$ is rewritten in Π and thus all intermediate variables in s' occur in $s \approx t, H_1$ and therefore also in $s \approx l, r \approx t, H_1$. Finally, **VC3** is proved in exactly the same way. □

Note that the above proof breaks down if we admit extra variables in the conditional rewrite rules. Further note that the proof remains valid if we would put the equation $r \approx t$ after the conditions c in G'.

Lemma 3. *Let $s = f(s_1, \dots, s_n)$ and $t \in \mathcal{V}$. If $\text{root}(t\theta) = f$ then there exists an admissible state $\phi_{[i]}(\underline{\Pi}) = \langle G', \theta', \Pi, X'\rangle$ with $G' = G\sigma_1$ such that $\sigma_1\theta' = \theta\ [W]$. Here $\sigma_1 = \{t \mapsto f(x_1, \dots, x_n)\}$ with $x_1, \dots, x_n \notin W$.*

Proof. Write $t\theta = f(t_1, \ldots, t_n)$ and define $\theta' = \theta \cup \{x_i \mapsto t_i \mid 1 \leqslant i \leqslant n\}$. One easily verifies that $\sigma_1\theta' = \theta\ [W]$. We have $G'\theta' = G\sigma_1\theta' = G\theta$ and thus Π is a rewrite proof of $G'\theta'$. We define $X' = \cup_{x \in X} \mathcal{V}\mathrm{ar}(x\sigma_1)$. Equivalently,

$$X' = \begin{cases} (X \setminus \{t\}) \cup \{x_1, \ldots, x_n\} & \text{if } t \in X, \\ X & \text{otherwise.} \end{cases}$$

It remains to show that $\phi_{[i]}(\underline{\Pi})$ is admissible. First we show that $\theta' \lceil_{X'}$ is normalized. We consider two cases. If $t \in X$ then $\theta' \lceil_{X'} = \theta \lceil_{X \setminus \{t\}} \cup \{x_i \mapsto t_i \mid 1 \leqslant i \leqslant n\}$. The substitution $\theta \lceil_{X \setminus \{t\}}$ is normalized because $\theta \lceil_X$ is normalized. Furthermore, since every t_i is a subterm of $t\theta$ and $t\theta$ is a normal form because $\underline{\Pi}$ is normal and $t \in X$, $\{x_i \mapsto t_i \mid 1 \leqslant i \leqslant n\}$ is normalized as well. If $t \notin X$ then $\theta' \lceil_{X'} = \theta \lceil_X$ is normalized by assumption. Next we show that every equation in G' satisfies the variable condition. Again we consider two cases.

1. Suppose that $t \in X$. Then $x_1, \ldots, x_n$ belong to X' and thus the right-hand side $t\sigma_1 = f(x_1, \ldots, x_n)$ of the leftmost equation $s\sigma_1 \approx t\sigma_1$ in G' does not contain X'-intermediate variables. Hence $s\sigma_1 \approx t\sigma_1$ satisfies **VC1** and **VC3**. Suppose $s\sigma_1\theta'$ is rewritten in Π. Then, as $\underline{\Pi}$ is admissible, s does not contain X-intermediate variables. We have to show that $s\sigma_1$ does not contain X'-intermediate variables. Since the variables $x_1, \ldots, x_n$ are of interest, it follows that every X'-intermediate variable in $s\sigma_1$ is X-intermediate in s. Therefore $s\sigma_1 \approx t\sigma_1$ satisfies **VC3**.
   Next consider an equation $s'\sigma_1 \approx t'\sigma_1$ in $H\sigma_1 = (H_1, s' \approx t', H_2)\sigma_1$. Let V_1 be the set of X'-intermediate variables in $s'\sigma_1$ and V_2 the set of X'-intermediate variables in $t'\sigma_1$. Since the variables $x_1, \ldots, x_n$ are not X'-intermediate and t is not X-intermediate, V_1 (V_2) coincides with the set of X-intermediate variables in s' (t'). Since $\underline{\Pi}$ is admissible, $V_1 \subseteq \mathcal{V}\mathrm{ar}(s \approx t, H_1)$ or $V_2 \subseteq \mathcal{V}\mathrm{ar}(s \approx t, H_1)$. Because $t \notin V_1 \cup V_2$, $V_1 \subseteq \mathcal{V}\mathrm{ar}((s \approx t, H_1)\sigma_1)$ or $V_2 \subseteq \mathcal{V}\mathrm{ar}((s \approx t, H_1)\sigma_1)$. This concludes the proof of **VC1**. Next we prove **VC2**. If $s'\sigma_1\theta' = s'\theta$ is rewritten in Π then $V_1 \subseteq \mathcal{V}\mathrm{ar}(s \approx t, H_1)$ and as $t \notin V_1$ also $V_1 \subseteq \mathcal{V}\mathrm{ar}((s \approx t, H_1)\sigma_1)$. The proof of **VC3** is just as easy.
2. Suppose that $t \notin X$. Then t is $\underline{\Pi}$-intermediate and $x_1, \ldots, x_n$ are $\phi_{[i]}(\underline{\Pi})$-intermediate. First consider the equation $s\sigma_1 \approx t\sigma_1$. Since t is intermediate, s cannot contain intermediate variables. In particular, t does not occur in s and therefore $s\sigma_1 = s$. So $s\sigma_1 \approx t\sigma_1$ satisfies **VC1** and **VC2**. Since t is a variable, $t\sigma_1\theta' = t\theta$ cannot be rewritten in Π as a consequence of Lemma 1(2) and hence **VC3** is satisfied too.
   Next consider an equation $s'\sigma_1 \approx t'\sigma_1$ in $H\sigma_1 = (H_1, s' \approx t', H_2)\sigma_1$. Let V_1' (V_2') be the set of $\phi_{[i]}(\underline{\Pi})$-intermediate variables in $s'\sigma_1$ ($t'\sigma_1$) and let V_1 (V_2) be the set of $\underline{\Pi}$-intermediate variables in s' (t'). We have

$$V_1' = \begin{cases} (V_1 \setminus \{t\}) \cup \{x_1, \ldots, x_n\} & \text{if } t \in \mathcal{V}\mathrm{ar}(s'), \\ V_1 & \text{otherwise,} \end{cases}$$

and

$$V_2' = \begin{cases} (V_2 \setminus \{t\}) \cup \{x_1, \dots, x_n\} & \text{if } t \in \mathcal{V}\mathrm{ar}(t'), \\ V_2 & \text{otherwise.} \end{cases}$$

Because $\underline{\Pi}$ is admissible, $V_1 \subseteq \mathcal{V}\mathrm{ar}(s \approx t, H_1)$ or $V_2 \subseteq \mathcal{V}\mathrm{ar}(s \approx t, H_1)$. We consider the former. To conclude **VC1** it is sufficient to show that $V_1' \subseteq \mathcal{V}\mathrm{ar}((s \approx t, H_1)\sigma_1)$. We distinguish two cases. If $t \in \mathcal{V}\mathrm{ar}(s')$ then $t \in V_1$ and thus $x_1, \dots, x_n \in \mathcal{V}\mathrm{ar}((s \approx t, H_1)\sigma_1)$. Since we also have the inclusion $V_1 \setminus \{t\} \subseteq \mathcal{V}\mathrm{ar}((s \approx t, H_1)\sigma_1)$, $V_1' \subseteq \mathcal{V}\mathrm{ar}((s \approx t, H_1)\sigma_1)$ holds. If $t \notin \mathcal{V}\mathrm{ar}(s')$ then $t \notin V_1$ and thus $V_1' = V_1 \subseteq \mathcal{V}\mathrm{ar}((s \approx t, H_1)\sigma_1)$. This proves **VC1**. For **VC2** we reason as follows. Suppose $s'\sigma_1\theta' = s'\theta$ is rewritten in Π. This implies that $V_1 \subseteq \mathcal{V}\mathrm{ar}(s \approx t, H_1)$ and hence $V_1' \subseteq \mathcal{V}\mathrm{ar}((s \approx t, H_1)\sigma_1)$ by using similar arguments as before. The proof of **VC3** is again very similar. □

Lemma 4. *Let $s = f(s_1, \dots, s_n)$, $t = f(t_1, \dots, t_n)$, and suppose that no reduct of $s\theta \approx t\theta$ in Π is rewritten at position 1 or 2. There exists an admissible state $\phi_{[\mathrm{d}]}(\underline{\Pi}) = \langle G', \theta, \Pi', X\rangle$ with $G' = s_1 \approx t_1, \dots, s_n \approx t_n, H$.*

Proof. The given rewrite proof Π is of the form

$$G\theta \rightarrowtail^* f(u_1, \dots, u_n) \approx f(u_1, \dots, u_n), C, H\theta \rightarrowtail \mathtt{true}, C, H\theta \rightarrowtail^* \top.$$

Here C are the instantiated conditions of the rewrite rules applied in the rewrite sequence from $s\theta \approx t\theta$ to $f(u_1, \dots, u_n) \approx f(u_1, \dots, u_n)$. The first part of Π can be transformed into

$$G'\theta' \rightarrowtail^* u_1 \approx u_1, C_1, \dots, u_n \approx u_n, C_n, H\theta \rightarrowtail^* \mathtt{true}, C_1, \dots, \mathtt{true}, C_n, H\theta.$$

Here $C_1, \dots, C_n$ and C consist of the same equations in possibly different order. Hence by rearranging the steps in the latter part of Π we obtain

$$\mathtt{true}, C_1, \dots, \mathtt{true}, C_n, H\theta \rightarrowtail^* \top.$$

Concatenating these two derivations yields the rewrite proof Π' of $G'\theta$. It remains to show that the state $\phi_{[\mathrm{d}]}(\underline{\Pi}) = \langle G', \theta, \Pi', X\rangle$ is admissible. Since $\underline{\Pi}$ has the same θ and X, normality is obvious. Because $\underline{\Pi}$ satisfies condition **VC1**, s or t does not contain intermediate variables. Hence there are no intermediate variables in $s_1, \dots, s_n$ or in $t_1, \dots, t_n$. Consequently, the equations $s_1 \approx t_1, \dots, s_n \approx t_n$ in G' satisfy **VC1**. The conditions **VC2** and **VC3** are also easily verified. For instance, suppose that $t_i\theta$ is rewritten in Π'. Then, by construction of Π', $t\theta$ is rewritten in Π. According to Lemma 1, t does not contain intermediate variables and since t_i is a subterm of t, t_i also lacks intermediate variables. By using similar arguments one easily verifies that the equations in H satisfy the three conditions. □

Lemma 5. *Let $t \in \mathcal{V}$, $s \neq t$, and suppose that in the first step of Π $s\theta \approx t\theta$ is rewritten at the root position. There exists an admissible state $\phi_{[\mathrm{v}]}(\underline{\Pi}) = \langle G', \theta, \Pi', X'\rangle$ with $G' = H\sigma_1$ such that $\sigma_1\theta = \theta$ $[W]$. Here $\sigma_1 = \{t \mapsto s\}$.*

Proof. Since $s\theta \approx t\theta$ is rewritten to $\mathtt{true}$ by the rule $x \approx x \to \mathtt{true}$, we must have $s\theta = t\theta$. Hence $t\sigma_1\theta = s\theta = t\theta$. For variables y different from t we have $y\sigma_1\theta = y\theta$. Hence $\sigma_1\theta = \theta\ [W]$. Since $\mathcal{V}\mathrm{ar}(H) \subseteq W$, $G'\theta = H\sigma_1\theta = H\theta$ and thus from the tail of the rewrite proof Π:

$$G\theta \rightarrowtail \mathtt{true}, H\theta \rightarrowtail^* \top$$

we can extract a rewrite proof Π' of $G'\theta$. We define $X' = \bigcup_{x \in X} \mathcal{V}\mathrm{ar}(x\sigma_1)$. Clearly

$$X' = \begin{cases} (X \setminus \{t\}) \cup \mathcal{V}\mathrm{ar}(s) & \text{if } t \in X, \\ X & \text{otherwise.} \end{cases}$$

It remains to show that $\phi_{[\mathrm{v}]}(\underline{\Pi})$ is admissible. First we show that $\theta\lceil_{X'}$ is normalized. We consider two cases. If $t \in X$ then $\theta\lceil_{X'} = \theta\lceil_{X\setminus\{t\}\cup\mathcal{V}\mathrm{ar}(s)}$. The substitution $\theta\lceil_{X\setminus\{t\}}$ is normalized because $\theta\lceil_X$ is normalized. If $x \in \mathcal{V}\mathrm{ar}(s)$ then $x\theta$ is a subterm of $s\theta = t\theta$. Since $t\theta$ is a normal form by the normality of $\underline{\Pi}$, so is $x\theta$. Hence $\theta\lceil_{\mathcal{V}\mathrm{ar}(s)}$ is normalized as well. If $t \notin X$ then $\theta\lceil_{X'} = \theta\lceil_X$ is normalized by assumption. Next we show that every equation in G' satisfies the variable condition. Let $s'\sigma_1 \approx t'\sigma_1$ be an equation in $H\sigma_1 = (H_1, s' \approx t', H_2)\sigma_1$. Let V_1' (V_2') be the set of X'-intermediate variables in $s'\sigma_1$ ($t'\sigma_1$) and let V_1 (V_2) be the set of intermediate variables in s' (t'). We consider two cases.

1. Suppose that $t \in X$. Then $\mathcal{V}\mathrm{ar}(s) \subseteq X'$. So the variables in $\mathcal{V}\mathrm{ar}(s)$ are not X'-intermediate and t is not X-intermediate. It follows that $V_1' = V_1$ and $V_2' = V_2$. Since $\underline{\Pi}$ is admissible, $V_1 \subseteq \mathcal{V}\mathrm{ar}(H_1)$ or $V_2 \subseteq \mathcal{V}\mathrm{ar}(H_1)$. Because $t \notin V_1 \cup V_2$, $V_1' \subseteq \mathcal{V}\mathrm{ar}(H_1\sigma_1)$ or $V_2' \subseteq \mathcal{V}\mathrm{ar}(H_1\sigma_1)$. This concludes the proof of **VC1**. The proofs of **VC2** and **VC3** also easily follow from the identities $V_1' = V_1$ and $V_2' = V_2$ and the fact that $t \notin V_1 \cup V_2$.
2. Suppose that $t \notin X$. Then t is $\underline{\Pi}$-intermediate and all variables in $\mathcal{V}\mathrm{ar}(s)$ are $\phi_{[\mathrm{v}]}(\underline{\Pi})$-intermediate. We have

$$V_1' = \begin{cases} (V_1 \setminus \{t\}) \cup \mathcal{V}\mathrm{ar}(s) & \text{if } t \in \mathcal{V}\mathrm{ar}(s'), \\ V_1 & \text{otherwise,} \end{cases}$$

and

$$V_2' = \begin{cases} (V_2 \setminus \{t\}) \cup \mathcal{V}\mathrm{ar}(s) & \text{if } t \in \mathcal{V}\mathrm{ar}(t'), \\ V_2 & \text{otherwise.} \end{cases}$$

Because $\underline{\Pi}$ is admissible, $V_1 \subseteq \mathcal{V}\mathrm{ar}(H_1)$ or $V_2 \subseteq \mathcal{V}\mathrm{ar}(H_1)$. We consider the latter. To conclude **VC1** it is therefore sufficient to show that $V_2' \subseteq \mathcal{V}\mathrm{ar}(H_1\sigma_1)$. We distinguish two cases. If $t \in \mathcal{V}\mathrm{ar}(t')$ then $t \in V_2$ and thus $\mathcal{V}\mathrm{ar}(s) \subseteq \mathcal{V}\mathrm{ar}(H_1\sigma_1)$. Since the inclusion $V_2 \setminus \{t\} \subseteq \mathcal{V}\mathrm{ar}(H_1\sigma_1)$ also holds, $V_2' \subseteq \mathcal{V}\mathrm{ar}(H_1\sigma_1)$ as desired. If $t \notin \mathcal{V}\mathrm{ar}(t')$ then $t \notin V_2$ and thus $V_2' = V_2 \subseteq \mathcal{V}\mathrm{ar}(H_1\sigma_1)$. This completes the proof of **VC1**. The proofs of **VC2** and **VC3** are based on similar arguments and omitted.

□

Lemma 6. *Let $t \in \mathcal{V}$, $s = t$, and suppose that in the first step of Π $s\theta \approx t\theta$ is rewritten at the root position. There exists an admissible state $\phi_{[t]}(\underline{\Pi}) = \langle G', \theta, \Pi', X \rangle$ with $G' = H$.*

Proof. The given rewrite proof Π has the form

$$G\theta \;\rightarrowtail\; \mathtt{true}, H\theta \;\rightarrowtail^*\; \top.$$

From the tail of Π we extract a rewrite proof Π' of $G'\theta = H\theta$. It is easy to show that $\phi_{[t]}(\underline{\Pi})$ is admissible. □

Lemma 7. *There exists an admissible state $\phi_{\mathsf{swap}}(\underline{\Pi}) = \langle G', \theta, \Pi', X \rangle$ with $G' = t \approx s, H$.*

Proof. The given rewrite proof $\Pi\colon (s \approx t, H)\theta \rightarrowtail^* \top$ is transformed into a rewrite proof Π' of $(t \approx s, H)\theta$ by simply swapping the two sides of every reduct of $s\theta \approx t\theta$. This clearly does not affect normality and since the variable condition is symmetric with respect the two sides of an equation it follows that $\phi_{\mathsf{swap}}(\underline{\Pi})$ is admissible. □

We want to stress that swapping different equations (as opposed to the two sides of a single equation as in the preceding lemma) does *not* preserve the variable condition. This makes a lot of sense, since if it would preserve the variable condition then we could prove strong completeness of LCNC but from [23] we already know that the LNC is not strongly complete.

In the proof of the main theorem below, we use induction on admissible states with respect to the well-founded order defined below. This order is essentially the same as the one used in the completeness proofs of [23, 12].

Definition 2. *The complexity $|\underline{\Pi}|$ of a state $\underline{\Pi} = \langle G, \theta, \Pi, X \rangle$ is defined as the triple consisting of (1) the number of rewrite steps in Π at non-root positions, (2) the multiset $|\mathcal{MV}\mathrm{ar}(G)\theta|$, and (3) the number of occurrences of symbols different from $\approx$ and $\mathtt{true}$ in G. Here $\mathcal{MV}\mathrm{ar}(G)$ denotes the multiset of variable occurrences in G, and for any multiset $M = \{t_1, \ldots, t_n\}$ of terms, $M\theta$ and $|M|$ denote the multisets $\{t_1\theta, \ldots, t_n\theta\}$ and $\{|t_1|, \ldots, |t_n|\}$, respectively. The well-founded order $\gg$ on states is defined as follows: $\underline{\Pi_1} \gg \underline{\Pi_2}$ if $|\underline{\Pi_1}|$ $\mathsf{lex}(>, >_{\mathsf{mul}}, >)$ $|\underline{\Pi_2}|$. Here $\mathsf{lex}(>, >_{\mathsf{mul}}, >)$ denotes the lexicographic product of $>$, $>_{\mathsf{mul}}$, and $>$.*

Lemma 8. *Let $\underline{\Pi}$ be a state and $\alpha \in \{\mathrm{o}, \mathrm{i}, \mathrm{d}, \mathrm{v}, \mathrm{t}\}$. We have $\underline{\Pi} \gg \phi_{[\alpha]}(\underline{\Pi})$ whenever the latter is defined. Moreover, $|\underline{\Pi}| = |\phi_{\mathsf{swap}}(\underline{\Pi})|$.*

Proof. Basically the same as the proof of Lemma 20 in [23]. For $\alpha = \mathrm{o}$ we observe a decrease in the first component of $|\underline{\Pi}|$. Here it is essential that we work with $\rightarrowtail$ instead of the ordinary rewrite relation $\rightarrow$; in this way steps that take place in the conditional part of the applied rewrite rule are already accounted for in $|\underline{\Pi}|$. For $\alpha \in \{\mathrm{i}, \mathrm{d}, \mathrm{v}, \mathrm{t}\}$ the number of rewrite steps at non-root positions remains the same. For $\alpha \in \{\mathrm{i}, \mathrm{v}, \mathrm{t}\}$ the second component of $|\underline{\Pi}|$ decreases. For $\alpha = \mathrm{d}$ the second component remains the same while the third component of $|\underline{\Pi}|$ decreases. □

Theorem 1. *Let $\mathcal{R}$ be a confluent CTRS without extra variables and G a goal. For every normalized solution θ of G there exists an* LCNC*-refutation $G \Rightarrow_\sigma^* \Box$ respecting $\mathcal{S}_{\text{left}}$ such that $\sigma \leqslant \theta$ $[\mathcal{V}\text{ar}(G)]$.*

Proof. Because $\mathcal{R}$ is confluent, $G\theta$ admits a rewrite proof Π. Consider the state $\underline{\Pi} = \langle G, \theta, \Pi, X\rangle$ with $X = \mathcal{V}\text{ar}(G)$. By assumption $\theta\lceil_X$ is normalized. Since all variables of G are of interest, G does not contain intermediate variables and hence the variable condition is trivially satisfied. Therefore $\underline{\Pi}$ is admissible. We use induction on the complexity of $\underline{\Pi}$. In order to make the induction work we prove $\sigma \leqslant \theta$ $[W]$ for a finite set of variables W that includes $\mathcal{V}\text{ar}(G)$. The base case is trivial since G must be the empty goal (and thus we can take $\sigma = \epsilon$, the empty substitution). For the induction step we proceed as follows. We prove the existence of an LCNC-step $\Psi_1 \colon G \Rightarrow_{\sigma_1} G'$ that respects $\mathcal{S}_{\text{left}}$ and an admissible state $\underline{\Pi'} = \langle G', \theta', \Pi', X'\rangle$ such that $\sigma_1\theta' = \theta$ $[W]$. Let $G = s \approx t, H$. We distinguish the following cases, depending on what happens to $s\theta \approx t\theta$ in Π.

1. Suppose no reduct of $s\theta \approx t\theta$ is rewritten at position 1 or 2. We distinguish five further cases.
   (a) Suppose $s, t \notin \mathcal{V}$. We may write $s = f(s_1, \ldots, s_n)$ and $t = f(t_1, \ldots, t_n)$. From Lemma 4 we obtain an admissible state $\phi_{[\mathsf{d}]}(\underline{\Pi}) = \langle G', \theta', \Pi', X'\rangle$ with $G' = s_1 \approx t_1, \ldots, s_n \approx t_n, H$, $\theta' = \theta$, and $X' = X$. We have $\Psi_1 \colon G \Rightarrow_{[\mathsf{d}]} G'$. Take $\sigma_1 = \epsilon$ and $\underline{\Pi'} = \phi_{[\mathsf{d}]}(\underline{\Pi})$.
   (b) Suppose $t \in \mathcal{V}$ and $s = t$. According to Lemma 1 no $s\theta$ and $t\theta$ are not rewritten and hence in the first step of Π $s\theta \approx t\theta$ is rewritten at the root position. Hence Lemma 6 is applicable, yielding an admissible state $\phi_{[\mathsf{t}]}(\underline{\Pi}) = \langle G', \theta', \Pi', X'\rangle$ with $G' = H$, $\theta' = \theta$, and $X' = X$. We have $\Psi_1 \colon G \Rightarrow_{[\mathsf{t}]} G'$. Take $\sigma_1 = \epsilon$ and $\underline{\Pi'} = \phi_{[\mathsf{t}]}(\underline{\Pi})$.
   (c) Suppose $t \in \mathcal{V}$, $s \neq t$, and a reduct of $s \approx t$ is rewritten at a non-root position. From Lemma 1 we infer that s is not a variable and moreover that $t\theta$ is not rewritten in Π. Hence we may write $s = f(s_1, \ldots, s_n)$ and we have $\text{root}(t\theta) = f$. Consequently, Lemma 3 is applicable, yielding an admissible state $\phi_{[\mathsf{i}]}(\underline{\Pi}) = \langle G'', \theta'', \Pi'', X''\rangle$ with $G'' = G\sigma_1$, $\Pi'' = \Pi$, and $\sigma_1\theta'' = \theta$ $[W]$ for the substitution $\sigma = \{t \mapsto f(x_1, \ldots, x_n)\}$. We have $G'' = (f(s_1, \ldots, s_n) \approx f(x_1, \ldots, x_n), H)\sigma_1$. By assumption no reduct of $s\sigma\theta'' \approx t\sigma\theta''$ is rewritten at position 1 or 2. Hence we can apply Lemma 4. This yields an admissible state $\phi_{[\mathsf{d}]}(\phi_{[\mathsf{i}]}(\underline{\Pi})) = \langle G', \theta', \Pi', X'\rangle$ with $G' = (s_1 \approx x_1, \ldots, s_n \approx x_n, H)\sigma_1$, $\theta' = \theta''$, and $X' = X''$. We have $\Psi_1 \colon G \Rightarrow_{[\mathsf{i}],\sigma_1} G'$ and $\sigma_1\theta' = \sigma_1\theta'' = \theta$ $[W]$. Take $\underline{\Pi'} = \phi_{[\mathsf{d}]}(\phi_{[\mathsf{i}]}(\underline{\Pi}))$.
   (d) Suppose $t \in \mathcal{V}$, $s \neq t$, and the first rewrite step takes place at the root position of $s \approx t$. Lemma 5 yields an admissible state $\phi_{[\mathsf{v}]}(\underline{\Pi}) = \langle G', \theta', \Pi', X'\rangle$ with $G' = G\sigma$, $\Pi' = \Pi$, and $\sigma_1\theta' = \theta$ $[W]$ for the substitution $\sigma_1 = \{t \mapsto s\}$. We have $\Psi_1 \colon G \Rightarrow_{[\mathsf{v}],\sigma_1} G'$. Take $\underline{\Pi'} = \phi_{[\mathsf{v}]}(\underline{\Pi})$.
   (e) In the remaining case we have $t \notin \mathcal{V}$ and $s \in \mathcal{V}$. This case reduces to case 1(c) or 1(d) by an appeal to Lemma 7.

2. Suppose a reduct of $s\theta \approx t\theta$ is rewritten at position 1. Let $l = f(l_1, \ldots, l_n) \to r \Leftarrow c$ be the employed rewrite rule the first time this happens. From Lemma 2 we obtain an admissible state $\phi_{[o]}(\underline{\Pi}) = \langle G'', \theta'', \Pi'', X'' \rangle$ with $G'' = s \approx l, r \approx t, c, H$, $X'' = X$, and $\theta'' = \theta\ [W]$. According to Lemma 1, s cannot be a variable. Hence we may write $s = f(s_1, \ldots, s_n)$. Let $G' = s_1 \approx l_1, \ldots, s_n \approx l_n, r \approx t, c, H$. We have $\Psi_1 \colon G \Rightarrow_{[o]} G''$. Note that Lemma 4 is applicable to $\phi_{[o]}(\underline{\Pi})$ since by construction no reduct of $s\theta'' \approx l\theta''$ is rewritten at position 1 and 2. This results in an admissible state $\phi_{[d]}(\phi_{[o]}(\underline{\Pi})) = \langle G', \theta', \Pi', X' \rangle$ with $\theta' = \theta''$ and $X' = X$. Clearly $\theta' = \theta\ [W]$. Take $\sigma_1 = \epsilon$ and $\underline{\Pi'} = \phi_{[d]}(\phi_{[o]}(\underline{\Pi}))$.
3. Suppose a reduct of $s\theta \approx t\theta$ is rewritten at position 2. This case reduces to the previous one by an appeal to Lemma 7.

In all cases we obtain $\underline{\Pi'}$ from $\underline{\Pi}$ by applying one or two transformation steps $\phi_{[o]}$, $\phi_{[i]}$, $\phi_{[d]}$, $\phi_{[v]}$, $\phi_{[t]}$ together with an additional application of ϕ_{swap} in case 1(e) and 3. According to Lemma 8 $\underline{\Pi'}$ has smaller complexity than $\underline{\Pi}$. Let $W' = \mathcal{V}\mathrm{ar}_W(\sigma_1) \cup \mathcal{V}\mathrm{ar}(G')$. We have $\mathcal{V}\mathrm{ar}(G') \subseteq W'$ and thus we can apply the induction hypothesis to $\underline{\Pi'}$. This yields an LCNC-refutation $\Psi' \colon G' \Rightarrow^*_{\sigma'} \Box$ respecting $\mathcal{S}_{\mathrm{left}}$ such that $\sigma' \leqslant \theta'\ [W']$. Define $\sigma = \sigma_1\sigma'$. From $\sigma_1\theta' = \theta\ [W]$, $\sigma' \leqslant \theta'\ [W']$, and $\mathcal{V}\mathrm{ar}_W(\sigma_1) \subseteq W'$ we infer that $\sigma \leqslant \theta\ [W]$. Concatenating the LCNC-step Ψ_1 and the LCNC-refutation Ψ' yields the desired LCNC-refutation Ψ. □

4 Conclusion

In this paper we showed that the lazy conditional narrowing calculus LCNC is complete for arbitrary confluent 1-CTRSs and normalized solutions with respect to the leftmost selection function. As we suggested in the text following Lemma 2, this result remains true if in the outermost narrowing rule [o] of LCNC we would interchange $r \approx t$ and c in the new goal $G', s_1 \approx l_1, \ldots, s_n \approx l_n, r \approx t, c, G''$. Even with the restriction to $\mathcal{S}_{\mathrm{left}}$ the search space of LCNC is still very large, owing mainly to the non-determinism due to the choice of the inference rule. We should investigate under what conditions we can eliminate this non-determinism. In the unconditional case this question has been fully answered ([22]), but it seems doubtful whether the same conditions work for arbitrary confluent 1-CTRSs. Nevertheless, the result presented in this paper is an important step towards a complete deterministic version of LCNC. In [10] Ida and Hamada present an implementation of $\mathrm{LCNC}_{\mathrm{d}}$ in the symbolic computation language Mathematica. $\mathrm{LCNC}_{\mathrm{d}}$ is the conditional counterpart of the deterministic calculus $\mathrm{LNC}_{\mathrm{d}}$ ([22]) and incorporates leftmost selection. It is unknown for which classes of CTRSs and solutions this calculus is complete. (No completeness results are reported in [10].)

Our result answers affirmatively one of the two open problems mentioned in [12]. The other open problem refers to the following completeness result of [12] that we already mentioned in the introduction: LCNC is complete for arbitrary terminating and level-confluent 3-CTRSs. Level-confluence is a stronger notion than confluence but sufficient syntactic criteria are known ([26]). The proof of this result in [12] relies on a complicated selection function which is not effective. In particular, completeness with respect to the leftmost selection function is unknown and it is even open whether or not LCNC is strongly complete for terminating and level-confluent 3-CTRSs.[1]

It is worthwhile to obtain completeness results (for LCNC as well as for ordinary conditional narrowing) for CTRSs with extra variables that do not rely on some kind of termination requirement. Examples in [21, 11] show that this is a highly non-trivial task.

Acknowledgements

Taro Suzuki is partially supported by the Grant-in-Aid for Encouragement of Young Scientist 11780204. Aart Middeldorp is partially supported by the Grant-in-Aids for Scientific Research B 12480066 and C(2) 11680338 of the Ministry of Education, Science, Sports and Culture of Japan.

References

1. S. Antoy, R. Echahed, and M. Hanus. A needed narrowing strategy. *Journal of the ACM*, 47(4):776–822, 2000.
2. F. Baader and Nipkow. T. *Term Rewriting and All That.* Cambridge University Press, 1998.
3. A. Bockmayr. *Beiträge zur Theorie des Logisch-Funktionalen Programmierens.* PhD thesis, Universität Karlsruhe, 1990. In German.
4. N. Dershowitz and J.-P. Jouannaud. Rewrite systems. In J. van Leeuwen, editor, *Handbook of Theoretical Computer Science*, volume B, pages 243–320. North-Holland, 1990.
5. M. Fay. First-order unification in equational theories. In *Proceedings of the 4th Conference on Automated Deduction*, pages 161–167, 1979.
6. J. Gallier and W. Snyder. Complete sets of transformations for general *E*-unification. *Theoretical Computer Science*, 67:203–260, 1989.
7. E. Giovannetti and C. Moiso. A completeness result for *E*-unification algorithms based on conditional narrowing. In *Proceedings of the Workshop on Foundations of Logic and Functional Programming*, volume 306 of *LNCS*, pages 157–167, 1986.
8. J.C. González-Moreno, M.T. Hortalá-González, and M. Rodríguez-Artalejo. A higer-order rewriting logic for functional logic programming. In *Proceedings of the International Conference on Logic Programming*, pages 153–167. The MIT Press, 1997.
9. M. Hamada. Strong completeness of a narrowing calculus for conditional rewrite systems with extra variables. In *Proceedings of the 6th Australasian Theory Symposium, Electronic Notes in Theoretical Computer Science*, volume 31. Elsevier Science Publishers, 2000.

[1] In [9] Hamada recently claimed to have solved this open problem. However, his proof contains a fatal mistake.

10. M. Hamada and T. Ida. Deterministic and non-deterministic lazy conditional narrowing and their implementations. *Transactions of Information Processing Society of Japan*, 39(3):656–663, 1998.
11. M. Hamada and A. Middeldorp. Strong completeness of a lazy conditional narrowing calculus. In *Proceedings of the 2nd Fuji International Workshop on Functional and Logic Programming*, pages 14–32, Shonan Village, 1997. World Scientific.
12. M. Hamada, A. Middeldorp, and T. Suzuki. Completeness results for a lazy conditional narrowing calculus. In *Combinatorics, Computation and Logic: Proceedings of 2nd Discrete Mathematics and Theoretical Computer Science Conference and the 5th Australasian Theory Symposium*, pages 217–231, Auckland, 1999. Springer-Verlag Singapore.
13. M. Hanus. The integration of functions into logic programming: From theory to practice. *Journal of Logic Programming*, 19 & 20:583–628, 1994.
14. M. Hanus. Lazy unification with simplification. In *Proceedings of the 5th European Symposium on Programming*, volume 788 of *LNCS*, pages 272–286, 1994.
15. S. Hölldobler. *Foundations of Equational Logic Programming*, volume 353 of *LNAI*. 1989.
16. J.-M. Hullot. Canonical forms and unification. In *Proceedings of the 5th Conference on Automated Deduction*, volume 87 of *LNCS*, pages 318–334, 1980.
17. S. Kaplan. Conditional rewrite rules. *Theoretical Computer Science*, 33:175–193, 1984.
18. J.W. Klop. Term rewriting systems. In S. Abramsky, D. Gabbay, and T. Maibaum, editors, *Handbook of Logic in Computer Science*, volume 2, pages 1–116. Oxford University Press, 1992.
19. M. Marin, T. Ida, and T. Suzuki. On reducing the search space of higer-order lazy narrowing. In *Proceedings of the 4th Fuji International Symposium on Functional and Logic Programming*, volume 1722 of *LNCS*, pages 319–334, 1999.
20. A. Martelli, C. Moiso, and G.F. Rossi. Lazy unification algorithms for canonical rewrite systems. In H. Aït-Kaci and M. Nivat, editors, *Resolution of Equations in Algebraic Structures, Vol. II, Rewriting Techniques*, pages 245–274. Academic Press Press, 1989.
21. A. Middeldorp and E. Hamoen. Completeness results for basic narrowing. *Applicable Algebra in Engineering, Communication and Computing*, 5:213–253, 1994.
22. A. Middeldorp and S. Okui. A deterministic lazy narrowing calculus. *Journal of Symbolic Computation*, 25(6):733–757, 1998.
23. A. Middeldorp, S. Okui, and T. Ida. Lazy narrowing: Strong completeness and eager variable elimination. *Theoretical Computer Science*, 167(1,2):95–130, 1996.
24. C. Prehofer. *Solving Higher-Order Equations: From Logic to Programming.* Progress in Theoretical Computer Science. Birkäuser, 1998.
25. W. Snyder. *A Proof Theory for General Unification*, volume 11 of *Progress in Computer Science and Applied Logic.* Birkäuser, 1991.
26. T. Suzuki, A. Middeldorp, and T. Ida. Level-confluence of conditional rewrite systems with extra variables in right-hand sides. In *Proceedings of the 6th International Conference on Rewriting Techniques and Applications*, volume 914 of *Lecture Notes in Computer Science*, pages 179–193, Kaiserslautern, 1995. Springer-Verlag.
27. A. Werner. *Untersuchung von Strategien für das logisch-funktionale Programmieren.* Shaker-Verlag Aachen, March 1998.

An Abstract Machine Based System for a Lazy Narrowing Calculus *

Teresa Hortalá-González and Eva Ullán

Departamento de Sistemas Informáticos y Programación
Facultad de Ciencias Matemáticas
Universidad Complutense de Madrid
Avda. Complutense s/n, 28040 Madrid, Spain
teresa@sip.ucm.es, evah@sip.ucm.es

Abstract. CLNC is a lazy narrowing calculus for goal solving in the context of CRWL, a rewriting logic for functional logic programming that deals with non-deterministic functions. The JUMP-machine is an abstract machine model for the efficient implementation of functional logic languages. In this paper, we propose the integration of these two abstract models into an experimental system, for which extensibility and modifiability are major concerns. This leads us to the selection of an object-oriented approach and the use of design patterns for the system design and implementation.

1 Introduction

The rewriting logic CRWL (Constructor-based conditional ReWriting Logic [9, 10]) constitutes an approach to the integration of higher-order functional programming and logic programming, supporting non-deterministic lazy functions (with call-time choice semantics). Associated to CRWL, the authors also propose CLNC, a sound and complete lazy narrowing calculus, able to support sharing. Rather than a concrete operational model, CLNC is an abstract description of goal solving.

Our aim is to define an experimental language and system that implements the CRWL paradigm. Such a language and system does already exist: $\mathcal{TOY}$ [16] and —the Prolog [5] implementation of— Curry [12] are Prolog implementations that support all aspects of CRWL programming, as well as some interesting extensions. Roughly, source programs are translated into Prolog code, and then the systems rely on the Prolog operational mechanism. Our implementation purposes are completely different. The development of our system is motivated by the implementation of an abstract machine for CLNC. The experimental aspect of the system is involved with being able to try out different implementation issues of functional logic languages. Hence, we are interested in an extensible and modifiable design of the system.

* This work has been partially supported by the Spanish National Project TIC98-0445-C03-02 'TREND'.

H. Kuchen and K. Ueda (Eds.): FLOPS 2001, LNCS 2024, pp. 216–232, 2001.

Chakravarty and Lock summarize their research on the abstract machine based implementation of functional logic languages in [7]. They present the JUMP-machine, an abstract machine model "that integrates the execution mechanisms underlying efficient implementations of functional and logic programming languages." Compared to the standard approach to abstract machines, the machine code of the JUMP-machine, called JCode, is rather high-level (in the same way of STG, a very small functional language used as the abstract machine code for the Spineless Tagless G-machine in [18]). In essence, the abstraction level eases code generation and transformational code optimizations.

The main ingredients used in our work are the lazy narrowing calculus CLNC and the JUMP-machine. Both have to be refined in some sense. Regarding the calculus, some notion of strategy is needed in order to obtain an operational model. Regarding the JUMP-machine, it has to be adapted to the CRWL setting. For instance, we have to deal with non-deterministic functions, and hence with a non-deterministic version of strict equality.

The rest of the paper runs as follows. In Sect. 2, we introduce the different languages used by the system: the source language, the intermediate language and the JUMP-machine language. In Sect. 3, we formally specify the operational semantics of the intermediate language, along with the, informally stated, relation of each calculus rule to abstract machine code constructs. Section 4 is devoted to sketch out some implementation decisions, and conclusions are given in Sect. 5.

2 Preliminaries

The following process is accomplished by the system: CRWL programs are transformed into TFL programs, an intermediate language defined to suit our interests. Next, TFL programs are translated into —a modified version of— JCode, the JUMP-machine code. The next subsections describe each language.

2.1 CRWL Programs

We use constructor-based signatures $\Sigma = \langle DC, FS \rangle$, where $DC = \bigcup_{n\in\mathbb{N}} DC^n$ and $FS = \bigcup_{n\in\mathbb{N}} FS^n$ are ranked sets of *data constructors* and *defined function symbols*, respectively. Assuming a countable set $DVar$ of data variables, *expressions* $e \in Exp$ are defined as follows:

$$e ::= X \quad (X \in DVar) \quad | \quad h \quad (h \in DC \cup FS) \quad | \quad (e_1\ e_2) \quad \text{(application)}$$

Two important subclasses of expressions are *data terms* $t \in Term$, used to represent data values, and *patterns* $p \in Pat$, a generalization of data terms. Patterns of the form $f\ p_1\ \ldots\ p_m$ $(f \in FS^n, m < n)$ are not data terms and can be used as an intensional representation of functions. They are defined as:

$$\begin{array}{lllll} t & ::= & X \quad (X \in DVar) & | & c\, t_1 \ldots t_n \quad (c \in DC^n) \\ p & ::= & X \quad (X \in DVar) & | & c\ p_1\ \ldots\ p_m \quad (c \in DC^n,\ m \le n) \\ & & & | & f\ p_1\ \ldots\ p_m \quad (f \in FS^n,\ m < n) \end{array}$$

A *CRWL program* is a set of well-typed[1] defining rules for function symbols f. Each *defining rule* for f must have the following form:

$$\underbrace{f\ p_1\ \ldots\ p_n}_{\text{left hand side } (l)} \quad = \quad \underbrace{e}_{\text{right hand side}} \quad \Leftarrow \quad \underbrace{C}_{\text{condition}}$$

where l must be linear, p_i must be patterns, e must be an expression such that $var(e) \subseteq var(l)^2$, and C must consist of finitely many so-called *joinability statements* $a == b$, where a and b are expressions. *Goals* are syntactically identical to conditions. A joinability statement is similar to a strict equality, a pattern t is needed as a common value for a and b, but t is not required to be unique. Function-typed variables in goals or conditions that involve guessing a binding operationally, such as $X\ 0 == Y$, are not yet covered by the implementation. Neither termination nor confluence is imposed, and the latter allows us to cope with the definition of non-deterministic functions.

Example 1. This CRWL program will be the basis of the next two examples.

```
data nat = zero | suc nat                -- data type declaration

coin = zero                              -- non-deterministic
coin = suc zero                          -- nullary function

zeros = [zero|zeros]                     -- infinite list

take zero     Ys      = []               -- case distinction
take (suc X) []       = []               -- in patterns
take (suc X) [Y|Ys]   = [Y|take X Ys]
```

The first line introduces the user defined data constructors $zero/0$ and $suc/1$. Next, the functions $coin/0$, $zeros/0$, and $take/2$ are defined. Note that we use Prolog notation for lists, but this is just syntactic sugar, i.e., $nil/0$ and $cons/2$ are predefined constructors, instead of $[\ ]/0$ and $[.|.]/2$. Thus, we are using the signature $\Sigma = \langle\{zero/0, nil/0, suc/1, cons/2\}, \{coin/0, zeros/0, take/2\}\rangle$.

We propose the goal `take coin zeros == X`, for which the expected answers are $X = [\ ]$ and $X = [zero]$.

2.2 TFL Programs

The source language is translated into a tiny functional logic (TFL) intermediate language. TFL emerged as a way of abstracting from peculiarities of the source language. Hence, its use could help to consider different declarative source languages. Our hope is that TFL (or some extension of it) could be used to implement different computation models and extensions for CWRL. Up to now,

[1] For simplicity, we are not considering types in this paper.

[2] This is not a CRWL restriction, but a restriction of the current implementation.

we have implemented the demand driven strategy from [15], closely related to needed narrowing [3, 4] and its non-deterministic extension [2]. The current syntax of TFL has been designed to express the *definitional trees* used in [2–4, 15]. Being CLNC an abstract description of goal solving, with the use of a concrete strategy we get a concrete operational model that enables the implementation of CRWL.

A *TFL program* is a set of defining rules for function symbols. The multiple CRWL defining rules for a given function symbol $f \in FS^n$ are transformed into a single TFL *defining rule*:

$$f\ X_1\ \ldots\ X_n\ =\ te$$

where X_i must be n new distinct variables and te must be a TFL expression.

TFL expressions $te \in TExp$ are defined as follows:

$$\begin{array}{llll}
te & ::= & \mathsf{case}\ X\ \mathsf{of}\ \{alt_1 \mid \ldots \mid alt_n\} & (X \in DVar) \\
 & \mid & \mathsf{when}\ C\ \mathsf{then}\ e & (C \in TCond, e \in Exp) \\
 & \mid & \mathsf{try}\ \{te_1 \mid \ldots \mid te_n\} & \\
 & \mid & e & (e \in Exp) \\
alt & ::= & c\ Y_1\ \ldots\ Y_m\ \texttt{->}\ te & (c \in CS^n,\ m \leq n,\ Y_i \in DVar) \\
 & \mid & f\ Y_1\ \ldots\ Y_m\ \texttt{->}\ te & (f \in FS^n,\ m < n,\ Y_i \in DVar)
\end{array}$$

Each case alternative is formed by a flat linear pattern (with new local variables) and an expression (the above variables can only occur within the expression). Each pattern has the same type that the case variable X. The alternatives of a case expression are exclusive: the symbols c or f must be pairwise different.

Thus, TFL expressions make possible to explicitly express case distinctions, conditional expressions, non-deterministic choices, and CRWL expressions. For inductively sequential [3, 4] CRWL source programs, the corresponding TFL programs do not include the try construct.

TFL conditions $C \in TCond$ are like CRWL ones, but those variables that have their first occurrence in the condition are explicitly represented by means of the extra construct. Regarding *TFL goals*, the extra part include all their variables. They are defined as:

$$\begin{array}{llll}
C & ::= & \mathsf{extra}\ V_1\ \ldots\ V_n\ \mathsf{in}\ Cs & (V_i \in DVar) \\
 & \mid & Cs & \\
Cs & ::= & e_1 == e_2 & (e_1,\ e_2 \in Exp) \\
 & \mid & e_1 == e_2 \wedge Cs & (e_1,\ e_2 \in Exp)
\end{array}$$

Example 2. The CRWL program from Example 1 is translated into the following TFL program:

```
coin = try {zero | suc zero}

zeros = cons zero zeros
```

```
take N L = case N of
           { zero   -> nil
           | suc N1 -> case L of
                       { nil       -> nil
                       | cons Y Ys -> cons Y (take N1 Ys)}}
```

In addition, the proposed goal is transformed into the TFL goal:

```
extra X in take coin zeros == X
```

The use of an intermediate language is not new in the literature, neither in this area. TFL is quite similar to FlatCurry [13], an intermediate representation of Curry [12] programs, used by the Curry2Prolog compiler [5]. Albert et al. [1] use a "maximally simplified abstract representation of programs", also very close to TFL, for the specialization of functional logic languages. Their technique for partial evaluation, restricted to inductively sequential systems, could be directly applied in our system —to TFL programs without any occurrence of the try construct.

2.3 JCode Programs

JCode "resembles a block-structured, imperative language with a very restricted control and data flow, i.e., no explicit loops are possible (only recursion) and only single-assignment variables are allowed" [7]. Due to space restrictions, we do not detail the JCode syntax (neither the translations from CRWL to TFL, and from TFL to JCode). The most important JCode statements are assignments, `SWITCH` that implements case selection, `CHOICES` that realizes non-determinism, `JUMP` is used for tail calls, and `JOIN` for joinability (this statement was not part of the original JUMP-machine). There are also several return instructions that will be introduced later.

Active objects. They are a central tool for the integration of functional and logic computations in the JUMP-machine framework. Active objects constitute a uniform object representation, which was first proposed for the Spineless Tagless G-machine [18], with the name of closures. Data objects are represented by a pointer to a method table and an environment (also called the active object arguments). In this presentation, the only provided method for active objects is their evaluation method (also called code). The different treatment of different objects is encapsulated in the code, avoiding the traditional use of tags.

An active object is represented as

$$\langle(\texttt{FUN}\ mode\ as\ bs\ block),\ ws\rangle$$

where as is a list that contains the formal parameters, bs is a list that includes the free variables, that are not formal parameters, that appear within the code $block$ (its evaluation method) . Finally, ws is a list that contains values for the variables in bs. Before executing the code in $block$, $length(as)$ arguments are taken from the argument stack and bound to the elements of as.

Assignments. An *assignment* associates variables or function symbols to active objects, and has the following form:

$$f \text{ (or } X) \;:=\; \texttt{FUN}\ \mathit{mode}\ [A_1, \ldots, A_n]\ [B_1, \ldots, B_m]\ \mathit{block};$$

It can be understood as a function definition: its name is f (or X), its n formal parameters are A_i, and its code is *block*. On execution, an assignment creates a new active object in the heap. Its heap reference is assigned to f (or X). The *mode* (UPD or NOUPD) indicates whether the object has to be updated with the result obtained after evaluating it the first time.

A *JCode program* is a collection of assignments for function symbols. Each of them has the following form:

$$f \;:=\; \texttt{FUN NOUPD}\ [A_1, \ldots, A_n]\ [\,]\ \mathit{block};$$

Apart from the assignments defining function symbols, two other types of assignment are possible: for "external" and "internal" variables. An *external* variable is just one of the extra variables from goals or from rule conditions (explicitly represented in the TFL transformation). Assignments for external variables will always be like:

$$X \;:=\; \texttt{FUN NOUPD}\ [\,]\ [X]\ \{\texttt{RET LVAR}\ X\}$$

They are needed to ensure that these variables will be created in the heap before using them. *Internal* variables[3] are new variables generated during the compilation process to JCode. They are needed because JCode does not support nested expressions. An internal variable assignment is of the following form:

$$\texttt{\#i} \;:=\; \texttt{FUN}\ \mathit{mode}\ [\,]\ [B_1, \ldots, B_n]\ \mathit{block}$$

Internal variables can give rise to *updatable* active objects (*mode* is set to UPD instead of NOUPD). They permit to implement sharing and laziness, by ensuring that an updatable active object is evaluated at most once (updating the active object with the result of the evaluation).

Abstract machine architecture. A state of the non-optimized JUMP-machine comprises nine components:

- The *code component* specifies the next operation to be executed.
- The *argument stack* stores the currently supplied arguments.
- The *return stack* keeps track of what remains to be done after performing a sub-computation.
- The *update stack* is used to update an updatable active object with the obtained result after executing its code for the first time.
- The *choice point stack* helps to manage the search through alternative computations.

[3] They are noted as #i, where i is just a counter.

- The *trail* records the updates of suspensions and variable bindings, in order to be able to undo them on backtracking.
- The *heap* is a collection of active objects.
- The *global environment* is a mapping of function symbols, and goal variables, to the references denoting the associated active objects in the heap.
- The *joinability stack* is used to solve joinabilities, and was not present in the original JUMP-machine.

The *initial state* of the machine stores the goal code block in the code component, the active objects for goal variables and defined function symbols are put into the heap, and their references are stored in the global environment. Everything else is initially empty.

Example 3. The TFL program from Example 2 is translated into the following JCode program:

```
coin := FUN NOUPD [] []
  {CHOICES
     {RET TERM zero []}
    ||
     {#6 := FUN NOUPD [] [] {RET TERM zero []};
      RET TERM suc [#6]}
  }
```

Remember that nested expressions are not allowed in JCode. For instance, in `suc zero`, `zero` is a nested expression, and thus it has to be translated to an internal variable assignment.

```
zeros := FUN NOUPD [] []
  {#4 := FUN UPD [] [] {JUMP zeros []};
   #5 := FUN NOUPD [] [] {RET TERM zero []};
   RET TERM cons [#5, #4]}
```

The same happens with `cons zero zeros`. The difference with respect to the previous function definition is that one of the nested expressions is a function call; the code block reflects this fact by using a `JUMP` statement.

```
take := FUN NOUPD [N, L] []
  {SWITCH N OF
     TERM zero [] : {RET TERM nil []}
     TERM suc [N1] :
       {SWITCH L OF
          TERM nil [] : {RET TERM nil []}
          TERM cons [Y, Ys] :
             {#0 := FUN UPD [] [N1, Ys]
                {#1 := FUN UPD [] [Ys] {JUMP Ys []};
                 #2 := FUN UPD [] [N1] {JUMP N1 []};
                 JUMP take [#2, #1]}
```

```
                #3 := FUN UPD [] [Y] {JUMP Y []};
                RET TERM cons [#3, #0]}
        }
}
```

The machine initial state includes the goal code block in its code component.

```
{#7 := FUN UPD [] [X] {JUMP X []};
 #8 := FUN UPD [] []
   {#9 := FUN UPD [] [] {JUMP zeros []};
    #10 := FUN UPD [] [] {JUMP coin []};
    JUMP take [#10, #9]};
 JOIN #7 #8;
 RET }
```

Goal variables (like X in this example) and defined function symbols are explicitly represented in the heap, before execution begins.

3 TFL Operational Semantics

Along this section, we will present a calculus that formally specifies the TFL operational semantics. Our aim for defining the calculus was to show the JCode operational behavior in a simpler context. The machine is intended to explore all the possible computations, while the calculus is intended to perform a single computation. Along the calculus presentation, we will —rather informally— state the relation of the JCode constructs behavior with the different rules.

Notation, definitions, and assumptions. The calculus manages *configurations* $(E,\ C,\ \sigma)$ (or $(E,\ e,\ \sigma)$), where E is an *environment* where we store variable bindings, C is a TFL goal (or a TFL condition) to be solved (or $e \in TExp$ is an expression to be evaluated to head normal form), and σ is the *computed substitution*. We assume that for every configuration, the substitution has been applied to the other components:

- $C\sigma \equiv C$ (or $e\sigma \equiv e$)
- $E\sigma \equiv E$, where $E\sigma = \{X \mapsto e\sigma \text{ for all } X \mapsto e \in E\}$

We also assume that the computed substitutions are idempotent: the rules that involve a modification on the substitution replace a variable by a pattern that does not include any occurrence of the substituted variable. Hence, applying again the same substitution has no effect.

It's worth noting that a variable, say X, that occurs in an environment E, say $X \mapsto e \in E$, is always a fresh variable, that comes from a function rule application (renaming with fresh variables is required). Such a variable can act as a parameter or as a pattern local variable in a function rule. Hence, environments do not contain extra variables (except as bindings for an environment variable).

The notation ($\mathtt{HNF}_E\ e$) is used to indicate that an expression $e \in TExp$ is in *head normal form* with respect to an environment E, i.e.,

- $e \equiv c\ \overline{e_m}$ $(c \in CS^n,\ m \leq n)$, or
- $e \equiv f\ \overline{e_m}$ $(f \in FS^n,\ m < n)$, or
- $e \equiv X$ if X does not have a binding in E.

Roughly, head normal forms are expressions with the outermost appearance of a pattern.

We also use the notation $e\ \overline{e_m}$ to abbreviate $e\ e_1 \ldots e_m$.

Goal solving $\longrightarrow_{\texttt{solve}}$. The *initial configuration* $(\emptyset,\ C,\ id)$ starts with the empty environment, the TFL goal C to be solved, and the identity substitution. If the goal is solvable, we will be able to apply different rules until we reach a *final configuration* $(E,\ \mathsf{true},\ \sigma)$. By restricting the computed substitution to the goal variables, we get the *answer substitution*. This process is guided by the SOLVE rule, which simply states that a goal is solved like a condition:

$$[\textsc{solve}]\ \frac{(\emptyset,\ C,\ id) \longrightarrow_{\mathsf{C}} (E,\ \mathsf{true},\ \sigma)}{(\emptyset,\ C,\ id) \longrightarrow_{\texttt{solve}} (E,\ \mathsf{true},\ \sigma)}$$

The machine initial state stores the goal code in its code component. The execution begins with this code until a success final state is reached (if any).

Condition solving $\longrightarrow_{\mathsf{C}}$. The presence of extra variables in a condition is ignored in the calculus configuration. Note that there is no name conflicts due to the use of rule variants, and to the fact that when we have a choice, only one of the alternatives is selected[4].

$$[\textsc{ex}]\ \frac{(E,\ C,\ \sigma) \longrightarrow_{\mathsf{C}} (E',\ \mathsf{true},\ \sigma')}{(E, \mathsf{extra}\ \overline{X_n}\ \mathsf{in}\ C,\ \sigma) \longrightarrow_{\mathsf{C}} (E',\ \mathsf{true},\ \sigma')}$$

Notwithstanding, in the machine side, we need JCode statements of the form

$$X_i\ := \texttt{FUN NOUPD}\ [\,]\ [X_i]\ \{\texttt{RET LVAR}\ X_i\}$$

to ensure that these variables will be created in the heap before using them.

Up to now, we deal with conjunctions of joinability conditions by solving them sequentially.

$$[\textsc{and}]\ \frac{(E,\ e_1 == e_2,\ \sigma) \longrightarrow_{\mathsf{C}} (E',\ \mathsf{true},\ \sigma')\quad (E',\ C\sigma',\ \sigma') \longrightarrow_{\mathsf{C}} (E'',\ \mathsf{true},\ \sigma'')}{(E,\ e_1 == e_2 \wedge C,\ \sigma) \longrightarrow_{\mathsf{C}} (E'',\ \mathsf{true},\ \sigma'')}$$

[4] A calculus intended to explore all the possible computations, should not ignore extra variables.

The translation process of TFL to JCode ensures this sequential behavior. When a joinability condition is solved, the success is indicated by a special return statement `RET`. If something remains to be done (the return stack will not be empty), the machine proceeds with the execution.

A joinability condition is solved by computing the head normal form of both sides, and then solving a joinability condition between head normal forms.

$$[\text{EQ}]\ \frac{(E,\ e_1,\ \sigma) \longrightarrow_{\mathtt{HNF}} (E',\ e_1',\ \sigma') \qquad (E',\ e_2\sigma',\ \sigma') \longrightarrow_{\mathtt{HNF}} (E'',\ e_2',\ \sigma'') \qquad (E'',\ (e_1'\sigma'') == e_2',\ \sigma'') \longrightarrow_{\mathrm{J}} (E''',\ \mathsf{true}, \sigma''')}{(E,\ e_1 == e_2,\ \sigma) \longrightarrow_{\mathrm{C}} (E''',\ \mathsf{true}, \sigma''')}$$

The `JOIN` statement performs the head normal form computations, stores the results in the heap, and proceed to compare them, as will be explained later.

Head normal forms $\longrightarrow_{\mathtt{HNF}}$. In some of the previous rules, TFL expressions need to be evaluated to head normal form. Expressions are evaluated gradually until a head normal form is obtained. The rules that accomplish this task are the following ones:

$$[\text{NO-HNF}]\ \frac{(E,\ e,\ \sigma) \longrightarrow (E',\ e',\ \sigma') \qquad (E',\ e',\ \sigma') \longrightarrow_{\mathtt{HNF}} (E'',\ e'',\ \sigma'')}{(E,\ e,\ \sigma) \longrightarrow_{\mathtt{HNF}} (E'',\ e'',\ \sigma'')}$$

if not $(\mathtt{HNF}_E\ e)$.

$$[\text{HNF}] \qquad (E,\ e,\ \sigma) \longrightarrow_{\mathtt{HNF}} (E,\ e,\ \sigma) \qquad \text{if } (\mathtt{HNF}_E\ e).$$

When the machine returns a value, it always corresponds to a head normal form evaluation. At this point, the code component of the state will keep a return statement: `RET LVAR X`, `RET TERM c as`, `RET PAPC c as` or `RET PAPF f as`, corresponding to a variable, a data term or a partial application.

TFL expressions $\longrightarrow$. Those TFL expressions that are not in head normal form are handled by the following rules that help to obtain head normal forms.

- This rule allows the non-deterministic selection of a TFL expression e_i from the rest of them.

  $$[\text{TRY}] \qquad (E, \mathsf{try}\ \{\ldots \mid e_i \mid \ldots\}\ \overline{a_k},\ \sigma) \longrightarrow (E,\ e_i\ \overline{a_k},\ \sigma)$$

  Up to now, the machine implements this kind of non-determinism by the use of *rule choice points* (similar to the WAM [19] choice points) that sequentially select the code blocks, storing the remaining alternatives in the choice point stack. This roughly corresponds to the execution of a statement:

  $$\mathtt{CHOICES}\ \{\ldots\ \|\ block_i\ \|\ \ldots\};$$

  where $block_i$ would be the translation to JCode of the TFL expression e_i.

- Conditional expressions require solving the condition, and only in case of success to proceed with the guarded expression.

$$[\text{WHEN}]\ \frac{(E,\ C,\ \sigma) \longrightarrow_{\mathsf{C}} (E',\ \mathsf{true},\ \sigma')}{(E,\ \mathsf{when}\ C\ \mathsf{then}\ e\ \overline{a_k},\ \sigma) \longrightarrow (E',\ (e\ \overline{a_k})\sigma',\ \sigma')}$$

The translation to JCode ensures this behavior. After returning from the condition solving process, the return stack will store a return continuation with the needed information to proceed with the execution by evaluating the expression.

- The variable on which a case distinction is performed has to be evaluated to head normal form. It's worth noting that we are able to ensure that any variable that appears within a case is always bound to some expression in the environment. Hence, the binding expression has to be evaluated. If the obtained head normal form is a non-variable pattern, say $h\ e_1\ \ldots\ e_n$, at most one of the case alternative guard patterns, say $h\ X_1\ \ldots\ X_n$, will match the result. In this case, pattern matching is performed: the X_i variables are bound to the e_i expressions and stored in the environment, and the alternative guarded expression e' is selected. We call this situation a deterministic case application.

$$[\text{CASE}]\ \frac{(E,\ X,\ \sigma) \longrightarrow_{\mathsf{HNF}} (E',\ h\ \overline{e_n},\ \sigma')}{\begin{array}{l}(E,\ \mathsf{case}\ X\ \mathsf{of}\ \{\ldots\ h\ \overline{X_n} \to e'\ \ldots\}\ \overline{a_k},\ \sigma)\\ \qquad \longrightarrow (E' \cup \{\overline{X_n} \mapsto \overline{e_n}\},\ (e'\ \overline{a_k})\sigma',\ \sigma')\end{array}}$$

The obtained head normal form can also be a variable Y (this means that there is no binding for Y in the environment E'). This situation will lead to a non-deterministic case application, in the sense that a variable unifies with each alternative pattern. Thus, any of the alternative expressions may be non-deterministically selected.

$$[\text{ND-CASE}]\ \frac{(E,\ X,\ \sigma) \longrightarrow_{\mathsf{HNF}} (E',\ Y,\ \sigma')}{\begin{array}{l}(E,\ \mathsf{case}\ X\ \mathsf{of}\ \{\ldots\ h\ \overline{X_n} \to e'\ \ldots\}\ \overline{a_k},\ \sigma)\\ \qquad \longrightarrow ((E' \cup \{\overline{X_n} \mapsto \overline{Y_n}\})\sigma'_0,\ (e'\ \overline{a_k})\sigma'_0,\ \underbrace{\sigma' \cdot \{Y \mid h\ \overline{Y_n}\}}_{\sigma'_0})\end{array}}$$

where $\overline{Y_n}$ are fresh variables.

Case selection is performed by the JCode statement

`SWITCH` X `OF` *alts*;

It puts the code of the alternatives *alts* into the return stack, and "calls" X, by means of a `JUMP` statement, that will get the active object for X. Depending on the kind of active object, it executes its evaluation method (for the

first time) or it gets a previously computed result. The return continuation put by a `SWITCH` instruction into the return stack stores all the relevant information to continue, depending on the kind of head normal form returned by the sub-computation.
If a non-variable is returned, the matching alternative is selected. If a logical variable is returned, a *variable choice point* is created on top of the choice point stack. Its task is to sequentially generate all possible bindings for the variable according to the patterns of the `SWITCH`.
In the case of inductively sequential programs, choice points are only built in order to manage the different bindings of a variable, leading to an on-the-fly detection of deterministic computations.

– The function call rule performs parameter passing binding the arguments e_i to the formal parameters X_i in the environment, without evaluating them. The function definition right hand side substitutes the function call.

$$[\text{APP-FUN}]\quad (E,\ f\ \overline{e_n}\ \overline{a_k},\ \sigma) \longrightarrow (E \cup \{\overline{X_n} \mapsto \overline{e_n}\},\ r\ \overline{a_k},\ \sigma)$$

where $(f\ \overline{X_n} = r)$ is a renaming of the TFL program rule for f with fresh variables.

The translation process to JCode ensures that the arguments are processed before the call to the function. They are just allocated into the heap, without evaluating them, and their heap addresses are put onto the argument stack. When the function call is performed by means of a `JUMP` statement, the evaluation method for f is executed.

– A variable needs evaluation (i.e., is not in head normal form) when it has an associated binding in the environment. For instance, a variable that represents a formal parameter could be evaluated (only if necessary). When this is the case, the environment binding expression should be evaluated to head normal form. We remember that computed substitutions are always applied to environments: this fact ensures sharing and that evaluation is done at most once.

$$[\text{VAR}]\quad \frac{(E,\ e,\ \sigma) \longrightarrow_{\texttt{HNF}} (E',\ e',\ \sigma')}{\begin{array}{l}(E \supseteq \{X \mapsto e\},\ X\ \overline{a_k},\ \sigma)\\ \qquad \longrightarrow ((E' \backslash \{X \mapsto e\sigma'\}) \cup \{X \mapsto e'\},\ e'\ \overline{a_k}\ \sigma',\ \sigma')\end{array}}$$

As mentioned above, this is performed by a `JUMP` statement.
Note that we are not considering variable applications because they are not yet handled by the system.

Condition solving between head normal forms $\longrightarrow_{\texttt{J}}$. TFL and JCode joinability deal with head normal forms to guarantee laziness: as soon as a mismatch is detected, the whole process fails.

The following rules (decomposition, imitation, binding, variable binding, and identity) control condition solving between expressions in head normal form, say e_1 and e_2. Their obvious symmetrical counterparts are omitted.

$$[\text{DEC}]\ \frac{(E,\ a_1 == b_1 \wedge \ldots \wedge a_m == b_m,\ \sigma) \longrightarrow_{\text{C}} (E',\ \mathsf{true},\ \sigma')}{(E,\ h\ \overline{a_m} == h\ \overline{b_m},\ \sigma) \longrightarrow_{\text{J}} (E',\ \mathsf{true},\ \sigma')}$$

$$[\text{IMI}]\ \frac{(E\sigma_X,\ \overline{Y_m} == \overline{b_m}\sigma_X,\ \sigma \cdot \overbrace{\{X \mid h\ \overline{Y_m}\}}^{\sigma_X}) \longrightarrow_{\text{C}} (E',\ \mathsf{true},\ \sigma')}{(E,\ X == h\ \overline{b_m},\ \sigma) \longrightarrow_{\text{J}} (E',\ \mathsf{true},\ \sigma')}$$

if X does not occur in $h\ \overline{b_m}$ at any position outside the scope of evaluable function calls. $\overline{Y_m}$ are fresh variables.

$$[\text{BD}]\quad (E,\ X == h,\ \sigma) \longrightarrow_{\text{J}} (E\sigma_h,\ \mathsf{true},\ \sigma \cdot \underbrace{\{X \mid h\}}_{\sigma_h})$$

$$[\text{VBD}]\ (E,\ X == Y,\ \sigma) \longrightarrow_{\text{J}} (E\sigma_X,\ \mathsf{true},\ \sigma \cdot \underbrace{\{X \mid Y\}}_{\sigma_X}) \qquad \text{if } X \neq Y.$$

$$[\text{ID}]\quad (E,\ X == X,\ \sigma) \longrightarrow_{\text{J}} (E,\ \mathsf{true},\ \sigma)$$

One of the tasks of the `JOIN` statement is to lazily compare for joinability the two expressions it has previously reduced to head normal form. This means that only special types of active objects are to be compared: those that represent head normal forms, i.e., `RET LVAR X`, `RET TERM c as`, `RET PAPC c as` and `RET PAPF f as`.

Failure rules. If none of the rules can be applied, the computation fails. As usual in non-deterministic settings, we consider that the overall goal solving process fails if all the possible computations fail.

The machine implementation incorporates explicit fail situations, in order to fail as soon as possible. In this case, if alternative computations remain to be explored, backtracking is automatically performed. After a successful goal solving process, asking for more solutions would also lead to backtrack. When the choice point stack is empty, the machine execution stops indicating that the last attempt to solve the goal has failed.

4 Implementation Outline

Due to our interest on experimenting with different computation models, as well as the corresponding compilation schemes for TFL programs, extensibility and modifiability were major concerns for the implementation. This led us to the selection of an object-oriented approach and the use of design patterns (e.g., [8]) for the system design and implementation. In particular, we are using Java, which is available on a wide range of platforms. We have a running implementation extended with a graphical user interface, that is depicted in Fig. 1. Apart from

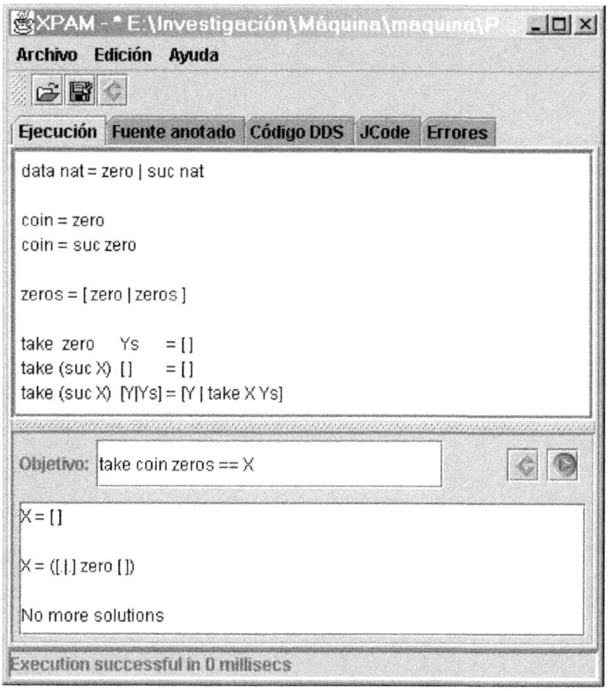

Fig. 1. System graphical user interface

the CRWL source program, the user can see different translations performed by the system while compiling to JCode: the source program with type annotations (after performing type inference), the TFL resulting program and the JCode program.

The Java language portability leads, at present, to an interpreted virtual machine that handicaps performance. Furthermore, we have not considered any kind of optimization: neither dedicated optimizations to the generated JCode, nor the details on how to obtain an efficient implementation of the JUMP-machine given in [7], nor performance considerations of the different Java constructs. Hence it is evident that we are far from other more mature abstract machine based implementations, even developed in Java such as the Curry2Java implementation [14], and even further from the Münster Curry implementation by Lux and Kuchen [17], that compiles into native machine code using the well-known "C as portable assembler technique".

Our design heavily relies on the Visitor pattern. Each visitor represents an operation to be performed on the elements of an object structure (in our case, the program representation in the different languages). Visitor lets us define operations without changing the classes of the elements on which it operates. This way, the classes that implement program structures remain untouched when different processing strategies are applied. For instance, Fig. 2 shows the class diagrams

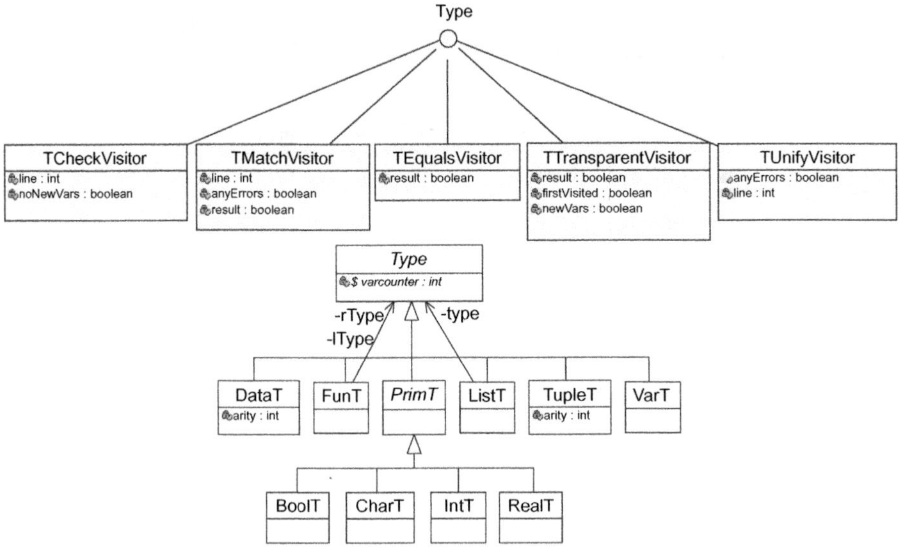

Fig. 2. Types representation and types visitors class diagrams

for the representation of types and (part of) the different visitors operating on them.

Just by switching the strategy visitor that operates on the type annotated internal source program representation, we can consider a very simple alternative computation model. Standard lazy functional languages use textual order rule selection and left to right pattern matching. Although such a naïve strategy is clearly worse than the implemented one, it makes sense to consider it in the context of functional logic languages.

The only change to our setting is to follow a different translation from CRWL source programs to TFL. A straightforward approach is to translate a CRWL function definition, composed by m rules, into a single TFL rule whose right hand side is a `try` expression (if $m > 1$), with m `case` expressions inside, corresponding to the rules individual translations (if, for a concrete rule, the left-hand side patterns were variables, no `case` expression is obtained). A clear disadvantage of the above simple translation is that for CRWL functions with at least two rules, a choice point would always be generated, even for non-overlapping left-hand sides. Taking into account this observation, one could conceive a better translation, as illustrated in the following example.

Example 4. Consider the CRWL program

```
f 1 2 = 1                g 1 = 0
f 2 X = 2                g 2 = 3
f 1 2 = 3
```

Taking into account overlapping, we get this translation to TFL:

```
g X1 = case X1 of { 1 -> 0 | 2 -> 3 }

f X1 X2 = try { case X1 of { 1 -> case X2 of { 2 ->1 } }
              | case X1 of {
                               2 -> 2
                             | 1 -> case X2 of { 2 -> 3 } } }
```

Opposed to this ideal situation, that would enable to offer two alternative lazy narrowing strategies, considering more interesting computation models would obviously involve more substantial changes. Our hope is that the current system design will ease the modifications.

5 Conclusions and Future Work

We have defined an intermediate language that allows us to implement CRWL programs [9, 10] using a demand driven lazy narrowing strategy [15]. A calculus that formally specifies the operational semantics of this intermediate language has also been defined. We have adapted the JUMP-machine to the CRWL framework, taking into account non-deterministic functions and joinability statements. Completeness of CLNC is not realized by our current implementation. This could be mended by adopting some fair search strategy.

Although we have a running implementation, the current state of the system is far from being over. Besides all the optimizations that should be performed, we are mainly interested in extending the system to implement different computation models and extensions of the CRWL framework. Regarding the computation models, we plan to consider simplification, residuation, and dynamic type checking that has been proposed in [11] for higher-order narrowing computations in the CRWL framework, and suggested in [6] for a polymorphic setting. The latter will enable us to accept any kind of function-typed variables in conditions and goals. We are also considering different CRWL extensions, such as algebraic datatypes, type classes, constraints, and a declarative debugger.

Another interesting line of future work is to formalize the relationship between TFL and JCode, which would help to prove the soundness of the implementation.

Acknowledgments The authors are very grateful to Rafa Caballero, Pedro A. González-Calero, Mario Rodríguez-Artalejo, and Jaime Sánchez-Hernández for their interest in our work, and for making many valuable comments on the contents of this paper. Our thanks also to the referees, whose detailed comments on earlier versions of this paper enabled us to improve it considerably.

References

1. E. Albert, M. Hanus, G. Vidal. *Using an Abstract Representation to Specialize Functional Logic Programs.* Procs. 7th Int. Conf. on Logic Programming and Automated Reasoning (LPAR 2000), Springer LNCS 1955, pp. 381–398, 2000.

2. S. Antoy. *Optimal Non-Deterministic Functional Logic Computations.* Procs. 6th Int. Conf. on Algebraic and Logic Programming (ALP'97), Springer LNCS 1298, pp. 16–30, 1997.
3. S. Antoy, R. Echahed, M. Hanus. *A Needed Narrowing Strategy.* Procs. ACM Symp. on Principles of Programming Languages (POPL'94), ACM Press, pp. 268–279, 1994.
4. S. Antoy, R. Echahed, M. Hanus. *A Needed Narrowing Strategy.* Journal of the ACM **47** (4), pp. 776–822, 2000.
5. S. Antoy, M. Hanus. *Compiling Multi-Paradigm Declarative Programs into Prolog.* Procs. 3rd Int. Work. on Frontiers of Combining Systems (FroCoS 2000), Springer LNCS 1794, pp. 171–185, 2000.
6. S. Antoy, A. Tolmach. *Typed Higher-order Narrowing without Higher-order Strategies.* Procs. 4th Fuji Int. Symp. on Functional and Logic Programming (FLOPS'99), Springer LNCS 1722, pp. 335–350, 1999.
7. M.M.T. Chakravarty, H.C.R. Lock. *Towards the Uniform Implementation of Declarative Languages.* Computer Languages **23** (2-4), Pergamon Press, pp. 121–160, 1997.
8. E. Gamma, R. Helm, R. Johnson, J. Vlissides. *Design Patterns: Elements of Reusable Object-Oriented Software.* Addison-Wesley, 1995.
9. J.C. González-Moreno, M.T. Hortalá-González, F.J. López-Fraguas, M. Rodríguez-Artalejo. *An Approach to Declarative Programming Based on a Rewriting Logic.* Journal of Logic Programming **40** (1), pp. 47–87, 1999.
10. J.C. González-Moreno, M.T. Hortalá-González, M. Rodríguez-Artalejo. *A Higher Order Rewriting Logic for Functional Logic Programming.* Procs. 14th Int. Conf. on Logic Programming (ICLP'97), MIT Press, pp. 153–167, 1997.
11. J.C. González-Moreno, M.T. Hortalá-González, M. Rodríguez-Artalejo. *Semantics and Types in Functional Logic Programming.* Procs. 4th Fuji Int. Symp. on Functional and Logic Programming (FLOPS'99), Springer LNCS 1722, pp. 1–20, 1999.
12. M. Hanus (ed.). *Curry: An Integrated Functional Logic Language, Version 0.7.1.* Available at `http://www.informatik.uni-kiel.de/~curry`, 2000.
13. M. Hanus (ed.). *PACKS 1.3: The Portland Aachen Kiel Curry System, User Manual.* Available at `http://www.informatik.uni-kiel.de/~curry`, 2000.
14. M. Hanus, R. Sadre. *An Abstract Machine for Curry and its Concurrent Implementation in Java.* Journal of Functional and Logic Programming, Volume 1999, Special Issue on Parallelism and Implementation Technologies for (Constraint) Logic Programming, Article 6, 1999.
15. R. Loogen, F.J. López-Fraguas, M. Rodríguez-Artalejo. *A Demand Driven Computation Strategy for Lazy Narrowing.* Procs. Int. Symp. on Programming Language Implementation and Logic Programming (PLILP'93), Springer LNCS 714, pp. 184–200, 1993.
16. F.J. López-Fraguas, J. Sánchez-Hernández. *$\mathcal{TOY}$: A Multiparadigm Declarative System.* Procs. 10th Int. Conf. on Rewriting Techniques and Applications (RTA'99), Springer LNCS 1631, pp. 244–247, 1999. System available at `http://titan.sip.ucm.es/toy`.
17. W. Lux, H. Kuchen. *An Efficient Abstract Machine for Curry.* Procs. 8th Int. Work. on Functional and Logic Programming (WFLP'99), pp. 171–181, 1999.
18. S.L. Peyton Jones. *Implementing lazy functional languages on stock hardware: the Spineless Tagless G-machine, Version 2.5.* Journal of Functional Programming **2** (2), pp. 127–202, 1992.
19. D.H.D. Warren. *An Abstract Prolog Instruction Set.* Technical Note 309, SRI International, 1983.

Incremental Learning of Functional Logic Programs

C. Ferri-Ramírez, J. Hernández-Orallo, M.J. Ramírez-Quintana *

DSIC, UPV, Camino de Vera s/n, E-46022 Valencia, Spain,
E-mail:{cferri,jorallo,mramirez}@dsic.upv.es.

Abstract. In this work, we consider the extension of the Inductive Functional Logic Programming (IFLP) framework in order to learn functions in an incremental way. In general, incremental learning is necessary when the number of examples is infinite, very large or presented one by one. We have performed this extension in the FLIP system, an implementation of the IFLP framework. Several examples of programs which have been induced indicate that our extension pays off in practice. An experimental study of some parameters which affect this efficiency is performed and some applications for programming practice are illustrated, especially small classification problems and data-mining of semi-structured data.

Keywords: Inductive functional logic programming (IFLP), inductive logic programming (ILP), incremental learning, theory revision.

1 Introduction

Since the beginning of the last decade, Inductive Logic Programming (ILP) [14] has been a very important area of research as an appropriate framework for the inductive inference of first-order clausal theories from facts. As a machine learning paradigm, the general aim of ILP is to develop tools, theories and techniques to induce hypotheses from examples and background knowledge. ILP inherits the representational formalism, the semantical orientation and the well-established techniques of logic programming. The ILP learning task can be defined as the inference process of a theory (a logic program) P from facts (in general, positive and negative evidence) using a background knowledge theory B (another logic program). More formally, a program P is a solution to the ILP problem if it covers all positive examples ($B \cup P \models E^+$) and does not cover any negative examples ($B \cup P \not\models E^-$).

ILP has provided an outstanding advantage in the inductive machine learning field by increasing the applicability of learning systems to theories with more expressive power than propositional frameworks. Functional logic languages fully exploit the facilities of logic programming in a general sense: functions, predicates and equality. The inductive functional logic approach (IFLP) [9] is inspired

* This work has been partially supported by CICYT under grant TIC 98-0445-C03-C1 and by Generalitat Valenciana under grant GV00-092-14.

H. Kuchen and K. Ueda (Eds.): FLOPS 2001, LNCS 2024, pp. 233–247, 2001.

by the idea of bringing these facilities to the mainstream of ILP [13]. From a representational point of view, IFLP is at least as suitable for many applications as ILP, since FLP programs subsume LP programs. Moreover, many problems can be stated in a more natural way by using a function than a predicate. For instance, classification problems are solved in ILP by using predicate symbols such that one of their arguments represents the class.

A learning system is incremental if the examples are supplied one (or a few) at a time and after each one the system induces, maintains or revises a hypothesis. This operation mode is opposite to that of non-incremental systems (known as batch systems) for which the whole evidence is given initially and does not change afterwards.

Incrementality in machine learning is a powerful and useful technique that tends to improve performance by reducing the use of resources. In regard to spatial resources, many problems can consist of a large evidence, which cannot fit in memory, and an incremental handling of this evidence is a straightforward and convenient solution (there are, of course, other solutions, such as sampling or caching). Secondly, there is also a temporal resources improvement, since induction is much more computationally expensive than deduction. Incrementality allows the establishment of a hypothesis in the early stages of the learning process. If this hypothesis is stable, the next work will be deductive in order to check that the following evidence is consistent with the current hypothesis. Moreover, there are other reasons for using an incremental learning approach[2]: it may be impossible to have all examples initially or even its number cannot be known. In this sense, incrementality is essential when the number of examples is infinite or very large. This is the case of knowledge discovery from databases [6].

Incrementality has been studied by the ILP community. Some incremental ILP systems are CLINT [17], MOBAL [12], FORTE [19] and CIGOL [15]. On the other hand, predicates which are already known (learned) can be used as background knowledge in learning new predicates, and so on. This allows the learning of programs which define more than one concept at the same time in a way that is also incremental [18].

In this paper we present an incremental algorithm for the induction of functional logic programs. Starting with the IFLP general framework defined in [8], we focus on the case of learning one target concept from an evidence whose examples are given one by one. The IFLP framework has been implemented as the FLIP system [5]. We extend its main algorithm in order to make it incremental.

The paper is organised as follows. In Section 2, we review the IFLP framework and the FLIP system. Section 3 defines an incremental IFLP algorithm and extends the FLIP system according to this improvement. From this point, the system can operate not only as an incremental or non-incremental theory inducer but as a theory evaluator/reviser if one or more initial theories are provided. Some results and running examples are presented in Section 4. Finally, Section 5 concludes the paper and discusses future work.

2 IFLP Framework

IFLP can be defined as the functional (or equational) extension of ILP[1]. The goal is the inference of a theory (a functional logic program[2] P) from evidence (a set of positive and optionally negative equations E). The (positive and negative) examples are expressed as pairs of ground terms or ground equations whose right hand sides are in normal form wrt. B and P. Positive examples represent pairs of terms that will have to be proven equal using the induced program, whereas negative examples consist of pairs of terms, where the lhs term has a normal form different from the rhs term. In this section we briefly review the IFLP framework and its implementation. More complete descriptions of the framework and the system can be found in [8][9][5].

The IFLP framework is based on a bottom-up iterative search which generalises the positive examples. The generalisation process is limited by a number of restrictions that eliminate many rules that would be inconsistent with old and new examples or useless for the induction process. We name this limited generalisation *Consistent Restricted Generalisation* (CRG). More specifically, a CRG of an equation e is defined as a new equation e' which is a generalisation of e (i.e. there exists a substitution σ such that $e'\sigma = e$), and there are no fresh variables on the rhs of e' and e' is consistent wrt. the positive and negative evidence.

The basic IFLP algorithm works with an initial set of equations (we denote EH, Equations Hypothesis) and a set of programs (PH, Program Hypothesis) composed exclusively of equations of EH. The new generalised equations obtained from a first stage are added to EH (removing duplicates) and new unary programs from each equation are generated, which are added to PH (removing duplicates). From this new set PH, the main loop of the algorithm selects first a pair of programs according to the selection criterion (currently, the pair which covers more positive examples with the minimum length of the rules) and then combines them.

Two operators for the combination of rules of each pair of programs have been developed: a *Union Operator*, whose use is restricted in order to avoid non-coherent solutions, and an *Inverse Narrowing* operator, which is able to introduce recursion in the programs to be induced. The union operator just gives the program resulting from the union of other two programs. The inverse narrowing, on the contrary, is more sophisticated. This operator is inspired by Muggleton's inverse resolution operator [13]. An inverse narrowing step has as input a pair of equations: the receiver equation e_r and the sender equation e_s. In an informal way, the sender rule is reversed and a narrowing step is performed

---

[1] It is obvious that any problem expressed in the ILP framework can also be expressed in the IFLP framework, because all the positive facts e_i^+ of an ILP problem can be converted into equations of the form $e_i^+ = true$ and all the negative facts e_j^- can be expressed as $e_j^- = false$.

[2] A functional logic program is a logic program augmented with a Horn equational theory. The operational semantics most widely accepted for functional logic languages is based on the narrowing mechanism [7].

to each of the occurrences of the rhs of the receiver rule. In this way, there are as many resulting terms as occurrences to which the sender rule can be applied. Each of these terms are used as rhs of new rules whose lhs's are the lhs's of the receiver rule. These rules are the output of the inverse narrowing step. For instance, consider $e_r : X + s(0) = s(X)$ and $e_s : X + 0 = X$. Reversely using the sender equation in two different occurrences of the rhs of the receiver equation we can construct two different terms: $s(X + 0)$ and $s(X) + 0$. The resulting equations are $X + s(0) = s(X + 0)$ and $X + s(0) = s(X) + 0$. This mechanism allows the generation of new programs starting with two different rules. The new rules and programs produced by the application of inverse narrowing are added to the set of rules and programs EH and PH.

The loop finishes when the stop criterion ($StopCrit$) becomes true, usually when a desired value of optimality has been obtained for the best solution or a maximum number of loops has taken place. In the first case, one or more solutions to the induction problem can be found in a rated PH. In the latter case, partial solutions can be found in PH.

For the induction of programs using background knowledge we use the following method. It permits the introduction of function symbols from background knowledge into the program that is being induced. Briefly, the method consists of applying the inverse narrowing operator with a rule from the background theory. In this way it is possible to obtain new equations with the background function in their rhs. For instance, if the background theory B contains the equation $sum(X, 0) = X$, then the equation $prod(X, 0) = 0$ can be used to generate $prod(X, 0) = sum(0, 0)$ by the application of inverse narrowing. In this way, we have introduced a function from the background theory into the induction process.

2.1 The FLIP system.

To implement this algorithm we have built the FLIP system. FLIP is a project built in C, that implements the Inductive Functional Logic Programming framework. The system includes an interface, a simple parser, a narrowing solver, an inverse narrowing method, and a CRG generator (see [5] for details).

We have tested our system with several examples of different kinds. FLIP usually finds the solution after a few loops, but, logically, this depends mainly on the number of rules of the solution program and on the 'quality' of the initial examples. The length of the induced program is not limited. However, each new rule requires at least one iteration of the main loop. Consequently, FLIP deals better with shorter hypotheses. The main interest (and complexity) appears when learning recursive functions. In this sense, some relevant recursive functional logic programs induced without the use of background knowledge can be seen in Table 1.

Functions such as *app* are more naturally defined as a function than as a predicate. No mode information is then necessary. It should be highlighted that

Induced program	Description	Steps
sum(s(X),Y) = s(sum(X,Y)) sum(0,Y)=Y	Sum of two natural numbers	1
length(·(X,Y)) = s(length(X)) length(λ)=0	Length of a list	2
consec(·(X,Y)) = consec(X) consec(·(·(X,Y),Y)) = true	Returns true if there exist two consecutive elements in a list	1
drop(0,X) = X drop(s(X),·(Y,Z)) = drop(X,Y)	Drops the N last elements of a list	1
app(·(X,Y),Z) = ·(app(X,Z),Y) app(λ,X) = X	Appends two lists	1
member(·(X,Y),Z) = member(X,Z) member(·(X,Y),Y) = true	Returns true if Z is in a list	1
last(·(X,Y)) = last(X) last(·(λ,X)) = X	Last element of a list	1
geq(s(X),s(Y)) = geq(X,Y) geq(X,0) = true	Returns true if the first element is equal or greater than the second	1
sum(s(X),Y) = s(sum(X,Y)) sum(0,Y)=Y prod(s(X0),X1) = sum(prod(X0,X1),X1) prod(0,X0) = 0	Addition and Multiplication at the same time	3
mod3(0) = 0 mod3(s(0)) = s(mod3(0)) mod3(s(s(0))) = s(s(mod3(0))) mod3(s(s(s(X0)))) = mod3(X0)	The mod 3 operation	3
even(s(s(X)) = even(X) even(0) = true	Returns true if natural number is even	1

Table 1. Recursive programs induced without background knowledge[3]

the FLIP system is not restricted to learn one function at a time, as can be shown for the *sum&prod* functions, which are induced together from a mixed evidence.

Finally, with the use of background knowledge, more complex problems can be generated, as is illustrated in Table 2.

The results presented in this section were obtained by randomly selected examples. Evidence was relatively small in all cases: from 3 to 12 positive examples and from 2 to 11 negative examples. For a more extensive account of results, examples used, etc. please visit [4].

[3] The constructor symbols s, $\cdot$ and λ represent the *successor*, *insert* and the *empty list* function symbols, respectively.

Induced program	Description	Bkg.	Steps
rev(·(X0,X1)) = app(rev(X0),·(λ,X1)) rev(λ) = λ	Reversal of a list	append	2
suml(·(X0,X1)) = sum(suml(X0),X1) suml(·(λ,X0)) = X0	Sum of a list of natural numbers	sum	1
maxl(·(X0,X1)) = max(X1,maxl(X0)) maxl(·(λ,X0)) = X0	Max of a list of natural numbers	max	1
prod(s(X0),X1) = sum(prod(X0,X1),X1) prod(0,X0) = 0	Product of two natural numbers	sum	1
fact(s(X0)) = prod(fact(X0),s(X0)) fact(0) = s(0)	Product of two natural numbers	prod sum	4
sort(·(X0,X1)) = inssort(X1,sort(X0)) sort(λ) = λ	Inefficient sort of a list	inssort, gt, if	1

Table 2. Some programs induced with background knowledge

3 Incrementality in IFLP

In this section we present an extension of the IFLP algorithm in order to make it incremental.

Given the current best hypothesis P selected by the algorithm, three possible situations can now arise each time that a new positive example e is presented:

Definition 1. HIT. *e is correctly covered by P, i.e., $P \models e$.*

Definition 2. NOVELTY. *Given the old evidence OE, a novelty situation is given when e is not covered by P but consistent, i.e., $P \not\models e \land \forall e' \in OE : P \cup \{e\} \models e'$.*

Definition 3. ANOMALY. *e is inconsistent with P i.e., $P \models \neg e$.*

Both novelty and anomaly situations will require the revision of the current best hypothesis in order to match the new examples. In the first case, the theory must be generalised in order to cover the new evidence, whereas in the other case, it must be specialised in order to eliminate the inconsistency. Hence, the topic known as theory refinement [21, 22] is a central operation for incremental learning. The incremental reading of negative examples can also be contemplated, but in this case only hits and anomalies are possible.

As has been commented in the introduction, incremental learning forces the introduction of a revision process. Let us denote by `CoreAlgorithm` the algorithm which induced a solution problem from an old and new positive (and negative) evidence and a background knowledge given an initial set of hypotheses and an initial set of theories (programs). The calling specification of the algorithm is:

`CoreAlgorithm`$(OE^+, OE^-, NE^+, NE^-, B, EH, PH, StopCrit)$
This algorithm generates the CRGs from the new positive evidence (although consistency is checked wrt. both old and new evidence: OE^+, OE^-, NE^+ and NE^-).

The algorithm starts with the initial sets EH and PH which can be both empty. The first process is the generalisation of the new positive evidence NE^+. The old positive evidence OE^+ is only used for checking consistence of these generalisations, as well as the old and new negative evidence OE^- and NE^-. When learning non-incrementally, OE^+ and OE^- are usually empty. The result of the CRGs is added then to EH (removing duplicates) and generates unary programs which are added to PH. Then, the algorithm enters a loop which has been described in the previous section until a program in PH covers both OE^+ and NE^+ (and consistent with old and new negative evidence) with a certain optimality value given in the $StopCrit$.

In any incremental framework the number of examples that should be read in each iteration must be specified. The most flexible approach is the use of adaptable values, which can be adjusted by the use of heuristics. The simplest case, on the contrary, is the use of a constant value, which is usually 1. In our case, we have adopted an intermediate but still simple approach. We use an initial incrementality value (*start-up* value) which is different from the next incrementality value. The reason for different initial incrementality values is the CRG stage, which may require greater start-up values than the next incrementality value, which is usually 1.

According to the previous rationale, new additional parameters are required in our algorithm: i_0^+ is the initial positive incrementality value (*start-up* value), which determines how many positive examples are read initially. i_0^- is the initial negative incrementality value. i^+ is the positive incrementality value and i^- is the negative incrementality value, which determine how many positive and negative examples are read at each incremental step. With these four parameters, the overall algorithm can be generalised as follows:

`OverallAlgorithm`$(E^+, E^-, B, PH, StopCrit, OptimalityCrit, i_0^+, i_0^-, i^+, i^-, no\_rev)$
begin
  $OE^+ := \emptyset$, $OE^- := \emptyset$ // old examples
  $IE^+ := \emptyset$, $IE^- := \emptyset$ // ignored examples
  $EH :=$ ExtractAllEquationsFrom(PH)
  $PH := PH \cup \{EH\}$ // adds equations from EH as unary programs
  $NE^+ :=$ Remove($\&E^+, i_0^+$) // extracts the first i_0^+ elements from E^+
  $NE^- :=$ Remove($\&E^-, i_0^-$) // extracts the first i_0^- elements from E^-
  CoreAlgorithm($OE^+, OE^-, NE^+, NE^-, B, \&EH, \&PH, StopCrit$)
  while ($E^+ \neq \emptyset$) or ($E^- \neq \emptyset$) **do**
    BestSolution:= SelectBest($PH, OptimalityCrit$)
    $NE^+ :=$ Remove($\&E^+, i^+$) // extracts the first i^+ elements from E^+
    $NE^- :=$ Remove($\&E^-, i^-$) // extracts the first i^- elements from E^-
    if Bestsolution $\models NE^+$ **and** Bestsolution $\not\models NE^-$ **then** // Hit
      $IE^+ := IE^+ \cup NE^+$ // the new + and - examples are ignored
      $IE^- := IE^- \cup NE^-$ // and the Best Solution is maintained
  else // Novelty or Anomaly. The sets are revised
      RecomputeCoverings($\&EH, \&PH, IE^+, IE^-, NE^+, NE^-$)

```
          // recomputes the coverings of equations and programs wrt.
          // the new examples and (optionally) the ignored examples
        { NE+ := IE+ ∪ NE+ } // Option. Ignored + examples are reconsidered
        { NE- := IE- ∪ NE- } // Option. Ignored - examples are reconsidered
        BestSolution:= SelectBest(PH, OptimalityCrit)
        if not (Bestsolution ⊨ NE+ and Bestsolution ⊭ NE-) then
          if not no-rev then
            CoreAlgorithm(OE+, OE-, NE+, NE-, B, &EH, &PH, StopCrit)
    endif
    OE+ := OE+ ∪ NE+; // the new + examples are now added to old
    OE- := OE- ∪ NE-; // the new - examples are now added to old
  endwhile
  return BestSolution:= SelectBest(PH, OptimalityCrit)
end
```

Plainly, the algorithm considers two cases (if-else). The first one is given when the best solution covers and is consistent with the new examples. In this case, the new examples are ignored (included in the sets IE^+ and IE^-) and nothing else happens. This has been done in this way because if the right solution is found soon, the algorithm is highly accelerated as it only performs a deductive checking of subsequent examples.

In the case of a novelty or anomaly, the EH and PH sets are re-evaluated. The existing information for old evidence is reused, but the values are recomputed for the new examples. Ignored examples of previous iteration can be taken into account, depending on a user option. The result is that some equations and programs can be removed because they are inconsistent. The optimality of the elements of both EH and PH is recomputed from the old ones and the covering of the new examples. Then the best solution is obtained again in order to see whether there is a solution to the problem. In this case, nothing is done. Otherwise, the procedure `CoreAlgorithm` is activated, which will generate the CRG's for the new examples as we have seen before and will work with the old EH and PH jointly with the new CRG's until a solution is found.

This new algorithm allows a much richer functionality for FLIP. This can now accept a set PH of initial programs or theories P_1, P_2, ..., P_s, a background theory B and the examples. If these initial programs are not specified, FLIP begins with no initial program set. If one or more initial programs are provided, FLIP will build EH from all the equations that form the initial programs (avoiding duplicate equations) and will generate a PH for each program.

In this way, FLIP is at the same time:

- a **pure inducer**: when there are no initial programs.
- a **theory reviser**: when a unique initial program is given. The program will be preserved until an example forces to 'launch' the `CoreAlgorithm`.
- a **theory reviser/evaluator**: when several initial programs are given and n examples are provided with a value of (positive) incrementality $i_0^+ < n$. In this case, the SelectBest function selects the best one wrt. the i_0^+ first examples. This program will be compared with subsequent examples and

could be changed accordingly. In the end, FLIP will indicate which initial program (or a new derived program) is better wrt. the n examples. If $i_0^+ \geq n$ FLIP will be just an evaluator if the theories are consistent with all the examples.

- a **theory evaluator**: when the `no-rev` option is selected, several initial programs are given and n examples are given with a value of (positive) incrementality $i_0^+ \geq n$. In this case, the optimality criterion is applied and the best program wrt. the n examples is chosen. Consequently, FLIP simply indicates which of the initial programs is the best wrt. the evidence. The additional condition `no-rev` of the overall algorithm precludes the theories to be revised and new equations and programs to be generated.

Initial theories, negative examples and background knowledge are optional for the incremental FLIP system. The positive examples are also optional because FLIP can also work as a theory evaluator for negative evidence only.

At the present FLIP implementation, both i_0^+ and i_0^- are specified by the user, and $i^+ = 1$ and $i^- = 0$. The use of $i^- > 0$ does not affect considerably the efficiency of the algorithm since the CRG's are generated only for the positive examples. Moreover, negative examples are not necessary for classification problems with a finite number of classes, due to the nature of functional logic languages. In any case, the parts of a theory which the user wants to be fixed should be specified in the background knowledge.

With regard to the automated evaluation possibilities of FLIP, it is possibly the most direct application for programming practice. As has been commented in [10], selection criteria from machine learning can be used to automatically choose the most predictive model of requirements, in order to reduce modification probability of software systems. Although in the next subsections we will center on generation and revision for small problems, the scalability of FLIP for large problems can be shown in the evaluation stage of software development.

4 Results and applications

To study the usefulness of our approach, we have performed some experiments using the FLIP system.

4.1 Extending ILP and IFLP applications

Apart from classical ILP problems, the first kind of application for which IFLP is advantageous is the dealing with semi-structured data, an area that is becoming increasingly more important. Most information in the web is unstructured or semi-structured. In order to do this, learning tools should be able to cope with this kind of data.

FLIP is able to handle these problems because it can learn recursive functions and can work with complex arguments (tree terms).

Example 1. Given an eXtended Mark-up Language (XML) document [1] which contains information about the good customers of a car insurance company (customers with a 30% gratification):

```
<goodc> <name>john</name> <has_children/> </goodc>
<goodc> <married/> <teacher/> <has_cellularphone/> </goodc>
<goodc> <sex>male</sex> <teacher/> <name>jimmy</name> </goodc>
...
```

this document cannot be addressed by usual data-mining tools, because the data are not structured within a relation. Moreover the possible attributes are unordered and of different number and kind for each example. Nonetheless, it can be processed by our IFLP system FLIP by automatically converting XML documents into functional terms trees. In this case, the resulting trees would be:

```
goodc(·(·(λ,name(john)),has_children))=30
goodc(·(·(·(λ,married),teacher),has_phone))=30,
goodc(·(·(·(λ,sex(male),teacher),name(jimmy))))=30,
goodc(·(·(λ,sex(female)),tall))=30,
goodc(·(·(λ,nurse),sex(female)))=30,
goodc(·(·(·(λ,browneye),likes_coffee),has_children))=30,
goodc(·(·(·(λ,has_children),nurse),has_phone))=30,
goodc(·(·(·(λ,name(jane)),plays_chess),has_children))=30,
goodc(·(·(·(λ,has_children),name(joan)),speaks_spanish))=30,
goodc(·(·(·(λ,name(jane)),sex(female))tall))=30,
goodc(·(·(·(·(λ,name(jimmy)),teacher),sex(male)),tall))=30,
goodc(·(·(·((λ,teacher),low_income),is_atheist),married))=30,
goodc(·(·(·(λ,name(mary)),has_children),has_phone))=30
```

and the evidence for the other classes (customers with a 10% or 20% gratification), extracted from bad customers:

```
goodc(·(·(λ,sex(male)),tall))=10,
goodc(·(·(λ,nurse),sex(male)))=20,
goodc(·(·(λ,name(peter)),married))=20,
goodc(·(·(·(λ,married),policeperson),has_phone))=10,
goodc(·(·(·(λ,name(charlie)),sex(male)),butcher))=10,
goodc(·(·(·(λ,browneye),likes_coffee),sex(male)))=20,
goodc(·(·(·(λ,plays_football),nurse),has_phone))=10,
goodc(·(·(·(λ,susan),plays_chess),married))=20,
goodc(·(·(·(·(λ,butcher),sex(male)),name(paul)),speaks_spanish))=10,
goodc(·(·(·(λ,name(steve)),sex(male)),speaks_portuguese))=10,
goodc(·(·(·(·(λ,name(pat)),married),sex(male)),high_income))=20,
goodc(·(·(·(·(λ,policeperson),atheist),has_phone),married))=10
```

The FLIP system returns the following solution:

```
goodc(·(X0,X1)) = goodc(X0)
goodc(·(X0,has_children)) = 30
goodc(·(X0,sex(female))) = 30
goodc(·(X0,teacher)) = 30
```

Note that the solution is recursive and covers semi-structured datasets.

The next example, originally appeared in [3], can illustrate the application of the revision abilities of FLIP:

Example 2. An optician requires a program to determine which kind of contact lenses should be used first on a new young client/patient. The optician has many previous cases available where s/he has finally fitted the correct lenses (either soft or hard) to each young client/patient or has just recommended glasses. The evidence is composed of 8 examples with the following attributes, parameter ordering and possible values for them:

`Age`:	#1	*young*
`SpectaclePrescription`:	#2	*myopia, hypermetropia*
`Astigmatism`:	#3	*no, yes*
`TearProductionRate`:	#4	*reduced, normal*

The goal is to construct a program that classifies a new patient into the following three classes *soft*, *hard*, *no*. After feeding FLIP with the 8 lens examples of young patients from the database, it returns:

```
lens(X0, X1, no, normal)  = soft
lens(X0, X1, yes, normal) = hard
lens(X0, X1, X2, reduced) = no
```

Consider that the optician wants to extend the potential clients. Now s/he deals with three different kinds of age: *young*, *prepresbyopic* and *presbyopic*. S/he adds 16 new examples to the database with the results of the new clients. Using the new and old examples, FLIP revises the old program into the following one:

```
lens(X0, hypermetropia, no, normal)             = soft
lens(young, myopia, no, normal)                 = soft
lens(X0, myopia, yes, normal)                   = hard
lens(young, hypermetropia, yes, normal)         = hard
lens(prepresbyopic, myopia, no, normal)         = soft
lens(prepresbyopic, hypermetropia, yes, normal) = no
lens(presbyopic, myopia, no, normal)            = no
lens(X0, X1, X2, reduced)                       = no
lens(presbyopic, hypermetropia, yes, normal)    = no
```

4.2 Speed-up analysis

We have performed several other experiments with the new incremental version of FLIP to learn well-known problems with and without knowledge (see [4] for the source code of the problems). The inclusion of incrementality can highly improve the induction speed. Table 3 shows the speed-ups reached when inducing these problems running FLIP. Times were measured on a Pentium III processor (450 Mhz) with 64 MBytes of RAM under Linux version 2.2.12-20. They are expressed in seconds and are the average of 10 executions. The column Speed-up shows the

Benchmarks	Non-inc.	Inc.	Speed-up	#Rules	#Attributes
`sum`	6.01	0.42	14.30	2	2
`length`	13.96	5.51	2.53	2	2
`lenses`	12.17	2.15	5.66	9	4
`prod`	10.57	2.22	4.76	2 + 2 bkg	2
`maxlist`	39.66	2.27	17.47	2 + 3 bkg	2

Table 3. Benchmark results for $i_0 = 6$ and 24 examples. The accuracy for all of them is 100%

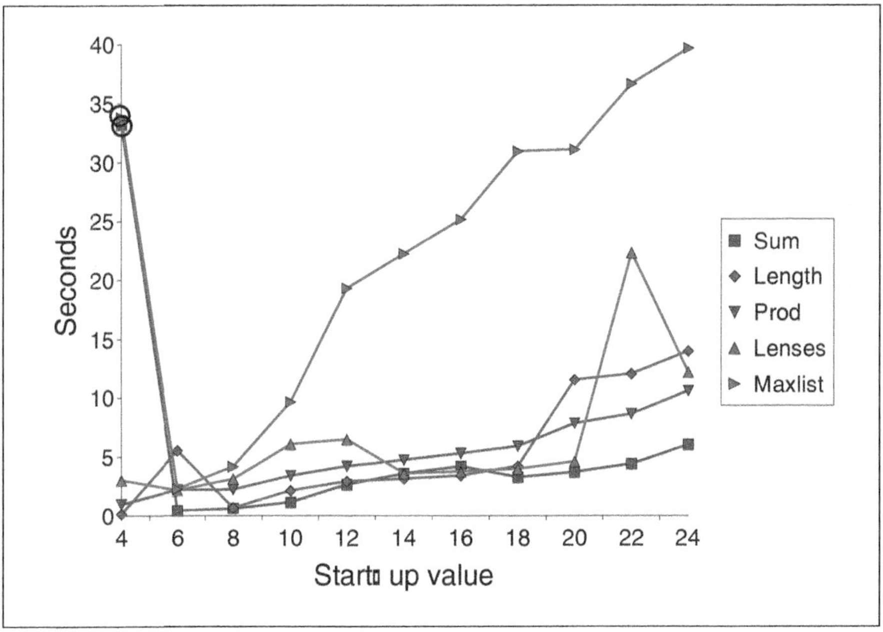

Fig. 1. Times obtained in the induction of some problems depending on the start-up value.[5]

relative improvement achieved by the incremental approach for $i_0 = 6$, obtained as the ratio Non-Incremental ÷ Incremental.

One can think that the time can strongly oscillate depending on the start-up value. Nevertheless, as we illustrate in Figure 1, the use of incrementality generally improves induction time whereas the start-up value only affects the speed-up. Figure 1 expresses the performances of rules of the resulting programs induced for different problems, depending on the start-up value. The results show that increasing start-up values give increasing times, because induction, especially CRG's, are used more intensively. This is especially noticeable in the case of the *maxlist* problem, because the size of examples is large, and CRG's are very time consuming. Although lower i values give the most efficient results,

[5] The points surrounded by a circle indicate experiments where the accuracy is below 100%.

there is also a risk of missing the good solution. This value is very dependent on the number of attributes. For instance, in the case of the problems with 2 attributes, the optimal start-up value could be between 4 and 8 with some risk of missing the target program at low values. For the lenses problem (4 attributes) the optimal start-up value could be between 7 and 20. This suggests that the start-up value can be estimated from the number of attributes (which, moreover, is the only parameter that is known a priori).

Let us perform a more detailed study for a larger problem: the monks1 problem. This problem is a popular problem from the UCI ML dataset repository [16] which defines a function such that $monks1(\_,\_,\_,\_,1,\_)$ and $monks1(X,X,\_,\_,\_,\_)$. It has a larger number of examples to essay and the function depends on 6 attributes. The following table shows, as expected, that the speed-up increases as long as the number of examples increases:

Benchmarks	Non-inc.	Inc.	Speed-up	#Examples	#Rules	#Attributes
monks1	528	345	1.53	25	2	6
monks1	1075	344	3.13	50	2	6
monks1	2012	347	5.8	100	2	6
monks1	3286	350	9.39	150	2	6
monks1	4598	351	13.10	216	2	6

Table 4. Benchmark results for $i_0 = 14$, and variable number of examples for the monks1 problem. The accuracy for all of them is 100%

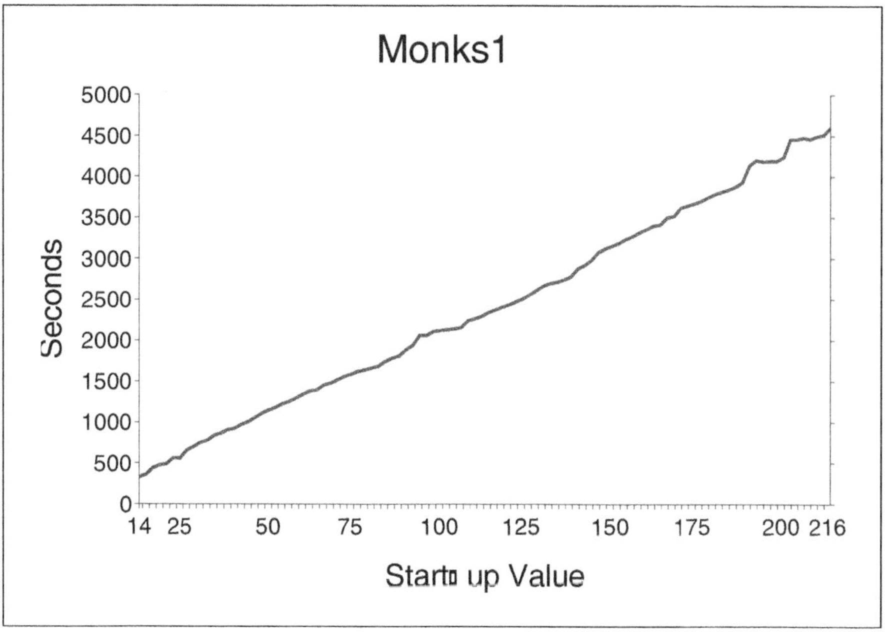

Fig. 2. Times obtained in the induction of the *monks1* problem depending on the start-up value.

We have also measured the speed-up for different values of the start-up value, from 14 to 216. Figure 2 shows the results. Values below 14 are quite irregular but, in general, are worse than those for 14.

5 Conclusions and future work

In this paper we have extended the induction of functional logic programs to an incremental framework. Incremental learning allows the handling of large volumes of data and can be used in interactive situations, when all the data are not received a priori.

Although incrementality forces the introduction of revision processes, these can be of different kinds. According to the complexity of revision, many approaches [20] [22] have been based on minimal revisions, which usually 'patch' the theory with some factual cases to cover the exceptions. These approaches are more efficient in the short term but, since revisions are minimal, the resulting theories tend to be more a patchwork and more frequently revised with time [11] than a coherent hypothesis. On the contrary, our approach is based on deep revisions (the whole inductive core algorithm is reactivated) until the best hypothesis reaches a good score according to the evaluation criterion. This motivates that theories can be revised either by anomalies or novelties, and the resulting theories output by FLIP are more coherent.

As future work we plan to implement 'oblivion' criteria in order to forget old data that are redundant or that have been used in theories which are well reinforced. 'Stopping' criteria should also be introduced in order to increase the speed-up. Currently the speed-up is obtained because in the moment that a hypothesis is stable, the rest of positive evidence is just checked deductively, and the inductive process (the costly one) is not used. Among the stopping criteria we are investigating two heuristics: one based on the number of iterations that the hypothesis has remained unchanged and the other one based on the optimality of the hypothesis. These could also be used in order to work with non-constant incrementality values (currently $i^+ = 1$). In the same way, we want to study the relation between FLIP performance and the use of different evaluation criteria by using the evaluation mode of FLIP and a generator of examples that has been recently developed. More ambitiously, we are working on an incremental redesign of the CRGs in order to cope with a great number of attributes. In this way, incrementality would be horizontal as well as vertical, allowing the use of complex and large examples (lists, trees, etc.) that in many cases cannot be handled non-incrementally. This would extend the range of applications of the FLIP system to other kinds of problems: data-mining and program synthesis.

References

1. S. Abiteboul, P. Buneman, and D. Suciu. *Data on the web: from relations to semistructured data and XML*. Morgan Kaufmann Publishers, 1999.

2. F. Bergadano and D. Gunetti. *Inductive Logic Programming: from Machine Learning to Software Engineering.* The MIT Press, Cambridge, Mass., 1995.
3. J. Cendrowska. Prism: An algorithm for inducing modular rules. *International Journal of Man-Machines Studies*, 27:349–370, 1987.
4. C. Ferri, J. Hernández, and M.J. Ramírez. The FLIP system homepage. `http://www.dsic.upv.es/~jorallo/flip/`, 2000.
5. C. Ferri, J. Hernández, and M.J. Ramírez. The FLIP user's manual (v0.7). Technical report, Department of Information Systems and Computation, Valencia University of Technology, 2000/24, 2000.
6. R. Godin and R. Missaoui. An incremental concept formation approach for learning from databases. *Theoretical Computer Science*, 133:387–419, 1994.
7. M. Hanus. The Integration of Functions into Logic Programming: From Theory to Practice. *Journal of Logic Programming*, 19-20:583–628, 1994.
8. J. Hernández and M.J. Ramírez. Inverse Narrowing for the Induction of Functional Logic Programs. In *Proc. Joint Conference on Declarative Programming, APPIA-GULP-PRODE'98*, pages 379–393, 1998.
9. J. Hernández and M.J. Ramírez. A Strong Complete Schema for Inductive Functional Logic Programming. In *Proc. of the Ninth International Workshop on Inductive Logic Programming, ILP'99*, volume 1634 of *Lecture Notes in Artificial Intelligence*, pages 116–127, 1999.
10. J. Hernández and M.J. Ramírez. Predictive Software. *Automated Software Engineering*, to appear, 2001.
11. H. Katsuno and A. O. Mendelzon. On the difference between updating a knowledge base and revising it. In *Proc of the 2nd Intern. Conf. on Princip. of Knowledge Representation and Reasoning*, pages 387–394. M. Kaufmann Publishers, 1991.
12. J. U. Kietz and S. Wrobel. Controlling the complexity of learning in logic through syntactic and task-oriented models. In S. Muggleton, editor, *Inductive Logic Programming*. Academic Press, 1992.
13. S. Muggleton. Inductive Logic Programming. *New Generation Computing*, 8(4):295–318, 1991.
14. S. Muggleton. Inductive logic programming: Issues, results, and the challenge of learning language in logic. *Artificial Intelligence*, 114(1–2):283–296, 1999.
15. S. Muggleton and W. Buntine. Machine invention of first-order predicates by inverting resolution. In S. Muggleton, editor, *Inductive Logic Programming*, pages 261–280. Academic Press, 1992.
16. University of California. UCI Machine Learning Repository Content Summary. `http://www.ics.uci.edu/~mlearn/MLSummary.html`.
17. L. De Raedt. *Interactive Theory Revision: An Inductive Logic Programming Approach.* Academic Press, 1992.
18. M. Krishna Rao. A framework for incremental learning of logic programs. *Theoretical Computer Science*, 185:191–213, 1997.
19. B. L. Richards and R. J. Mooney. First order theory revision. In *Proc. of the 8th International Workshop on Machine Learning*, pages 447–451. Morgan Kaufmann, 1991.
20. B. L. Richards and R. J. Mooney. Automated refinement of first-order horn-clause domain theories. *Machine Learning*, 19:95–131, 1995.
21. S. Wrobel. On the proper definition of minimality in spezialization and theory revision. In P.B. Brazdil, editor, *Proc. of ECML-93*, volume 667 of *Lecture Notes in Computer Science*, pages 65–82. Springer-Verlag, 1993.
22. S. Wrobel. First order theory refinement. In L. De Raedt, editor, *Advances in Inductive Logic Programming*, pages 14–33. IOS Press, 1996.

A General Type Inference Framework for Hindley/Milner Style Systems

Martin Sulzmann

Dept. of Computer Science and Software Engineering,
The University of Melbourne
sulzmann@cs.mu.oz.au

Abstract. We propose a constraint-based formulation of Hindley/Milner style type inference system as opposed to the standard substitution-based formulation. This allows us to make important distinctions between different phases of type inference: Constraint generation/propagation, constraint solving, constraint simplification and term reconstruction. The inference system is parametric in the constraint domain, covering a wide range of application domains. A problem, incompleteness of substitution-based inference, identified by A. J. Kennedy can be solved naturally by employing a constraint-based view of type inference. In addition, our formulation of type inference can easily be tailored to different inference algorithms such as $\mathcal{W}$ and $\mathcal{M}$. On the technical side, we present concise soundness and completeness results.

1 Introduction

Type systems are important in the design of programming languages and type-based program analyses. The Hindley/Milner system has proved to be one of the most popular and successful type systems. One of the most important features of the Hindley/Milner system [Mil78] is decidable type inference. Type inference algorithm $\mathcal{W}$, introduced by Milner, reports a type for a given program. Milner could prove that algorithm $\mathcal{W}$ is sound, i.e. every reported type is a valid type. In [Dam85], Damas proved that algorithm $\mathcal{W}$ is complete, i.e. for any typable program algorithm $\mathcal{W}$ will report an answer or otherwise will report failure. Most notably, algorithm $\mathcal{W}$ infers principal types. A principal type subsumes all other types we can possibly assign to a given program.

In [LY98], Lee and Yi prove soundness and completeness of algorithm $\mathcal{M}$ which is a top-down formulation of algorithm $\mathcal{W}$. Both algorithms yield the same result but algorithm $\mathcal{M}$ seems to be the better choice if the program is ill-typed. Lee and Yi formally prove that algorithm $\mathcal{M}$ reports type errors earlier than algorithm $\mathcal{W}$. In [LY00], Lee and Yi propose a generic scheme for inference algorithms for the standard Hindley/Milner system which contains algorithms $\mathcal{W}$ and $\mathcal{M}$ as special instances.

Extensions of the Hindley/Milner system with equational theories and its inference systems were studied in [Rém92,Ken96]. A more general approach was considered by Odersky/Sulzmann/Wehr. In [OSW99], Odersky *et al.* introduce a generic version of algorithm $\mathcal{W}$ parameterized in the constraint domain. Under certain conditions on the constraint domain, type inference yields principal

H. Kuchen and K. Ueda (Eds.): FLOPS 2001, LNCS 2024, pp. 248–263, 2001.

types. Several application domains such as [DHM95,Oho95,NP95,AW93] have been studied in [OSW99] and [Sul00a].

As observed by Kennedy, algorithm $\mathcal{W}$ is incomplete in case of a variation of the Hindley/Milner system that deals with physical dimensions.

Our work extends the approaches of Lee/Yi, Rémy, Kennedy and Odersky/Sulzmann/Wehr. We present a constraint-based inference scheme for Hindley/Milner style systems which allows for flexibility in the following different components of type inference:

1. Constraint generation: We need to generate a correct set of constraints which represents the possible solutions to the typing problem.
2. Constraint solving: Our inference system is parametric in the constraint solver. Solving of constraints must be decidable to retain decidable type inference.
3. Constraint propagation: Different inference algorithms such as $\mathcal{W}$ and $\mathcal{M}$ can be modelled by different constraint propagation policies.
4. Constraint simplification: By simplification, we mean the task of achieving certain optimal syntactic representation forms of constraints. This is important to ensure efficient type inference.
5. Term reconstruction: Type inference keeps all typing information in constraint form. However, the type system itself might enforce certain term representations of types. Completeness holds if we can reconstruct best term solutions to constraint problems.

Specific inference algorithms fall out by instantiating the individual components appropriately. We believe it is important to make a distinction among the different components. This helps in establishing concise soundness and completeness results which are parametric in the individual components. In particular, our new formulation of type inference provides a natural solution to Kennedy's problem.

We start in Section 2 with some background information about constraint systems and HM(X). HM(X) is a general framework to study Hindley/Milner style type systems parameterized in the constraint domain X. Section 3 introduces our general inference scheme formulated as a constraint-based inference system. We give an axiomatic description of sound and complete constraint propagation policies and provide a range of possible instances. In Section 4, we review Kennedy's problem and present a new formulation of term-based inference systems. We conclude in Section 5.

A detailed exposition including full proofs can be found in [Sul00b].

2 Preliminaries

2.1 Constraints and Substitutions

Constraint systems are defined in terms of a first-order logic where $\wedge$ stands for logical conjunction and $\exists\bar{\alpha}.$ for existential quantification of a sequence of variables $\alpha_1, \ldots, \alpha_n$. Given a set Var of type variables and a subset U of Var, we define $\bar{\exists} U.C = \exists V.C$ where $V = Var \backslash U$. The domain is defined by a term algebra $\mathcal{T}$ which also describes the language of types. We assume that at least we are given a primitive predicate $(=)$ which expresses type equality between members of the term algebra $\mathcal{T}$. $C \models D$ and $C \equiv D$ denote model-theoretic consequence and equivalence among constraints. We will always assume that for a given constraint system there exists a model $\mathcal{M}$ which satisfies the laws of the constraint system. However, we leave the specific model $\mathcal{M}$ implicit. For example, we write $\models C$ to denote that C is valid under $\mathcal{M}$. Given a constraint C, then $fv(C) = \{\alpha \mid \exists\alpha.C \not\equiv C\}$ is the set of *free variables* in C. A constraint C is *satisfiable* iff $\models \exists fv(C).C$.

A substitution $\phi = [\bar{\tau}/\bar{\alpha}]$ mapping type variables α_i to (monomorphic) types τ_i can always be viewed as the constraint $(\alpha_1 = \tau_1) \wedge \ldots \wedge (\alpha_n = \tau_n)$. In the same way, a type τ can be viewed as the type variable α under the constraint $(\alpha = \tau)$. Applying substitution $\phi = [\bar{\tau}/\bar{\alpha}]$ to constraint C can be expressed within the language of constraints via conjunction and existential quantification $\exists\bar{\alpha}$. We have the following identity: $\phi C \equiv \exists\bar{\alpha}.((\bar{\tau} = \bar{\alpha}) \wedge C)$. We use the convention that constraints $\phi, \psi, \ldots$ refer to substitutions in constraint form. The domain of a substitution equals the set of free variables of a constraint. We have the following identity $dom(\phi) = fv(\phi)$. Syntactic substitutions can easily be expressed in terms of the constraint language. We define $\phi(\alpha) = \tau$ iff $\models \exists U.(\phi \wedge (\alpha = \tau))$ where $U = fv(\phi)$.

2.2 Normalization

We introduce the concept of normalization as an extension of constraint solving and unification. Note that we only consider constraints over Herbrand terms, therefore we do not need to rely on more advanced solving methods such as semi-unification and higher-order unification.

Given a constraint system X over a term algebra $\mathcal{T}$, we say $\mathcal{S}$ is the set of *solved forms* in X iff $\mathcal{S}$ is a subset of all satisfiable constraints in X.

Given constraints C, D and ϕ in X, then $C \wedge \phi$ is a *normal form* of D iff $C \in \mathcal{S}$ and $C \wedge \phi \models D$. We say $C \wedge \phi$ is *principal* if for all normal forms $C' \wedge \phi'$ it holds that $\bar{\exists}U.(C' \wedge \phi') \models \bar{\exists}U.(C \wedge \phi)$ where $U = fv(D)$.

Example 1. Consider the standard Herbrand constraint system. We take $\mathcal{S}$ to be the set consisting only of true, which is represented by the empty token set $\{\}$. Then, a principal normal form corresponds to a most general unifier and a normal form corresponds to a unifier of a constraint problem.

Principal normal forms are unique modulo semantic equivalence. Hence, it is possible to define a well-defined function *normalize* from constraints C to normal forms:

$$
\begin{aligned}
& normalize(D) \\
& = C \wedge \psi \text{ if } C \wedge \psi \text{ is a principal normal form of } D \\
& = fail \quad \text{if no normal form exists}
\end{aligned}
$$

The property of having a principal normal form extends to constraint systems. Given a constraint system X over a term algebra $\mathcal{T}$ and a set of solved constraints $\mathcal{S}$ in X, we say the constraint system X has the *principal constraint property* if for every constraint C in X, either C does not have a normal form or C has a principal normal form.

2.3 The HM(X) Framework

We assume, we are given a constraint system X over a term algebra $\mathcal{T}$ and a set $\mathcal{S}$ of solved forms in X. The typing rules and a description of the language of expressions and types can be found in Fig. 1. Types are members of the term algebra $\mathcal{T}$ where there might be other constructors besides $\rightarrow$. This is expressed by the symbol $\supseteq$. Type schemes include a constraint component C which restricts the types that can be substituted for the type variable α. The language of terms is exactly as in [DM82]. That is, we assume that any language constructs that make use of type constraints are expressible as predefined values, whose names and types are recorded in the initial type environment Γ_0.

Typing judgments are of the form $C, \Gamma \vdash e : \sigma$ where C is in X, Γ is a type environment associating free variables with their type, and σ is a type scheme. A typing judgment is *valid* if it can be derived by application of the typing rules.

We restrict the set of constraints allowed to appear in typing judgments and type schemes to the set $\mathcal{S}$ of solved forms. Given a constraint C appearing on the left-hand side of the turnstile or in a type scheme, then there must be a constraint $D \in \mathcal{S}$ such that C and D are equivalent.

Most rules are straightforward extensions of the standard Hindley/Milner rules. In rules (Abs) and (Let), the type environment Γ_x denotes the type environment obtained from Γ by excluding variable x. The formulation of the ($\forall$ Elim) rule is similar to previous formulations. The only valid instances of a type scheme $\forall\bar{\alpha}.D \Rightarrow \tau$ are those that satisfy the constraint part of the type scheme. The formulation of the ($\forall$ Intro) rule is one of the novelties of the HM(X) system. Type variables are not only bound in the type component but in addition also in the constraint component through the existential quantifier. Rule ($\exists$ Intro) is motivated by the following logical rule: $\forall\alpha.(P \rightarrow Q) = (\exists\alpha.P) \rightarrow Q$ where $\alpha \notin fv(Q)$. The outermost universal quantification of the free type variable α in the judgment $C, \Gamma \vdash e : \sigma$ can be moved to the constraint part, if α does only appear in the constraint part. This allows type variables that only appear in the constraint part of typing judgments to be hidden.

Unlike standard treatments of Hindley/Milner style systems, there is also a subsumption rule (Sub), which allows us to derive term e with type τ' if we can derive term e with type τ and type τ subsumes type τ'. The subsumption relation $\preceq$ is determined by the constraint system X, and is assumed to satisfy the standard axioms for a partial ordering plus the contra-variance rule, see Fig. 1. Except for these conditions, the choice of $\preceq$ is arbitrary. Note that the subsumption relation $\preceq$ is a generalization of other relations such as type equality or subtyping.

The relation $C \vdash^i \sigma \preceq \sigma'$ states that type scheme σ is smaller than type scheme σ' with respect to the constraint C. Rule (SubI) connects the relation $\vdash^i$ to the entailment relation $\models$. Rules ($\forall \preceq$) and ($\preceq \forall$) describe how to deal with type schemes. The definition is standard.

We maintain that an instance of the HM(X) system is defined by the five-tuple $(\mathrm{X}, \preceq, \mathcal{T}, \mathcal{S}, \Gamma_0)$ which we commonly refer to as HM(X) or simply X.

Example 2. The Hindley/Milner system is an instance of our HM(X) type system framework. Take X to be the Herbrand constraint system HERBRAND over the algebra of types τ. HERBRAND consists only of primitive constraints of the

Expressions

$v ::= x \mid \lambda x.e$

$e ::= v \mid e\,e \mid \mathsf{let}\ x = e\ \mathsf{in}\ e$

Types

$\tau ::\supseteq \alpha \mid \tau \to \tau$

$\sigma ::= \tau \mid \forall \bar{\alpha}.C \Rightarrow \tau$

Typing rules

$$\text{(Var)}\ C, \Gamma \vdash x : \sigma \quad (x : \sigma \in \Gamma) \qquad \text{(Sub)}\ \frac{C, \Gamma \vdash e : \tau \quad C \models (\tau \preceq \tau')}{C, \Gamma \vdash e : \tau'}$$

$$\text{(Abs)}\ \frac{C, \Gamma_x.x : \tau \vdash e : \tau'}{C, \Gamma_x \vdash \lambda x.e : \tau \to \tau'} \qquad \text{(App)}\ \frac{\begin{array}{c} C, \Gamma \vdash e_1 : \tau_1 \to \tau_2 \\ C, \Gamma \vdash e_2 : \tau_1 \end{array}}{C, \Gamma \vdash e_1 e_2 : \tau_2}$$

$$\text{(Let)}\ \frac{\begin{array}{c} C, \Gamma_x \vdash e : \sigma \\ C, \Gamma_x.x : \sigma \vdash e' : \tau' \end{array}}{C, \Gamma_x \vdash \mathsf{let}\ x = e\ \mathsf{in}\ e' : \tau'} \qquad (\forall\ \text{Intro})\ \frac{\begin{array}{c} C \wedge D, \Gamma \vdash e : \tau \\ \bar{\alpha} \notin fv(C, \Gamma) \end{array}}{C \wedge \exists \bar{\alpha}.D, \Gamma \vdash e : \forall \bar{\alpha}.D \Rightarrow \tau}$$

$$(\forall\ \text{Elim})\ \frac{\begin{array}{c} C, \Gamma \vdash e : \forall \bar{\alpha}.D \Rightarrow \tau \\ C \models [\bar{\tau}/\bar{\alpha}]D \end{array}}{C, \Gamma \vdash e : [\bar{\tau}/\bar{\alpha}]\tau} \qquad (\exists\ \text{Intro})\ \frac{\begin{array}{c} C, \Gamma \vdash e : \sigma \\ \bar{\alpha} \notin fv(\Gamma, \sigma) \end{array}}{\exists \bar{\alpha}.C, \Gamma \vdash e : \sigma}$$

Subsumption rules

$$\frac{C \models (\alpha = \alpha')}{C \models (\alpha \preceq \alpha') \wedge (\alpha' \preceq \alpha)} \qquad \frac{C \models (\alpha \preceq \alpha') \wedge (\alpha' \preceq \alpha)}{C \models (\alpha = \alpha')}$$

$$\frac{C \models (\alpha_1 \preceq \alpha_2) \quad C \models (\alpha_2 \preceq \alpha_3)}{C \models (\alpha_1 \preceq \alpha_3)} \qquad \frac{C \models (\alpha_1' \preceq \alpha_1) \quad C \models (\alpha_2 \preceq \alpha_2')}{C \models (\alpha_1 \to \alpha_2 \preceq \alpha_1' \to \alpha_2')}$$

Instance relation

$$\text{(SubI)}\ \frac{C \models (\tau \preceq \tau')}{C \vdash^i \tau \preceq \tau'}$$

$$(\preceq \forall)\ \frac{C \wedge D \vdash^i \sigma \preceq \tau \quad \bar{\alpha} \notin tv(\sigma, C)}{C \wedge \exists \bar{\alpha}.D \vdash^i \sigma \preceq (\forall \bar{\alpha}.D \Rightarrow \tau)} \qquad (\forall \preceq)\ \frac{C \vdash^i [\bar{\tau}/\bar{\alpha}]\tau \preceq \tau' \quad C \models [\bar{\tau}/\bar{\alpha}]D}{C \vdash^i (\forall \bar{\alpha}.D \Rightarrow \tau) \preceq \tau'}$$

Fig. 1. Logical Type System

form ($\tau = \tau'$) where τ and τ' are elements of a term algebra $\mathcal{T}$. Equality in HERBRAND is syntactic, $\mathcal{T}$ is a free algebra. Take ($\preceq$) to be ($=$). Take the set of solved forms to be the set consisting only of true, which is represented by the empty token set $\{\}$. Then the only type schemes arising in proof trees of valid typing judgments are of the form $\forall\alpha.\{\} \Rightarrow \sigma$, which we equate with Hindley/Milner type schemes $\forall\alpha.\sigma$. It is easy to convince oneself that a judgment $\Gamma \vdash e : \sigma$ is derivable in Hindley/Milner if and only if $\{\}, \Gamma \vdash e : \sigma$ is derivable in HM(HERBRAND).

For the purpose of this paper we omit a further discussion and refer to previous work [Sul00a,OSW99].

3 Constraint-Based Inference

We consider type inference in the purely constraint-based fragment of HM(X) where the set $\mathcal{S}$ of solved forms consists of all satisfiable constraints in X. Constraint solving requires only a satisfiability check.

$$\text{(Var)}\quad \frac{x : (\forall\bar{\alpha}.D \Rightarrow \tau) \in \Gamma}{C, \Gamma, x : \alpha \vdash^{inf} (C \wedge \exists\bar{\alpha}.((\alpha = \tau) \wedge D))}$$

$$\text{(Abs)}\quad \frac{\begin{array}{c} C_1, \Gamma_x.x : \alpha_1, e : \alpha_2 \vdash^{inf} D \quad (C_1, \alpha_2) \in \mathit{PartSol}(\Gamma.x : \alpha_1, e) \\ D' = D \wedge (\alpha_1 \to \alpha_2 \preceq \alpha) \wedge C \end{array}}{C, \Gamma_x, \lambda x.e : \alpha \vdash^{inf} D'}$$

$$\text{(App)}\quad \frac{\begin{array}{c} C_1, \Gamma, e_1 : \alpha_1 \vdash^{inf} D_1 \quad (C_1, \alpha_1) \in \mathit{PartSol}(\Gamma, e_1 \,|\, \Gamma, e_1 e_2) \\ C_2, \Gamma, e_2 : \alpha_2 \vdash^{inf} D_2 \quad (C_2, \alpha_2) \in \mathit{PartSol}(\Gamma, e_2 \,|\, \Gamma, e_1 e_2) \\ D = D_1 \wedge D_2 \wedge (\alpha_1 \preceq \alpha_2 \to \alpha) \wedge C \end{array}}{C, \Gamma, e_1 e_2 : \alpha \vdash^{inf} D}$$

$$\text{(Let)}\quad \frac{\begin{array}{c} C_1, \Gamma, e : \alpha_1 \vdash^{inf} D_1 \quad (C_1, \alpha_1) \in \mathit{PartSol}(\Gamma, e) \\ D_1, \Gamma, \alpha_1 \vdash^{gen} (D_1', \sigma_1') \\ C_2, \Gamma_x.x : \sigma_1', e' : \alpha_2 \vdash^{inf} D_2 \quad (C_2, \alpha_2) \in \mathit{PartSol}(\Gamma_x.x : \sigma_1', e') \\ D = D_1' \wedge D_2 \wedge C \wedge (\alpha_2 \preceq \alpha) \end{array}}{C, \Gamma_x, \mathsf{let}\ x = e\,\mathsf{in}\ e' : \alpha \vdash^{inf} D}$$

$$(\exists\ \text{Intro})\quad \frac{C, \Gamma, e : \alpha \vdash^{inf} D \quad \bar{\alpha} \notin \mathit{fv}(\Gamma, \alpha)}{C, \Gamma, e : \alpha \vdash^{inf} \exists\bar{\alpha}.D}$$

Fig. 2. Constraint-Based Inference

3.1 A General Inference Scheme

The inference system is given in Figure 2. Inference clauses are of the form

$$C, \Gamma, e : \alpha \vdash^{inf} D$$

with constraint C, type environment Γ, expression e and type variable α as input values and constraint D as output value. Premises of inference clauses should be read as logical premises which need to be fulfilled in order to derive the conclusion. Note that input constraints are passed up in the inference tree whereas output constraints are passed down in the inference tree. We consider the inference tree to be up-side down with the root node at the bottom. Commonly, C constraints denote input constraints and D constraints denote output constraints. The inference rules preserve satisfiability of the output constraints. Therefore, satisfiability can be checked at any stage of the inference process at latest when reporting the result to the user.

All rules except ($\exists$ Intro) are syntax-directed. This rule allows us to hide some set of type variables and is justified by the logical typing rule ($\exists$ Intro) from Figure 1. Commonly, rule ($\exists$ Intro) is applied aggressively, so that useless variables do not appear in the final result.

The novelty of our formulation is that we allow *partial solutions* to be passed up in the inference tree in rules (Abs), (App) and (Let). As an example, we consider the standard Hindley/Milner system.

Example 3. We are given the following program:

$$e \quad = \quad \underbrace{(\lambda f.f\,3)}_{e_1}\underbrace{(\lambda x.x\,+\,1)}_{e_2}$$

Inference in style of algorithm $\mathcal{W}$ proceeds by inferring the type for the two subexpressions e_1 and e_2. We find $e_1 : (\mathsf{Int} \rightarrow \alpha) \rightarrow \alpha$ and $e_2 : \mathsf{Int} \rightarrow \mathsf{Int}$ where α is a new type variable. The final result for expression e is formed by generating the type constraint $(\mathsf{Int} \rightarrow \alpha) \rightarrow \alpha = (\mathsf{Int} \rightarrow \mathsf{Int}) \rightarrow \beta$ where β is a new type variable.

In contrast, inference in style of algorithm $\mathcal{M}$ carries a type constraint from the context of the expression. This imposes the constraint that expression e_1 must be a function type. Given the result $(\mathsf{Int} \rightarrow \alpha) \rightarrow \alpha$ for expression e_1, algorithm $\mathcal{M}$ imposes the constraint that $\mathsf{Int} \rightarrow \alpha$ must be a partial solution of the result of expression e_2.

We find that both algorithms yield the same result, however they differ in the way type information is propagated during type inference.

Given our constraint-based formulation of type inference, it immediately follows that there are a wide range of different inference algorithms possible. A discussion can be found in the following section.

First, we need to characterize all valid partial solutions we are allowed to pass up in the inference tree. To ensure completeness of inference, a partial solution must subsume all other possible solutions for a given typing context.

Definition 1 (Ordering Relation). *Given a typing problem* (Γ, e) *and constraints* C_1, C_2 *and types* τ_1, τ_2. $(C_1, \tau_1) \leq_\Gamma (C_2, \tau_2)$ *iff* $C_2 \models \bar{\exists} U.(C_1 \wedge (\tau_1 \preceq \tau_2))$ *where* $U = fv(C_2, \Gamma, \tau_2)$.

For a fixed typing problem (Γ, e), *we write* $(C_1, \tau_1) \leq (C_2, \tau_2)$ *for simplicity.*

The next lemma states that our ordering relation preserves solutions.

Lemma 1. *Given* $(C_1, \tau_1) \leq_\Gamma (C_2, \tau_2)$ *such that* $C_1, \Gamma \vdash e : \tau_1$ *is valid. Then* $C_2, \Gamma \vdash e : \tau_2$ *is valid as well.*

Definition 2 (Partial Solutions). *Given constraints* C *and* C', *types* τ *and* τ', *expression* e *and type environment* Γ. *Then,* $(C, \tau) \in PartSol(C', \Gamma \vdash e : \tau')$ *iff (1)* $C', \Gamma \vdash e : \tau'$ *is valid and there exists a constraint* D *such that (2)* $C \wedge D, \Gamma \vdash e : \tau$ *is valid and (3)* $(C \wedge D, \tau) \leq_\Gamma (C', \tau')$.

$(C, \tau) \in PartSol(C', \Gamma \vdash e : \sigma')$ *iff for each* τ' *if* $C' \vdash^i \sigma' \preceq \tau'$ *then* $(C, \tau) \in PartSol(C', \Gamma \vdash e : \tau')$.

$(C, \tau) \in PartSol(\Gamma, e)$ *iff* $(C, \tau) \in PartSol(C'', \Gamma \vdash e : \tau'')$ *for each* (C'', τ'').

Example 4. Consider expression $\lambda x.x + 1$ in Example 3. We immediately know that $((\alpha_1 = \alpha_2 \rightarrow \alpha_3), \alpha_1)$ is a partial solution.

Definition 3 (Partial Solutions and Context Information). *Given constraints* C_1, C *and* C', *types* τ_1, τ *and* τ', *expressions* e *and* e' *and type environments* Γ, Γ'. *Then,* $(C_1, \tau_1) \in PartSol(\Gamma', e' \mid \Gamma, e)$ *iff* $(C_1, \tau_1) \in PartSol(C', \Gamma' \vdash e' : \tau' \mid \Gamma, e)$ *for each* (C', τ').

$(C_1, \tau_1) \in PartSol(C', \Gamma' \vdash e' : \tau' \mid \Gamma, e)$ *iff* $(C_1, \tau_1) \in PartSol(C', \Gamma' \vdash e' : \tau')$ *and there exists a derivation with final judgment* $C'', \Gamma \vdash e : \tau''$ *for some constraint* C'' *and type* τ'' *such that judgment* $C', \Gamma' \vdash e' : \tau'$ *appears in an intermediate step.*

Example 5. In Example 3, the expression e_1 has $((\alpha_1 = \alpha_2 \rightarrow \alpha_3), \alpha_1)$ as a partial solution given the context information $e_1 e_2$.

To ensure soundness, we need to generate constraints $(\alpha_1 \rightarrow \alpha_2 \preceq \alpha)$ (in case of the (Abs) rule), $(\alpha_1 \preceq \alpha_2 \rightarrow \alpha)$ (App) and $(\alpha_2 \preceq \alpha)$ (Let) and pass these constraints down the inference tree. Note that these constraints might already be entailed by the propagated constraints, and therefore need not be generated again when forming the output constraints. In general, we assume that constraints can always be replaced by semantically equivalent constraints.

Quantification of type variables is tied to the (Let) rule. We need to introduce a generalization relation that yields the generalized type scheme and the generalized constraint. Given constraints $C, C_o \in \mathcal{S}$, a type environment Γ and types τ, σ_o. Then $C, \Gamma, \tau \vdash^{gen} (C_o, \sigma_o)$ iff $C_o \equiv \exists \bar{\alpha}.C \equiv C_1 \wedge \exists \bar{\alpha}.C_2$, $\sigma_o = \forall \bar{\alpha}.C_2 \Rightarrow \tau$, $\bar{\alpha} \notin fv(C_1, \Gamma)$ for some constraints C_1, C_2. Note that the above requirements can always be fulfilled by taking C_1 to be true. However, depending on the actual constraint system used, there might exist better strategies, which keep the constraint in the generalized type scheme smaller.

3.2 Soundness and Completeness Results

Soundness of inference is straightforward.

Theorem 1 (Soundness of Inference). *Given a type environment Γ, an expression e, two constraints C, D and a type variable α. If $C, \Gamma, e : \alpha \vdash^{inf} D$ then $D, \Gamma \vdash e : \alpha$ and $D \models C$.*

The completeness result is restricted to type schemes that have a type instance. We say σ is *realizable* in C if there exists a type τ such that $C \vdash^{i} \sigma \preceq \tau$. This extends to type environments.

Theorem 2 (Completeness of Inference). *Given $C', \Gamma \vdash e : \tau'$ such that Γ is realizable in C' and $(C, \alpha) \in PartSol(C', \Gamma \vdash e : \tau')$. Then $C, \Gamma, e : \alpha \vdash^{inf} D$ such that $C' \models \bar{\exists}_{\Gamma}.(D \wedge (\alpha \preceq \tau'))$ for some constraint D.*

3.3 Constraint Propagation Policies

$$(\text{Abs-}\mathcal{W})\ \frac{\begin{array}{c}\mathsf{true}, \Gamma_x.x : \alpha_1, e : \alpha_2 \vdash^{inf} D \\ D' = D \wedge (\alpha_1 \to \alpha_2 \preceq \alpha) \\ \alpha_1, \alpha_2 \text{ new}\end{array}}{\mathsf{true}, \Gamma_x, \lambda x.e : \alpha \vdash^{inf} D}$$

$$(\text{App-}\mathcal{W})\ \frac{\begin{array}{c}\mathsf{true}, \Gamma, e_1 : \alpha_1 \vdash^{inf} D_1 \\ \mathsf{true}, \Gamma, e_2 : \alpha_2 \vdash^{inf} D_2 \\ D = D_1 \wedge D_2 \wedge (\alpha_1 \preceq \alpha_2 \to \alpha) \\ \alpha_1, \alpha_2 \text{ new}\end{array}}{\mathsf{true}, \Gamma, e_1 e_2 : \alpha \vdash^{inf} D}$$

$$(\text{Abs-}\mathcal{M})\ \frac{\begin{array}{c}C', \Gamma_x.x : \alpha_1, e : \alpha_2 \vdash^{inf} D \\ C' = C \wedge (\alpha_1 \to \alpha_2 \preceq \alpha) \\ \alpha_1, \alpha_2 \text{ new}\end{array}}{C, \Gamma_x, \lambda x.e : \alpha \vdash^{inf} D}$$

$$(\text{App-}\mathcal{M})\ \frac{\begin{array}{c}C', \Gamma, e_1 : \alpha_1 \vdash^{inf} D_1 \\ C' = C \wedge (\alpha_1 \preceq \alpha_2 \to \alpha) \\ C'', \Gamma, e_2 : \alpha_2' \vdash^{inf} D_2 \\ C'' = D_1 \wedge (\alpha_2' \preceq \alpha_2) \\ \alpha_1, \alpha_2, \alpha_2' \text{ new}\end{array}}{C, \Gamma, e_1 e_2 : \alpha \vdash^{inf} D_2}$$

$$(\text{App-}\mathcal{M}')\ \frac{\begin{array}{c}C', \Gamma, e_1 : \alpha_1 \vdash^{inf} D_1 \\ C' = \exists \alpha', \alpha''.C \wedge (\alpha_1 \preceq \alpha' \to \alpha'') \\ \mathsf{true}, \Gamma, e_2 : \alpha_2 \vdash^{inf} D_2 \\ D = D_1 \wedge D_2 \wedge C \wedge \\ (\alpha_1 \preceq \alpha_2 \to \alpha) \\ \alpha_1, \alpha_2 \text{ new}\end{array}}{C, \Gamma, e_1 e_2 : \alpha \vdash^{inf} D}$$

$$(\text{App-}\mathcal{M}'')\ \frac{\begin{array}{c}\mathsf{true}, \Gamma, e_2 : \alpha_2 \vdash^{inf} D_1 \\ C', \Gamma, e_1 : \alpha_1 \vdash^{inf} D_2 \\ C' = D_1 \wedge C \wedge \\ (\alpha_1 \preceq \alpha_2 \to \alpha) \\ \alpha_1, \alpha_2 \text{ new}\end{array}}{C, \Gamma, e_1 e_2 : \alpha \vdash^{inf} D_2}$$

Fig. 3. Inference in $\mathcal{W}$ and $\mathcal{M}$ Style

In [LY00], Lee and Yi propose a generic scheme for inference algorithms for the standard Hindley/Milner system. It is straightforward to incorporate their inference algorithm scheme into our inference system. Note that in addition our inference scheme applies to a much wider range of Hindley/Milner style systems.

In Figure 3, rules (Abs-$\mathcal{W}$) and (App-$\mathcal{W}$) model inference in $\mathcal{W}$ style. Rules (Abs-$\mathcal{M}$) and (App-$\mathcal{M}$) model inference in $\mathcal{M}$ style. Note that the constraint ($\alpha_2' \preceq \alpha_2$) is essential for subtyping but could be omitted in the case of an HM(X) instance where $\preceq$ models type equality.

Our formulation allows for several variations of inference in $\mathcal{M}$ style. A more conservative propagation policy is formulated by rule (App-$\mathcal{M}'$). With the existential quantifier, we can hide any specific details of e_1's argument and function type. The only information that we propagate up the inference tree is that expression e_1 must be a function type. It is also possible to let information flow from the argument to the function site, see rule (App-$\mathcal{M}''$). This kind of constraint propagation policy does not seem to be covered in [LY00].

Soundness and completeness of inference can be re-established if the inference rules preserve partial solutions and generate a correct set of constraints. A proof can be found in the Appendix.

An alternative proof method would be proving a new inference algorithm correct wrt. a standard algorithm, i.e. for any given program both algorithms generate equivalent constraints. However, this method does not work well if we propagate typing information up in the inference tree. To ensure completeness, it is crucial to formally prove that the propagated typing information does not restrict the set of possible solutions.

4 Term-Based Inference

We consider inference for the term-based fragment of HM(X) where the set $\mathcal{S}$ of solved forms is possibly more restricted.

As observed by Kennedy, algorithm $\mathcal{W}$ is incomplete in case solutions to constraints (substitutions in his case) are represented in the language of types (or terms in our terminology).

We cite the following example given by Kennedy [Ken96]. He introduces a Hindley/Milner style system that deals with physical dimensions. In addition to the usual types there are dimension types. [1] We find the following type language:

$$\begin{array}{lll}\textbf{Dimensions} & d & ::= \alpha \mid i(d) \mid prod(d,d) \mid 1 \mid \mathrm{M} \mid \mathrm{T} \\ \textbf{Types} & \tau & ::= \alpha \mid \dim d \mid \tau \to \tau\end{array}$$

where the dimension constructor $i(\cdot)$ corresponds to the inverse of a dimension and $prod(\cdot,\cdot)$ to the product of two dimensions. Dimension constants are 1 for the unit measure, M for the mass dimension and T for the time dimension.

Example 6. Consider the following initial type environment:

$$\begin{array}{ll}\Gamma = \{ & kg : \dim \mathrm{M}, s : \dim \mathrm{T}, pair : \forall t_1, t_2 . t_1 \to t_2 \to (t_1, t_2) \\ & div : \forall d_1, d_2 . \dim prod(d_1, d_2) \to \dim d_1 \to \dim d_2 \}\end{array}$$

[1] Please note, we consider physical dimensions such as mass, time, length, etc. It would also be possible to consider unit types such as feet, meter and so on which are simply finer-grained versions of dimensions.

where kg and s are some basic dimensions, $pair$ is the pairing operator and div is a primitive operation on dimensions. Consider the program:

$$e \quad = \quad \lambda x.\mathsf{let}\ y = div\,x\ \mathsf{in}\ pair(y\,kg)(y\,s)$$

Note that function y is applied to arguments of different type, hence must be polymorphic. Consider typing e under the type environment Γ. In an intermediate step we find:

$$\Gamma.x : \dim prod(d_1, d_2) \vdash div\,x : \dim d_1 \rightarrow \dim d_2 \tag{1}$$

It is not possible to quantify over the type variables d_1 and d_2 because d_1 and d_2 also appear in the type environment. Hence, we can not give function y a polymorphic type. This suggests that program e is not typable in the dimension type system. However, we can derive another type for $div\,x$ under the same type environment:

$$\Gamma.x : \dim prod(d_1, d_2) \vdash div\,x : \dim prod(d_1, d_3) \rightarrow \dim prod(i(d_3), d_2) \tag{2}$$

We have simply instantiated d_1 with $prod(d_1, d_3)$ and d_2 with $prod(i(d_3), d_2)$. Dimension types obey the laws of an Abelian group. For details we refer to [Ken96]. For instance, it holds that

$$\models (prod(prod(d_1, d_3), prod(i(d_3), d_2)) = prod(d_1, d_2))$$

This ensures that the type environment remains unchanged. However, it is now possible to quantify over the free type variable d_3 in typing judgment (2). Then program e becomes typable. We find that

$$\Gamma \vdash e : \forall d_1, d_2.\, \dim prod(d_1, d_2) \rightarrow \begin{array}{l}(\dim prod(i(\mathrm{M}), prod(d_1, d_2)),\\ \dim prod(i(\mathrm{T}), prod(d_1, d_2)))\end{array} \tag{3}$$

The above example shows that the standard substitution-based inference algorithm is incomplete. This can be fixed by switching to a constraint-based inference algorithm where substitutions are represented in the domain of constraints.

The dimension type system belongs to a class of systems where constraint solving relies on a unification-based approach. In addition to the inference rules in Figure 2 we introduce an additional term reconstruction step:

$$(\text{Normalize})\ \frac{C, \Gamma, e : \alpha \vdash^{inf} D \quad D' \wedge \phi = normalize(D)}{C, \Gamma, e : \alpha \vdash^{inf} D' \wedge \phi}$$

The above rule invokes a normalization function which returns the normalized constraint represented as a constraint and residual substitutions. We assume that rule (Normalize) is applied at latest in the final inference step. Note that substitutions are represented in the domain of constraints and not in the domain of types. This is crucial to circumvent problems such as demonstrated by Kennedy's example.

Results of this section directly follow from the results in Section 3, hence are independent of a specific constraint propagation policy. We explicitly switch from a constraint representation to a term representation, when presenting the result of inference.

Theorem 3 (Soundness of Inference). *Given an* HM(X) *type system instance where* X *satisfies the principal constraint property. Given a type environment* Γ, *an expression* e, *constraints* C, D', ψ', *a type variable* α *and* $C, \Gamma, e : \alpha \vdash^{inf} D' \wedge \psi'$. *Then* $D', \psi'\Gamma \vdash e : \psi'(\alpha)$.

Term-based inference computes principal types if minimal term solutions (i.e. principal normal forms) exist.

Given an instance $\mathcal{X}$ of the HM(X) type system. $\mathcal{X}$ satisfies the *principal type property* iff the following holds: Given a pair (Γ, e) such that $C', \Gamma \vdash e : \sigma'$ for some constraint C' and type scheme σ'. Then there is a constraint C and a type scheme σ such that (1) $C, \Gamma \vdash e : \sigma$ and (2) Given $C', \Gamma \vdash e : \sigma'$ then $C' \models C$ and $C' \vdash^{i} \sigma \preceq \sigma'$.

The pair (C, σ) is called a *principal type*. Commonly, the constraint component equals true.

Theorem 4 (Principal Types). *Given an instance of the* HM(X) *system where* X *satisfies the principal constraint property. Given a closed typing judgment* $\mathsf{true}, \Gamma \vdash e : \sigma$ *where* Γ *is realizable in* true *and a fresh type variable* α. *Then, there exist constraints* D *and* ϕ *such that* $\mathsf{true}, \Gamma, e : \alpha \vdash^{inf} D \wedge \phi$, $C, \phi\Gamma, \phi(\alpha) \vdash^{gen} (\mathsf{true}, \sigma_o)$ *and* $\vdash^{i} \sigma_o \preceq \sigma$ *for some type scheme* σ_o.

Note that this is a straightforward extension of the notion of principal types found in the Hindley/Milner system. In the standard Hindley/Milner system, principality states there is one unique type (a principal type) from which all other types can be generated (by building generic instances). In contrast, a principal type in HM(X) represents rather a class of types which are semantically equivalent.

Example 7. Consider the program $\lambda x.x$ in a variation of the Hindley/Milner system where the set of solved forms equals all satisfiable constraints. One obvious principal type would be $\sigma_1 = \forall \alpha.\alpha \to \alpha$. However, the type $\sigma_2 = \forall \alpha, \beta.(\alpha = \beta) \Rightarrow \alpha \to \beta$ would be another possible candidate. It holds that $\mathsf{true}, \emptyset \vdash \lambda x.x : \sigma_1$ and $\mathsf{true}, \emptyset \vdash \lambda x.x : \sigma_2$ and $\vdash^{i} \sigma_1 \preceq \sigma_2$ but also $\vdash^{i} \sigma_2 \preceq \sigma_1$. This shows there is no unique principal type in a variation of the Hindley/Milner type system where the set of solved forms equals all satisfiable constraints.

A unique principal type can be computed if principal normal forms are syntactically unique. It is straightforward to prove that principal normal forms are syntactically unique if for each constraint $C \in \mathcal{S}$ there is no other constraint $D \in \mathcal{S}$ such that C and D are semantically equivalent.

Finally, we come back to Kennedy's example.

Example 8. The theory of dimension types possesses most general unifiers, see [LBB84]. In case of dimension types we are faced with the problem of having several different term representations of a type for a given term under the same type environment, see judgments (1) and (2) in Example 6. Both judgments have the same information content but a different syntactic representation. The inference algorithm simply picks the wrong syntactic representation and gets stuck.

If we allow dimension types to appear in constraint form, we find the following variation of typing judgment (1):

$$(\alpha = prod(d_1, d_2)), \Gamma.x : \alpha \vdash div\, x : \dim d_1 \to \dim d_2.$$

If we unify with the constraint $(\alpha = \mathit{prod}(d_1, d_2))$ we would obtain judgment (1) again. The representation of substitutions in constraint form leaves type variables d_1 and d_2 free in the type environment. Hence, we can quantify over these type variables. The function y has now the desired polymorphic type $\forall d_1, d_2.(\alpha = \mathit{prod}(d_1, d_2)) \Rightarrow \dim d_1 \rightarrow \dim d_2$. The following typing judgment is a variation of judgment (3):

$$\begin{array}{l}(\alpha = \mathit{prod}(d_1', d_2')) \wedge (d_1' = \mathrm{M}) \wedge (d_2' = \beta)\wedge \\ (\alpha = \mathit{prod}(d_1'', d_2'')) \wedge (d_1'' = \mathrm{T}) \wedge (d_2'' = \gamma)\end{array}, \Gamma \vdash e : \dim \alpha \rightarrow (\dim \beta, \dim \gamma)$$

Unification would result in judgment (3).

5 Conclusion

We have showed how to extend and combine the approaches of Odersky *et al.* [OSW99] and Lee and Yi [LY98]. Our motivation was to provide a flexible and general Hindley/Milner inference system which allows us to separate the essential components of type inference: Constraint generation, constraint solving, constraint propagation, constraint simplification and term reconstruction.

The main idea of our approach was to represent all typing information in the domain of constraints. We believe that issues such as syntactic representation forms of types are important for user interaction but are irrelevant when performing type inference. In particular, our constraint-based formulation of type inference leads to a natural solution of the problem pointed out by Kennedy. We could improve the inference results in [OSW99] and can finally state that the principal types property implies principal types (see Theorem 4).

Our constraint-based formulation of type inference has also proved to be useful when considering different inference algorithms such as $\mathcal{W}$ and $\mathcal{M}$. We gave an axiomatic description of sound and complete constraint generation/propagation policies which improves work by Lee and Yi [LY00].

In this work, we focussed on the abstract inference framework. We believe that our general inference scheme makes it easier to design new Hindley/Milner style inference algorithms and furthermore allows to re-establish corresponding soundness and completeness results in a uniform and concise way.

There are many possible avenues for future research. We consider it particularly interesting to apply our inference scheme to type-based program analyses.

Acknowledgments

This work gained from fruitful discussions with Kevin Glynn, Peter Stuckey, Harald Søndergaard, Kwangkeun Yi and Christoph Zenger. Thanks goes also to the anonymous referres for their valuable feedback. In particular, I would like to thank Martin Müller for stimulating discussions about HM(X). He also contributed to the observation to separate the different type inference phases. Parts of this work were carried out while the author was at Yale University supported by DARPA Grant F30602-96-2-0232.

References

[AW93] A. Aiken and E. L. Wimmers. Type inclusion constraints and type inference. In *FPCA '93: Conference on Functional Programming Languages and Computer Architecture, Copenhagen, Denmark*, pages 31–41, New York, June 1993. ACM Press.

[Dam85] L. Damas. *Type Assignment in Programming Languages*. PhD thesis, Edinburgh University, 1985.

[DHM95] D. Dussart, F. Henglein, and C. Mossin. Polymorphic recursion and subtype qualifications: Polymorphic binding-time analysis in polynomial time. In A. Mycroft, editor, *Proc. Second Int. Symp. Static Analysis*, volume 983 of *Lecture Notes in Computer Science*, pages 118–135. Springer-Verlag, 1995.

[DM82] L. Damas and R. Milner. Principal type-schemes for functional programs. In *Conference Record of the Ninth Annual ACM Symposium on Principles of Programming Languages*, pages 207–212. ACM, ACM, January 1982.

[Ken96] A. J. Kennedy. Type inference and equational theories. Technical Report LIX/RR/96/09, LIX, Ecole Polytechnique, 91128 Palaiseau Cedex, France, September 1996.

[LBB84] D. S. Lankford, G. Butler, and B. Brady. Abelian group unification algorithms for elementary terms. In W. Bledsoe and W. Loveland, editors, *Automated Theorem Proving: After 25 Years*. AMS, 1984.

[LY98] O. Lee and K. Yi. Proofs about a folklore let-polymorphic type inference algorithm. *ACM Transactions on Programming Languages and Systems*, 20(4):707–723, 1998.

[LY00] O. Lee and K. Yi. A generalized let-polymorphic type inference algorithm. Technical Memorandum ROPAS-2000-5, Research on Program Analysis System, Korea Advanced Institute of Science and Technology, March 2000.

[Mil78] R. Milner. A theory of type polymorphism in programming. *Journal of Computer and System Sciences*, 17:348–375, Dec 1978.

[NP95] T. Nipkow and C. Prehofer. Type reconstruction for type classes. *Journal of Functional Programming*, 5(2):201–224, 1995.

[Oho95] A. Ohori. A polymorphic record calculus and its compilation. *ACM TOPLAS*, 6(6):805–843, November 1995.

[OSW99] M. Odersky, M. Sulzmann, and M Wehr. Type inference with constrained types. *Theory and Practice of Object Systems*, 5(1):35–55, 1999.

[Rém92] D. Rémy. Extending ML type system with a sorted equational theory. Technical Report 1766, INRIA, October 1992.

[Sul00a] M. Sulzmann. *A General Framework for Hindley/Milner Type Systems with Constraints*. PhD thesis, Yale University, Department of Computer Science, May 2000.

[Sul00b] M. Sulzmann. A general type inference framework for Hindley/Milner style systems. Technical report, Dept. of Computer Science and Software Engineering, The University of Melbourne, 2000. URL: *http://www.cs.mu.oz.au/ sulzmann/publications/inference.ps*.

A Basic Lemmas

The following lemmas are used in the correctness proof of inference in $\mathcal{M}$ style. Proofs are straightforward by induction over the derivation $\vdash$.

We say a subsitution ϕ is *consistent* in Γ if for each $(x : \sigma) \in \Gamma$ the constraint component in $\phi\sigma$ is satisfiable.

Lemma 2 (Substitution). *Given $C, \Gamma \vdash e : \tau$ and a substitution ϕ such that ϕC is satisfiable and ϕ is consistent in Γ. Then $\phi C, \phi\Gamma \vdash e : \phi\tau$.*

Lemma 3 (Weakening). *Given $C, \Gamma \vdash e : \tau$ and a constraint D such that $C \wedge D$ is satisfiable. Then $C \wedge D, \Gamma \vdash e : \tau$.*

Lemma 4 (Canonical). *Given $C, \Gamma \vdash e : \tau$. Then $C \wedge (\alpha = \tau), \Gamma \vdash e : \alpha$ where α is a new type variable.*

Lemma 5 (Replacement). *Given $C, \Gamma_x.x : \tau \vdash e : \tau'$. Then $C \wedge (\alpha = \tau), \Gamma_x.x : \alpha \vdash e : \tau'$ where α is a new type variable.*

B Proof of Correctness of Inference in $\mathcal{M}$-style

We show that the inference rules in Figure 3 are correct, i.e. preserve partial solutions and generate a correct set of constraints. For simplicity, we only prove correctness of rules (Abs-$\mathcal{M}$) and (App-$\mathcal{M}$). The other proofs are similar.

An easy observation shows that rules (Abs-$\mathcal{M}$) and (App-$\mathcal{M}$) generate a correct set of constraints. It remains to prove that both rules preserve partial solutions. In case of the (Abs-$\mathcal{M}$) rule we find the following situation:

$$\frac{C', \Gamma_x.x : \alpha_1, e : \alpha_2 \vdash^{inf} D \quad C' = C \wedge (\alpha_1 \to \alpha_2 \preceq \alpha) \quad \alpha_1, \alpha_2 \text{ new}}{C, \Gamma_x, \lambda x.e : \alpha \vdash^{inf} D}$$

By assumption $(C, \alpha) \in \mathit{PartSol}(\Gamma_x, \lambda x.e)$. We have to show that $(C \wedge (\alpha_1 \to \alpha_2 \preceq \alpha), \alpha_2) \in \mathit{PartSol}(\Gamma_x.x : \alpha_1, e)$.

By assumption we have the following (normalized) derivation

$$\frac{\dfrac{C \wedge D, \Gamma_x.x : \tau_1 \vdash e : \tau_2}{C \wedge D, \Gamma_x \vdash \lambda x.e : \tau_1 \to \tau_2} \quad C \wedge D \models (\tau_1 \to \tau_2 \preceq \alpha)}{C \wedge D, \Gamma_x \vdash \lambda x.e : \alpha} \tag{4}$$

for some constraint D and types τ_1, τ_2. Application of the Weakening, Canonical and Replacement Lemmas (see Appendix A) yields $C \wedge (\alpha_1 \to \alpha_2 \preceq \alpha) \wedge (\alpha_1 = \tau_1) \wedge (\alpha_2 = \tau_2) \wedge D, \Gamma_x.x : \alpha_1 \vdash e : \alpha_2$. This shows part (2) of the definition of partial solutions.

For part (3), we assume given a valid $C', \Gamma_x.x : \alpha_1 \vdash e : \tau'$. We can derive that $C', \Gamma_x \vdash \lambda x.e : \alpha_1 \to \tau'$. (C, α) is a partial solution. We find that $C' \models \bar{\exists} U'.(C \wedge D \wedge (\alpha \preceq \alpha_1 \to \tau'))$ where $U' = \mathit{fv}(\Gamma_x, C', \alpha_1 \to \tau')$. From 4 we have that $C \wedge D \models (\tau_1 \to \tau_2 \preceq \alpha)$. We conclude that $C' \models \bar{\exists} U'.(\alpha_1 = \tau_1)$. We maintain that every solution to α_1 in C' must consist of τ_1.

Starting from $C', \Gamma_x.x : \alpha_1 \vdash e : \tau'$ we can derive (by application of the Substitution Lemma) $[\tau_1/\alpha_1]C', \Gamma_x \vdash \lambda x.e : \tau_1 \to [\tau_1/\alpha_1]\tau'$. Note that the constraint $[\tau_1/\alpha_1]C'$ is satisfiable. (C, α) is a partial solution. We find that $[\tau_1/\alpha_1]C' \models \bar{\exists} U''.C \wedge D \wedge (\alpha \preceq \tau_1 \to [\tau_1/\alpha_1]\tau')$ where $U'' = \mathit{fv}(\Gamma_x, [\tau_1 \alpha_1]C', \tau_1 \to [\tau_1/\alpha_1]\tau')$. We can conclude that $[\tau_1/\alpha_1]C' \models \bar{\exists} U.(C \wedge (\tau_1 \to \tau_2 \preceq \alpha) \wedge D \wedge (\tau_2 \preceq [\tau_1/\alpha_1]\tau'))$ where $U = \mathit{fv}(\Gamma_x.x : \alpha_1, C', \tau')$. Note that $[\tau_1/\alpha_1]C' \models \bar{\exists} U.(C \wedge (\tau_1 \to \tau_2 \preceq \alpha) \wedge D \wedge (\tau_2 \preceq [\tau_1/\alpha_1]\tau'))$ iff $C' \models \bar{\exists} U.(C \wedge (\alpha_1 \to \alpha_2 \preceq \alpha) \wedge (\alpha_1 = \tau_1) \wedge (\alpha_2 =$

$\tau_2) \wedge D \wedge (\alpha_2 \preceq \tau'))$ because every solution to α_1 in C' must consist of τ_1, i.e. for every τ_1' we have that $[\tau_1'/\alpha_1]C' \models [[\bar{\tau}/\bar{\alpha}]\tau_1/\alpha_1]C'$ for some types $\bar{\tau}$ and type variables $\bar{\alpha}$. We established the left part of the iff therefore the right part holds as well, i.e. we can establish part (3) in the definition of partial solutions. This concludes the correctness proof for rule (Abs-$\mathcal{M}$).

In case of rule (App-$\mathcal{M}$) we find the following situation:

$$\frac{C', \Gamma, e_1 : \alpha_1 \vdash^{inf} D_1 \quad C' = C \wedge (\alpha_1 \preceq \alpha_2 \to \alpha) \quad C', \Gamma, e_2 : \alpha_2' \vdash^{inf} D_2 \quad C'' = D_1 \wedge (\alpha_2' \preceq \alpha_2) \quad \alpha_1, \alpha_2, \alpha_2' \text{ new}}{C, \Gamma, e_1 e_2 : \alpha \vdash^{inf} D_2}$$

By assumption $(C, \alpha) \in \mathit{PartSol}(\Gamma, e_1 e_2)$. First, we show that $(C \wedge (\alpha_1 \preceq \alpha_2 \to \alpha), \alpha_1) \in \mathit{PartSol}(\Gamma, e_1 \mid \Gamma, e_1 e_2)$.

We assume we are given $C', \Gamma \vdash e_1 : \tau'$. The context information enforces that we have the following (normalized) derivation

$$\frac{C', \Gamma \vdash e_1 : \tau' \quad C', \Gamma \vdash e_2 : \tau_1' \quad C' \models (\tau' \preceq \tau_1' \to \tau_2')}{C', \Gamma \vdash e_1 e_2 : \tau_2'}$$

(C, α) is a partial solution. We find that $C' \models \bar{\exists} U'.(C \wedge D \wedge (\alpha \preceq \tau_2'))$ where $U' = \mathit{fv}(\Gamma, C', \tau_2')$. This ensures that $C' \wedge C$ is satisfiable. Weakening yields $C' \wedge C, \Gamma \vdash e_1 : \tau'$. From that we obtain $C \wedge (\alpha_1 \preceq \alpha_2 \to \alpha) \wedge C' \wedge (\alpha_1 = \tau') \wedge (\alpha_2 = \tau_1') \wedge (\alpha \preceq \tau_2'), \Gamma \vdash e_1 : \alpha_1$ which establishes part (2).

Part (3) follows straightforwardly. We have that

$$C' \models \bar{\exists} U.(C \wedge (\alpha_1 \preceq \alpha_2 \to \alpha) \wedge C' \wedge (\alpha_1 = \tau') \wedge (\alpha_2 = \tau_1') \wedge (\alpha \preceq \tau_2') \wedge (\alpha_1 \preceq \tau'))$$

where $U = \mathit{fv}(\Gamma, C', \tau')$.

It remains to prove that $(D_1 \wedge (\alpha_2' \preceq \alpha_2), \alpha_2') \in \mathit{PartSol}(\Gamma, e_2 \mid \Gamma, e_1 e_2)$. We assume we are given $C', \Gamma \vdash e_2 : \tau_1'$. The context information enforces that we have the following (normalized) derivation

$$\frac{C', \Gamma \vdash e_1 : \tau' \quad C', \Gamma \vdash e_2 : \tau_1' \quad C' \models (\tau' \preceq \tau_1' \to \tau_2')}{C', \Gamma \vdash e_1 e_2 : \tau_2'}$$

Then, we can derive that $D_1 \wedge (\alpha_2' \preceq \alpha_2) \wedge C' \wedge (\alpha_2' = \tau_1'), \Gamma \vdash e : \alpha_2'$. By induction we assume that all inference nodes above preserve partial solutions. Hence, we can apply the inference result (completeness) and obtain $C' \models \bar{\exists} \Gamma.(D_1 \wedge (\alpha_1 \preceq \tau'))$. Finally, we can conclude that $C' \models \bar{\exists} U.(D_1 \wedge (\alpha_2' \preceq \alpha_2) \wedge C' \wedge (\alpha_2' = \tau_1') \wedge (\alpha_2' \preceq \tau_1'))$ where $U = \mathit{fv}(\Gamma, C', \tau_1')$ and we are done.

Monadic Encapsulation with Stack of Regions

Koji KAGAWA

RISE, Kagawa University
2217-20 Hayashi-cho, Takamatsu 761-0396, JAPAN
kagawa@eng.kagawa-u.ac.jp

Abstract. Many modern programming languages use garbage collection for the sake of reliability and productivity. On the other hand, garbage collection causes several difficulties in some situations, for example, in real-time systems.
Tofte and Talpin's region and effect system for ML infers lifetime of objects at compile time and makes it possible to reclaim memory safely without using garbage collectors at run time. Programmers do not have to provide any explicit directives about lifetime of objects. However, it is sometimes necessary for programmers to transform programs specially in order to make the system infer as they intend. As a result, programmers have to know, to some extent, how the system infers about regions.
In this paper, we introduce a type system for an ML-like language which also aims for compile-time lifetime inference. It, however, lets programmers delimit lifetime of objects explicitly and makes the system check the correctness of programmers' directives.

1 Introduction

Most functional languages such as ML and Haskell, and many object-oriented languages such as Smalltalk and Java use garbage collection to reclaim memory automatically. Programmers are freed from worry about memory management and they can enjoy more safety and productivity than in conventional languages such as C. On the other hand, garbage collection causes several difficulties in real-time systems and very small systems, since it is difficult for us to predict execution time of particular parts of programs and since garbage collection requires certain amount of memory in order to be performed efficiently.

Tofte and Talpin's region and effect system for ML [8] is an alternative to run-time garbage collection. It *infers* lifetime of objects at compile time and makes it possible to reclaim memory safely without using garbage collectors at run time. Then, objects can be allocated in a stack (to be exact, in a stack of *regions*). The system uses an ordinary ML program as input, and annotates it with region operators such as **`letregion`** and **`at`**. Here, "**`letregion`** ρ **`in`** e" is a computation which allocates a new region ρ on top of the stack, computes e and then deallocates ρ, and "e **`at`** ρ" means that the result of e is allocated in region ρ. Programmers do not have to provide any explicit directives about lifetime of objects. It is sometimes necessary, however, for programmers to transform programs specially in order to make the system infer as they want. Therefore, programmers have to know, to some extent, how the system infers about regions.

The following example is reported in [7].

H. Kuchen and K. Ueda (Eds.): FLOPS 2001, LNCS 2024, pp. 264–279, 2001.

```
(* A *)
fun length ([], acc)      = acc
  | length (_::xs, acc) = length (xs, acc+1)

(* B *)
fun length l =
   let fun loop (p as ([], acc)) = p
         | loop (_::xs, acc) = loop (xs, acc+1)
   in snd (loop (l, 0)) end
```

If we define `length` as `(* A *)`, contrary to programmers' intention, every time `length` is called recursively, a new tuple for the argument is allocated in a new region. The stack size becomes proportional to the length of the list. On the other hand, in `length (* B *)`, a new region is not created for each recursive call thanks to "as" pattern in the second line. And a further analysis called *storage mode analysis* detects that even in-place updating of the tuple is possible. As a result, `length (* B *)` can be computed in a constant size of memory.

Instead of a system which infers all about regions automatically, it might be convenient to have a semi-automatic system which lets programmers delimit lifetime of objects explicitly and checks safety of such directives. This is what we want to propose here. In principle, such an explicit style would be possible in Tofte and Talpin's system by just allowing programmers to use region annotations explicitly. In practice, however, it would be difficult to do so, since region annotations tend to be lengthy and complex.

For example, the following program:

```
(let x = (2, 3) in λy. (fst x, y) end) 5
```

is region-annotated by Tofte and Talpin's system as follows [8]:

```
letregion ρ4, ρ5
in letregion ρ6
   in let x = (2 at ρ2, 3 at ρ6) at ρ4
      in (λy. (fst x, y) at ρ1) at ρ5
      end
   end
   5 at ρ3
end
```

There are too many annotations (**letregion** and **at**) about regions to be used explicitly by programmers. Moreover, type expressions may be also lengthy and complex.

On the other hand, Launchbury and Peyton Jones proposed a special construct **runST** [4] for Haskell, which encapsulates *stateful computations* in pure computations. "State" in Launchbury and Peyton Jones's terminology corresponds to "region" in Tofte and Talpin's. Semmelroth and Sabry [5] studied and formalized the connection between Launchbury and Peyton Jones's monadic state encapsulation and the region and effect system. They showed that monadic operators and **runST** can be used as "a cheap form of" region and effect system, that is, they can be used in order to delimit lifetime of objects in *call-by-value* functional languages. It is "cheap" because it can handle only a single region at a time and cannot handle stacks of regions like Tofte and Talpin's.

The system which will be proposed in this paper extends the system of monadic encapsulation of Semmelroth and Sabry. In addition to **`runST`**, which simply encapsulates the state, it provides an operator which *extends* the current state with a new region and makes a stack of regions. In most cases, programmers do not have to specify regions. Then, the current default region which is passed around implicitly is used. However, sometimes programmers want to access older regions instead of the current newest region. In such cases, programmers are able to explicitly specify the region. *Compositional references*, which the author proposed in [2] in order to manipulate general mutable data structures in Haskell, are used for this purpose. Our region actually corresponds to a set of regions of Tofte and Talpin's. A newer region contains older regions and there is a kind of a subtyping relation between old and new regions, which is helpful to keep type expressions simple. When our region primitive named **`letextend`** allocates a new region and makes it the default region, it passes to the inner expression a reference to the *old* default region. This is contrary to Tofte and Talpin's **`letregion`**, which passes to the expression a reference to the *newly* created region.

We do not discuss issues such as dynamic semantics and type safety of the proposed extension in this paper. Instead, we will mainly focus on type inference. One of the important points of Tofte and Talpin's system is type inference of recursive functions. Recursive functions must be given region polymorphic types in order for the system to be practical. In general, however, ML-style type inference algorithm cannot infer the most general type for polymorphic recursion. Tofte and Talpin's system treats region parameters in a special way to deal with polymorphic recursion. However, since our system treats regions explicitly and shows information about regions to programmers as a part of type expressions, it is not natural to treat regions specially in type inference. Therefore, in our system, regions and effects are not distinguished from ordinary type parameters in type inference of recursive functions. We will present another way of inferring types of recursive functions when polymorphic recursion is necessary.

2 Our Language

In this section, we present our language which is basically a variant of EML (Encapsulated ML) of Semmelroth and Sabry [5]. We, however, choose a simpler form. For example, **`let`**-binding is restricted to values.

Our language is a call-by-value functional language and its syntax and type system are shown in Figure 1. Here, an overline (*e.g.* $\overline{\alpha}$) is a sequence of something, $FV(\tau)$ means *free variables* of τ as usual and $\sigma \succ \tau$ means "σ instantiates to τ."

In these rules, the type expression after "!" is *the effect* of the expression. We use a notational convention here that if an expression does not have any effects, this effect is written as underscore (_) (as in (Var) and (Lambda) rules and in the premise of (Let) rule) meaning a fresh variable. This convention is analogous to the use of underscore in pattern matching in many functional languages. We will refer to the typing rule for recursive definitions (LetRec) later.

$$
\begin{array}{lll}
v \in \mathit{Value} & v & ::= x \mid \lambda x \to e \\
x \in \mathit{Id} & & \\
e \in \mathit{Expr} & e & ::= v \mid e\,e' \mid \texttt{let}\ x = e\ \texttt{in}\ e' \mid \texttt{encap}\ e \\
 & & \quad \mid \texttt{letrec}\ x = e\ \texttt{in}\ e' \mid \texttt{letextend}\ x\ \texttt{in}\ e \mid e\ \texttt{at}\ e'
\end{array}
$$

$$
\begin{array}{lll}
m \in \mathit{Effect} & m & ::= \alpha \mid \mathtt{ST}\ \tau \\
\tau \in \mathit{Type} & \tau & ::= \alpha \mid \tau \xrightarrow{m} \tau' \mid \mathtt{Ta}\ \tau\ \tau' \\
\alpha \in \mathit{TypeVar} & & \\
\pi \in \mathit{TypeWithEff} & \pi & ::= \tau\,!\,m
\end{array}
$$

$$
\sigma \in \mathit{TypeScheme} \quad \sigma ::= \tau \mid \forall\overline{\alpha}.\,\tau
$$

$$
\frac{x :: \sigma \in \Gamma \quad \sigma \succ \tau}{\Gamma \vdash x :: \tau\,!\,\_}\ (\text{Var}) \qquad \frac{\Gamma \vdash e_1 :: (\tau_1 \xrightarrow{m} \tau_2)\,!\,m \quad \Gamma \vdash e_2 :: \tau_1\,!\,m}{\Gamma \vdash e_1\,e_2 :: \tau_2\,!\,m}\ (\text{App})
$$

$$
\frac{\Gamma, x :: \tau_1 \vdash e :: \tau_2\,!\,m}{\Gamma \vdash \lambda x \to e :: (\tau_1 \xrightarrow{m} \tau_2)\,!\,\_}\ (\text{Lambda})
$$

$$
\frac{\Gamma \vdash e_1 :: \tau_1\,!\,\_ \ \ (e_1 : \text{value}) \quad \Gamma, x :: \forall\overline{\alpha}.\,\tau_1 \vdash e_2 :: \tau_2\,!\,m \quad (\overline{\alpha} = \mathit{FV}(\tau) \setminus \mathit{FV}(\Gamma))}{\Gamma \vdash \texttt{let}\ x = e_1\ \texttt{in}\ e_2 :: \tau_2\,!\,m}\ (\text{Let})
$$

$$
\frac{\Gamma \vdash e :: \tau\,!\,\mathtt{ST}\ s \quad s \notin \mathit{FV}(\Gamma) \cup \mathit{FV}(\tau)}{\Gamma \vdash \texttt{encap}\ e :: \tau\,!\,\_}\ (\text{Encap})
$$

Fig. 1. Typing Rules

(Encap) explains the encapsulation construct which corresponds to Launchbury and Peyton Jones's **`runST`**. Usually, **`encap`** is used with the primitive operators on ML-style references:

$$
\begin{array}{lll}
\mathtt{ref} & :: & \tau \xrightarrow{\mathtt{ST}\ s} \mathtt{Ref}\ s\ \tau \\
\mathtt{deref} & :: & \mathtt{Ref}\ s\ \tau \xrightarrow{\mathtt{ST}\ s} \tau \\
\mathtt{setref} & :: & \mathtt{Ref}\ s\ \tau \xrightarrow{\_} \tau \xrightarrow{\mathtt{ST}\ s} \mathtt{Unit}
\end{array}
$$

In this paper, however, in-place updating is not a main topic and we introduce other primitives later. It would be straightforward to add in-place updating to our proposal, though.

As a generalization of **`encap`**, we introduce a new operator **`letextend`** which also has a special typing rule:

$$
\frac{\Gamma, x :: \mathtt{Ta}\ s\ t \vdash e :: \tau\,!\,\mathtt{ST}\ s \quad s \notin \mathit{FV}(\Gamma) \cup \mathit{FV}(\tau\,!\,\mathtt{ST}\ t)}{\Gamma \vdash \texttt{letextend}\ x\ \texttt{in}\ e :: \tau\,!\,\mathtt{ST}\ t}\ (\text{Letextend})
$$

A condition similar to **`encap`** should hold for s and τ. Intuitively, s is a region which extends a region t. In **`letextend`** x **`in`** e, though e is computed using the region s, s is not visible from outside and the expression behaves as a computation on the region t. Objects allocated in $s \setminus t$ become unnecessary and get reclaimed when the execution of **`letextend`** x **`in`** e is finished.

For example,

```
letextend x in var a = newArray n 0 in
                   foo a
```

An array a is allocated in the new region created by **letextend** (new objects are allocated in the newest region by default), used in foo and is reclaimed after the evaluation of **letextend** ... is finished. (Here, we use **var** $v = e_1$ **in** e_2 as a shorthand for $(\lambda v \rightarrow e_2)\ e_1$. Since **let** is restricted to values in our language, we cannot write **let** $v = e_1$ **in** e_2 when e_1 is a computation.)

Though x is not used in the example above, it is bound to a reference to old region which was active just before **letregion** ... is executed. Ta is the type constructor for compositional references. Compositional references are abstract data which represent (the position of) an inner object relative to some base object. If the type of the inner object is t and the type of the base object is s, the type of the compositional reference is Ta s t. (Ta s t reads "t at region s." Ta s t is written as Mut s t in [2]. We use a new name Ta, since it seems Mut(able) is not an appropriate name here — it is only used in order to associate objects with regions.)

At a glance, **letextend** resembles Tofte and Talpin's **letregion**, however, note that the value given to the variable of **letextend** (*e.g.* x in the above example) points to the old region instead of the new region.

Another new primitive for compositional references is **at**:

$$\frac{\Gamma \vdash e_1 :: \mathtt{Ta}\ s\ t\ !\ \mathtt{ST}\ s \quad \Gamma \vdash e_2 :: \tau\ !\ \mathtt{ST}\ t}{\Gamma \vdash e_2\ \mathbf{at}\ e_1 :: \tau\ !\ \mathtt{ST}\ s}\ \text{(At)}$$

"e_2 **at** e_1" intuitively means that e_2 is computed in the region whose position is given by e_1. Though we use the same name as Tofte and Talpin's operator, its meaning is slightly different. Our **at** may be used even when e_2 is not a constructor application as is shown soon later. The construct **at** corresponds to appR in [2]. We use **at** when we want to take $\tau\ !\ \mathtt{ST}\ t$ — an expression using region t as $\tau\ !\ \mathtt{ST}\ s$ — an expression using region s where s is bigger than t. See [2] for details. Later, we will introduce a simple form of subtyping, in order to do without using **at** explicitly in most cases.

We give primitive functions for pairs and lists as follows.

$$\begin{array}{ll}
\mathtt{mkPair} & :: a \xrightarrow{-} b \xrightarrow{\mathtt{ST}\ s} \mathtt{Ta}\ s\ (a,\ b) \\
\mathtt{fst} & :: \mathtt{Ta}\ s\ (a,\ b) \xrightarrow{\mathtt{ST}\ s} a \\
\mathtt{snd} & :: \mathtt{Ta}\ s\ (a,\ b) \xrightarrow{\mathtt{ST}\ s} b
\end{array}$$

$$\begin{array}{ll}
\mathtt{nil} & :: \mathtt{Unit} \xrightarrow{\mathtt{ST}\ s} \mathtt{Ta}\ s\ (\mathtt{List}\ s\ a) \\
\mathtt{cons} & :: a \xrightarrow{-} \mathtt{Ta}\ s\ (\mathtt{List}\ s\ a) \xrightarrow{\mathtt{ST}\ s} \mathtt{Ta}\ s\ (\mathtt{List}\ s\ a) \\
\mathtt{isNull} & :: \mathtt{Ta}\ s\ (\mathtt{List}\ s\ a) \xrightarrow{\mathtt{ST}\ s} \mathtt{Bool} \\
\mathtt{head} & :: \mathtt{Ta}\ s\ (\mathtt{List}\ s\ a) \xrightarrow{\mathtt{ST}\ s} a \\
\mathtt{tail} & :: \mathtt{Ta}\ s\ (\mathtt{List}\ s\ a) \xrightarrow{\mathtt{ST}\ s} \mathtt{Ta}\ s\ (\mathtt{List}\ s\ a)
\end{array}$$

`Ta` s `(List` s a`)` is the type of lists allocated in region s. Since `List` is a recursive type constructor, `List` must have a region parameter s as one of its parameters. The following is the declaration of `List` written in the notation of Haskell.

```
data List s a = Cons a (Ta s (List s a)) | Nil
```

When we are computing on region s and a list is in region t where s includes t, we have to use a compositional reference and **at** to access the list as follows.

```
var xs = cons 1 (nil ()) in
letextend t in var x = head xs at t in ...
```

However, we will soon find that using **at** in this way is tedious and makes programs clumsy. Therefore, we introduce a kind of subtyping as follows.

$$
\begin{array}{lll}
\texttt{cons} & :: s \supset t \Rightarrow a \longrightarrow \texttt{Ta}\ t\ \texttt{(List}\ t\ a\texttt{)} \stackrel{\texttt{ST}\ s}{\longrightarrow} \texttt{Ta}\ t\ \texttt{(List}\ t\ a\texttt{)} \\
\texttt{isNull} & :: s \supset t \Rightarrow \texttt{Ta}\ t\ \texttt{(List}\ t\ a\texttt{)} \stackrel{\texttt{ST}\ s}{\longrightarrow} \texttt{Bool} \\
\texttt{head} & :: s \supset t \Rightarrow \texttt{Ta}\ t\ \texttt{(List}\ t\ a\texttt{)} \stackrel{\texttt{ST}\ s}{\longrightarrow} a \\
\texttt{tail} & :: s \supset t \Rightarrow \texttt{Ta}\ t\ \texttt{(List}\ t\ a\texttt{)} \stackrel{\texttt{ST}\ s}{\longrightarrow} \texttt{Ta}\ s\ \texttt{(List}\ s\ a\texttt{)}
\end{array}
$$

$$
\begin{array}{lll}
\texttt{fst} & :: s \supset t \Rightarrow \texttt{Ta}\ t\ (a,\ b) \stackrel{\texttt{ST}\ s}{\longrightarrow} a \\
\texttt{snd} & :: s \supset t \Rightarrow \texttt{Ta}\ t\ (a,\ b) \stackrel{\texttt{ST}\ s}{\longrightarrow} b
\end{array}
$$

Here, $s \supset t$ is a type constraint which means s is an extension of t. Then, **at** is inserted automatically where the constraint $s \supset t$ is used. Explicit use of **at** is rarely necessary. The type of **letextend** is changed accordingly.

$$
\frac{\Gamma, x :: \texttt{Ta}\ s\ t \vdash e :: P \Rightarrow \tau \,!\, \texttt{ST}\ s \quad s \notin FV(\Gamma) \cup FV(P' \Rightarrow \tau \,!\, \texttt{ST}\ t) \\ \{s \supset t\} + P' \Vdash P}{\Gamma \vdash \textbf{letextend}\ x\ \textbf{in}\ e :: P' \Rightarrow \tau \,!\, \texttt{ST}\ t}
$$

Here, $\Vdash$ is the standard entailment relation for subtyping constraints consisting of reflectivity and transitivity rules.

$$
\frac{\pi \in P}{P \Vdash \pi} \qquad \frac{}{P \Vdash s \supset s} \qquad \frac{P \Vdash s \supset t \quad P \Vdash t \supset u}{P \Vdash s \supset u}
$$

The typing rules for the other constructs are also changed straightforwardly in order to carry over type constraints.

3 Recursive Functions and `letextend`

Since **letextend** requires one of region parameters to be polymorphic, it is impossible for the ordinary ML-style type inference algorithm to infer the type of a recursive function which calls itself inside **letextend**.

It is well-known that type checking, instead of type inference, is possible even for *polymorphic recursion* as in the following rule.

$$\frac{\Gamma, x :: \forall\overline{\alpha}.\, P_1 \Rightarrow \tau_1 \vdash e_1 :: P_1 \Rightarrow \tau_1 \,!\, \_ \quad \Gamma, x :: \forall\overline{\alpha}.\, P_1 \Rightarrow \tau_1 \vdash e_2 :: P_2 \Rightarrow \tau_2 \,!\, m}{\Gamma \vdash \mathbf{letrec}\; x = e_1 \;\mathbf{in}\; e_2 :: P_2 \Rightarrow \tau_2 \,!\, m} \quad \text{(LetRec)}$$

(Here, we restrict e_1 to values.)

However, it would be a burden for programmers to explicitly give a type to every recursive function. It would be better if we could define recursive functions which use **letextend** without supplying their types explicitly.

Tofte and Birkedal's type inference algorithm [6] for polymorphic recursion (**letrec** $x = e_1$ **in** e_2) is summarized as follows.

- First, we infer the type of e_1 ignoring region parameters.
- Next, we give it the most general region type. That is, we use a fresh region variable everywhere a region parameter is required. Assuming that x has this very general type, we infer the type of e_1 again. If the type of x and the type of e_1 are identical, type inference is finished.
- If they are not identical, we assume that x has now the new type of e_1 and process e_1 again. And repeat this until the types of x and e_1 agree.

They proved that this iteration always terminates in their system.

This proof, however, depends on the properties characteristic to their system. Since, in their system, effects and regions are used only internally in the compiler, this approach seems feasible. However, in our system, effects and regions are explicit and they are shown to programmers as part of type expressions. It seems unnatural to treat region parameters specially in type inference.

Instead, we take another approach to type inference of recursive functions (**letrec** $x = e_1$ **in** e_2), which is roughly summarized as follows:

- When we check the condition of **encap** ($s \notin FV(\Gamma) \cup FV(\tau)$) and **letextend** ($s \notin FV(\Gamma) \cup FV(\tau \,!\, \mathrm{ST}\; t)$) in e_1, we do not take into account occurrences of the type variable s in the type of the **letrec**-bound variable x in the environment Γ. Instead, we just keep track of such occurrences. Such occurrences do not do harm, if later it is found that they can be replaced with a more generic type.
- When we unify the type of e_1 and x, we check whether the positions of the occurrences recorded in the above process can be made generic. We also check **encap** and **letextend** in e_1 again so that the region variable (s) to be confined does not appear free in the type environment (Γ) or the type of the result (τ).

That is, we postpone the check of the special condition of **encap** and **letextend** until the check of enclosing **letrec**'s. It is an ad-hoc extension of the usual ML-style type inference. However, it seems to work and is sufficient for our purpose. Our type inference algorithm *TC* is shown in Figure 2, 3 and 4. Letrec-bound variables are written as $x ::_r \tau$ and are distinguished from other variables written as $x ::_n \tau$ in the environment. Figure 5 shows auxiliary functions used in Figure 3 and 4.

The soundness of this algorithm with respect to the type system ($\vdash$) is shown by considering another type system ($\vdash'$). See the appendix (Section A) for the definition of $\vdash'$ and part of the proof of the soundness of *TC*.

TC takes an environment Γ and an expression e, and returns a triple of a substitution, a type expression and the third component that is explained soon later. Figure 2 shows type inference for variables, applications, λ-abstractions and **`let`**-expressions, which does not differ so much from ordinary type inference algorithm for ML except the third component of return values. Figure 3 explains type inference for **`encap`** and **`letextend`**. In type-checking **`encap`** and **`letextend`**, the region part of the type expression is assigned an expression $\kappa[\tau]$ — κ is a fresh *special type constructor*, and τ is a parameter representing its direct subregion (*i.e.*, $\kappa[\tau] \supset \tau$ holds). For technical reason, we define $FV(\kappa[\tau]) = \emptyset$ whatever the type expression τ is. This special constructor indicates that it must become generic type variable later. This is very similar to the use of *skolem* constructors in the theory of existential types [3]. $FS(\tau)$ means a set of such special constructors occurring in τ and $FSV(\tau)$ is defined as $FS(\tau) \cup FV(\tau)$. Furthermore, we keep track of free variables of the environment and the type in the third component (I) of the result of *TC* when type-checking **`encap`** and **`letextend`**. (Here I ranges over sets of pairs of a special constructor and a set of (free) variables and special constructors.) This is necessary because otherwise later in type-checking **`letrec`**, it is possible that such free variables be unified with type expressions containing κ. The type checking rule for **`letrec`** ensures that this does not happen.

In type-checking **`encap`** and **`letextend`**, if there exists some variable α such that $\alpha \supset \kappa[\tau] \in UP$, such α should be checked in the same way as $\kappa[\tau]$ so that it does not escape, though in order to keep the presentation simple, we do not make this explicit in the rules.

Figure 4 shows type inference for **`letrec`**-expression. First, we begin with replacing each occurrence of x with fresh variables $\{x_i\}$, for due to polymorphic recursion they might be instantiated to different types. Then x_i's are assigned types Sa_i which may contain special constructors. Before performing unification, we replace each occurrence of such special constructors (along with their parameters) in Sa_i with a fresh type variable and obtain σ_i. Let U be the most general unifier of σ_i and τ. Since $U\sigma_i = U\tau$ by definition of U, USa_i and $U\tau$ are almost the same except special constructors in Sa_i. Z_i maps variables in $U\tau$ to special constructors in Sa_i. Moreover, if there are variables in Sa_i that are unified with new variables in σ_i, they should also be mapped to special constructors. This mapping is done by Y. Y must be consistently defined for all i and should not affect variables in $FV(US\Gamma|_N) \cup FV(U\tau)$.

Note that Z_i and therefore Y_i are not substitutions in the usual sense, since they are not idempotent, that is, Z_i maps a variable v to a type expression containing v itself (*e.g.* $\kappa[v]$). The condition $\forall i.dom(Z_i) \subset FV(U\tau) \setminus FV(YUS\Gamma)$ means that special constructors that appear in the environment are actually thought of as instances of generic types. $\mathsf{OK}(\mathsf{AddVar}((YU \star I), \sigma))$ checks whether the condition of **`encap`** and **`letextend`** holds still true. The condition $Z_i v \supset v$ is necessary because otherwise the number of subtyping constraints of the type of the **`letrec`**-expression might increase in an unexpectable way due to polymorphic recursion.

$TC(\Gamma, x) =$

if $x ::_{\mathcal{L}} \forall\overline{\alpha}.P \Rightarrow \tau \in \Gamma$ ($\mathcal{L}$ can be either n or r) then $(Id, (P \Rightarrow \tau\,!\,\_)[\overline{t}/\overline{\alpha}], \emptyset)$ ($\overline{t}$: fresh)

$TC(\Gamma, e\,e') =$

let $(S, P \Rightarrow \tau\,!\,m, I) = TC(\Gamma, e)$

$(S', P' \Rightarrow \tau'\,!\,m', I') = TC(S\Gamma, e')$

μ and β are new type variables.

$U = mgu(\{S'\tau, \tau' \xrightarrow{\mu} \beta\})$

$U' = mgu(\{US'm, Um', \mu\}) \cdot U$

in $(U'S'S, U'(S'P \cup P' \Rightarrow \beta\,!\,\mu), U' \star ((S' \star I) \cup I'))$

$TC(\Gamma, \lambda x \to e) =$

let β is a new type variable.

$(S, P \Rightarrow \tau\,!\,m, I) = TC(\Gamma + \{x ::_n \beta\}, e)$

in $(S,\ P \Rightarrow S\beta \xrightarrow{m} \tau\,!\,\_,\ I)$

$TC(\Gamma, \mathbf{let}\ x = e\ \mathbf{in}\ e') =$

let $(S, P \Rightarrow \tau\,!\,\_, I) = TC(\Gamma, e)$

$(S', P' \Rightarrow \tau'\,!\,m, I') = TC(S\Gamma + \{x ::_n gen(S\Gamma, P \Rightarrow \tau)\}, e')$

in $(S'S, P' \Rightarrow \tau'\,!\,m, (S' \star I) \cup I')$

Fig. 2. Type Inference Algorithm (Part 1)

$TC(\Gamma, \textbf{encap}\, e) =$

$\texttt{let}\quad (S, P \Rightarrow \tau \,!\, m, I) = TC(\Gamma, e)$

$\qquad U = mgu(\{\tau \,!\, m, a \,!\, \mathrm{ST}\ (\kappa[\texttt{Unit}])\})$

$\qquad$ (κ is a new special constructor, and a is a new type variable.)

$\qquad P' = \mathsf{Simplify}(UP, \{\kappa[\texttt{Unit}] \supset \texttt{Unit}\})$

$\texttt{if}\quad \kappa \notin FS(P' \Rightarrow Ua) \cup FS(US\Gamma|_N)$

$\texttt{then}\ (US,\ P' \Rightarrow U\ a \,!\, \_),$

$\qquad (U \star I) \cup \{(\kappa, FSV(P' \Rightarrow Ua) \cup FSV(US\Gamma|_N))\})$

$TC(\Gamma, \textbf{letextend}\, x\ \textbf{in}\, e) =$

$\texttt{let}\quad (S, P \Rightarrow \tau \,!\, m, I) = TC(\Gamma + \{x :: \mathrm{Ta}\ (\kappa[t])\ t\}, e)$

$\qquad U = mgu(\{\tau \,!\, m, a \,!\, \mathrm{ST}\ (\kappa[t])\})$

$\qquad$ (κ is a new special constructor, a and t are new type variables.)

$\qquad P' = \mathsf{Simplify}(UP, \{U(\kappa[t]) \supset Ut\})$

$\qquad \tau = P' \Rightarrow U(a \,!\, \mathrm{ST}\, t)\ \ \texttt{in}$

$\texttt{if}\quad \kappa \notin FS(\tau) \cup FS(US\Gamma|_N)$

$\texttt{then}\ (US,\ \tau,\ (U \star I) \cup \{(\kappa, FSV(\tau) \cup FSV(US\Gamma|_N))\})$

Fig. 3. Type Inference Algorithm (Part 2)

$TC(\Gamma, \texttt{letrec}\ x = e\ \texttt{in}\ e') =$

`let` e^* is an expression obtained by replacing each occurrence of x in e by a new variable x_i. (*i.e.* $e = e^*[x/x_i]$)

$(S, Q \Rightarrow \tau\ !\ \_, I) = TC(\Gamma + \bigcup_{i=1}^{n} \{x_i ::_r a_i\}, e^*)$

where a_i is a new type variable.

σ_i is a type expression obtained by replacing each occurrence of applications of special constructors in Sa_i with a new variable.

i.e. $\exists\ B_i.\ B_i\sigma_i = Sa_i$

$U = mgu(\bigcup_{i=1}^{n} \{\sigma_i\} \cup \{\tau\})$

Z_i is a substitution $s.t.$ $Z_iU = B_i$ on $dom(B_i)$

$Y_i = Z_i|_{FV(USa_i)}$ and $Y = \oplus_{i=1}^{n} Y_i$

(Y_i's must be all disjoint. Also note that $YUSa_i = Z_iU\tau$)

$\sigma = gen(YUS\Gamma, U(Q \Rightarrow \tau))$ `in`

`if` $\forall i.dom(Z_i) \subset FV(U\tau) \setminus FV(YUS\Gamma)$

`and` $dom(Y) \cap (FV(US\Gamma|_N) \cup FV(U\tau)) = \emptyset$

`and` $\mathsf{OK}(\mathsf{AddVar}((YU \star I), \sigma))$ `and` $\forall i.\ \forall v \in dom(Z_i).\ Z_iv \supset v$

`then let` $(S', \tau', I') = TC(YUS\Gamma + \{x ::_n \sigma\}, e')$ `in`

$(S'YUS,\ \tau',\ S' \star (\mathsf{AddVar}(YU \star I, \sigma)) \cup I')$

Fig. 4. Type Inference Algorithm (Part 3)

$$\Gamma|_R = \{x ::_r \tau \mid (x ::_r \tau) \in \Gamma\}$$
$$\Gamma|_N = \{x ::_n \tau \mid (x ::_n \tau) \in \Gamma\}$$
$$gen(\Gamma, \tau) = \forall(FV(\tau) \setminus FV(\Gamma)).\tau$$
$$S \star I = \{(\kappa, \{v \mid t \in vs, v \in FSV(S\,t)\}) \mid (\kappa, ss) \in I\}$$
$$\mathsf{AddVar}(I, \sigma) = \{(\kappa, ss \cup FSV(\sigma)) \mid (\kappa, ss) \in I\}$$
$$\mathsf{OK}(I) = \forall(\kappa, ss) \in I.\ \kappa \notin ss$$
$$\mathsf{Simplify}(P, Q) = \texttt{if}\ \kappa[s]\supset t \in Q\ \texttt{and}\ \kappa[s]\supset\alpha \in P\ \texttt{then}\ \mathsf{Simplify}((P \setminus \{\kappa[s]\supset\alpha\}) \cup \{t\supset\alpha\}, Q)\ \texttt{else}\ P$$

Fig. 5. Auxiliary Functions

4 Examples

In this section, we show examples type-checked by the above algorithm. All the examples are taken from [7] and are translated to our language straightforwardly.

First, we show the definition of `msort` (merge sort) function (Figure 6). As we do not use pattern matching here, the definition becomes a little lengthy. However, except the use of **`letextend`** and **`at`** (and hence `copyD` function), this is a straightforward (and maybe naïve) implementation of merge sort algorithm.

We use **`letextend`** and **`at`** as follows. When we split list in `msort` by calling `split`, we put the two lists obtained as the result in the extended part of the region created by **`letextend`**, since they only have to survive during the recursive call of `msort`. The function `copyD` which is called from `merge` uses **`at`** explicitly to allocate a new list in the old region. This is necessary because the return value of `merge` in the definition of `msort` must be used outside the surrounding **`letextend`**.

```
split xs l r = if      isNull xs then mkPair l r
               else if isNull (tail xs) then
                  mkPair (cons (head xs) l) r
               else split (tail (tail xs)) (cons (head xs) l)
                          (cons (head (tail xs)) r)

copyD t xs = if isNull xs then (nil ()) at t
             else var a  = head xs in
                  var as = copyD t (tail xs) in cons a as

merge t xs0 ys0 = if      isNull xs0 then copyD t ys0
                  else if isNull ys0 then copyD t xs0
                  else var y = head ys0 in
                       var x = head xs0 in
                       if x<y then
                         var xs1 = merge t (tail xs0) ys0 in
                         cons x xs1
                       else
                         var ys1 = merge t xs0 (tail ys0) in
                         cons y ys1

msort xs0 = if      isNull xs0 then nil ()
            else if isNull (tail xs0) then xs0
            else letextend t in
                   var p = split xs0 (nil ()) (nil ()) in
                   var l = fst p    in var r = snd p    in
                   var l1 = msort l in var r1 = msort r in
                   merge t l1 r1
```

Fig. 6. The definitions of `split`, `merge` and `msort`

The types of these functions are inferred as follows:

$$\begin{aligned}\texttt{split} &: s \supset t \Rightarrow \texttt{Ta}\ t\ (\texttt{List}\ t\ a)\\ &\quad \xrightarrow{\texttt{ST}\ s} \texttt{Ta}\ s\ (\texttt{List}\ s\ a) \xrightarrow{\texttt{ST}\ s} \texttt{Ta}\ s\ (\texttt{List}\ s\ a)\\ &\quad \xrightarrow{\texttt{ST}\ s} \texttt{Ta}\ s\ (\texttt{Ta}\ s\ (\texttt{List}\ s\ a),\ \texttt{Ta}\ s\ (\texttt{List}\ s\ a))\end{aligned}$$

$$\begin{aligned}\texttt{merge} &: \texttt{s} \supset \texttt{t} \Rightarrow \texttt{Ta}\ s\ t \xrightarrow{\texttt{ST}\ s} \texttt{Ta}\ s\ (\texttt{List}\ s\ a)\\ &\quad \xrightarrow{\texttt{ST}\ s} \texttt{Ta}\ s\ (\texttt{List}\ s\ a) \xrightarrow{\texttt{ST}\ s} \texttt{Ta}\ t\ (\texttt{List}\ t\ a)\end{aligned}$$

$$\texttt{msort} : \texttt{Ta}\ s\ (\texttt{List}\ s\ a) \xrightarrow{\texttt{ST}\ s} \texttt{Ta}\ s\ (\texttt{List}\ s\ a)$$

The second example is a version of Eratosthenes's sieves using lists (Figure 7). The

```
sift n xs = if isNull xs then nil ()
            else var y  = head xs in var ys = tail xs in
                 if mod n y == 0 then sift n ys
                 else cons y (sift n ys)

sieve xs p = if isNull xs then p
             else letextend t in
                  var z  = head xs in var zs = tail xs in
                  var rest = sift z zs in
                  sieve rest (cons z p)
```

Fig. 7. Eratosthenes

intermediate list `rest` is allocated in the new region created by **`letextend`**. The type of `sieve` is inferred as follows.

$$\begin{aligned}\texttt{sieve} &: s \supset t \Rightarrow \texttt{Ta}\ s\ (\texttt{List}\ s\ \texttt{Int}) \xrightarrow{\texttt{ST}\ s} \texttt{Ta}\ t\ (\texttt{List}\ t\ \texttt{Int})\\ &\qquad\qquad \xrightarrow{\texttt{ST}\ s} \texttt{Ta}\ t\ (\texttt{List}\ t\ \texttt{Int})\end{aligned}$$

Both examples show that it is relatively easy to insert **`letextend`** at appropriate places, and that the output produced by the type inference algorithm is readable.

In Tofte and Talpin's system, a further optimization called *region resetting* [1] is inserted by storage mode analysis. Then `sieve` above can be executed with a single region. In our system, no operator that corresponds to region resetting is offered. Anyhow, it is obvious that if we use destructive update and iteration instead of recursion, the above two examples can be made more space efficient. Nonetheless, it does not mean that our attempt is meaningless. Since recursive and non-destructive definition is easier to write in general, it would be often the case that first we define a recursive and non-destructive version of an algorithm and then gradually rewrite it into a more space-efficient version.

5 Concluding Remarks

We presented a type system where programmers can give explicit directives about lifetime of objects. Regions are hierarchical and are given a kind of subtyping relations between them. This fact simplifies representation of regions. We explained type inference of recursive functions and showed the results for some short examples. Compositional references play an implicit role in our system. They are actually used when we use subtyping of the form $s \supset t$.

We should remark that, in this paper, allocation of function closures is disregarded and that partial function application such as `map f` is not used. Creating a function closure might actually consumes memory. Therefore, it might be necessary that the type constructor $\rightarrow$ also be associated with `Ta` s. Then, if we define a curried function (*e.g.* `map`) and give it a full number of actual arguments (*e.g.* `map f xs`), at least conceptually, closures for intermediate partial applications (*e.g.* `map f`) are created and used immediately. Intuitively, however, full function applications do not consume the heap nor the regions for intermediate closures. It seems that this sort of memory reclamation can not be expressed as a typing rule like the one presented in this paper. However, it should be noted that our main objective in this paper is to simplify the representation of regions. Then, associating regions to even such short-lived closures seems incompatible to our approach. There would be several workarounds however, for example, to separate partial and full function applications syntactically and to associate regions only to such explicit partial applications.

It is necessary to prove that our new operator **`letextend`** can safely deallocate the extended region. Semmelroth and Sabry [5] defined dynamic semantics and proved *subject reduction property* for a language which includes **`runST`**. The author believes that their technique can be extended to our language which includes **`letextend`**.

Acknowledgement

I would like to thank the anonymous reviewers for their valuable comments. This research is partially supported by Japan Society for the Promotion of Science, Grant-in-Aid for Encouragement of Young Scientists, 10780196.

References

1. Lars Birkedal, Mads Tofte, and Magnus Vejlstrup. From region inference to von neumann machines via region representation inference. In *23rd ACM Symposium on Principles of Programming Languages*, January 1996.
2. Koji Kagawa. Compositional references for stateful functional programming. In *Proc. of the International Conference on Functional Programming 1997*. ACM Press, June 1997.
3. Konstantin Läufer and Martin Odersky. Polymorphic type inference and abstract data types. *ACM Transactions on Programming Languages and Systems (TOPLAS)*, 16(5):1411–1430, September 1994.
4. John Launchbury and Simon L. Peyton Jones. State in Haskell. *Lisp and Symbolic Computation*, 8(4):293–341, 1995.

5. Miley Semmelroth and Amr Sabry. Monadic encapsulation in ML. In *The 1999 International Conference on Functional Programming (ICFP)*, 1999.
6. Mads Tofte and Lars Birkedal. A region inference algorithm. *ACM Transactions on Programming Languages and Systems*, 20(5):724–767, July 1998.
7. Mads Tofte, Lars Birkedal, Martin Elsman, Niels Hallenberg, Tommy Højfeld Olesen, Peter Sestoft, and Peter Bertelsen. Programming with regions in the ML kit. Technical Report 97/12, Department of Computer Science, University of Copenhagen, April 1997.
8. Mads Tofte and Jean-Pierre Talpin. Implementation of typed call-by-value λ-calculus using a stack of regions. In *Annual ACM Symp. on Principles of Prog. Languages*, pages 188–201, January 1994.

A Soundness of *TC*

In this section, we will prove the soundness of *TC* with respect to $\vdash$. Of course, the completeness cannot be proved, since $\vdash$ permits polymorphic recursion (LetRec).

First, we need a new form of typing rules ($\vdash'$) which bridges the gap between *TC* and ($\vdash$).

Definition 1.

$$\frac{x ::_{(n \text{ OR } r)} \sigma \in \Gamma \quad \sigma \succ P \Rightarrow \tau}{\Gamma \vdash' x :: P \Rightarrow \tau \,!\, \_, \emptyset}\ (\text{Var'}) \qquad \frac{\Gamma, x ::_n \tau_1 \vdash' e :: P \Rightarrow \tau_2 \,!\, m, I}{\Gamma \vdash' \lambda x \to e :: P \Rightarrow \tau_1 \xrightarrow{m} \tau_2 \,!\, \_, I}\ (\text{Lambda'})$$

$$\frac{\Gamma \vdash' e_1 :: P_1 \Rightarrow \tau_1 \xrightarrow{m} \tau_2 \,!\, m, I_1 \quad \Gamma \vdash' e_2 :: P_2 \Rightarrow \tau_1 \,!\, m, I_2}{\Gamma \vdash' e_1\, e_2 :: P_1 \cup P_2 \Rightarrow \tau_2 \,!\, m, I_1 \cup I_2}\ (\text{App'})$$

$$\frac{\begin{array}{l}\Gamma \vdash' e_1 :: P_1 \Rightarrow \tau_1 \,!\, \_, I_1 \\ \Gamma, x ::_n \forall\overline{\alpha}.\, P_1 \Rightarrow \tau_1 \vdash' e_2 :: P_2 \Rightarrow \tau_2 \,!\, m, I_2 \quad (\overline{\alpha} = FV(\tau_1) \setminus FV(\Gamma))\end{array}}{\Gamma \vdash' \texttt{let}\ x = e_1\ \texttt{in}\ e_2 :: P_2 \Rightarrow \tau_2 \,!\, m, I_1 \cup I_2}\ (\text{Let'})$$

$$\frac{\begin{array}{l}\Gamma, x ::_n \forall\overline{\alpha}.\, P_1 \Rightarrow \tau_1 \vdash' e_1 :: P_1 \Rightarrow \tau_1 \,!\, \_, I_1 \\ \Gamma, x ::_n \forall\overline{\alpha}.\, P_1 \Rightarrow \tau_1, \vdash' e_2 :: P_2 \Rightarrow \tau_2 \,!\, m, I_2 \quad (\overline{\alpha} = FV(\tau_1) \setminus FV(\Gamma))\end{array}}{\Gamma \vdash' \texttt{letrec}\ x = e_1\ \texttt{in}\ e_2 :: P_2 \Rightarrow \tau_2 \,!\, m, I_1 \cup I_2}\ (\text{LetRec'})$$

$$\frac{\begin{array}{l}\Gamma \vdash' e :: P \Rightarrow \tau \,!\, \mathit{ST}(\kappa[\texttt{Unit}]), I \\ P' = \mathsf{Simplify}(P, \{\kappa[\texttt{Unit}] \supset \texttt{Unit}\}) \quad \kappa \notin FS(P' \Rightarrow \tau \,!\, m) \cup FS(\Gamma|_N)\end{array}}{\begin{array}{l}\Gamma \vdash' \texttt{encap}\ e :: P' \Rightarrow \tau \,!\, m, I' \\ (I' = I \cup \{(\kappa, FSV(P' \Rightarrow \tau \,!\, m) \cup FSV(\Gamma|_N))\})\end{array}}$$

(Encap')

$$\frac{\begin{array}{l}\Gamma, x ::_n \texttt{Ta}\ (\kappa[t])\ t \vdash' e :: P \Rightarrow \tau \,!\, \mathit{ST}(\kappa[t]), I \\ P' = \mathsf{Simplify}(P, \{\kappa[t] \supset t\}) \quad \kappa \notin FS(P' \Rightarrow \tau \,!\, \mathit{ST}\, t) \cup FS(\Gamma|_N)\end{array}}{\begin{array}{l}\Gamma \vdash' \texttt{letextend}\ x\ \texttt{in}\ e :: P' \Rightarrow \tau \,!\, \mathit{ST}\, t, I' \\ (I' = I \cup \{(\kappa, FSV(P' \Rightarrow \tau \,!\, \mathit{ST}\, t) \cup FSV(\Gamma|_N))\})\end{array}}$$

(Letextend')

Note that, if $\Gamma \vdash' e :: P \Rightarrow \tau, I$ and $\Gamma|_R = \emptyset$, then $\Gamma \vdash e :: P \Rightarrow \tau$ holds. For $\vdash'$, we can prove some desirable properties.

Lemma 1. *If* $\Gamma \vdash' e :: P \Rightarrow \tau, I$ *and* $\mathsf{OK}(S \star I)$, *then* $S\Gamma \vdash' e :: S(P \Rightarrow \tau), S \star I$.

Proof. By induction on the structure of the derivation.

Lemma 2. *If* $\Gamma, \bigcup_i \{x_i ::_r \tau_i\} \vdash' e :: P \Rightarrow \tau, I$ *and* $\forall i.\ \sigma \succ \tau_i$ *and* $\mathsf{OK}(\mathsf{AddVar}(I, \sigma))$ *then* $\Gamma, x ::_n \sigma \vdash' e[x/x_i] :: P \Rightarrow \tau, \mathsf{AddVar}(I, \sigma)$.

Proof. By induction on the structure of the derivation.

Lemma 3. *(Soundness of TC)*
If $TC(\Gamma, e) = (S, \tau, I)$, *then* $S\Gamma \vdash' e :: \tau, I$.

Proof. We show the case of (LetRec).

Let $(S^*, \tau^*, I^*) = TC(\Gamma, \mathtt{letrec}\ x = e\ \mathtt{in}\ e')$. By the definition of *TC*, there exists S, τ_1, I s.t.

$$(S, Q \Rightarrow \tau_1 \,!\, \_, I) = TC(\Gamma + \textstyle\bigcup_{i=1}^{n} \{x_i ::_r a_i\}, e^*)$$

where e^* is an expression as is defined in the algorithm. By induction,

$$S\Gamma + \textstyle\bigcup_{i=1}^{n} \{x_i ::_r Sa_i\} \vdash' e^* :: Q \Rightarrow \tau_1 \,!\, \_, I$$

By lemma 1,

$$YUS\Gamma + \textstyle\bigcup_{i=1}^{n} \{x_i ::_r YUSa_i\} \vdash' e^* :: U(Q \Rightarrow \tau_1 \,!\, \_), YU \star I$$

By the condition $\forall i.\ \forall v \in dom(Z_i).\ Z_i v \supset v$, adding constraints $Z_i UQ$ to the type of x_i does not actually add new constraints to the type of e^* because they are finally simplified to UQ.

$$YUS\Gamma + \textstyle\bigcup_{i=1}^{n} \{x_i ::_r Z_i UQ \Rightarrow YUSa_i\} \vdash' e^* :: U(Q \Rightarrow \tau_1 \,!\, \_), YU \star I$$

By the definition of Y, $YUSa_i = Z_i U \sigma_i = Z_i U \tau_1$. Then, by lemma 2,

$$YUS\Gamma + \{x ::_n \sigma\} \vdash' e :: U(Q \Rightarrow \tau_1 \,!\, \_), \mathsf{AddVar}(YU \star I, \sigma)$$

By the definition of *TC*, there exists S', τ', I' s.t.

$$(S', \tau', I') = TC(YUS\Gamma + \{x ::_n \sigma\}, e')$$

By induction,

$$S'(YUS\Gamma + \{x ::_n \sigma\}) \vdash' e' :: \tau', I'$$

Moreover, by lemma 1,

$$S'(YUS\Gamma + \{x ::_n \sigma\}) \vdash' e :: S'U(Q \Rightarrow \tau_1 \,!\, \_), S' \star (\mathsf{AddVar}(YU \star I, \sigma))$$

By (LetRec'),

$$S'YUS\Gamma \vdash' \mathtt{letrec}\ x = e\ \mathtt{in}\ e' :: \tau', S' \star (\mathsf{AddVar}(YU \star I, \sigma)) \cup I'$$

where $S^* = S'YUS$, $\tau^* = \tau'$ and $I^* = S' \star (\mathsf{AddVar}(YU \star I, \sigma)) \cup I'$.

Well-Typed Logic Programs Are not Wrong

Pierre Deransart[1] and Jan-Georg Smaus[2]

[1] INRIA-Rocquencourt, BP105, 78153 Le Chesnay Cedex, France
pierre.deransart@inria.fr
[2] CWI, Kruislaan 413, 1098 SJ Amsterdam, The Netherlands, jan.smaus@cwi.nl

Abstract. We consider prescriptive type systems for logic programs (as in Gödel or Mercury). In such systems, the typing is *static*, but it guarantees an operational property: if a program is "well-typed", then all derivations starting in a "well-typed" query are again "well-typed". This property has been called *subject reduction*. We show that this property can also be phrased as a property of the *proof-theoretic* semantics of logic programs, thus abstracting from the usual operational (top-down) semantics. This proof-theoretic view leads us to questioning a condition which is usually considered necessary for subject reduction, namely the *head condition*. It states that the head of each clause must have a type which is a variant (and not a proper instance) of the declared type. We provide a more general condition, thus reestablishing a certain symmetry between heads and body atoms. The condition ensures that in a derivation, the types of two unified terms are themselves unifiable. We discuss possible implications of this result. We also discuss the relationship between the head condition and *polymorphic recursion*, a concept known in functional programming.

1 Introduction

Prescriptive types are used in logic programming (and other paradigms) to restrict the underlying syntax so that only "meaningful" expressions are allowed. This allows for many programming errors to be detected by the compiler. Moreover, it ensures that once a program has passed the compiler, the types of arguments of predicates can be ignored at runtime, since it is guaranteed that they will be of correct type. This has been turned into the famous slogan [19, 20]

Well-typed programs cannot go wrong.

Adopting the terminology from the theory of the λ-calculus [29], this property of a typed program is called *subject reduction*. For the simply typed λ-calculus, subject reduction states that the type of a λ-term is invariant under reduction. Translated to logic programming, this means that resolving a "well-typed" query with a "well-typed" clause will always result in a "well-typed" query, and so the successive queries obtained during a derivation are all "well-typed".

From this observation, it is clear that subject reduction is a property of the *operational* semantics of a logic program, i.e., SLD resolution [17]. In this paper,

H. Kuchen and K. Ueda (Eds.): FLOPS 2001, LNCS 2024, pp. 280–295, 2001.

we show that it is also a property of the proof-theoretic semantics based on *derivation trees*. This is obtained by showing that using "well-typed" clauses, only "well-typed" derivation trees can be constructed, giving rise to the new slogan:

Well-typed programs *are* not wrong.

The *head condition*, which is a condition on the program (clauses) [13], is usually considered to be crucial for subject reduction. The second objective of this paper is to analyse the head condition in this new light and open the field for generalisations, of which we introduce one.

The head condition, also called *definitional genericity* [16], states that the types of the arguments of a clause head must be a variant[1] (and not a proper instance) of the declared type of the head predicate. This condition imposes a distinction between "definitional" occurrences (clause heads) and "applied" occurrences (body atoms) of a predicate. In contrast, the proof-theoretic view of subject reduction we propose reestablishes a certain symmetry between the different occurrences. By this generalisation, the class of programs for which subject reduction is guaranteed is enlarged.

This paper is organised as follows. Section 2 contains some preliminaries. Section 3 introduces our proof-theoretic notion of subject reduction. Section 4 gives conditions for subject reduction, and in particular, a generalisation of the head condition. In Section 5, we discuss, in the light of these results, the usefulness of the head condition and its generalisation. We also exhibit an interesting relationship between the head condition and *polymorphic recursion* [15]. Section 6 concludes by mentioning possible applications of these results.

2 Preliminaries

We assume familiarity with the standard concepts of logic programming [17]. To simplify the notation, a vector such as $o_1, \dots, o_m$ is often denoted by $\bar{o}$. The restriction of a substitution θ to the variables in a syntactic object o is denoted as $\theta\lceil_o$, and analogously for type substitutions (see Subsec. 2.2). The relation symbol of an atom a is denoted by $Rel(a)$.

When we refer to a *clause in a program*, we usually mean a copy of this clause whose variables are renamed apart from variables occurring in other objects in the context. A query is a sequence of atoms. A query Q' is **derived from** a query Q, denoted $Q \rightsquigarrow Q'$, if $Q = a_1, \dots, a_m$, $Q' = (a_1, \dots, a_{k-1}, B, a_{k+1}, \dots, a_m)\theta$, and $h \leftarrow B$ is a clause (in a program usually clear from the context) such that h and a_k are unifiable with MGU θ. A **derivation** $Q \rightsquigarrow^* Q'$ is defined in the usual way. Given a program P, the **immediate consequence operator** T_P is defined by $T_P(M) = \{h\theta \mid h \leftarrow a_1, \dots, a_m \in P,\ a_1\theta, \dots, a_m\theta \in M\}$.

[1] A variant is obtained by renaming the type parameters in a type.

2.1 Derivation Trees

A key element of this work is the proof-theoretic semantics of logic programs based on derivation trees [6]. We recall some important notions and basic results.

Definition 2.1. An **instance name** of a clause C is a pair of the form $\langle C, \theta \rangle$, where θ is a substitution.

Definition 2.2. Let P be a program. A **derivation tree** for P is a labelled ordered tree [6] such that:

1. Each leaf node is labelled by $\perp$ or an instance name $\langle C, \theta \rangle$ of a clause[2] in P; each non-leaf node is labelled by an instance name $\langle C, \theta \rangle$ of a clause in P.
2. If a node is labelled by $\langle h \leftarrow a_1, \ldots, a_m, \theta \rangle$, where $m \geq 0$, then this node has m children, and for $i \in \{1, \ldots, m\}$, the ith child is labelled either $\perp$, or $\langle h' \leftarrow B, \theta' \rangle$ where $h'\theta' = a_i\theta$.

Nodes labelled $\perp$ are **incomplete**, all other nodes are **complete**. A derivation tree containing only complete nodes is a **proof tree**.

To define the semantics of logic programs, it is useful to associate an atom with each node in a derivation tree in the following way.

Definition 2.3. Let T be a derivation tree. For each node n in T, the **node atom** of n, denoted $atom(n)$, is defined as follows: If n is labelled $\langle h \leftarrow B, \theta \rangle$, then $h\theta$ is the node atom of n; if n is labelled $\perp$, and n is the ith child of its parent labelled $\langle h \leftarrow a_1, \ldots, a_m, \theta \rangle$, then $a_i\theta$ is the node atom of n. If n is the root of T then $atom(n)$ is the **head of** T, denoted $head(T)$.

Derivation trees are obtained by grafting instances of clauses of a program. To describe this construction in a general way, we define the following concept.

Definition 2.4. Let P be a program. A **skeleton (tree)** for P is a labelled ordered tree such that:

1. Each leaf node is labelled by $\perp$ or a clause in P, and each non-leaf node is labelled by a clause in P.
2. If a node is labelled by $h \leftarrow a_1, \ldots, a_m$, where $m \geq 0$, then this node has m children, and for $i \in \{1, \ldots, m\}$, the ith child is labelled either $\perp$, or $h' \leftarrow B$ where $Rel(h') = Rel(a_i)$.

The **skeleton of a tree** T, denoted $Sk(T)$, is the skeleton obtained from T by replacing each label $\langle C, \theta \rangle$ with C. Conversely, we say that T is a **derivation tree based on** $Sk(T)$.

---

[2] Recall that C is renamed apart from any other clause in the same tree.

$$
\begin{array}{l}
\text{h}(X) \leftarrow \text{q}(X), \text{p}(X). \\
\text{q}([]). \\
\text{p}(X) \leftarrow \text{r}(X).
\end{array}
$$

$$
\langle \text{h}(X) \leftarrow \text{q}(X), \text{p}(X), \{x/[]\} \rangle
$$

$$
\langle \text{q}([]), \emptyset \rangle \qquad \langle \text{p}(X') \leftarrow \text{r}(X'), \{x'/[]\} \rangle
$$

$$
\bot
$$

$$
\text{h}(X) \leftarrow \text{q}(X), \text{p}(X)
$$

$$
\text{q}([]) \qquad \text{p}(X') \leftarrow \text{r}(X')
$$

$$
\bot
$$

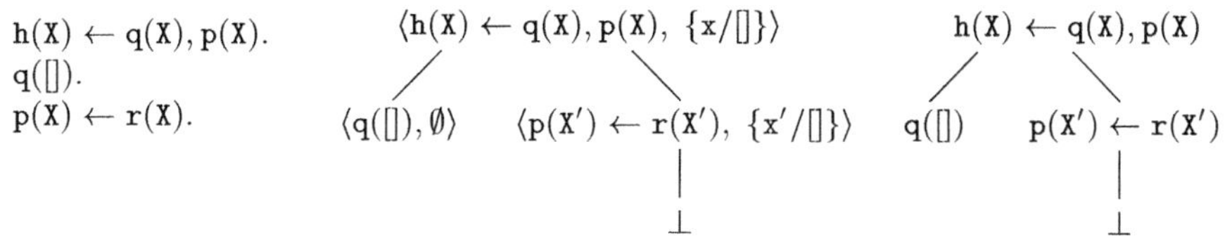

Fig. 1. A program, a derivation tree and its skeleton

Definition 2.5. Let S be a skeleton. We define

$$
Eq(S) = \{a_i = h' \mid \text{there exist complete nodes } n, n' \text{ in } S \text{ such that}
$$

- n' is the ith child of n,
- n is labelled $h \leftarrow a_1, \ldots, a_m$,
- n' is labelled $h' \leftarrow B\}$

Abusing notation, we frequently identify the set of equations with the conjunction or sequence of all equations contained in it. If $Eq(S)$ has a unifier then we call S a **proper** skeleton.

Proposition 2.1. [6, Prop. 2.1] Let S be a skeleton. A derivation tree based on S exists if and only if S is proper.

Theorem 2.2. [6, Thm. 2.1] Let S be a skeleton and θ an MGU of $Eq(S)$. Let $D(S)$ be the tree obtained from S by replacing each node label C with the pair $\langle C, \theta\!\restriction_C \rangle$. Then $D(S)$ is a most general derivation tree based on S (i.e., any other derivation tree based on S is an instance of $D(S)$).

Example 2.1. Figure 1 shows a program, one of its derivation trees, and the skeleton of the derivation tree.

To model derivations for a program P and a query Q, we assume that P contains an additional clause go $\leftarrow Q$, where go is a new predicate symbol.

We recall the following straightforward correspondences between derivations, the T_P-semantics and derivation trees.

Proposition 2.3. Let P be a program. Then

1. $a \in lfp(T_P)$ if and only if $a = head(T)$ for some proof tree T for P,
2. $Q \rightsquigarrow^* Q'$ if and only if Q' is the sequence of node atoms of incomplete nodes of a most general derivation tree for $P \cup \{\text{go} \leftarrow Q\}$ with head go, visited left to right.

2.2 Typed Logic Programming

We assume a type system for logic programs with parametric polymorphism but without subtyping, as realised in the languages Gödel [12] or Mercury [27].

Table 1. Rules defining a typed language

(Var)	$\{x:\tau,\ldots\}\vdash x:\tau$	
(Func)	$\dfrac{U\vdash t_1{:}\tau_1\Theta \ \cdots\ U\vdash t_m{:}\tau_m\Theta}{U\vdash f_{\tau_1\ldots\tau_m\to\tau}(t_1,\ldots,t_m){:}\tau\Theta}$	Θ is a type substitution
(Atom)	$\dfrac{U\vdash t_1{:}\tau_1\Theta \ \cdots\ U\vdash t_m{:}\tau_m\Theta}{U\vdash p_{\tau_1\ldots\tau_m}(t_1,\ldots,t_m)\ \mathit{Atom}}$	Θ is a type substitution
(Query)	$\dfrac{U\vdash A_1\ \mathit{Atom}\ \cdots\ U\vdash A_m\ \mathit{Atom}}{U\vdash A_1,\ldots,A_m\ \mathit{Query}}$	
(Clause)	$\dfrac{U\vdash A\ \mathit{Atom}\quad U\vdash Q\ \mathit{Query}}{U\vdash A\leftarrow Q\ \mathit{Clause}}$	
(Program)	$\dfrac{\_\vdash C_1\ \mathit{Clause}\ \cdots\ \_\vdash C_m\ \mathit{Clause}}{\_\vdash\{C_1,\ldots,C_m\}\ \mathit{Program}}$	
(Queryset)	$\dfrac{\_\vdash Q_1\ \mathit{Query}\ \cdots\ \_\vdash Q_m\ \mathit{Query}}{\_\vdash\{Q_1,\ldots,Q_m\}\ \mathit{Queryset}}$	

The set of types $\mathcal{T}$ is given by the term structure based on a finite set of **constructors** $\mathcal{K}$, where with each $K\in\mathcal{K}$ an arity $m\geq 0$ is associated (by writing K/m), and a denumerable set $\mathcal{U}$ of **parameters**. A **type substitution** is an idempotent mapping from parameters to types which is the identity almost everywhere. The set of parameters in a syntactic object o is denoted by $pars(o)$.

We assume a denumerable set $\mathcal{V}$ of **variables**. The set of variables in a syntactic object o is denoted by $vars(o)$. A **variable typing** is a mapping from a finite subset of $\mathcal{V}$ to $\mathcal{T}$, written as $\{x_1:\tau_1,\ldots,x_m:\tau_m\}$.

We assume a finite set $\mathcal{F}$ (resp. $\mathcal{P}$) of **function** (resp. **predicate**) symbols, each with an arity and a **declared type** associated with it, such that: for each $f\in\mathcal{F}$, the declared type has the form $(\tau_1,\ldots,\tau_m,\tau)$, where m is the arity of f, $(\tau_1,\ldots,\tau_m)\in\mathcal{T}^m$, and τ satisfies the *transparency condition* [13]: $pars(\tau_1,\ldots,\tau_m)\subseteq pars(\tau)$; for each $p\in\mathcal{P}$, the declared type has the form $(\tau_1,\ldots,\tau_m)$, where m is the arity of p and $(\tau_1,\ldots,\tau_m)\in\mathcal{T}^m$. We often indicate the declared types by writing $f_{\tau_1\ldots\tau_m\to\tau}$ and $p_{\tau_1\ldots\tau_m}$, however we assume that the parameters in $\tau_1,\ldots,\tau_m,\tau$ are fresh for each occurrence of f or p. We assume that there is a special predicate symbol $=_{u,u}$ where $u\in\mathcal{U}$.

Throughout this paper, we assume $\mathcal{K}$, $\mathcal{F}$, and $\mathcal{P}$ arbitrary but fixed. The **typed language**, i.e. a language of terms, atoms etc. based on $\mathcal{K}$, $\mathcal{F}$, and $\mathcal{P}$, is defined by the rules in Table 1. All objects are defined relative to a variable typing U, and $\_\vdash\ldots$ stands for "there exists U such that $U\vdash\ldots$". The expressions below the line are called **type judgements**.

Formally, a proof of a type judgement is a tree where the nodes are labelled with judgements and the edges are labelled with rules (e.g. see Fig. 2) [29]. From the form of the rules, it is clear that in order to prove any type judgement, we must, for each occurrence of a term t in the judgement, prove a judgement $\ldots\vdash t:\tau$ for some τ. We now define the most general such τ. It exists and can be computed by *type inferencing algorithms* [2].

$$\dfrac{\dfrac{\vdots}{U \vdash \bar{t} : \bar{\tau}}}{U \vdash p(\bar{t})\ Atom} \quad \dfrac{\dfrac{\dfrac{\vdots}{U \vdash \bar{t}_1 : \bar{\tau}_1}}{U \vdash p_1(\bar{t}_1)\ Atom} \cdots \dfrac{\dfrac{\vdots}{U \vdash \bar{t}_m : \bar{\tau}_m}}{U \vdash p_m(\bar{t}_m)\ Atom}}{U \vdash p_1(\bar{t}_1), \ldots, p_m(\bar{t}_m)\ Query}$$
$$\overline{U \vdash p(\bar{t}) \leftarrow p_1(\bar{t}_1), \ldots, p_m(\bar{t}_m)\ Clause}$$

Fig. 2. Proving a type judgement

Definition 2.6. Consider a judgement $U \vdash p(\bar{t}) \leftarrow p_1(\bar{t}_1), \ldots, p_m(\bar{t}_m)$ *Clause* and a proof of this judgement containing judgements $U \vdash \bar{t} : \bar{\tau}$, $U \vdash \bar{t}_1 : \bar{\tau}_1$, $\ldots$, $U \vdash \bar{t}_m : \bar{\tau}_m$ (see Fig. 2) such that $(\bar{\tau}, \bar{\tau}_1, \ldots, \bar{\tau}_m)$ is most general (wrt. all such proofs). We call $(\bar{\tau}, \bar{\tau}_1, \ldots, \bar{\tau}_m)$ the **most general type** of $p(\bar{t}) \leftarrow p_1(\bar{t}_1), \ldots, p_m(\bar{t}_m)$ **wrt.** U.

Moreover, consider the variable typing U' and the proof of $U' \vdash p(\bar{t}) \leftarrow p_1(\bar{t}_1), \ldots, p_m(\bar{t}_m)$ *Clause* containing judgments $U' \vdash \bar{t} : \bar{\tau}$, $U' \vdash \bar{t}_1 : \bar{\tau}_1$, $\ldots$, $U' \vdash \bar{t}_m : \bar{\tau}_m$ such that $(\bar{\tau}, \bar{\tau}_1, \ldots, \bar{\tau}_m)$ is most general (wrt. all such proofs and all possible U'). We call $(\bar{\tau}, \bar{\tau}_1, \ldots, \bar{\tau}_m)$ the **most general type** of $p(\bar{t}) \leftarrow p_1(\bar{t}_1), \ldots, p_m(\bar{t}_m)$.

The following example explains the difference between the most general type wrt. a fixed variable typing, and the most general type as such.

Example 2.2. Consider function $\mathtt{nil}_{\to \mathtt{list(U)}}$ and clause $C = \mathtt{p} \leftarrow \mathtt{X}{=}\mathtt{nil}, \mathtt{nil}{=}\mathtt{nil}$. Fixing $U = \{\mathtt{X} : \mathtt{list(int)}\}$, the judgement $U \vdash C$ *Clause* can be proven using the judgements $U \vdash \mathtt{X} : \mathtt{list(int)}$ and then $U \vdash \mathtt{nil} : \mathtt{list(int)}$ for *each* occurrence of nil. It can also be proven using the judgements $U \vdash \mathtt{X} : \mathtt{list(int)}$ and then $U \vdash \mathtt{nil} : \mathtt{list(int)}$ (for the first occurrence of nil) and then $U \vdash \mathtt{nil} : \mathtt{list(V)}$ (for the other two occurrences of nil). In the latter case, we obtain $(\mathtt{list(int)}, \mathtt{list(int)}, \mathtt{list(V)}, \mathtt{list(V)})$, the most general type of C wrt. U. Moreover, $(\mathtt{list(V')}, \mathtt{list(V')}, \mathtt{list(V)}, \mathtt{list(V)})$ is the most general type of C (choose $U' = \{\mathtt{X} : \mathtt{list(V')}\}$).

Definition 2.7. If $U \vdash x_1 = t_1, \ldots, x_m = t_m$ *Query* where $x_1, \ldots, x_m$ are distinct variables and for each $i \in \{1, \ldots, m\}$, t_i is a term distinct from x_i, then $(\{x_1/t_1, \ldots, x_m/t_m\}, U)$ is a **typed (term) substitution**.

3 Subject Reduction for Derivation Trees

We first define subject reduction as a property of derivation trees and show that it is equivalent to the usual operational notion. We then show that a sufficient condition for subject reduction is that the types of all unified terms are themselves unifiable.

3.1 Proof-Theoretic and Operational Subject Reduction

Subject reduction is a well-understood concept, yet it has to be defined formally for each system. We now provide two fundamental definitions.

Definition 3.1. Let $\_ \vdash P$ *Program* and $\_ \vdash \mathcal{Q}$ *Queryset*. We say P has **(proof-theoretic) subject reduction wrt.** $\mathcal{Q}$ if for every $Q \in \mathcal{Q}$, for every most general derivation tree T for $P \cup \{\mathtt{go} \leftarrow Q\}$ with head go, there exists a variable typing U' such that for each node atom a of T, $U' \vdash a$ *Atom*.

P has **operational subject reduction wrt.** $\mathcal{Q}$ if for every $Q \in \mathcal{Q}$, for every derivation $Q \leadsto^* Q'$ of P, we have $\_ \vdash Q'$ *Query*.

The reference to $\mathcal{Q}$ is omitted if $\mathcal{Q} = \{Q \mid \_ \vdash Q \text{ } \mathit{Query}\}$. The following theorem states a certain equivalence between the two notions.

Theorem 3.1 (Proof see [8]). Let $\_ \vdash P$ *Program* and $\_ \vdash \mathcal{Q}$ *Queryset*. If P has subject reduction wrt. $\mathcal{Q}$, then P has operational subject reduction wrt. $\mathcal{Q}$. If P has operational subject reduction, then P has subject reduction.

The following example shows that in the second statement of the above theorem, it is crucial that P has operational subject reduction wrt. *all* queries.

Example 3.1. Let $\mathcal{K} = \{\mathtt{list}/1, \mathtt{int}/0\}$, $\mathcal{F} = \{\mathtt{nil}_{\to \mathtt{list(U)}}, \mathtt{cons}_{\mathtt{U},\mathtt{list(U)} \to \mathtt{list(U)}}, -1_{\to \mathtt{int}}, 0_{\to \mathtt{int}}, \ldots\}$, $\mathcal{P} = \{\mathtt{p}_{\mathtt{list(int)}}, \mathtt{r}_{\mathtt{list(U)}}\}$, and P be

```
p(X) <- r(X).                    r([X]) <- r(X).
```

For each derivation $\mathtt{p(X)} \leadsto^* Q'_0$, we have $Q'_0 = \mathtt{p(Y)}$ or $Q'_0 = \mathtt{r(Y)}$ for some $\mathtt{Y} \in \mathcal{V}$, and so $\{\mathtt{Y} : \mathtt{list(int)}\} \vdash \mathtt{p(Y)}$ *Query* or $\{\mathtt{Y} : \mathtt{list(U)}\} \vdash \mathtt{r(Y)}$ *Query*. Therefore P has operational subject reduction wrt. $\{\mathtt{p(X)}\}$. Yet the derivation trees for P have heads p(Y), p([Y]), p([[Y]]) etc., and $\_ \nvdash$ p([[Y]]) *Query*.

3.2 Unifiability of Types and Subject Reduction

We now lift the notion of skeleton to the type level.

Definition 3.2. Let $\_ \vdash P$ *Program* and S be a skeleton for P. The **type skeleton corresponding to** S is a tree obtained from S by replacing each node label $C_n = p(\bar{t}) \leftarrow p_1(\bar{t}_1), \ldots, p_m(\bar{t}_m)$ with $p(\bar{\tau}) \leftarrow p_1(\bar{\tau}_1), \ldots, p_m(\bar{\tau}_m)$, where $(\bar{\tau}, \bar{\tau}_1, \ldots, \bar{\tau}_m)$ is the most general type of C_n.[3] For a type skeleton TS, the **type equation set** $Eq(TS)$ and a **proper** type skeleton are defined as in Def. 2.5.

The following theorem states that subject reduction is ensured if terms are unified only if their types are also unifiable.

Theorem 3.2. Let $\_ \vdash P$ *Program* and $\_ \vdash \mathcal{Q}$ *Queryset*. P has subject reduction wrt. $\mathcal{Q}$ if for each proper skeleton S of $P \cup \{\mathtt{go} \leftarrow Q\}$ with head go, where $Q \in \mathcal{Q}$, the *type* skeleton corresponding to S is proper.

The proof uses a statement that unification of terms of the same type yields a typed substitution [8].

[3] Recall that the variables in C_n and the parameters in $\bar{\tau}, \bar{\tau}_1, \ldots, \bar{\tau}_m$ are renamed apart from other node labels in the same (type) skeleton.

```
go ← p(X)                      go ← p(list(int))
   |                                  |
p(X') ← r(X')                  p(list(int)) ← r(list(int))
   |                                  |
r([X'']) ← r(X'')              r(list(U'')) ← r(U'')
   |                                  |
r([X''']) ← r(X''')            r(list(U''')) ← r(U''')
```

Fig. 3. A skeleton and the corresponding *non-proper* type skeleton for Ex. 3.1

```
app([],Ys,Ys).                 %app(list(U),list(U),list(U))
app([X|Xs],Ys,[X|Zs]) <-       %app(list(U),list(U),list(U))
  app(Xs,Ys,Zs).               %app(list(U),list(U),list(U))

r([1]).                        %r(list(int))


go <-
  app(Xs,[],Zs),               %app(list(int),list(int),list(int))
  r(Xs).                       %r(list(int))
```

Fig. 4. A program used to illustrate type skeletons

Example 3.2. Figure 3 shows a proper skeleton and the corresponding *non-proper* type skeleton for the program in Ex. 3.1.

In contrast, let $\mathcal{K}$ and $\mathcal{F}$ be as in Ex. 3.1, and $\mathcal{P} = \{\mathtt{app}_{\mathtt{list(U)},\mathtt{list(U)},\mathtt{list(U)}}, \mathtt{r}_{\mathtt{list(int)}}\}$. Let P be the program shown in Fig. 4. The most general type of each clause is indicated as comment. Figure 5 shows a skeleton S and the corresponding type skeleton TS for P. A solution of $Eq(TS)$ is obtained by instantiating all parameters with `int`.

4 Conditions for Subject Reduction

By Thm. 3.2, a program has subject reduction if for each proper skeleton, the corresponding type skeleton is also proper. A more general sufficient condition consists in ensuring that *any* type skeleton is proper. We call this property **type unifiability**. Arguably, type unifiability is in the spirit of prescriptive typing, since subject reduction should be independent of the unifiability of terms, i.e., success or failure of the computation. However this view has been challenged in the context of higher-order logic programming [21].

We conjecture that both subject reduction and type unifiability are undecidable. Proving this is a topic for future work.

4.1 The Head Condition

The head condition is the standard way [13] of ensuring type unifiability.

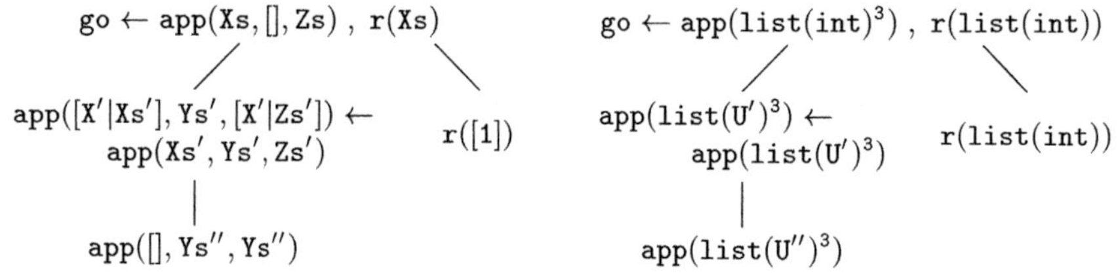

Fig. 5. A skeleton and the corresponding type skeleton for Ex. 3.2

Definition 4.1. A clause $C = p_{\bar{\tau}}(\bar{t}) \leftarrow B$ fulfills the **head condition** if its most general type has the form $(\bar{\tau}, \ldots)$.

Note that by the typing rules in Table 1, clearly the most general type of C must be $(\bar{\tau}, \ldots)\Theta$ for some type substitution Θ. Now the head condition states that the type of the head arguments must be the declared type of the predicate, or in other words, $\Theta\lceil_{\bar{\tau}} = \emptyset$. It has been shown previously that typed programs fulfilling the head condition have operational subject reduction [13, Thm. 1.4.7]. By Thm. 3.1, this means that they have subject reduction.

4.2 Generalising the Head Condition

To reason about the existence of a solution for the equation set of a type skeleton, we give a sufficient condition for unifiability of a finite set of term equations.

Proposition 4.1. Let $E = \{l_1 = r_1, \ldots, l_m = r_m\}$ be a set of oriented equations, and assume an order relation on the equations such that $l_1 = r_1 \rightarrow l_2 = r_2$ if r_1 and l_2 share a variable. E is unifiable if

1. for all $1 \leq i < j \leq m$, r_i and r_j have no variable in common, and
2. the graph of $\rightarrow$ is a partial order, and
3. for all $i \in \{1, \ldots, m\}$, l_i is an instance of r_i.

In fact, the head condition ensures that $Eq(TS)$ meets the above conditions for any type skeleton TS. The equations in $Eq(TS)$ have the form $p(\bar{\tau}_a) = p(\bar{\tau}_h)$, where $\bar{\tau}_a$ is the type of an atom and $\bar{\tau}_h$ is the type of a head. Taking into account that the "type clauses" used for constructing the equations are renamed apart, all the head types (r.h.s.) have no parameter in common, the graph of $\rightarrow$ is a tree isomorphic to TS, and, by the head condition, $\bar{\tau}_a$ is an instance of $\bar{\tau}_h$. In the next subsection, we show that by decomposing each equation $p(\bar{\tau}_a) = p(\bar{\tau}_h)$, one can refine this condition.

4.3 Semi-generic Programs

In the head condition, all arguments of a predicate in clause head position are "generic" (i.e. their type is the declared type). One might say that all arguments are "head-generic". It is thus possible to generalise the head condition by partitioning the arguments of each predicate into those which stay head-generic and those which one requires to be generic for body atoms. The latter ones will be called *body-generic*. If we place the head-generic arguments of a clause head and the body-generic arguments of a clause body on the right hand sides of the equations associated with a type skeleton, then Condition 3 in Prop. 4.1 is met.

The other two conditions can be obtained in various ways, more or less complex to verify (an analysis of the analogous problem of not being subject to occur check (NSTO) can be found in [6]). Taking into account the renaming of "type clauses", a relation between two equations amounts to a shared parameter between a generic argument (r.h.s.) and a non-generic argument (l.h.s.) of a clause. We propose here a condition on the clauses which implies that the equations of any skeleton can be ordered.

In the following, an atom written as $p(\bar{s}, \bar{t})$ means: $\bar{s}$ and $\bar{t}$ are the vectors of terms filling the head-generic and body-generic positions of p, respectively. The notation $p(\bar{\sigma}, \bar{\tau})$, where σ and τ are types, is defined analogously.

Definition 4.2. Let $\_ \vdash P$ *Program* and $\_ \vdash C$ *Clause* where

$$C = p_{\bar{\tau}_0, \bar{\sigma}_{m+1}}(\bar{t}_0, \bar{s}_{m+1}) \leftarrow p^1_{\bar{\sigma}_1, \bar{\tau}_1}(\bar{s}_1, \bar{t}_1), \ldots, p^m_{\bar{\sigma}_m, \bar{\tau}_m}(\bar{s}_m, \bar{t}_m),$$

and Θ the type substitution such that $(\bar{\tau}_0, \bar{\sigma}_{m+1}, \bar{\sigma}_1, \bar{\tau}_1, \ldots, \bar{\sigma}_m, \bar{\tau}_m)\Theta$ is the most general type of C. We call C **semi-generic** if

1. for all $i, j \in \{0, \ldots, m\}$, $i \neq j$, $pars(\tau_i\Theta) \cap pars(\tau_j\Theta) = \emptyset$,
2. for all $i \in \{1, \ldots, m\}$, $pars(\bar{\sigma}_i) \cap \bigcup_{i \leq j \leq m} pars(\bar{\tau}_j) = \emptyset$,
3. for all $i \in \{0, \ldots, m\}$, $\tau_i\Theta = \tau_i$.

A query Q is **semi-generic** if the clause go $\leftarrow Q$ is semi-generic. A program is **semi-generic** if each of its clauses is semi-generic.

Note that semi-genericity has a strong resemblance with *nicely-modedness*, where head-generic corresponds to input, and body-generic corresponds to output. Nicely-modedness has been used, among other things, to show that programs are free from unification [1]. Semi-genericity serves a very similar purpose here. Note also that a typed program which fulfills the head condition is semi-generic, where all argument positions are head-generic.

The following theorem states subject reduction for semi-generic programs.

Theorem 4.2 (Proof see [8]). Every semi-generic program P has subject reduction wrt. the set of semi-generic queries.

The following example shows that our condition extends the class of programs that have subject reduction.

Example 4.1. Suppose $\mathcal{K}$ and $\mathcal{F}$ define lists as usual (see Ex. 3.1). Let $\mathcal{P} = \{\mathtt{p_{U,V}}, \mathtt{q_{U,V}}\}$ and assume that for $\mathtt{p}, \mathtt{q}$, the first argument is head-generic and the second argument is body-generic. Consider the following program.

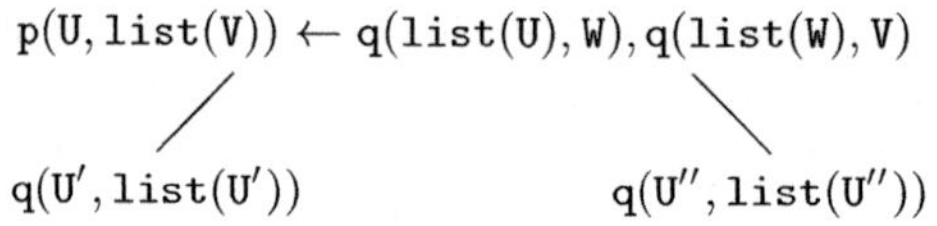

Fig. 6. A type skeleton for a semi-generic program

```
p(X,[Y]) <-                      %p(U,list(V)) <-
  q([X],Z), q([Z],Y).            %  q(list(U),W), q(list(W),V).
q(X,[X]).                        %q(U,list(U)).
```

This program is semi-generic. E.g. in the first type clause the terms in generic positions are U, W, V; all generic arguments have the declared type (condition 3); they do not share a parameter (condition 1); no generic argument in the body shares a parameter with a non-generic position to the left of it (condition 2). A type skeleton is shown in Fig. 6.

As another example, suppose now that $\mathcal{K}$ and $\mathcal{F}$ define list and integers, and consider the predicate r/2 specified as r(1, []), r(2, [[]]), r(3, [[[]]]) .... Its obvious definition would be

```
r(1,[]).
r(J,[X]) <-  r(J-1,X).
```

One can see that this program must violate the head condition no matter what the declared type of r is. However, assuming declared type (int, list(U)) and letting the second argument be body-generic, the program is semi-generic.

One can argue that in the second example, there is an intermingling of the typing and the computation, which contradicts the spirit of prescriptive typing. However, as we discuss in the next section, the situation is not always so clearcut.

5 What is the Use of the Head Condition?

The above results shed new light on the head condition. They allow us to view it as just one particularly simple condition guaranteeing type unifiability and consequently subject reduction and "well-typing" of the result, and hence a certain correctness of the program. This raises the question whether by generalising the condition, we have significantly enlarged the class of "well-typed" programs.

However, the head condition is also sometimes viewed as a condition inherent in the type system, or more specifically, an essential characteristic of *generic* polymorphism, as opposed to *ad-hoc* polymorphism. Generic polymorphism means that predicates are defined on an infinite number of types and that the definition is independent of a particular instance of the parameters. Ad-hoc polymorphism, often called *overloading* [19], means, e.g., to use the same symbol + for integer addition, matrix addition and list concatenation. Ad-hoc polymorphism is in fact forbidden by the head condition.

One way of reconciling ad-hoc polymorphism with the head condition is to enrich the type system so that types can be passed as parameters, and the definition of a predicate depends on these parameters [18]. Under such conditions, the head condition is regarded as natural.

So as a second, more general question, we discuss the legitimacy of the head condition briefly, since the answer justifies the interest in our first question.

In favour of the head condition, one could argue (1) that a program typed in this way does not compute types, but only propagates them; (2) that it allows for separate compilation since an imported predicate can be compiled without consulting its definition; and (3) that it disallows certain "unclean" programs [22].

In reality, these points are not, strictly speaking, fundamental arguments in favour of the head condition. Our generalisation does not necessarily imply a confusion between computation and typing (even if the result type does not depend on the result of a computation, it may be an instance of the declared type). Moreover, if the type declarations of the predicates are accompanied by declarations of the head- and body-generic arguments, separate compilation remains possible. Finally, Hanus [11] does not consider the head condition to be particularly natural, arguing that it is an important feature of logic programming that it allows for *lemma generation*.

We thus believe that the first question is, after all, relevant. So far, we have not been able to identify a "useful", non-contrived, example which clearly shows the interest in the class of semi-generically typed programs. The following example demonstrates the need for a generalisation, but also the insufficiency of the class defined in Def. 4.2.

Example 5.1. Let $\mathcal{K} = \{\mathtt{t}/1, \mathtt{int}/0\}$ and

$$\mathcal{F} = \{-1_{\to\mathtt{int}}, 0_{\to\mathtt{int}}, \ldots, \mathtt{c}_{\to\mathtt{t(U)}}, \mathtt{g}_{\mathtt{U}\to\mathtt{t(U)}}, \mathtt{f}_{\mathtt{t(t(U))}\to\mathtt{t(U)}}\}.$$

For all $i \geq 0$, we have $\_ \vdash \mathtt{g}^i(\mathtt{c}) : \mathtt{t}^{i+1}(\mathtt{U})$ and $\_ \vdash \mathtt{f}^i(\mathtt{g}^i(\mathtt{c})) : \mathtt{t(U)}$. This means that the set $\{\sigma \mid \exists s,t.\ s \text{ is subterm of } t,\ \_ \vdash s : \sigma,\ \_ \vdash t : \mathtt{t(U)}\}$ is infinite, or in words, there are infinitely many types that a subterm of a term of type $\mathtt{t(U)}$ can have. This property of the type $\mathtt{t(U)}$ is very unusual. In [26], a condition is considered (the *Reflexive Condition*) which rules out this situation.

Now consider the predicate $\mathtt{fgs}/2$ specified as $\mathtt{fgs}(i, \mathtt{f}^i(\mathtt{g}^i(\mathtt{c})))$ ($i \in \mathbb{N}$). Figure 7 presents three potential definitions of this predicate. The declared types are given by $\mathcal{P} = \{\mathtt{fgs1}_{\mathtt{int},\mathtt{t(U)}}, \mathtt{gs1}_{\mathtt{int},\mathtt{t(U)}}, \mathtt{fgs2}_{\mathtt{int},\mathtt{t(U)}}, \mathtt{fgs3}_{\mathtt{int},\mathtt{t(U)}}, \mathtt{fs1}_{\mathtt{int},\mathtt{t(U)},\mathtt{int}}, \mathtt{fs2}_{\mathtt{int},\mathtt{t(U)},\mathtt{int}}, \mathtt{gs2}_{\mathtt{int},\mathtt{t(U)},\mathtt{t(V)}}, \mathtt{fgs3\_aux}_{\mathtt{int},\mathtt{t(U)},\mathtt{t(U)}}\}$. The first solution is the most straightforward one, but its last clause does not fulfill the head condition. For the second solution, the fact clause `gs2(0,x,x).` does not fulfill the head condition. The third program fulfills the head condition but is the least obvious solution.

For the above example, the head condition is a real restriction. It prevents a solution using the most obvious algorithm, which is certainly a drawback of any type system. We suspected initially that it would be impossible to write a program fulfilling the specification of `fgs` without violating the head condition.

```
fgs1(I,Y) <-
  fs1(I,Y,I).

fs1(I,f(X),J) <-
  fs1(I-1,X,J).
fs1(0,X,J) <-
  gs1(J,X).

gs1(J,g(X)) <-
  gs1(J-1,X).
gs1(0,c).
```

```
fgs2(I,Y) <-
  fs2(I,Y,I).

fs2(I,f(X),J) <-
  fs2(I-1,X,J).
fs2(0,X,J) <-
  gs2(J,X,c).

gs2(J,X,Y) <-
  gs2(J-1,X,g(Y)).
gs2(0,X,X).
```

```
fgs3(I,X) <-
  fgs3_aux(I,c,X).

fgs3_aux(I,X,f(Y)) <-
  fgs3_aux(I-1,g(X),Y).
fgs3_aux(0,X,X).
```

Fig. 7. Three potential solutions for Ex. 5.1

Now it would of course be interesting to see if the first two programs, which violate the head condition, are semi-generic. Unfortunately, they are not. We explain this for the first program. The second position of gs1 must be body-generic because of the second clause for gs1. This implies that the second position of fs1 must also be body-generic because of the second clause for fs1 (otherwise there would be two generic positions with a common parameter). That however is unacceptable for the first clause of fs1 (X has type t(t(U)), instance of t(U)).

It can however be observed that both programs have subject reduction wrt. the queries fgs$j$(i, Y) for $i \in \mathbb{N}$ and $j = 1, 2$. In fact for these queries all type skeletons are proper, but it can be seen that the equations associated with the type skeletons cannot be ordered. This shows that the condition of semi-genericity is still too restrictive.

There is a perfect analogy between gs1 and r in Ex. 4.1.

To conclude this section, note that our solution to the problem in Ex. 5.1 uses *polymorphic recursion*, a concept previously discussed for functional programming [15]: In the recursive clause for fgs3_aux, the arguments of the recursive call have type (int, t(t(U)), t(t(U))), while the arguments of the clause head have type (int, t(U), t(U)). If we wrote a function corresponding to fgs3_aux in Miranda [30] or ML, the type checker could not infer its type, since it assumes that recursion is monomorphic, i.e., the type of a recursive call is identical to the type of the "head". In Miranda, this problem can be overcome by providing a type declaration, while in ML, the function will definitely be rejected. This limitation of the ML type system, or alternatively, the ML type checker, has been studied by Kahrs [14].

There is a certain duality between the head condition and monomorphic recursion. When trying to find a solution to our problem, we found that we either had to violate the head condition or use polymorphic recursion. For example, in the recursive clause for gs1, the arguments of the recursive call have type (int, t(U)), while the arguments of the clause head have type (int, t(t(U))), which is in a way the reverse of the situation for fgs3_aux. Note that this implies a violation of the head condition for *any* declared type of gs1. It would be interesting to investigate this duality further.

6 Conclusion

In this paper we redefined the notion of *subject reduction* by using derivation trees, leading to a proof-theoretic view of typing in logic programming. We showed that this new notion is equivalent to the operational one (Thm. 3.1).

We introduced *type skeletons*, obtained from skeletons by replacing terms with their types. We showed that a program has subject reduction if for each proper skeleton, the type skeleton is also proper. Apart from clarifying the motivations of the head condition, it has several potential applications:

- It facilitates studying the semantics of typed programs by simplifying its formulation in comparison to other works (e.g. [16]). Lifting the notions of derivation tree and skeleton on the level of types can help formulate proof-theoretic and operational semantics, just as this has been done for untyped logic programming with the classical trees [3, 6, 9].
- The approach may enhance program analysis based on abstract interpretation. Proper type skeletons could also be modelled by fixpoint operators [4, 5, 10]. Abstract interpretation for prescriptively typed programs has been studied by [24, 26], and it has been pointed out that the head condition is essential for ensuring that the abstract semantics of a program is finite, which is crucial for the termination of an analysis. It would be interesting to investigate the impact of more general conditions.
- This "proof-theoretic" approach to typing could also be applied for synthesis of typed programs. In [28], the authors propose the automatic generation of lemmas, using synthesis techniques based on resolution. It is interesting to observe that the generated lemmas meet the head condition, which our approach seems to be able to justify and even generalise.
- The approach may help in combining *prescriptive* and *descriptive* approaches to typing. The latter are usually based on partial correctness properties. Descriptive type systems satisfy certain criteria of type-correctness [7], but subject reduction is difficult to consider in such systems. Our approach is a step towards potential combinations of different approaches.

We have presented a condition for type unifiability which is a refinement of the head condition (Thm. 4.2). Several observations arise from this:

- Definition 4.2 is decidable. If the partitioning of the arguments is given, it can be verified in polynomial time. Otherwise, finding a partitioning is exponential in the number of argument positions.
- The refinement has a cost: subject reduction does not hold for arbitrary (typed) queries. The head condition, by its name, only restricts the clause heads, whereas our generalisation also restricts the queries, and hence the ways in which a program can be used.
- As we have seen, the proposed refinement may not be sufficient. Several approaches can be used to introduce further refinements based on abstract interpretation or on properties of sets of equations. Since any sufficient condition for type unifiability contains at least an NSTO condition, one could

also benefit from the refinements proposed for the NSTO check [6]. Such further refined conditions should, in particular, be fulfilled by all solutions of Ex. 5.1.

We have also studied *operational* subject reduction for type systems with subtyping [25]. As future work, we want to integrate that work with the *proof-theoretic* view of subject reduction of this paper. Also, we want to prove the undecidability of subject reduction and type unifiability, and design more refined tests for type unifiability.

Acknowledgements

We thank François Fages for interesting discussions. Jan-Georg Smaus was supported by an ERCIM fellowship.

References

1. K. R. Apt and S. Etalle. On the unification free Prolog programs. In A. Borzyszkowski and S. Sokolowski, editors, *Proceedings of the Conference on Mathematical Foundations of Computer Science*, volume 711 of *LNCS*, pages 1–19. Springer-Verlag, 1993.
2. C. Beierle. Type inferencing for polymorphic order-sorted logic programs. In L. Sterling, editor, *Proceedings of the Twelfth International Conference on Logic Programming*, pages 765–779. MIT Press, 1995.
3. A. Bossi, M. Gabbrielli, G. Levi, and M. Martelli. The *s*-semantics approach: theory and applications. *Journal of Logic Programming*, 19/20:149–197, 1991.
4. M. Comini, G. Levi, M. C. Meo, and G. Vitiello. Proving properties of logic programs by abstract diagnosis. In M. Dams, editor, *Analysis and Verification of Multiple-Agent Languages, 5th LOMAPS Workshop*, volume 1192 of *LNCS*, pages 22–50. Springer-Verlag, 1996.
5. P. Cousot and R. Cousot. Abstract interpretation: A unified lattice model for static analysis of programs by construction or approximation of fixpoints. In *Proceedings of the 4th Symposium on Principles of Programming Languages*, pages 238–252. ACM Press, 1977.
6. P. Deransart and J. Małuszyński. *A Grammatical View of Logic Programming.* MIT Press, 1993.
7. P. Deransart and J. Małuszyński. Towards soft typing for CLP. In F. Fages, editor, *JICSLP'98 Post-Conference Workshop on Types for Constraint Logic Programming.* École Normale Supérieure, 1998. Available at `http://discipl.inria.fr/TCLP98/`.
8. P. Deransart and J.-G. Smaus. Well-typed logic programs are not wrong. Technical Report RR-4082, INRIA, 2000. Available via CoRR: `http://arXiv.org/archive/cs/intro.html`.
9. M. Falaschi, G. Levi, M. Martelli, and C. Palamidessi. Declarative modeling of the operational behavior of logic languages. *Theoretical Computer Science*, 69(3):289–318, 1989.
10. R. Giacobazzi, S. K. Debray, and G. Levi. Generalized semantics and abstract interpretation for constraint logic programs. *Journal of Logic Programming*, 25(3):191–247, 1995.

11. M. Hanus. *Logic Programming with Type Specifications*, chapter 3, pages 91–140. In [23].
12. P. M. Hill and J. W. Lloyd. *The Gödel Programming Language*. MIT Press, 1994.
13. P. M. Hill and R. W. Topor. *A Semantics for Typed Logic Programs*, chapter 1, pages 1–61. In [23].
14. S. Kahrs. Limits of ML-definability. In H. Kuchen and S. D. Swierstra, editors, *Proceedings of the 8th Symposium on Programming Language Implementations and Logic Programming*, volume 1140 of *LNCS*, pages 17–31. Springer-Verlag, 1996.
15. A. J. Kfoury, J. Tiuryn, and P. Urzyczyn. Type reconstruction in the presence of polymorphic recursion. *ACM Transactions on Programming Languages and Systems*, 15(2):290–311, 1993.
16. T.K. Lakshman and U.S. Reddy. Typed Prolog: A semantic reconstruction of the Mycroft-O'Keefe type system. In V. Saraswat and K. Ueda, editors, *Proceedings of the 1991 International Symposium on Logic Programming*, pages 202–217. MIT Press, 1991.
17. J. W. Lloyd. *Foundations of Logic Programming*. Springer-Verlag, 1987.
18. P. Louvet and O. Ridoux. Parametric polymorphism for Typed Prolog and λProlog. In H. Kuchen and S. D. Swierstra, editors, *Proceedings of the 8th Symposium on Programming Language Implementations and Logic Programming*, volume 1140 of *LNCS*, pages 47–61. Springer-Verlag, 1996.
19. R. Milner. A theory of type polymorphism in programming. *Journal of Computer and System Sciences*, 17(3):348–375, 1978.
20. A. Mycroft and R. O'Keefe. A polymorphic type system for Prolog. *Artificial Intelligence*, 23:295–307, 1984.
21. G. Nadathur and F. Pfenning. *Types in Higher-Order Logic Programming*, chapter 9, pages 245–283. In [23].
22. R. A. O'Keefe. *The Craft of Prolog*. MIT Press, 1990.
23. F. Pfenning, editor. *Types in Logic Programming*. MIT Press, 1992.
24. O. Ridoux, P. Boizumault, and F. Malésieux. Typed static analysis: Application to groundness analysis of Prolog and λProlog. In A. Middeldorp and T. Sato, editors, *Proceedings of the 4th Fuji International Symposium on Functional and Logic Programming*, volume 1722 of *LNCS*, pages 267–283. Springer-Verlag, 1999.
25. J.-G. Smaus, F. Fages, and P. Deransart. Using modes to ensure subject reduction for typed logic programs with subtyping. In S. Kapoor and S. Prasad, editors, *Proceedings of the 20th Conference on the Foundations of Software Technology and Theoretical Computer Science*, volume 1974 of *LNCS*. Springer-Verlag, 2000.
26. J.-G. Smaus, P. M. Hill, and A. M. King. Mode analysis domains for typed logic programs. In A. Bossi, editor, *Proceedings of the 9th International Workshop on Logic-based Program Synthesis and Transformation*, volume 1817 of *LNCS*, pages 83–102, 2000.
27. Z. Somogyi, F. Henderson, and T. Conway. The execution algorithm of Mercury, an efficient purely declarative logic programming language. *Journal of Logic Programming*, 29(1–3):17–64, 1996.
28. P. Tarau, K. De Bosschere, and B. Demoen. On Delphi lemmas and other memoing techniques for deterministic logic programs. *Journal of Logic Programming*, 30(2):145–163, 1997.
29. Simon Thompson. *Type Theory and Functional Programming*. Addison-Wesley, 1991.
30. Simon Thompson. *Miranda: The Craft of Functional Programming*. Addison-Wesley, 1995.

A Framework for Analysis of Typed Logic Programs

Vitaly Lagoon and Peter J. Stuckey

Dept. of Computer Science and Software Engineering
University of Melbourne, Parkville 3052, Australia
{lagoon,pjs}@cs.mu.oz.au

Abstract. The paper presents a novel approach to the analysis of typed logic programs. We assume regular type descriptions of logic program variables provided by *regular tree grammars*. Types are used to identify components of terms which can be equated during the programs execution. This information is reflected in form of *set constraints* in the generic abstract domain called Type(X). The domain allows for abstract compilation of typed logic programs into *set logic programs*. We demonstrate how the analyzers of *groundness* and *sharing* of typed logic programs are obtained by applying the existing (untyped) techniques based on Pos and Sharing to set logic programs. The corresponding analyses in Type(Pos) and Type(Sharing) are more precise than those in Pos and Sharing.

1 Introduction

Recent logic programming languages Gödel [10], Mercury [19] and HAL [5] are strongly typed, using variations of Hindley-Milner [15] type systems. Prescriptive type information is useful for detecting many simple programming errors, and gives a new source of information to use in optimizing compilation. The advantages of type information in efficient execution are well illustrated by the performance of Mercury programs. Additionally systems [6] exist for automatically inferring regular tree types from programs. Once such a type is inferred we can use the information in later analyses to improve the accuracy of the results.

In this paper we examine how we can analyze (regular-tree) typed logic programs. Analysis of typed logic programs is important for optimizing compilation of Mercury and HAL.

Types allow analyses to be more accurate than analyses of the corresponding untyped programs. For example consider the analysis of the typed "append" program shown in Figure 1. The types of A, B, C, D and E are lists. A typed analysis separates a list variable v into two parts, the skeleton of the list L_v, and the elements of the list E_v. The analysis creates a CLP(B) program relating the boundness of these different parts of the list. The bottom-up abstract evaluation of abstract "append" results in:

$$\mathsf{append}(\langle L_A, E_A\rangle, \langle L_B, E_B\rangle, \langle L_C, E_C\rangle) \texttt{ :- } L_A,\ L_B \leftrightarrow L_C,\ E_C \leftrightarrow E_A \wedge E_B.$$

H. Kuchen and K. Ueda (Eds.): FLOPS 2001, LNCS 2024, pp. 296–310, 2001.

```
append(A,B,C) :-
    A = [],
    B = C.

append(A,B,C) :-
    A = [X|D],
    C = [X|E],
    append(D,B,E).
```

$$\begin{array}{l}\text{append}(\langle L_A, E_A\rangle, \langle L_B, E_B\rangle, \langle L_C, E_C\rangle) \text{ :-}\\ \quad L_A \leftrightarrow \top,\ E_A \leftrightarrow \top,\\ \quad L_B \leftrightarrow L_C,\ E_B \leftrightarrow E_C.\end{array}$$

$$\begin{array}{l}\text{append}(\langle L_A, E_A\rangle, \langle L_B, E_B\rangle, \langle L_C, E_C\rangle) \text{ :-}\\ \quad L_A \leftrightarrow L_D,\ E_A \leftrightarrow E_X \wedge E_D,\\ \quad L_C \leftrightarrow L_E,\ E_C \leftrightarrow E_X \wedge E_E,\\ \quad \text{append}(\langle L_D, E_D\rangle, \langle L_B, E_B\rangle, \langle L_E, E_E\rangle).\end{array}$$

Fig. 1. Abstraction of append

showing that on success the list skeleton of A is fixed and the skeleton of B is fixed if and only if that of C is, and the elements are related in the usual way. This more specific information can be used to improve program optimizations. The usual groundness analysis of "append" only gives the answer $C \leftrightarrow A \wedge B$, i.e. C is ground if and only if A and B are ground. With this information it is not possible to determine that the goal `append([A,B],[C,D],E),append(E,F,G)` will result in the list skeleton of E being fixed. This might prevent a partial evaluator evaluating the second call to "append".

It is important to stress that the type-based analyses proposed in this paper are not only more expressive as can be seen from the above example but also more precise in a strict sense. As a simplest example consider the unification $f(A, B) = f(C, D)$. While the standard Pos approximation of groundness produces $(A \wedge B) \leftrightarrow (C \wedge D)$, in our type-based analysis we may get $(A \leftrightarrow C) \wedge (B \leftrightarrow D)$, which is clearly a more precise Pos approximation.

The rest of the paper is organized as follows. In the next section we give some preliminary definitions, in particular those for deterministic tree automata and deterministic regular tree grammars. In Section 3 we define how we can relate the types of variables occurring in constraints. In Section 4, we present the parametric abstract domain Type(X) which adds type information to an abstract domain X, as well as the corresponding abstraction of typed logic programs into programs over set constraints. In Sections 5 and 6 we present the techniques of groundness and sharing analysis of typed logic programs based on Type(X). Finally, in Section 7 we provide a brief comparison with some related works and conclude.

2 Preliminaries

In the following we assume a familiarity with the standard definitions and notation for logic programs as described in [13] and with the framework of abstract interpretation [4]. For a set of function symbols Σ and variables $\mathcal{V}$, we let $T(\Sigma, \mathcal{V})$ denote the set of *terms* constructed using symbols from Σ and variables from $\mathcal{V}$. The set of atoms constructed using predicate symbols from Π and terms from $T(\Sigma, \mathcal{V})$ is denoted by $\mathcal{B}$. The set of variables occurring in a syntactic object s is denoted vars(s). We say that a term t is ground if vars$(t) = \emptyset$.

We assume the rules of the program are in *canonical form*. That is, procedure calls and rule heads are normalized such that parameters are distinct variables, unifications are broken into sequences of simple *unification constraints* and nested terms are flattened by introducing intermediate variables. Unification constraints are elements of the set $\mathcal{C}$ and can be either in the form $X = Y$, where both X and Y are variables, or in the form $X = f(Y_1, \ldots, Y_n)$, where $f/n \in \Sigma$, $n \geq 0$ and $X, Y_1, \ldots, Y_n$ are variables. A body of a rule in canonical form contains only unification constraints and procedure calls in the form $p(X_1, \ldots, X_n)$ where $p/n \in \Pi$ is a predicate symbol and $X_1, \ldots, X_n$ are distinct variables (parameters). In addition, the heads of each rule for predicate p are required to be identical atoms $p(X_{p1}, \ldots, X_{pn})$, and every variable not appearing in the head of a rule is required to appear in exactly one rule. It is straightforward to convert any logic program to this canonical form. The concrete (left-hand) side of "append" shown in Figure 1 is in canonical form. The domain of *facts* is denoted by $\mathcal{B}_\mathcal{C}$ and consists of rules of the form $p(X_1, \ldots, X_n) \leftarrow C_1, \ldots, C_k$, where $C_1 \ldots C_k$ are unification constraints.

Regular Types Deterministic regular types are defined as a class of languages accepted by top-down deterministic regular tree automata [7]. The analysis presented below can be performed if such regular types are either given explicitly as in Mercury,[1] or inferred through any mechanism (for example [6]).

Definition 1 (Top-Down Deterministic Tree Automata). *A top-down deterministic finite tree automaton (top-down DFTA) is a tuple* $\mathcal{A} = \langle q_0, Q, \Sigma, \Delta \rangle$, *where* Q *is a set of states,* $q_0 \in Q$ *is an initial state and* Δ *is a set of transition rules in the form:* $q(f(x_1, \ldots, x_n)) \rightarrow f(q_1(x_1), \ldots, q_n(x_n))$, *such that no two rules have the same left-hand side.*

Top-down deterministic tree automata accept the class of languages called *regular types*, which is a proper subset of regular tree languages and is closed under intersection.

Example 1. The deterministic tree automata $A = \langle q_L, \{q_L, q_E\}, \{cons/2, a/0, b/0\}, \Delta \rangle$, where $\Delta = \{q_L(\text{nil}) \rightarrow \text{nil},\ q_L(\text{cons}(x, y)) \rightarrow \text{cons}(q_E(x), q_L(y)),\ q_E(a) \rightarrow a,\ q_E(b) \rightarrow b\}$ accepts ground lists of a's and b's.

Definition 2 (Regular Tree Grammar). *A regular tree grammar is a tuple* $\mathcal{G} = \langle S, W, \Sigma, \Delta \rangle$, *where:* S *is a starting non-terminal,* W *is a finite set of non-terminal symbols, s.t.* $S \in W$, Σ *is a set of function symbols,* Δ *is a set of productions in the form* $X \rightarrow f(Y_1, \ldots, Y_n)$ *s. t.* $X, Y_1 \ldots Y_n \in W$ *and* $f/n \in \Sigma$.

Definition 2 is more restrictive than in the standard definitions (e.g. [7]). We assume a *normal form* of productions which allows only one function symbol in each rule. However, this restriction is merely syntactic since productions with two or more function symbols can always be converted into a normal form by introducing new non-terminals. For instance, $A \rightarrow f(g(X))$ can be rewritten using a new non-terminal G as $A \rightarrow f(G)$, $G \rightarrow g(X)$.

[1] It is straightforward to convert the Hindley-Milner types of Mercury to (weaker) deterministic regular types.

Definition 3 (Deterministic Regular Tree Grammars). *A regular tree grammar* $\mathcal{G} = \langle V, W, \Sigma, \Delta \rangle$ *as given by Definition 2 is deterministic if for a non-terminal* $X \in W$ *and any two corresponding productions* $(X \to f(Y_1, \ldots, Y_n)) \in \Delta$ *and* $(X \to g(Z_1, \ldots, Z_m)) \in \Delta$ *we always have* $f/n \neq g/m$.

Deterministic regular tree grammars define the same class of languages as top-down deterministic tree automata. Moreover, by assuming the normal form of grammar we achieve the syntactic uniformity of the two formalisms. Transitions of an automaton can be converted into grammar productions and vice versa by associating each non-terminal symbol with a corresponding state of the automaton.

Example 2. The following regular tree grammar clearly defines the same language as accepted by the tree automaton in Example 1: $L \to nil \mid cons(E, L)$, $E \to a \mid b$.

The equivalence of regular tree grammars and tree automata allows us for the clear and expressive representation of derivations as transitions of a *deterministic rewriting system* in the form $N(c) \longrightarrow c$ for a constant c or in the form $N(f(t_1, \ldots, t_n)) \longrightarrow f(N_1(t_1), \ldots, N_n(t_n))$ for $f/n \in \Sigma$ and $n > 0$. Using this notation we say that the grammar $\mathcal{G} = \langle S, W, \Sigma, \Delta \rangle$ accepts (derives) a term t if $S(t) \stackrel{*}{\longrightarrow}_{\mathcal{G}} t$. Sometimes we restrict our attention to a single path or a segment of a path of a derivation tree starting from the root (S) and reaching a non-terminal N with a subterm t' of t: $S(t) \stackrel{*}{\longrightarrow}_{\mathcal{G}} N(t')$.

Definition 4 (Acceptance of Non-Ground Terms). *A regular tree grammar* $\mathcal{G}$ *accepts a non-ground term* t*, denoted* $t \in \mathcal{L}(\mathcal{G})$*, if and only if it accepts some ground instance of* t.

Example 3. The grammar shown in Example 2 accepts the terms $\mathrm{cons}(a, \mathrm{cons}(C, \mathrm{nil}))$ and $\mathrm{cons}(C, D)$ but not $\mathrm{cons}(\mathrm{cons}(C, \mathrm{nil}), \mathrm{nil})$.

We assume through the rest of this paper that the term "grammar" refers to a deterministic regular tree grammar provided by Definition 3. We also treat the terms "state" and "non-terminal" as equivalent and interchangeable due to the uniformity of the corresponding formalisms. As a consequence, we make no distinction between a "run" of a top-down deterministic tree automaton and a "derivation" using a deterministic regular tree grammar.

3 Properties of Typed Logic Programs

A *typed logic program* is a program in canonical form, together with an association of the variables of the program to regular tree grammars. For a variable $V \in \mathcal{V}$ we assume a deterministic regular tree grammar $\mathcal{G}_V = \langle S_V, W_V, \Sigma, \Delta_V \rangle$, conforming to Definitions 2 and 3. We assume grammars associated with different variables do not involve the same non-terminal symbol (if not we can rename appropriately).

In addition we require that all calls to a predicate name $p/n \in \Pi$ have the same type (a renaming of the grammar) as the head. This means that all

```
p(X) :- q(X).                    p(X) :- X = Z, q(Z).
q(Y) :- ...                      q(Y) :- ...
```

Assuming the types of X, Y and Z are:

$$\begin{array}{ll} \mathcal{G}_X: & L_X \rightarrow nil \mid cons(E_X, L'_X),\ L'_X \rightarrow cons(E_X, L_X),\ E_X \rightarrow a \mid b. \\ \mathcal{G}_Y: & L_Y \rightarrow nil \mid cons(E_Y, L_Y),\ E_Y \rightarrow a \mid b. \\ \mathcal{G}_Z: & L_Z \rightarrow nil \mid cons(E_Z, L_Z),\ E_Z \rightarrow a \mid b. \end{array}$$

Fig. 2. Modifying a program so that each predicate call has the same type as the head.

implicit type casts of procedure parameters are converted into explicit unification constraints. For example the program in the left of Figure 2 must be rewritten as on the right.

The analyses presented in this paper assume that the program is well-typed in the sense of Mycroft and O'Keefe [17]. That is, the results of analyses approximate semantics computed through a sequence of type-correct resolution steps. A type-correct resolution step, whether it is top-down or bottom-up, is restricted to considering only a type-correct subset of the result.

Types of Terms Satisfying Program Constraints Let us now lift the concept of typing of program variables to the level of unification constraints. In particular, we are interested in the internal structure of grammars providing the types of terms satisfying the unification constraints.

The type of terms satisfying a constraint $X = Y$ is naturally computed from the associated grammars $\mathcal{G}_X = \langle S_X, W_X, \Sigma, \Delta_X \rangle$ and $\mathcal{G}_Y = \langle S_Y, W_Y, \Sigma, \Delta_Y \rangle$ as a grammar $\mathcal{G}_\cap = \langle S_\cap, W_\cap, \Sigma, \Delta_\cap \rangle$ for the intersection of (languages of) $\mathcal{G}_X$ and $\mathcal{G}_Y$, where $S_\cap = \langle S_X, S_Y \rangle$, $W_\cap$ is a reachable (through the rules of $\Delta_\cap$) subset of $W_X \times W_Y$ and $\langle N_X, N_Y \rangle \rightarrow f(\langle N_1, N'_1 \rangle, \ldots \langle N_n, N'_n \rangle) \in \Delta_\cap$ iff $N_X \rightarrow f(N_1, \ldots, N_n) \in \Delta_X$ and $N_Y \rightarrow f(N'_1, \ldots, N'_n) \in \Delta_Y$.

The type of terms satisfying a constraint $X = f(Y_1, \ldots, Y_n)$ is computed in two steps. First, the types of $Y_1 \ldots Y_n$ are combined into a new grammar $\mathcal{G}_Y = \langle S_f, W_Y, \Sigma, \Delta_Y \rangle$, defining the type of $f(Y_1, \ldots, Y_n)$, s.t. S_f is a new starting symbol, $W_Y = \{S_f\} \cup W_{Y_1} \cup \cdots \cup W_{Y_n}$ and $\Delta_Y = \{S_f \rightarrow f(S_{Y_1}, \ldots, S_{Y_n})\} \cup \Delta_{Y_1} \cup \cdots \cup \Delta_{Y_n}$. Then the intersection of (languages of) $\mathcal{G}_X$ and $\mathcal{G}_Y$ is computed as shown above.

It follows that the type of terms satisfying a program constraint corresponds to an intersection of (languages of) the grammars of two sides of the constraints. Each state of the grammar for this type is in the form $\langle A, B \rangle$, where A and B are non-terminals of the left-hand side and right-hand side grammars respectively.

Labelling The concept of labelling of non-terminals introduced in this paper is a basis for reasoning about the properties of possibly non-ground objects with respect to their types. The idea of labelling consists in associating the non-terminals of type grammars with sets of variables. In general, the need for augmenting the type information with some additional attributes naturally arises in the context of any analysis based on regular types. It is motivated by the insufficient expressive power of the underlying type mechanism. For instance, dependencies such as "two subterms are identical" or "two variables can share" are non-regular and thus, cannot be expressed as regular types.

Definition 5 (Labelling). *A variable V of a non-ground term t labels a non-terminal N of a grammar $\mathcal{G}$ if there exists a path in the run of $\mathcal{G}$ on t such that $S(t) \xrightarrow{*}_{\mathcal{G}} N(V)$, where S is a starting symbol of $\mathcal{G}$.*

In the following we assume a function $\zeta(\mathcal{G}, N, t)$ returning the set of labels of a non-terminal N of the grammar $\mathcal{G}$ on its run on a term t. By our assumption different grammars have different sets of non-terminal symbols and thus, it is always unambiguous to use the more compact notation $\zeta(N, t)$.

Example 4. Consider the labelling imposed by the term $t = [A, B|D]$ on the non-terminals for the regular tree grammar accepting lists: $L_X \rightarrow \text{nil} \mid \text{cons}(E_X, L_X)$. We can see that $\zeta(L_X, t) = \{D\}$ since $L_X(t) \xrightarrow{*} L_X(D)$ and $\zeta(E_X, t) = \{A, B\}$ since $L_X(t) \xrightarrow{*} E_X(A)$ and $L_X(t) \xrightarrow{*} E_X(B)$.

The concept of labelling of states (non-terminals) is a basis for the analyses shown below in this paper. Labelling allows us to associate different variables of a term with different non-terminals of the corresponding regular tree grammar. Thus, we can analyze the presence (or absence) of variables, groundness dependencies, sharing of variables, etc. on the *per-role* basis, computing more precise results than traditional untyped analyses usually operating on the *per-term* basis. For instance, this allows us to analyze groundness of "append" separately for list structure and list elements.

Labelling in Constraint Types Let's now apply the notion of labelling to the results about types of terms satisfying unification constraints. Assume a grammar $\mathcal{G}_\cap$ defining the type of terms satisfying a unification constraint C. Recall that all non-terminals of $\mathcal{G}_\cap$ can be viewed as pairs $\langle A, B\rangle$ where A and B are non-terminals of the left-hand side grammar $\mathcal{G}_X$ and right-hand side grammar $\mathcal{G}_Y$ respectively. Assume that a term t satisfying C labels some non-terminal A of $\mathcal{G}_X$ by a set of variables S on the run of $\mathcal{G}_X$ on t, i.e. $\zeta(\mathcal{G}_X, A, t) = S$. Now consider a run of $\mathcal{G}_\cap$ on t. Since $\mathcal{G}_\cap$ defines the intersection of (languages of) $\mathcal{G}_X$ and $\mathcal{G}_Y$, the elements of S can label only the non-terminals $\langle A, B\rangle$ of $\mathcal{G}_\cap$, i.e. the pairs with A in the first position. Thus, in a run of $\mathcal{G}_Y$ on t, the labels of S are divided between all such non-terminals B for which there exists a reachable non-terminal $\langle A, B\rangle$ of $\mathcal{G}_\cap$. Naturally, the same arguments can be applied in the opposite direction, i.e. by fixing a non-terminal $B \in W_Y$ and reasoning about its labels. Thus, for a term $t \in \mathcal{L}(\mathcal{G}_\cap)$ we have:

$$\forall A \in W_X.\ \zeta(A, t) \subseteq \bigcup_{\langle A,B\rangle \in W_\cap} \zeta(B, t) \tag{1}$$

$$\forall B \in W_Y.\ \zeta(B, t) \subseteq \bigcup_{\langle A,B\rangle \in W_\cap} \zeta(A, t). \tag{2}$$

Partitions of Non-Terminals As we can see, the sharing of labels by non-terminals of grammars $\mathcal{G}_X$ and $\mathcal{G}_Y$ is merely determined by the presence of particular pairs $\langle A, B\rangle$ in the set of reachable states of the intersection—the grammar $\mathcal{G}_\cap$. The two non-terminals $X \in W_X$ and $Y \in W_Y$ can have some labels in common if they can be related by some chain of states of $\mathcal{G}_\cap$, e.g. $\langle X, W\rangle \ldots \langle Z, W\rangle \ldots \langle Z, Y\rangle$. The more important fact is that a most general solution of the unification constraint cannot introduce sharing of labels between non-terminals that cannot be related through a chain of states of $\mathcal{G}_\cap$. In the following we formalize these two claims as theorems.

The notion of related states is formalized as the equivalence relation partitioning the state space W of $\mathcal{G}_\cap$ into the (disjoint) classes of states $W_\cap^{\mathcal{P}} = \{W_\cap^1, \ldots W_\cap^k\}$. The partitioning is induced by the following relation:

$$\forall \langle A, B\rangle \in W_\cap^i\ \forall \langle A', B'\rangle \in W_\cap^j.\ i \neq j \Rightarrow A \neq A' \wedge B \neq B'. \tag{3}$$

We say that two non-terminals $X, Y \in (W_X \cup W_Y)$ are *dependent* if the states of $\mathcal{G}_\cap$ including X and the states of $\mathcal{G}_\cap$ including Y appear in the same partition of $W_\cap$. We say that the non-terminals are *independent* otherwise.

Theorem 1. *Assume a unification constraint C, the grammars $\mathcal{G}_X$ and $\mathcal{G}_Y$ defining respectively the types of the left-hand side and the right-hand side of C, the grammar $\mathcal{G}_\cap$ such that $\mathcal{L}(\mathcal{G}_\cap) = \mathcal{L}(\mathcal{G}_X) \cap \mathcal{L}(\mathcal{G}_Y)$ and the partitioning $W_\cap^{\mathcal{P}} = \{W_\cap^1, \ldots, W_\cap^k\}$ of states of $\mathcal{G}_\cap$. Then for any $t \in \mathcal{L}(\mathcal{G}_\cap)$ and $i \in \{1 \ldots k\}$:*

$$\bigcup_{\langle X,Y\rangle \in W_\cap^i} \zeta(X, t) = \bigcup_{\langle X,Y\rangle \in W_\cap^i} \zeta(Y, t)$$

Proof. *In two directions using Equations (1) and (2).*

Theorem 1 provides us with the basic relation for the dependency between labelling sets of classes of non-terminals. This relation is based entirely on types of variables participating in the corresponding constraints and thus, can be computed statically. Now let us investigate the other side, i.e. the statically-known facts about independence of (labelling of) non-terminals.

Assume without loss of generality a constraint $C : X = f(Y_1, \ldots, Y_n)$, the grammars $\mathcal{G}_X$ and $\mathcal{G}_Y$ defining respectively the types of the left-hand side and the right-hand side of C and the grammar $\mathcal{G}_\cap$ defining the intersection of (languages of) $\mathcal{G}_X$ and $\mathcal{G}_Y$. Assume that the constraint C is solved in the environment $\psi = \{X/t_X, Y_1/t_1, \ldots Y_n/t_n\}$. Thus, solving C consists in finding the most general unifier of two terms: t_X and t_Y, where $t_Y = f(t_1, \ldots, t_n)$. Let $\theta = \mathrm{mgu}(t_X, t_Y)$. Now assume that A and B are two independent non-terminals of $\mathcal{G}_X$ and $\mathcal{G}_Y$ respectively. We claim that solving C cannot introduce any new sharing of labels of A and B. In other words, solving C cannot unify a variable from $\zeta(A, t_X)$ with a variable from $\zeta(B, t_Y)$.

Theorem 2. *For a unification problem $t_X \doteq t_Y$ with the types of t_X and t_Y given by the grammars $\mathcal{G}_X$ and $\mathcal{G}_Y$, the constraint solution $\theta = \mathrm{mgu}(t_X, t_Y)$ and two independent non-terminals A and B of $\mathcal{G}_X$ and $\mathcal{G}_Y$ respectively:*

$$\zeta(A, t_X) \cap \zeta(B, t_Y) = \emptyset \Rightarrow \zeta(A, t_X\theta) \cap \zeta(B, t_Y\theta) = \emptyset$$

Corollary 1. *Most general solutions of unification constraints never unify variables labelling independent non-terminals of type grammars.*

The results of Theorems 1 and 2 lead us to what we see as the main contribution of this work. Namely, the fact that by analyzing set constraints similar to the one in the claim of Theorem 1 we can obtain correct static approximations of properties such as groundness and sharing imposed by the corresponding unification constraint. Indeed, Theorem 1 approximates the ways in which labels (variables) can be unified when solving the corresponding unification constraint. Theorem 2 serves as a safety statement for Theorem 1 claiming that there are no other ways in which labels can be unified. Thus, correct descriptions of groundness and sharing dependencies can be derived using Theorem 1. Moreover, these descriptions are in general more precise than the results of traditional untyped analyses. This is because in our case the analysis is performed independently on the corresponding components of terms (i.e. per-role) and not on whole terms as in the traditional approach (e.g. [14]).

Note that in general the relations as shown in Theorem 1 may not include all non-terminals of the corresponding left-hand side and right-hand side grammars. Assume without loss of generality a non-terminal N of the left-hand side grammar $\mathcal{G}_X$. It is possible that the grammar defining the intersection does not contain any state in the form $\langle N, N' \rangle$. It means that no term satisfying the constraint can reach the state N on its run (derivation) in $\mathcal{G}_X$. Thus, $\zeta(N, t) = \emptyset$ for any t. We want to preserve this information in the abstract domains shown in the following sections. Thus, assuming the sets W_X, W_Y and $W_\cap$ of non-terminals of the left-hand side, right-hand side and the intersection grammars respectively we define a set of unreachable non-terminals:

$$W_\emptyset = \begin{array}{l} \{\, A \in W_X \mid \forall B \in W_Y .\ \langle A, B \rangle \notin W_\cap \,\} \cup \\ \{\, B \in W_Y \mid \forall A \in W_X .\ \langle A, B \rangle \notin W_\cap \,\} . \end{array} \tag{4}$$

4 Abstraction of Typed Logic Programs

The analyses described in this paper are constructed using a first order language, similar to that of logic programs, called *set logic programs*. In the previous works [2, 3] set logic programs are shown to be a clean and powerful formalism for designing program analyses.

Syntactically, we assume a set of variables $\mathcal{V}$ and an underlying alphabet $\Sigma^\oplus = \{\oplus/2, \emptyset/0\}$ consisting of a single binary function symbol $\oplus$ which "glues" elements together and a single constant symbol $\emptyset$ to represent the empty set. Abstract terms, or *set expressions*, are elements of the term algebra $\mathcal{T}(\Sigma^\oplus, \mathcal{V})$ modulo an equality theory consisting of the following axioms:

$$\begin{array}{llll} (x \oplus y) \oplus z = x \oplus (y \oplus z) & \text{(associativity)} & x \oplus x = x & \text{(idempotence)} \\ x \oplus y = y \oplus x & \text{(commutativity)} & x \oplus \emptyset = x & \text{(unity)} \end{array} \tag{5}$$

This equality theory is sometimes referred to as ACI1 and the corresponding equivalence relation on terms denoted $\approx$. This notion of equivalence suggests that abstract terms can be viewed as flat sets of variables. For example, the terms $x_1 \oplus x_2 \oplus x_3$, $x_1 \oplus x_2 \oplus x_3 \oplus \emptyset$, and $x_1 \oplus x_2 \oplus x_3 \oplus x_2$ can each be viewed as representing the set $\{x_1, x_2, x_3\}$ of three variables.

In this work we introduce the abstraction of unification constraints of typed logic programs into set constraints (ACI1-unification constraints). Set constraints are the elements of the set $\mathcal{C}^{\oplus} = \mathcal{T}(\Sigma^{\oplus}, \mathcal{V}) \times \mathcal{T}(\Sigma^{\oplus}, \mathcal{V})$ and are in the form $x \approx y$, where x and y are set expressions. The constraints are derived from the result of Theorem 1 as follows. Assuming a most general instance t satisfying the unification constraint we abstract each $\varsigma(N, t)$ to an abstract variable also named N. This variable denotes the set of possible labels of the non-terminal N. We also let "$\oplus$" replace "$\cup$" in abstract constraints. This is done mainly because our abstract operations deal with abstract constraints literally and do not attach to the binary combinator "$\oplus$" any other meaning than prescribed by ACI1-axioms of Equation (5). The resulting set constraints reflect the relations between sets of concrete variables corresponding to dependent non-terminals of the type grammars, i.e. classes of variables which can interfere during the program execution.

Abstraction of Program Constraints Function σ_1, defined below, maps constraints of the form $X = Y$ to corresponding set constraints. We assume we are given the partition $W_{\cap}^{\mathcal{P}} = \{W_{\cap}^1, \dots W_{\cap}^k\}$ of non-terminals of the grammar $\mathcal{G}_{\cap}$ defining the type of terms satisfying the constraint and the set of unreachable non-terminals $W_{\emptyset}$ as defined by Equation (4).

$$\sigma_1(C) = \left\{ \bigoplus_{\langle A,B\rangle \in W_{\cap}^i} A \approx \bigoplus_{\langle A,B\rangle \in W_{\cap}^i} B \;\middle|\; i = 1 \dots k \right\} \cup \{ N \approx \emptyset \mid N \in W_{\emptyset} \} \quad (6)$$

Example 5. Consider the abstraction of the constraint $B = C$ from the first rule of concrete "append" (Figure 1). Assume that B and C are lists with the types defined as $L_A \to nil \mid cons(E_A, L_A)$ and $L_B \to nil \mid cons(E_B, L_B)$. Here we assume that E_A and E_B derive all possible terms thus, effectively providing the "any" type of elements. The grammar defining the intersection is: $\langle L_B, L_C\rangle \to \text{nil} \mid \text{cons}(\langle E_B, E_C\rangle, \langle L_B, L_C\rangle)$. Each of $\langle L_B, L_C\rangle$ and $\langle E_B, E_C\rangle$ forms an independent partition of the state space of this grammar. Thus, application of σ_1 of Equation (6) to the constraint produces: $\{L_B \approx L_C,\ E_B \approx E_C\}$. Note that the set $W_{\emptyset}$ is empty in this example.

The abstraction of constraints in the form $X = f(Y_1, \dots, Y_n)$ is almost the same as for $X = Y$. In addition we take into account the fact that only bound terms can satisfy the constraint. Thus, for any term t satisfying the constraint we have $\varsigma(S_f, t) = \emptyset$, where S_f is a starting symbols of the right-hand side grammar. The function of abstraction σ_2 is defined for this case as:

$$\sigma_2(C) = \sigma_1(C) \cup \{S_f \approx \emptyset\} \quad (7)$$

Example 6. Consider the abstraction of the constraint $A = [X|D]$ from the second rule of concrete "append" (Figure 1). Assume that A and D are lists defined respectively by the grammars $L_A \to \text{nil} \mid \text{cons}(E_A, L_A)$ and $L_D \to \text{nil} \mid \text{cons}(E_D, L_D)$. The intersection of the grammar for the right-hand side of the constraint with the grammar for A results in:

$$\begin{aligned} \mathcal{G}_{\cap} : \langle L_A, S_{\text{cons}}\rangle &\to \text{cons}(\langle E_A, S_X\rangle, \langle L_A, L_D\rangle) \\ \langle L_A, L_D\rangle &\to \text{nil} \mid \text{cons}(\langle E_A, E_D\rangle, \langle L_A, L_D\rangle), \end{aligned}$$

where S_{cons} is a starting non-terminal of the grammar for the right-hand side. The partition of states of $\mathcal{G}_\cap$ is $\{\{\langle L_A, S_{\text{cons}}\rangle, \langle L_A, L_D\rangle\}, \{\langle E_A, S_X\rangle, \langle E_A, E_D\rangle\}\}$. Thus, $\sigma_2(A = [X|D]) = \{L_A \oplus L_A \approx S_{\text{cons}} \oplus L_D,\ E_A \oplus E_A \approx S_X \oplus E_D,\ S_{\text{cons}} \approx \emptyset\}$, which is simplified to $\{L_A \approx L_D,\ E_A \approx S_X \oplus E_D\}$ by substituting $\emptyset$ for S_{cons} and applying the idempotence and unity axioms.

Finally, the abstraction of unification constraints is formalized as a function σ based on the two cases of Equations (6) and (7):

$$\sigma : \mathcal{C} \rightarrow \wp(\mathcal{C}^{\oplus})$$
$$\sigma(C) = \begin{cases} \sigma_1(C) & \text{if } C \text{ is in the form } X = Y \\ \sigma_2(C) & \text{if } C \text{ is in the form } X = f(Y_1, \ldots, Y_n) \end{cases} \tag{8}$$

Note that $\sigma(C)$ constrains all non-terminals of the corresponding left-hand and right-hand side grammars of C. This is because each non-terminal of these grammars appears either as "reachable", i.e. as a part of some combined non-terminal of the intersection, or as "unreachable", i.e. as a member of $W_\emptyset$.

Program Abstraction Our goal is to obtain refined view of properties of program variables by considering the interaction of the corresponding components (non-terminals) of their associated types. Thus, the abstraction of concrete literals naturally replaces each variable with the corresponding tuple of non-terminals. Let function $\omega(\mathcal{G})$ return the non-terminals of $\mathcal{G}$ in an ordered tuple. The abstraction of literals is then defined as:

$$\begin{aligned} &\delta : \mathcal{B} \rightarrow \mathcal{B}^{\oplus} \\ &\delta(p(X_1, \ldots, X_n)) = p(\omega(\mathcal{G}_{X_1}), \ldots, \omega(\mathcal{G}_{X_n})). \end{aligned} \tag{9}$$

The concept of abstraction of literals and unification constraints is naturally lifted for abstracting programs. A *set logic program* is obtained by applying δ to all literals and σ to all unification constraints. The example of abstraction of "append" into a set logic program is shown in Figure 3.

In Section 3 we assume that all rule heads and calls corresponding to a predicate name $p/n \in \Pi$ have the same type. Thus, all abstract literals corresponding to p/n have the same form. This is important for evaluating semantics of abstract program since the corresponding parameters, i.e. tuples of non-terminals can be unified directly on the syntactic basis.

The Abstract Domain of Set Logic Programs The abstract domain is formalized as a lattice $\text{Type}(\mathsf{X}) = \langle \wp(\mathcal{B}^{\oplus}_{\mathcal{C}}), \subseteq \rangle$, where $\mathcal{B}^{\oplus}_{\mathcal{C}}$ is a set of *constrained abstract literals* in the form: $\pi \leftarrow \varphi_1 \wedge \cdots \wedge \varphi_n$. The mapping from concrete literals to abstract literals is provided by $\alpha^{\oplus}$:

$$\begin{aligned} &\alpha^{\oplus} : \mathcal{B}_{\mathcal{C}} \rightarrow \mathcal{B}^{\oplus}_{\mathcal{C}} \\ &\alpha^{\oplus}([p(X_1 \ldots, X_n) \leftarrow C_1 \wedge \cdots \wedge C_m]) = \\ &\quad = p(\omega(\mathcal{G}_{X_1}), \ldots, \omega(\mathcal{G}_{X_n})) \leftarrow \left[\bigwedge_{\varphi \in \sigma(C_1)} \varphi \wedge \cdots \wedge \bigwedge_{\varphi \in \sigma(C_m)} \varphi \right] \end{aligned} \tag{10}$$

```
append(A,B,C) :-
    A = [],
    B = C.

append(A,B,C) :-
    A = [X|D],
    C = [X|E],
    append(D,B,E).
```

$\text{append}(\langle L_A, E_A\rangle, \langle L_B, E_B\rangle, \langle L_C, E_C\rangle)$:-
  $L_A \approx \emptyset$, $E_A \approx \emptyset$,
  $L_B \approx L_C$, $E_B \approx E_C$.

$\text{append}(\langle L_A, E_A\rangle, \langle L_B, E_B\rangle, \langle L_C, E_C\rangle)$:-
  $L_A \approx L_D$, $E_A \approx E_X \oplus E_D$,
  $L_C \approx L_E$, $E_C \approx E_X \oplus E_E$,
  $\text{append}(\langle L_D, E_D\rangle, \langle L_B, E_B\rangle, \langle L_E, E_E\rangle)$.

Fig. 3. Abstraction of append to set logic program

Finally the Galois insertion between the $\wp(\mathcal{B}_C)$ and $\wp(\mathcal{B}_C^{\oplus})$ is provided by the following pair of *abstraction* and *concretization* functions:

$$\begin{array}{ll} \alpha : \wp(\mathcal{B}_C) \to \wp(\mathcal{B}_C^{\oplus}) & \gamma : \wp(\mathcal{B}_C^{\oplus}) \to \wp(\mathcal{B}_C) \\ \alpha(I) = \{\, \alpha^{\oplus}(a) \,|\, a \in I \,\} & \gamma(\mathcal{I}) = \bigcup \{\, I \,|\, \alpha(I) \subseteq \mathcal{I} \,\} \end{array} \tag{11}$$

5 Groundness Analysis of Typed Logic Programs

Groundness is probably the best-understood and most developed application of abstract analysis of logic programs. Most of the known optimizations found in compilers of (constraint) logic programming languages require some approximation of groundness to operate.

The best-known method of groundness analysis of logic programs consists in approximating groundness dependencies using the domain of *positive boolean formulas* called Pos. This method is proposed in [14]. Without loss of generality the abstraction of unification constraint $t_1 = t_2$ is defined by the following function α_{Pos}:

$$\begin{array}{l} \alpha_{\mathsf{Pos}} : \mathcal{C} \to \mathsf{Pos} \\ \alpha_{\mathsf{Pos}}([t_1 = t_2]) = \left[\bigwedge_{V \in \text{vars}(t_1)} V \leftrightarrow \bigwedge_{W \in \text{vars}(t_2)} W \right] \end{array} \tag{12}$$

Thus, the abstraction of ground t_1 or ground t_2 results in T (true) on the corresponding side of the formula. The notion of Pos-based groundness abstraction is naturally lifted for all syntactic objects such as constrained literals, rules and programs. The semantics of a CLP(B) program resulting from program abstraction provides a correct approximation of groundness dependencies of the original program. The abstract domain for groundness analysis is thus formalized in terms of (sets of) Pos-constrained literals ordered by logical consequence.

Example 7. The abstraction of "append" for Pos-based groundness analysis.

$\text{append}(A, B, C)$:- $A \leftrightarrow \mathsf{T}$, $B \leftrightarrow C$.
$\text{append}(A, B, C)$:- $A \leftrightarrow X \wedge D$, $C \leftrightarrow X \wedge E$, $\text{append}(D, B, E)$.

The bottom-up evaluation of this program results in the well-known groundness approximation: $\text{append}(A, B, C)$:- $C \leftrightarrow A \wedge B$. Note that this result is less precise than the result for typed "append" shown in Section 1.

It's clear that given type descriptions we can adopt a more refined view of groundness than in the untyped case. Namely, groundness of a term can be expressed in terms of *boundness* of all non-terminals of the corresponding grammar. If we can prove, for instance, that for some non-terminal N and for any t satisfying the constraint we have $\zeta(N,t) = \emptyset$, it means that the subterm corresponding to N is always instantiated. Consequently proving that $\zeta(N,t) = \emptyset$ for any N means that all terms satisfying the constraint are ground. The following two definitions formalize the concepts of boundness and groundness:

Definition 6 (Boundness). *Non-terminal N of the grammar $\mathcal{G}_V$ associated with a variable V is bound by a substitution θ if $\zeta(N, V\theta) = \emptyset$.*

Definition 7 (Groundness). *A variable V is ground under a substitution θ if all non-terminals of the associated grammar $\mathcal{G}_V$ are bound by θ.*

The domain for groundness analysis of typed logic programs is called Type(Pos). It is a proper abstraction of the generic domain Type(X) presented in Section 4 obtained by application of α_{Pos} of Equation (12) to ACI1-constraints of a set logic program. As an example, the application of α_{Pos} to the abstract "append" shown in Figure 3 results in the program shown earlier in Figure 1.

The semantics of the resulting abstract CLP(B) program is then evaluated either in a top-down or a bottom-up way. Thus, the approximation of boundness of a program is obtained by its abstraction into a set logic program followed by direct application of Pos-based groundness analysis.

Clearly, the analysis in Type(Pos) is at least as precise as the analysis in Pos. We formalize this relation showing that given a description in Type(Pos) we can always "abstract away" the types and get a description in Pos domain. In other words, we are showing that Pos is a proper abstraction of Type(Pos). Intuitively this claim is supported by the fact that groundness of a program variable V can be expressed as Pos-formula $V \leftrightarrow \bigwedge_{N \in W_V} N$, where W_V is the set of non-terminals of the type grammar $\mathcal{G}_V$.

Theorem 3. Pos *is a proper abstraction of* Type(Pos).

Example 8. The groundness description of typed "append" shown in Section 1 can be mapped onto the original program variables as

$$\begin{aligned}\texttt{append}(A,B,C)\ \texttt{:-}\ & L_A \leftrightarrow \mathsf{T},\ L_B \leftrightarrow L_C,\ E_C \leftrightarrow E_A \wedge E_B,\\ & A \leftrightarrow L_A \wedge E_A,\ B \leftrightarrow L_B \wedge E_B,\ C \leftrightarrow L_C \wedge E_C.\end{aligned}$$

This description implies the standard result for untyped "append".

6 Sharing Analysis of Typed Logic Programs

Two or more variables in a logic program are said to *share* if in some execution of the program they are bound to terms which contain a common variable. The information about sharing of program variables provides the basis for many optimizations, such as occur check reduction [20] or elimination of run-time dataflow checks in and-parallel execution [9].

One of the more widely applied sharing analyses reported in the literature is the so called *set-sharing* analysis based on Sharing domain originally proposed by Jacobs and Langen [11]. The alternative domain for set-sharing analysis is recently presented in [3]. This domain denoted by $\mathsf{Sh}^{\oplus}$ is isomorphic to Sharing and based on set expressions. Sharing descriptions are obtained by abstracting original programs into set logic programs and evaluating their meaning using standard top-down or bottom-up semantics extended with ACI1-unification.

In this work we show how both both Sharing and $\mathsf{Sh}^{\oplus}$ can be upgraded with type information of Type(X) domain resulting respectively in Type(Sharing) and Type($\mathsf{Sh}^{\oplus}$). It turns out similarly to the case of groundness analysis that the abstract operations of Sharing and $\mathsf{Sh}^{\oplus}$ can be applied to set logic programs resulting from Type(X) abstraction. Moreover, sharing analysis based on $\mathsf{Sh}^{\oplus}$ can be applied directly to a result of Type(X) abstraction because of the same syntax used in both domains.

Similarly as groundness can be viewed as a combination of the corresponding boundness dependencies, set-sharing between program variables can be viewed as a combination of *aliasing* of labels of corresponding non-terminals. The following two definitions formalize the concepts of aliasing and sharing:

Definition 8 (Aliasing). *Non-terminals* $N_1 \ldots N_n$ *of the respective grammars* $\mathcal{G}_1 \ldots \mathcal{G}_n$ *associated with variables* $V_1 \ldots V_n$ *are aliased by a substitution* θ *if* $\zeta(N_1, V_1\theta) \cap \cdots \cap \zeta(N_n, V_n\theta) \neq \emptyset$.

Definition 9 (Sharing). *Program variables* $V_1 \ldots V_n$ *share under a substitution* θ *if there is a set of non-terminals* $N_1 \ldots N_n$ *of the respective grammars* $\mathcal{G}_1 \ldots \mathcal{G}_n$ *aliased by* θ.

Example 9. Consider the bottom-up sharing analysis of abstract "append" shown in Figure 3 using $\mathsf{Sh}^{\oplus}$. The result is:

$$\mathsf{append}(\langle L_A, E_A\rangle, \langle L_B, E_B\rangle, \langle L_C, E_C\rangle) \text{ :- } L_A \approx \emptyset,\ L_B \approx L_C,\ E_C \approx E_A \oplus E_B.$$

showing that L_A is ground; L_B and L_C can share; E_C can share with each of E_A and E_B, but E_A and E_B are independent. The analysis based on Sharing domain can also be applied producing the same (upto isomorphism) result. The abstraction in Sharing treats terms as sets of variables and thus can be applied to set constraints. The result of the analysis in Sharing is naturally $\psi = \{\emptyset, \{L_B, L_C\}, \{E_C, E_A\}, \{E_C, E_B\}\}$.

Note that the information computed in Example 9 approximates possible aliasing between the labels of the corresponding non-terminals. The information about actual sharing of program variables can be extracted by projecting the aliasing back on the type description. For instance, variables A and C of "append" can share because the elements of the lists can be aliased. Variables B and C can share because of two possible reasons: the structures can be aliased, provided by the aliasing of L_B and L_C or the elements can be aliased, provided by the aliasing of E_B and E_C. In general, if we adopt the syntax of $\mathsf{Sh}^{\oplus}$, the information about sharing of the original variables can be captured by introducing new set constraints in the form $V \approx N_1 \oplus \cdots \oplus N_k$, where V is a program variable and $N_1 \ldots N_k$ are non-terminals of the corresponding grammar $\mathcal{G}_V$. Thus, similarly to the case of groundness analysis we can show that the analysis in Type($\mathsf{Sh}^{\oplus}$) is at least as precise as in $\mathsf{Sh}^{\oplus}$. The similar result for Sharing follows by the isomorphism.

Theorem 4. $\mathsf{Sh}^{\oplus}$ *is a proper abstraction of* Type($\mathsf{Sh}^{\oplus}$).

7 Related Work and Conclusion

We briefly compare the approach proposed in this paper with some previous works presenting abstract domains based on regular types.

Janssens and Bruynooghe present in [12] a framework for program type and mode analysis of Prolog programs based on type graphs. The abstract domains based on *rigid types* and *integrated types* are capable of inferring types and modes of a program. The later domain can track *freeness* as an additional mode, thus significantly improving the precision of analysis for programs manipulating partially instantiated structures. The work of Mulkers *et al.* [16] applies the framework of [12] for tracking *liveness* of Prolog structures. The abstract domain developed in this work models the execution environment of a predicate using type graphs and special arcs representing structure sharing. In Bruynooghe *et al.* [1] the framework of [16] is further extended and applied to liveness analysis of statically typed languages such as Mercury.

The work of Van Hentenryck *et al.* [8] presents the systematic approach to the construction of abstract domains using the generic domain Pat($\mathcal{R}$). In particular, authors describe how the domain of type graphs Type can be integrated into Pat($\mathcal{R}$) producing Pat(Type). The resulting domain provides type and mode inference similarly to the domain of Janssens and Bruynooghe [12].

The main difference of our approach from the mentioned works is in the way we deal with regular types. In all cited works the abstract representation includes regular types as a component. Abstract operations presented in these works normally involve complex and costly manipulations with type graphs during the analysis. In contrast, our approach fully handles the type descriptions on the stage of program abstraction, i.e. by type-based abstract compilation into set logic programs. The most similar approach in a technical sense is that proposed by Naish [18]. In this work the problem of modes validation of a typed and moded logic program is reduced to checking the entailment on multiset constraints composed from parameters of polymorphic types.

We have presented an approach to analysing typed logic programs by mapping to a set logic program. It is a straightforward syntax-directed translation which can increase the size of the program by a factor d^2, where d is the largest number of nonterminals in a grammar, although in practice it is usually linear.

A practical advantage of the approach is that the type-based analyzer does not need to manipulate automata or graphs during the analysis. Instead, the actual analysis which comes after the type-based abstraction can be delegated to the existing analyzers thus reusing their expertise together with their code and optimizations.

An obvious direction for the future research is to extend our approach to directly handle parametric polymorphism in types. Another direction for the research consists in formalizing and extending the class of abstract domains that can be upgraded with type information using our method. Here we show that two important abstract domains in logic program analysis, Pos and Sharing, fall into this class.

References

1. M. Bruynooghe, G. Janssens, and A. Kågedal. Live-structure analysis for logic programming languages with declarations. In *Procs. 14th ICLP*, 33–47. MIT Press, 1997.
2. M. Codish and V. Lagoon. Type dependencies for logic programs using ACI-unification. *Theoretical Computer Science*, 238(1-2):131–159, 2000.
3. M. Codish, V. Lagoon, and F. Bueno. An algebraic approach to sharing analysis of logic programs. *JLP*, 42(2):111–149, 2000.
4. P. Cousot and R. Cousot. Abstract interpretation: A unified lattice model for static analysis of programs by construction or approximation of fixpoints. In *Proceedings of the 4th ACM Symp. on Principles of Programming Languages*, 238–252, 1977.
5. B. Demoen, M. Garcia de la Banda, W. Harvey, K. Marriott, and P. Stuckey. An overview of HAL. In *Procs. CP99. LNCS* 1713, 174–188, 1999.
6. J. Gallagher and D. Waal. Fast and precise regular approximations of logic programs. In *Procs. 11th ICLP*, 599–613. MIT Press, 1994.
7. F. Gécseg and M. Steinby. *Tree Automata*. Akadémiai Kiadó, Budapest, 1984.
8. P. Van Hentenryck, A. Cortesi, and B. Le Charlier. Type analysis of Prolog using type graphs. *JLP*, 22(3):179–209, 1995.
9. M. V. Hermenegildo and K. J. Greene. &-Prolog and its performance: Exploiting independent And-Parallelism. In *Procs. 7th ICLP*, 253–268. MIT Press, 1990.
10. P. Hill and J. Lloyd. *The Gödel Language*. MIT Press, 1994.
11. D. Jacobs and A. Langen. Static analysis of logic programs for independent AND-parallelism. *JLP*, 13(2 & 3):291–314, 1992.
12. G. Janssens and M. Bruynooghe. Deriving descriptions of possible values of program variables by means of abstract interpretation. *JLP*, 13(2 & 3):205–258, 1992.
13. J. Lloyd. *Foundations of Logic Programming*. Springer-Verlag, 2nd edition, 1988.
14. K. Marriott and H. Søndergaard. Precise and efficient groundness analysis for logic programs. *ACM TOPLAS*, 2(4):181–196, 1993.
15. R. Milner. A theory of type polymorphism in programming. *Journal of Computer and System Sciences*, 17:348–375, 1978.
16. A. Mulkers, W. Winsborough, and M. Bruynooghe. Live-structure dataflow analysis for Prolog. *ACM TOPLAS*, 16(2):205–258, 1994.
17. A. Mycroft and R.A. O'Keefe. A polymorphic type system for Prolog. *Artificial Intelligence*, 23:295–307, 1984.
18. L. Naish. Mode checking using constrained regular trees. Technical Report 98/3, Department of Computer Science, University of Melbourne, Australia, 1998.
19. Z. Somogyi, F. Henderson, and T. Conway. The execution algorithm of Mercury, an efficient purely declarative logic programming language. *JLP*, 29(1–3):17–64, 1996.
20. H. Søndergaard. An application of abstract interpretation of logic programs: Occur check reduction. In *Procs. ESOP86*, *LNCS* 213, 327–338, 1986.

Abstract Compilation for Sharing Analysis

Gianluca Amato[1] and Fausto Spoto[2]

[1] Dipartimento di Informatica, Corso Italia, 40, I-56100 Pisa, Italy
amato@di.unipi.it
Ph.: +39-050887248 Fax: +39-050887226
[2] IRISA, Campus universitaire de Beaulieu, 35042 Rennes Cedex, France
spoto@irisa.fr

Abstract. An abstract domain for non pair-sharing and freeness analysis of logic programs has been recently developed by using the *automatic* technique of linear refinement. W.r.t. previously available domains, it can be used for abstract compilation, which allows a modular and goal-independent analysis of logic programs. In this paper, we describe our implementation of an analyser which uses that domain. Sometimes, we have sacrificed precision for efficiency. We evaluate it over a set of benchmarks and we compare the results with those obtained through a goal-dependent analysis. Not surprisingly, our goal-independent analysis is slower. However, it is almost always as precise as the goal-dependent one. To the best of our knowledge, this is the first goal-independent implementation of sharing analysis based on abstract interpretation, as well as the first implementation of a linearly refined domain.

Keywords: *Abstract interpretation, domain theory, linear refinement, linear logic, logic programming.*

1 Introduction

Pair-sharing analysis [1, 16] determines those pairs of variables which, in a given program point, can be bound to two terms which share some variable. It is a particular case of set-sharing analysis [12]. In set-sharing analysis, indeed, sets of variables are considered, and not just pairs. It is useful for avoiding occur-check [16] and for automatic program parallelisation [12, 15]. As stressed in [1], pair-sharing information is actually needed in program analysis and transformation, set-sharing information being redundant w.r.t. pair-sharing information.

Freeness analysis [4, 15] determines those variables which are always bound to a variable in a given program point. It is useful for optimising unification, for goal reordering and for avoiding type checking. It is well known that performing sharing and freeness analysis together improves the precision of both [12, 15].

When the fixpoint computation is based on a compositional definition, the $(i+1)$-th iteration can re-use any intermediate results already computed during the i-th iteration that are known not to change across iterations. Such results

H. Kuchen and K. Ueda (Eds.): FLOPS 2001, LNCS 2024, pp. 311–325, 2001.

are usually the denotations of some program parts which do not contain recursive procedure calls. Therefore, these parts can be replaced by their denotation and the fixpoint computed on this modified (partially *compiled*) program. This technique is traditionally known as *abstract compilation* [5, 11], since it is an application of abstract interpretation [9] where a program is iteratively compiled to its abstract denotation. This leads, in general, to a more efficient computation of the abstract fixpoint. Moreover, modular analysis is allowed. This means that procedures or libraries can be analysed separately, and their analyses can *then* be combined to obtain the analysis of a large program.

Linear refinement [10] is a technique for systematically improving abstract domains for program analysis. It has been defined as a slight generalisation of Cousot's reduced power operation [8]. Given a basic abstract domain representing just the property of interest and a concrete operation $\boxtimes$ (in the case of logic programming, unification) the new refined domain is constructed, and allows us to define an abstract operation which is more precise than that of the basic domain. This is achieved by enriching the basic domain with linear logic implications $i \multimap o$ representing the propagation of the abstract property of interest through the concrete operator $\boxtimes$. Namely, if the abstract property i holds for the input of the operator $\boxtimes$ then the abstract property o holds for its output. In this way, the development of new domains becomes almost automatic and we can define the denotation for a procedure as a function from abstract properties of the input to abstract properties of the output. Thus, static analysis can be applied even if the source code of some procedures is not known (which can be the result of some copyright policy), provided that its abstract denotation is available.

In [13] an abstract domain for non pair-sharing and freeness analysis has been developed through linear refinement. It is more precise than the traditional domain of [12] and correct abstract operators have been explicitly defined. However, no experimental results are provided. Since the abstract operations are not optimal, the usefulness of the domain was left unclear.

Our contribution is the implementation of the domain of [13], which is the first implementation of a goal-independent sharing and freeness analysis of logic programs based on abstract interpretation, as well as of a linearly refined domain. Note that the traditional domains for groundness did exist before it became clear they could be obtained through refinement. Beyond the implementation, this paper contains a piece of theory about *reduction rules*, necessary for an efficient analysis, and which can be tuned in such a way to avoid any loss of precision.

1.1 Related Works

Almost all works about sharing analysis are not amenable to abstract compilation and have been developed without any automatic technique like linear refinement. To the best of our knowledge, only [4, 6, 7] provide abstract domains for sharing analysis which can be used for abstract compilation. The domain in [4] models sharing, freeness and groundness. It is not based on abstract interpretation. Its authors claim that its precision is no more than that of the

Sharing × *Free* domain of [12]. An implementation exists. The domain in [6] is isomorphic to the *Sharing* domain of [12]. The domain in [7] is isomorphic to the domain *Pos* for groundness analysis. Since in both cases the authors provided an abstract unification algorithm over the abstract domain only (in contrast with an abstract unification algorithm between an element of the abstract domain and a concrete substitution, like in [12]), abstract compilation is allowed in both cases. However, the domains in [6] and [7] induce abstraction maps which are too coarse for practical applications. Namely, those maps cannot distinguish between concrete substitutions like $\{x = y\}$ and $\{x = \mathtt{f}(y, y)\}$ (as implied by Equation (7) of [6] and Observation 4.1 of [7]). However, those substitutions must be distinguished in order to provide decent precision, as shown in Example 8 of [13]. Other sources of imprecision are shown by Examples 4 and 5 of [13]. Some of those problems can be solved by adding *freeness* and *linearity* to the abstract domain, but we are not aware of any implementation of the domains in [6] and [7] coupled with freeness and linearity.

2 Preliminaries

We denote by $\wp(S)$ the powerset of a set S, by $\#S$ its cardinality and by $\wp_f(S)$ the set of all finite subsets of S.

Given a set of variables V and a set of function symbols Σ with associated arity, containing at least a symbol of arity 0, we define $\mathsf{terms}(\Sigma, V)$ as the minimal set of terms built from V and Σ, i.e., $V \subseteq \mathsf{terms}(\Sigma, V)$ and if $t_1, \ldots, t_n \in \mathsf{terms}(\Sigma, V)$ and $\mathtt{f}^n \in \Sigma$, then $\mathtt{f}(t_1, \ldots, t_n) \in \mathsf{terms}(\Sigma, V)$. We denote by $\mathsf{vars}(t)$ the set of variables which occur in a term t. When $\mathsf{vars}(t) = \emptyset$ we say that t is ground. If x is a variable, $V \cup x$ means $V \cup \{x\}$ and $V \setminus x$ means $V \setminus \{x\}$. The set of idempotent substitutions θ ($\mathsf{dom}(\theta) \cup \mathsf{rng}(\theta) \subseteq V$ and $\mathsf{dom}(\theta) \cap \mathsf{rng}(\theta) = \emptyset$) is denoted by Θ_V.

Let $\mathcal{V}$ be an infinite set of variables and $V \in \wp_f(\mathcal{V})$. We define the set $C_V = \wp_f\{t^1 = t^2 \mid t^1, t^2 \in \mathsf{terms}(\Sigma, V)\}$ of *Herbrand constraints*. Let $\mathcal{W}$ be an infinite set of variables disjoint from $\mathcal{V}$. For each $V \in \wp_f(\mathcal{V})$, we have the set of *existential Herbrand constraints*

$$H_V = \left\{ \exists_W c \,\middle|\, \begin{array}{l} W \in \wp_f(\mathcal{W}),\ c \in C_{V \cup W} \text{ and there exists} \\ \theta \in \Theta_{V \cup W} \text{ s.t. } \mathsf{rng}(\theta) \subseteq V \text{ and } c\theta \text{ holds} \end{array} \right\} .$$

Here, $\mathcal{V}$ are called the *program variables* and $\mathcal{W}$ the *existential variables*, which are a formalisation of the unnamed variables of Prolog. The condition about the existence of θ such that $c\theta$ holds, means that we consider satisfiable constraints only.

Four operations, called *conjunction*, *restriction*, *expansion* and *renaming*, are defined over H_V.

Definition 1. *We define* $\star^{H_V} : H_V \times H_V \mapsto H_V$, $\mathsf{restrict}_n^{H_V} : H_V \mapsto H_{V \setminus n}$ *with* $n \in V$, $\mathsf{expand}_x^{H_V} : H_V \mapsto H_{V \cup x}$ *with* $x \notin V$, *and* $\mathsf{rename}_{x \to n}^{H_V} : H_V \mapsto H_{(V \setminus x) \cup n}$, *with* $x \in V$ *and* $n \notin V$ *as*[1]

$$(\exists_{W_1} c_1) \star^{H_V} (\exists_{W_2} c_2) = \begin{cases} \exists_{W_1 \cup W_2} \mathsf{mgu}(c_1 \cup c_2) & \textit{if } \mathsf{mgu}(c_1 \cup c_2) \textit{ exists,} \\ \textit{undefined} & \textit{otherwise} \end{cases}$$

$$\mathsf{restrict}_n^{H_V}(\exists_W c) = \exists_{W \cup N} c[N/n] \qquad \textit{with } N \in \mathcal{W} \setminus W,$$

$$\mathsf{expand}_x^{H_V}(\exists_W c) = \exists_W c\ ,$$

$$\mathsf{rename}_{x \to n}^{H_V}(\exists_W c) = \exists_W (c[n/x])\ .$$

Note that in the definition of $\star^{H_V}$ *we put the constraint in normal form through the Martelli and Montanari unification algorithm [14]. The other operations are closed on the set of existential Herbrand constraints in normal form.*

Our concrete domain is the collecting version [9] of H_V, i.e., the lattice $\langle \wp(H_V), \cap, \cup, H_V, \emptyset \rangle$. The operations on H_V are point-wise extended to $\wp(H_V)$. The new operation $\cup^{\wp(H_V)}(S_1, S_2) = S_1 \cup S_2$ is defined. It is used to merge the results of different branches of execution.

3 Non Pair-Sharing and Freeness Analysis

We briefly recall the definition of the abstract domain for non pair-sharing and freeness described in [13]. Its abstract elements are sets of arrows.

Definition 2. *Given* $V \in \wp_f(\mathcal{V})$, *we denote by* V_2 *the set of* unordered *pairs of elements of* V. *We define* $ShF_V = \wp(V \cup V_2)$ *as the domain used to express the freeness of variables and the non-sharing of pairs of variables. We define* $Abs_V = \wp(ShF_V \times (V \cup V_2))$. *We write the elements of* V_2 *as* (v_1, v_2), *with* $\{v_1, v_2\} \subseteq V$ *and a pair* $(\{l_1, \ldots, l_n\}, r) \in Abs_V$ *as* $l_1 \cdots l_n \Rightarrow r$, *for* $n \geq 0$. *The* dimension $\mathsf{dim}(s)$ *of* $s \in ShF$ *is its cardinality. If* $A \in Abs_V$, $\mathsf{dim}(A) = \sum_{l \Rightarrow r \in A} \mathsf{dim}(l)$.

For instance, the object $x(y, z) \in ShF_V$ means that x is free and that y and z do not share any variable. The arrow $l_1 \cdots l_n \Rightarrow r$ represents the set of existential Herbrand constraints which, when unified with a constraint satisfying $l_1 \cdots l_n$ (i.e., whose freeness and non pair-sharing properties are consistent with those expressed by $l_1 \cdots l_n$), give a result satisfying r.

We can approximate the operations of Definition 1. *Entailment* and *tautological* arrows are defined in [13]. Roughly speaking, $l \in ShF_V$ entails $l' \in ShF_V$ when every existential Herbrand constraint satisfying l satisfies l', i.e., its freeness and non pair-sharing properties, when consistent with those expressed by l are also consistent with those expressed by l'. For instance, we have that $x(y, x)$ entails (y, x) and x, and that (x, x) entails (x, y) (since (x, x) means that x is ground). A tautological arrow is an arrow which is satisfied by every constraint.

[1] In the definition of $\star^{H_V}$ we assume $W_1 \cap W_2 = \emptyset$, since a constraint $\exists_W c$ is equivalent to $\exists_{W'} c[W'/W]$, with W' made of fresh variables. Similarly, different choices of N in $\mathsf{restrict}_n^{H_V}$ lead to equivalent constraints.

Definition 3. *Let $A_1, A_2 \in Abs_V$. Let T be made of tautological arrows*[2]. *Then*

$$A_1 \star^{Abs_V} A_2 = \left\{ l_1 \cdots l_n \Rightarrow r \;\middle|\; \begin{array}{l} r_1 \cdots r_n \Rightarrow r \in A_2 \cup T,\ l_i \Rightarrow r'_i \in A_1 \cup T \\ \text{and } r'_i \text{ entails } r_i \text{ for } i = 1, \ldots, n, \text{ or} \\ r_1 \cdots r_n \Rightarrow r \in A_1 \cup T,\ l_i \Rightarrow r'_i \in A_2 \cup T \\ \text{and } r'_i \text{ entails } r_i \text{ for } i = 1, \ldots, n \end{array} \right\} .$$

In our implementation, in Definition 3 we use $T = \{(v, v) \Rightarrow (v, v) \mid v \in V\}$.

Example 1. In Definition 3, let $T = \{\}$, $V = \{x, y, z\}$ and

$$A_1 = \{xy \Rightarrow x, (x, y)(x, z) \Rightarrow (x, y), (x, x) \Rightarrow (z, z)\} ,$$
$$A_2 = \{x(x, y) \Rightarrow x, \ \Rightarrow (y, y)\} .$$

Then

$$A_1 \star^{Abs_V} A_2 = \{xy(x, y)(x, z) \Rightarrow x, \ \Rightarrow (y, y)\} .$$

Note that we do not obtain the arrow $\{(x, x) \Rightarrow (z, z)\}$, since the set T is empty. But this arrow must hold for $A_1 \star^{Abs_V} A_2$, since it holds for A_1 and groundness dependencies cannot be lost. By using $T \supseteq \{(v, v) \Rightarrow (v, v) \mid v \in V\}$ we would include that arrow in the conjunction.

Definition 4. *Let $V \in \wp_f(\mathcal{V})$ and $n \in V$. Let $X = \{n\} \cup \{(v, n) \mid v \in V\}$ and $A, A_1, A_2 \in Abs_V$. We define*

$$\mathsf{restrict}_n^{Abs_V}(A) = \left\{ l \setminus X \Rightarrow r \;\middle|\; \begin{array}{l} l \Rightarrow r \in A,\ (n, n) \notin l, \\ r \not\equiv n \text{ and } r \not\equiv (n, v) \text{ for every } v \in V \end{array} \right\} .$$

If $x \in V$, $n \notin V$ and $A \in Abs_V$, we define

$$\mathsf{rename}_{x \to n}^{Abs_V}(A) = A[n/x] .$$

Finally, we define

$$\cup^{Abs_V}(A_1, A_2) = \{l_1 l_2 \Rightarrow r \mid l_1 \Rightarrow r \in A_1,\ l_2 \Rightarrow r \in A_2\} .$$

Example 2. Let $V = \{x, y, z\}$ and

$$A = \{xy \Rightarrow x, xy \Rightarrow y, (x, x) \Rightarrow (y, z), (y, z)(x, y)(x, z) \Rightarrow (y, z)\} .$$

Then

$$\mathsf{restrict}_x^{Abs_V}(A) = \{y \Rightarrow y, (y, z) \Rightarrow (y, z)\} .$$

For the expansion, we use a distinguished variable $?_1 \in V$ which stands for all the variables which do not occur in the Herbrand constraints. In order to compute $\mathsf{expand}_x^{Abs_V}(A)$, we substitute x for $?_1$ in A. Since non pair-sharing is a property of pairs of variables, we wish to know how this new x behaves in conjunction with the distinguished variable itself. Thus we use two distinguished variables $?_1$ and $?_2$. By using the abstraction map (Definition 6) with $\{?_1, ?_2\} \subseteq V$, we introduce these variables in the constraints.

[2] The larger T is, the more precise $\star^{Abs_V}$ is.

Definition 5. *Let $V \in \wp_f(\mathcal{V})$ and $x \in \mathcal{V} \setminus V$. Let $\{?_1, ?_2\} \subseteq V$ and $A \in Abs_V$. We define*

$$\mathsf{expand}_x^{Abs_V}(A) = A \cup \{l[x/?_1][?_1/?_2] \Rightarrow r[x/?_1][?_1/?_2] \mid l \Rightarrow r \in A\} .$$

Example 3. Let $V = \{x, y, z\}$ and

$$A = \{?_1(x, ?_1) \Rightarrow ?_1, (?_1, x)(?_1, z)(?_1, ?_2) \Rightarrow (?_1, ?_2), xyz \Rightarrow z\} .$$

Given $n \in \mathcal{V} \setminus V$ we have

$$\mathsf{expand}_n^{Abs_V}(A) = \left\{ \begin{array}{l} xyz \Rightarrow z, n(x, n) \Rightarrow n, (n, x)(n, z)(n, ?_1) \Rightarrow (n, ?_1), \\ ?_1(x, ?_1) \Rightarrow ?_1, (?_1, x)(?_1, z)(?_1, ?_2) \Rightarrow (?_1, ?_2) \end{array} \right\} .$$

We show here how to compute an approximation of the abstraction map. It considers separately the information of groundness, non pair-sharing and freeness contained in a binding. A substitution is then abstracted by combining through $\star^{Abs_V}$ the abstraction of every binding of which it is composed.

Definition 6. *Let $V \in \wp_f(\mathcal{V})$, $v \in V$ and $t \in \mathsf{terms}(\Sigma, V)$. We define*

$$\alpha^V(v = t) = \alpha^V_{gr}(v = t) \cup \alpha^V_{nsh}(v = t) \cup \alpha^V_{fr}(v = t) ,$$

where α^V_{gr}, α^V_{nsh} and α^V_{free} are defined below. We write $t(v_1, \ldots, v_n)$ for t if $\mathsf{vars}(t) = \{v_1, \ldots, v_n\}$. If $n = 0$ then $t(v_1, \ldots, v_n)$ is ground. Variables with different names are different variables.

$$\alpha^V_{gr}(v = t(v_1, \ldots, v_n)) = \bigcup_{v' \in V} \left\{ \begin{array}{l} (v_1, v_1) \cdots (v_n, v_n) \Rightarrow (v, v'), \\ (v, v) \Rightarrow (v_1, v'), \ldots, (v, v) \Rightarrow (v_n, v') \end{array} \right\}$$

$$\alpha^V_{nsh}(x = t) = \cup_{\{v,v'\} \subseteq V} \alpha^{(v,v')}_{nsh}(x = t)$$

$$\alpha^{(v,v')}_{nsh}(v = t(v', v_1, \ldots, v_n)) = \{\} = \alpha^{(v,v')}_{nsh}(v = t') \quad t' \text{ ground}$$

$$\alpha^{(v,v')}_{nsh}(x = t(v, v', v_1, \ldots, v_n)) = \{x(v, v') \Rightarrow (v, v')\}$$

$$\alpha^{(v,v')}_{nsh}(v = t(v_1, \ldots, v_n)) = \{(v', v)(v', v_1) \cdots (v', v_n) \Rightarrow (v', v)\} \quad t(v_1, \ldots, v_n) \text{ non ground}$$

$$\alpha^{(v,v')}_{nsh}(x = t(v, v_1, \ldots, v_n)) = \left\{ \begin{array}{l} (v', v)(v', x)(v', v_1) \cdots (v', v_n) \Rightarrow (v', v), \\ (v', v)(v', x)x \Rightarrow (v', v) \end{array} \right\}$$

$$\alpha^{(v,v')}_{nsh}(x = t) = \{(v, v') \Rightarrow (v, v')\} \quad t \text{ ground}$$

$$\alpha^{(v,v')}_{nsh}(x = t(v_1, \ldots, v_n)) = \left\{ \begin{array}{l} (v, v')(v, x)(v, v_1) \cdots (v, v_n) \Rightarrow (v, v'), \\ (v, v')(v', x)(v', v_1) \cdots (v', v_n) \Rightarrow (v, v'), \\ (v, v')(v, x)(v', x)x \Rightarrow (v, v') \end{array} \right\} \quad t(v_1, \ldots, v_n) \text{ non ground}$$

$$
\begin{aligned}
\alpha_{fr}^{V}(x = t) &= \cup_{v \in V} \alpha_{fr}^{v}(x = t) \\
\alpha_{fr}^{v}(v = x) &= \{vx \Rightarrow v\} = \alpha_{fr}^{v}(x = t(v, v_1, \ldots, v_n)) \\
\alpha_{fr}^{v}(v = t(v_1, \ldots, v_n)) &= \{\} \quad t(v_1, \ldots, v_n) \notin \mathcal{V} \\
\alpha_{fr}^{v}(x = y) &= \{v(x, v)(v, y) \Rightarrow v, vxy \Rightarrow v\} \\
\alpha_{fr}^{v}(x = t(v_1, \ldots, v_n)) &= \{vx(x, v) \Rightarrow v, v(x, v)(v_1, v) \cdots (v_n, v) \Rightarrow v\} \\
& \qquad t(v_1, \ldots, v_n) \notin \mathcal{V} \ .
\end{aligned}
$$

We can compute the abstract information contained in an abstract constraint, i.e., the set of variables which are free and the set of pairs of variables which do not share in any existential Herbrand constraint belonging to the concretisation of the abstract constraint.

Definition 7. *Given* $V \in \wp_f(\mathcal{V})$, *we define* $\mathsf{free}_V : Abs_V \mapsto \wp(V)$ *and* $\mathsf{nsh}_V : Abs_V \mapsto V_2$ *as*

$$
\begin{aligned}
\mathsf{free}_V(A) &= \{v \in V \mid l \Rightarrow v \in A \text{ and } v'(v', v') \not\subseteq l \text{ for any } v' \in V\} \ , \\
\mathsf{nsh}_V(A) &= \{(v_1, v_2) \in V_2 \mid l \Rightarrow (v_1, v_2) \in A \text{ and } (v, v) \notin l \text{ for any } v \in V\} \ .
\end{aligned}
$$

4 Implementation

We describe now our prototypical implementation[3] of the domain of Section 3. We did not aim at efficiency, though much care has been taken to avoid the explosion of the computational cost of the abstract conjunction operator (Definition 3).

Constraints are manipulated by C procedures, while the normalisation, abstraction and fixpoint computation phases (see below) are written in Prolog. The choice of C as implementation language for the constraints is a consequence of efficiency considerations. Indeed, constraints are represented by arrays of bitmaps. Every basic *token* of information, i.e., the freeness of a variable or the non-sharing of a pair of variables, is associated with a bit position. Elements of ShF_V (Definition 2) are then implemented as strings of bits.

4.1 Normalisation, Abstraction and Fixpoint Computation

We describe the three phases of our analysis, normalisation, abstraction and fixpoint calculation of the abstract s-semantics for computed answers [3] (a call-pattern or resultant semantics could be used here), by using the traditional `member/2` program as a running example:

```
member(X,[X|Xs]).
member(X,[Y|Ys]):-member(X,Ys).
```

[3] Downloadable at `http://www.di.unipi.it/~amato/papers/flops01.tgz`.

Normalisation transforms a program in such a way that procedure calls are made only in their most general form, i.e., with variables `v(0)`, `v(1)`, and so on, as arguments. Moreover, the structure of the program (disjunctions, conjunctions, expansions and similar) is made apparent, which simplifies the subsequent fixpoint iteration. For instance, the normalisation of `member/2` is

```
member(2):-
   rename(v(16), v(0), rename(v(17), v(1), or(
      restrict(v(18), bi_eq(v(17), [v(16)|v(18)])),
      restrict(v(20), and(
          expand(v(16), restrict(v(19), bi_eq(v(17), [v(19)|v(20)]))),
          expand(v(17), rename(v(0), v(16), rename(v(1), v(20),
              call(member(2)))))
      ))
   )))
```

The program has been compiled in a code which contains calls to the abstract operations of the domain, as well as built-in's, like `bi_eq`, which unifies two terms, and procedure calls, like `call(member(2))`, where 2 is the arity of the procedure. This preliminary transformation has the advantage of keeping the set of variables used for the analysis of a given program point as small as possible. For instance, if a variable is not used in a constraint, then it will be added (through `expand`) *after* the analysis (i.e., the abstraction) of the constraint. See the case of `v(16)` and `v(17)` in the normalisation of `member/2` above. If a variable is not used after a conjunction, then it can be removed (through `restrict`). See the case of `v(20)` in the normalisation of `member/2` above. This reduces the complexity of the analysis, since the abstract operations have computational complexities which are proportional to the dimension of the elements of the abstract domain, and this dimension is in its turn proportional to the number of variables used.

Note that the normalisation phase above is not abstract compilation. Instead, abstract compilation substitutes the built-in's with their abstract behaviour, i.e., a constraint of the abstract domain. In the case of `bi_eq` it applies the abstraction map of Definition 6. Moreover, it applies partial evaluation when the operands of an abstract operation are known (i.e., if they do not contain any procedure call), by substituting the operation with its result. In our case, we obtain

```
member(2):-
   rename(v(16), v(0), rename(v(17), v(1), or(
       abs(177072),
       restrict(v(20), and(
           abs(203050),
           expand(v(17), rename(v(0), v(16), rename(v(1), v(20),
               call(member(2)))))
       ))
   )))
```

An element of Abs_V is written as abs(N), N being the pointer in memory where the constraint is stored. Indeed, as we have said, constraints are manipulated by C procedures.

The calculation of the abstract fixpoint is just an iterated depth-first evaluation of the abstract program, by using the operations of Section 3. The call graph of the program is used. Namely, if a procedure p is called by a procedure q but not vice versa (even through intermediate procedures), the denotation of p is computed first, and that of q later. In the case of `member/2`, this machinery is of no help.

Even for a procedure as simple as `member/2`, our abstract analyser would not reach the abstract fixpoint in a reasonable time, since the computational cost of the analysis explodes. We show now how to obtain a reasonable performance.

4.2 Reduction Rules and Widening

Since several elements of Abs_V may have the same concretisation (γ_{Rep} is defined in the proofs appendix) and the computational complexity of the abstract operators of Section 3 depends on the dimension of their operands, we wish to use the elements of Abs_V of smallest dimension. This is the goal of *reduction rules.*

Definition 8. *A* reduction rule *is a family of maps* $\{\rho_V\}_{V\in\wp_f(\mathcal{V})}$ *such that, for every* $V \in \wp_f(\mathcal{V})$,

i) $\rho_V : Abs_V \mapsto Abs_V$,
ii) $\mathsf{dim}(\rho_V(A)) \leq \mathsf{dim}(A)$ *and*
iii) $\gamma_{Rep}(\rho_V(A)) = \gamma_{Rep}(A)$ *for every* $A \in Abs_V$.

The last two conditions say that a reduction rule reduces the dimension of a constraint without losing any information. Though it can be shown that not all the operations of Section 3 are monotonic w.r.t. dim, our evaluation (Section 5) suggests that reduction rules are useful in practice. If we apply a reduction rule after every abstract operator, Definition 8 guarantees that we obtain a correct result. The following condition entails that we do not lose any precision, which was not obvious, since the abstract operators are not optimal.

Proposition 1. *For* $V \in \wp_f(\mathcal{V})$ *and* $A_1, A_2 \in Abs_V$, *let* $A_1 \preceq A_2$ *if and only if for every* $l_2 \Rightarrow r \in A_2$ *there is* $l_1 \Rightarrow r \in A_1$ *with*

$$l_1 \subseteq l_2 \cup \{(v, v') \mid v, v' \in V,\ v \neq v' \text{ and } (v, v) \in l_2\} .$$

Every reduction rule ρ *which is reductive w.r.t.* $\preceq$ *(i.e.,* $\rho(A) \preceq A$ *for every* $A \in Abs_V$*) does not introduce any loss of precision.*

We show now two examples of reduction rules which are reductive w.r.t. $\preceq$.

Proposition 2. *Let* $\rho^1 = \{\rho^1_V\}_{V\in\wp_f(\mathcal{V})}$, *where*

$$\rho^1_V(A) = \left\{ l \Rightarrow r \in A \,\middle|\, \begin{array}{l} \text{there is no } l' \Rightarrow r \in A \text{ s.t.} \\ l' \subset l \cup \{(v, v') \mid v, v' \in V,\ v \neq v' \text{ and } (v, v) \in l\} \end{array} \right\}$$

for any $V \in \wp_f(\mathcal{V})$ *and* $A \in Abs_V$. *Then* ρ^1 *is a reduction rule and is reductive w.r.t.* $\preceq$. *Moreover, it is possible to prove that* $\rho^1_V(A) = \bigcap\{X \subseteq A \mid X \preceq A\}$, *i.e.,* $\rho^1(A)$ *is the smallest set of* A *to precede* A *w.r.t.* $\preceq$.

Example 4. Let $V = \{v, x, y, z\}$ and

$$A = \{x(x, y)(x, z)(x, v) \Rightarrow (x, v), x(v, v) \Rightarrow (x, v), xy \Rightarrow y, x(x, v) \Rightarrow (x, v)\} .$$

Then

$$\rho^1_V(A) = \{xy \Rightarrow y, x(x, v) \Rightarrow (x, v)\} .$$

Proposition 3. *Let* $\rho^2 = \{\rho^2_V\}_{V \in \wp_f(\mathcal{V})}$*, where*

$$\rho^2_V(A) = \{l \setminus (\{(v, v') \mid v, v' \in V,\ v \neq v' \text{ and } (v, v) \in l\} \Rightarrow r) \mid l \Rightarrow r \in A\}$$

for any $V \in \wp_f(\mathcal{V})$ *and* $A \in Abs_V$*. Then* ρ^2 *is a reduction rule and is reductive w.r.t.* $\preceq$*.*

Example 5. Let $V = \{v, x, y, z\}$ and

$$A = \{x(x, y)(y, y)(y, z)(x, z) \Rightarrow (x, z), xy \Rightarrow y, y(y, z)(z, z)(v, v) \Rightarrow y\} .$$

Then

$$\rho^2_V(A) = \{x(y, y)(x, z) \Rightarrow (x, z), xy \Rightarrow y, y(z, z)(v, v) \Rightarrow y\} .$$

The efficiency of the analysis can be obviously improved by removing some arrows from the elements of Abs_V, possibly introducing some imprecision, like with every widening operation [9]. In our implementation we use syntactical equality for the entailment test of Definition 3, which means that some arrows allowed by the theory are not generated by the implementation.

4.3 The Result of the Analysis

By using the techniques of Subsection 4.2, our analyser computes the following denotation for `member/2`:

```
?1,(a1,?1),(a0,?1),(a0,a1)=>?1
?1,a1,(a1,?1)=>?1
(?1,?2),(a1,?1),(a0,?1),(a0,a1)=>(?1,?2)
(?1,?1)=>(?1,?1)
(a1,?1),(a0,?1),(a0,a1)=>(a1,?1)
(a1,a1)=>(a1,a1)
a1,a0,(a0,a1)=>a0
(a1,?1),(a0,?1),(a0,a1)=>(a0,?1)
(a1,a1)=>(a0,?1)
(a0,a0)=>(a0,a0)
(a1,a1)=>(a0,a0)
```

The variables `a0` and `a1` are the two argument positions of the procedure. Beyond simple groundness dependencies, note that the analyser concludes that $a1, a0, (a0, a1) \Rightarrow a0$. Indeed, if `member/2` is called with two different free variables, then the freeness of the first variable cannot be lost. Note that the simple freeness of `a1` and `a2` is not judged enough to this purpose. Indeed, a call like `member(X,X)` binds `X` to the term `[X|_]` if the occur-check is not applied. If the occur-check is applied, the freeness of `a1` and `a2` would be enough.

Benchmark	Bytes	Prepr.	Fix.	Conj.	Others	Shell
ackermann.pl	139	0.06	0.10	35.0%	7.2%	57.8%
append.pl	62	0.03	0.52	77.5%	6.9%	16.5%
eliza.pl	1400	0.42	2.20	70.1%	6.0%	23.9%
hanoi.pl	199	0.09	2.91	88.9%	4.3%	5.7%
heapify.pl	508	0.16	106.67	99.5%	0.0%	0.5%
map_coloring.pl	419	0.08	0.49	57.6%	12.9%	29.5%
queens.pl	735	0.24	1.01	52.7%	14.9%	33.3%
quicksort.pl	431	0.18	18.45	97.0%	1.0%	2.0%
openlist.pl	159	0.76	0.48	80.3%	10.5%	9.2%

Fig. 1. The analysis times.

5 Experimental Evaluation

We show now the behaviour of our analyser on some benchmarks. We have used SWI-Prolog 3.3.2 over an AMD K5 100Mhz processor with 64Mbytes of memory, running Linux 2.2. The techniques of Subsection 4.2 have been applied.

In Figure 1, for every benchmark, we report its dimension in bytes, the time in seconds spent in the preprocessing phase (normalisation, abstraction and call graph construction), that spent for the fixpoint calculation, and the relative computational cost of the conjunction operation (Definition 3) w.r.t. the other operations of the domain and the shell (preprocessor) which normalises, abstracts and computes the fixpoint. As you can see, the preprocessing time is always small, while the fixpoint calculation is sometimes expensive and is much more related to the number of variables in the clauses of the program than to its dimension (compare the lucky case of `eliza.pl` with that of `heapify.pl`). Indeed, when that number becomes large, the time spent for the abstract conjunction explodes, as the fifth column shows. Thus a clever implementation of the conjunction is welcome.

We have compared our analyser with a goal-dependent analysis performed by using the *Sharing* × *Free* domain [12] inside the China analyser[4] [2]. The result is shown in Figure 2. The goal-dependent analysis is definitely more efficient, but must be re-executed for every query. W.r.t. precision, we have run some abstract queries with the goal-dependent analyser and we have compared the resulting abstract information with what we get by instantiating our goal-independent denotation on the queries.

In the third column, "`A`" means "`A` free", while "`(A,B,C)`" means that `A`, `B` and `C` are mutually independent, and is a compact notation for `(A,B)(A,C)(B,C)`. The last two columns show the results of the analysis with our analyser and with China, expressed in our domain. Our analyser is always as precise as China except for `app/6`, a version of `append/3` for incomplete lists.

[4] We thank Roberto Bagnara for his help with this experiment.

Benchmark	Predicate call	Input constraint	Our response	China's
ackermann.pl	ackermann(A,B,C)	ABC(A,B,C)	(A,A)	(A,A)
		(B,B)	(A,A)(B,B) (C,C)	(A,A)(B,B) (C,C)
append.pl	append(A,B,C)	ABC(A,B,C)	B(A,B)	B(A,B)
		BC(A,B,C)	B(A,B)	B(A,B)
		C(A,B,C)	(A,B)	(A,B)
		(C,C)	(A,A)(B,B) (C,C)	(A,A)(B,B) (C,C)
eliza.pl	eliza(A)	A	true	true
hanoi.pl	hanoi(A,B,C,D,E)	ABCDE(A,B,C,D,E)	(A,A)	(A,A)
		(E,E)	(A,A)(B,B) (C,C)(E,E)	(A,A)(B,B) (C,C)(E,E)
heapify.pl	heapify(A,B)	AB(A,B)	true	true
		(A,A)	(A,A)(B,B)	(A,A)(B,B)
map_coloring.pl	color_map(A,B)	AB(A,B)	true	true
queens.pl	queens(A,B)	AB(A,B)	(A,A)(B,B)	(A,A)(B,B)
		(A,A)	(A,A)(B,B)	(A,A)(B,B)
quicksort.pl	quicksort(A,B)	AB(A,B)	(A,A)(B,B)	(A,A)(B,B)
		(A,A)	(A,A)(B,B)	(A,A)(B,B)
openlist.pl	nil(A,B)	AB(A,B)	B	B
	cons(A,B,C,D,E)	CDE(A,A)(B,D,E) (C,D,E)	CE(A,A)	CE(A,A)
	app(A,B,C,D,E,F)	BDEF(A,C,E,F) (A,D,E,F)(B,C,E,F) (B,D,E,F)	true	DF
	list2open(A,B,C)	BC(B,C)(A,A)	C(A,A)	C(A,A)

Fig. 2. The comparison of our analysis with that done through China.

6 Conclusion

We have described the implementation of a static analyser based on the abstract domain for non pair-sharing and freeness of [13]. It shows that linear refinement can be used to devise practically useful domains. We do not know of any other implementation of a static analysis developed through linear refinement.

We have shown that reduction rules are necessary in order to obtain an efficient analysis. We have studied a sufficient condition which entails that a reduction rule does not introduce any loss of precision.

A promising widening operation would delete all the arrows whose dimension is too big. They are the cause of the computational cost of the analysis and are seldom useful in practice. Preliminary experiments have shown that a drastic performance improvement can be obtained.

Our analysis is almost always as precise as a traditional goal-dependent analysis. This justifies the research of more efficient implementations. At the same time, it challenges us to exploit the full power of the domain.

References

1. R. Bagnara, P. M. Hill, and E. Zaffanella. Set-Sharing is Redundant for Pair-Sharing. In P. Van Hentenryck, editor, *Proc. of the 4th Int. Symp. on Static Analysis*, volume 1302 of *Lecture Notes in Computer Science*, pages 53–67, Paris, France, 1997. Springer-Verlag, Berlin.
2. Roberto Bagnara. *Data-Flow Analysis for Constraint Logic-Based Languages*. PhD thesis, Dipartimento di Informatica, Università di Pisa, 1997.
3. A. Bossi, M. Gabbrielli, G. Levi, and M. Martelli. The s-semantics approach: Theory and applications. *Journal of Logic Programming*, 19–20:149–197, 1994.
4. M. Bruynooghe, B. Demoen, D. Boulanger, M. Denecker, and A. Mulkers. A Freeness and Sharing Analysis of Logic Programs Based on a Pre-Interpretation. In R. Cousot and D. A. Schmidt, editors, *3rd Int. Symp. on Static Analysis*, volume 1145 of *Lecture Notes in Computer Science*, pages 128–142, Aachen, Germany, 1996. Springer Verlag.
5. M. Codish and B. Demoen. Deriving Polymorphic Type Dependencies for Logic Programs Using Multiple Incarnations of Prop. In *Proc. of the first International Symposium on Static Analysis*, volume 864 of *Lecture Notes in Computer Science*, pages 281–296. Springer-Verlag, 1994.
6. M. Codish, V. Lagoon, and F. Bueno. An Algebraic Approach to Sharing Analysis of Logic Programs. *Journal of Logic Programming*, 42(2):110–149, February 2000.
7. M. Codish, H. Søndergaard, and P. J. Stuckey. Sharing and Groundness Dependencies in Logic Programs. *ACM Transactions on Programming Languages and Systems*, 21(5):948–976, 1999.
8. P. Cousot and R. Cousot. Systematic Design of Program Analysis Frameworks. In *Proc. Sixth ACM Symp. Principles of Programming Languages*, pages 269–282, 1979.
9. P. Cousot and R. Cousot. Abstract Interpretation and Applications to Logic Programs. *Journal of Logic Programming*, 13(2 & 3):103–179, 1992.
10. R. Giacobazzi and R. Ranzato. The Reduced Relative Power Operation on Abstract Domains. *Theoretical Computer Science*, 216:159–211, 1999.
11. M. Hermenegildo, W. Warren, and S. K. Debray. Global Flow Analysis as a Practical Compilation Tool. *Journal of Logic Programing*, 13(2 & 3):349–366, 1992.
12. D. Jacobs and A. Langen. Static Analysis of Logic Programs for Independent AND Parallelism. *Journal of Logic Programming*, 13(2 & 3):291–314, 1992.
13. Giorgio Levi and Fausto Spoto. Non Pair-Sharing and Freeness Analysis through Linear Refinement. In *Proc. of the Partial Evaluation and Program Manipulation Workshop*, pages 52–61, Boston, Mass., January 2000. ACM Press. Available at `http://strudel.di.unipi.it/papers`.
14. A. Martelli and U. Montanari. An efficient unification algorithm. *ACM Transactions on Programming Languages and Systems*, 4:258–282, 1982.
15. K. Muthukumar and M. Hermenegildo. Combined Determination of Sharing and Freeness of Program Variables through Abstract Interpretation. In K. Furukawa, editor, *Proceedings of the 8th International Conference on Logic Programming*, pages 49–63, Paris, 1991. The MIT Press.
16. H. Søndergaard. An Application of Abstract Interpretation of Logic Programs: Occur Check Reduction. In B. Robinet and R. Wilhelm, editors, *Proc. ESOP 86*, volume 213 of *Lecture Notes in Computer Science*, pages 327–338. Springer-Verlag, 1986.

PROOFS

We recall from [13] the following definitions.

Definition 9. *Given $V \in \wp_f(\mathcal{V})$ and $\{v, v_1, v_2\} \subseteq V$, we define $(\mathbf{v_1}, \mathbf{v_2})_V = \{\exists_W c \in H_V \mid \mathsf{vars}(c(v_1)) \cap \mathsf{vars}(c(v_2)) = \emptyset\}$ and $\mathbf{v}_V = \{\exists_W c \in H_V \mid c(v) \in V \cup W\}$. When the set V is obvious from the context, we write $(\mathbf{v_1}, \mathbf{v_2})$ for $(\mathbf{v_1}, \mathbf{v_2})_V$ and $\mathbf{v}$ for $\mathbf{v}_V$. Given $\{(v_1^1, v_1^2), \ldots, (v_n^1, v_n^2), v_1, \ldots, v_m\}$, we write $(\mathbf{v_1^1}, \mathbf{v_1^2}) \ldots (\mathbf{v_n^1}, \mathbf{v_n^2})\mathbf{v_1} \ldots \mathbf{v_m}$ (the order is irrelevant) for $(\cap_{i=1,\ldots,n}(\mathbf{v_i^1}, \mathbf{v_i^2})) \cap (\cap_{i=1,\ldots,m}\mathbf{v_i})$.*

The linear arrow $\mathbf{l} \multimap \mathbf{r}$ is defined as

$$\mathbf{l} \multimap \mathbf{r} = \{h \in H_V \mid \textit{for every } h' \in \mathbf{l} \textit{ if } h \star^{H_V} h' \textit{ is defined then } h \star^{H_V} h' \in \mathbf{r}\}$$

for every $\mathbf{l}, \mathbf{r} \in \wp(H_V)$.

We define the concretisation map $\gamma_{Rep} : Abs_V \mapsto \wp(H_V)$ as

$$\gamma_{Rep}(A) = \bigcap_{l \Rightarrow r \in A} \mathbf{l} \multimap \mathbf{r}$$

for any $A \in Abs_V$.

The following definition formalises the intuitive concept of computation.

Definition 10. *A* computation *is whether an element of Abs_V, for any $V \in \wp_f(\mathcal{V})$, or a term of the form $\mathsf{op}(c_1, \ldots, c_n)$, where the c_i's are computations, op is the name of one of the abstract operators defined in Section 3 and its signature is respected. The evaluation of a computation is defined as $[\![A]\!] = A$ if $A \in Abs_V$ for some $V \in \wp_f(\mathcal{V})$ and $[\![\mathsf{op}(c_1, \ldots, c_n)]\!] = \mathsf{op}([\![c_1]\!], \ldots, [\![c_n]\!])$. Moreover, if ρ is a reduction rule, we define $[\![A]\!]^\rho = \rho_V(A)$ if $A \in Abs_V$ for some $V \in \wp_f(\mathcal{V})$ and $[\![\mathsf{op}(c_1, \ldots, c_n)]\!]^\rho = \rho_V(\mathsf{op}([\![c_1]\!]^\rho, \ldots, [\![c_n]\!]^\rho))$ if $\mathsf{op}([\![c_1]\!]^\rho, \ldots, [\![c_n]\!]^\rho) \in Abs_V$ for some $V \in \wp_f(\mathcal{V})$.*

*Proof (**Proof of Proposition 1**).* We have to prove that every computation c is such that $\mathsf{free}_V([\![c]\!]) \subseteq \mathsf{free}_V([\![c]\!]^\rho)$ and $\mathsf{nsh}_V([\![c]\!]) \subseteq \mathsf{nsh}_V([\![c]\!]^\rho)$. We prove that all the abstract operators of Section 3 are monotonic w.r.t. $\preceq$. This will entail the thesis by induction on c, since $\rho_V(A) \preceq A$ and it is easy to check that $A_1 \preceq A_2$ entails $\mathsf{free}_V(A_2) \subseteq \mathsf{free}_V(A_1)$ and $\mathsf{nsh}_V(A_2) \subseteq \mathsf{nsh}_V(A_1)$.

Assume $V \in \wp_f(\mathcal{V})$ and $A, A_1, A_2 \in Abs_V$ such that $A_1 \preceq A_2$.

We have trivially $\mathsf{rename}_{x \to n}^{Abs_V}(A_1) \preceq \mathsf{rename}_{x \to n}^{Abs_V}(A_2)$.

For $\mathsf{restrict}^{Abs_V}$, consider $l_2 \Rightarrow r \in \mathsf{restrict}_x^{Abs_V}(A_2)$. Then $l_2 = l_2' \setminus X$ with $l_2' \Rightarrow r \in A_2$, $(x, x) \notin l_2'$ and X as defined in Definition 4. Then there exists $l_1' \Rightarrow r \in A_1$ such that $l_1' \subseteq l_2' \cup \{(v, v') \mid v, v' \in V,\ v \neq v',\ (v, v) \in l_2'\}$. Since $(x, x) \notin l_2'$, we have $(x, x) \notin l_1'$. Therefore, $l_1' \setminus X \Rightarrow r \in \mathsf{restrict}_x^{Abs_V}(A_1)$, and $l_1' \setminus X \subseteq l_2' \cup \{(v, v') \mid v, v' \in V,\ v \neq v',\ (v, v) \in l_2'\} \setminus X = (l_2' \setminus X) \cup \{(v, v') \mid v, v' \in V \setminus x,\ v \neq v',\ (v, v) \in l_2' \setminus X\}$, since $(x, x) \notin l_2'$.

For expand^{Abs_V}, let $l_2 \Rightarrow r \in \mathsf{expand}_n^{Abs_V}(A_2)$ with $l_2 \Rightarrow r \in A_2$. Then there exists $l_1 \Rightarrow r \in A_1$ with $l_1 \subseteq l_2 \cup \{(v, v') \mid v, v' \in V,\ v \neq v',\ (v, v) \in l_2\}$ and $l_1 \Rightarrow r \in \mathsf{expand}_n^{Abs_V}(A_1)$. If $l_2[n/?_1][?1/?2] \Rightarrow r[n/?_1][?1/?2] \in \mathsf{expand}_n^{Abs_V}(A_2)$

with $l_2 \Rightarrow r \in A_2$, then there exists $l_1 \Rightarrow r \in A_1$ with $l_1 \subseteq l_2 \cup \{(v,v') \mid v,v' \in V,\ v \neq v',\ (v,v) \in l_2\}$. Therefore, $l_1[n/?_1][?1/?2] \subseteq l_2[n/?_1][?1/?2] \cup \{(v,v') \mid v,v' \in V,\ v \neq v',\ (v,v) \in l_2\}[n/?_1][?1/?2] \subseteq l_2[n/?_1][?1/?2] \cup \{(v,v') \mid v,v' \in V \cup n,\ v \neq v',\ (v,v) \in l_2[n/?_1][?1/?2]\}$. Since $l_1[n/?_1][?1/?2] \Rightarrow r[n/?_1][?1/?2] \in \mathsf{expand}_n^{Abs_V}(A_1)$, we have the thesis.

For $\cup^{Abs_V}$, consider $l_2 l \Rightarrow r \in \cup^{Abs_V}(A_2, A)$, with $l_2 \Rightarrow r \in A_2$ and $l \Rightarrow r \in A$. There exists $l_1 \Rightarrow r \in A_1$ with $l_1 \subseteq l_2 \cup \{(v,v') \mid v,v' \in V,\ v \neq v',\ (v,v) \in l_2\}$. Therefore, $l_1 l \subseteq l_2 l \cup \{(v,v') \mid v,v' \in V,\ v \neq v',\ (v,v) \in l_2\} \subseteq l_2 l \cup \{(v,v') \mid v,v' \in V,\ v \neq v',\ (v,v) \in l_2 l\}$. Since $l_1 l \Rightarrow r \in \cup^{Abs_V}(A_1, A)$ and the same argument can be used for the symmetrical case of the definition of $\cup^{Abs_V}$, we have the thesis.

For $\star^{Abs_V}$, consider $l_1 \cdots l_n \Rightarrow r \in A_2 \star^{Abs_V} A$, with $r_1 \cdots r_n \Rightarrow r \in A \cup T$ (T is the set of Definition 3), $l_i \Rightarrow r'_i \in A_2 \cup T$ and $\mathbf{r'_i} \subseteq \mathbf{r_i}$ for $i = 1, \ldots, n$. Then $l'_i \Rightarrow r'_i \in A_1 \cup T$ with $l'_i \subseteq l_i \cup \{(v,v') \mid v,v' \in V,\ v \neq v',\ (v,v) \in l_i\}$ and $l'_1 \cdots l'_n \Rightarrow r \in A_1 \star^{Abs_V} A$ with $l'_1 \cdots l'_n \subseteq l_1 \cdots l_n \cup \{(v,v') \mid v,v' \in V,\ v \neq v',\ (v,v) \in l_1 \cdots l_n\}$. Consider now $l_1 \cdots l_n \Rightarrow r \in A_2 \star^{Abs_V} A$ with $r_1 \cdots r_n \Rightarrow r \in A_2 \cup T$, $l_i \Rightarrow r'_i \in A \cup T$ and $\mathbf{r'_i} \subseteq \mathbf{r_i}$. There exists $l' \Rightarrow r \in A_1 \cup T$ such that $l' \subseteq r_1 \cdots r_n \cup \{(v,v') \mid v,v' \in V,\ v \neq v', (v,v) \in r_1 \cdots r_n\}$. Given $k \in l'$, whether $k \in r_1 \cdots r_n$ or $k = (v,v')$ with $(v,v) \in r_1 \cdots r_n$. In both cases there exists i, $1 \leq i \leq n$, such that $\mathbf{r'_i} \subseteq \mathbf{r_i} \subseteq \mathbf{k}$, and we can select a set S of natural numbers between 1 and n such that $\cup_{i \in S} l_i \Rightarrow r \in A_1 \star^{Abs_V} A$ and $\cup_{i \in S} l_i \subseteq l_1 \cdots l_n \subseteq l_1 \cdots l_n \cup \{(v,v') \mid v,v' \in V,\ v \neq v',\ (v,v) \in l_1 \cdots l_n\}$. The other case of $\star^{Abs_V}$ is symmetrical.

Given $V \in \wp_f(\mathcal{V})$ and two arrows $l \Rightarrow r$ and $l' \Rightarrow r'$, we write $l \Rightarrow r \preceq l' \Rightarrow r'$ if and only if $r = r'$ and $l \subseteq l' \cup \{(v,v') \mid v,v' \in V, v \neq v', (v,v) \in l'\}$. The relation $\preceq$ turns out to be a well founded partial order. It is obvious that $A \preceq A'$ if and only if for each arrow $a' \in A'$ there exists an arrow $a \in A$ such that $a \preceq a'$.

Proof (**Proof of Proposition 2**). Given an arrow $a \in A$, let us consider the set of all the arrows $b \in A$ with $b \preceq a$, which we denote by $\downarrow a$. If $A' \preceq A$, the least element of $\downarrow a$, namely $\bigcap \downarrow a$ has to be in A'. It turns out that $\bar{A} = \{\bigcap(\downarrow a) \mid a \in A\}$ is the least subset of A according to the $\preceq$ ordering. It is easy to check that $\bar{A} = \rho^1(A)$.

Now, we want to prove that $\gamma_{Rep}(\rho^1(A)) = \gamma_{Rep}(A)$. It is enough to prove that, given two arrows a and a', if $a \preceq a'$ then $\gamma_{Rep}(a) \subseteq \gamma_{Rep}(a')$. If $a \preceq a'$, then $a = l \Rightarrow r$, $a' = l' \Rightarrow r$ and $\gamma_{Rep}(l) \supseteq \gamma_{Rep}(l')$. By properties of the linear refinement, $\gamma_{Rep}(a) \subseteq \gamma_{Rep}(a')$ follows.

Proof (**Proof of Proposition 3**). Given $V \in \wp_f(\mathcal{V})$, the map ρ^2_V, applied to $A \in Abs_V$, removes (v,v') from the left hand side of $l \Rightarrow r$ if and only if $(v,v) \in l$ and $v \neq v'$. Therefore it is reductive w.r.t. $\preceq$. Moreover, $\mathsf{dim}(\rho^2_V(A)) \leq \mathsf{dim}(A)$ and $\gamma_{Rep}(A) = \gamma_{Rep}(\rho^2_V(A))$. Indeed, given $h \in H_V$, if $h \in (\mathbf{v},\mathbf{v})$ then h is ground and $h \in (\mathbf{v},\mathbf{v'})$ for any $v' \in V$.

A Practical Partial Evaluator for a Multi-Paradigm Declarative Language*

Elvira Albert[1], Michael Hanus[2], and Germán Vidal[1]

[1] DSIC, UPV, Camino de Vera s/n, E-46022 Valencia, Spain
{ealbert,gvidal}@dsic.upv.es
[2] Institut für Informatik, CAU Kiel, Olshausenstr. 40, D-24098 Kiel, Germany
mh@informatik.uni-kiel.de

Abstract. Partial evaluation is an automatic technique for program optimization which preserves program semantics. The range of its potential applications is extremely large, as witnessed by successful experiences in several fields. This paper summarizes our findings in the development of partial evaluation tools for Curry, a modern multi-paradigm declarative language which combines features from functional, logic and concurrent programming. From a practical point of view, the most promising approach appears to be a recent partial evaluation framework which translates source programs into a maximally simplified representation. We support this statement by extending the underlying method in order to design a practical partial evaluation tool for the language Curry. The process is fully automatic and can be incorporated into a Curry compiler as a source-to-source transformation on intermediate programs. An implementation of the partial evaluator has been undertaken. Experimental results confirm that our partial evaluator pays off in practice.

1 Introduction

Curry [13, 15] is a modern multi-paradigm declarative language which integrates features from functional, logic and concurrent programming. The most important features of the language include lazy evaluation, higher-order functions, non-deterministic computations, concurrent evaluation of constraints with synchronization on logical variables, and a unified computation model which integrates *narrowing* and *residuation*. Furthermore, Curry is a complete programming language which has been used to implement distributed applications (e.g., Internet servers [14], dynamic web pages [17]) or graphical user interfaces [16]. Several efficient implementations of the language already exist (see, e.g., [7, 18, 25]), although there is still room for further improvements. Existing compilers for pure functional languages have been successfully improved by semantics-based program transformation techniques. For instance, the Glasgow Haskell Compiler includes a number of source-to-source program transformations which are able

* This work has been partially supported by CICYT TIC 98-0445-C03-01, by Acción Integrada hispano-alemana HA1997-0073, and by the DFG under grant Ha 2457/1-2.

H. Kuchen and K. Ueda (Eds.): FLOPS 2001, LNCS 2024, pp. 326–342, 2001.

to optimize the quality of code in many different aspects [27]. Encouraged by these successful experiences, we develop an automatic program transformation technique to improve the efficiency of Curry functional logic programs.

For instance, consider functions defined by higher-order combinators such as `map`, `foldr`, etc. Although such functions can be simply defined in a concise way, some overhead is introduced at runtime which can be eliminated by program transformation techniques. As an example, consider the following function `foo`:

```
foo xs = foldr (+) 0 (map (+1) xs)
```

to add `1` to the elements of a given list `xs` and then compute their total sum. From the programmer point of view, this definition is perfectly right, but there exist more efficient definitions for `foo`, like the following one:

```
foo []       = 0
foo (x : xs) = (x + 1) + (foo xs)
```

In contrast to the original definition, it is a first-order function and, over existing functional logic compilers, it can be executed more efficiently (since it is completely "deforested" [30]). Therefore, we are concerned with program transformations which, given a program, output a *residual* program from which the overhead has been removed at compile time. Partial evaluation (PE) is an automatic technique for program optimization which preserves program semantics. Optimization is achieved by specializing programs w.r.t. parts of their input (hence also called *program specialization*). We note that several PE techniques are able to perform deforestation automatically and, thus, they can be useful to optimize functions like the above one. Informally, a partial evaluator is a mapping which takes a program P and a function call C and derives a more efficient, specialized program P_C which gives the same answers for C (and any of its instances) as P does.

PE techniques have been intensively studied in the context of a wide variety of declarative programming paradigms, specially in both the functional and logic programming communities (see, e.g., [9,11,20,23] and references herein). Recently, a unified framework for the PE of languages which integrate features from functional and logic programming has been introduced in [4]. The original framework is defined for languages whose operational semantics is based solely on narrowing, although it has been extended to deal with residuation in [2]. The Indy partial evaluator [1] is a prototype implementation based on the above framework. The system is written in Prolog and accepts unconditional term rewriting systems as programs. The narrowing-driven approach to PE has the same potential for specialization as *positive supercompilation* [29] of functional programs and *conjunctive partial deduction* [10] of logic programs (it has been experimentally tested in [2,4]).

Unfortunately, the use of Indy within a realistic functional logic language (e.g., Curry [15], Escher [22] or Toy [24]) becomes impractical since there are many facilities of these languages (e.g., higher-order functions, constraints, I/O, built-in's, etc.) which are not covered neither by Indy nor by the underlying PE framework. For instance, Indy cannot be used to optimize the above function `foo` due to occurrences of the built-in function + and the higher-order functions `map` and `foldr`. Furthermore, the PE framework of [4] suffers from some limitations, e.g., within a lazy (call-by-name) semantics, terms in head normal form (i.e., rooted by a constructor symbol) cannot be evaluated during the PE process. This can drastically reduce the optimization power of the method in many cases. To overcome this problem, [3] introduces a novel approach for the PE of functional logic languages. The new scheme considers a maximally simplified representation into which programs written in a higher-level language (i.e., inductively sequential programs [5] with evaluation annotations) can be automatically translated. The restriction to not evaluate terms in head normal form is avoided by defining a non-standard semantics which is well-suited to perform computations at PE time.

The aim of this work is to show how—in contrast to [4] and INDY—the framework of [3] can be successfully applied in practice. To this end, we first enrich the intermediate representation considered in [3] in order to cover all the facilities of the language Curry. The resulting representation is essentially equivalent to the standard intermediate language FlatCurry [18], which has been proposed to provide a common interface for connecting different tools working on Curry programs, e.g., back ends for various compilers [7]. Then, the non-standard semantics of [3] is carefully extended in order to cover the additional language features. This extension is far from trivial, since the underlying calculus does not compute bindings but represents them by "residual" case expressions. However, there are a number of functions, like equalities, (concurrent) conjunctions, some arithmetic functions, etc., in which the propagation of bindings between their arguments is crucial to achieve a good level of specialization. Therefore, we are constrained to define a specific treatment for these important features. Finally, in order to make the resulting framework practically applicable, we define appropriate control strategies which take into account the particularities of the considered language and (non-standard) semantics. The resulting method is able to transform realistic Curry programs in contrast to other existing partial evaluators. For instance, the "higher-order" definition of `foo` can be automatically transformed into the more efficient version (see Sect. 5).

The structure of this paper is as follows. Section 2 recalls the basic notions and techniques associated to the PE of functional logic programs. Section 3 extends the previous approach in order to cover all the facilities provided by the language Curry. A description of the control issues involved in the PE process is presented in Sect. 4. Some experiments with the partial evaluator are described in Sect. 5 before we conclude in Sect. 6.

2 The Basic Approach

For the sake of completeness, in this section we briefly recall the approach presented in [3] for the PE of functional logic programs. Informally speaking, the process is based on two steps: firstly, the source program is translated into a maximally simplified representation (Sect. 2.1); then, function calls are partially evaluated using a non-standard semantics, the RLNT calculus, which is specially well-suited for performing computations at PE time (Sect. 2.2). To be precise, for each finite (possibly partial) computation of the form $e_1 \Rightarrow^+ e_2$ performed with the RLNT calculus, we generate a residual rule—a *resultant*—of the form: $e_1 = e_2$. Additionally, a post-processing of renaming is often required to recover the same class of programs.

2.1 The Flat Representation

Following [13], we consider inductively sequential rewrite systems [5] (with evaluation annotations) as programs and an operational semantics which integrates (needed) narrowing and residuation. In order to simplify the underlying semantics, a *flat* representation for programs is introduced. This representation is based on the formulation of [19] to express pattern-matching by case expressions. As it will become apparent in Sect. 3, it corresponds to a subset of the FlatCurry syntax [18], a standard intermediate representation for Curry programs.

$$
\begin{array}{ll}
\mathcal{R} ::= D_1 \ldots D_m & e ::= x \quad \text{(variable)} \\
D ::= f(x_1, \ldots, x_n) = e & \quad\mid c(e_1, \ldots, e_n) \quad \text{(constructor)} \\
 & \quad\mid f(e_1, \ldots, e_n) \quad \text{(function call)} \\
p \;::= c(x_1, \ldots, x_n) & \quad\mid \mathit{case}\ e_0\ \mathit{of}\ \{p_1 \to e_1; \ldots; p_n \to e_n\} \quad \text{(rigid case)} \\
 & \quad\mid \mathit{fcase}\ e_0\ \mathit{of}\ \{p_1 \to e_1; \ldots; p_n \to e_n\} \quad \text{(flexible case)}
\end{array}
$$

A program $\mathcal{R}$ consists of a sequence of function definitions D such that each function is defined by one rule whose left-hand side contains only variables as parameters. The right-hand side is an expression e composed by variables, constructors, function calls, and case expressions for pattern-matching. The form of a case expression is:[1]

$$(f)\mathit{case}\ e\ \mathit{of}\ \{c_1(\overline{x_{n_1}}) \to e_1; \ldots; c_k(\overline{x_{n_k}}) \to e_k\}$$

where e is an expression, $c_1, \ldots, c_k$ are different constructors of the type of e, and $e_1, \ldots, e_k$ are expressions (possibly containing $(f)\mathit{case}$'s). The variables $\overline{x_{n_i}}$ are local variables which occur only in the corresponding subexpression e_i. The difference between *case* and *fcase* only shows up when the argument e is a free variable: *case* suspends (which corresponds to residuation) whereas *fcase* nondeterministically binds this variable to a pattern in a branch of the case expression (which corresponds to narrowing). Functions defined only by *fcase* (resp. *case*) expressions are called *flexible* (resp. *rigid*). Thus, flexible functions act as generators (like predicates in logic programming) and rigid functions act as consumers.

For example, consider the rules defining the (rigid) function "$\leqslant$":[2]

$$
\begin{array}{lcl}
\texttt{0} \leqslant \texttt{n} & = & \texttt{True} \\
(\texttt{Succ m}) \leqslant \texttt{0} & = & \texttt{False} \\
(\texttt{Succ m}) \leqslant (\texttt{Succ n}) & = & \texttt{m} \leqslant \texttt{n}
\end{array}
$$

Using case expressions, they can be represented by the following rewrite rule:

[1] We write $\overline{o_n}$ for the *sequence of objects* $o_1, \ldots, o_n$.

[2] Although we consider in this work a first-order representation for programs, we use a curried notation in concrete examples (as usual in functional languages).

```
x ≤ y =  case x of {0         → True;
                    (Succ x1) → case y of {0 → False;
                                          (Succ y1) → x1 ≤ y1} }
```

An automatic transformation from inductively sequential programs [5] to programs using case expressions is introduced in [19].

2.2 The Residualizing Semantics

The operational semantics of flat programs becomes simpler, since *definitional trees* [5] (used to guide the needed narrowing strategy [6]) have been compiled in the program by means of case expressions. The LNT calculus [19] (Lazy Narrowing with definitional Trees) is an operational semantics for inductively sequential programs expressed in terms of case expressions, which has been proved equivalent to needed narrowing. This calculus has been also extended to cover programs containing evaluation annotations in [3]; namely, flexible (resp. rigid) functions are translated by using only *fcase* (resp. *case*) expressions. In the following, we refer to the LNT calculus to mean the LNT calculus of [3].

In [3], it was shown that, by using the standard semantics during PE, one would have the same problems of previous approaches. In particular, one of the main problems comes from the *backpropagation* of variable bindings to the left-hand sides of residual rules (see Example 2 of [3]). Therefore, they propose a *residualizing* version of the LNT calculus which avoids this restriction. In this calculus, variable bindings are encoded by case expressions (and are considered "residual" code). The inference rules of the residualizing calculus, RLNT (Residualizing LNT), can be seen in Fig. 1. In the following, we consider a (*many-sorted*) *signature* partitioned into a set $\mathcal{C}$ of *constructors* and a set $\mathcal{F}$ of defined *functions* or *operations*.

Let us recall the six inference rules defining the one-step relation $\Rightarrow$.[3]

(1) HNF. The HNF (Head Normal Form) rules are used to evaluate terms in head normal form. If the expression is a variable or a constructor constant, the square brackets are removed and the evaluation process stops. Otherwise, the evaluation proceeds with the arguments.

(2) Case Function. This rule can be only applied when the argument of the case is operation-rooted. In this case, it allows the *unfolding* of the function call.

(3) Case Select. This rule selects the appropriate branch of a case expression and continues with the evaluation of this branch.

(4) Case Guess. The treatment of case expressions with variable arguments distinguishes it from the LNT calculus. In the standard semantics, these expressions are evaluated by means of the following rules:

– fcase: $[\![fcase\ x\ of\ \{\overline{p_k \to e_k}\}]\!] \Rightarrow^{\sigma} [\![\sigma(e_i)]\!]$ if $\sigma = \{x \mapsto p_i\},\ i = 1, \ldots, k$
– case: $[\![case\ x\ of\ \{\overline{p_k \to e_k}\}]\!] \Rightarrow^{\{\}} case\ x\ of\ \{\overline{p_k \to e_k}\}$

[3] The symbols "$[\![$" and "$]\!]$" in an expression like $[\![e]\!]$ do not denote a semantic function but are only used to identify which part of an expression should be still evaluated.

HNF

$$[\![t]\!] \Rightarrow t \quad \text{if } t \in \mathcal{V} \text{ or } t = c() \text{ with } c/0 \in \mathcal{C}$$
$$[\![c(t_1, \ldots, t_n)]\!] \Rightarrow c([\![t_1]\!], \ldots, [\![t_n]\!])$$

Case-of-Case

$$[\![(f)case\ ((f)case\ t\ of\ \{\overline{p_k \to t_k}\})\ of\ \{\overline{p'_j \to t'_j}\}]\!]$$
$$\Rightarrow [\![(f)case\ t\ of\ \{\overline{p_k \to (f)case\ t_k\ of\ \{\overline{p'_j \to t'_j}\}}\}]\!]$$

Case Function

$$[\![(f)case\ g(\overline{t_n})\ of\ \{\overline{p_k \to t'_k}\}]\!] \Rightarrow [\![(f)case\ \sigma(r)\ of\ \{\overline{p_k \to t'_k}\}]\!]$$
$$\text{if } g(\overline{x_n}) = r \in \mathcal{R} \text{ is a rule with fresh variables and } \sigma = \{\overline{x_n \mapsto t_n}\}$$

Case Select

$$[\![(f)case\ c(\overline{t_n})\ of\ \{\overline{p_k \to t'_k}\}]\!] \Rightarrow [\![\sigma(t'_i)]\!] \quad \text{if } p_i = c(\overline{x_n}),\ c \in \mathcal{C},\ \sigma = \{\overline{x_n \mapsto t_n}\}$$

Case Guess

$$[\![(f)case\ x\ of\ \{\overline{p_k \to t_k}\}]\!] \Rightarrow (f)case\ x\ of\ \{\overline{p_k \to [\![\sigma_k(t_k)]\!]}\}$$
$$\text{if } \sigma_i = \{x \mapsto p_i\},\ i = 1, \ldots, k$$

Function Eval

$$[\![g(\overline{t_n})]\!] \Rightarrow [\![\sigma(r)]\!] \quad \text{if } g(\overline{x_n}) = r \in \mathcal{R} \text{ is a rule with fresh variables and } \sigma = \{\overline{x_n \mapsto t_n}\}$$

Fig. 1. RLNT Calculus

However, in this case, one would inherit the limitations of previous approaches. Therefore, it has been modified in order not to backpropagate the bindings of variables. In particular, the new Case Guess rule "residualizes" the case structure and continues with the evaluation of the different branches (by applying the corresponding substitution in order to propagate bindings forward in the computation). It imitates the instantiation of variables in the standard evaluation of a flexible case but keeps the case structure. Due to this modification, no distinction between flexible and rigid case expressions is needed in the RLNT calculus. Moreover, the resulting calculus does not compute "answers". Rather, they are represented in the derived expressions by means of case expressions with variable arguments. Also, the calculus becomes deterministic, i.e., there is no don't know nondeterminism involved in the computations. This means that only one derivation can be issued from a given expression (thus, there is no need to introduce a notion of RLNT "tree").

(5) Case-of-Case. An undesirable effect of the Case Guess rule is that nested case expressions may suspend unnecessarily. Take, for instance, the expression:

```
⟦case (case x of { 0 → True
                   (Succ y) → False}) of {True → C x}⟧
```

The evaluation of this expression suspends since the outer case can be only evaluated if the argument is a variable (Case Guess), a function call (Case Eval) or a constructor-rooted term (Case Select). To avoid such premature suspensions, the Case-of-Case rule moves the outer case inside the branches of the inner one and, thus, the evaluation of some branches can now proceed (similar rules can be found in the Glasgow Haskell Compiler as well as in Wadler's deforestation

[30]). By using the Case-of-Case rule, the above expression can be reduced to:

$$[\![\texttt{case x of } \{\texttt{0} \to \texttt{case True of } \{\texttt{True} \to \texttt{C x}\} \\ \qquad\qquad (\texttt{Succ y}) \to \texttt{case False of } \{\texttt{True} \to \texttt{C x}\}]\!]$$

(which can be further simplified with the Case Guess and Case Select rules). Rigorously speaking, this rule can be expanded into four rules (with the different combinations for *case* and *fcase*), but we keep the above (less formal) presentation for simplicity. Observe that the outer case expression may be duplicated several times, but each copy is now (possibly) scrutinizing a known value, and so the Case Select rule can be applied to eliminate some case constructs.

(6) Function Eval. This rule performs the unfolding of a function call. As in proof procedures for logic programming, we assume that we take a program rule with fresh variables in each such evaluation step.

The correctness of the PE scheme for flat programs based on the RLNT calculus can be found in [3].

3 Extending the Basic Framework

The aim of this section is to extend the basic approach in order to cover the facilities of a realistic multi-paradigm language: Curry [15]. To this end, we first enrich the flat representation of Sect. 2.1 with some additional features which constitute the most useful facilities of the language. Then, we correspondingly extend the rules of the RLNT calculus to properly deal with these new features.

3.1 An Intermediate Representation for Curry Programs

Our extended flat representation essentially coincides with the standard intermediate representation, FlatCurry [18], used during the compilation of Curry programs. It contains all the necessary information about a Curry program with all "syntactic sugar" compiled out and type-checking and lambda-lifting performed. In the extended representation, we allow the following expressions:

$$\begin{array}{lll}
e ::= & x & \text{(variable)} \\
\mid & c(e_1,\ldots,e_n) & \text{(constructor)} \\
\mid & f(e_1,\ldots,e_n) & \text{(function call)} \\
\mid & (f)case\ e_0\ of\ \{p_1 \to e_1; \ldots; p_n \to e_n\} & \text{(case expression)} \\
\mid & external(e) & \text{(external function call)} \\
\mid & partcall(f, e_1,\ldots,e_k) & \text{(partial application)} \\
\mid & apply(e_1, e_2) & \text{(application)} \\
\mid & constr(\{x_1,\ldots,x_n\}, e) & \text{(constraint)} \\
\mid & or(e_1, e_2) & \text{(disjunction)} \\
\mid & guarded(\{x_1,\ldots,x_n\}, e_1, e_2) & \text{(guarded expression)}
\end{array}$$

The right-hand side of each function definition is now an expression e composed by variables, constructors, function calls, case expressions, and additional features like: non user-defined ("external") functions, higher-order features like partial application and an application of a functional expression to an argument, constraints (like equational constraints $e_1 =:= e_2$, possibly containing existentially quantified variables), disjunctions (to represent functions with overlapping left-hand sides), and guarded expressions (to represent conditional rules, i.e., the first expression is always a constraint and the list of variables are the local variables which are visible in the constraint and the right-hand side). A detailed description of these features and their intended semantics can be found in [15].

3.2 Extending the RLNT Calculus

In principle, one could extend the RLNT calculus in order to deal with all the facilities of FlatCurry in a simple way. The naive idea is to treat all the additional features of the language as constructor symbols at PE time. This means that they are never partially evaluated but their original definitions are returned by the PE process. However, in realistic Curry programs, the presence of these additional features is perfectly common, hence it is an unacceptable restriction just to residualize them. Our experimental tests have shown that no specialization is obtained in most cases if we follow this simple approach.

On the other hand, extending the RLNT calculus of Sect. 2.2 with the standard semantics for the additional features of FlatCurry is not a good solution either. The problem stems from the fact that the RLNT calculus only propagates bindings forward into the branches of a case expression. However, there are a number of functions, like equalities, (concurrent) conjunctions, some arithmetic functions, etc., in which the propagation of bindings between their arguments is crucial to achieve a good level of specialization. In order to propagate bindings[4] between different arguments, we permit to lift some case expressions from argument positions to the top level while propagating the corresponding bindings to the remaining arguments. For example, the expression[5]

$$[\![(\texttt{x} =:= 1)\ \&\ (\texttt{fcase x of } \{1 \to \texttt{success}\})]\!]$$

can be transformed into

$$[\![\texttt{fcase x of } \{1 \to (\texttt{x} =:= 1\ \&\ \texttt{success})\}]\!]$$

The transformed expression can be now evaluated by the Case Guess rule, thus propagating the binding $\{\texttt{x} \mapsto 1\}$ to the first conjunct:

$$\texttt{fcase x of } \{1 \to [\![1 =:= 1\ \&\ \texttt{success}]\!]\}$$

We notice that this transformation cannot be applied over arbitrary expressions since the intended (lazy) semantics is only preserved when the given function is *strict* in the position of the case expression. Nevertheless, typical FlatCurry programs contain many elements where the evaluation order is fixed. For instance, the condition of a guard is strict, since it must be reduced to `True` (or "`success`") before applying a conditional rule, the arguments of most external functions are also strict, because they must be reduced to ground constructor terms before executing the external call, etc.

---

[4] Recall that bindings are represented by case expressions with a variable argument.

[5] Following [15], "`success`" denotes a constraint which is always solvable.

Furthermore, there are a number of situations in which an expression cannot be evaluated until all (or some) of its arguments have some particular form. For example, a call of the form $apply(e_1, e_2)$ can be only reduced if the first argument e_1 is of the form $partcall(\ldots)$. In these cases, we will try to evaluate the arguments of the function to achieve the required form. For the sake of a simpler presentation, we introduce the auxiliary function *try_eval*. Given a function call $f(\overline{e_n})$ and a set of natural numbers I which represents the set of strict arguments of function f, we define *try_eval* as follows:

$$try\_eval(f(\overline{e_n}), I) = \begin{cases} [\![(f)case\ x\ of\ \{\overline{p_k \to f(e_1,\ldots,e_{i-1},e'_k,e_{i+1},\ldots,e_n)}\}]\!] \\ \quad \text{if } e_i = (f)case\ x\ of\ \{\overline{p_k \to e'_k}\} \text{ for some } i \in I \\ [\![f(e_1,\ldots,e_{i-1},e'_i,e_{i+1},\ldots,e_n)]\!] \\ \quad \text{if } \exists i \in \{1,\ldots,n\}.\ [\![e_i]\!] \Rightarrow e''_i,\ e'_i = del_{sq}(e''_i),\ e_i \neq e'_i \\ f(\overline{e_n}) \text{ otherwise} \end{cases}$$

Here we denote by $del_{sq}(e)$ the expression which results from deleting all occurrences of "$[\![$" and "$]\!]$" from e. We use it to test syntactic equality between expressions without taking into account the relative positions of "$[\![$" and "$]\!]$". Let us informally explain the function above. First, *try_eval* tries to float a case expression in the i-th argument (with $i \in I$) out of this argument. If this is not possible, it tries to evaluate some argument and, if this does not lead to a progress, the expression is just residualized. Since this definition of *try_eval* is ambiguous, we additionally require that the different cases are tried in their textual order and the arguments are evaluated from left to right.

Non User-Defined Functions. FlatCurry programs often contain functions which are not defined in Curry but implemented in another language (*external* functions, like arithmetic operators, basic input/output facilities, etc). Such functions are executed only if all arguments are evaluated to ground constructor terms.[6] The same restriction seems reasonable when computing the PE of an external function. This implies that all arguments of external functions are assumed to be strict and, thus, the call to *try_eval* is performed with the complete set of argument positions:

$$[\![external(f(\overline{e_n}))]\!] \Rightarrow \begin{cases} ext\_call(f(\overline{e_n})) & \text{if } e_1,\ldots,e_n \text{ are ground constructor} \\ [\![external(e')]\!] & \text{if } try\_eval(f(\overline{e_n}), \{1,\ldots,n\}) = [\![e']\!] \\ external(f(\overline{e_n})) & \text{otherwise} \end{cases}$$

where $ext\_call(e)$ evaluates e according to its predefined semantics. Basically, the partial evaluator first tries to execute the external function and, if this is not possible because all arguments are not ground constructor terms, then it tries to evaluate its arguments. Furthermore, we need to add the rule:

$$[\![external((f)case\ x\ of\ \{\overline{p_k \to e_k}\})]\!] \Rightarrow [\![(f)case\ x\ of\ \{\overline{p_k \to external(e_k)}\}]\!]$$

to move a case expression obtained by *try_eval* outside the external call (in order to allow further evaluation of the branches).

[6] There are few exceptions to this general rule but typical external functions (like arithmetic operators) fulfill this condition. We assume it for the sake of simplicity.

The only exception to the above rule are I/O actions, for which Curry follows the monadic approach to I/O. These functions act on the current "state of the outside world". They are residualized since this state is not known at PE time.

Constraints. The treatment for constraints heavily depends on the associated constraint solver. In the following, we only consider *equational* constraints. An elementary constraint is an equation e_1 =:= e_2 between two expressions which is solvable if both sides are reducible to unifiable constructor terms. This notion of equality, the so-called *strict* equality, is incorporated in our calculus by

$$[\![e_1 \ =:= \ e_2]\!] \Rightarrow \begin{cases} case_\sigma(\texttt{success}) & \text{if } \sigma = mgu(e_1, e_2) \text{ and } e_1, e_2 \\ & \quad \text{are constructor terms} \\ try\_eval(e_1 \ =:= \ e_2, \{1,2\}) & \text{otherwise} \end{cases}$$

Note that we call to *try_eval* with the set of positions $\{1,2\}$ since function "=:=" is strict in its two arguments. Here, we use $case_\sigma$(`success`) as a shorthand for denoting the encoding of σ by nested (flexible) case expressions with `success` at the final branch. For example, the expression $[\![$`C x 2` =:= `C 1 y`$]\!]$, whose *mgu* is $\{\texttt{x} \mapsto 1, \texttt{y} \mapsto 2\}$ is evaluated to: `fcase x of` $\{1 \rightarrow$ `fcase y of` $\{2 \rightarrow$ `success`$\}\}$. This simple treatment of constraints is not sufficient in practical programs since they are often used in concurrent conjunctions, written as c_1 & ... & c_n ("&" is a built-in operator which evaluates its arguments concurrently). In this case, constraints may instantiate variables and the corresponding bindings should be propagated to the remaining conjuncts. The problematic point is that we cannot move arbitrary case expressions to the top level, but only flexible case expressions (otherwise, we could change the floundering behavior of the program). Consider, for instance, the following simple functions:

```
f x = case x of {1 → success}
g x = fcase x of {1 → success}
```

where `f` is rigid and `g` is flexible. Given the expression $[\![$`f x & g x`$]\!]$, if we allow to float out arbitrary case expressions, we could perform the following evaluation:

$$\begin{aligned} [\![\texttt{f x \& g x}]\!] &\Rightarrow [\![\texttt{case x of } \{1 \rightarrow \texttt{success}\} \ \& \ \texttt{g x}]\!] \\ &\Rightarrow [\![\texttt{case x of } \{1 \rightarrow \texttt{success \& g x}\}]\!] \\ &\Rightarrow \texttt{case x of } \{1 \rightarrow [\![\texttt{success \& g 1}]\!]\} \end{aligned}$$

which ends up in `case x of` $\{1 \rightarrow$ `success`$\}$. Note that this residual expression suspends if variable `x` is not instantiated, whereas the original expression could be reduced by evaluating first function `g` and then function `f`. Therefore, we handle concurrent conjunctions as follows:

$$[\![c_1 \ \& \ \ldots \ \& \ c_n]\!] \Rightarrow$$

$$\begin{cases} \texttt{success} & \text{if } c_i = \texttt{success for all } i \in \{1,\ldots,n\} \\ [\![fcase\ x\ of\ \{\overline{p_k \rightarrow (c_1 \ \& \ldots \ \& \ c_{i-1} \ \& \ e'_k \ \& \ c_{i+1} \ \& \ \ldots \ \& \ c_n)}\}]\!] \\ & \text{if } c_i = fcase\ x\ of\ \{\overline{p_k \rightarrow e'_k}\} \text{ for some } i \in \{1,\ldots,n\} \\ [\![c_1 \ \& \ldots \ \& \ c_{i-1} \ \& \ c'_i \ \& \ c_{i+1} \ \& \ \ldots \ \& \ c_n]\!] \\ & \text{if } \exists i \in \{1,\ldots,n\}.\ [\![c_i]\!] \Rightarrow c''_i,\ c'_i = del_{sq}(c''_i), c_i \neq c'_i \\ c_1 \ \& \ \ldots \ \& \ c_n & \text{otherwise} \end{cases}$$

Note that, in contrast to external functions, only flexible case expressions are moved to the top level. Equational constraints can also contain local existentially quantified variables. In this case they take the form $constr(vars, c)$, where $vars$ are the existentially quantified variables in the constraint c. We treat these constraints as follows:

$$[\![constr(vars, c)]\!] \Rightarrow \begin{cases} \texttt{success} & \text{if } c = \texttt{success} \\ try\_eval(constr(vars, c), \{2\}) & \text{otherwise} \end{cases}$$

Note that the above rule moves all bindings to the top level, even those for the local variables in $vars$. In practice, case expressions denoting bindings for the variables in $vars$ are removed since they are local, but we keep the above formulation for simplicity.

Guarded Expressions. In Curry, functions can be defined by conditional rules of the form

$$f\ e_1 \ldots e_n \mid c \;=\; e$$

where c is a constraint (rules with multiple guards are also allowed but considered as syntactic sugar for denoting a sequence of rules). Conditional rules are represented in FlatCurry by the *guarded* construct. At PE time, we are interested in inspecting not only the guard but also the right-hand side of the guard. However, only bindings produced from the evaluation of the guard can be floated out (since this is the unique strict argument):

$$[\![guarded(vars, gc, e)]\!] \Rightarrow \begin{cases} [\![e]\!] & \text{if } gc = \texttt{success} \\ try\_eval(guarded(vars, gc, e), \{2\}) & \text{otherwise} \end{cases}$$

As in the case of constraints, the application of *try_eval* can unnecessarily move some bindings (i.e., those for the variables in $vars$) outside the guarded expression. A precise treatment can be easily defined, but we preserve the above presentation for the sake of readability.

Higher-Order Functions. The higher-order features of functional programming are implemented in Curry by providing a (first-order) definition of the application function (*apply*). Since Curry excludes higher-order unification, the operational semantics of Curry covers the usual higher-order features of functional languages by adding the following axiom [15]:

$$[\![apply(f(e_1, \ldots, e_m), e)]\!] \Rightarrow f(e_1, \ldots, e_m, e)$$

if f has arity $n > m$. Thus, an application is evaluated by simply adding the argument to a partial call. In FlatCurry, we distinguish partial applications from total functions; namely, partial applications are represented by means of the *partcall* symbol. We treat higher-order features as follows:

$$[\![apply(e_1, e_2)]\!] \Rightarrow \begin{cases} [\![f(\overline{c_k}, e_2)]\!] & \text{if } e_1 = partcall(f, \overline{c_k}),\ k+1 = ar(f) \\ partcall(f, \overline{c_k}, e_2) & \text{if } e_1 = partcall(f, \overline{c_k}),\ k+1 < ar(f) \\ try\_eval(apply(e_1, e_2), \{1\}) & \text{otherwise} \end{cases}$$

where $ar(f)$ denotes the arity of the function f. Roughly speaking, we allow a partial function to become a total function by adding the missing argument, if possible. If the function does not have the right number of arguments after adding the new argument, we maintain it as a partial function. In the remaining cases, we evaluate the *apply* arguments in hopes of achieving a partial call after evaluation. Note that *try_eval* is called with the set $\{1\}$ in order to avoid the propagation of bindings from the evaluation of non-strict arguments (i.e., from the second argument of *apply*).

Overlapping Left-Hand Sides. Overlapping left-hand sides in Curry programs produce a disjunction where the different alternatives have to be considered. Similarly, we treat *or* expressions in FlatCurry as follows:

$$[\![or(e_1, e_2)]\!] \;\Rightarrow\; or([\![e_1]\!], [\![e_2]\!])$$

4 The Partial Evaluator in Practice

In this section, we describe the structure of a simple *on-line* partial evaluator in the style of [11] which follows the ideas presented so far. Essentially, the partial evaluator proceeds as follows:

Unfolding phase. Firstly, given a program and a set of function calls, we compute a finite (possibly incomplete) RLNT derivation for each call of the set according to an *unfolding rule* $\mathcal{U}$. Roughly speaking, the unfolding rule determines how to stop RLNT derivations in order to avoid infinite computations. Formally, given a program $\mathcal{R}$ and a set of function calls $T = \{t_1, \ldots, t_n\}$, $\mathcal{U}$ is a (total) function such that, whenever $\mathcal{U}(T, \mathcal{R}) = S$, then $S = \{s_1, \ldots, s_n\}$ and there exist finite RLNT derivations of the form $[\![t_i]\!] \Rightarrow^+ s_i$ in $\mathcal{R}$, with $i = 1, \ldots, n$.

Abstraction phase. Since some of the derived expressions $S = \{s_1, \ldots, s_n\}$ may contain function calls which are not covered by the already (partially) evaluated calls T, this process is iteratively repeated for any term of S which is not *closed* w.r.t. the set T. Informally, a term s is closed w.r.t. a set of terms T (or, simply, T-closed) if the maximal operation-rooted subterms of s are instances of some terms in T and the terms in the matching substitution are recursively T-closed (see [4] for a precise definition). In order to avoid repeating this process infinitely, an *abstraction operator* is commonly used. In particular, we consider a mapping *abstract* which takes two sets of terms T and S (which represent the set of terms already evaluated and the set of terms to be added to this set, respectively) and returns a *safe* approximation $abstract(T, S)$ of $T \cup S$. Here, by "safe" we mean that each term in $T \cup S$ is closed w.r.t. the result of $abstract(T, S)$ (i.e., no function call is lost during the abstraction process).

Following the structure of many on-line partial evaluators (see, e.g., [11]), we sketch a PE algorithm which is parametric w.r.t. an unfolding rule $\mathcal{U}$ and an abstraction operator *abstract*:

> **Input**: a program $\mathcal{R}$ and a set of terms T / **Output**: a set of terms S
> **Initialization**: $i := 0;\ T_0 := T$
> **Repeat** $S := \mathcal{U}(T_i, \mathcal{R});\ \ T_{i+1} := abstract(T_i, S);\ \ i := i + 1$
> **Until** $T_i = T_{i-1}$ (modulo renaming)
> **Return** $S := T_i$

The above PE algorithm involves two control issues: the so-called *local* control, which concerns the definition of an unfolding rule $\mathcal{U}$ to compute finite partial evaluations, and the *global* control, which consists of defining a safe abstraction operator *abstract* to ensure the termination of the iterative process.

Local Control. In the local control, the main novelty w.r.t. previous partial evaluators for functional logic programs is the use of a non-standard semantics, the RNLT calculus, to perform computations at PE time. Since RLNT computations do not produce bindings, the restriction to not evaluate terms in head normal form of previous partial evaluators is avoided.

In order to ensure the finiteness of RLNT derivations, there exist a number of well-known techniques in the literature, e.g., depth-bounds, loop-checks, well-founded (or well-quasi) orderings (see, e.g., [8, 21, 28]). For instance, an unfolding rule based on the use of the homeomorphic embedding ordering was used in the INDY partial evaluator. Informally, expression e_1 *embeds* expression e_2 if e_2 can be obtained from e_1 by deleting some operators. For example, $Succ\ (\underline{Succ}\ ((\underline{u}+w)\underline{\times}(\underline{u+}(Succ\ \underline{v}))))$ embeds $Succ\ (u \times (u + v))$. However, in the presence of an infinite signature (e.g., natural numbers in Curry), this unfolding rule can lead to non-terminating computations. For example, consider the following Curry program which generates a list of natural numbers within two given limits:

```
enum a b  =  if a > b then [] else (a : enum (a + 1) b)
```

During its specialization w.r.t. the call `enum 1 n`, the following calls are produced: `enum 1 n`, `enum 2 n`, `enum 3 n`, ..., and no call embeds some previous call.

Therefore, in our partial evaluator we have chosen a safe (and "cheap") unfolding rule: only the unfolding of one function call is allowed (the positive supercompiler of [20] employs a similar strategy). The main advantage of this approach is that expressions can be "folded back" (i.e., can be proved closed) w.r.t. any partially evaluated call. In practice, this generates optimal recursive functions in many cases. As a counterpart, many (unnecessary) intermediate functions may appear in the residual program. This does not mean that we incur in a "code explosion" problem since this kind of redundant rules can be easily removed by a post-unfolding phase (similarly to [20]). Our experiments with the one-step unfolding rule and the post-unfolding phase indicate that this leads to optimal (and concise) residual functions in many cases.

Global Control. As for global control, an abstraction operator usually relies on a concrete ordering over terms in order to keep the sequence of partially evaluated terms finite. As discussed above, a well-quasi ordering like the homeomorphic embedding ordering cannot be used since we consider an infinite signature. Therefore, we implement an abstraction operator which uses a *well-founded* order to ensure termination and generalizes those calls which do not satisfy this ordering by using the *msg* (*most specific generalization*). Abstraction operators based on this relation are defined in, e.g., [26].

The main novelty of our abstraction operator w.r.t. previous operators is that it is *guided* by the RLNT calculus. The key idea is to take into account the position of the square brackets of the calculus in expressions; namely, subterms within square brackets should be added to the set of partially evaluated terms (if possible, otherwise generalized) since further evaluation is still required, while subterms which are not within square brackets should be definitively residualized (i.e., ignored by the abstraction operator, except for operation-rooted terms). The combination of this strategy with the above unfolding rule gives rise to efficient residual programs in many cases, while still guaranteeing termination.

5 Experimental Results

This section describes some experiments with an implementation of a partial evaluator for Curry programs which follows the guidelines presented in previous sections. Our PE tool is implemented in Curry itself and it is publicly available at `http://www.dsic.upv.es/users/elp/soft.html`. The implemented partial evaluator first translates the subject program into a FlatCurry program. To do this, we use the module `Flat` for meta-programming in Curry (included in the current distribution of PAKCS [18]). This module contains datatype definitions to treat FlatCurry programs as data objects (using a kind of *ground representation*). In particular, the I/O action `readFlatCurry` reads a Curry program, translates it to the intermediate language FlatCurry, and finally returns a data structure representing the input program.

The effectiveness of the narrowing-driven approach to PE is out of question (see, e.g., [2–4] for typical PE benchmarks). Unfortunately, these ad-hoc programs do not happen very frequently in real Curry applications. This motivated us to benchmark more realistic examples where the most important features of Curry programs appear. One of the most useful features of functional languages are higher-order functions since they improve code reuse and modularity in programming. Thus, such features are often used in practical Curry programs (much more than in Prolog programs, which are based on first-order logic and offer only weak features for higher-order programming). Furthermore, almost every practical program uses built-in arithmetic functions which are available in Curry as external functions (but, for instance, not in purely narrowing-based functional logic languages). These practical features were not treated in previous approaches to PE of functional logic languages.

The following functions `map` (for applying a function to each element of a list) and `foldr` (for accumulating all list elements) are often used in functional (logic) programs:

```
map _ []       = []                   foldr _ z []      = z
map f (x : xs) = f x : map f xs       foldr f z (h : t) = f h (foldr f z t)
```

For instance, the expression `foldr (+) 0 [1,2,3]` is the sum of all elements of the list [1, 2, 3]. Due to the special handling of higher-order features (*apply* and *partcall*) and built-in functions (*external*), our partial evaluator is able to reduce occurrences of this expression to `6`. However, instead of such constant expressions, realistic programs contain calls to higher-order functions which are partially instantiated. For instance, the expression `foldr (+) 0 xs` is specialized

Benchmark	original		specialized		speedup
	time	heap	time	heap	
`foldr (+) 0 xs`	210	2219168	60	619180	3.5
`foldr (+) 0 (map (+1) xs)`	400	4059180	100	859180	4.0
`foldr (+) 0 (map square xs)`	480	4970716	170	1770704	2.8
`foldr (++) [] xs` (*concat*)	290	2560228	110	560228	2.6
`filter (>100) (map (*3) xs)`	750	6639908	430	3120172	1.7
`map (iterate (+1) 2) xs`	1730	17120280	600	6720228	2.9

Table 1. Benchmark results

by our partial evaluator to `f xs` where `f` is a first-order function defined by:

$$\begin{array}{lll} \texttt{f []} & = & \texttt{0} \\ \texttt{f (x : xs)} & = & \texttt{x + f xs} \end{array}$$

Calls to this residual function run 3.5 times faster (in the Curry→Prolog compiler [7] of PAKCS [18]) than calls to the original definitions; also, memory usage has been reduced significatively (see Table 1, first row). Similarly, the expression `foldr (+) 0 (map (+1) xs)` has been successfully specialized to the efficient version of Sect. 1. Note that our partial evaluator neither requires function definitions in a specific format (like "foldr/build" in short cut deforestation [12]) nor it is restricted to "higher-order macros" (as in [30]), but can handle arbitrary higher-order functions. For instance, the higher-order function

$$\texttt{iterate f n} \ = \ \texttt{if n == 0 then f else iterate (f.f) (n - 1)}$$

which modifies its higher-order argument in each recursive call (`f.f` denotes function composition) can be successfully handled by our partial evaluator. Table 1 shows the results of specializing some calls to higher-order and built-in functions with our partial evaluator. For each benchmark, we show the execution time and heap usage for the original and specialized calls and the speedups achieved. The input list `xs` contains 20,000 elements in each call. Times are expressed in milliseconds and measured on a 700 MHz Linux-PC (Pentium III, 256 KB cache). The programs were executed with the Curry→Prolog compiler [7] of PAKCS.

Another important feature of Curry is the use of (concurrent) constraints. Consider, for instance, the following function `arith`:

```
digit 0   = success
...
digit 9   = success
arith x y = x + x =:= y & x * x =:= y & digit x
```

Calls to "`arith`" might be completely evaluated at PE time. Actually, our partial evaluator returns the residual function `arith'` for the call `arith x y` :

```
arith' 0 0 = success
arith' 2 4 = success
```

In this section, we have shown the specialization of calls to some small functions. However, this does not mean that only the specialization of small programs is feasible in our PE tool. Actually, in the specialization of larger programs the programmer would include some annotations indicating the function calls to be specialized (which usually only involve calls to small functions). In this case, the same program would be returned by the system except for the annotated calls, which are replaced by new calls to the specialized functions, together with the definitions of such specialized functions. The PE tool is not fully integrated into PAKCS yet and, thus, transformed programs cannot be directly executed in Curry (since they are in FlatCurry format). Our aim is to incorporate the partial evaluator in PAKCS as a source-to-source transformation on FlatCurry programs. The process would be automatic and transparent to the user.

6 Conclusions

This paper describes a successful experience in the development of a program transformation technique for a realistic multi-paradigm declarative language. Our method builds on the theoretical basis of [3] for the PE of functional logic languages. We have shown how this framework can be successfully applied in practice by extending the underlying method in order to cover the facilities of the language Curry. A partial evaluator has been implemented which is able to generate efficient (and reasonably small) specialized programs.

Future work in partial evaluation of multi-paradigm functional logic languages should still address several issues. For a more effective deployment, *off-line* partial evaluators perform a binding-time analysis which annotates each function call in the source program as either reducible or subject to residualize. Although our PE scheme is essentially *on-line*, we think that it could be also improved with the information gathered by a pre-processing consisting of a binding-time analysis. In particular, this will allow us to use the standard semantics of the language over those expressions which can be fully evaluated in a finite number of steps, thus improving the effectiveness of the PE process.

References

1. E. Albert, M. Alpuente, M. Falaschi, and G. Vidal. Indy User's Manual. Technical Report DSIC-II/12/98, UPV, 1998. Available at `http://www.dsic.upv.es/users/elp/papers.html`.
2. E. Albert, M. Alpuente, M. Hanus, and G. Vidal. A Partial Evaluation Framework for Curry Programs. In *Proc. of LPAR'99*, pages 376–395. Springer LNAI 1705, 1999.
3. E. Albert, M. Hanus, and G. Vidal. Using an Abstract Representation to Specialize Functional Logic Programs. In *Proc. of LPAR'2000*, pages 381–398. Springer LNAI 1955, 2000.
4. M. Alpuente, M. Falaschi, and G. Vidal. Partial Evaluation of Functional Logic Programs. *ACM Trans. on Programming Lang. and Systems*, 20(4):768–844, 1998.
5. S. Antoy. Definitional trees. In *Proc. of the 3rd Int'l Conference on Algebraic and Logic Programming, ALP'92*, pages 143–157. Springer LNCS 632, 1992.
6. S. Antoy, R. Echahed, and M. Hanus. A Needed Narrowing Strategy. *Journal of the ACM*, 47(4):776–822, 2000.

7. S. Antoy and M. Hanus. Compiling Multi-Paradigm Declarative Programs into Prolog. In *Proc. of FroCoS'2000*, pages 171–185. Springer LNCS 1794, 2000.
8. M. Bruynooghe, D. De Schreye, and B. Martens. A General Criterion for Avoiding Infinite Unfolding. *New Generation Computing*, 11(1):47–79, 1992.
9. C. Consel and O. Danvy. Tutorial notes on Partial Evaluation. In *Proc. of POPL'93*, pages 493–501. ACM, New York, 1993.
10. D. De Schreye, R. Glück, J. Jørgensen, M. Leuschel, B. Martens, and M.H. Sørensen. Conjunctive Partial Deduction: Foundations, Control, Algorihtms, and Experiments. *Journal of Logic Programming*, 41(2&3):231–277, 1999.
11. J. Gallagher. Tutorial on Specialisation of Logic Programs. In *Proc. of PEPM'93*, pages 88–98. ACM, New York, 1993.
12. A.J. Gill, J. Launchbury, and S.L. Peyton Jones. A Short Cut to Deforestation. In *Proc. of the FPCA'93*, pages 223–232, New York, NY, USA, 1993. ACM Press.
13. M. Hanus. A unified computation model for functional and logic programming. In *Proc. of POPL'97*, pages 80–93. ACM, New York, 1997.
14. M. Hanus. Distributed Programming in a Multi-Paradigm Declarative Language. In *Proc. of PPDP'99*, pages 376–395. Springer LNCS 1702, 1999.
15. M. Hanus. Curry: An Integrated Functional Logic Language. Available at: `http://www.informatik.uni-kiel.de/~curry/`, 2000.
16. M. Hanus. A Functional Logic Programming Approach to Graphical User Interfaces. In *Proc. of PADL'00*, pages 47–62. Springer LNCS 1753, 2000.
17. M. Hanus. High-Level Server Side Web Scripting in Curry. In *Proc. of PADL'01*, Springer LNCS (to appear), 2001.
18. M. Hanus, S. Antoy, J. Koj, R. Sadre, and F. Steiner. PAKCS 1.3: The Portland Aachen Kiel Curry System User Manual. University of Kiel, Germany, 2000.
19. M. Hanus and C. Prehofer. Higher-Order Narrowing with Definitional Trees. *Journal of Functional Programming*, 9(1):33–75, 1999.
20. N.D. Jones, C.K. Gomard, and P. Sestoft. *Partial Evaluation and Automatic Program Generation*. Prentice-Hall, Englewood Cliffs, NJ, 1993.
21. M. Leuschel. On the Power of Homeomorphic Embedding for Online Termination. In G. Levi, editor, *Proc. of SAS'98*, pages 230–245. Springer LNCS 1503, 1998.
22. J.W. Lloyd. Combining Functional and Logic Programming Languages. In *Proc. of the International Logic Programming Symposium*, pages 43–57, 1994.
23. J.W. Lloyd and J.C. Shepherdson. Partial Evaluation in Logic Programming. *Journal of Logic Programming*, 11:217–242, 1991.
24. F. López-Fraguas and J. Sánchez-Hernández. TOY: A Multiparadigm Declarative System. In *Proc. of RTA'99*, pages 244–247. Springer LNCS 1631, 1999.
25. W. Lux and H. Kuchen. An Efficient Abstract Machine for Curry. In *Proc. of WFLP'99*, pages 171–181, 1999.
26. B. Martens and J. Gallagher. Ensuring Global Termination of Partial Deduction while Allowing Flexible Polyvariance. In L. Sterling, editor, *Proc. of ICLP'95*, pages 597–611. MIT Press, 1995.
27. S.L. Peyton-Jones. Compiling Haskell by Program Transformation: a Report from the Trenches. In *Proc. of ESOP'96*, pages 18–44. Springer LNCS 1058, 1996.
28. M.H. Sørensen and R. Glück. An Algorithm of Generalization in Positive Supercompilation. In *Proc. of ILPS'95*, pages 465–479. MIT Press, 1995.
29. M.H. Sørensen, R. Glück, and N.D. Jones. A Positive Supercompiler. *Journal of Functional Programming*, 6(6):811–838, 1996.
30. P.L. Wadler. Deforestation: Transforming programs to eliminate trees. *Theoretical Computer Science*, 73:231–248, 1990.

A Simple Take on Typed Abstract Syntax in Haskell-like Languages *

Olivier Danvy and Morten Rhiger

BRICS**
Department of Computer Science
University of Aarhus
Ny Munkegade, Building 540, DK-8000 Aarhus C, Denmark
E-mail: {danvy,mrhiger}@brics.dk
Home pages: `http://www.brics.dk/~{danvy,mrhiger}`

Abstract. We present a simple way to program typed abstract syntax in a language following a Hindley-Milner typing discipline, such as Haskell and ML, and we apply it to automate two proofs about normalization functions as embodied in type-directed partial evaluation for the simply typed lambda calculus: normalization functions (1) preserve types and (2) yield long beta-eta normal forms.

Keywords. Type-directed partial evaluation, normalization functions, simply typed lambda-calculus, higher-order abstract syntax, Haskell.

1 Introduction

Programs (implemented in a *meta language*) that manipulate programs (implemented in an *object language*) need a representation of the manipulated programs. Examples of such programs include interpreters, compilers, partial evaluators, and logical frameworks.

When the meta language is a functional language with a Hindley-Milner type system, such as Haskell [2] or ML [7], a data type is usually chosen to represent object programs. In functional languages, data types are instrumental in representing sum types and inductive types, both of which are needed to represent even the simplest programs such as arithmetic expressions.

However, the *object-language types* of object-language terms represented by data types cannot be inferred from the representation if the meta language does not provide dependent types. Hence, regardless of any typing discipline in the object language, when the meta language follows a Hindley-Milner type discipline, it cannot prevent the construction of object-language terms that are untyped, and correspondingly, it cannot report the types of object-language terms that are well-typed. This typeless situation is familiar to anyone who has represented λ-terms using a data type in an Haskell-like language.

* Extended version available as the technical report BRICS RS-00-34.
** Basic Research in Computer Science (`http://www.brics.dk/`), Centre of the Danish National Research Foundation.

H. Kuchen and K. Ueda (Eds.): FLOPS 2001, LNCS 2024, pp. 343–358, 2001.

In this article we consider a simple way of representing monomorphically typed λ-terms in an Haskell-like language. We describe a typeful representation of terms that prevents one from constructing untyped object-language terms in the meta language and that makes the type system of the meta language report the types of well-typed object-language terms.

We apply this typeful representation to *type-directed partial evaluation* [1, 3], using Haskell [9]. In Haskell, the object language of type-directed partial evaluation is a subset of the meta language, namely the monomorphically typed λ-calculus. Type-directed partial evaluation is an implementation of *normalization functions.* As such, it maps a meta-language value that is simply typed into a (textual) representation of its *long beta-eta normal form.*

All previous implementations of type-directed partial evaluation in Haskell-like languages have the type $t \to \mathsf{Term}$, for some t and where Term denotes the typeless representation of object programs. This type does not express that the output of type-directed partial evaluation is a representation of an object of the same type as the input. In contrast, our implementation has the more expressive type $t \to \mathsf{Exp}(t)$, where Exp denotes our typeful representation of object programs. This type proves that type-directed partial evaluation preserves types. Furthermore, using the same technique, we also prove that the output of type-directed partial evaluation is indeed in long beta-eta normal form.

The rest of this article is organized as follows. In Section 2 we review a traditional, typeless data-type representation of λ-terms in Haskell. In Section 3, we review higher-order abstract syntax, which is a stepping stone towards our typeful representation. Section 4 presents our main result, namely an extension of higher-order abstract syntax that only allows well-typed object-language terms to be constructed. In Section 5, we review type-directed partial evaluation, which is our chosen domain of application. Section 6 presents our first application, namely an implementation of type-directed partial evaluation preserving types. Section 7 presents our second application, namely another implementation of type-directed partial evaluation demonstrating that it produces long beta-eta normal forms. Section 8 concludes.

2 Typeless first-order abstract syntax

We consider the simply typed λ-calculus with integer constants, variables, applications, and function abstractions:

$$\begin{array}{ll} \text{(Types)} & t ::= \alpha \mid \mathsf{int} \mid t_1 \to t_2 \\ \text{(Terms)} & e ::= i \mid x \mid e_0\, e_1 \mid \lambda x.e \end{array}$$

Other base types (booleans, reals, etc.) and other type constructors (products, sums, lists, etc.) are easy to add. So our object language is the λ-calculus.

Our meta language is Haskell. We use the following data type to represents λ-terms. Its constructors are: integers (`INT`), variables (`VAR`), applications (`APP`), and functional abstractions (`LAM`).

```
data Term = INT Int
          | VAR String
          | APP Term Term
          | LAM String Term
```

Object-language terms are constructed in Haskell using the translation below. Note that the type of $\lceil e \rceil_0$ is Term regardless of the type of e in the λ-calculus.

$$\begin{aligned}
\lceil i \rceil_0 &= \texttt{INT}\ i \\
\lceil x \rceil_0 &= \texttt{VAR}\ \texttt{"}x\texttt{"} \\
\lceil e_0\, e_1 \rceil_0 &= \texttt{APP}\ \lceil e_0 \rceil_0\ \lceil e_1 \rceil_0 \\
\lceil \lambda x.e \rceil_0 &= \texttt{LAM}\ \texttt{"}x\texttt{"}\ \lceil e \rceil_0
\end{aligned}$$

The constructors of the data type are typed in Haskell: The term `INT 9` is valid whereas `INT "a"` is not. However, Haskell knows nothing of the λ-terms we wish to represent. In other words, the translation $\lceil \cdot \rceil_0$ is not surjective: Some well-typed *encodings* of object-language terms do not correspond to any legal object-language term. For example, the term `APP (INT 1) (LAM "x" (VAR "x"))` has type Term in Haskell, even though it represents the term $1(\lambda x.x)$ which has no type in the λ-calculus.

The fact that we can represent untyped λ-terms is not a shortcoming of the meta language. One might want to represent programs in an untyped object language like Scheme [6] or even structures for which no notion of type exists.

3 Typeless higher-order abstract syntax

To the data type Term we add an interface using *higher-order abstract syntax* [8]. In higher-order abstract syntax, object-language variables and bindings are represented by meta-language variables and bindings. The interface to the data type Term is shown in Figure 1.

The interface consists of syntax constructors for integers, applications, and abstractions. There is no constructor for variables. Instead, fresh variable names are generated and passed to the higher-order representation of abstractions. A λ-expression is represented by a function accepting the next available fresh-variable name, using de Bruijn levels.

Object-language terms are constructed in the meta language using the following translation. Note again that the type of $\lceil e \rceil_1$ is Term regardless of the type of e in the λ-calculus.

$$\begin{aligned}
\lceil i \rceil_1 &= \texttt{int}\ i \\
\lceil x \rceil_1 &= x \\
\lceil e_0\, e_1 \rceil_1 &= \texttt{app}\ \lceil e_0 \rceil_1\ \lceil e_1 \rceil_1 \\
\lceil \lambda x.e \rceil_1 &= \texttt{lam}\ (\texttt{\textbackslash}x\ \texttt{->}\ \lceil e \rceil_1)
\end{aligned}$$

```
module TypelessExp(int, app, lam, Exp) where

  data Term = INT Int | VAR String | APP Term Term | LAM String Term

  type Exp = Int -> Term

  int i      j = INT i
  app e0 e1 j = APP (e0 j) (e1 j)
  lam f      j = LAM v (f (\_ -> VAR v) (j + 1))
                 where v = "x" ++ show j
```

Fig. 1. Typeless higher-order abstract syntax in Haskell

This translation is also not surjective in the sense outlined in Section 2. Indeed, the types of the three higher-order constructors in Haskell still allow untypable λ-terms to be constructed. These three constructors are typed as follows.

$$\texttt{int} :: \mathsf{Int} \to \mathsf{Exp}$$
$$\texttt{app} :: \mathsf{Exp} \to (\mathsf{Exp} \to \mathsf{Exp})$$
$$\texttt{lam} :: (\mathsf{Exp} \to \mathsf{Exp}) \to \mathsf{Exp}$$

Therefore, the term `app (int 1) (lam (\x -> x))` still has a type in Haskell, namely Exp.

4 Typeful higher-order abstract syntax

Let us restrict the three higher-order constructors above to only yield well-typed terms. To this end, we make the following observations about constructing well-typed terms.

- The constructor `int` produces a term of object-language type Int.
- The first argument to `app` is a term of object-language type $\alpha \to \beta$, the second argument is a term of object-language type α, and `app` produces a term of object-language type β.
- The argument to `lam` must be a function mapping a term of object-language type α into a term of object-language type β, and `lam` produces a term of object-language type $\alpha \to \beta$.

These observations suggest that the (polymorphic) types of the three constructors actually could reflect the object-language types. We thus parameterize the type Exp with the object-language type and we restrict the types of the constructors according to these observations. In Haskell we implement the new type constructor as a data type, not just as an alias for Int $\to$ Term as in Figure 1. In this way the internal representation is hidden. The result is shown in Figure 2. The three constructors are typed as follows.

```
module TypefulExp (int, app, lam, Exp) where

  data Term = INT Int | VAR String | APP Term Term | LAM String Term

  data Exp t = EXP (Int -> Term)

  int :: Int -> Exp Int
  app :: Exp (a -> b) -> Exp a -> Exp b
  lam :: (Exp a -> Exp b) -> Exp (a -> b)

  int i                 = EXP (\x -> INT i)
  app (EXP e0) (EXP e1) = EXP (\x -> APP (e0 x) (e1 x))
  lam f                 = EXP (\x -> let v     = "x" ++ show x
                                         EXP b = f (EXP (\_ -> VAR v))
                                     in  LAM v (b (x + 1)))
```

Fig. 2. Typeful higher-order abstract syntax in Haskell

$$\texttt{int} :: \mathsf{Int} \to \mathsf{Exp}(\mathsf{Int})$$
$$\texttt{app} :: \mathsf{Exp}(\alpha \to \beta) \to (\mathsf{Exp}(\alpha) \to \mathsf{Exp}(\beta))$$
$$\texttt{lam} :: (\mathsf{Exp}(\alpha) \to \mathsf{Exp}(\beta)) \to \mathsf{Exp}(\alpha \to \beta)$$

The translation from object-language terms to meta-language terms is the same as the one for the typeless higher-order abstract syntax. However, unlike for the typeless version, if e is an (object-language) term of type t then the (meta-language) type of $\lceil e \rceil_1$ is $\mathsf{Exp}(t)$.

As an example, consider the λ-term $\lambda f.f(1)$ of type $(\mathsf{Int} \to \alpha) \to \alpha$. It is encoded in Haskell by $\lceil \lambda f.f(1) \rceil_1 =$ `lam (\f -> app f (int 1))` of type $\mathsf{Exp}((\mathsf{Int} \to \alpha) \to \alpha)$. Now consider the λ-term $1(\lambda x.x)$ which is not well-typed in the λ-calculus. It is encoded by $\lceil 1(\lambda x.x) \rceil_1 =$ `app 1 (lam (\x -> x))` which is rejected by Haskell.

In the remaining sections, we apply typeful abstract syntax to type-directed partial evaluation.

5 Type-directed partial evaluation

The goal of *partial evaluation* [5] is to specialize a program p of type $t_1 \to t_2 \to t_3$ to a fixed first argument v of type t_1. The result is a *residual* program p_v that satisfies $p_v(w) = p(v)(w)$ for all w of type t_2, if both expressions terminate. The motivation for partial evaluation is that running $p_v(w)$ is more efficient than running $p(v)(w)$.

In *type-directed partial evaluation* [1, 3, 9, 10], specialization is achieved by normalization. For simply typed λ-terms, the partial application $p(v)$ is residualized into (the text of) a program p_v in *long beta-eta normal form*. That is,

```
module TypelessTdpe where

  import TypelessExp  -- from Figure 1

  data Reify_Reflect(a) =
    RR { reify   :: a -> Exp,
         reflect :: Exp -> a }

  rra =                 -- atomic types
    RR { reify   = \x -> x,
         reflect = \x -> x }

  rrf (t1, t2) =        -- function types
    RR { reify   = \v -> lam (\x -> reify t2 (v (reflect t1 x))),
         reflect = \e -> \x -> reflect t2 (app e (reify t1 x)) }

  normalize t v = reify t v
```

Fig. 3. A typeless implementation of type-directed partial evaluation

the residual program contains no beta-redexes and it is fully eta-expanded with respect to its type.

5.1 Type-directed partial evaluation in Haskell

Figure 3 displays a typeless implementation of type-directed partial evaluation for the simply typed λ-calculus in Haskell. To normalize a polymorphic value v of type t, one applies the main function `normalize` to the value, v, and a *representation* of the type, $|t|$, defined as follows.

$$|\alpha| = \texttt{rra}$$
$$|t_1 \to t_2| = \texttt{rrf}(|t_1|,\ |t_2|)$$

To analyze the type of the representations of types, we first define the *instance* of a type as follows.

$$[\alpha]_0 = \mathsf{Exp}$$
$$[t_1 \to t_2]_0 = [t_1]_0 \to [t_2]_0$$

Then, for any type t, the type of $|t|$ is $\mathsf{Reify\_Reflect}([t]_0)$. Haskell infers the following type for the main function.

$$\texttt{normalize} :: \mathsf{Reify\_Reflect}(\alpha) \to \alpha \to \mathsf{Exp}$$

This type shows that `normalize` maps a α-typed input value into an Exp-typed output value, i.e., a term. This type, however, does not show that the input (meta-language) value and the output (object-language) term have the same type. In Section 6, we show that type-directed partial evaluation is type-preserving, and in Section 7, we show that the output term is in normal form.

5.2 Example: Church numerals, typelessly

As an example, we apply type-directed partial evaluation to specialize the addition of two Church numerals with respect to one argument. The Church numeral zero, the successor function, and addition are defined as follows.

```
zero     :: (a -> a) -> a -> a
zero     = \s -> \z -> z
suc n    = \s -> \z -> s (n s z)
add m n = \s -> \z -> m s (n s z)
```

Specializing `add` **with respect to 0:** We specialize the addition function with respect to the Church numeral 0 by normalizing the partial application `add zero`. This expression has the following type.

$$t_{\text{add}} = ((\alpha \to \alpha) \to \beta \to \alpha) \to (\alpha \to \alpha) \to \beta \to \alpha$$

This type is represented in Haskell as follows.

$|t_{\text{add}}| =$ `rrf(rrf(rrf(rra, rra), rrf(rra, rra)),`
`rrf(rrf(rra, rra), rrf(rra, rra)))`

Thus, evaluating the Haskell expression

`normalize` $|t_{\text{add}}|$ `(add zero) 37`

(taking 37, for example, as the first de Bruijn level) yields a representation of the following residual term.

$$\lambda x_{37}.\lambda x_{38}.\lambda x_{39}.x_{37}(\lambda x_{40}.x_{38}\; x_{40})x_{39}$$

For readability, let us rename this residual term:

$$\lambda n.\lambda s.\lambda z.n(\lambda n'.s\, n')z$$

This term is the (η-expanded) identity function over Church numerals, reflecting that 0 is neutral for addition.

Haskell infers the following type of the expression `normalize` $|t_{\text{add}}|$.

$$(((t' \to t') \to t' \to t') \to (t' \to t') \to t' \to t') \to t', \quad \text{where } t' = \mathsf{Int} \to \mathsf{Term}$$

This type does not express any relationship between the type of the input term and the type of the residual term.

Specializing `add` **with respect to 5:** We specialize the addition function with respect to the Church numeral 5 by normalizing the partial application `add five`, where `five` is defined as follows.

```
five     = suc (suc (suc (suc (suc zero))))
```

The expression `add five` also has the type t_{add}. Thus, evaluating the Haskell expression

$$\texttt{normalize}\ |t_{\text{add}}|\ \texttt{(add five) 57}$$

(taking 57 this time as the first de Bruijn level) yields a representation of the following residual term.

$$\lambda x_{57}.\lambda x_{58}.\lambda x_{59}.x_{58}(x_{58}(x_{58}(x_{58}(x_{58}(x_{57}(\lambda x_{60}.x_{58}\ x_{60})x_{59})))))$$

For readability, let us rename this residual term:

$$\lambda n.\lambda s.\lambda z.s(s(s(s(s(n(\lambda n'.s\,n')z)))))$$

In this term, the successor function is applied five times, reflecting that the addition function has been specialized with respect to five.

6 Application 1: Type-directed partial evaluation preserves types

In this section, we use the type inferencer of Haskell as a theorem prover to show that type-directed partial evaluation preserves types. To this end, we implement type-directed partial evaluation using typed abstract syntax.

6.1 Typeful type-directed partial evaluation (first variant)

We want the type of `normalize` to be $\text{Reify\_Reflect}(\alpha) \to \alpha \to \text{Exp}(\alpha)$. As a first step to achieve this more expressive type, we shift to the typeful representation of terms from Figure 2. The parameterized type constructor $\text{Exp}(\alpha)$ replaces the type Exp. Thus, we change the data type $\text{Reify\_Reflect}(\alpha)$ from Figure 3 to the following.

```
data Reify_Reflect a =
  RR { reify   :: a -> Exp a,
       reflect :: Exp a -> a }
```

This change, however, makes the standard definition of `rra` untypable: The identity function does not have type $\alpha \to \text{Exp}(\alpha)$ (or $\text{Exp}(\alpha) \to \alpha$ for that matter). We solve this problem by introducing two identity functions in the module of typed terms.

$$\texttt{coerce} :: \text{Exp}(\alpha) \to \text{Exp}(\text{Exp}(\alpha))$$
$$\texttt{uncoerce} :: \text{Exp}(\text{Exp}(\alpha)) \to \text{Exp}(\alpha)$$

At first it might seem that a function of type $\text{Exp}(\alpha) \to \text{Exp}(\text{Exp}(\alpha))$ cannot be the identity. However, internally $\text{Exp}(t)$ is an alias for $\text{Int} \to \text{Term}$, thus discarding t, so in effect we are looking at two identity functions of type $(\text{Int} \to \text{Term}) \to (\text{Int} \to \text{Term})$. Figure 4 shows the required changes to the typeful representation of Figure 2.

```
module TypefulExpCoerce (int, app, lam, coerce, uncoerce, Exp) where

  [...]

  coerce   :: Exp a -> Exp (Exp a)
  uncoerce :: Exp (Exp a) -> Exp a

  coerce   (EXP f) = EXP f
  uncoerce (EXP f) = EXP f
```

Fig. 4. Typeful higher-order abstract syntax with coercions for atomic types

```
module TypefulTdpe where

  import TypefulExpCoerce   -- from Figure 4

  data Reify_Reflect(a) =
    RR { reify   :: a -> Exp a,
         reflect :: Exp a -> a }

  rra =                       -- atomic types
    RR { reify   = \x -> coerce x,
         reflect = \x -> uncoerce x }

  rrf (t1, t2) =              -- function types
    RR { reify   = \v -> lam (\x -> reify t2 (v (reflect t1 x))),
         reflect = \e -> \x -> reflect t2 (app e (reify t1 x)) }

  normalize t v = reify t v
```

Fig. 5. A typeful implementation of type-directed partial evaluation

We can now define `rra` using `coerce` and `uncoerce`. The complete implementation is shown in Figure 5. Types are represented as in Section 5, but the types of the represented types differ. We define the instance as follows.

$$[\alpha]_1 = \mathsf{Exp}(\alpha)$$
$$[t_0 \to t_1]_1 = [t_0]_1 \to [t_1]_1$$

Then the type of $|t|$ is $\mathsf{Reify\_Reflect}([t]_1)$. Haskell infers the following type for the main function.

$$\texttt{normalize} :: \mathsf{Reify\_Reflect}(\alpha) \to \alpha \to \mathsf{Exp}(\alpha)$$

This type proves that type-directed partial evaluation preserves types.

N.B. The typeless implementation in Figure 3 and the typeful implementation in Figure 5 are as efficient. Indeed, they differ only in the two occurrences of `coerce` and `uncoerce` in `rra` in Figure 5, which are defined as the identity function.

6.2 Typeful type-directed partial evaluation (second variant)

The two auxiliary functions `coerce` and `uncoerce` are only necessary to obtain an automatic proof of the type-preservation property of type-directed partial evaluation: They are artefacts of the typeful encoding. But could one do without them? In this section, we present an alternative proof of the typing of type-directed partial evaluation without using these coercions. Instead, we show that when type-directed partial evaluation is applied to a correct representation of the type of the input value, the residual term has the same type as the input value.

To this end, we implement `rra` as a pair of identity functions, as in Figure 3, and we modify the data type Reify_Reflect by weakening the connection between the domains and the codomains of the reify / reflect pairs.

```
module TypefulTdpe where
  import TypefulExp   -- from Figure 2

  data Reify_Reflect a b =
    RR { reify   :: a -> Exp b,
         reflect :: Exp b -> a }

  [...]
```

These changes make all of `rra`, `rrf`, and `normalize` well-typed in Haskell. Their types read as follows.

$$\begin{aligned} \texttt{rra} &:: \mathsf{Reify\_Reflect}(\mathsf{Exp}(\alpha))(\alpha) \\ \texttt{rrf} &:: (\mathsf{Reify\_Reflect}(\alpha)(\gamma), \mathsf{Reify\_Reflect}(\beta)(\delta)) \rightarrow \\ &\qquad\qquad\qquad\qquad \mathsf{Reify\_Reflect}(\alpha \rightarrow \beta)(\gamma \rightarrow \delta) \\ \texttt{normalize} &:: \mathsf{Reify\_Reflect}(\alpha)(\beta) \rightarrow \alpha \rightarrow \mathsf{Exp}(\beta) \end{aligned}$$

The type of `normalize` no longer proves that it preserves types. However, we can fill in the details by hand using the inferred types of `rra` and `rrf`: We prove by induction on the type t that the type of $|t|$ is $\mathsf{Reify\_Reflect}([t]_1)(t)$. For $t = \alpha$, we have $|t| = \texttt{rra}$ which has type $\mathsf{Reify\_Reflect}(\mathsf{Exp}(\alpha))(\alpha)$ as required. For $t = t_1 \rightarrow t_2$, we have $|t| = \texttt{rrf}(|t_1|, |t_2|)$. By hypothesis, $|t_i|$ has type $\mathsf{Reify\_Reflect}([t_i]_1)(t_i)$ for $i \in \{1, 2\}$. Hence, by the inferred type for `rrf` we have that $\texttt{rrf}(|t_1|, |t_2|)$ has type $\mathsf{Reify\_Reflect}([t_1]_1 \rightarrow [t_2]_1)(t_1 \rightarrow t_2)$ as required. As a corollary we obtain that for all types t,

$$\texttt{normalize}\ |t| :: [t]_1 \rightarrow \mathsf{Exp}(t)$$

This proof gives a hint about how to prove (by hand) that typeless type-directed partial evaluation preserves types.

6.3 Example: Church numerals, typefully

Let us revisit the example of Section 5.2. We specialize the addition function with respect to a fixed argument using the two typeful variants of type-directed partial evaluation. In both cases the residual terms are the same as in Section 5.2. The Haskell expression `normalize` $|t_{\mathrm{add}}|$ has type $[t_{\mathrm{add}}]_1 \rightarrow \mathsf{Exp}([t_{\mathrm{add}}]_1)$ using the first variant and it has type $[t_{\mathrm{add}}]_1 \rightarrow \mathsf{Exp}(t_{\mathrm{add}})$ using the second variant.

7 Application 2: Type-directed partial evaluation yields normal forms

In this section, we use the type inferencer of Haskell as a theorem prover to show that type-directed partial evaluation yields long beta-eta normal forms. We first specify long beta-eta normal forms, both typelessly and typefully (Section 7.1). Then we revisit type-directed partial evaluation, both typelessly (Section 7.2) and typefully (Sections 7.3 and 7.4).

7.1 Long beta-eta normal forms

We consider explicitly typed λ-terms:

$$\begin{array}{ll} \text{(Types)} & t ::= \mathsf{a} \mid t_1 \rightarrow t_2 \\ \text{(Terms)} & e ::= x \mid e_0\, e_1 \mid \lambda x :: t.\, e \end{array}$$

Definition 1 (long beta-eta normal forms [3, 4]). *A closed term e of type t is in* long beta-eta normal form *if and only if it satisfies $\cdot \vdash_{\mathrm{nf}} e :: t$ where "$\cdot$" denotes the empty environment and where terms in normal form and atomic form are defined by the following rules:*

$$\frac{\Delta, x :: t_1 \vdash_{\mathrm{nf}} e :: t_2}{\Delta \vdash_{\mathrm{nf}} \lambda x :: t_1.\, e :: t_1 \rightarrow t_2}[\mathsf{lam}] \qquad \frac{\Delta \vdash_{\mathrm{at}} e :: \mathsf{a}}{\Delta \vdash_{\mathrm{nf}} e :: \mathsf{a}}[\mathsf{coerce}]$$

$$\frac{\Delta \vdash_{\mathrm{at}} e_0 :: t_1 \rightarrow t_2 \quad \Delta \vdash_{\mathrm{nf}} e_1 :: t_1}{\Delta \vdash_{\mathrm{at}} e_0\, e_1 :: t_2}[\mathsf{app}] \qquad \frac{\Delta(x) = t}{\Delta \vdash_{\mathrm{at}} x :: t}[\mathsf{var}]$$

No term containing β-redexes can be derived by these rules, and the coerce rule ensures that the derived terms are fully η-expanded.

Figure 6 displays a typeless representation of normal forms in Haskell. Figure 7 displays a typeful representation of normal forms in Haskell.

7.2 Typeless type-directed partial evaluation and normal forms

We now reexpress type-directed partial evaluation as specified in Figure 8 to yield typeless terms, as also done by Filinski [3]. The type of `normalize` reads as follows.

$$\texttt{normalize} :: \mathsf{Reify\_Reflect}(\alpha) \rightarrow \alpha \rightarrow \mathsf{Nf}$$

```
module TypelessNf where

  data Nf_ = AT_ At_
           | LAM String Nf_
  data At_ = VAR String
           | APP At_ Nf_

  type Nf = Int -> Nf_
  type At = Int -> At_

  app e1 e2  x = APP (e1 x) (e2 x)
  lam f      x = LAM v (f (\_ -> VAR v) (x + 1))
                 where v = "x" ++ show x
  at2nf e x = AT_ (e x)
```

Fig. 6. Typeless representation of normal forms

```
module TypefulNf where

  data Nf_ = AT_ At_
           | LAM String Nf_
  data At_ = VAR String
           | APP At_ Nf_

  data Nf t = NF (Int -> Nf_)
  data At t = AT (Int -> At_)

  app      :: At (a -> b) -> Nf a -> At b
  lam      :: (At a -> Nf b) -> Nf (a -> b)

  coerce   :: Nf a -> Nf (Nf a)
  uncoerce :: At (Nf a) -> Nf a

  at2nf    :: At a -> Nf a

  app (AT e1) (NF e2) = AT (\x -> APP (e1 x) (e2 x))
  lam f               = NF (\x -> let v    = "x" ++ show x
                                      NF b = f (AT (\_ -> VAR v))
                                  in  LAM v (b (x + 1)))

  coerce   (NF f) = NF f
  uncoerce (AT f) = NF (\x -> AT_ (f x))

  at2nf    (AT f) = NF (\x -> AT_ (f x))
```

Fig. 7. Typeful representation of normal forms

```
module TypelessTdpeNf where

  import TypelessNf  -- from Figure 6

  data Reify_Reflect a =
    RR { reify   :: a -> Nf,
         reflect :: At -> a }

  rra =                 -- atomic types
    RR { reify   = \x -> x,
         reflect = \x -> at2nf x }

  rrf (t1, t2) =        -- function types
    RR { reify   = \v -> lam (\x -> reify t2 (v (reflect t1 x))),
         reflect = \e -> \x -> reflect t2 (app e (reify t1 x)) }

  normalize t v = reify t v
```

Fig. 8. Typeless implementation of type-directed partial evaluation with normal forms

This type proves that type-directed partial evaluation yields residual terms in beta normal form since the representation of Figure 6 does not allow beta redexes. These residual terms are also in eta normal form because `at2nf` is only applied at base type: residual terms are thus fully eta expanded.

7.3 Typeful type-directed partial evaluation and normal forms (first variant)

We now reexpress type-directed partial evaluation to yield typeful terms as specified in Figure 9. The type of `normalize` reads as follows.

$$\texttt{normalize} :: \mathsf{Reify\_Reflect}(\alpha) \rightarrow \alpha \rightarrow \mathsf{Nf}(\alpha)$$

This type proves that type-directed partial evaluation (1) preserves types and (2) yields terms in normal form.

7.4 Typeful type-directed partial evaluation and normal forms (second variant)

On the same ground as Section 6.2, i.e., to bypass the artefactual coercions of the typeful encoding of abstract syntax, we now reexpress type-directed partial evaluation to yield typeful terms as specified in Figure 10. The type of `normalize` reads as follows.

$$\texttt{normalize} :: \mathsf{Reify\_Reflect}(\alpha)(\beta) \rightarrow \alpha \rightarrow \mathsf{Nf}(\beta)$$

```
module TypefulTdpeNf1 where

  import TypefulNf  -- from Figure 7

  data Reify_Reflect a =
    RR { reify   :: a -> Nf a,
         reflect :: At a -> a }

  rra =                 -- atomic types
    RR { reify   = \x -> coerce x,
         reflect = \x -> uncoerce x }

  rrf (t1, t2) =     -- function types
    RR { reify   = \v -> lam (\x -> reify t2 (v (reflect t1 x))),
         reflect = \e -> \x -> reflect t2 (app e (reify t1 x)) }

  normalize t v = reify t v
```

Fig. 9. Typeful implementation of type-directed partial evaluation with normal forms (first variant)

```
module TypefulTdpeNf2 where

  import TypefulNf  -- from Figure 7

  data Reify_Reflect a b =
    RR { reify   :: a -> Nf b,
         reflect :: At b -> a }

  rra =                 -- atomic types
    RR { reify   = \x -> x,
         reflect = \x -> at2nf x }

  rrf (t1, t2) =     -- function types
    RR { reify   = \v -> lam (\x -> reify t2 (v (reflect t1 x))),
         reflect = \e -> \x -> reflect t2 (app e (reify t1 x)) }

  normalize t v = reify t v
```

Fig. 10. Typeful implementation of type-directed partial evaluation with normal forms (second variant)

This type only proves that type-directed partial evaluation yields terms in normal form. As in Section 6.2, we can prove type preservation by hand, i.e., that

$$\texttt{normalize}\ |t| :: [t]_2 \rightarrow \mathsf{Nf}(t)$$

where the instance of a type is defined by

$$[\alpha]_2 = \mathsf{Nf}(\alpha)$$
$$[t_1 \rightarrow t_2]_2 = [t_1]_2 \rightarrow [t_2]_2$$

8 Conclusions and issues

We have presented a simple way to express typed abstract syntax in a Haskell-like language, and we have used this typed abstract syntax to demonstrate that type-directed partial evaluation preserves types and yields residual programs in normal form. The encoding is limited because it does not lend itself to programs taking typed abstract syntax as input—as, e.g., a typeful transformation into continuation-passing style. Nevertheless, the encoding is sufficient to establish two key properties of type-directed partial evaluation automatically.

These two properties could be illustrated more directly in a language with dependent types such as Martin-Löf type theory. In such a language, one can directly represent typed abstract syntax and program type-directed partial evaluation typefully.

Acknowledgments: This work is supported by the ESPRIT Working Group APPSEM (`http://www.md.chalmers.se/Cs/Research/Semantics/APPSEM/`). Part of it was carried out while the second author was visiting Jason Hickey at Caltech, in the summer and fall of 2000. We are grateful to the anonymous reviewers and to Julia Lawall for perceptive comments.

References

1. Olivier Danvy. Type-directed partial evaluation. In John Hatcliff, Torben Æ. Mogensen, and Peter Thiemann, editors, *Partial Evaluation – Practice and Theory; Proceedings of the 1998 DIKU Summer School*, number 1706 in Lecture Notes in Computer Science, pages 367–411, Copenhagen, Denmark, July 1998. Springer-Verlag.
2. Joseph H. Fasel, Paul Hudak, Simon Peyton Jones, and Philip Wadler (editors). Haskell special issue. *SIGPLAN Notices*, 27(5), May 1992.
3. Andrzej Filinski. A semantic account of type-directed partial evaluation. In Gopalan Nadathur, editor, *International Conference on Principles and Practice of Declarative Programming*, number 1702 in Lecture Notes in Computer Science, pages 378–395, Paris, France, September 1999. Springer-Verlag. Extended version available as the technical report BRICS RS-99-17.
4. Gérard Huet. Résolution d'équations dans les langages d'ordre 1, 2, ..., ω. Thèse d'État, Université de Paris VII, Paris, France, 1976.

5. Neil D. Jones, Carsten K. Gomard, and Peter Sestoft. *Partial Evaluation and Automatic Program Generation.* Prentice-Hall International, 1993. Available online at `http://www.dina.kvl.dk/~sestoft/pebook/pebook.html`.
6. Richard Kelsey, William Clinger, and Jonathan Rees, editors. Revised^5 report on the algorithmic language Scheme. *Higher-Order and Symbolic Computation*, 11(1):7–105, 1998. Also appears in ACM SIGPLAN Notices 33(9), September 1998.
7. Robin Milner, Mads Tofte, Robert Harper, and David MacQueen. *The Definition of Standard ML (Revised).* The MIT Press, 1997.
8. Frank Pfenning and Conal Elliott. Higher-order abstract syntax. In *Proceedings of the ACM SIGPLAN'88 Conference on Programming Languages Design and Implementation*, SIGPLAN Notices, Vol. 23, No 7, pages 199–208, Atlanta, Georgia, June 1988. ACM Press.
9. Morten Rhiger. Deriving a statically typed type-directed partial evaluator. In *Proceedings of the ACM SIGPLAN Workshop on Partial Evaluation and Semantics-Based Program Manipulation*, Technical report BRICS-NS-99-1, University of Aarhus, pages 25–29, San Antonio, Texas, January 1999.
10. Zhe Yang. Encoding types in ML-like languages. In Paul Hudak and Christian Queinnec, editors, *Proceedings of the 1998 ACM SIGPLAN International Conference on Functional Programming*, pages 289–300, Baltimore, Maryland, September 1998. ACM Press. Extended version available as the technical report BRICS RS-98-9.

A simply typed context calculus with first-class environments

Masahiko Sato[1], Takafumi Sakurai[2], and Yukiyoshi Kameyama[1]

[1] Graduate School of Informatics, Kyoto University
{masahiko,kameyama}@kuis.kyoto-u.ac.jp
[2] Department of Mathematics and Informatics, Chiba University
sakurai@math.s.chiba-u.ac.jp

Abstract. We introduce a simply typed λ-calculus $\lambda\kappa\varepsilon$ which has both contexts and environments as first-class values. In $\lambda\kappa\varepsilon$, holes in contexts are represented by ordinary variables of appropriate types and hole filling is represented by the functional application together with a new abstraction mechanism which takes care of packing and unpacking of the term which is used to fill in the holes of the context. $\lambda\kappa\varepsilon$ is a conservative extension of the simply typed $\lambda\beta$-calculus, enjoys subject reduction property, is confluent and strongly normalizing.
The traditional method of defining substitution does not work for our calculus. So, we also introduce a new method of defining substitution. Although we introduce the new definition of substitution out of necessity, the new definition turns out to be conceptually simpler than the traditional definition of substitution.

1 Introduction

Informally speaking, a context (in λ-calculus) is a λ-term with some holes in it. For example, writing [ ] for a hole, $\lambda y.$ [ ] is a context, and by filling the hole in it with $x + y$, we get $\lambda y.\ x + y$. By this operation, the variable y in $x + y$ gets *captured* and becomes bound in $\lambda y.\ x + y$, and the variable x remains to be free. So, unlike substitution, hole filling may introduce new and intended bound variables.

Recently there have been several attempts to formalize the notion of context and thereby make computing with contexts possible. For example, Talcott [16], Lee-Friedman [8], Dami [5], Hashimoto-Ohori [7], Sands [13], Mason [9] and Bognar-de Vrijer [3] made notable contributions. However, as far as we know, there is as yet no proposal of a language which has contexts as first-class values and which is at the same time *pure* in the following sense. We understand that a functional language is *pure*[1] if (i) it is a conservative extension of the untyped or simply typed $\lambda\beta$-calculus, (ii) confluent and (iii) strongly normalizing (SN) if the language is typed and has preservation of strong normalization (PSN) property if the language is untyped. The conservative extension property guarantees that

[1] We have introduced this notion of purity in [15].

H. Kuchen and K. Ueda (Eds.): FLOPS 2001, LNCS 2024, pp. 359–374, 2001.

the language is logically well-behaved and the confluence property and SN or PSN would guarantee that the language is computationally well-behaved.

In this paper, we introduce the calculus $\lambda\kappa\varepsilon$ (κ is for context and ε is for environment) which is pure in the above sense and which has contexts and environments as its first class values, so that we can bind contexts and environments to variables and return them as the values of computations. $\lambda\kappa\varepsilon$ is a simply typed calculus, and in $\lambda\kappa\varepsilon$, holes are represented by ordinary variables of appropriate types (which we will call hole types) and hole filling is represented by the functional application together with a new abstraction mechanism which takes care of packing and unpacking of the term which is used to fill in the holes of the context.

We now illustrate some of the difficulties we face in formalizing the notion of context, and explain our solution informally by relating it to previous works. First, let us consider the context:

$$a[\,] \equiv \lambda x.\ (\lambda y.\ x + [\,])3.$$

If we fill the hole in $a[\,]$ with the term $x + y$, we get

$$a[x + y] \equiv \lambda x.\ (\lambda y.\ x + (x + y))3.$$

By β-reducing it, we can convert $a[x + y]$ to $\lambda x.\ x + (x + 3)$. Since we wish to compute with contexts, we would also like to reduce the β-redex $(\lambda y.\ x + [\,])3$ in $a[\,]$. If we reduce it naïvely, we get $x + [\,]$, so that $a[\,]$ reduces to $\lambda x.\ x + [\,]$. Now, if we fill the hole in $\lambda x.\ x + [\,]$ with $x + y$, we get $\lambda x.\ x + (x + y)$. This shows that hole filling and β-reduction do not commute if we define hole filling and β-reduction as above. In this example, we can note that the hole in the original context $a[\,]$ is within the scope of λx and λy, while the hole in the β-reduced context is only within the scope of λx. This means that a part of the information as to which variables should be captured at the hole is lost if one reduces a β-redex which has a hole in it. Hashimoto-Ohori [7] did not solve this problem. Instead they put restriction on the β-reduction rule in their system and prohibited such β-reductions like the above example.

To solve this problem, we introduce the type A^E which represents the set of objects obtained by abstracting objects of type A with respect to a set $E = \{x_1, \ldots, x_n\}$ of variables. Canonical objects of type A^E are abstracts of the form $\kappa E.\ a$ where a is of type A and the κE binder declares that the variables in E should be understood as local in a. Moreover, E is also a type and its canonical elements are *environments* of the form $\{a_1/x_1, \ldots, a_n/x_n\}$. Then, an object a of type A^E can be instantiated to an object b of type A by applying the abstract a to an environment $e = \{a_1/x_1, \ldots, a_n/x_n\}$. We write $a{\cdot}e$ for the application of the abstract a to the environment e. For example, $(\kappa\{x, y\}.\ x + y){\cdot}\{1/x, 2/y\}$ can be reduced to 3.

In this setting, we can represent the above context $a[\,]$ as

$$C \equiv \lambda x.\ (\lambda y.\ x + X{\cdot}\{x/x, y/y\})3$$

where X represents the hole and its type is of the form $A^{\{x,y\}}$. Now, suppose that we wish to fill the hole X with the term $x + y$. Then, we can achieve this hole filling by substituting $\kappa\{x, y\}.\ x + y$ for X in C. By this substitution, we have:

$$D \equiv \lambda x.\ (\lambda y.\ x + (\kappa\{x, y\}.\ x + y)\cdot\{x/x, y/y\})3.$$

D can be reduced to $\lambda x.\ (\lambda y.\ x + (x + y))3$, which can be further reduced to $\lambda x.\ x + (x + 3)$ as expected. Let us now see what happens if we reduce the β-redex in C first and then fill the hole with $x + y$. By β-reducing C, we get $\lambda x.\ x + X\cdot\{x/x, 3/y\}$. Substituting $\kappa\{x, y\}.\ x + y$ for X in this term, we have

$$\lambda x.\ x + (\kappa\{x, y\}.\ x + y)\cdot\{x/x, 3/y\},$$

which we can further reduce to $\lambda x.\ x + (x + 3)$. We can thus see that hole filling and β-reduction commute in this case.

The idea of decorating a hole with an environment is due to Talcott [16], and Mason [9] also used this idea in his calculus of contexts that has contexts as first-class values. However, in Mason's system, environments appear in a term containing holes only as annotations. This means that such environments are objects outside the system. We present our calculus $\lambda\kappa\varepsilon$ as an extension of $\lambda\varepsilon$ [15] which is a simply typed λ-calculus that has environments as first class values. So, environments are first-class objects in $\lambda\kappa\varepsilon$. Moreover, Mason defines hole filling only as a meta-level operation. Therefore, although contexts are first-class values in his system, one cannot compute hole filling within his system. In contrast to this, we can compute hole filling within our system. For example, we can express the above example of filling $a[\,]$ with $x + y$ as follows:

$$(\lambda X.\ \lambda x.\ (\lambda y.\ x + X\cdot\{x/x, y/y\})3)(\kappa\{x, y\}.\ x + y).$$

We can compute the above term in $\lambda\kappa\varepsilon$, and we get $\lambda x.\ x + (x + 3)$.

We now turn to another problem in the formalization of contexts. Consider the informal context $\lambda x.\ [\,]$. If we fill the hole in this context with x, we get the term $\lambda x.\ x$. This term is α-equivalent to $\lambda y.\ y$. What is the context which is α-equivalent to $\lambda x.\ [\,]$ and which, when filled with x, becomes $\lambda y.\ y$? It is certainly preferable that such a context exists, since, otherwise, hole filling and α-conversion will not always commute. A naïve attempt is to α-convert $\lambda x.\ [\,]$ to $\lambda y.\ [\,]$. But this does not work, since filling $\lambda y.\ [\,]$ with x results in $\lambda y.\ x$ which is not α-equivalent to $\lambda y.\ y$. We can solve this problem easily in our setting as follows. In $\lambda\kappa\varepsilon$, the context $\lambda x.\ [\,]$ is written as $\lambda x.\ X\cdot\{x/x\}$ and this context is α-equivalent to $\lambda y.\ X\cdot\{y/x\}$. Filling these holes in these two contexts with x is achieved by substituting $\kappa\{x\}.\ x$ for X in these contexts, and the results are $\lambda x.\ (\kappa\{x\}.\ x)\cdot\{x/x\}$ and $\lambda y.\ (\kappa\{x\}.\ x)\cdot\{y/x\}$ respectively. Then they are reduced to $\lambda x.\ x$ and $\lambda y.\ y$ as expected.

In this paper we also introduce a new method of defining substitution. As we explain below, the traditional method of defining substitution does not work for our calculus. We are therefore forced to use the new method, but, we believe our new definition of substitution is mathematically cleaner than the traditional method of defining substitution. We now give an example where the traditional method of defining substitution fails to work. By way of comparison, we first consider the λ term $a \equiv \lambda x.\ x + y$. What is the result of substituting x for y in a? We must be careful enough to avoid the variable clash and rename the bound variable x in a to a fresh variable, say, z, and we get $\lambda z.\ z + x$ as the result of the substitution. Now consider the abstract $b \equiv \kappa\{x\}.\ x + y$. What will be the result c of substituting x for y in b? If we perform substitution by the same method as above, we get $\kappa\{z\}.\ z + x$ which is wrong for the following reason. Note that $b{\cdot}\{2/x\}$ reduces to $2 + y$. So, $c{\cdot}\{2/x\}$ must reduce to $2 + x$. However, we cannot reduce $(\kappa\{z\}.\ z + x){\cdot}\{2/x\}$ since the argument $\{2/x\}$ does not match the binder $\kappa\{z\}$. By the same token, the term $(\kappa\{z\}.\ z + x){\cdot}\{2/x\}$ is not even typable. We can thus see that, unlike variables bound by the λ binder, we cannot rename variables bound by the κ binder. To cope with this situation, we introduce a new method of defining substitution where we rename *free* variables (if necessary) to achieve the capture avoiding substitution. So, our substitution will yield $\kappa\{x\}.\ x + \sharp x$ as the result of substituting x for y in b, where $\sharp x$ in the scope of the $\kappa\{x\}$ binder is a renamed form of the *free* variable x and it stands for the free variable x.

The paper is organized as follows. In section 2, we introduce the type system of $\lambda\kappa\varepsilon$, and introduce derivation rules that are used to define (typed) terms together with their types and free variables. There, we define variables so that they naturally contain both ordinary variables with names and variables as de Bruijn indices. In section 3, we define substitution as a meta-level operation. In section 4, we give reduction rules of $\lambda\kappa\varepsilon$ and give some examples of computations in $\lambda\kappa\varepsilon$. In section 5, we show that $\lambda\kappa\varepsilon$ enjoys a number of desirable properties such as confluence and strong normalizability. In section 6, we give concluding remarks. Due to lack of space, we have omitted almost all proofs. A full version of this paper with proofs is accessible at `http://www.sato.kuis.kyoto-u.ac.jp/~masahiko/index-e.html`.

2 The Type System

In this section, we define the type system of $\lambda\kappa\varepsilon$ by defining the notion of a derivation of a typing judgment. A typing judgement is an expression of the form $\Gamma \vdash a : A$, and if it is derivable then it means that the expression a is a term whose type is A and whose set of free variables is Γ.

In the following we assume that we have given a finite set of atomic types which we do not specify further in this paper. We also assume that we have infinitely many *identifiers* (i). Then, we define *variables* and *types* simultaneously as follows.

A *variable* (we will use x, y, z, u, v as meta-variables for variables) is a triple $\langle k, i, A\rangle$ where k is a natural number, i is an identifier and A is a type. A variable $\langle k, i, A\rangle$ is called a *pure variable* if $k = 0$. *Types* (A, B) are defined by the following grammar:

$$A, B ::= K \mid E \mid A \Rightarrow B \mid A^E$$

where K ranges over atomic types and E over finite sets of pure variables.

In the following, we will use *declaration* as a synonym for a finite set of variables and *pure declaration* as a synonym for a finite set of pure variables. We use Γ, Δ etc. as meta variables for declarations and E, F as meta variables for pure declarations. A pure declaration $\{x_1, \ldots, x_n\}$ will also be called an *environment type* since it is the type of environments whose canonical forms are elements of the form $\{a_1/x_1, \ldots, a_n/x_n\}$.

If $x \equiv \langle k, i, A\rangle$, then we call k the *level* of x, i the *name* of x and A the *type* of x. In this case, we sometimes write x^A for x and also write $\sharp^l x$ for $\langle k+l, i, A\rangle$, $\sharp x$ for $\sharp^1 x$, and $\bar{x}$ for $\langle 0, i, A\rangle$.

We write V for the set of all the variables. Let E be a pure declaration. We define a function $\Uparrow^E : \mathsf{V} \to \mathsf{V} - E$ by $\Uparrow^E(x) := \sharp x$ if $\bar{x} \in E$ and $\Uparrow^E(x) := x$ if $\bar{x} \notin E$. We also define $\Downarrow_E$ as the inverse function of $\Uparrow^E$. Note that $\Downarrow_E(x)$ is defined only when $x \notin E$. For example, if E is empty, then $\Uparrow^E(x) = x$ for any variable x. If E is $\{x, y\}$, then $\Uparrow^E(x) = \sharp^1 x$, $\Uparrow^E(\sharp^1 x) = \sharp^2 x$, $\Uparrow^E(z) = z$, $\Downarrow_E(\sharp^2 x) = \sharp^1 x$, and $\Downarrow_E(x)$ is undefined. We will use $\Uparrow^E$ later to systematically rename variables to avoid collision with the variables in E.

Let Γ be a declaration and E, F be pure declarations. We define the declarations $\Gamma\Uparrow^E$ and $\Gamma\Downarrow_E$ as follows:

$$\Gamma\Uparrow^E := \{\Uparrow^E(x) \mid x \in \Gamma\}, \qquad \Gamma\Downarrow_E := \{\Downarrow_E(x) \mid x \in \Gamma\},$$

where $\Gamma\Downarrow_E$ is defined only when $\Gamma \cap E$ is empty. Furthermore, given two declarations E and F, we define a function $\Updownarrow_F^E : \mathsf{V} \to \mathsf{V}$ as follows.

$$\Updownarrow_F^E(x) := \begin{cases} \Uparrow^E(x) \text{ if } x \in F, \\ \Downarrow_F(x) \text{ if } x \in E\Uparrow^F, \\ x \qquad\quad \text{otherwise.} \end{cases}$$

We give a few examples here. If E is $\{x\}$, then $\Updownarrow_E^E(x) = \sharp x$, $\Updownarrow_E^E(\sharp x) = x$, and $\Updownarrow_E^E(\sharp^2 x) = \sharp^2 x$. If E is $\{x, y\}$ and F is $\{x\}$, then $\Updownarrow_F^E(x) = \sharp x$, $\Updownarrow_F^E(\sharp x) = x$, $\Updownarrow_F^E(y) = y$, and $\Updownarrow_F^E(z) = z$. As we will see in the next section, we will use $\Updownarrow_F^E$ to rename variables when the order of two binders are exchanged.

Using the function $\Updownarrow_F^E$, we define the declaration $\Gamma\Updownarrow_F^E$ as follows.

$$\Gamma\Updownarrow_F^E := \{\Updownarrow_F^E(x) \mid x \in \Gamma\}.$$

Lemma 1. *We have the following equations.*

1. $\Gamma\Uparrow^E \cap E = \emptyset$.
2. $\Gamma\Uparrow^E\Downarrow_E = \Gamma$. *If* $\Gamma \cap E = \emptyset$, *then* $\Gamma\Downarrow_E\Uparrow^E = \Gamma$.
3. $((\Gamma - E)\Downarrow_E - F)\Downarrow_F = ((\Gamma\Updownarrow_E^F - F)\Downarrow_F - E)\Downarrow_E$.

A *typing judgment* is an expression of the form $\Gamma \vdash a : A$ where Γ is a declaration and A is a type. We have the typing rules in Figure 1 that are used to derive typing judgments, where those rules whose names end with '*I*' ('*E*') introduce (eliminate, respectively) the types mentioned in the rule names.

An expression a is said to be a *term* if a typing judgment of the form $\Gamma \vdash a : A$ is derivable for some Γ and A. In this case, we say that Γ is the set of *free*

$$\frac{}{\{x\} \vdash x^A : A}\ (\mathsf{axiom})$$

$$\frac{\Gamma \vdash b : B}{(\Gamma - \{x\})\Downarrow_{\{x\}} \vdash \lambda x^A.\, b : A \Rightarrow B}\ ({\Rightarrow}I) \qquad \frac{\Gamma \vdash b : A \Rightarrow B \quad \Delta \vdash a : A}{\Gamma \cup \Delta \vdash ba : B}\ ({\Rightarrow}E)$$

$$\frac{\Gamma \vdash a : A}{(\Gamma - E)\Downarrow_E \vdash \kappa E.\, a : A^E}\ (\mathsf{abs}I) \qquad \frac{\Gamma \vdash a : A^E \quad \Delta \vdash e : E}{\Gamma \cup \Delta \vdash a{\cdot}e : A}\ (\mathsf{abs}E)$$

$$\frac{\Gamma_1 \vdash a_1 : A_1 \quad \cdots \quad \Gamma_n \vdash a_n : A_n}{\Gamma_1 \cup \ldots \cup \Gamma_n \vdash \{a_1/x_1^{A_1}, \ldots, a_n/x_n^{A_n}\} : \{x_1, \ldots, x_n\}}\ (\mathsf{env}I)$$

$$\frac{\Gamma \vdash e : E \quad \Delta \vdash a : A}{\Gamma \cup (\Delta - E)\Downarrow_E \vdash e[\![a]\!] : A}\ (\mathsf{env}E)$$

In $({\Rightarrow}I)$, the variable x must be pure.
In $(\mathsf{env}I)$, the variables $x_1, \ldots, x_n$ must be pure and mutually distinct.

Fig. 1. Typing rules of $\lambda\kappa\varepsilon$

variables in a and write $\mathrm{FV}(a)$ for it and also say that A is the *type* of a and write $\mathrm{TY}(a)$ for it. Note that if $e \equiv \{a_1/x_1, \ldots, a_n/x_n\}$, then $\mathrm{TY}(e)$ is $\{x_1, \ldots, x_n\}$. We will say that these variables are *bound by* e. We also write T for the set of all the terms. A term is *canonical* if it is of the form $\lambda x.b$, $\{a_1/x_1, \ldots, a_n/x_n\}$ or $\kappa E.\ a$, that is, if it is obtained by one of the introduction rules. A term is said to be an *environment term* if its type is an environment type.

In $({\Rightarrow}I)$, since free variables in b are within the scope of λx^A, $\Downarrow_{\{x\}}$ should be applied to $\Gamma - \{x\}$ to refer to the variables in b from the outside of the binder. By the same reason, $\Downarrow_E$ is used in $(\mathsf{abs}I)$ and $(\mathsf{env}E)$. We have explained the intuitive meaning of the typing rules $(\mathsf{abs}I)$ and $(\mathsf{abs}E)$ for introducing and eliminating abstractions in section 1. The remaining typing rules come from $\lambda\varepsilon$, and the reader is referred to [15] for the detailed explanation of these rules. Here, we only remark that the term $e[\![a]\!]$ in the $(\mathsf{env}E)$ rule means to evaluate a in the environment e. So, for example, if $e \equiv \{\lambda x.\ \lambda y.\ x + y/z,\ 1/x,\ 2/u\}$, then $e[\![zxy]\!]$ is evaluated to $1 + y$. Note that z and x in zxy are bound by e and y is free in $e[\![zxy]\!]$.

We give below a simple example of a derivation. In the example below, we assume that x and y are distinct pure variables.

$$\dfrac{\dfrac{\dfrac{\dfrac{\dfrac{}{\{y\} \vdash y : A \Rightarrow A \Rightarrow B}\ (\mathsf{axiom}) \quad \dfrac{}{\{\sharp x\} \vdash \sharp x : A}\ (\mathsf{axiom})}{\{y, \sharp x\} \vdash y(\sharp x) : A \Rightarrow B}\ ({\Rightarrow}E) \quad \dfrac{}{\{x\} \vdash x : A}\ (\mathsf{axiom})}{\{y, \sharp x, x\} \vdash y(\sharp x)x : B}\ ({\Rightarrow}E)}{\{y, x\} \vdash \lambda x.\ y(\sharp x)x : A \Rightarrow B}\ ({\Rightarrow}I)}{\{\} \vdash \kappa\{x, y\}.\ \lambda x.\ y(\sharp x)x : (A \Rightarrow B)^{\{x,y\}}}\ (\mathsf{abs}I)\ .$$

It is easy to see that if $\Gamma \vdash a : A$ is derivable, then we can completely recover the entire derivation tree uniquely by inspecting the typed term a[2].

We have two kinds of abstractions λ and κ — λ abstracts nameless variables and κ abstracts named variables. We can eliminate λ by taking the distinguished named variable ι, replacing λ by $\kappa\{\iota\}$, and using the de Bruijn index method that we explain in the next section. But we did not do so, because we want to design $\lambda\kappa\varepsilon$ so that it extends the traditional λ-calculus directly. (See also the comments at the end of section 3.)

3 Substitution

In this section we define substitution as a meta-level syntactic operation. Our definition is conceptually simpler than the ordinary definition of substitution where α-conversion is sometimes necessary to avoid the unwanted capture of variables. Our method of defining substitution is a simple extension of the method due to de Bruijn [4].

Before going into technical details, we explain our method by comparing it with the traditional method of defining substitution for terms with named variables [1] and also with the method invented by de Bruijn [4]. In the traditional method, for example, substitution of x for y in $\lambda x.\ y$ is done by first α-converting $\lambda x.\ y$ to, say, $\lambda z.\ y$ and then replacing y by x. Thus, the result of substitution is $\lambda z.\ x$. The α-conversion was necessary to avoid unwanted capturing of x by the λx binder in the original term. So, in this approach, one has to define terms as equivalence classes of concrete terms modulo α-equivalence, and therefore, we have to check the well-definedness of the substitution, since we first define the substitution operation on concrete terms. Also, in this approach, one has to define α-equivalence before substitution, but the definition of α-conversion requires the notion of renaming variables which is similar to substitution.

We think that such complication in the traditional definition of substitution comes from the fact that avoidance of capturing free variables was achieved by the renaming of the name of the λ-binder. Our approach here is to avoid the capture of free variables by systematically renaming the free variables which would otherwise be captured[3]. For instance, in case of the above example of substituting x for y in $\lambda x.\ y$, we rename x to $\sharp x$ and substitute $\sharp x$ for y, so that the result of the substitution becomes $\lambda x.\ \sharp x$. We note that in the resulting term $\lambda x.\ \sharp x$, the variable $\sharp x$ is different from x within the scope of λx, and that $\sharp x$ refers to x outside the scope of λx. From this explanation, it should be easy to understand that the result of substituting $x * z$ for y in $\lambda x.\ \lambda x.\ x + y$ is $\lambda x.\ \lambda x.\ x + (\sharp^2 x * z)$. As can be seen from this example, we rename only those variables that would otherwise be captured. Therefore, in case capturing does

[2] Strictly speaking, in order to have this property, we have to identify those derivations which are the same up to the difference of ordering of the premises of the (env$I$) rule.

[3] We have introduced this idea of renaming free variables in [14].

not occur, the result of substitution obtained by our method is the same as that obtained by the traditional method.

We give another example to clarify the intuitive idea. Suppose that x, y, z are distinct pure variables. Then the following terms are all α-equivalent with each other.

$$\begin{aligned}&\lambda x.\ \lambda y.\ (\lambda z.\ y(zx))(yx)\\ &\equiv_\alpha \lambda \sharp^0 x.\ \lambda \sharp^0 x.\ (\lambda \sharp^0 x.\ \sharp^1 x(\sharp^0 x\ \sharp^2 x))(\sharp^0 x\ \sharp^1 x)\\ &\equiv_\alpha \lambda x.\ \lambda y.\ (\lambda x.\ y(x\ \sharp x))(yx).\end{aligned}$$

If we write $0, 1$ and 2 for $\sharp^0 x, \sharp^1 x$ and $\sharp^2 x$, respectively, in the second term above, we get $\lambda 0.\ \lambda 0.\ (\lambda 0.\ 1(02))(01)$. Therefore, this term is essentially the same as the representation of the first term in de Bruijn indices. We can therefore see that our terms are natural extensions of both traditional concrete terms with variable names and name free terms á la de Bruijn that use indices.

Let $\phi : \mathsf{V} \to \mathsf{V}$ be a (possibly) partial function such that $\phi(x)$ may be undefined for some $x \in \mathsf{V}$. We extend this function to the function $\overline{\phi} : \mathsf{T} \to \mathsf{T}$ as follows. $\overline{\phi}$ will be total if and only if ϕ is total.

1. $\overline{\phi}(x) := \phi(x)$.
2. $\overline{\phi}(\lambda x.\ a) := \lambda x.\ \overline{\phi_{\{x\}}}(a)$.
3. $\overline{\phi}(ba) := \overline{\phi}(b)\overline{\phi}(a)$.
4. $\overline{\phi}(\kappa F.\ a) := \kappa F.\ \overline{\phi_F}(a)$.
5. $\overline{\phi}(a \cdot f) := \overline{\phi}(a) \cdot \overline{\phi}(f)$.
6. $\overline{\phi}(\{a_1/x_1, \ldots, a_n/x_n\}) := \{\overline{\phi}(a_1)/x_1, \ldots, \overline{\phi}(a_n)/x_n\}$.
7. $\overline{\phi}(e[\![a]\!]) := \overline{\phi}(e)[\![\overline{\phi_{\mathrm{TY}(e)}}(a)]\!]$.

where, for each declaration E, $\phi_E : \mathsf{V} \to \mathsf{V}$ is defined by

$$\phi_E(x) := \begin{cases} x & \text{if } x \in E,\\ \Uparrow^E(\phi(\Downarrow_E(x))) & \text{otherwise.}\end{cases}$$

(We note that if ϕ is not total, ϕ_E is also not total.)

We define the push operation $\uparrow^E$ by putting $a\!\uparrow^E := \overline{\Uparrow^E}(a)$, the pull operation $\downarrow_E$ by putting $a\!\downarrow_E := \overline{\Downarrow_E}(a)$, and the exchange operation $\updownarrow_F^E$ by putting $a\!\updownarrow_F^E := \overline{\Updownarrow_F^E}(a)$.

Let us give a few examples here. Let E be $\{x, y\}$.

$$\begin{aligned}(\lambda x.\ x(\sharp^3 x))\!\uparrow^E &\equiv \overline{\Uparrow^E}(\lambda x.\ x(\sharp^3 x))\\ &\equiv \lambda x.\ \overline{\Uparrow^E{}_{\{x\}}}(x(\sharp^3 x))\\ &\equiv \lambda x.\ (\overline{\Uparrow^E{}_{\{x\}}}(x))(\overline{\Uparrow^E{}_{\{x\}}}(\sharp^3 x))\\ &\equiv \lambda x.\ x(\Uparrow^{\{x\}}\Uparrow^E\Downarrow_{\{x\}}(\sharp^3 x))\\ &\equiv \lambda x.\ x(\sharp^4 x).\end{aligned}$$

Note that $\mathrm{FV}(\lambda x.\ x(\sharp^3 x)) = \{\sharp^2 x\}$, and $\{\sharp^2 x\}\!\Uparrow^E = \{\sharp^3 x\}$, which is equal to $\mathrm{FV}(\lambda x.\ x(\sharp^4 x))$. Similarly, we have $(\lambda x.\ x(\sharp^3 x))\!\downarrow_E \equiv \lambda x.\ x(\sharp^2 x)$.

For the exchange operation, we have:

$$(\lambda x.\ (\sharp x)(\sharp^2 x))\updownarrow^{\{x\}}_{\{x\}} \equiv \lambda x.\ (\sharp^2 x)(\sharp x),$$
$$(\lambda x.\ (\sharp x)(\sharp^2 x))\updownarrow^{\{y\}}_{\{x\}} \equiv \lambda x.\ (\sharp x)(\sharp^2 x),$$

where x and y are distinct pure variables.

We now define the substitution operation as follows. Let $s \equiv \{c_1/x_1, \ldots, c_n/x_n\}$ be a canonical environment term. Note that $\mathrm{TY}(s) = \{x_1, \ldots, x_n\}$ in this case. For each term a we define a term $a[s]$ inductively as follows. (We think that the 2nd clause below corresponds to the 2nd clause of the definition of the substitution operation $\sigma : \delta\Lambda \times \Lambda \to \Lambda$ in Fiore-Plotkin-Turi [6], and we think that it should be possible to establish a precise correspondence.)

1. $x[s] := \begin{cases} c_i & \text{if } x \equiv x_i \text{ for some } i, \\ \Downarrow_{\mathrm{TY}(s)}(x) & \text{otherwise.} \end{cases}$
2. $(\lambda x.\ b)[s] := \lambda x.\ b\updownarrow^{\mathrm{TY}(s)}_{\{x\}}[s\uparrow^{\{x\}}]$.
3. $(ba)[s] := b[s]a[s]$.
4. $(\kappa E.\ a)[s] := \kappa E.\ a\updownarrow^{\mathrm{TY}(s)}_{E}[s\uparrow^{E}]$.
5. $(a{\cdot}e)[s] := a[s]{\cdot}e[s]$.
6. $(\{a_1/x_1, \ldots, a_n/x_n\})[s] := \{a_1[s]/x_1, \ldots, a_n[s]/x_n\}$.
7. $(e[\![a]\!])[s] := e[s][\![(a\updownarrow^{\mathrm{TY}(s)}_{\mathrm{TY}(e)})[s\uparrow^{\mathrm{TY}(e)}]]\!]$.

We call $a[s]$ the result of *substituting* $c_1, \ldots, c_n$ *for* $x_1, \ldots, x_n$ *in* a.

Again we give a few examples. Let s be $\{\sharp^3 x/y,\ (x\ \sharp x)/x\}$. Then we have:

$$\begin{aligned}(\lambda x.\ x\ \sharp x)[s] &\equiv \lambda x.\ (x\ \sharp x)\updownarrow^{\{y,x\}}_{\{x\}}[s\uparrow^{\{x\}}] \\ &\equiv \lambda x.\ (\sharp x\ x)[\{\sharp^4 x/y,\ (\sharp x\ \sharp^2 x)/x\}] \\ &\equiv \lambda x.\ (\Downarrow_{\{y,x\}}\sharp x)(\sharp x\ \sharp^2 x) \\ &\equiv \lambda x.\ x(\sharp x\ \sharp^2 x), \\ (\lambda x.\ xy)[\{z/y\}] &\equiv \lambda x.\ xz,\end{aligned}$$

where x, y, z are distinct pure variables.

In the first example, x in $\lambda x.\ x\ \sharp x$ is bound by λx and $\sharp x$ is bound by s. When s goes into the scope of λx, x and $\sharp x$ should be renamed to $\sharp x$ and x, respectively so that they are bound by λx and $s\uparrow^{\{x\}}$.

We can now define the α-equivalence using substitution as follows.

1. $x \equiv_\alpha x$
2. If $a[\{z/x\}] \equiv_\alpha a'[\{z/x'\}]$, then $\lambda x.\ a \equiv_\alpha \lambda x'.\ a'$ where z is a variable such that $z \notin \mathrm{FV}(a) \cup \mathrm{FV}(a') \cup \{x, x'\}$.
3. If $b \equiv_\alpha b'$ and $a \equiv_\alpha a'$, then $ba \equiv_\alpha b'a'$.
4. If $a \equiv_\alpha a'$, then $\kappa E.\ a \equiv_\alpha \kappa E.\ a'$.
5. If $a \equiv_\alpha a'$ and $e \equiv_\alpha e'$, then $a{\cdot}e \equiv_\alpha a'{\cdot}e'$.
6. If $a_1 \equiv_\alpha a'_1, \cdots, a_n \equiv_\alpha a'_n$, then $\{a_1/x_1, \ldots, a_n/x_n\} \equiv_\alpha \{a_1/x_1, \ldots, a_n/x_n\}$.

7. If $a \equiv_\alpha a'$ and $e \equiv_\alpha e'$, then $e[\![a]\!] \equiv_\alpha e'[\![a']\!]$.

Note that variables bound by κ are not renamed in the 4th clause because κ abstracts named variables. On the other hand, variables bound by λ may be renamed in the 2nd clause bacause λ plays the same role as λ in the traditional λ-calculus.

4 Reduction Rules

In this section we give reduction rules of the $\lambda\kappa\varepsilon$ calculus. We first define $\mapsto_{\lambda\kappa\varepsilon}$ as the union of the following three relations $\mapsto_\lambda$, $\mapsto_\kappa$ and $\mapsto_\varepsilon$.

The relation $\mapsto_\lambda$ is defined by the following single rule:

$$(\lambda)\ \ (\lambda x.\ b)a \mapsto_\lambda \{a/x\}[\![b]\!],$$

and the relation $\mapsto_\kappa$ is defined by the following single rule:

$$(\kappa)\ \ (\kappa E.\ a)\cdot e \mapsto_\kappa e[\![a]\!].$$

The relation $\mapsto_\varepsilon$ is defined by the following 8 conversion rules.

$$\begin{array}{rl}
(\mathsf{gc}) & e[\![a]\!] \mapsto_\varepsilon a\!\downarrow_{\mathrm{TY}(e)},\ \text{if } \mathrm{TY}(e) \cap \mathrm{FV}(a) = \emptyset. \\
(\mathsf{var}) & \{a_1/x_1, \ldots, a_n/x_n\}[\![x_i]\!] \mapsto_\varepsilon a_i\ (1 \leq i \leq n). \\
(\mathsf{fun}) & e[\![\lambda x.\ b]\!] \mapsto_\varepsilon \lambda x.\ (e\!\uparrow^{\{x\}})[\![b\!\updownarrow^{\mathrm{TY}(e)}_{\{x\}}]\!] \\
(\mathsf{funapp}) & e[\![ba]\!] \mapsto_\varepsilon e[\![b]\!]e[\![a]\!]. \\
(\mathsf{abs}) & e[\![\kappa E.\ a]\!] \mapsto_\varepsilon \kappa E.\ (e\!\uparrow^{E})[\![a\!\updownarrow^{\mathrm{TY}(e)}_{E}]\!]. \\
(\mathsf{absapp}) & e[\![a\cdot f]\!] \mapsto_\varepsilon e[\![a]\!]\cdot e[\![f]\!]. \\
(\mathsf{env}) & e[\![\{a_1/x_1, \ldots, a_n/x_n\}]\!] \mapsto_\varepsilon \{e[\![a_1]\!]/x_1, \ldots, e[\![a_n]\!]/x_n\}. \\
(\mathsf{eval}) & e[\![f[\![x]\!]]\!] \mapsto_\varepsilon e[\![f]\!][\![x]\!],\ \text{if } x \in \mathrm{TY}(f).
\end{array}$$

The rules other than (eval) are internalized forms of the clauses 1–6 of the definition of substitution in section 3. In these rules we have the environment term e in place of the canonical environment term s, and the rule (gc) is a generalization of the second case of clause 1. We can also internalize clause 7 directly and get a correct rule. But, we do not do so since it will result in a system where the strong normalization property does not hold. Instead we have the (eval) rule which corresponds to a special case of clause 7. Although the (eval) rule is a weak version of clause 7, we will see in Theorem 1 that we can faithfully compute substitution internally by using these reduction rules, and at the same time the system enjoys the strong normalizability (Theorem 6). In fact, as can be seen in, e.g., Melliès [10] and Bloo [2], the strong normalizability of calculi of explicit substitutions and explicit environments is a subtle problem. The reader is referred to [15] for a detailed discussion on our choice of the (eval) rule.

We write $a \to_\lambda b$ if b is obtained from a by replacing a subterm c in a by d such that $c \mapsto_\lambda d$. Similarly $\to_\kappa$, $\to_\varepsilon$ and $\to_{\lambda\kappa\varepsilon}$ are defined. The transitive closures of these reductions are denoted with asterisk (*), such as $\stackrel{*}{\to}_\varepsilon$. The equivalence relation generated by $\rightarrow_{\lambda\kappa\varepsilon}$ is denoted by $=_{\lambda\kappa\varepsilon}$, namely, the reflexive, symmetric, and transitive closure of $\rightarrow_{\lambda\kappa\varepsilon}$. Similarly $=_{\varepsilon}$ is defined.

We give a few examples of reduction sequences. Let $s \equiv \{(x\ \sharp x)/x,\ \sharp^3 x/y\}$ in the second example.

$$\begin{aligned}(\lambda x.\ \lambda y.\ x)y &\rightarrow_{\lambda} \{y/x\}[\![\lambda y.\ x]\!]\\ &\rightarrow_{\varepsilon} \lambda y.\ (\{y/x\}\uparrow^{\{y\}})[\![x \updownarrow^{\{x\}}_{\{y\}}]\!]\\ &\equiv \lambda y.\ \{\sharp y/x\}[\![x]\!] \rightarrow_{\varepsilon} \lambda y.\ \sharp y.\end{aligned}$$

$$\begin{aligned}s[\![\lambda x.\ x\ \sharp x]\!] &\rightarrow_{\varepsilon} \lambda x.\ (s\uparrow^{\{x\}})[\![(x\ \sharp x)\updownarrow^{\{x,y\}}_{\{x\}}]\!]\\ &\equiv \lambda x.\ \{(\sharp x\ \sharp^2 x)/x,\ \sharp^4 x/y\}[\![(\sharp x\ x)]\!]\\ &\xrightarrow{*}_{\varepsilon} \lambda x.\ (\Downarrow_{\{x,y\}}\sharp x)(\sharp x\ \sharp^2 x)\\ &\equiv \lambda x.\ x(\sharp x\ \sharp^2 x).\end{aligned}$$

$$\begin{aligned}(\lambda X.\ \lambda y.\ X\cdot\{y/y\})(\kappa\{y\}.\ y) &\rightarrow_{\lambda} \{\kappa\{y\}.\ y/X\}[\![\lambda y.\ X\cdot\{y/y\}]\!]\\ &\xrightarrow{*}_{\varepsilon} \lambda y.\ (\kappa\{y\}.\ y)\cdot\{y/y\}\\ &\rightarrow_{\kappa} \lambda y.\ \{y/y\}[\![y]\!] \xrightarrow{*}_{\varepsilon} \lambda y.\ y.\end{aligned}$$

In the first example, y is renamed to $\sharp y$ so that it is not captured by the λy binder. The second example corresponds to the example given after the definition of substitution. The third example shows the hole-filling operation where y is captured by the λy binder.

We take an example from Hashimoto-Ohori's paper [7]. Consider the term $(\lambda z.\ C[x+z])x$ where C is an (informal) context $(\lambda x.\ [\ ]+y)3$ and $C[x+z]$ represents the hole-filling operation in the λ-calculus. In Hashimoto-Ohori's calculus, this term can be written as

$$a \equiv (\lambda z.\ (\delta X.(\lambda u.\ X^{\{u/x\}} + y)3) \odot_{\{x/v\}} (v+z))x$$

where X represents a hole, δX abstracts the hole X, and $\odot$ is a hole-filling operator. $\{u/x\}$ and $\{x/v\}$ (called renamers) annotate X and $\odot$ respectively. They are introduced to solve the problem of variable capturing. In our system, the above term can be written as

$$a \equiv (\lambda z.\ (\lambda X.\ (\lambda u.\ X\cdot\{u/x\} + y)3)(\kappa\{x\}.\ (x+z)))x.$$

We can compute this term in many ways, but, here we give two reduction sequences.

$$\begin{aligned}a &\rightarrow_{\lambda} \{x/z\}[\![(\lambda X.\ (\lambda u.\ X\cdot\{u/x\}+y)3)(\kappa\{x\}.\ x+z)]\!]\\ &\xrightarrow{*}_{\varepsilon} (\lambda X.\ (\lambda u.\ X\cdot\{u/x\}+y)3)(\kappa\{x\}.\ x+\sharp x)\\ &\rightarrow_{\lambda} \{\kappa\{x\}.\ x+\sharp x/X\}[\![(\lambda u.\ X\cdot\{u/x\}+y)3]\!]\\ &\xrightarrow{*}_{\varepsilon} (\lambda u.\ (\kappa\{x\}.\ x+\sharp x)\cdot\{u/x\}+y)3\end{aligned}$$

$$\begin{aligned}
&\to_\kappa (\lambda u.\ \{u/x\}[\![x + \sharp x]\!] + y)3 \\
&\xrightarrow{*}_\varepsilon (\lambda u.\ u + x + y)3 \\
&\to_\lambda \{3/u\}[\![u + x + y]\!] \xrightarrow{*}_\varepsilon 3 + x + y.
\end{aligned}$$

$$\begin{aligned}
a &\to_\lambda (\lambda z.\ (\lambda X.\ \{3/u\}[\![X{\cdot}\{u/x\} + y]\!])(\kappa\{x\}.\ x + z))x \\
&\xrightarrow{*}_\varepsilon (\lambda z.\ (\lambda X.\ X{\cdot}\{3/x\} + y)(\kappa\{x\}.\ x + z))x \\
&\to_\lambda (\lambda z.\ \{\kappa\{x\}.\ x + z/X\}[\![X{\cdot}\{3/x\} + y]\!])x \\
&\xrightarrow{*}_\varepsilon (\lambda z.\ (\kappa\{x\}.\ x + z){\cdot}\{3/x\} + y)x \\
&\to_\kappa (\lambda z.\ \{3/x\}[\![x + z]\!] + y)x \\
&\xrightarrow{*}_\varepsilon (\lambda z.\ 3 + z + y)x \\
&\to_\lambda \{x/z\}[\![3 + z + y]\!] \xrightarrow{*}_\varepsilon 3 + x + y.
\end{aligned}$$

We remark that, in the second reduction sequence above, we have first reduced the innermost β-redex $(\lambda u.\ X{\cdot}\{u/x\} + y)3$. Such a reduction is not possible in Hashimoto-Ohori's calculus since in their system the β-conversion is prohibited when the redex contains a free hole. Though the roles of $X^{\{u/x\}}$ and $X{\cdot}\{u/x\}$ are similar, u in $X^{\{u/x\}}$ should always be a variable, while u in $X{\cdot}\{u/x\}$ can be substituted by an arbitrary term. This is the reason why our calculus need not put any restriction to the (λ)-reduction rule (the β-conversion).

We also remark on the hole-filling operations without going into the technical details. In Hashimoto-Ohori's calculus, the renamer ν in $\odot_\nu$ works as a variable binder to the second operand of $\odot$ (i.e. to the term to be filled into the hole). Because their typing rule of $M \odot_\nu N$ causes a side effect to the type of the free hole in N, they had to put the restriction that each free hole may occur at most once. Our κE binder, which plays the similar role to the renamer ν in $\odot_\nu$, does not have such a problem, because it is merely an abstraction.

Therefore, our calculus $\lambda\kappa\varepsilon$ can be regarded as a natural and flexible extension to Hashimoto-Ohori's calculus.

5 Properties of $\lambda\kappa\varepsilon$

In this section, we show that $\lambda\kappa\varepsilon$ enjoys a number of desirable properties. We first show that the meta-level operation of substitution is internally realized by the operation of evaluation (Theorem 1), and show some properties of substitution. We also show that $\lambda\kappa\varepsilon$ enjoys subject reduction property (Theorem 3), confluence property (Theorem 4), conservativity over the simply typed $\lambda\beta$-calculus (Theorem 5), and strong normalizability (Theorem 6). Theorems 4–6 establish the purity of $\lambda\kappa\varepsilon$, and as a corollary to the confluence of $\lambda\kappa\varepsilon$, we see that the operations of hole filling and β-reduction always commute.

As we have studied in [15], we can internalize the meta-level operation of substitution by means of evaluation terms which are of the form $e[\![a]\!]$. We can show that the meta-level substitution and the internalized substitution coincide, that is, $a[s] =_{\kappa\varepsilon} s[\![a]\!]$ holds.

Theorem 1. *Let s be a canonical environment term. Then, for any term a, $a[s] =_{\kappa\varepsilon} s[\![a]\!]$ holds.*

Lemma 2 corresponds to the Substitution Lemma [1] in the λ-calculus, that is, $M[x := K][y := L] \equiv M[y := L][x := K[y := L]]$ if $x \not\equiv y$ and $x \notin \mathrm{FV}(L)$.

Lemma 2 (Substitution Lemma). *Let s and t be canonical environment terms. Then, for any term a, $a[s][t] \equiv a \updownarrow^{\mathrm{TY}(t)}_{\mathrm{TY}(s)} [t \uparrow^{\mathrm{TY}(s)}][s[t]]$ holds.*

Note that the effect of exchanging the order of two substitutions s and t is adjusted by applying the exchange operation $\updownarrow^{\mathrm{TY}(t)}_{\mathrm{TY}(s)}$ to a and the push operation $\uparrow^{\mathrm{TY}(s)}$ to t. For example, let a be $x \;\sharp x$, s be $\{z/x\}$, and t be $\{\sharp^3 x/y,\ (x \;\sharp x)/x\}$ in the Lemma. Then, we have

$$\begin{aligned}
(x \;\sharp x)[s][t] &\equiv (z\ x)[t] \\
&\equiv z\ (x \;\sharp x), \\
(x \;\sharp x) \updownarrow^{\{y,x\}}_{\{x\}} [t \uparrow^{\{x\}}][s[t]] &\equiv (\sharp x\ x)[\{\sharp^4 x/y,\ (\sharp x\ \sharp^2 x)/x\}][s[t]] \\
&\equiv (x\ (\sharp x\ \sharp^2 x))[\{z/x\}] \\
&\equiv z\ ((\sharp x\ \sharp^2 x) \downarrow_{\{x\}}) \\
&\equiv z\ (x \;\sharp x).
\end{aligned}$$

(See also the example below the definition of the substitution in seciton 3.)

The reduction is compatible with substitution.

Theorem 2. *If $a \xrightarrow{*}_{\lambda\kappa\varepsilon} b$, then $a[s] \xrightarrow{*}_{\lambda\kappa\varepsilon} b[s]$.*

The following theorems will establish the purity of our calculus.

Theorem 3 (Subject Reduction). *If $\Gamma \vdash a : A$ and $a \to_{\lambda\kappa\varepsilon} b$, then $\Delta \vdash b : A$ for some $\Delta \subseteq \Gamma$.*

Theorem 4 (Confluence). *$\to_{\lambda\kappa\varepsilon}$ on $\lambda\kappa\varepsilon$-terms is confluent.*

Proof. The proof is a straightforward extension of that for $\lambda\varepsilon$, and we omit the details here. 2

We remark that from the confluence of $\lambda\kappa\varepsilon$, we see that the operations of hole filling and β-reduction always commute, since in $\lambda\kappa\varepsilon$, hole filling is computed by reducing a term of the form $(\lambda X.\ a)(\kappa E.\ b)$.

We next prove that $\lambda\kappa\varepsilon$ is a conservative extension of the simply typed lambda calculus $\lambda\beta$. For this purpose, we embed the $\lambda\beta$-terms in the $\lambda\kappa\varepsilon$-terms. A $\lambda\beta$-term is a $\lambda\kappa\varepsilon$-term such that its typing derivation uses the (axiom), ($\Rightarrow I$), ($\Rightarrow E$) rules only, and all the variables used in the (axiom) rule are pure variables. The α- and β-conversions over $\lambda\beta$ terms are defined as usual.

Theorem 5 (Conservativity). *Let a and b be $\lambda\beta$-terms. We have $a \xrightarrow{*}_{\alpha\beta} b$ in $\lambda\beta$ if and only if $a \xrightarrow{*}_{\lambda\kappa\varepsilon} b'$ and $b \equiv_\alpha b'$ for some term b' in $\lambda\kappa\varepsilon$.*

Proof. (Only-if part) easily follows from the fact that the β-conversion can be simulated by the $\lambda\varepsilon$-reduction rules up to the α-equivalence.

(If-part) can be proved in the same way as in [15], which uses the translation from $\lambda\varepsilon$-terms to $\lambda\beta$-terms. 2

Theorem 6 (Strong Normalizability). *If $\Gamma \vdash a : A$, then a is strongly normalizable.*

Proof. We can prove this theorem in the same way as the strongly normalizability theorem of $\lambda\varepsilon$ [15], because we can treat the cases of (abs) and (absapp) similarly to the cases of (fun) and (funapp). 2

6 Conclusion

We have introduced a simply typed λ-calculus which has both contexts and environments as first-class values. We have shown that our calculus, $\lambda\kappa\varepsilon$, is a conservative extension of the simply typed $\lambda\beta$-calculus, enjoys subject reduction property, is confluent and strongly normalizing. Thus we have shown that our language is pure in the sense of [15] and also we have realized our hope, which we stated in the conclusion of [15], to design a pure language that has both contexts and environments as first-class values. To the best of our knowledge, $\lambda\kappa\varepsilon$ is the first such language.

We have also introduced a new method of defining substitution which is conceptually simpler than traditional methods. We think that our method is also suitable for representing terms and computing substitutions on the computer.

We conclude the paper by comparing our calculus with some related works. The style of the presentation of our paper is very close to that of Hashimoto-Ohori [7]. Both our calculus and the calculus presented in [7] are simply typed calculi which include simply typed $\lambda\beta$-calculus as their subcalculus. The system in [7] enjoys subject reduction property and is confluent. However, neither conservativity over simply typed $\lambda\beta$-calculus nor strong normalizability are shown in the paper. Therefore, it is not known whether their system is pure in our sense[4]. Also, their calculus has severe restrictions in that (i) each context may have at most one hole in it, and (ii) as we have explained in section 1, the application of the β-reduction is allowed only when the β-redex has no hole in it. Our calculus does not have such restrictions and β-reduction and hole-filling always commute.

Dami's calculus λN [5] is a very simple and powerful calculus with named variables. It is possible to represent both contexts and hole-filling in λN. However, this is done by a translation of $\lambda\beta$ calculus into λN. Therefore, it is hard to read the translated terms as contexts. On the other hand, Mason [9] introduces a system with first-class contexts in which contexts are directly represented as terms in his calculus. However, he defines hole-filling as a meta-level operation.

[4] Sakurada [12] proved the strong normalizability of Hashimoto-Ohori's calculus by interpreting it in $\lambda\varepsilon$.

It is therefore not possible to compute hole-filling within his system. Unlike these systems, in $\lambda\kappa\varepsilon$, contexts are directly representable as terms of $\lambda\kappa\varepsilon$, and we can compute hole-filling within $\lambda\kappa\varepsilon$.

Sands [13] uses Pitts' [11] definition of contexts and shows that hole-filling commutes with many relations on terms including α-equivalence. Pitts defines contexts by representing holes by (higher-order) function variables where each function variable has a fixed arity, and by representing hole-filling by substitution of a meta-abstraction for a function variable. For example, the term

$$\lambda x.\ (\lambda y.\ x + X \cdot \{x/x, y/y\})3$$

in $\lambda\kappa\varepsilon$ can be expressed by

$$\lambda x.\ (\lambda y.\ x + \xi(x, y))3$$

where ξ is a binary function variable, and the substitution

$$\{\kappa\{x, y\}.\ x + y/X\}$$

in $\lambda\kappa\varepsilon$ can be expressed by

$$[(x, y)(x + y)/\xi].$$

As can be seen by this example, Pitts' representation of contexts is structurally similar to ours, but the statuses of contexts are quite different. That is, Pitts' contexts are meta-level objects outside the object language (λ calculus in case of the above example) and our contexts are internal objects of our language $\lambda\kappa\varepsilon$. Because of this meta-level status of Pitts' contexts, Sands [13] could successfully attach contexts to many languages and could prove that hole-filling commutes with many rules in a uniform way. In contrast to this, we have been interested in internalizing such meta-level objects as contexts and environments so that we can enrich λ-calculus to a more powerful programming language.

References

1. Barendregt, H. P., *The Lambda Calculus, Its Syntax and Semantics*, North-Holland, 1981.
2. Bloo, R. and Rose, K.H., Preservation of Strong Normalization in Named Lambda Calculi with Explicit Substitution and Garbage Collection, *Proceedings of CSN'95 (Computer Science in Netherlands)*, van Vliet J.C. (ed.), 1995. (`ftp://ftp.diku.dk/diku/semantics/papers/D-246.ps`)
3. Bognar, M. and de Vrijer, R., A calculus of lambda calculus contexts, available at: `http://www.cs.vu.nl/~mirna/new.ps.gz`.
4. de Bruijn, D. G., Lambda Calculus Notation with Nameless Dummies, a Tool for Automatic Formula Manipulation, with Application to the Church-Rosser Theorem, *Indag. Math.* 34, pp. 381-392, 1972.
5. Dami, L., A Lambda-Calculus for Dynamic Binding, pp. 201-231, *Theoretical Computer Science* **192**, 1998.

6. Fiore, M., Plotkin, G., and Turi, D., Abstract Syntax and Variable Binding (Extended Abstract), *Proc. 14th Symposium on Logic in Computer Science*, pp. 193-202, 1999.
7. Hashimoto, M. and Ohori, A., A typed context calculus, Preprint RIMS-1098, Res. Inst. for Math. Sci., Kyoto Univ., 1996, Journal version is to appear in *Theoretical Computer Science.*
8. Lee, S.-R., and D. P. Friedman, Enriching the Lambda Calculus with Contexts: Toward a Theory of Incremental Program Construction, *ACM SIGPLAN Notices, Proc. International Conference on Functional Programming*, pp. 239-250, 1996.
9. Mason, I., Computing with Contexts, *Higher-Order and Symbolic Computation* 12, pp. 171-201, 1999.
10. Melliès, P.-A., Typed λ-calculi with explicit substitutions may not terminate, Typed Lambda Calculi and Applications, *Lecture Notes in Computer Science* **902**, pp. 328-349, 1995.
11. Pitts, A.M., Some notes on inductive and co-inductive techniques in the semantics of functional programs, Notes Series BRICS-NS-94-5, Department of Computer Science, University of Aarhus, 1994.
12. Sakurada, H., An interpretation of a context calculus in an environment calculus, Master Thesis, Dept. of Information Science, Kyoto Univ., 1999 (in Japanese).
13. Sands, D., Computing with Contexts - a simple approach, Proc. Higher-Order Operational Techniques in Semantics, HOOTS II, 16 pages, *Electronic Notes in Theoretical Computer Science* **10**, 1998.
14. Sato, M., Theory of Symbolic Expressions, II, *Publ. of Res. Inst. for Math. Sci.*, Kyoto Univ., **21**, pp. 455-540, 1985.
15. Sato, M., Sakurai T., and Burstall, R., Explicit Environments, Typed Lambda Calculi and Applications, *Lecture Notes in Computer Science* **1581**, pp. 340-354, 1999.
16. Talcott, C., A Theory of binding structures and applications to rewriting, *Theoretical Computer Science* **112**:1, pp. 99-143, 1993.

Refining the Barendregt Cube using Parameters*

Fairouz Kamareddine**[1], Twan Laan[2], and Rob Nederpelt[3]

[1] Computing and Electrical Engineering, Heriot-Watt Univ., Riccarton, Edinburgh EH14 4AS, Scotland, fairouz@cee.hw.ac.uk

[2] Molenstraat 208, 5701 KL Helmond, the Netherlands, twan.laan@wxs.nl

[3] Mathematics and Computing Science, Eindhoven Univ. of Technology, P.O.Box 513, 5600 MB Eindhoven, the Netherlands, r.p.nederpelt@tue.nl

Abstract. The Barendregt Cube (introduced in [3]) is a framework in which eight important typed λ-calculi are described in a uniform way. Moreover, many type systems (like AUTOMATH [18], LF [11], ML [17], and system F [10]) can be related to one of these eight systems. Furthermore, via the propositions-as-types principle, many logical systems can be described in the Barendregt Cube as well (see for instance [9]). However, there are important systems (including AUTOMATH, LF and ML) that cannot be adequately placed in the Barendregt Cube or in the larger framework of Pure Type Systems. In this paper we add a parameter mechanism to the systems of the Barendregt Cube. In doing so, we obtain a refinement of the Cube. In this refined Barendregt Cube, systems like AUTOMATH, LF, and ML can be described more naturally and accurately than in the original Cube.

1 Introduction

In [3], Barendregt proposes a framework, now often called the Barendregt Cube, in which eight important and well-known type systems are presented in a uniform way. This makes a detailed comparison of these systems possible. The weakest systems of the Cube is Church's simply typed λ-calculus $\lambda\!\to$ [7], and the strongest system is the Calculus of Constructions λC [8]. Girard's well-known System F [10] figures on the Cube between $\lambda\!\to$ and λC. Moreover, via the Propositions-as-Types principle (see [13]), many logical systems can be described in the systems of the Cube, see [9].

In the Cube, we have in addition to the usual λ-abstraction, a type forming operator Π. Briefly, if A is a type, and B is a type possibly containing the variable x, then $\Pi x{:}A.B$ is the type of functions that, given a term $a : A$, output a value of type $B[x := a]$. Here $a : A$ expresses that a is of type A, and $B[x := a]$ means the result of the substitution of a for x in B. If x does

* This work has been partially supported by EPSRC grant numbers GR/L36963 and GR/L15685, by a Royal Society ESEP grant and by the British council and the Dutch research council NWO.

** Kamareddine is grateful to Eindhoven University of Technology for its hospitality and support during the preparation of this article.

H. Kuchen and K. Ueda (Eds.): FLOPS 2001, LNCS 2024, pp. 375–389, 2001.

not occur in B, then $\Pi x{:}A.B$ is the type of functions from A to B, written $A \to B$. To the Π-abstraction at the level of types corresponds λ-abstraction at the level of objects. Roughly speaking, if M is a term of type B (M and possibly B containing x), then $\lambda x{:}A.M$ is a term of type $\Pi x{:}A.B$. The Cube has two sorts $*$ (the set of types) and $\square$ (the set of kinds) with $* : \square$. If $A : *$ (resp. $A : \square$) we say A is a type (resp. a kind). All systems of the Cube have the same typing rules. What distinguishes one system from another however is the set $\boldsymbol{R}$ of pairs of sorts (s_1, s_2) allowed in the so-called *type-formation* or *Π-formation* rule, simply referred to as the rule (Π). Each system of the Cube has its own set $\boldsymbol{R}$ (which must contain $(*, *)$). A Π-type can only be formed in a specific system of the Cube if rule (Π) is satisfied for some (s_1, s_2) in the set $\boldsymbol{R}$ of that system. The rule (Π) is as follows:

$$(\Pi) \qquad \frac{\Gamma \vdash A : s_1 \qquad \Gamma, x{:}A \vdash B : s_2}{\Gamma \vdash (\Pi x{:}A.B) : s_2} \qquad (s_1, s_2) \in \boldsymbol{R}$$

Note that as there are only two sorts, $*$ and $\square$, and as each set $\boldsymbol{R}$ must contain $(*, *)$, there are only eight possible different systems of the Cube. With the rule (Π), an important aspect of the Cube is that it provides a factorisation of the expressive power of the Calculus of Constructions into three features: *polymorphism, type constructors*, and *dependent types*:

- $(*, *)$ is the basic rule that forms types. All type systems of the Cube have this rule.
- $(\square, *)$ is the rule that takes care of polymorphism. Girard's System (also known as $\lambda 2$) is the weakest system on the Cube that features this rule.
- $(\square, \square)$ takes care of type constructors. The system $\lambda\underline{\omega}$ is the weakest system on the Cube that features this rule.
- $(*, \square)$ takes care of term dependent types. The system λP is the weakest system on the Cube that features this rule.

Figures 1... 3 illustrate the various systems of the Cube.

Many other well-known type systems, like AUTOMATH [18], LF [11], and ML [17] can be more or less related to one of the systems of the Barendregt Cube. However, the relations between systems from "practice", and systems of the Cube are not always perfect. Here are some examples illustrating this point:

Example 1 (AUTOMATH) All the AUTOMATH systems have a relatively restricted typed λ-calculus. But they are more expressive than their λ-calculus suggests at first sight. This is due to a strong parameter mechanism. Even if one removes the typed λ-calculus from AUTOMATH, a quite expressive system "PAL", fully based on parameters, remains. See [18]. On the other hand, both AUT-68 and AUT-QE have been related to the Cube. But the corresponding Cube-systems are too weak to properly describe these AUTOMATH-systems (see below). We will be able to place both AUT-68 and AUT-QE on our refined Cube.

Example 2 (LF) The system LF (see [11]) is often described as the system λP of the Barendregt Cube. However, Geuvers [9] shows that the use of the Π-formation rule $(*, \Box)$ is very restricted in the practical use of LF. We will see that this use is in fact based on a parametric construct rather than on a Π-formation rule. Here again, we will be able to find a more precise position of LF on the Cube which will be the center of the line whose ends are $\lambda\!\rightarrow$ and λP.

Example 3 (ML) In ML (see [17]), types are written implicitly à la Curry. For example, instead of writing $\lambda x{:}A.B$, one writes $\lambda x.B$ and the type checker in ML looks for the type. It is well-known however from [4] that the implicit and explicit type schemes can be related. In any case, for the purposes of our paper, we only consider an explicit version of a subset of ML. Furthermore, we do not treat recursive types nor the Y combinator. In ML, one can define the polymorphic identity by:

$$\mathtt{Id}(\alpha{:}*) = (\lambda x{:}\alpha.x) : (\alpha \rightarrow \alpha). \tag{1}$$

But in ML, it is not possible to make an explicit λ-abstraction over $\alpha : *$ by:

$$\mathtt{Id} = (\lambda\alpha{:}*.\lambda x{:}\alpha.x) : (\Pi\alpha{:}*.\alpha \rightarrow \alpha) \tag{2}$$

Those familiar with ML know that the type $\Pi\alpha{:}*.\alpha \rightarrow \alpha$ does not belong to the language of ML and hence the λ-abstraction of equation (2) is not possible in ML. Therefore, we can state that ML does not have a Π-formation rule $(\Box, *)$. Nevertheless, it clearly has some parameter mechanism (α acting as parameter of `Id`) and hence ML has limited access to the rule $(\Box, *)$ enabling equation (1) to be defined. This means that ML's type system is none of those of the eight systems of the Cube. We will find a place for the type system of ML on our refined Cube. That place will be the intersection of the diagonals of the square (of the Barendregt Cube) whose corners are $\lambda\!\rightarrow$, $\lambda 2$, $\lambda\underline{\omega}$, and $\lambda\omega$ (cf. Figure 5).

The above examples show that the Barendregt Cube of [4] cannot accommodate well-known and practical type systems in a precise manner. In this paper, we refine the Barendregt Cube by extending it with a parameter mechanism. Such a mechanism allows the construction of terms of the form $c(b_1, \ldots, b_n)$ where c is a constant and $b_1, \ldots .b_n$ are terms. In traditional typed λ-calculus such a term would be written as $cb_1 \ldots b_n$. This last term is constructed step by step. First, c gets typed, then it is applied to b_1, then the result is applied to b_2, and so on. This means that c, cb_1, cb_1b_2, $\ldots$, $cb_1 \ldots b_n$ are all legal terms of the system. Hence, the attempt to internalise the parameter mechanism into typed λ-calculus as described above, is going too far. In the parametric situation, only $c(b_1, \ldots, b_n)$ is a term. Partial constructions of this term like $c(b_1, \ldots, b_i)$ (for $i < n$) are not a part of the syntax.

Adding parameters *is* an extension, and a useful one, since parametric constructs occur in many practical systems:

Example 4 As explained in Example 1, AUTOMATH has a parametric system.

Example 5 First-order predicate logic has no λ-calculus. It only has parametric constructs. In [15] it is shown that parametric constructs make it possible to give a description of first-order predicate logic in type theory that is much more accurate than the traditional approach in typed λ-calculus.

Example 6 Parameters occur in many parts of computer science. For example, look at the following Pascal fragment P with the function `double`:

```
function double(z : integer) : integer;
begin
  double := z + z
end;
```

P could be represented by the definition

$$\mathtt{double} = (\lambda \mathtt{z{:}Int}.(\mathtt{z}+\mathtt{z})) : (\mathtt{Int} \rightarrow \mathtt{Int}). \tag{3}$$

Of course, this declaration can imitate the behaviour of the function perfectly well. But the construction has the following disadvantages:

- The declaration has as subterm the type `Int` $\rightarrow$ `Int`. This subterm does not occur in P itself. More general, Pascal does not have a mechanism to construct types of the form $A \rightarrow B$. Hence, the representation contains terms that do not occur in Pascal;
- `double` itself is not a separate expression in Pascal: you can't write $x :=$ `double` in a program body. One may only use the expression `double` in a program, if one specifies a parameter p that serves as an argument of `double`.

We conclude that the translation of P as given above is not fully to the point. A parameter mechanism allows us to translate P in the parametric form

$$\mathtt{double}(z : \mathtt{Int}) = (z + z) : \mathtt{Int}. \tag{4}$$

This declaration in (4) does not have the disadvantages of (3) described above.

So for an optimal description of practical systems it may be an advantage to study the "mild" extension with parametric constructs only.

In Section 2, we give a short description of the Barendregt Cube. In Section 3, we extend the syntax of the Cube with parametric constructs, and propose types systems that can type these new constructs. In Section 4 we show that the proposed extension in fact leads to a refinement of the Barendregt Cube: it is split into eight smaller cubes. Section 5 places systems like LF, ML, and AUTOMATH in the Refined Barendregt Cube. We conclude in Section 6.

2 The Barendregt Cube

In this section we shortly repeat the definition of the systems in the Cube. For background information the reader may consult [4].

$\lambda{\to}$	$(*,*)$			
$\lambda 2$	$(*,*)$	$(\Box,*)$		
λP	$(*,*)$		$(*,\Box)$	
$\lambda\underline{\omega}$	$(*,*)$			$(\Box,\Box)$
$\lambda P2$	$(*,*)$	$(\Box,*)$	$(*,\Box)$	
$\lambda\omega$	$(*,*)$	$(\Box,*)$		$(\Box,\Box)$
$\lambda P\underline{\omega}$	$(*,*)$		$(*,\Box)$	$(\Box,\Box)$
λC	$(*,*)$	$(\Box,*)$	$(*,\Box)$	$(\Box,\Box)$

Fig. 1. Different type formation conditions

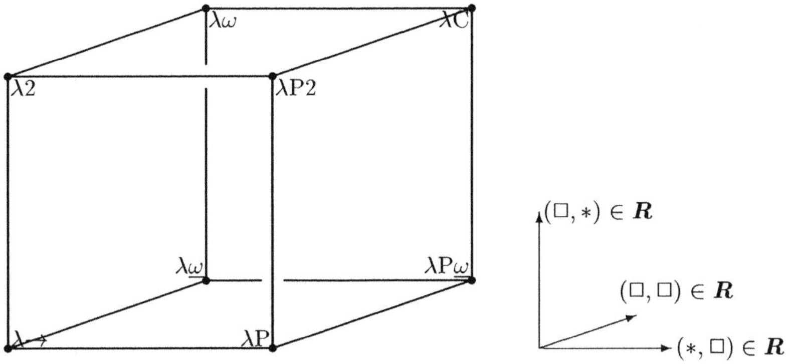

Fig. 2. The Barendregt Cube

System	Related system	Names, references
$\lambda{\to}$	λ^{τ}	simply typed λ-calculus; [7], [2] (Appendix A), [12] (Chapter 14)
$\lambda 2$	F	second order typed λ-calculus; [10], [20]
λP	AUT-QE	[6]
	LF	[11]
$\lambda P2$		[16]
$\lambda\underline{\omega}$	POLYREC	[19]
$\lambda\omega$	$F\omega$	[10]
λC	CC	Calculus of Constructions; [8]

Fig. 3. Systems of the Barendregt Cube

Definition 7 (Terms) Let $\mathcal{V}$ be a set of variables. The set $\mathcal{T}$ of terms is defined by the following abstract syntax: $\mathcal{T} ::= * \mid \Box \mid \mathcal{V} \mid \lambda\mathcal{V}{:}\mathcal{T}.\mathcal{T} \mid \Pi\mathcal{V}{:}\mathcal{T}.\mathcal{T} \mid \mathcal{T}\mathcal{T}$.

Definition 8 (Contexts) A context is a finite (and possibly empty) list $x_1 : A_1, \ldots, x_n : A_n$ (shorthand: $\vec{x}{:}\vec{A}$) of declarations of typed variables where x_i has type A_i. The set $\{x_1, \ldots, x_n\}$ of distinct variables is called the *domain* $\text{DOM}\left(\vec{x}{:}\vec{A}\right)$ of the context. The *empty context* is denoted $\langle\rangle$. We use Γ, Δ as meta-variables for contexts.

Definition 9 (Systems of the Barendregt Cube) Let $\mathbf{R}$ be a subset of $\{(*,*), (*,\Box), (\Box,*), (\Box,\Box)\}$ such that $(*,*) \in \mathbf{R}$. The type system $\lambda\mathbf{R}$ describes in which ways judgments $\Gamma \vdash_{\mathbf{R}} A : B$ (or $\Gamma \vdash A : B$, if it is clear which $\mathbf{R}$ is used) can be derived. $\Gamma \vdash A : B$ states that A has type B in context Γ. The typing rules are inductively defined as follows:

$$\text{(axiom)} \qquad \langle\rangle \vdash * : \Box$$

$$\text{(start)} \qquad \frac{\Gamma \vdash A : s}{\Gamma, x{:}A \vdash x : A} \qquad x \notin \text{DOM}(\Gamma)$$

$$\text{(weak)} \qquad \frac{\Gamma \vdash A : B \qquad \Gamma \vdash C : s}{\Gamma, x{:}C \vdash A : B} \qquad x \notin \text{DOM}(\Gamma)$$

$$(\Pi) \qquad \frac{\Gamma \vdash A : s_1 \qquad \Gamma, x{:}A \vdash B : s_2}{\Gamma \vdash (\Pi x{:}A.B) : s_2} \qquad (s_1, s_2) \in \boldsymbol{R}$$

$$(\lambda) \qquad \frac{\Gamma, x{:}A \vdash b : B \qquad \Gamma \vdash (\Pi x{:}A.B) : s}{\Gamma \vdash (\lambda x{:}A.b) : (\Pi x{:}A.B)}$$

$$\text{(appl)} \qquad \frac{\Gamma \vdash F : (\Pi x{:}A.B) \qquad \Gamma \vdash a : A}{\Gamma \vdash Fa : B[x{:=}a]}$$

$$\text{(conv)} \qquad \frac{\Gamma \vdash A : B \qquad \Gamma \vdash B' : s \qquad B =_\beta B'}{\Gamma \vdash A : B'}$$

There are eight different possibilities for $\mathbf{R}$ leading to the systems in Figure 1.

The dependencies between these systems can be depicted in the Barendregt Cube (see Figure 2). Furthermore, the systems in the Cube are related to other type systems as is shown in the overview of Figure 3 which is taken from [4].

3 Parameters

We extend the eight systems of the Barendregt Cube with parametric constructs. Parametric constructs are of the form $c(b_1, \ldots, b_n)$ where $b_1, \ldots, b_n$ are terms of certain prescribed types. Just as we can allow several kinds of Π-constructs (via the set $\mathbf{R}$) in the Barendregt Cube, we can also allow several kinds of parametric constructs. This is indicated by a set $\mathbf{P}$, consisting of tuples (s_1, s_2) where $s_1, s_2 \in \{*, \Box\}$. $(s_1, s_2) \in \mathbf{P}$ means that we allow parametric constructs $c(b_1, \ldots, b_n) : A$ where $b_1, \ldots, b_n$ have types $B_1, \ldots, B_n$ of sort s_1, and A is of type s_2. However, if both $(*, s_2) \in \mathbf{P}$ and $(\Box, s_2) \in \mathbf{P}$ then combinations of parameters are possible. For example, it is allowed that B_1 has type $*$, whilst B_2 has type $\Box$.

First we describe the extended syntax.

Definition 10 The set $\mathcal{T}_P$ of *parametric terms* is defined together with the set $\mathcal{L}_V$ of *lists of variables* and the set $\mathcal{L}_T$ of *lists of terms* as follows:

$$\mathcal{T}_P ::= \mathcal{V} \mid \boldsymbol{S} \mid \mathcal{C}(\mathcal{L}_T) \mid \mathcal{T}_P\mathcal{T}_P \mid \lambda\mathcal{V}{:}\mathcal{T}_P.\mathcal{T}_P \mid \Pi\mathcal{V}{:}\mathcal{T}_P.\mathcal{T}_P;$$
$$\mathcal{L}_T ::= \varnothing \mid \langle \mathcal{L}_T, \mathcal{T}_P \rangle.$$

where, as usual, $\mathcal{V}$ is a set of variables, $\mathcal{C}$ is a set of constants, and $\boldsymbol{S} = \{*, \Box\}$ is a set of sorts. Formally, lists of terms are of the form $\langle \dots \langle\langle \varnothing, A_1\rangle, A_2\rangle \dots A_n\rangle$. We usually write $\langle A_1, \dots, A_n\rangle$ or even $A_1, \dots, A_n$. In a parametric term of the form $c(b_1, \dots, b_n)$, the subterms $b_1, \dots, b_n$ are called the *parameters* of the term.

Let $\vec{x}{:}\vec{A}$ denote $x_1{:}A_1, \dots, x_n{:}A_n$. We extend the usual definition of $\mathrm{FV}(A)$, the set of *free variables* of a term A, to parametric terms:

$$\mathrm{FV}(c(a_1, \dots, a_n)) = \textstyle\bigcup_{i=1}^{n} \mathrm{FV}(a_i);$$

Convention 11 Names of bound variables and constants will always be chosen such that they differ from the free ones in a term.

Hence, we do not write $(\lambda \mathrm{x}{:}A.\mathrm{x})\mathrm{x}$ but $(\lambda \mathrm{y}{:}A.\mathrm{y})\mathrm{x}$.

We extend the definition of substitution of a term a for a variable x in a term b, $b[x{:=}a]$, to parametric terms, assuming that x is not a bound variable of either b or a:

$$c(b_1, \dots, b_n)[x{:=}a] \equiv c(b_1[x{:=}a], \dots, b_n[x{:=}a]);$$

Definition 12 Given the set of parametric terms, we define the set $\mathcal{C}_P$ of *parametric contexts* (which we denote by $\Gamma, \Gamma', \dots$) and the set $\mathcal{L}_D$ of *lists of variable declarations* as follows:

$$\mathcal{C}_P ::= \varnothing \mid \langle \mathcal{C}_P, \mathcal{V}{:}\mathcal{T}_P\rangle \mid \langle \mathcal{C}_P, \mathcal{C}(\mathcal{L}_V){:}\mathcal{T}_P\rangle$$
$$\mathcal{L}_D ::= \varnothing \mid \langle \mathcal{L}_D, \mathcal{V}{:}\mathcal{T}_P\rangle.$$

Notice that $\mathcal{L}_D \subseteq \mathcal{C}_P$: all lists of variable declarations are contexts, as well.

Now we extend the typing rules of the Cube as follows:

Definition 13 (The Barendregt Cube with parametric constants) Let $\mathbf{R}$ be as in Definition 9 and let $\mathbf{P}$ be a subset of $\{(*, *), (*, \Box), (\Box, *), (\Box, \Box)\}$, such that $(*, *) \in \mathbf{P}$. The judgments that are derivable in $\lambda\mathbf{RP}$ are determined by the rules for $\lambda\mathbf{R}$ of Definition 9 and the following two rules where $\Delta \equiv x_1{:}B_1, \dots, x_n{:}B_n$ and $\Delta_i \equiv x_1{:}B_1, \dots, x_{i-1}{:}B_{i-1}$:

$$(\vec{\mathbf{C}}\textbf{-weak}) \quad \frac{\Gamma \vdash b : B \qquad \Gamma, \Delta_i \vdash B_i : s_i \qquad \Gamma, \Delta \vdash A : s}{\Gamma, c(\Delta) : A \vdash b : B} \quad (s_i, s) \in \mathbf{P}$$

$$(\vec{\mathbf{C}}\textbf{-app}) \quad \frac{\begin{array}{ll} \Gamma_1, c(\Delta){:}A, \Gamma_2 \vdash b_i{:}B_i[x_j{:=}b_j]_{j=1}^{i-1} & (i = 1, \dots, n) \\ \Gamma_1, c(\Delta){:}A, \Gamma_2 \vdash A : s & (\text{if } n = 0) \end{array}}{\Gamma_1, c(\Delta){:}A, \Gamma_2 \vdash c(b_1, \dots, b_n) : A[x_j{:=}b_j]_{j=1}^{n}}$$

where the c that is introduced in the $\vec{\mathrm{C}}$-weakening rule is assumed to be Γ-fresh.

At first sight one might miss a $\vec{\mathrm{C}}$-introduction rule. Such a rule, however, is not necessary, as c (on its own) is not a term. c can only be (part of) a term in the form $c(b_1,\ldots,b_n)$, and such terms can be typed by the ($\vec{\mathrm{C}}$-app) rule.

Constant weakening ($\vec{\mathrm{C}}$-weak) explains how we can introduce a declaration of a parametric constant in the context. The context Δ indicates the arity of the parametric constants (the number of declarations in Δ), and of which type each parameter must be ($x_j : B_j$ in Δ means the j-th parameter must be of type B_j).

The extra condition $\Gamma_1, c(\Delta){:}A, \Gamma_2 \vdash A : s$ in the ($\vec{\mathrm{C}}$-app) for $n = 0$ is necessary to prevent an empty list of premises. Such an empty list of premises would make it possible to have almost arbitrary contexts in the conclusion. The extra condition is needed to assure that the context in the conclusion is a legal.

A term a is *legal* (with respect to a certain type system) if there are Γ, b such that either $\Gamma \vdash a : b$ or $\Gamma \vdash b : a$ is derivable (in that type system). Similarly, a context Γ is *legal* if there are a, b such that $\Gamma \vdash a : b$.

The parametric type system of Definition 13 has similar meta-theoretical properties as the systems of the Barendregt Cube. We list them below. The proofs are similar to those of the Barendregt Cube (see [14]).

Lemma 14 *Assume* $\Gamma \vdash b : B$. *Then* $\mathrm{DOM}(b), \mathrm{DOM}(B) \subseteq \mathrm{DOM}(\Gamma)$;

Lemma 15 (Generation Lemma)

1. *If* $\Gamma \vdash s : C$ *then* $s \equiv *$, $C =_\beta \square$ *and if* $C \not\equiv \square$ *then* $\Gamma \vdash C : s'$ *for some sort* s'.
2. *If* $\Gamma \vdash x : C$ *then there is* $s \in \boldsymbol{S}$ *and* $B =_\beta C$ *such that* $\Gamma \vdash B : s$ *and* $(x{:}B) \in \Gamma$;
3. *If* $\Gamma \vdash (\Pi x{:}A.B) : C$ *then there is* $(s_1, s_2) \in \boldsymbol{R}$ *such that* $\Gamma \vdash A : s_1$, $\Gamma, x{:}A \vdash B : s_2$ *and* $C =_\beta s_2$;
4. *If* $\Gamma \vdash (\lambda x{:}A.b) : C$ *then there is* $s \in \boldsymbol{S}$ *and* B *such that* $\Gamma \vdash (\Pi x{:}A.B) : s$; $\Gamma, x{:}A \vdash b : B$; *and* $C =_\beta (\Pi x{:}A.B)$;
5. *If* $\Gamma \vdash Fa : C$ *then there are* A, B *such that* $\Gamma \vdash F : (\Pi x{:}A.B)$, $\Gamma \vdash a : A$ *and* $C =_\beta B[x{:=}a]$.
6. *If* $\Gamma \vdash c(b_1,\ldots,b_n) : D$ *then there exist* s, $\Delta \equiv x_1 : B_1, \ldots, x_n : B_n$ *and* A *such that* $\Gamma \vdash D =_\beta A[x_j{:=}b_j]_{j=1}^{n}$, *and* $\Gamma \vdash b_i{:}B_i[x_j{:=}b_j]_{j=1}^{i-1}$. *Moreover,* $\Gamma \equiv \Gamma_1, c(\Delta) : A, \Gamma_2$ *and* $\Gamma_1, \Delta \vdash A : s$. *Finally, there are* $s_i \in S$ *such that* $\Gamma, \Delta_i \vdash B_i : s_i$ *and* $(s_i, s) \in \mathbf{P}$.

Lemma 16 (Correctness of Types) *If* $\Gamma \vdash A : B$ *then* $B \equiv s$ *or* $\Gamma \vdash B : s$ *for some* $s \in \boldsymbol{S}$.

Lemma 17 (Subterm Lemma) *If* A *is legal and* B *is a subterm of* A, *then* B *is legal.*

Lemma 18 (Subject Reduction) *If* $\Gamma \vdash A : B$ *and* $A \to_\beta A'$ *then* $\Gamma \vdash A' : B$.

Lemma 19 (Unicity of Types) *If $\Gamma \vdash A : B_1$ and $\Gamma \vdash A : B_2$, then $B_1 =_\beta B_2$.*

Theorem 20 (Strong Normalisation) *If $\Gamma \vdash A : B$ then A and B are β-strongly normalising, that is: any β-reduction path of A or B is finite.*

4 The Refined Barendregt Cube

The systems of Definition 13 have six degrees of freedom: three for the possible choices of $(*, \Box)$, $(\Box, *)$ and $(\Box, \Box) \in \mathbf{R}$ and three for the possible choices of $(*, \Box)$, $(\Box, *)$, and $(\Box, \Box) \in \mathbf{P}$. However, these choices are not independent since constructs that can be made with **P**-rule (s_1, s_2) can be imitated in a typed λ-calculus with **R**-rule (s_1, s_2). This means that the parameter-free type system with $\mathbf{R} = \{(*, *), (*, \Box)\}$ is at least as strong as the type system with parameters with the same set **R**, but with $\mathbf{P} = \{(*, *), (*, \Box)\}$. We make this precise in Theorem 26.

The insight of Theorem 26 can be expressed by depicting the systems with parameters of Definition 13 as a *refinement* of the Barendregt Cube. As in the Barendregt Cube, we start with the system $\lambda\!\rightarrow$, which has $\mathbf{R} = \{(*, *)\}$ and $\mathbf{P} = \{(*, *)\}$. Adding an extra element (s_1, s_2) to **R** still corresponds to moving in one dimension in the Cube. Now we add the possibility of moving in one dimension in the Cube but stopping half-way. We let this movement correspond to extending **P** with (s_1, s_2). This "going only half-way" is in line with the intuition that Π-formation with (s_1, s_2) can imitate the construction of a parametric construct with (s_1, s_2). In other words, the system obtained by "going all the way" is at least as strong as the system obtained by "going only half-way".

The refinement of the Barendregt Cube is depicted in Figure 4. We now make the above intuition that "**R** can imitate **P**" precise.

Definition 21 Consider the system $\lambda\mathbf{RP}$. We call this system *parametrically conservative* if $(s_1, s_2) \in \boldsymbol{P}$ implies $(s_1, s_2) \in \boldsymbol{R}$.

Let $\lambda\mathbf{RP}$ be parametrically conservative. In order to show that the parameter-free system $\lambda\mathbf{R}$ is at least as powerful as $\lambda\mathbf{RP}$, we need to remove the parameters from the syntax of $\lambda\mathbf{RP}$. To do so, we replace the parametric application in a term $c(b_1, \ldots, b_n)$ by function application $cb_1, \ldots, b_n$:

Definition 22 Define the parameter-free translation $\{t\}$ of a term $t \in \mathcal{T}_P$ by:

$$\begin{aligned} \{a\} &\equiv a \quad \text{if } a \equiv x \text{ or } a \equiv s; \\ \{c(b_1, \ldots, b_n)\} &\equiv c\,\{b_1\} \cdots \{b_n\}\,; \\ \{ab\} &\equiv \{a\}\,\{b\}\,; \\ \{\mathcal{O}x{:}A.B\} &\equiv \mathcal{O}x{:}\,\{A\}\,.\,\{B\} \quad \text{if } \mathcal{O} \text{ is } \lambda \text{ or } \Pi \end{aligned}$$

Definition 23 We extend the definition of $\{\_\}$ to contexts:

$$\begin{aligned} \{\langle\rangle\} &\equiv \langle\rangle; \\ \{\Gamma, x{:}A\} &\equiv \{\Gamma\}\,, x{:}\,\{A\}\,; \\ \{\Gamma, c(\Delta){:}A\} &\equiv \{\Gamma\}\,, c(){:}\,\{\textstyle\prod \Delta.A\}\,. \end{aligned}$$

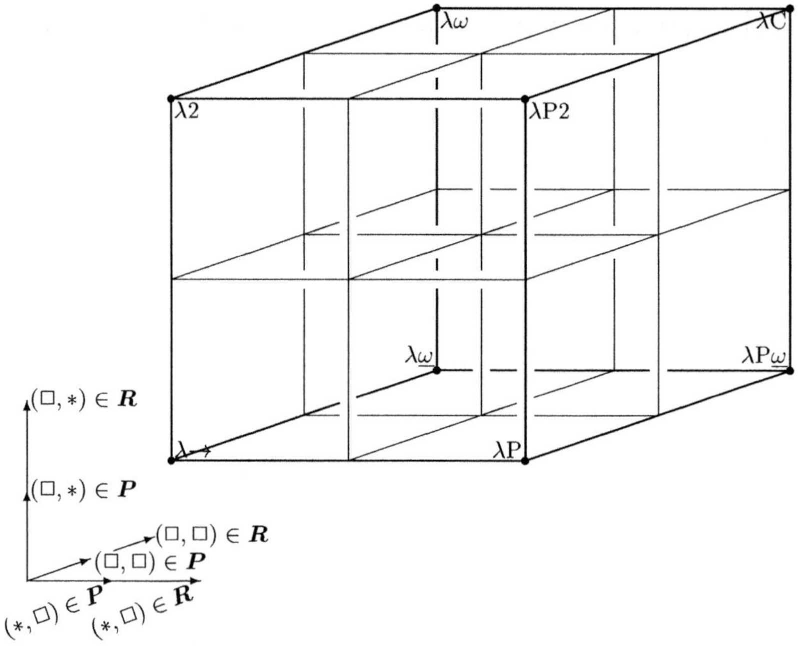

Fig. 4. The refined Barendregt Cube

Here, $\Delta \equiv x_1 : B_1, \dots, x_n : B_n$, and $\prod \Delta.A$ is shorthand for $\prod_{i=1}^{n} x_n : B_i.A$.

To demonstrate the behaviour of $\{\_\}$ under β-reduction, we need a lemma that shows how to manipulate with substitutions and $\{\_\}$. The proof is straightforward, using induction on the structure of a.

Lemma 24 *For* $a, b \in \mathcal{T}_{\mathbf{P}}$: $\{a[x{:=}b]\} \equiv \{a\}\,[x{:=}\,\{b\}]$. ⊠

The mapping $\{\_\}$ maintains β-reduction:

Lemma 25 $a \rightarrow_\beta a'$ *if and only if* $\{a\} \rightarrow_\beta \{a'\}$.

PROOF: Follows easily by induction on the structure of a, and Lemma 24. ⊠

Now we show that $\{\_\}$ embeds the parametrically conservative $\lambda\mathbf{RP}$ in the parameter-free $\lambda\mathbf{R}$:

Theorem 26 *Let* $\lambda\mathbf{RP}$ *be parametrically conservative. If* $\Gamma \vdash_{\mathbf{RP}} a : A$ *then* $\{\Gamma\} \vdash_{\mathbf{R}} \{a\} : \{A\}$.

PROOF: Induction on the derivation of $\Gamma \vdash_{\mathbf{RP}} a : A$. By Lemma 24, all cases are easy except for ($\vec{\mathrm{C}}$-weak). So: assume the last step of the derivation was

$$\frac{\Gamma \vdash_{\mathbf{RP}} b : B \qquad \Gamma, \Delta_i \vdash_{\mathbf{RP}} B_i : s_i \qquad \Gamma, \Delta \vdash_{\mathbf{RP}} A : s}{\Gamma, c(\Delta){:}A \vdash_{\mathbf{RP}} b : B} \qquad (s_i, s) \in \boldsymbol{P}.$$

By the induction hypothesis, we have:

$$\{\Gamma\} \vdash_{\mathbf{R}} \{b\} : \{B\}; \tag{5}$$

$$\{\Gamma, \Delta_i\} \vdash_{\mathbf{R}} \{B_i\} : s_i; \tag{6}$$

$$\{\Gamma, \Delta\} \vdash_{\mathbf{R}} \{A\} : s. \tag{7}$$

λ**RP** is parametrically conservative, so $(s_i, s) \in \boldsymbol{R}$ for $i = 1, \ldots, n$. Therefore, we can repeatedly use the Π-formation rule, starting with (7) and (6), obtaining

$$\{\Gamma\} \vdash_{\mathbf{R}} \textstyle\prod_{i=1}^{n} x_i{:}\, \{B_i\} \,.\, \{A\} : s. \tag{8}$$

Notice that $\prod_{i=1}^{n} x_i{:}\, \{B_i\} \,.\, \{A\} \equiv \{\prod \Delta.A\}$. Using ($\vec{\mathrm{C}}$-weak) on (5) and (8) gives

$$\{\Gamma\}, c(){:}\, \{\textstyle\prod \Delta.A\} \vdash_{\mathbf{R}} \{b\} : \{B\}\,. \qquad \boxtimes$$

5 Systems in the Refined Barendregt Cube

In this section, we show that the Refined Barendregt Cube enables us to compare some well-known type systems with systems from the Barendregt Cube. In particular, we show that AUT-68, and AUT-QE, LF, and ML, can be seen as systems in the Refined Barendregt Cube. This is depicted in Figure 5 on page 14, and motivated in the three subsections below.

5.1 AUTOMATH

The AUTOMATH-systems (see [18]) all heavily rely on parametric constructs.
1) AUT-68: The typed λ-calculus of one of the most elementary systems of AUTOMATH, AUT-68, is relatively simple and corresponds to $\lambda\!\!\rightarrow$: it has only $(*, *)$ as a Π-formation rule. This should suggest that AUT-68 has comparable expressiveness $\lambda\!\!\rightarrow$. But for the parametrical constructions there are no limitations in AUT-68 whose parameter mechanism has the following features:

- A line $(\Gamma; k; \mathrm{PN}; \mathtt{type})$ in a book is nothing more that the declaration of a parametric constant $k(\Gamma){:}*$. There are no demands on the context Γ, and this means that for a declaration $x{:}A \in \Gamma$ we can have either $A \equiv \mathtt{type}$ (in Cube-terminology: $A \equiv *$, so $A : \Box$) or $A{:}\mathtt{type}$ (in Cube-terminology: $A : *$). We conclude that AUT-68 has the parameter rules $(*, \Box)$ and $(\Box, \Box)$;
- Similarly, lines of the form $(\Gamma; k; \mathrm{PN}; \Sigma_2)$ where $\Sigma_2{:}\mathtt{type}$, represent parametric constants that are constructed using the parameter rules $(*, *)$ and $(\Box, *)$.

This suggests that AUT-68 can be represented by the parametric system with $\mathbf{R} = \{(*, *)\}$ and $\mathbf{P} = \{*, \Box\} \times \{*, \Box\}$. The AUT-68 system can be found in the exact middle of the refined Barendregt Cube.

2) AUT-QE: Something similar holds for the more extensive system AUT-QE. This system has an extra Π-formation rule: $(*, \Box)$ additionally to the rules of

AUT-68. This means that for representing this system, we need the Π-formation rules $\mathbf{R} = \{(*,*),(*,\Box)\}$, and parametric rules (s_1, s_2) for $s_1, s_2 \in \{*,\Box\}$. This system is located in the middle of the right side of the Refined Barendregt Cube, exactly in between λC and λP.

3) PAL: It should be noted that the AUTOMATH languages are all based on two concepts: typed λ-calculus and a parameter/definition mechanism. Both concepts can be isolated: it is possible to study λ-calculus without a parameter/definition mechanism (for instance via the format of Pure Type Systems or the Barendregt Cube of [4]), but one can also isolate the parameter/definition mechanism from AUTOMATH. One then obtains a language that is called PAL, the "Primitive AUTOMATH Language". It cannot be described within the Refined Barendregt Cube (as all the systems in that cube have at least some basic λ-calculus in it), but it can be described as a system with the following parametric specification: $\boldsymbol{R} = \varnothing$; $\boldsymbol{P} = \{(*,*),(*,\Box),(\Box,*),(\Box,\Box)\}$.

This parametric specification corresponds to the parametric specifications that were given for the AUTOMATH systems above, from which the Π-formation rules are removed.

5.2 LF

Geuvers [9] initially describes the system LF (see [11]) as the system λP of the Cube. However, the use of the Π-formation rule $(*,\Box)$ is quite restrictive in most applications of LF. Geuvers splits the λ-formation rule in two:

$$(\lambda_0)\frac{\Gamma, x{:}A \vdash M : B \qquad \Gamma \vdash \Pi x{:}A.B : *}{\Gamma \vdash \lambda_0 x{:}A.M : \Pi x{:}A.B};$$

$$(\lambda_P)\frac{\Gamma, x{:}A \vdash M : B \qquad \Gamma \vdash \Pi x{:}A.B : \Box}{\Gamma \vdash \lambda_P x{:}A.M : \Pi x{:}A.B}.$$

System LF without rule (λ_P) is called LF^-. β-reduction is split into β_0-reduction and β_P-reduction:

$$(\lambda_0 x{:}A.M)N \to_{\beta_0} M[x{:=}N];$$

$$(\lambda_P x{:}A.M)N \to_{\beta_P} M[x{:=}N].$$

Geuvers then shows that

- If $M : *$ or $M : A : *$ in LF, then the β_P-normal form of M contains no λ_P;
- If $\Gamma \vdash_{\mathrm{LF}} M : A$, and Γ, M, A do not contain a λ_P, then $\Gamma \vdash_{\mathrm{LF}^-} M : A$;
- If $\Gamma \vdash M : A(:*)$, all in β_P-normal form, then $\Gamma \vdash_{\mathrm{LF}^-} M : A(:*)$.

This means that the only real need for a type $\Pi x{:}A.B : \Box$ is to be able to declare a variable in it. The only point at which this is really done is where the bool-style implementation of the Propositions-As-Types principle PAT is made: the construction of the type of the operator Prf (in an unparameterised form) has to be made as follows:

$$\frac{\mathtt{prop}{:}* \vdash \mathtt{prop}: * \qquad \mathtt{prop}{:}*, \alpha{:}\mathtt{prop} \vdash *{:}\Box}{\mathtt{prop}{:}* \vdash (\Pi\alpha{:}\mathtt{prop}.*) : \Box}.$$

In the practical use of LF, this is the only point where the Π-formation rule $(*,\Box)$ is used. No λ_P-abstractions are used, either, and the term Prf is only used when it is applied to a term p:`prop`. This means that the practical use of LF would not be restricted if we introduced Prf in a parametric form, and replaced the Π-formation rule $(*,\Box)$ by a parameter rule $(*,\Box)$. This puts (the practical applications of) LF in between the systems $\lambda\!\to$ and λP in the Refined Barendregt Cube.

5.3 ML

In ML (cf. [17]) one can define the polymorphic identity by (we use the notation of this paper, whereas in ML, the types and the parameters are left implicit):

$$\mathtt{Id}(\alpha{:}*) = (\lambda\mathtt{x}{:}\alpha.\mathtt{x}) : (\alpha \to \alpha).$$

But we cannot make an explicit λ-abstraction over $\alpha{:}*$. That is, the expression

$$\mathtt{Id} = (\lambda\alpha{:}*.\lambda x{:}\alpha.x) : (\Pi\alpha{:}*.\alpha \to \alpha)$$

cannot be constructed in ML, as the type $\Pi\alpha{:}*.\alpha \to \alpha$ does not belong to the language of ML. Therefore, we can state that ML does not have a Π-formation rule $(\Box,*)$, but that it does have the parametric rule $(\Box,*)$.

Similarly, one can introduce the type of lists and some operations by:
$\mathtt{List}(\alpha{:}*) : *$;
$\mathtt{nil}(\alpha{:}*) \ : \mathtt{List}(\alpha)$;
$\mathtt{cons}(\alpha{:}*) : \alpha \to \mathtt{List}(\alpha) \to \mathtt{List}(\alpha)$,
but the expression $\Pi\alpha{:}*.*$ does not belong to ML, so introducing `List` by

$$\mathtt{List} : \Pi\alpha{:}*.*$$

is not possible in ML. We conclude that ML does not have a Π-formation rule $(\Box,\Box)$, but only the parametric rule $(\Box,\Box)$. Together with the fact that ML has a Π-formation rule $(*,*)$, this places ML in the middle of the left side of the refined Barendregt Cube, exactly in between $\lambda\!\to$ and $\lambda\omega$.

6 Conclusion

In this paper, we observed that many existing type systems do not fit exactly in the Barendregt Cube. In particular, we explained that previous attempts to describe LF and AUTOMATH were not very successfull. We noted that AUTOMATH uses parameters heavily, and that there are some types that are only used in special situations by LF and that those types and situations could be covered by parameters. In addition, we considered an explicitly typed version of ML and noted that there too, ML cannot occupy any of the corners of the cube. The reason being that, ML (as well as LF and AUTOMATH) allows Π-types, but not all of them. In any corner of the Cube, as soon as an abstraction of a sort is allowed, all abstractions of that sort are allowed too.

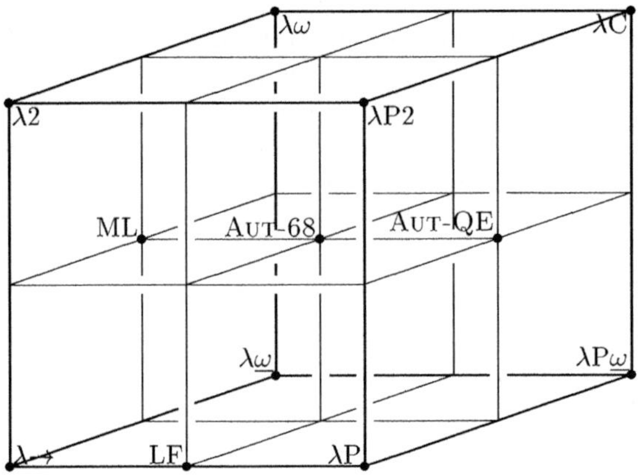

Fig. 5. LF, ML, Aut-68, and Aut-QE in the refined Barendregt Cube

Our above reasoning led us to propose a refinement of the Cube where not only the eight corners can be inhabited, but also points half way between these corners. This way, Automath, LF, and ML find more accurate locations on the Cube to represent their typing systems. We described an extension of the Barendregt Cube with parameters. This is more a *refinement* than an *extension*, as new systems that are introduced can be depicted by dividing the traditional Barendregt Cube into eight sub-cubes. This is due to the fact that parametric constructs can be imitated by constructions of typed λ-calculus (see Theorem 26) but not the other way around.

We showed that our refinement makes it possible to:

- Give a better description of practical type systems like LF and ML than the systems in the usual Cube.
- Position systems that could not be placed in the usual Cube (several Automath-systems).

This makes it possible to give a more detailed comparison between the expressiveness of several type systems.

Not only can we add parameters to the Barendregt Cube resulting in an elegant and more refined hierarchy of systems, but we can follow a similar construction to the more generalised notion of Pure Type Systems (PTSs) (see [4]). In addition, we can add definitions (see [5, 22]) and parametric definitions to our above refinement of the Cube and even to the refinements of PTSs, giving a very general hierarchy that can express more precisely and elegantly many practical systems and that give a full description of Automath.

References

1. S. Abramsky, Dov M. Gabbay, and T.S.E. Maibaum, editors. *Handbook of Logic in Computer Science, Volume 2: Background: Computational Structures.* Oxford

University Press, 1992.
2. H.P. Barendregt. *The Lambda Calculus: its Syntax and Semantics.* Studies in Logic and the Foundations of Mathematics **103**. North-Holland, Amsterdam, revised edition, 1984.
3. H.P. Barendregt. Introduction to generalised type systems. *Functional Programming*, 1:125–154, 1991.
4. H.P. Barendregt. Lambda calculi with types. In [1], pages 117–309. Oxford University Press, 1992.
5. R. Bloo, F. Kamareddine, and R. P. Nederpelt. The Barendregt Cube with Definitions and Generalised Reduction. *Information and Computation*, 126 (2):123–143, 1996.
6. N.G. de Bruijn. The mathematical language AUTOMATH, its usage and some of its extensions. In M. Laudet, D. Lacombe, and M. Schuetzenberger, editors, *Symposium on Automatic Demonstration*, pages 29–61, IRIA, Versailles, 1968. Springer Verlag, Berlin, 1970. Lecture Notes in Mathematics **125**; also in [18], pages 73–100.
7. A. Church. A formulation of the simple theory of types. *The Journal of Symbolic Logic*, 5:56–68, 1940.
8. T. Coquand and G. Huet. The calculus of constructions. *Information and Computation*, 76:95–120, 1988.
9. J.H. Geuvers. *Logics and Type Systems.* PhD thesis, Catholic University of Nijmegen, 1993.
10. J.-Y. Girard. *Interprétation fonctionelle et élimination des coupures dans l'arithmétique d'ordre supérieur.* PhD thesis, Université Paris VII, 1972.
11. R. Harper, F. Honsell, and G. Plotkin. A framework for defining logics. In *Proceedings Second Symposium on Logic in Computer Science*, pages 194–204, Washington D.C., 1987. IEEE.
12. J.R. Hindley and J.P. Seldin. *Introduction to Combinators and λ-calculus*, volume 1 of *London Mathematical Society Student Texts.* Cambridge University Press, 1986.
13. W.A. Howard. The formulas-as-types notion of construction. In [21], pages 479–490, 1980.
14. T. Laan. *The Evolution of Type Theory in Logic and Mathematics.* PhD thesis, Eindhoven University of Technology, 1997.
15. Twan Laan and Michael Franssen. Parameters for first order logic. *Logic and Computation*, 2001.
16. G. Longo and E. Moggi. Constructive natural deduction and its modest interpretation. Technical Report CMU-CS-88-131, Carnegie Mellono University, Pittsburgh, USA, 1988.
17. R. Milner, M. Tofte, and R. Harper. *Definition of Standard ML.* MIT Press, Cambridge (Massachusetts)/London, 1990.
18. R.P. Nederpelt, J.H. Geuvers, and R.C. de Vrijer, editors. *Selected Papers on Automath.* Studies in Logic and the Foundations of Mathematics **133**. North-Holland, Amsterdam, 1994.
19. G.R. Renardel de Lavalette. Strictness analysis via abstract interpretation for recursively defined types. *Information and Computation*, 99:154–177, 1991.
20. J.C. Reynolds. *Towards a theory of type structure*, volume 19 of *Lecture Notes in Computer Science*, pages 408–425. Springer, 1974.
21. J.P. Seldin and J.R. Hindley, editors. *To H.B. Curry: Essays on Combinatory Logic, Lambda Calculus and Formalism.* Academic Press, New York, 1980.
22. P. Severi and E. Poll. Pure type systems with definitions. In A. Nerode and Yu.V. Matiyasevich, editors, *Proceedings of LFCS'94 (LNCS **813**)*, pages 316–328, New York, 1994. LFCS'94, St. Petersburg, Russia, Springer Verlag.

Author Index

Lecture Notes in Computer Science

For information about Vols. 1–1920
please contact your bookseller or Springer-Verlag

Vol. 1921: S.W. Liddle, H.C. Mayr, B. Thalheim (Eds.), Conceptual Modeling for E-Business and the Web. Proceedings, 2000. X, 179 pages. 2000.

Vol. 1922: J. Crowcroft, J. Roberts, M.I. Smirnov (Eds.), Quality of Future Internet Services. Proceedings, 2000. XI, 368 pages. 2000.

Vol. 1923: J. Borbinha, T. Baker (Eds.), Research and Advanced Technology for Digital Libraries. Proceedings, 2000. XVII, 513 pages. 2000.

Vol. 1924: W. Taha (Ed.), Semantics, Applications, and Implementation of Program Generation. Proceedings, 2000. VIII, 231 pages. 2000.

Vol. 1925: J. Cussens, S. Džeroski (Eds.), Learning Language in Logic. X, 301 pages 2000. (Subseries LNAI).

Vol. 1926: M. Joseph (Ed.), Formal Techniques in Real-Time and Fault-Tolerant Systems. Proceedings, 2000. X, 305 pages. 2000.

Vol. 1927: P. Thomas, H.W. Gellersen, (Eds.), Handheld and Ubiquitous Computing. Proceedings, 2000. X, 249 pages. 2000.

Vol. 1928: U. Brandes, D. Wagner (Eds.), Graph-Theoretic Concepts in Computer Science. Proceedings, 2000. X, 315 pages. 2000.

Vol. 1929: R. Laurini (Ed.), Advances in Visual Information Systems. Proceedings, 2000. XII, 542 pages. 2000.

Vol. 1931: E. Horlait (Ed.), Mobile Agents for Telecommunication Applications. Proceedings, 2000. IX, 271 pages. 2000.

Vol. 1658: J. Baumann, Mobile Agents: Control Algorithms. XIX, 161 pages. 2000.

Vol. 1756: G. Ruhe, F. Bomarius (Eds.), Learning Software Organization. Proceedings, 1999. VIII, 226 pages. 2000.

Vol. 1766: M. Jazayeri, R.G.K. Loos, D.R. Musser (Eds.), Generic Programming. Proceedings, 1998. X, 269 pages. 2000.

Vol. 1791: D. Fensel, Problem-Solving Methods. XII, 153 pages. 2000. (Subseries LNAI).

Vol. 1799: K. Czarnecki, U.W. Eisenecker, Generative and Component-Based Software Engineering. Proceedings, 1999. VIII, 225 pages. 2000.

Vol. 1812: J. Wyatt, J. Demiris (Eds.), Advances in Robot Learning. Proceedings, 1999. VII, 165 pages. 2000. (Subseries LNAI).

Vol. 1932: Z.W. Raś, S. Ohsuga (Eds.), Foundations of Intelligent Systems. Proceedings, 2000. XII, 646 pages. (Subseries LNAI).

Vol. 1933: R.W. Brause, E. Hanisch (Eds.), Medical Data Analysis. Proceedings, 2000. XI, 316 pages. 2000.

Vol. 1934: J.S. White (Ed.), Envisioning Machine Translation in the Information Future. Proceedings, 2000. XV, 254 pages. 2000. (Subseries LNAI).

Vol. 1935: S.L. Delp, A.M. DiGioia, B. Jaramaz (Eds.), Medical Image Computing and Computer-Assisted Intervention – MICCAI 2000. Proceedings, 2000. XXV, 1250 pages. 2000.

Vol. 1936: P. Robertson, H. Shrobe, R. Laddaga (Eds.), Self-Adaptive Software. Proceedings, 2000. VIII, 249 pages. 2001.

Vol. 1937: R. Dieng, O. Corby (Eds.), Knowledge Engineering and Knowledge Management. Proceedings, 2000. XIII, 457 pages. 2000. (Subseries LNAI).

Vol. 1938: S. Rao, K.I. Sletta (Eds.), Next Generation Networks. Proceedings, 2000. XI, 392 pages. 2000.

Vol. 1939: A. Evans, S. Kent, B. Selic (Eds.), «UML» – The Unified Modeling Language. Proceedings, 2000. XIV, 572 pages. 2000.

Vol. 1940: M. Valero, K. Joe, M. Kitsuregawa, H. Tanaka (Eds.), High Performance Computing. Proceedings, 2000. XV, 595 pages. 2000.

Vol. 1941: A.K. Chhabra, D. Dori (Eds.), Graphics Recognition. Proceedings, 1999. XI, 346 pages. 2000.

Vol. 1942: H. Yasuda (Ed.), Active Networks. Proceedings, 2000. XI, 424 pages. 2000.

Vol. 1943: F. Koornneef, M. van der Meulen (Eds.), Computer Safety, Reliability and Security. Proceedings, 2000. X, 432 pages. 2000.

Vol. 1944: K.R. Dittrich, G. Guerrini, I. Merlo, M. Oliva, M.E. Rodriguez (Eds.), Objects and Databases. Proceedings, 2000. X, 199 pages. 2001.

Vol. 1945: W. Grieskamp, T. Santen, B. Stoddart (Eds.), Integrated Formal Methods. Proceedings, 2000. X, 441 pages. 2000.

Vol. 1946: P. Palanque, F. Paternò (Eds.), Interactive Systems. Proceedings, 2000. X, 251 pages. 2001.

Vol. 1947: T. Sørevik, F. Manne, R. Moe, A.H. Gebremedhin (Eds.), Applied Parallel Computing. Proceedings, 2000. XII, 400 pages. 2001.

Vol. 1948: T. Tan, Y. Shi, W. Gao (Eds.), Advances in Multimodal Interfaces – ICMI 2000. Proceedings, 2000. XVI, 678 pages. 2000.

Vol. 1949: R. Connor, A. Mendelzon (Eds.), Research Issues in Structured and Semistructured Database Programming. Proceedings, 1999. XII, 325 pages. 2000.

Vol. 1950: D. van Melkebeek, Randomness and Completeness in Computational Complexity. XV, 196 pages. 2000.

Vol. 1951: F. van der Linden (Ed.), Software Architectures for Product Families. Proceedings, 2000. VIII, 255 pages. 2000.

Vol. 1952: M.C. Monard, J. Simão Sichman (Eds.), Advances in Artificial Intelligence. Proceedings, 2000. XV, 498 pages. 2000. (Subseries LNAI).

Vol. 1953: G. Borgefors, I. Nyström, G. Sanniti di Baja (Eds.), Discrete Geometry for Computer Imagery. Proceedings, 2000. XI, 544 pages. 2000.

Vol. 1954: W.A. Hunt, Jr., S.D. Johnson (Eds.), Formal Methods in Computer-Aided Design. Proceedings, 2000. XI, 539 pages. 2000.

Vol. 1955: M. Parigot, A. Voronkov (Eds.), Logic for Programming and Automated Reasoning. Proceedings, 2000. XIII, 487 pages. 2000. (Subseries LNAI).

Vol. 1956: T. Coquand, P. Dybjer, B. Nordström, J. Smith (Eds.), Types for Proofs and Programs. Proceedings, 1999. VII, 195 pages. 2000.

Vol. 1957: P. Ciancarini, M. Wooldridge (Eds.), Agent-Oriented Software Engineering. Proceedings, 2000. X, 323 pages. 2001.

Vol. 1960: A. Ambler, S.B. Calo, G. Kar (Eds.), Services Management in Intelligent Networks. Proceedings, 2000. X, 259 pages. 2000.

Vol. 1961: J. He, M. Sato (Eds.), Advances in Computing Science – ASIAN 2000. Proceedings, 2000. X, 299 pages. 2000.

Vol. 1963: V. Hlaváč, K.G. Jeffery, J. Wiedermann (Eds.), SOFSEM 2000: Theory and Practice of Informatics. Proceedings, 2000. XI, 460 pages. 2000.

Vol. 1964: J. Malenfant, S. Moisan, A. Moreira (Eds.), Object-Oriented Technology. Proceedings, 2000. XI, 309 pages. 2000.

Vol. 1965: Ç. K. Koç, C. Paar (Eds.), Cryptographic Hardware and Embedded Systems – CHES 2000. Proceedings, 2000. XI, 355 pages. 2000.

Vol. 1966: S. Bhalla (Ed.), Databases in Networked Information Systems. Proceedings, 2000. VIII, 247 pages. 2000.

Vol. 1967: S. Arikawa, S. Morishita (Eds.), Discovery Science. Proceedings, 2000. XII, 332 pages. 2000. (Subseries LNAI).

Vol. 1968: H. Arimura, S. Jain, A. Sharma (Eds.), Algorithmic Learning Theory. Proceedings, 2000. XI, 335 pages. 2000. (Subseries LNAI).

Vol. 1969: D.T. Lee, S.-H. Teng (Eds.), Algorithms and Computation. Proceedings, 2000. XIV, 578 pages. 2000.

Vol. 1970: M. Valero, V.K. Prasanna, S. Vajapeyam (Eds.), High Performance Computing – HiPC 2000. Proceedings, 2000. XVIII, 568 pages. 2000.

Vol. 1971: R. Buyya, M. Baker (Eds.), Grid Computing – GRID 2000. Proceedings, 2000. XIV, 229 pages. 2000.

Vol. 1972: A. Omicini, R. Tolksdorf, F. Zambonelli (Eds.), Engineering Societies in the Agents World. Proceedings, 2000. IX, 143 pages. 2000. (Subseries LNAI).

Vol. 1973: J. Van den Bussche, V. Vianu (Eds.), Database Theory – ICDT 2001. Proceedings, 2001. X, 451 pages. 2001.

Vol. 1974: S. Kapoor, S. Prasad (Eds.), FST TCS 2000: Foundations of Software Technology and Theoretical Computer Science. Proceedings, 2000. XIII, 532 pages. 2000.

Vol. 1975: J. Pieprzyk, E. Okamoto, J. Seberry (Eds.), Information Security. Proceedings, 2000. X, 323 pages. 2000.

Vol. 1976: T. Okamoto (Ed.), Advances in Cryptology – ASIACRYPT 2000. Proceedings, 2000. XII, 630 pages. 2000.

Vol. 1977: B. Roy, E. Okamoto (Eds.), Progress in Cryptology – INDOCRYPT 2000. Proceedings, 2000. X, 295 pages. 2000.

Vol. 1978: B. Schneier (Ed.), Fast Software Encryption. Proceedings, 2000. VIII, 315 pages. 2001.

Vol. 1979: S. Moss, P. Davidsson (Eds.), Multi-Agent-Based Simulation. Proceedings, 2000. VIII, 267 pages. 2001. (Subseries LNAI).

Vol. 1983: K.S. Leung, L.-W. Chan, H. Meng (Eds.), Intelligent Data Engineering and Automated Learning – IDEAL 2000. Proceedings, 2000. XVI, 573 pages. 2000.

Vol. 1984: J. Marks (Ed.), Graph Drawing. Proceedings, 2001. XII, 419 pages. 2001.

Vol. 1987: K.-L. Tan, M.J. Franklin, J. C.-S. Lui (Eds.), Mobile Data Management. Proceedings, 2001. XIII, 289 pages. 2001.

Vol. 1989: M. Ajmone Marsan, A. Bianco (Eds.), Quality of Service in Multiservice IP Networks. Proceedings, 2001. XII, 440 pages. 2001.

Vol. 1991: F. Dignum, C. Sierra (Eds.), Agent Mediated Electronic Commerce. VIII, 241 pages. 2001. (Subseries LNAI).

Vol. 1992: K. Kim (Ed.), Public Key Cryptography. Proceedings, 2001. XI, 423 pages. 2001.

Vol. 1993: E. Zitzler, K. Deb, L. Thiele, C.A.Coello Coello, D. Corne (Eds.), Evolutionary Multi-Criterion Optimization. Proceedings, 2001. XIII, 712 pages. 2001.

Vol. 1995: M. Sloman, J. Lobo, E.C. Lupu (Eds.), Policies for Distributed Systems and Networks. Proceedings, 2001. X, 263 pages. 2001.

Vol. 1998: R. Klette, S. Peleg, G. Sommer (Eds.), Robot Vision. Proceedings, 2001. IX, 285 pages. 2001.

Vol. 2000: R. Wilhelm (Ed.), Informatics: 10 Years Back, 10 Years Ahead. IX, 369 pages. 2001.

Vol. 2003: F. Dignum, U. Cortés (Eds.), Agent Mediated Electronic Commerce III. XII, 193 pages. 2001. (Subseries LNAI).

Vol. 2004: A. Gelbukh (Ed.), Computational Linguistics and Intelligent Text Processing. Proceedings, 2001. XII, 528 pages. 2001.

Vol. 2006: R. Dunke, A. Abran (Eds.), New Approaches in Software Measurement. Proceedings, 2000. VIII, 245 pages. 2001.

Vol. 2009: H. Federrath (Ed.), Designing Privacy Enhancing Technologies. Proceedings, 2000. X, 231 pages. 2001.

Vol. 2010: A. Ferreira, H. Reichel (Eds.), STACS 2001. Proceedings, 2001. XV, 576 pages. 2001.

Vol. 2024: H. Kuchen, K. Ueda (Eds.), Functional and Logic Programming. Proceedings, 2001. X, 391 pages. 2001.

GPSR Compliance

The European Union's (EU) General Product Safety Regulation (GPSR) is a set of rules that requires consumer products to be safe and our obligations to ensure this.

If you have any concerns about our products, you can contact us on ProductSafety@springernature.com

In case Publisher is established outside the EU, the EU authorized representative is:

Springer Nature Customer Service Center GmbH
Europaplatz 3
69115 Heidelberg, Germany

Batch number: 09624486

Printed by Printforce, the Netherlands